A Survey of
Contemporary
Economics

The participation of The American Economic Association in the presentation of this material consists in the appointment of a Committee on the Development of Economic Thinking and Information to plan a periodic review of economics, established in April, 1945, and of an appropriation of Association funds for this purpose.

A Survey of

Contemporary

Economics

Edited by
HOWARD S. ELLIS
University of California
Berkeley

VOLUME I

Published for

THE AMERICAN ECONOMIC ASSOCIATION

RICHARD D. IRWIN, INC.
HOMEWOOD, ILLINOIS

Second Printing, March, 1949
Third Printing, June, 1952
Fourth Printing, February, 1954
Fifth Printing, January, 1956
Sixth Printing, November, 1957
Seventh Printing, February, 1959

PRINTED IN THE UNITED STATES OF AMERICA

PREFACE

As READERS of *The Wealth of Nations* know, the gain in product from the division of labor "is owing to three different circumstances; first, to the *increase of dexterity* in every particular workman; secondly, to the *saving of the time* which is commonly lost in passing from one species of work to another; and lastly, to the *invention of a great number of machines* which facilitate and abridge labor . . ."[1] Economists have undoubtedly increased their dexterity, saved time, and invented many machines by reason of the division of labor within their science. But they may also be uncomfortably aware of the picture drawn by Smith of the narrow specialist: "The torpor of his mind renders him, not only incapable of relishing or bearing a part in any rational conversation, but of conceiving any generous, noble, or tender sentiment, and consequently of forming any just judgment concerning many even of the ordinary duties of private life. Of the great and extensive interests of his country he is altogether incapable of judging."[2]

The American Economic Association would regard with dismay an incapacity of its members—because of a too confining division of labor—to conceive noble sentiments, judge of private duties, and assess the interests of their country. These qualities rest upon more than technical *expertise*: they require a knowledge of human history, philosophy, and politics. But, more immediately, they require that the economist look beyond the regression coefficients, propensities, balances of accounts, and equilibria of forces within his own laboratory to the whole arena of economic life. The primary purpose of the present volume is to provide to the economist outside a particular field an intelligible and reliable account of its main ideas—both analytical devices and their practical application to public policy—which have evolved during the last ten or fifteen years. For most of the less abstruse and technical subjects, it is hoped that the qualified layman, the beginning graduate student, and the public servant will also read with profit.

---

[1] Adam Smith, *The Wealth of Nations*, Cannan ed., Bk. I, Ch. 1; italics supplied.
[2] *Ibid.*, p. 734.

The period under review began in the worst depression in our history, continued through our biggest war, and extends into the time of our gravest concern for the future. It is little wonder that these years produced an amazing efflorescence of economic ideas. Like their fellow citizens, economists were confronted with changes of awesome extent and rapidity and with the inadequacy of many of their older patterns of thought. Probably no decade or score of years in the entire history of economics could match those just passed, in innovation, sharpness of controversy, and volume of writing.

To review the course of economic thinking in such a period and to appraise its results impose upon the writer of any of these surveys a task of formidable difficulty. It is unlikely that a qualified reviewer should not himself have taken an active part in recent discussions, and an active part is not generally quite neutral. And yet the expert is asked to withdraw himself from the fray and to take a detached view of his fellows and—still more inhuman—of himself. The reader of the essays which follow will not be surprised to discover that this feat has not always been achieved with equal success; but he may be disposed to treat this shortcoming with indulgence: sometimes because of the difficulty of the undertaking, occasionally because of the brilliance of the performance. Only within limits does economics partake of the character of an exact science, and the judgment of the observer inevitably plays a role. Consequently, there is no official economics. The views expressed in this book do not necessarily represent those of The American Economic Association, the editor, the two critics associated with each essay, and possibly not even the author if he were to have the benefit of ten instead of two sets of proof. What, then, *do* they represent?

These essays may fairly claim to present the considered thought and judgment of able scholars who are well aware of the trust involved in their delegation to the task. All of the authors have recognized their fallibility, and—so far as possible without the sacrifice of their own honest convictions—they have tried to incorporate or to meet the suggestions of critics and editor. In rare cases, the piece appeared from the mold without serious flaw at the first pouring. More frequently, the workman was content only after a second, third, or even fourth attempt. Ideally the qualifying or dissenting remarks of the critics should also appear in print, to give fair warning to the reader that complete unanimity does not prevail. But the book is a stout volume as matters stand; and the process of arriving at a *final* version by the author, to appear with a *final* statement by critics, would stretch out toward infinity. These practical considerations determined the actual procedure from the outset. If the book serves its purpose well, however, this will be attributable in large measure to the distinguished economists who accepted the difficult and delicate role of critic, without having their voices heard by the audience, in order to further the success of the Association's undertaking.

The present volume represents the fruition of extensive planning and preliminary work on the part of a Committee on the Development of Economic Thinking and Information, established by The American Economic Association in April 1945; and of an appropriation of Association funds for this purpose. Much of the arduous—and thankless—exploratory work was done by the chairman of the present committee, Professor J. J. Spengler, Duke University; by Dr. Eveline M. Burns, Columbia University; by a former president of the Association, Professor A. B. Wolfe, The Ohio State University; by the faithful secretary of the Association, Professor James W. Bell, Northwestern University; and by the other members of the reconstituted Review of Economics Committee—Dr. Corwin D. Edwards, Dr. Paul T. Homan, editor of the *American Economic Review*, Professor W. Blair Stewart, and Dr. Aryness J. Wickens. The editor gives grateful acknowledgment of valuable advice and help at numerous junctures given by his colleague Professor William Fellner, and also by Professors Frank L. Kidner and Earl R. Rolph.

Not all fields of economics worthy of inclusion in the present survey have actually been incorporated—population problems, social security, agricultural economics, etc.—to name only a few omitted. The somewhat arbitrary present selection of subjects, made by the Association's committee, was dictated by the desire to achieve a portable volume; and the same consideration imposed upon the writers the citing of representative and outstanding works rather than the construction of exhaustive bibliographies. The utilization of conventional fields in economics—overlapping and illogical as they may be in certain respects—seemed preferable, for ease of identification by the reader, to any newly decocted scheme. Finally, the choice of contributors and, in turn, their selection of subjects and substance answer to no grand design for a unified method or philosophy of economic thinking. The purpose of the book is not to impose an artful scheme upon the interpretation of recent analysis and policy, nor to influence their future course, but to review their substance and appraise their significance.

Whatever is lacking to economics through its limited access to the exact methods of the natural sciences has to be made good by the experience, breadth of knowledge, acumen, and judgment of the individual student. A systematic attempt to assess the progress of the various segments of economic research and thinking should afford valuable supplements to the intellectual resources of the individual economist in any field. For this reason, the editor of the present survey hopes that its character may be such as to lead to the periodic appearance of systematic reviews of economics, of even greater merit, in the future. Indeed, the subject matter of economics has become so vast and its techniques so specialized and difficult, that the day of the exhaustive treatise by a single Jovian figure, such as Mill, Marshall, or Pigou, may have passed. Its place may be taken by compendia of the present sort: less personal, less literary, and less unified, perhaps; but—it is to be hoped—less intuitive, less prescinded, and no less inspiring.

HOWARD S. ELLIS

CONTENTS

AUTHORS

JOE S. BAIN, Associate Professor of Economics, University of California, Berkeley. A.B. University of California at Los Angeles, 1935; Ph.D. Harvard University, 1940. LEARNED SOCIETIES, ETC.: Secretary, Pacific Coast Committee on Price Policies, Social Science Research Council, 1942–48. CHIEF PUBLICATIONS: *Economics of the Pacific Coast Petroleum Industry*, three volumes, University of California Press, Berkeley, 1944–47; *Pricing, Distribution and Employment*, Henry Holt, New York, 1948; *War and Post-war Developments in the Southern California Petroleum Industry*, Haynes Foundation, Los Angeles, 1945; "The Profit Rate as a Measure of Monopoly Power," *Quarterly Journal of Economics*, February 1941, LV, pp. 271–293.

ABRAM BERGSON, Associate Professor of Economics, Columbia University. A.B. Johns Hopkins University, 1933; Ph.D. Harvard University, 1940. GOVERNMENTAL POSITIONS: Office of Strategic Services: Economist, 1942–44; Chief, Economic Subdivision, Union of Soviet Socialist Republics Division, 1944–46. Department of State: Consultant, 1944–46; Member, American Delegation to Reparations Conference, Moscow, 1945. LEARNED SOCIETIES, ETC.: Conference on Research in Income and Wealth, National Bureau of Economic Research. CHIEF PUBLICATIONS: *Structure of Soviet Wages*, Harvard University Press, Cambridge, Mass., 1944; "A Problem in Soviet Statistics," *Review of Economic Statistics*, November 1947, XXIX, pp. 234–242; "A Reformulation of Welfare Economics," *Quarterly Journal of Economics*, February 1938, LII, pp. 310–334.

WILLIAM FELLNER, Professor of Economics, University of California, Berkeley. Ph.D. Berlin University, 1929. GOVERNMENTAL POSITIONS: Consulting Expert, Tax Division, Treasury Department, 1945. CHIEF PUBLICATIONS: *A Treatise on War Inflation*, University of California Press, Berkeley, 1942; *Monetary Policies and Full Employment*, University of California Press, Berkeley, 1946; joint editor, *Readings in the Theory of Income Distribution*, The Blakiston Company, Philadelphia, 1946; "The Technological Argument of the Stagnation Thesis," *Quarterly Journal of Economics*, August 1941, LV, pp. 636–651; "Prices and Wages under Bilateral Monopoly," *Quarterly Journal of Economics*, August 1947, LXI, pp. 503–532; "Monetary Policies and Hoarding in Periods of Stagnation," *Journal of Political Economy*, June 1943, LI, pp. 192–205.

J. K. GALBRAITH, Member of the Board of Editors, Fortune Magazine. B.S. University of Toronto, 1931; M.S. University of California, 1933; Ph.D. University of California, 1934. GOVERNMENTAL POSITIONS: Economic Adviser, National Defense Advisory Commission, 1940–41. Office of Price Administration: Assistant Administrator in Charge of Price Division, 1941–42; Department Administrator, 1942–43. Director of United States Strategic Bombing Survey, 1945. Director of Office of Economic Security Policy, State Department, 1946. LEARNED SOCIETIES, ETC.: Fellow, Social Science Research Council, 1937–38. CHIEF PUBLICATIONS: with H. D. Dennison, *Modern Competition and Business Policy*, Oxford University Press, New York, 1938; *The Economic Effects of the Federal Public Works Expenditures*, National Resources Planning Board, United States Government Printing Office, Washington, D. C., 1940.

BERNARD F. HALEY, Professor of Economics, Stanford University. A.B. Stanford University, 1922; A.M. Harvard University, 1926; Ph.D. Harvard University, 1933. GOVERNMENTAL POSITIONS: Office of Price Administration: Assistant Regional Price Executive, 1942; Director, Textile, Leather and Apparel Price Division, Washington, 1942–43. Department of State, 1943–45: Assistant Chief, Division of Economic Studies; Chief, Commodities Division; Director, Office of Economic Affairs; Director, Office of International Trade Policy. LEARNED SOCIETIES, ETC.: Chairman, Pacific Coast Regional Committee of the Social Science Research Council, 1941–42. Board of Editors, *American Economic Review*, 1938–40. American Economic Association: Executive Committee, 1948–; Chairman, Committee on Republications, 1948–. President, Pacific Coast Economic Association, 1942. CHIEF PUBLICATIONS: joint editor, *Readings in the Theory of Income Distribution*, The Blakiston Company, Philadelphia, 1946; "The Federal Budget: Economic Consequences of Deficit Financing," *American Economic Review*, February 1941, XXX, pp. 67–107; "The Relation Between Cartel Policy and Commodity Agreement Policy," *American Economic Review*, May 1946, XXXVI, pp. 717–734.

WASSILY LEONTIEF, Professor of Economics, Harvard University. University of Leningrad, 1921–25; Ph.D. University of Berlin, 1928. GOVERNMENTAL POSITIONS: Economic Adviser to the Chinese Government, 1929. Chief, Russian Economics Subdivision, Office of Strategic Services, 1943–45. Consultant, Bureau of Labor Statistics, 1942–45. LEARNED SOCIETIES, ETC.: Research Associate with National Bureau of Economic Research, 1931. Guggenheim Fellow, 1940. CHIEF PUBLICATIONS: *The Structure of the American Economy, 1919–1929*, Harvard University Press, Cambridge, Mass., 1941; "Essay on Statistical Analysis of Supply and Demand," *Weltwirtschaftliches Archiv*, 1929, pp. 1*–53*; "The Use of Indifference Curves in the Analysis of Foreign Trade," *Quarterly Journal of Economics*, May 1933, XLVII, pp. 493–503; "Exports and Imports, Domestic Output and Employment," *Quarterly Journal of Economics*, February 1946, LX, pp. 171–193; "Introduction to a Theory of the Internal Structure of Functional Relationships," *Econometrica*, October 1947, XV, pp. 361–373.

LLOYD A. METZLER, Associate Professor of Economics, University of Chicago. B.S. University of Kansas, 1935; M.A. Harvard University, 1941; Ph.D. Harvard University, 1942. GOVERNMENTAL POSITIONS: Economist, Office of Strategic Services, 1943–44. Economist, Board of Governors of the Federal Reserve System,

1944–46. Consultant, House of Representatives' Special Committee on Post-war Economic Policy and Planning, 1945. Member, Mission to Germany on German Currency Reform, American Military Government, 1946. CHIEF PUBLICATIONS: "The Transfer Problem Reconsidered," *Journal of Political Economy*, June 1942, .L, pp. 397–414; "Factors Governing the Length of Inventory Cycles," *Review of Economic Statistics*, February 1947, XXIX, pp. 1–15; "Exchange Rates and the International Monetary Fund," *International Monetary Policies*, Board of Governors of the Federal Reserve System, Washington, 1947, pp. 1–45.

LLOYD G. REYNOLDS, Professor of Economics and Associate Director of the Labor and Management Center, Yale University. B.A. University of Alberta, 1931; M.A. McGill University, 1933; Ph.D. Harvard University, 1936. GOVERNMENTAL POSITIONS: Regional Price Executive, Office of Price Administration, 1941–42. Public Panel Member and Public Member of the National Appeals Committee, National War Labor Board, 1943–45. Consultant, Bureau of the Budget, 1945–47. CHIEF PUBLICATIONS: *The Control of Competition in Canada*, Harvard University Press, Cambridge, Mass., 1940; *Labor and National Defense*, Twentieth Century Fund, New York, 1941; with C. C. Killingsworth, *Trade Union Publications, 1850–1941*, three volumes, Johns Hopkins University Press, Baltimore, 1944 and 1945.

PAUL A. SAMUELSON, Professor of Economics, Massachusetts Institute of Technology. B.A. University of Chicago, 1935; M.A. Harvard University, 1936; Ph.D. Harvard University, 1941. GOVERNMENTAL POSITIONS: Consultant, National Resources Planning Board, 1941–43. Consultant, War Production Board, 1945. LEARNED SOCIETIES, ETC.: American Economic Association, John Bates Clark Award, 1947. CHIEF PUBLICATIONS: *Foundations of Economic Analysis*, Harvard University Press, Cambridge, Mass., 1948; *Economics: An Introductory Analysis*, McGraw-Hill, New York, 1948; "The Gains from International Trade," *Canadian Journal of Economics and Political Science*, May 1939, V, pp. 195–205; "Interactions Between the Multiplier Analysis and the Principle of Acceleration," *Review of Economic Statistics*, May 1939, XXI, pp. 75–78.

CARL S. SHOUP, Professor of Economics in the School of Business and the Faculty of Political Science, Columbia University. A.B. Stanford University, 1924; Ph.D. Columbia University, 1939. GOVERNMENTAL POSITIONS: New York State Special Tax Commission, 1930–35. Consultant, U.S. Treasury Department, 1938–. Consultant, Council of Economic Advisers, 1946–. LEARNED SOCIETIES, ETC.: Director of the Survey of Taxation for the Twentieth Century Fund, 1937, *Facing the Tax Problem*. CHIEF PUBLICATIONS: *The Sales Tax in France*, Columbia University Press, New York, 1930; with Robert M. Haig, *The Sales Tax in the American States*, Columbia University Press, New York, 1934; with Milton Friedman and Ruth Mack, *Taxing to Prevent Inflation*, Columbia University Press, New York, 1943; *Principles of National Income Analysis*, Houghton Mifflin, Boston, 1947.

ARTHUR SMITHIES, Professor of Economics, Harvard University. B.A. Oxford University, 1932. Ph.D. Harvard University, 1934. GOVERNMENTAL POSITIONS:

Consultant, Board of Economic Warfare, 1942. Consultant, Office of Price Administration, 1942. Bureau of the Budget: Principal Fiscal Analyst, 1943–45; Chief Fiscal Analyst, 1945–46; Chief, Economics Branch, 1946. LEARNED SOCIETIES, ETC.: Tasmanian Rhodes Scholar, 1929. Commonwealth Fund Fellow, 1932. CHIEF PUBLICATIONS: "Equilibrium in Monopolistic Competition," *Quarterly Journal of Economics,* November 1940, LV, pp. 95–115; "The American Economy in the Thirties," *American Economic Review,* May 1946, XXXVI, pp. 11–27; "Effective Demand and Employment," Chapter XXXIX in *The New Economics,* Seymour Harris, editor, Alfred A. Knopf, New York, 1947.

HENRY H. VILLARD, Professor of Economics, Hofstra College. A.B. Yale University, 1932; A.M. Cambridge University, 1939; Ph.D. Columbia University, 1941. GOVERNMENTAL POSITIONS: Senior Economist, Division of Research and Statistics, Treasury Department, 1941. Chief Economist and Branch Chief, Service Trade Branch, Office of Price Administration, 1942–43. Economic Adviser, North African Economic Board, Department of State, 1943–44. Economist, Board of Governors of the Federal Reserve System, 1945–46. CHIEF PUBLICATIONS: *Deficit Spending and the National Income,* Farrar and Rinehart, New York, 1941; "The Federal Reserve System's Monetary Policy in 1931 and 1932," *Journal of Political Economy,* December 1937, XLV, pp. 721–739; "Dr. Moulton's Estimates of Saving and Investment," *American Economic Review,* September 1937, XXVII, pp. 479–489.

DAVID McC. WRIGHT, Professor of Economics, University of Virginia. LL.B. University of Virginia, 1935; M.A. Harvard University, 1939; Ph.D. Harvard University, 1940. GOVERNMENTAL POSITIONS: Consultant, National Resources Planning Board, 1943. CHIEF PUBLICATIONS: *The Creation of Purchasing Power,* Harvard University Press, Cambridge, Mass., 1942; *The Economics of Disturbance,* Macmillan Company, New York, 1947; *Democracy and Progress,* Macmillan Company, New York, 1948; "Internal Inconsistency in D. H. Robertson's 'Saving and Hoarding Concepts,'" *Economic Journal,* June–September 1941, LI, pp. 334–337.

CRITICS

James W. Angell, *Columbia University*
E. H. Chamberlin, *Harvard University*
J. M. Clark, *Columbia University*
M. A. Copeland, *Cornell University*
Joel P. Dean, *Columbia University*
R. A. Gordon, *University of California*
Frank D. Graham, *Princeton University*
Gottfried Haberler, *Harvard University*
E. E. Hagen, *Bureau of the Budget*
James K. Hall, *University of Washington*
Alvin H. Hansen, *Harvard University*
A. D. H. Kaplan, *Brookings Institution*
Clark Kerr, *University of California*
Frank H. Knight, *University of Chicago*
A. P. Lerner, *Roosevelt College*
Friedrich A. Lutz, *Princeton University*
Fritz Machlup, *Johns Hopkins University*
Joseph A. Schumpeter, *Harvard University*
Lawrence H. Seltzer, *Wayne University*
Edward S. Shaw, *Stanford University*
Sumner H. Slichter, *Harvard University*
Paul M. Sweezy, *Wilton Centre, N. H.*
Jacob Viner, *Princeton University*
Donald H. Wallace, *Princeton University*
W. Allen Wallis, *University of Chicago*
Elmer Wood, *University of Missouri*

1

VALUE AND DISTRIBUTION

Bernard F. Haley

An attempt is to be made, in the following pages, to review the more important contributions to value and distribution theory that have occurred in the past decade. In view of the volume of the literature that has appeared in the English language alone, with reference to these two phases of economic theory, this involves a highly selective process. Probably no two economists would agree as to all of the material that should be included, nor as to the material that, for lack of space, might most justifiably be excluded. The selective process must admittedly be a subjective one. The attempt will be made, however, to include those contributions that appear to have carried forward the development of theory in some significant respect, or that appear likely to stimulate further important theoretical analysis.

I. Value Theory

With respect to the theory of demand, the most significant developments have been the utilization of the indifference curve technique, and related concepts, for a restatement of particular and general equilibrium theory; and the kinked demand curve as applied to the case of oligopoly. The history of the indifference curve technique certainly antedates the period to be covered by the present review. The credit belongs, however, to J. R. Hicks and R. G. D. Allen for having made non-mathematically trained economists aware of the possibilities of this approach for the improvement of particular and general equilibrium theory. The most important single work in value theory that has appeared during the decade is Mr. Hicks' *Value and Capital*.[1] It has been followed by other able systematic treatments of equilibrium theory.[2]

With respect to analysis of the conditions of supply for the enterprise, empirical cost studies have suggested the necessity of revising previously accepted views as to the probable shape of the supply schedule for the

---

[1] Oxford, 1939.
[2] E.g., O. Lange, *Price Flexibility and Employment* (Bloomington, 1944); J. L. Mosak, *General-Equilibrium Theory in International Trade* (Bloomington, 1944).

firm, and have led to a re-examination of the assumptions underlying marginal analysis as applied to the behavior of the firm.

As to particular equilibrium theory, the most important developments have had reference to the cases of oligopoly and bilateral monopoly. In general, monopolistic competition theory has been improved by virtue of the increased attention that has been given to variables other than price and quantity, such as product variation, variation in location, and other manifestations of non-price competition. There has been more recognition of the need for tempering broad generalizations with respect to the behavior of a small number of variables by consideration for the institutional situation and the technical aspects of particular industries.

THE THEORY OF DEMAND

(1) The indifference curve approach to the theory of demand is based on the assumption that the individual, in planning his expenditures, so determines his outlay on any one commodity that he will be on the margin of indifference as between the last small increment of that commodity and an additional alternative increment of any other commodity that might be substituted.[3] Assume that the consumer is confronted with only two commodities upon which, in varying quantities, he may spend his income. In Figure 1, let the quantities of the two commodities be measured respectively on the OY and OX axes. Then I_1 and I_2 are indifference curves. Any combination of X and Y indicated by a point on I_1, for example, is equally desirable from the point of view of the consumer. Furthermore, since I_2 lies farther from O than I_1, it is assumed that any combination of X and Y indicated by a point on I_2 is preferred to any combination of X and Y indicated by a point on I_1. The ratio of exchange between X and Y may be shown by the slope of price lines, such as P_1, P_2, . . . If the individual's income in terms of Y is OM, and if the price of X in terms of Y is shown by the slope of P_2, the diagram shows that the consumer would wish to consume OX_2 of X, at a cost to him of FR of Y, since at this rate of consumption of X the price line corresponding to his income would be tangent to an indifference curve. His rate of consumption of X_2 places him on the highest indifference curve attainable for him, given the income OM and the price P_2. Given the whole map of the individual's indifference curves and given his income, it is possible to deduce his demand schedule for X.[4]

---

[3] J. R. Hicks and R. G. D. Allen, "A Reconsideration of the Theory of Value," *Economica*, February and May 1934, I, pp. 52–76, 196–219; H. Schultz, *The Theory and Measurement of Demand* (Chicago, 1938), Ch. 1; J. R. Hicks, *Value and Capital*, Ch. 1, 2.

[4] Analogous to the indifference curve in the theory of demand is the "isoquant" in production theory. If, in Figure 1, the two axes measured respectively quantities of two

One advantage claimed for this approach is that it is not necessary to assume that the consumer is capable of cardinally measuring the *amount* of utility attributable to any given increment of a commodity. All that is assumed is that the individual does weigh the *relative* desirability of different combinations of quantities of X and Y. Hence the concept of marginal utility is replaced by the concept of the marginal rate of substitution. The marginal rate of substitution of X for Y is the quantity of Y that would just

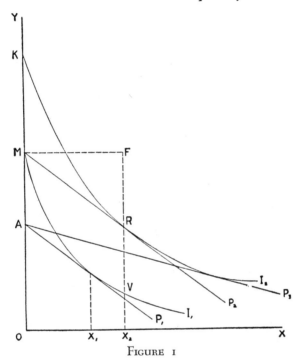

FIGURE 1

compensate the consumer for the loss of a marginal unit of X. For any combination of X and Y, it is measured by the slope of the indifference curve at the point which represents that combination. When the individual is in equilibrium with respect to his consumption of X and Y the marginal rate of substitution of X for Y will be equal to the price of X in terms of Y, and thus the price line must be tangent to the indifference curve at the equilibrium point.

---

factors of production, X and Y, the curve I_1 would be an isoquant, showing the various combinations of X and Y that would produce a given output. I_2 would be an isoquant with reference to a higher level of output. F. Y. Edgeworth early described a three-dimensional figure to illustrate the principle of varying proportions of the factors: "Contributions to the Theory of Railway Rates," *Economic Journal*, September 1911, XXI, pp. 362–363. Use of isoquants has been made by Frisch, Schneider, Hicks, Carlson, Boulding, and others. For references, see K. E. Boulding, "The Theory of the Firm," *American Economic Review*, December 1942, XXXII, p. 800.

Another advantage claimed for this approach is that it makes it easier to distinguish between the effect of a change in income and the effect of a change in relative prices upon the demand of an individual for a commodity. If the price of X falls relative to the price of Y, the increase in the quantity of X taken by the consumer may be broken down into two parts, one part attributable to the fact that the consumer's income is in effect increased by the fall in the price of X (the income effect), the other part attributable to the fact that the consumer will tend to increase his consumption of X at the expense of other commodities because of the relative cheapness of X (the substitution effect).

Hicks also utilizes the concept of the marginal rate of substitution for the definition of substitute and complementary goods so as to avoid the assumption of cardinally measurable utility. X and Y are substitute commodities if a decrease in the price of X has the effect of decreasing the marginal rate of substitution of Y for money; while X and Y are complementary goods if a decrease in the price of X has the reverse effect upon the marginal rate of substitution of Y for money.[5] That is, the tendency to consume more of X (because of the decrease in the price of X) will be accompanied by a tendency to consume less of Y, if X and Y are substitutes, or more of Y, if X and Y are complements, the price of Y assumed unchanged, and quite apart from any income effect of the decrease in the price of X.

Another by-product of the indifference curve analysis has been a revived interest in the concept of consumer's surplus, since it now becomes possible to define the concept without assuming either the cardinal measurability of utility by the consumer or the constancy of the marginal utility of money. In the course of the considerable discussion that has occurred, the advantage which a consumer gains from a given price situation, or which he obtains from a decrease in price, has been treated as measurable in terms of equivalent gains or losses of money income.[6] Once the assumption of a constant marginal utility of money is dropped, however, it becomes clear that there are several alternative ways of measuring consumer's surplus in terms of money income:

(a) The counterpart of the Marshallian concept: the difference between what the consumer actually pays for *a given quantity* of a com-

---

[5] Allowance being made for the income effect of the decrease in the price of X, which should not be permitted to affect the marginal rate of substitution of Y for money.

[6] J. R. Hicks, *Value and Capital*, pp. 38–41; H. W. Robinson, "Consumer's Surplus and Taxation: *ex ante or ex post?*" *South African Journal of Economics*, September 1939, VII, pp. 270–280; A. Henderson, "Consumer's Surplus and the Compensating Variation," *Review of Economic Studies*, February 1941, VIII, pp. 117–121; J. R. Hicks, "The Four Consumer's Surpluses," *ibid.*, Winter 1943, XI, pp. 31–41; *idem*, "The Generalised Theory of Consumer's Surplus," *ibid.*, 1945–46, XIII, pp. 68–74.

modity, and the maximum amount he could have been made to pay for it, *on an all or nothing basis*, without being made worse off than if he had not bought any of it at all.

(b) The compensating variation: the maximum deduction from the consumer's income which would leave him in a position still to consume *some* quantity of the commodity without being any worse off than if the commodity were not available to him at all.

(c) The equivalent variation: the amount of added income that would compensate the consumer for the loss of the opportunity to purchase any of the commodity.

If, in Figure 1, the individual's money income is OM and the price of X is shown by the slope of P_2, the Marshallian consumer's surplus is RV, the difference between FR and FV; the compensating variation is MA; and the equivalent variation is MK.[7]

It remains to be seen how useful the new tools will actually turn out to be.[8] It should be noted, however, that these new formulations are measures of satisfaction expressed in terms of money income, and consequently their employment for the appraisal of matters of economic policy involves nearly all of the risks that made the old concept of consumer's surplus of such questionable usefulness.

This brings us to the more important objections that have been made to the indifference curve approach to demand theory. These have mainly to do with the conception of human behavior presupposed by the analysis, and with its utilization of an "ordinal" rather than a "cardinal" concept of utility.[9]

Of those who object to the conception of human behavior presupposed, some maintain that the traditional concept of "cardinal" utility should not have been dropped, while others maintain that the new analysis has not gone far enough in breaking away from the traditional concept of a rational, calculating economic man carefully weighing "amounts" of utility or "satisfaction." According to the former, the individual does think in

---

[7] There are corresponding concepts of the *increment* of consumer's surplus attributable to a decrease in price. In addition to the Marshallian concept, there are the price-compensating variation, the quantity-compensating variation, the price-equivalent variation, and the quantity-equivalent variation. It is not possible, however, to examine these further refinements here.

[8] For some possible applications see: J. R. Hicks, "The Rehabilitation of Consumers' Surplus," *Review of Economic Studies*, February 1941, VIII, pp. 108–116; *idem*, "Consumers' Surplus and Index Numbers," *ibid.*, Summer 1942, IX, pp. 126–137.

[9] It has also been pointed out that the approach is not one which lends itself to empirical derivation of the values of the functions involved, any more than is possible with the older approach. Nor may the indifference function approach be used as a basis for empirical studies of consumption, income, prices, and their interrelationships. W. A. Wallis and M. Friedman, "The Empirical Derivation of Indifference Functions," *Studies in Mathematical Economics and Econometrics* (Chicago, 1942), pp. 175–189.

quantitative terms of the "subjective service" or satisfaction associated with successive increments of consumption of a particular good.[10] Hence "total satisfaction" is a cardinal magnitude and the individual does have a quantitative conception of diminishing marginal utility with respect to individual goods and total income. Since the individual does think in terms of cardinal utility and increments of total satisfaction, it is a mistake not to base the theory of demand upon these concepts.

Hicks would answer that there is no objection to retention of the quantitative conception of utility in the theory of demand if anyone cares to retain it. However, the notion of cardinal utility is not necessary to the explanation of price determination. "Therefore, on the principle of Occam's razor, it is better to do without it."[11]

The important question would appear to be: in which way does the individual consumer think his way through the problem of allocating his income? Does he think in terms of the *relative* importance of a small increment in his rate of consumption of one commodity vs. that of another? Or does he think in terms of an estimated quantity of satisfaction to be expected from a small increment in his rate of consumption of a particular commodity?

The question has also been raised, on the other hand, whether the indifference curve approach has not, after all, retained most of the objectionable features of the psychology presupposed in the older cardinal utility approach.[12] Although the theory of demand has been freed from dependence upon the assumption that utility is cardinally measurable by the individual and the assumption that the marginal utility of money is constant, it still seems to be assumed that the individual is able to measure his *preferences* quite precisely, and does so in a coldly rational way. There is no recognition of the way in which the individual's preferences may be shaped by advertising and other selling methods, no allowance for the effects of habit and custom, and no realization that the individual's map of indifference curves may be a very short-run phenomenon, subject to frequent and possibly capricious change.

(2) The high degree of simplification of the circumstances affecting demand characteristic of the indifference curve approach becomes evident when one comes to consider the conditions of demand in situations

---

[10] F. H. Knight, "Realism and Relevance in the Theory of Demand," *Journal of Political Economy*, December 1944, LII, pp. 289–318.

[11] J. R. Hicks, *Value and Capital*, p. 18.

[12] P. A. Samuelson, "A Note on the Pure Theory of Consumer's Behaviour," *Economica*, February 1938, V, pp. 61–62; R. T. Norris, *The Theory of Consumer's Demand* (New Haven, 1941), Ch. 3; J. M. Clark, "Realism and Relevance in the Theory of Demand," *Journal of Political Economy*, August 1946, LIV, pp. 347–353.

of oligopoly and monopolistic competition. Mrs. Norris has shown the way in which product differentiation has multiplied the number of "commodities" from which the consumer must choose.[13] From this wide variety of goods the consumer typically buys only one at a time of any one highly specialized and differentiated type of good. Hence the indifference curve apparatus, with its assumption of quantities of homogeneous goods measured on the respective axes, does not appear to be a very useful tool.[14] The theory of consumer's choice becomes very complicated indeed.

Most of the recent discussion of demand under conditions of monopolistic competition and oligopoly has, however, had reference to the demand curve as viewed by the individual concern.[15] What are the different types of situation, with respect to demand, that may occur under conditions of monopolistic competition and oligopoly; and what may be expected to be the price policy of the enterprise in each case?

The first, and most significant, of the developments has resulted from a recognition that the sales curve of the firm under conditions of oligopoly is not necessarily continuous but may be kinked or have an obtuse angle (as viewed from the axes) at the point representative of the current price.[16] The upper part of the sales curve is relatively elastic, reflecting the fear on the part of the enterprise that if it raises its price its competitors will not follow suit; while the lower part of the curve is relatively less elastic, on the basis that the enterprise expects any price cut it may make to be followed promptly by corresponding price cuts by its competitors. Such a situation may be particularly frequent in a period of depression,

---

[13] R. T. Norris, *The Theory of Consumer's Demand*, Ch. 1, 7–9.

[14] *Ibid.*, p. 45. Cf. J. M. Clark, *op. cit.*, p. 351.

[15] There has been some discussion as to whether the demand curve in question is the one "imagined" by the enterprise, or is the "real" or "objective" demand curve that the enterprise will in fact encounter when it sets its price. (The notion of the "imagined" demand curve is credited to N. Kaldor, "Mrs. Robinson's 'Economics of Imperfect Competition,'" *Economica*, August 1934, I, pp. 340–341.) As Triffin points out, the relevant sales or demand curve is the one which expresses the expectations of the enterprise. It may or may not correspond with the actual demand situation as the latter unfolds. Triffin also points out that economists writing in this field have usually assumed that the expectations of the enterprise are always in fact realized. Such an assumption may be appropriate to static analysis, but may not safely be made with respect to a dynamic economy. R. Triffin, *Monopolistic Competition and General Equilibrium Theory* (Cambridge, Mass., 1940), pp. 62–67. Some of the consequences of mistaken demand expectations, both on the assumption of stationary conditions and on the assumption of dynamic conditions, have been considered by R. H. Coase, "Some Notes on Monopoly Price," *Review of Economic Studies*, October 1937, V, pp. 17–31; and S. Weintraub, "Monopoly Equilibrium and Anticipated Demand," *Journal of Political Economy*, June 1942, L, pp. 427–434.

[16] R. L. Hall and C. J. Hitch, "Price Theory and Business Behaviour," *Oxford Economic Papers*, May 1939, No. 2, pp. 22–25; P. M. Sweezy, "Demand under Conditions of Oligopoly," *Journal of Political Economy*, August 1939, XLVII, pp. 568–573. The development has recently been reviewed by G. J. Stigler, "The Kinky Oligopoly Demand Curve and Rigid Prices," *ibid.*, October 1947, LV, pp. 432–437.

since at such a time the enterprise might well assume that its rivals were operating at less than capacity and were consequently in no mood to lose further business as a result of price-cutting by others, nor averse to acquiring additional business as a result of price increases by others.

The situation is illustrated in Figure 2, in which the sales curve is DD'D", and the corresponding marginal revenue curve is MQRM'. The prevailing price is XD'. There is a range of discontinuity in the marginal revenue curve, the extent of the discontinuity depending on the difference in elasticity of the two segments of the sales curve.

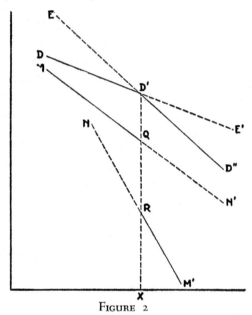

FIGURE 2

This kind of kinked demand curve is by no means the only possibility. Sweezy has also suggested the possibility of a kinked demand curve with an angle, as viewed from the axes, of more than 180 degrees.[17] In Figure 2, such a curve is ED'E', with the corresponding marginal revenue curve NRQN'. The upper stretch of the curve is now relatively inelastic, indicating the expectation on the part of the enterprise that price increases by it are likely to be followed by similar price increases on the part of rival firms. This might well be the expectation in a period in which the concerns are generally operating at close to capacity output. On the other hand, the lower section of the curve is relatively elastic, indicating the

---

[17] P. M. Sweezy, *op. cit.*, pp. 570–571. Efroymson has explored the possibility further, naming this curve the "reflex" curve, in contrast to the "obtusely kinked" curve considered earlier. C. W. Efroymson, "A Note on Kinked Demand Curves," *American Economic Review*, March 1943, XXXIII, pp. 104–107.

expectation that price decreases by the enterprise are *not* likely to be followed by rival concerns. This assumption also may be appropriate to a period of prosperity; it has also been suggested as appropriate to a situation in which price reductions take the form of secret concessions from list prices.[18]

Clearly the obtusely kinked and the reflex demand curves are only two of several forms that the sales curve of the individual enterprise may take under conditions of oligopoly, according to the assumptions that are made as to the probable reactions of rivals to the price policy of a given enterprise.[19] The cases considered above, however, appear rather more likely to occur than others.[20]

(3) In this review of developments in the theory of demand in recent years, some mention should be made of the empirical contributions in the field of statistical demand studies. Here the outstanding work of the past decade was, of course, the comprehensive and scholarly treatment of both the theory of demand and techniques of statistical analysis of demand provided by the late Henry Schultz.[21] The product of a ten-year program of research, this treatise is probably most valuable for its careful appraisal of the advantages and disadvantages of the different techniques of statistical analysis of demand, at all times considered in the light of demand theory. The work also includes, however, actual demand studies with respect to about fifteen agricultural commodities. Some of the most interesting, although not the most immediately fruitful, of his studies are those designed to measure the kind and degree of interrelations of the demands for several commodities (such as beef and pork).[22] Are the commodities complements or substitutes? What are the cross-elasticities of demand?[23]

There were other statistical demand studies during the past decade, probably the most important of which were those with respect to automobiles and steel—two of the few cases in which commodities were selected with respect to which more complex circumstances must be taken into

---

[18] As J. M. Clark has suggested in his critique of this chapter, it is hardly likely that a firm could, for long, expect to sell its full output secretly at a price lower than that of its competitors.

[19] Several other possible types are considered by S. Weintraub, "The Foundations of the Demand Curve," *American Economic Review*, September 1942, XXXII, pp. 547–549.

[20] The implications of the kinked sales curve for the analysis of particular equilibrium under conditions of oligopoly are considered below, pp. 19–20.

[21] H. Schultz, *op. cit.*

[22] *Ibid.*, Ch. 18, 19.

[23] What is the effect upon the quantity of beef taken by the market if there occurs a slight increase in the price of pork? Or more precisely, what is the relative change in the quantity taken of one commodity associated with a very small relative change in the price of the other commodity?

account than in the case of agricultural commodities seasonally produced.[24]

Little progress was made, however, in the methodology of statistical analysis of demand in the direction of bringing the statistically derived demand curve closer to the demand curve used by the economic theorist in his analysis.[25] It has to be recognized that the difficulties in the way of attaining such an objective may simply be insoluble. The continuing statistical studies of demand, however, cannot help but enrich the economist's knowledge of the conditions underlying the demand for individual commodities studied, and may also lead to improvements in his theoretical analysis.

CONDITIONS OF SUPPLY—THE ENTERPRISE

Developments in the analysis of the conditions of supply for the enterprise have mainly been concerned with the nature of the cost schedule for the individual concern. With respect to the short-run situation, these developments included: (1) a recognition of the fact that the cost of production of a commodity which constitutes its supply price in the short run cannot be regarded as independent of anticipated future prices and costs; (2) a considerable range of empirical studies of variations in short-run costs for individual enterprises; and (3) partly as a result of these empirical cost studies, a recognition of the multiplicity of forms that the cost functions of different enterprises may take in different types of technological situation. With respect to the long-run situation, (4) the principal developments had to do with the optimum size for the enterprise.

(1) The Keynesian concept of *user cost* is important as a more precise statement of the nature of the contribution of economic depreciation to prime cost in the short run.[26] The user cost of a unit of output consists of two elements: (a) the actual value of the materials used up in producing that unit of output (including any materials employed in the operation and maintenance of the equipment utilized), *plus* (b) the reduction in the discounted value of the expected future increments of income to be at-

---

[24] P. De Wolff, "The Demand for Passenger Cars in the United States," *Econometrica*, April 1938, VI, pp. 113–129; C. F. Roos and V. von Szeliski, "Factors Governing Changes in Domestic Automobile Demand," *The Dynamics of Automobile Demand* (New York, 1939), pp. 21–95; H. G. Lewis, "A Statistical Analysis of the Demand for Steel, 1919–1938," *United States Steel Corporation T.N.E.C. Papers* (New York, 1940), pp. 169–221.

[25] Cf. G. J. Stigler, "The Limitations of Statistical Demand Curves," *Journal of the American Statistical Association*, September 1939, XXXIV, pp. 469–481.

[26] J. M. Keynes, *The General Theory of Employment, Interest and Money* (London, 1936), pp. 52–73. Marshall's concept of prime cost included "the extra wear-and-tear of plant," but he touched upon it only lightly. A. Marshall, *Principles of Economics* (London, 1890; 8th ed., 1920), p. 360,

tributed to the equipment through using it for that unit of output instead of leaving it unused (but maintaining it).[27] We are mainly interested here in the second of the two elements in user cost, the part of depreciation of equipment which is properly to be included in prime cost and marginal cost in the short run.[28]

The concept of user cost serves to bring out the dependence of the current short-run supply schedule upon expectations as to the future course of costs and selling prices. The depreciation element in user cost, which enters into supply price, is in the nature of an opportunity cost. The cost attributable to the present use of the equipment is the net yield that, it is expected, could be obtained instead some time in the future if it were not to be used now.[29] Hence marginal cost may change without any variation in rate of output or in *immediately* anticipated costs of materials, rates of wages, etc., the change in marginal cost being attributable to a change in expectations as to, for example, future wage rates, future costs of materials, or future selling price.

There is some question, however, whether in most situations the depreciation element in user cost is very important.[30] Consequently this refinement in marginal cost analysis should not be overstressed. Furthermore, the business man's conception of cost of production only very roughly approximates at best the conception attributed to him by the theoretical economist.

(2) It was the objective of a group of Oxford economists under the leadership of R. L. Hall and C. J. Hitch to discover the way in which business men do decide what price to charge and what output to produce.[31] A considerable number of entrepreneurs were interviewed, and the answers of thirty-eight of these were selected for analysis. The principal conclusion was that most based their selling prices upon some sort

---

[27] J. M. Keynes, *op. cit.*, p. 53. See also A. P. Lerner, "User Cost and Prime User Cost," *American Economic Review*, March 1943, XXXIII, pp. 131–132.

[28] In an integrated economy this depreciation element in user cost would be the only element. Consequently the term is sometimes used to refer to the depreciation element alone. Cf. P. T. Bauer, "Notes on Cost," *Economica*, May 1945, XII, p. 96. J. S. Bain has made an excellent analysis of the components of the depreciation function, and of the relation between those components which are a part of supply price and those which are not. J. S. Bain, "Depression Pricing and the Depreciation Function," *Quarterly Journal of Economics*, August 1937, LI, pp. 705–715.

[29] The dependence of user cost upon expectations as to the future course of costs and selling price has been well illustrated from the behavior of the rubber plantations by P. T. Bauer, *op. cit.*, pp. 90–100. See also A. C. Neal, "Marginal Cost and Dynamic Equilibrium of the Firm," *Journal of Political Economy*, February 1942, L, pp. 45–64.

[30] Bain shows that, in industries in which the expected rate of obsolescence is high, the element of depreciation in user cost may be negligible. J. S. Bain, *op. cit.*, pp. 714–715.

[31] R. L. Hall and C. J. Hitch, *op. cit.*, pp. 12–45.

of full average cost including an allowance for profit, and did not think in terms of marginal cost or marginal revenue at all.[32] It should be noted that none of the cases considered approached even remotely the conditions of pure competition, and that most of the cases were characterized by oligopoly, with or without differentiation of product. It should also be noted that "full average cost" was not the same concept in all cases. In some cases, it turned out to be simply the price which the price leader regarded as covering his full cost; in others, it was a "standard" cost figure published by the trade association; in still others, it was actually computed independently by each concern. For some of the enterprises, however, it was a fairly flexible figure; some admitted "that they might charge more in periods of exceptionally high demand, and a greater number that they might charge less in periods of exceptionally depressed demand."[33] Furthermore, even when the individual concerns computed their costs independently, it appears that they varied their respective profit margins included in the "full cost" figure "so that approximately the same prices for similar products would rule within the 'group' of competing producers."[34]

As Machlup has shown, there appears to have been considerable attention paid by several of the entrepreneurs to what the economist has in mind when he uses the terms elasticity of demand and marginal revenue.[35] Machlup, however, is distrustful of the whole procedure of this study, since he does not believe that much information of value can be obtained from business men's answers to questions about their reasons for charging the prices they charge. The stress upon "full cost" may simply be a rationalization or justification of the price actually charged, or it may refer to the price arrived at by agreement of the members of the industry, or the price which the individual entrepreneur believes will yield him his fair share of the business without inducing his competitors to expand their businesses at his expense and without attracting new firms to the industry.[36]

[32] Cf. Committee on Price Determination, Conference on Price Research, *Cost Behavior and Price Policy* (New York, 1943), p. 286. The Committee discovered that the full cost principle appeared to be in fairly wide use among firms in the United States.

[33] R. L. Hall and C. J. Hitch, *op. cit.*, p. 19.

[34] *Ibid.*

[35] F. Machlup, "Marginal Analysis and Empirical Research," *American Economic Review*, September 1946, XXXVI, pp. 536–547. See also replies to Machlup by R. A. Lester, "Marginalism, Minimum Wages, and Labor Markets," *ibid.*, March 1947, XXXVII, pp. 135–142; and H. M. Oliver, Jr., "Marginal Theory and Business Behavior," *ibid.*, June, 1947, XXXVII, pp. 375–383.

[36] A study by R. A. Lester, "Shortcomings of Marginal Analysis for Wage-Employment Problems," *American Economic Review*, March 1946, XXXVI, pp. 63–82, based on questionnaires producing responses from thirty-six manufacturers, was interpreted to show that most of the replying firms believed that they were subject to decreasing varia-

Inadequate though these studies were in many respects, they may have served the useful purpose of making economic theorists more skeptical of the applicability, without great caution, of the traditional apparatus of cost curves, particularly in the cases of oligopoly and monopolistic competition. Those responsible for the studies have relied so heavily upon the answers of their respondents alone, however, that it probably would be unwise to give too much weight to their conclusions until these studies have been supplemented by further research in the behavior and motivation of entrepreneurs with respect to price policy.

Another important source of knowledge of the costs of the enterprise and, like the work of Lester and of Hall and Hitch, a stimulus to the re-examination of theoretical concepts, has been the series of statistical studies of costs which have appeared since 1933. Statistically derived cost curves designed to show the relation between variations in output and cost per unit of product have been constructed from accounting data for a considerable variety of industries.[37] Statistical procedures have been employed for the elimination of the effects upon cost of influences other than variations in output, such as changes in the prices of the factors, technological changes, and the lag of output behind costs; and the residual relationship between total cost and output has then been measured by a line of regression of best fit. In most cases the resulting cost curve has been representative, of necessity, of the behavior of costs for the aggregate of products of the concern rather than for a single undifferentiated commodity.

With only very few exceptions, the line of regression of best fit has been a straight line, and consequently the conclusion has been drawn that marginal cost within the range of variations of output covered by these studies has probably been constant. Such a conclusion is of course widely at variance with the economist's U-shaped marginal cost curve for

---

ble costs per unit of output within the range of 70 to 100 per cent of capacity. As Machlup has pointed out, the usefulness of the study must be seriously questioned, however, since Lester's questionnaire did not include any definition of "capacity," and it is therefore not possible, unfortunately, to determine the range of outputs the respondents might have had in mind when they reported decreasing variable costs. Other aspects of the replies indicate that little confidence can be placed in the evidence they represent. F. Machlup, *op. cit.*, pp. 550–552. See also R. A. Lester, "Marginalism, Minimum Wages, and Labor Markets," *ibid.*, March 1947, XXXVII, pp. 138–139.

[37] For example: J. P. Dean, *Statistical Determination of Cost with Special Reference to Marginal Cost* (Chicago, 1936); T. O. Yntema, "An Analysis of Steel Prices, Volume and Costs: Controlling Limitations on Price Reductions," *United States Steel Corporation T.N.E.C. Papers* (New York, 1940), I, pp. 223–323. For appraisal of these and other contributions, see: H. Staehle, "The Measurement of Statistical Cost Functions: An Appraisal of Some Recent Contributions," *American Economic Review*, June 1942, XXXII, pp. 321–333; Committee on Price Determination, Conference on Price Research, *op. cit.*, Ch. 5.

the individual concern in the short run as inferred from the principle of varying proportions.

Although there have now been several of these statistical cost studies that have yielded a constant marginal cost curve within the range of observations included, economists have not found the evidence by any means conclusive. In the first place, it has been pointed out, the accounting data and some of the methods of analysis employed (such as the computation of depreciation on a straight-line basis, the allocation of overhead over time, and the use of annual average figures for output) have introduced an important bias toward linearity.[38] Furthermore, the selection of the straight line as the line of regression of best fit for the corrected figures for cost and output may not in every case be justified. Very slight deviations from linearity in this statistically determined total cost function would yield a marginal cost curve of the traditional variety, and such a slightly curvilinear function might fit the corrected figures about as well as a straight line.[39]

It consequently appears premature to conclude that marginal cost, at least in the case of manufacturing enterprises, is typically constant instead of an increasing function of output. Furthermore, since these studies have not in general covered a range of outputs that included those in the neighborhood of capacity and beyond, they have been responsible for no doubts whatever as to the inevitability of rising marginal cost if the concern expands its output beyond "capacity." On the other hand, questionable though the conclusions of the studies may be, they have led to a re-examination of the assumptions on the basis of which the traditional marginal cost curve for the enterprise has been drawn, and to the consideration of possible situations in which marginal cost might, at least for outputs not departing very far from normal, be nearly constant.

(3) The conventional U-shaped marginal cost curve is probably applicable to the case in which the fixed plant is indivisible but is adaptable to the utilization of successive small increments of the variable factors. This, however, may be a special case. More likely cases will be those characterized by some degree of divisibility of fixed plant and some flexibility.[40] The greater the number of identical machines in the

---

[38] H. Staehle, *op. cit.*, pp. 328–330; C. A. Smith, "The Cost-Output Relation for the U.S. Steel Corporation," *Review of Economic Statistics*, November 1942, XXIV, pp. 168–171; Committee on Price Determination, Conference on Price Research, *op. cit.*, pp. 96–102.

[39] R. Ruggles, "The Concept of Linear Total Cost-Output Regressions," *American Economic Review*, June 1941, XXXI, pp. 332–335.

[40] G. Stigler, "Production and Distribution in the Short Run," *Journal of Political Economy*, June 1939, XLVII, pp. 305–322; also in W. Fellner and B. F. Haley, eds.,

plant, the greater the divisibility. The more divisible is the fixed plant, and the less each unit is adaptable to variations in the quantity of the variable factors, the greater will be the tendency toward constant marginal cost in the range of outputs short of full utilization, since increases in output up to that point will be obtained simply by bringing into operation successive additional units of the fixed plant together with the appropriate additional quantities of labor and materials to employ the new units. Of course perfect divisibility of fixed plant is probably a limiting case, but the existence of some degree of divisibility, Stigler suggests, should affect the shape of the marginal cost curve. Similarly, the presence of flexibility in the plant may work in the same direction. Flexibility of operations is obtained by various techniques that reduce the extent to which average cost increases for outputs greater than or less than the optimum.[41] One method of increasing flexibility is to increase the divisibility of fixed plant beyond the point that would be desirable if the plant were expected to operate continuously at the optimum. Another method is to reduce fixed plant relative to variable factors. Flexibility thus will probably involve a cost: the level of the average cost curve may be somewhat higher than for a less flexible plant designed to operate at the lowest possible minimum cost output. Variations in average cost with variations in output should not be so great, however, as in the less flexible plant, and consequently the marginal cost curve should also be flatter.

(4) Analysis of the determinants of the optimum size of the firm has profited from several contributions. First, there is the principle of increasing risk, which has been advanced as one source of limitation upon increase in scale of enterprise.[42] The larger the entrepreneur's own investment in the firm, the more is his total financial situation endangered in the event that the firm should fail. Furthermore, the larger his investment, the greater is the danger he incurs from sacrifice of liquidity. The applicability of this limitation upon size appears restricted, however, to the case of the individual proprietorship, and to a less extent, the partnership form of enterprise. The corporation, with its feature of limited liability of stockholders and with its ability to sell additional issues of stock to many investors, does not appear to be confronted with this sort of obstacle to increase in size.[43]

Readings in the Theory of Income Distribution (Philadelphia and Toronto, 1946), pp. 119–137.

[41] *Ibid.*, pp. 314–317. Cf. a subsequent discussion by J. Dean, *Statistical Cost Functions of a Hosiery Mill* (Chicago, 1941), pp. 7–15.

[42] M. Kalecki, "The Principle of Increasing Risk," *Economica*, November 1937, IV, pp. 440–447.

[43] N. S. Buchanan and R. D. Calkins, "A Comment on Mr. Kalecki's 'Principle of Increasing Risk,'" *Economica*, November 1938, V, pp. 455–458. Kalecki, in his reply

A limitation upon size somewhat similar to that suggested by Kalecki is the less than perfect elasticity of supply of enterprise that *may* characterize the attitude of entrepreneurs.[44] It has been generally assumed that the entrepreneur regularly seeks to maximize profits, and that he expands his enterprise to the point beyond which no increment of profit is to be obtained by further increase in output. The entrepreneur may not be indifferent, however, to other aspects of increase in size, such as the prestige and power that come from conduct of a large enterprise, or on the other hand the stress and strain, the heavy responsibility, and other possible disadvantages of bigness.

In the case of the large corporation it is particularly likely that the assumption that the entrepreneur seeks to maximize profit may not be valid.[45] One important case in point is the corporation whose entrepreneur regards retention of control as at least as important as the maximizing of profits. In this case, growth of the firm toward the technically optimum size may be checked by a fear of partial or complete loss of control as a consequence of resort to outsiders for additional capital.[46]

PARTICULAR EQUILIBRIUM

The principal contributions to particular equilibrium theory in recent years have had reference to the case of oligopoly and, to a less extent, to the case of bilateral monopoly.[47] Little has been added to previous analysis of the cases of pure competition and of the large group case under monopolistic competition. In this section, consideration will be given to:

(*ibid.*, pp. 459–460), maintains that there is a limit to the extent to which a corporation can raise new capital through common stock issues, and that this limit may affect the size of the corporation in the same way that increasing risk may affect the size of the individual proprietorship or partnership.

[44] T. de Scitovszky, "A Note on Profit Maximisation and Its Implications," *Review of Economic Studies*, Winter 1943, XI, pp. 57–60; K. E. Boulding, "The Incidence of a Profits Tax," *American Economic Review*, September 1944, XXXIV, pp. 567–572. Cf. B. Higgins, "Elements of Indeterminacy in the Theory of Non-Perfect Competition," *ibid.*, September 1939, XXIX, pp. 476–479.

[45] M. W. Reder, "A Reconsideration of the Marginal Productivity Theory," *Journal of Political Economy*, October 1947, LV, pp. 450–458. Cf. E. G. Nourse, *Price Making in a Democracy* (Washington, 1944), pp. 98–105.

[46] M. W. Reder, *op. cit.*, pp. 455–457. J. M. Clark, "Toward a Concept of Workable Competition," *American Economic Review*, June 1940, XXX, pp. 248–249, has found evidence to indicate that other factors than size appear to be principally responsible for differences in cost between plants, and that, consequently, there is typically no definite "optimum size" of plant but rather "a wide optimum range of size."

[47] Unfortunately, space does not permit more than mention of the considerable improvement in the diagrammatic apparatus for the exposition of the equilibrium conditions with respect to selling costs for the firm. The principal contributions are those of K. E. Boulding, *Economic Analysis* (New York and London, 1941), pp. 578–588, 616–618; and N. S. Buchanan, "Advertising Expenditures: A Suggested Treatment," *Journal of Political Economy*, August 1942, L, pp. 537–557.

(1) the position that particular equilibrium analysis is inappropriate to cases of oligopoly and monopolistic competition; (2) recent developments in the theory of oligopoly; and (3) recent developments in the theory of bilateral monopoly.

(1) Serious doubts have been raised as to whether it is appropriate or fruitful to attempt to develop particular equilibrium analysis for cases of oligopoly and monopolistic competition, particularly for a differentiated commodity.[48] Under pure competition an industry produces a homogeneous commodity, each producer of which realizes that his product is a perfect substitute for the product of each of his competitors in the industry. Under monopolistic competition, however, if the product is differentiated, the concept of an industry becomes necessarily vague. Each competitor is producing a somewhat unique product. He competes in varying degree with *all* other firms in the economy, and the competitiveness of technologically similar products has no peculiar significance that justifies theoretical analysis of particular equilibrium for the "industry." "In the general pure theory of value, the group and the industry are useless concepts."[49] It is urged, therefore, that attention be directed immediately to the problem of general equilibrium. Interdependence in selling should be measured simply by the cross-elasticities of demand, without regard to the technological similarities to be discerned among products.

Since, however, different brands or makes of the same "commodity" in general do compete with one another somewhat more closely than do different commodities, there appears to be empirical justification for retaining the concept of the industry, very much as Chamberlin has, as a highly flexible tool, and for continuing to employ a form of particular equilibrium analysis in monopolistic competition theory. Retention of the concept of the industry need in no way impede progress in the development of a general equilibrium approach such as Triffin urged, but which, thus far at least, has not proved particularly fruitful.

(2) "The theory of oligopoly has been aptly described as a ticket of admission to institutional economics."[50] One important development in the literature of oligopoly theory in recent years has been the increased emphasis given to the institutional aspects of the problem.[51] The stage of

[48] R. Triffin, *op. cit.*, pp. 78–108.
[49] *Ibid.*, p. 89.
[50] E. S. Mason, "Price and Production Policies of Large-Scale Enterprise," *American Economic Review*, March 1939, Proceedings, XXIX, pp. 64–65.
[51] For example, M. Abramovitz, "Monopolistic Selling in a Changing Economy," *Quarterly Journal of Economics*, February 1938, LII, pp. 191–214; E. S. Mason, *op. cit.*, pp. 61–74; J. M. Clark, "Toward a Concept of Workable Competition," *loc. cit.*, pp. 241–256; W. H. Nicholls, *A Theoretical Analysis of Imperfect Competition with Special Application to the Agricultural Industries* (Ames, 1941), Ch. 4–11.

development of the industry will to some extent determine entrepreneurs' knowledge of market conditions, the probable reactions to be expected from rival enterprises, and in general the intensity of competition. The different sizes of firms in the industry, the motivation of those in control (whether they are ambitious to expand their share of the market, or are content to let sleeping dogs lie), and the existence or lack of price leadership are other circumstances that have to be taken into account. Facilities for the spread of knowledge of the market may be a stabilizing element, reducing discrimination or price-cutting. In general, the tendency has been to recognize that each oligopolistic industry is to some extent unique, and not too much is to be gained from the multiplication of theoretical models.

It has also been suggested that the traditional approach to oligopoly makes a mistake in assuming that the firm necessarily seeks only to maximize profit. Other equally important objectives may necessitate a compromise with the profit objective. For example, the entrepreneur may be equally motivated by a desire for "security."[52] Furthermore, oligopoly theory must take into account the struggle for position that is constantly taking place, or threatening to take place. "To write a short manual on the *Principles of Oligopolistic War* would be a very important attempt towards a new approach to this aspect of price theory; . . ."[53]

As to the theoretical models that have been developed on the assumption that the firm does seek to maximize profits, the principal basis for classification has been the reaction which A expects from B as a result of what A does, not only as to price, but also as to the technological quality of his product, his outlay for selling efforts, and other circumstances pertaining to his product. Whatever the reaction of B assumed by A, further classification may be based on whether A's forecast of B's reaction is assumed to be correct or not. The classic Cournot and Bertrand models were based respectively on two different assumptions as to B's reactions to A's price policy, but in neither case was B's reaction in fact the one expected by A. These models, and others like them, involve of necessity a form of sequence analysis of which there obviously could be a large number of variations. During the period under review, not very much has been added to the analysis of this type of case.[54]

---

[52] K. W. Rothschild, "Price Theory and Oligopoly," *Economic Journal*, September 1947, LVII, pp. 299–320.

[53] *Ibid.*, p. 307. Reference should also be made, although no more than a reference is possible in spite of its importance, to the new approach to the analysis of oligopoly suggested by J. von Neumann and O. Morgenstern, *Theory of Games and Economic Behavior* (Princeton, 1944).

[54] Mention should be made, however, of A. Smithies, "Equilibrium in Monopolistic Competition," *Quarterly Journal of Economics*, November 1940, LV, pp. 95–115.

Much more attention has been directed to the type of model in which it is assumed that each oligopolist is, with somewhat more sophistication, capable of correctly anticipating the reactions of his rivals to his price policy. One such case, developed previously to the kinked demand curve cases, is that of the industry in which each producer correctly assumes that his rivals would match any price cut. If the cost functions of the rivals are assumed to be equal, the outcome is the monopoly price.[55]

By far the most attention, however, has been given to the case in which each enterprise conceives its sales curve to be obtusely kinked, with the consequence that its marginal revenue curve is discontinuous. In Figure 2, the case is illustrated by the sales curve DD'D", and the correspond-ing marginal revenue curve MQRM'.[56] On the assumption that the enterprise seeks to maximize its profit, it is in equilibrium at the current price XD' as long as the marginal cost curve cuts the marginal revenue curve at any point within the range of discontinuity. Hence the price XD' is likely to be very stable.[57]

An increase in demand for the product is likely to result in the upper part of the demand curve becoming less elastic and the lower part more elastic, since the firms will now be operating more nearly at capacity.[58] Hence the range of discontinuity will be reduced. The reverse will occur in a period of declining demand.

The kink may under certain circumstances temporarily disappear. If, for instance, there should occur a general increase in wage rates or mate-rials cost, affecting the whole industry, it might appear at first sight as though the consequent upward shift in the short-run supply schedule might not alter selling price and output, provided that the supply sched-ule continued to cut the marginal revenue curve within the zone of dis-continuity. If, however, the increase in costs is *general* for the whole in-dustry, the enterprise will now no longer regard the upper part of its sales

---

[55] M. Abramovitz, *op. cit.*, pp. 193–195; G. J. Stigler, "Notes on the Theory of Duopoly," *Journal of Political Economy*, August 1940, XLVIII, pp. 528–530. Other assumptions are involved, including probably the implicit assumption that each producer correctly anticipates that his rivals would also meet any price increase. The case in which the cost functions are not equal has also been considered by T. Kristensen, "A Note on Duopoly," *Review of Economic Studies*, October 1938, VI, pp. 56–59, and by Stigler, *loc. cit.*

[56] Above, p. 8.

[57] It has been suggested that the concept of the obtusely kinked sales curve is useful in the explanation of price rigidity, and in the analysis of the effects of open price agree-ments, cutthroat competition, and industrial racketeering. M. Bronfenbrenner, "Applica-tions of the Discontinuous Oligopoly Demand Curve," *Journal of Political Economy*, June 1940, XLVIII, pp. 420–427. See also G. J. Stigler, "The Kinky Oligopoly Demand Curve and Rigid Prices," *loc. cit.*, pp. 432–449.

[58] P. M. Sweezy, *op. cit.*, p. 571.

curve to be relatively elastic, since it will now expect other concerns to follow a price increase.[59] For the period of readjustment, the concern thinks of its sales curve as continuous and unkinked; but immediately the upward adjustment of price for the industry has been completed, the concern will revert to thinking in terms of a kinked sales curve, the kink now occurring of course at the new price.

The analysis does not appear reversible. If, in a period of depression for example, a decrease in wages or materials cost should occur, the enterprise is likely to resist downward revision of selling price since it will continue to think in terms of an inelastic sales curve with respect to lower prices on the assumption that other enterprises will promptly follow price cuts.[60] Price discrimination, particularly in the form of secret price concessions, may gradually bring about price reduction on a more general scale. Or the reduction of the prices of closely competitive commodities may finally necessitate a general reduction of prices in the industry.

A somewhat different type of model is concerned with the case in which each producer assumes that his rivals will insist on maintaining their respective "shares of the market."[61] If it is assumed that the cost functions are equal, the outcome must be the monopoly price. If marginal costs differ, the lower-cost firms may set slightly lower prices than the higher-cost firms. If the different firms' conceptions of their shares of the market add up to more than the total output that can be disposed of at the prices set, the situation is rendered unstable.

In the case of differentiated products, uniformity of price is not so likely to be the outcome as in the case of homogeneous commodities. In addition to price and output, variations in quality of product, selling costs, and other manifestations of non-price competition are involved in the process of reaching equilibrium for the industry. The most interesting contributions have been those which have taken differences in location of the enterprises constituting an industry as representative of differentiation of product.

The starting point for most of this sort of analysis is Hotelling's early article on the subject.[62] His analysis was devoted to a hypothetical community of consumers equally distributed along a straight line and each

---

[59] L. G. Reynolds, "Relations between Wage Rates, Costs, and Prices," *American Economic Review*, March 1942, Proceedings, XXXII, pp. 276–281; also in *Readings in the Theory of Income Distribution*, pp. 296–302.

[60] *Ibid.*, p. 280.

[61] G. J. Stigler, "Notes on the Theory of Duopoly," *loc. cit.*, pp. 530–531.

[62] H. Hotelling, "Stability in Competition," *Economic Journal*, March 1929, XXXIX, pp. 41–57.

having a perfectly inelastic demand per time unit for one unit of the commodity produced by two enterprises, A and B. The cost of transportation per unit of distance is constant, the cost of production per unit is also constant (at zero), and transport costs are paid by the buyer. The location of A being determined before B comes on the scene, B assumes that A will not change his location, and that A's price policy will be unaffected by the price which B charges.

Hotelling's case was remote from reality, but it has provided a point of departure for a number of writers who have successively brought the assumptions more nearly into accordance with the situation actually confronting a small number of concerns competing spatially in the sale of a commodity.[63] In particular, the introduction of a negatively inclined demand schedule for the commodity at each point in the linear market, recognition of the ability of each competitor to move his location at will, and consideration of various more likely price policies on the part of the rival concerns have made possible considerable improvements in the analysis. Further variations in the fundamental assumptions have produced a considerable number of models that collectively contribute substantially to an understanding of the complexities of oligopoly and monopolistic competition under conditions of differentiation of product. It is clear that the existence of transportation costs alone is sufficient to render competition less than pure. Furthermore the level of transportation costs has much to do with determining the spatial distribution of firms and the level of mill prices relative to cost of production. Even though the prices are quoted f.o.b. mill, there may be considerable freight absorption by the rival producers. If, however, each producer absorbs the whole of the freight to his customers within a given area (if, that is, prices are quoted on a free delivery basis), the pattern of distribution of the firms will be quite different. The analysis is not essentially affected by varying the assumption with regard to cost of production, whether marginal costs are assumed to rise or to fall with increases in output; but the assumption of different cost functions for the different concerns will result in different prices f.o.b. mill. The introduction of quality differentiation (in addition to spatial differentiation) and discrimination tends to increase scale of plant and to reduce

---

[63] Some of the more recent contributions: A. P. Lerner and H. W. Singer, "Some Notes on Duopoly and Spatial Competition," *Journal of Political Economy*, April 1937, XLV, pp. 145–186; M. A. Copeland, "Competing Products and Monopolistic Competition," *Quarterly Journal of Economics*, November 1940, LV, pp. 1–35; A. Smithies, "Optimum Location in Spatial Competition," *Journal of Political Economy*, June 1941, XLIX, pp. 423–439; W. A. Lewis, "Competition in Retail Trade," *Economica*, November 1945, XII, pp. 202–234.

monopoly profits.[64] In addition to throwing considerable light on the theory of location of industry and the effects of spatial differentiation upon price and output, the analysis has provided an approach to the examination of basing-point systems.[65]

(3) The theory of bilateral monopoly has reference to the situation in which a monopolistic seller confronts a monopsonistic buyer. The theory has focused attention mainly on three supposedly distinct types of case, which may be briefly summarized with reference to Figure 3.

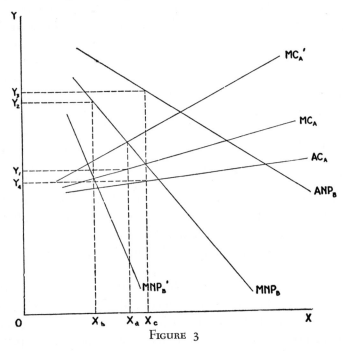

FIGURE 3

In the first case, the seller (A) is relatively weak, with the result that the buyer (B) fixes the price (OY_1) so that it is equal to A's marginal cost or supply price (shown by MC_A) for that amount sold (OX_a) for which the *increment* in supply price (shown by MC_A') is equal to B's marginal net product for this same amount of raw material purchased. (At the output OX_a, MC_A' intersects MNP_B. The supply price for this output, as shown by MC_A, is OY_1.)

[64] Copeland has paid particular attention to this case. He has also stressed the point that brand and quality competition are not precisely analogous to spatial competition. *Op. cit.*, pp. 17–28.

[65] See, for example, A. Smithies, "Aspects of the Basing-Point System," *American Economic Review*, December 1942, XXXII, pp. 705–726; V. A. Mund, "Monopolistic Competition Theory and Public Price Policy," *ibid.*, pp. 727–743; J. M. Clark, "Imperfect Competition Theory and Basing-Point Problems," *ibid.*, June 1943, XXXIII, pp. 283–300.

In the second case, the buyer is relatively weak, with the result that the seller (A) fixes the price (OY_2) so that it is equal to B's marginal net product for that amount of raw material purchased (OX_b) whose *increment* in marginal net product (shown by MNP_B') is equal to the seller's supply price (shown by MC_A).

In the third case, A and B are conceived to maximize their combined profits, the amount of raw material which changes hands being that amount (OX_c) for which A's marginal cost is equal to the marginal net product to B (i.e., the amount of X shown by the intersection of MC_A and MNP_B). The price paid would be indeterminate between OY_3, equal to the average net product of OX_c for B, and OY_4, equal to A's average cost for the amount sold.[66]

The first and second cases have generally been regarded as limiting cases, between which most actual situations of different degrees of relative bargaining power may be expected to fall. Leontief and Fellner, however, have drawn attention to the fact that either B, in the first case, or A, in the second case, could push his advantage still further by determining the quantity to be exchanged, on an all or nothing basis, as well as the price. In the first case, the result would be that B would fix the amount to be purchased at OX_c (on an all or nothing basis), and the price at OY_4, thus reducing A's profit to zero. In the second case, A would fix the amount to be sold at OX_c (on an all or nothing basis) and the price at OY_3, thus reducing B's profit to zero.[67]

It now becomes clear, as Fellner has pointed out, that what we really have is the third case; the first two cases do not appear to be genuine cases at all. Unless there should be some institutional obstacle which would prevent an all or nothing contract, both parties would gain by moving from the first or the second situation to the third, in which output would be increased and the joint profit maximized.[68] In the case of product markets there does not appear to be any such institutional obstacle, and consequently it is not likely that either of the first two cases will be found in these markets. Bilateral monopoly tends to establish

---

[66] The three cases have been summarized by G. Tintner, "Note on the Problem of Bilateral Monopoly," *Journal of Political Economy*, April 1939, XLVII, pp. 263–267; and W. Fellner, "Prices and Wages under Bilateral Monopoly," *Quarterly Journal of Economics*, August 1947, LXI, pp. 503–509. Both authors provide bibliographies of the earlier literature on the subject. In addition to the diagrams to be found in these two articles, ingenious diagrams have been developed by A. M. Henderson, "A Further Note on the Problem of Bilateral Monopoly," *Journal of Political Economy*, April 1940, XLVIII, pp. 238–243; and A. J. Nichol, "Monopoly Supply and Monopsony Demand," *ibid.*, December 1942, L, pp. 861–879.

[67] W. Leontief, "The Pure Theory of the Guaranteed Annual Wage Contract," *Journal of Political Economy*, February 1946, LIV, pp. 77–79; W. Fellner, *op. cit.*, pp. 506, 512–516.

[68] W. Fellner, *op. cit.*, pp. 524–528,

output at the level which maximizes the joint profit, the price paid by the monopsonistic buyer being indeterminate between two limits, the upper of which would eliminate profit for the buyer, the lower of which would eliminate profit for the seller.[69]

GENERAL EQUILIBRIUM

A revival of interest in analysis of the general equilibrium of the economy is largely to be credited to J. R. Hicks.[70] His contribution has been of some importance simply because he was willing to develop his analysis in a form accessible to the non-mathematical economist. Much more important, however, is the fact that he brought together in a single systematic treatment the theory of general equilibrium under static conditions and the analysis of the economy under dynamic conditions. This has been called "one of the most important achievements of modern economics."[71]

In fact, Hicks' interest in the analysis of general equilibrium under static conditions was primarily as a point of departure for the study of the instability which characterizes the dynamic economy. It is not surprising therefore that his principal contribution to static general equilibrium theory is his examination of the conditions necessary for the stability of the system.

There are several self-imposed limitations upon the analysis: (1) he assumes an economy in which competition is pure; (2) he abstracts from State interference in economic affairs; and (3) he abstracts from capital and interest, saving and investment, and speculation.[72] The third of these limitations is dropped in the later analysis of the dynamic economy.

Four markets are involved: (1) the market for products; (2) the market for factors; (3) the market for direct services; and (4) the market for intermediate products. In each case, Hicks recognizes that, if stability exists at all, it may be either perfect or imperfect stability. A market is perfectly stable if a fall in price below equilibrium results in an excess of demand over supply at the new price even after all other prices in the system have been readjusted to the new price. A market is imperfectly stable if a fall in price below equilibrium results

---

[69] Applications of the theory of bilateral monopoly to the wage bargain will be considered below, pp. 34–36.

[70] *Value and Capital*, Ch. 4, 5, 8.

[71] L. A. Metzler, "Stability of Multiple Markets: The Hicks Conditions," *Econometrica*, October 1945, XIII, p. 277.

[72] J. R. Hicks, *Value and Capital*, pp. 99–100. M. W. Reder has discussed the stability conditions under circumstances in which competition is not pure: "Monopolistic Competition and the Stability Conditions," *Review of Economic Studies*, February 1941, VIII, pp. 122–125.

in an excess of demand over supply at the new price *only after* all other prices have been readjusted to the new price.[73] In the former case, the market for a single commodity is not only stable taken by itself, but this stability is not disturbed by repercussions from changes in other prices resulting from a change in the price of the first commodity. In the latter case, the market for the first commodity is not stable taken by itself, but it is rendered stable by the repercussions from changes in other prices induced by the change in the price of the first commodity.

In the case of the market for products, Hicks' analysis led him to the conclusion that, if the market for a commodity was stable taken by itself, it was unlikely to be rendered unstable by repercussions from other price changes. Furthermore, the only element likely to render the market for a commodity unstable, taken by itself, was the income effect of the fall in price, and this was unlikely to be sufficiently important to affect stability in the case of products markets.[74] With regard to the case of imperfect stability, he was inclined to doubt whether the market for a commodity, unstable by itself, would be rendered stable by repercussions from other markets, although conceivably a large income effect in related markets might have this effect.[75] On the whole, he was inclined to conclude that a multiple product market was likely to be perfectly stable.

Of the other three types of market, the market for direct services behaves similarly to the market for products. Markets for intermediate products involve no income effects, and are therefore even more likely to be perfectly stable than markets for products and direct services. In the case of factor markets, however, such as the labor market, there is likely to be a considerable income effect in addition to the substitution effect of a fall in price, and this income effect may be a source of instability. Other stabilizing elements in the system, however, are probably more than adequate to offset such unstabilizing income effects as may exist.[76]

Hicks reasoned that if each individual market could be presumed to be stable, the whole complex of markets constituting the economic system would also be stable. This inference has been seriously criticized

---

[73] J. R. Hicks, *Value and Capital*, p. 67.

[74] A second source of instability, "extreme complementarity," was stressed in *Value and Capital*, but Hicks has since concluded that this part of his analysis was erroneous. See his "Consumers' Surplus and Index Numbers," *loc. cit.*, p. 133, note; and his "Recent Contributions to General Equilibrium Economics," *Economica*, November 1945, XII, p. 236.

[75] *Idem, Value and Capital*, p. 72.

[76] *Ibid.*, p. 103. A good summary of Hicks' analysis of the conditions of stability is to be found in F. Machlup, "Professor Hicks' Statics," *Quarterly Journal of Economics*, February 1940, LIV, pp. 284–293. See also O. Lange, *Price Flexibility and Employment*, pp. 91–109; and J. L. Mosak, *General-Equilibrium Theory in International Trade*, Ch. 2.

by Samuelson, and later by Metzler.[77] Metzler has summarized the criticism as follows:

> It cannot be assumed, as in the Hicks analysis, that when the price of one commodity is out of equilibrium the prices of all other commodities are either unchanged or are instantaneously adjusted to their new equilibria. For this reason, the Hicks stability conditions cannot be accepted unless it is shown that they are related to the stability of a true dynamic system. The errors of the Hicks method were first demonstrated by Samuelson in his pioneer article on the significance of dynamics to static analysis. It was there shown that imperfect stability, in the Hicks sense, is neither a necessary nor a sufficient condition for true dynamic stability. An example was given of a dynamic system which was unstable despite the fact that it was imperfectly stable in the Hicks sense. Another example was given of a system which was dynamically stable even though it was neither perfectly nor imperfectly stable according to Professor Hicks's definitions. In a later note, Professor Samuelson demonstrated that even perfect stability is insufficient to insure true dynamic stability under all circumstances.[78]

The criticism appears sound, and leads directly to the conclusion that the analysis of the stability conditions of equilibrium can only properly proceed as a part of the development of a dynamic economics.[79]

II. Distribution Theory

Distribution theory continued to be limited in the main to analysis of the determinants of the *per unit rate* of remuneration of the factors of production. Although such analysis should contribute to an understanding of the determinants of the corresponding functional *shares* of the national income, little progress is to be reported with respect to this higher stage of distribution analysis. The impact of the work of Keynes and his followers, however, may in time have the effect of directing more attention to this latter problem.

The concept of marginal productivity has continued to play a prominent part in the structure of distribution theory. It has, however, been subjected to vigorous attack with respect to its usefulness in the explanation of the demand for labor. Furthermore, proponents of the liquidity preference doctrine of interest do not regard the marginal productivity of capital as a determinant of the interest rate, although they do attribute

---

[77] P. A. Samuelson, "The Stability of Equilibrium: Comparative Statics and Dynamics," *Econometrica*, April 1941, IX, pp. 111–112; *idem*, "The Relation Between Hicksian Stability and True Dynamic Stability," *ibid.*, July–October 1944, XII, pp. 256–257; L. A. Metzler, *op. cit.*, p. 279.

[78] L. A. Metzler, *loc. cit.*

[79] Thus Lange considers the effect upon stability of the economy of the relative speeds of adjustment in the different markets. O. Lange, *op. cit.*, pp. 94–99. Cf. also L. A. Metzler, *op. cit.*, pp. 279–285.

to it the role of determining the amount of investment, given the rate of interest.

It is with respect to distribution theory rather than value theory that the impact of Keynesian doctrine has been important. The liquidity preference theory of interest is a case in point. Another closely related case is Keynes' treatment of saving. Economists already had had some doubts about the reliability of the concept of a positively inclined supply schedule of savings, treated as identical with the supply schedule of capital. Keynes strengthened those doubts, and gained general acceptance for the view that the relation between the rate of savings and the rate of flow of income is a more reliable relation, and probably a more useful one as well. The general theory of employment has also brought home to the economist the fact that the demand for labor, in the complex market in which the structure of wages is determined, depends in part upon the level of income which depends in part upon the level of employment, which is one of the variables supposed to be determined by the demand and supply of labor. So the determination of wages cannot be isolated from the numerous variables responsible for the determination of the level of employment and income. Finally, Keynes' work provided an important stimulus to more careful examination of the behavior of real and money wage rates in the short run or the business cycle.

The theory of rent has received relatively little attention. The tendency has been to associate both rent and profit with the working of the dynamic economy. A few contributions of genuine merit during the past decade may be credited with producing some progress toward clarification of the concept of profit, of the entrepreneurial function, and of the relation between the two.

Reference was made, at the beginning of this section, to the fact that little attention has been given, as yet, to the problem of the determinants of the proportion of the national product going to each of the functional shares. There are two contributions, however, which should receive mention. Kalecki undertook, on a rather fragile statistical basis, to investigate the relative share of manual labor in the national income.[80] He arrived at the conclusion that the relative share of manual labor tends to be affected adversely by (1) an increase in the (Lerner) degree of monopoly,[81] and (2) an increase in raw material prices relative to the

---

[80] M. Kalecki, "The Distribution of the National Income," *Essays in the Theory of Economic Fluctuations* (London, 1939), pp. 13–41. Cf. an earlier version of the same article, "The Determinants of Distribution of the National Income," *Econometrica,* April 1938, VI, pp. 97–112.

[81] The degree of monopoly, according to Lerner, is the ratio of price *minus* marginal cost to price. If marginal cost is equal to marginal revenue, the degree of monopoly is

wages bill, and *vice versa*.[82] Although it is not difficult to believe that these are important determinants of the proportion of wage income to total national income, the analysis is certainly far from satisfactory, as Kalecki would probably be the first to agree.[83]

With particular regard to the proportion of wages to income paid out in the short run (over the cycle), Dunlop has found that the ratio varied considerably from year to year in the period 1919–37. His analysis of the reasons for these variations stressed: "(a) extent of fluctuation in output, (b) the shape of the short-run labor cost function, (c) the relative price movements of variable factors and the possibilities of short-run substitution, (d) impact of the absolute fluctuation in variable factor prices on product prices, (e) the magnitude of technical change, and (f) the elasticity of product demand for the enterprise."[84]

THEORY OF WAGES

THE DEMAND FOR LABOR. (1) The utilization of the marginal productivity theory for the development of a systematic theory of exploitation under conditions of monopoly and monopsony has been followed by some further contributions in this same area. Defining exploitation as "the payment to labor of a wage less than its marginal revenue product," Bloom has turned up several types of exploitation in addition to those earlier developed.[85] First, there is the situation in which it is costly to change price, perhaps because of the additional advertising expense that would be involved in informing prospective buyers of the change. Under these circumstances a fall in wages may not be followed by any change in price unless the new rate of wages is below the marginal revenue product

---

the reciprocal of the elasticity of demand. A. P. Lerner, "The Concept of Monopoly and the Measurement of Monopoly Power," *Review of Economic Studies*, June 1934, I, pp. 157–175.

[82] See also M. Kalecki, "A Theory of Long-Run Distribution of the Product of Industry," *Oxford Economic Papers*, June 1941, No. 5, pp. 31–41, in which he considers the determinants of the proportion of wages to value added by an industry. The principal ones operative in the long run are: utilization of equipment, ratio of average wage to material cost, "quantitative and qualitative divergencies in the investment activity of various firms," changes in technique, degree of monopoly, degree of oligopoly, and the rate of prime selling cost.

[83] In addition to other criticisms of Kalecki's analysis, J. T. Dunlop points out that the part played by the degree of monopoly cannot properly be considered "causal," since the degree of monopoly is defined as the gap between price and marginal labor costs expressed as a ratio to price, and the proportion of the value product going to labor is the ratio of labor cost to price. J. T. Dunlop, *Wage Determination under Trade Unions* (New York, 1944), p. 187, note.

[84] *Ibid.*, pp. 176, 187.

[85] G. F. Bloom, "A Reconsideration of the Theory of Exploitation," *Quarterly Journal of Economics*, May 1941, LV, pp. 413–442; also in *Readings in the Theory of Income Distribution*, pp. 245–277.

by more than the cost of changing price. The case would appear limited to the mature oligopoly not confronted by a strong union, and Bloom therefore concludes that this type of exploitation will tend to disappear.

Second, there is the case in which labor receives less than its marginal revenue product because the firm is confronted by a discontinuous demand and marginal revenue curve for its product. If the marginal cost curve cuts the marginal revenue curve within the latter's discontinuous range (QR in Figure 2, p. 8) this means that the rate of wages is less than the marginal revenue product, and exploitation exists.[86]

(2) Hicks' classification of inventions, it will be recalled, was based upon the effect of the invention upon the ratio of the marginal productivities of the factors (labor and capital), the amounts of the factors assumed unchanged.[87] A labor-saving invention was one the effect of which was to increase the marginal product of capital relative to that of labor; a capital-saving invention had the reverse effect, and a neutral invention had no effect upon the ratio between the marginal productivities of labor and capital.

Mrs. Robinson has made the point that the ultimate effect of an invention upon the relative shares of labor and capital depends not only on the immediate effect of the invention upon the relative marginal productivities of the factors but also upon the elasticity of substitution which prevails as, for example, the supply of capital increases relative to the supply of labor in order to restore equilibrium in the capital market.[88] Thus the immediate effect of a labor-saving invention may be to increase the marginal productivity of capital relative to that of labor, and thus to increase the relative share of capital. If the rate of interest is assumed constant, the rise in the marginal productivity of capital, however, will presumably result in an increase in investment. The increase in the amount of capital relative to the amount of labor will now further change the relative marginal productivities of the two factors. If the elasticity of substitution is less than unity, for example, the increase in the ratio of capital to labor will tend to reduce the ratio of the marginal productivity of capital to that of labor and thus tend to offset the initial adverse effect of the labor-saving invention upon the share of labor.

---

[86] This case was earlier discussed by R. F. Mikesell, "Oligopoly and the Short-Run Demand for Labor," *Quarterly Journal of Economics*, November 1940, LV, pp. 161–166. It is also interesting to note in passing that the concept of the kinked demand curve inspired M. Bronfenbrenner to develop a correspondingly kinked *supply* curve for labor under conditions of oligopsony and a highly conventional wage structure. See his "Applications of the Discontinuous Oligopoly Demand Curve," *loc. cit.*, pp. 426–427.

[87] J. R. Hicks, *The Theory of Wages* (London, 1932), pp. 121–130.

[88] J. Robinson, *Essays in the Theory of Employment* (London, 1937), pp. 132–136.

Mrs. Robinson is thus led to suggest a classification of inventions slightly different from Hicks'.[89] If the *ultimate* effect of an invention is to leave the relative shares unchanged, the rate of interest being assumed constant, the invention is a neutral one; if the ultimate effect is to increase the share of capital, the invention is a capital-saving one; in the reverse case, it is a labor-saving one.[90]

G. F. Bloom has reported upon a series of field surveys on the nature of invention, and has offered some comments with regard to Hicks' analysis of the invention process.[91] Hicks had, in addition to his classification of inventions considered by Mrs. Robinson, a further classification into "induced" and "autonomous" inventions, the former being the result of a change in the relative prices of the factors.[92] Bloom's survey of business experience with inventions convinced him: (1) that relatively few inventions fit Hicks' definition of an induced invention; (2) that most labor-saving inventions are to be explained, not by *changes* in relative factor prices, as Hicks had maintained, but by the persistently high price of labor, and that this is the principal reason for the predominance of labor-saving inventions; (3) that, contrary to Hicks, the *very* labor-saving invention (which would have been profitable even without any change in relative factor prices, and which may result in a reduction of the absolute share of labor) is probably quite common; and (4) that, if sufficient time is permitted to elapse for the full effect of an invention to be obtained, the ultimate result will almost always be an increase in the real wage of labor, even though the initial effect is a reduction in the absolute share of labor.

O. Lange has considered the total effect of an innovation (he employs this term rather than invention) on the marginal cost of output and the marginal physical productivity of the input planned for the whole current or future period which the firm takes into consideration.[93] Thus he has output-neutral, output-increasing, or output-decreasing innovations on

---

[89] *Idem*, "The Classification of Inventions," *Review of Economic Studies*, February 1938, V, pp. 139–142; also in *Readings in the Theory of Income Distribution*, pp. 175–180.

[90] Alternatively, she defines a neutral invention as one which leaves the ratio of capital to product (the average productivity of capital) unchanged, after capital has increased in response to the initial increase in the marginal productivity of capital. A capital-saving invention is one which reduces the average productivity of capital; and a labor-saving invention is the opposite. The same definitions are also formulated in terms of the effect upon the elasticity of the average productivity curve for capital.

[91] G. F. Bloom, "A Note on Hicks's Theory of Invention," *American Economic Review*, March 1946, XXXVI, pp. 83–96.

[92] J. R. Hicks, *The Theory of Wages*, p. 125.

[93] O. Lange, "A Note on Innovations," *Review of Economic Statistics*, February 1943, XXV, pp. 19–25; also in *Readings in the Theory of Income Distribution*, pp. 181–196. Cf. also *idem*, *Price Flexibility and Employment*, Ch. 12.

the basis of the effect upon marginal cost, and factor-neutral, factor-using, and factor-saving innovations on the basis of the effect of the innovation upon the demand for input factors. An innovation may at the same time be output-increasing and factor-saving, etc., with regard to all factors at all dates. A special case which he considers, however, is the oligopoly case in which the demand curve is kinked. Only innovations which reduce marginal cost greatly would have the effect of increasing output, since the marginal cost curve would have to be lowered sufficiently to fall below the range of discontinuity in the marginal revenue curve.[94] Hence oligopoly exerts a selective effect in favor of factor-saving innovations, and against output-increasing innovations, except when the latter may *greatly* reduce marginal cost.

(3) For very much the same reasons that doubts have been raised about the assumption that management seeks to equate marginal cost and marginal revenue, the part played by marginal productivity in the analysis of the demand for labor has been subjected to severe criticism.[95] Lester, in the survey of business men's opinions mentioned earlier,[96] obtained answers from fifty-six firms as to the circumstances they regarded as most important in determining the number of individuals they respectively employed. Of the various circumstances suggested (market demand, wage rates, non-labor costs, profits, production techniques), market demand was selected as the *only* circumstance by half the firms, and it was given heavy weight by all of the others. Very little weight was given to "the level of wage rates or changes in the level of wage rates." Lester therefore concludes that most employers do not think of their demand for labor as a function of the wage rate, as the marginal productivity approach to the demand for labor would appear to imply, but rather as a function of expected sales.[97] One reason, he suggests, that business men do not respond to an increase in wage rates by curtailing employment is that they associate a reduction in output with an increase in variable cost per unit, as mentioned earlier.[98] Another reason is that,

---

[94] Cf. Figure 2, above, p. 8. Lange also considers the case of monopsony in which the supply curve of the factor is kinked. Cf. above, p. 29. In this case, factor-neutral innovations would be favored, because of the range of discontinuity in the marginal expenditure curve.

[95] R. A. Lester, "Shortcomings of Marginal Analysis for Wage-Employment Problems," *loc. cit.,* pp. 63–82; *idem,* "Marginalism, Minimum Wages, and Labor Markets," *loc. cit.,* pp. 135–148.

[96] Above, pp. 12–13.

[97] Machlup points to defects in Lester's questionnaire. He also quite rightly observes that the items, "market demand," "non-labor costs," "production techniques," are all elements affecting marginal productivity. F. Machlup, "Marginal Analysis and Empirical Research," *loc. cit.,* pp. 548–550.

[98] Above, pp. 12–13.

under existing techniques of production, the extent to which capital can be substituted for labor in a given enterprise is ordinarily very limited. He finds support for his conclusions in a study of the answers of forty-three southern firms to a question as to their probable reaction to an increase in their wage rates relative to those paid by competitors in other areas. Of the various possible reactions from which respondents might choose, the most frequently mentioned were improvements in efficiency through better management, incentives, etc., and the introduction of labor-saving machinery. "Reduce production by deliberately curtailing output" was mentioned by only four.[99]

(4) It is interesting to note that critics of the marginal productivity approach as well as its defenders made no reference to the considerable number of statistical studies of production as a function of the relative quantities of capital and labor, fathered mainly by Douglas and authors associated with him, that have continued to appear over the last decade.[100] One possible reason is the fact that these studies have been rather severely criticized with respect to the quality of data available, the statistical methods employed, and particularly the interpretation of the results.

THE LABOR MARKET. The most important institutional influence on the supply of labor, and thus on wage rates, comes from the organization of labor. It has been argued by some that existing wage theory is almost completely inadequate in the face of the complexities of the present-day labor market.[101] Contributions to the analysis of the part played by union organizations in the determination of wage rates have been made, however, with respect to the following types of labor market situation: (1) the open shop industry in which there is no employer discrimination; (2)

---

[99] In addition to differing with Lester as to the extent to which the proportion of factors can be altered, even in an enterprise already built, Machlup points out that, when competition is not pure, the firm's reaction to an increase in wage rates frequently will be, not a "deliberate" decrease in output, but an increase in price to a level at which, as it turns out, the quantity that can be sold is reduced. Hence the low score given to deliberate curtailment is not of any significance. On the other hand, the high scores given to the introduction of labor-saving machinery and to price-product changes are quite consistent with the marginal productivity approach. F. Machlup, *op. cit.*, pp. 552–553. See also Lester's reply, "Marginalism, Minimum Wages, and Labor Markets," *loc. cit.*, pp. 135–142. See also G. J. Stigler, "Professor Lester and the Marginalists," *American Economic Review*, March 1947, XXXVII, pp. 154–157.

[100] M. L. Handsaker and P. H. Douglas, "The Theory of Marginal Productivity Tested by Data for Manufacturing in Victoria," *Quarterly Journal of Economics*, November 1937 and February 1938, LII, pp. 1–36, 215–254; P. H. Douglas and G. Gunn, "Further Measurements of Marginal Productivity," *ibid.*, May 1940, LIV, pp. 399–428; and numerous others.

[101] For example, R. A. Lester, "Reflections on the 'Labor Monopoly' Issue," *Journal of Political Economy*, December 1947, LV, p. 513; A. M. Ross, "The Dynamics of Wage Determination under Collective Bargaining," *American Economic Review*, December 1947, XXXVII, pp. 793–798.

the closed shop industry; (3) the situation in which there is employer discrimination against union labor; (4) the case of bilateral monopoly.[102]

(1) In the case of the open shop industry in which there is no employer discrimination against union labor, let it be assumed that the union seeks to set that wage rate that would maximize the income of its employed members (i.e., the area under the demand curve for union labor).[103] If it is further assumed that, since there is no discrimination, the demand for union labor at all wage rates is a fixed fraction of the total demand for labor, then the union's policy would maximize the income of *all* labor employed. If the rate of wages fixed by the union is above the equilibrium level that would prevail in the absence of union action, there will be unemployment which will be shared by union and non-union workers alike.

(2) If the union enforces a closed or preferential shop, its wage policy will be the same as before, but in addition it will seek to provide the total of those employed. In the case of the preferential shop, unemployment will be concentrated in the non-union group. In the case of the closed shop, the union may restrict membership to a number less than adequate to provide the employment which would maximize the income of labor, thus changing its policy to one of maximizing income per member.

(3) There are two kinds of employer discrimination against union labor: (a) the employer may give a preference to non-union workers at any given wage; (b) the employer may decrease the rate of wages he is willing to offer for any given quantity of labor when the labor is unionized, as compared with what he would be willing to offer for that quantity of labor if it were not unionized.[104] Both kinds may exist simultaneously. If the first kind of discrimination exists, the union cannot do better

---

[102] The first three are considered by M. Bronfenbrenner, "The Economics of Collective Bargaining," *Quarterly Journal of Economics*, August 1939, LIII, pp. 535–561; the fourth, by W. Fellner, "Prices and Wages under Bilateral Monopoly," *ibid.*, August 1947, LXI, pp. 503–532; cf. the same author's *Monetary Policies and Full Employment* (Berkeley, 1946), pp. 103–111.

[103] Dunlop has pointed out that unions may have many important objectives of wage policy other than the maximizing of income: e.g., the promotion of membership, the allocation of available work, control of the rate of introduction of technical innovations. J. T. Dunlop, "Wage Policies of Trade Unions," *American Economic Review*, March 1942, Proceeding, XXXII, pp. 290–294; also in *Readings in the Theory of Income Distribution*, pp. 336–341. See also *idem*, *Wage Determination under Trade Unions*, pp. 45–54.

[104] It is assumed that both kinds of labor are paid the same rate of wages, but since the employer thinks of the union worker as costing him more than the non-union worker (because union workers are "troublesome" in some sense), the marginal productivity of the union workers employed must, as an offset, be correspondingly higher than the uniform rate of wages.

than seek to maximize the area under the demand curve for union labor, which will now equal the demand curve for all labor minus, at each wage rate, the supply of non-union labor available at that wage rate. If the supply of union labor is a relatively high proportion of the total supply, the union may still be able to increase the income of its employed members by raising the wage rate above the equilibrium level. The full burden of any resulting unemployment, however, would be borne by the union membership.

The effect of the second kind of discrimination, if it is assumed that the supply of non-union labor is not adequate to satisfy the demand for labor at all wage rates, is to reduce the effective demand for labor below the level that would otherwise prevail, and thus to reduce both the quantity of employment and the rate of wages. The union may still raise the rate of wages above the equilibrium level, but the optimum employment (from the union's point of view) will be less than it would be in the absence of discrimination, to the detriment of both union and non-union workers.[105]

(4) When there is a strong union confronted by a single large employer or employers' association, the theory of bilateral monopoly is applicable.[106] The application of the theory to the labor market, however, differs from its application to a commodity market since in the case of a unionized supply of labor, the concept of a supply schedule is inappropriate.[107] It may be assumed, however, that there is some level of wages below which the union would not accept employment for its members; and it also may be assumed that the union, to an extent which varies, weighs against one another the advantage of higher wages for its members and the disadvantage of increased unemployment that may accompany higher wages.

Analogous to application of the theory to commodity markets, three cases may be considered: (a) The employer is sufficiently strong to fix the rate of wages. In this case the rate of wages may be fixed at the lowest level at which members of the union would be willing to accept employment.

(b) The union is sufficiently strong to fix the rate of wages. If it has no regard for the effect upon employment, it will fix the wage at OY_1, in Figure 4, equal to the maximum average net product of labor (ANP). A vague fear of unemployment may temper union policy, however, and

---

[105] Bronfenbrenner also considers the case in which union labor is paid a different wage from that paid non-union labor. *Op. cit.*, pp. 551–561.

[106] Cf. above, pp. 22–24. The analysis which follows is Fellner's.

[107] There are special circumstances, however, which Fellner considers, in which the supply schedule of labor is significant.

result in a wage rate somewhat lower. If it is union policy to give equal weight to wage rate and employment, the situation may be pictured by an indifference map, the indifference curves I_1, I_2, I_3, showing that wages and employment are to some degree substitutes for one another. Under these circumstances, the union will, if it is sufficiently strong, fix the wage rate at OY_2, the rate at which the marginal net product curve (MNP) is tangent to an indifference curve (I_2).

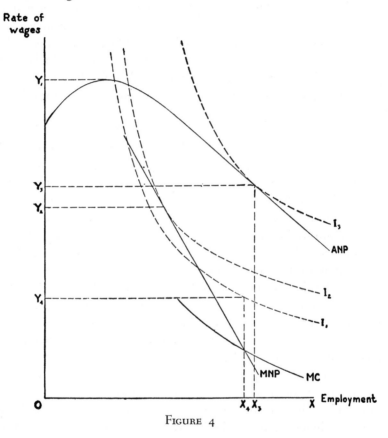

FIGURE 4

(c) As in the case of product markets, either of the two parties, if sufficiently strong, may push its advantage to the full by insisting not only on the most advantageous rate of wages but also on the most advantageous amount of employment, on an all or nothing basis. A case in point is the guaranteed annual wage contract.[108] If the union were the stronger party, it might insist on the wage rate OY_3 (indicated by the tangency of ANP to an indifference curve, I_3), at the same time requiring a guarantee

[108] Cf. W. Leontief, "The Pure Theory of the Guaranteed Annual Wage Contract," *loc. cit.*, pp. 76–79

of the corresponding amount of employment, OX_3. If, however, the employer were the stronger, he might drive the wage rate to the lowest possible indifference curve (any combination of wage rate and employment lying below this indifference curve being unacceptable to labor), which thus becomes, in a sense, the supply curve of labor as well as the average cost curve of labor to the employer. Let this lowest possible indifference curve be I_1, and let MC be drawn marginally to it, showing the marginal cost of labor to the employer. Then the employer will seek to equate the marginal cost of labor to his marginal net product. If he pushes his advantage to the full, he will require an amount of employment OX_4, on an all or nothing basis, at the wage rate OY_4. At this wage, the marginal cost of labor to the employer will be equal to his marginal net product for the amount of employment OX_4, and labor will be receiving its supply price for this same amount of employment.

It is clear that, as in the case of the all or nothing contract in a commodity market, this type of contract has advantages both for the union and the employer, provided that the union's indifference map is concave. From the point of view of the employer, however, there is a substantially increased risk involved in the fixed employment type of contract. Since the wage contract is likely to cover a considerable period, the disadvantage of the uncertainty involved may outweigh the bargaining advantage of the all or nothing type of contract. Similarly, from the point of view of the employees, the element of uncertainty for the employer in effect reduces the level of his marginal net product curve. Consequently there *may* be situations in which the union, even though it possesses the dominant position in the bargaining, would not find it to its advantage to insist on a contract that guaranteed a minimum volume of employment.

THE SHORT PERIOD. Mr. Keynes' treatment of the subject of wages in his *General Theory* was probably directly responsible for the exceedingly active discussion of short-run wage theory in the years that have followed.[109] There have really been two closely related branches to this discussion, one branch concerned with Mr. Keynes' assertion that, in general, as output increases or decreases, with given organization, equipment and technique, money wages will ordinarily also increase or decrease, but real wages will move in the opposite direction to money wages; the other

---

[109] J. M. Keynes, *The General Theory of Employment, Interest and Money*, pp. 5–17, 257–271. From the extended literature that has developed, the following are only a few of the contributions: A. C. Pigou, "Real and Money Wage Rates in Relation to Unemployment," *Economic Journal*, September 1937, XLVII, pp. 405–422; L. Tarshis, "Real Wages in the United States and Great Britain," *Canadian Journal of Economics and Political Science*, August 1938, IV, pp. 362–376; J. T. Dunlop, "The Movement of Real and Money Wage Rates," *Economic Journal*, September 1938, XLVIII, pp. 413–434; W. Fellner, *Monetary Policies and Full Employment*, pp. 94–103, 109–111.

branch concerned with the view that, subject to certain qualifications, "there may exist no expedient by which labour as a whole can reduce its *real* wage to a given figure by making revised *money* bargains with the entrepreneurs."[110]

The first of these two propositions clearly was based on the assumption that, with given organization, equipment, and technique, the supply curves of individual enterprises would be positively inclined in the short run, and the further assumption of pure competition. Under these circumstances, the increase in money wages that might ordinarily be expected to accompany an expansion in output would be more than matched by the increase in product prices, with the consequence that real wages would decline. The reverse sequence would apply in the case of a decrease in output.[111] The fact that real and money wages have not, in fact, behaved this way has suggested the necessity of modifying the underlying assumptions, and of taking into consideration circumstances not included in the Keynesian analysis. Out of this discussion there have emerged the following propositions with respect to the variables affecting real wages as output and money wages increase: (1) Money wages usually begin to rise while there is still considerable unemployment, and long before normal capacity output has been reached. On the other hand, marginal cost may be nearly constant for a considerable range of outputs and until peak production is approached. (2) There may be a decrease in the degree of monopsony as the business situation improves, as a result, for example, of increased strength of the unions. (3) As money wages rise there will tend to be, up to a point at least, an increase in the average productivity of labor. (4) The prices of factors other than labor that enter into variable cost may rise relatively slowly. (5) The degree of monopoly may decrease as business improves. All of these circumstances, if present, would affect real wages favorably as output increased, and might frequently more than offset the considerations that Keynes had in mind.[112]

Mr. Keynes' second proposition is the more important. It has reference to the effects of a policy of lowering money wages in a period of depression as a means of increasing employment.[113] On the assumption of pure

---

[110] J. M. Keynes, *op. cit.*, p. 13.

[111] Attention was directed to the proposition, first, by the showing that, historically, real and money wages have not in fact behaved in accordance with Mr. Keynes' expectation. L. Tarshis, *op. cit.*; J. T. Dunlop, "The Movement of Real and Money Wage Rates," *loc. cit.*; L. Tarshis, "Changes in Real and Money Wages," *Economic Journal,* March 1939, XLIX, pp. 150–154; also in *Readings in the Theory of Income Distribution,* pp. 330–335.

[112] The same analysis is applicable, inversely, to the case of declining output and decreasing money wages.

[113] The subject had, of course, been considered at length previously in the literature

competition and highly flexible prices, he held that a decrease in money wages, in a period of unemployment, will ordinarily result only in a corresponding reduction of prices with no increase in output or employment.[114] As in the former case, most of the later contributions to the discussion have had to do with considerations not involved in Mr. Keynes' presentation of the matter. The principal propositions that have been advanced are the following: (1) Prices will not necessarily fall in proportion to the decrease in wage rates. In the first place, even under conditions of competition, if the supply schedules of commodities are positively inclined at all, price would in any event fall less than in proportion even though wages were the whole of prime costs. If, in addition, prime costs include a considerable proportion of costs other than wages, the decline of prices will be still less in proportion to the decline in wages. In the second place, if competition is less than pure, prices may be "sticky" and may fall much less than the decrease in marginal costs—the extent of the fall depending essentially on the degree of monopoly, which is likely to be increasing. The net effect on employment is uncertain, but it might turn out to be a decrease.

(2) On the other hand, as money wages decrease there may, even in the short run, be some substitution of labor for other factors. (3) The reduction in money wages may favorably affect investment expenditure which is not related to consumer demand (which would not be expected to increase) but to expected investment activity in future periods. (4) Any such favorable effect upon employment may, however, be dampened somewhat by the decrease in the average propensity to consume that may accompany the change in distribution of money income, and by the increase in uncertainty for producers that may accompany the increase in the relative proportion of total demand that takes the form of producers' demand.[115] The net effect of all four sets of circumstances upon employment would certainly be difficult to forecast for the economy as a whole.

---

of business cycle theory. See, for example, A. C. Pigou, *Industrial Fluctuations* (London, 1927; 2nd ed., 1929), pp. 192–203, 306–313.

[114] He recognized the fact that employment might indirectly be affected favorably by a fall in the rate of interest as a result of a reduction in the schedule of liquidity preference. On the other hand, the effect on the propensity to consume of a transfer of income from laborers to entrepreneurs and rentiers is more likely to be unfavorable. If entrepreneurs are made more optimistic by the wage change, the schedule of the marginal efficiency of capital may increase. These and other less important qualifications are considered by Keynes, *op. cit.*, pp. 262–267.

[115] Fellner, who is primarily responsible for propositions (3) and (4), also points out that both of these effects may be dampened somewhat by the decrease in output per man-hour that is likely to occur. *Monetary Policies and Full Employment*, p. 101.

THEORY OF INTEREST

Two lines of development are to be noted. The first was the culmination in Hayek's *The Pure Theory of Capital*[116] of the discussions of the Austrian theory during the 'thirties. The second was the development of a theory of interest which comprehended monetary phenomena as having a direct bearing upon the determination of the rate of interest, and not merely responsible for temporary aberrations from the "real" situation.

(1) The essential features of Hayek's work had been revealed in the course of the extended debates which preceded the appearance of *The Pure Theory of Capital*.[117] The book added relatively little to the earlier discussions, except that it did constitute an orderly and systematic treatment of the Austrian theory of capital and interest in the form in which it survived the preceding debates. In a sense the book may be said to belong to an earlier period than that with which the present review is primarily concerned, and this fact justifies not giving this very important book more attention.

Hayek has been successful in developing an analysis of the capitalistic process for an economy which is neither stationary, on the one hand, nor fully dynamic, on the other. He is concerned with a sort of moving equilibrium for a moderately progressive economy, and is only to a minor extent concerned, in this volume, with the implications of his analysis for business cycle theory. He has avoided use of the concept of the average period of production and has made much less use of the idea of "stages" than he did in his earlier work, substituting in part input and output functions. His is still essentially a "time period" conception of productivity, however, and his interest rate in an equilibrium situation is partly dependent upon marginal productivity, partly upon time preference.[118] His theory is also still one which stresses the difference between the "real" forces as distinguished from the "more superficial monetary mechanism."[119]

(2) The development of a theory of interest which adequately comprehends the monetary elements was responsible for extraordinarily extended and fertile discussions.[120] The primary stimulus was provided by

[116] London, 1941.

[117] The issues discussed in these debates were well summarized in: N. Kaldor, "Annual Survey of Economic Theory: The Recent Controversy on the Theory of Capital," *Econometrica*, July 1937, V, pp. 201–233; F. H. Knight, "On the Theory of Capital: In Reply to Mr. Kaldor," *ibid.*, January 1938, VI, pp. 63–82.

[118] F. A. Hayek, "Time-Preference and Productivity: A Reconsideration," *Economica*, February 1945, XII, pp. 22–25.

[119] *Idem, The Pure Theory of Capital*, p. 409.

[120] In addition to Mr. Keynes' numerous and well-known contributions, the following

Mr. Keynes' theory of interest which stressed the relation between the supply of money and the demand for money for cash balances purposes as jointly responsible for the determination of the rate of interest. Apart from the not inconsiderable amount of subsequent attention devoted to determining what Keynes really meant, the contributions stimulated by the liquidity preference theory may be considered under the following headings: (a) the formulation of a competing theory in terms of the supply and demand for loanable funds;[121] (b) the reconciliation of, first, the liquidity preference with the loanable funds approach, on the one hand, and second, these two monetary theories with the "real" approach to the theory of interest, on the other hand; and (c) contributions that have improved the original formulations of the liquidity preference and the loanable funds theories.

(a) The theory which regards the rate of interest as determined by the supply of, and demand for, loanable funds includes in the supply of funds: current savings, funds released from embodiment in fixed or working capital, and net additional bank loans; in the demand for funds: requirements for new investment, and requirements for a net increase in cash balances ("hoardings").[122] From the very beginning, proponents of this type of interest theory have said that it does not lead to conclusions different from the Keynesian theory, although it does have the advantage over the Keynesian theory of corresponding somewhat more closely to the way in which the business world thinks of the determinants of the rate of interest, and it has the further advantage of showing more directly the relation between the marginal efficiency of investment and the rate of interest. Both theories, however, have the advantage over the "real" theories that they recognize the part played by the banking system, as well as the part played by the demand for speculative and precautionary balances, in the determination of the rate of interest. Both theories, fur-

---

should be especially noted: B. Ohlin, "Some Notes on the Stockholm Theory of Savings and Investment," *Economic Journal,* March and June 1937, XLVII, pp. 53–69, 221–240; also in *Readings in Business Cycle Theory* (Philadelphia, 1944), pp. 87–130; O. Lange, "The Rate of Interest and the Optimum Propensity to Consume," *Economica,* February 1938, V, pp. 12–32; also in *Readings in Business Cycle Theory,* pp. 169–192; J. R. Hicks, *Value and Capital,* Ch. 11–13, 19; D. H. Robertson, "Mr. Keynes and the Rate of Interest," *Essays in Monetary Theory* (London, 1940), pp. 1–38; also in *Readings in the Theory of Income Distribution,* pp. 425–460; H. M. Somers, "Monetary Policy and the Theory of Interest," *Quarterly Journal of Economics,* May 1941, LV, 488–507; also in *Readings in the Theory of Income Distribution,* pp. 477–498.

[121] It should be noted, however, that such a theory had been formulated before Mr. Keynes' liquidity preference theory came along. Also, such a theory was employed in G. Haberler, *Prosperity and Depression* (Geneva, 1937), which appeared very shortly after Keynes' *General Theory.*

[122] If, of course, a net decrease in cash balances, rather than an increase, was to be expected, the item might appropriately be listed on the supply side.

thermore, agree that the rate of saving is directly related to variations in the rate of interest, if at all, in a way that is not at present definable. They also agree that the level of saving is positively related to the level of income, the Keynesians maintaining furthermore that the marginal propensity to save probably increases as the level of income increases.[123]

(b) The loanable funds theory of interest can also be formulated in terms of the supply of, and demand for, securities and claims. If, to simplify the exposition, it is assumed that all borrowing and lending takes the form of the sale and purchase of a single type of security (say, a consol without maturity value and perfectly safe, bearing a fixed interest payment per period), then the rate of interest is the rate of yield of this security and it is determined, in any given time interval, by the supply of such securities coming on the market and the demand for them. The conditions of supply are determined by the urgency of the needs and the promise of the investment opportunities available to prospective borrowers, and the conditions of demand depend upon the volume of saving, the extent of funds released from embodiment in fixed and circulating capital, and the lending policy of the banking system.

It should be noted, however, that the total supply of securities potentially coming on the market must include old securities as well as new, since old securities may well change hands and may thus have their effect upon the determination of equilibrium in the market. In fact, in view of the relatively high proportion of existing stocks of securities to new securities appearing on the market in any time interval, the conditions of supply of securities may be affected relatively little by the volume of flow of new issues.[124]

It now appears evident that the loanable funds theory, thus stated, is entirely reconcilable with the liquidity preference theory. According to the former theory, the rate of interest is the rate of yield on securities, old as well as new, determined by the conditions of supply and demand for securities in a given time interval. According to the liquidity preference theory, the equilibrium rate of interest is the rate at which the demand for cash balances will be equal to the supply of cash available for cash

---

[123] There is a difference between the Ohlin and the Robertson versions of the loanable funds theory which can be illustrated by their treatment of savings. For Robertson, the supply of savings in period 2 is related to the income earned in period 1, while for Ohlin the supply of savings in period 2 is related to the income *expected* in period 2. In fact, there is a haziness about Ohlin's handling of *ex ante* savings and investment that raises considerable doubt as to the proper interpretation of his determinants of the rate of interest.

[124] Cf. H. Townshend, "Liquidity-premium and the Theory of Value," *Economic Journal*, March 1937, XLVII, pp. 157–158; T. de Scitovszky, "A Study of Interest and Capital," *Economica*, August 1940, VII, pp. 299–300.

balances. The alternative to the holding of cash, for the individual, is conceived to be the holding of securities. Hence the theory could equally well be stated as follows: At the end of trading in any time interval, if equilibrium is achieved, the prices of securities will be such that all individuals in the market will be content with their *holdings* of securities and their *holdings* of cash. Hence, if the liquidity preference theory is restated as a sort of "security preference" theory, it is not difficult to see that it involves the same determinants of the interest rate as the loanable funds theory.

A more formal way of showing the relation between the two theories is Hicks' method of counting the equations involved in an equilibrium situation and demonstrating that either the equation for the supply and demand for claims or that for the supply and demand for money may be ignored, since there will be one more than the necessary number of equations.[125] He draws the inference that, if the supply and demand for loans equation is retained, it is this equation which determines the rate of interest, while if the supply and demand for money equation is retained, the appropriate interest theory is the liquidity preference theory.[126]

Strictly speaking, the rate of interest is affected in some degree by *all* of the elements expressed in the equations in the Walras-Hicks system. Hence either the loanable funds approach or the liquidity preference approach represents a form of partial equilibrium analysis of the determinants of the rate of interest.[127] The reconciliation of the two monetary theories and the "real" theory can best be effected, therefore, by taking a somewhat broader view of the economy than any one of these three theories ordinarily takes.[128] In the use of resources, the individual or firm may be conceived to be concerned with the equalization of various sorts of marginal rates of return: on securities, cash, production, and consump-

---

[125] There are n — 1 equations for the prices of the same number of commodities and factors, one equation for the supply and demand for loans, and one equation for the supply and demand for money. This gives us n + 1 equations for the determination of n prices (the prices of n — 1 commodities and the rate of interest). Hence, one of the two last equations may be ignored. J. R. Hicks, "Mr. Keynes' Theory of Employment," *Economic Journal*, June 1936, XLVI, p. 246; also his *Value and Capital*, Ch. 12. Cf. also J. M. Fleming, "The Determination of the Rate of Interest," *Economica*, August 1938, V, pp. 333-341.

[126] But the supply and demand for money equation has reference to *all* monetary transactions, and could be applied to the determination of the rate of interest only on the assumption that the prices and quantities exchanged of all commodities and factors are assumed given. Cf. W. Fellner and H. M. Somers, "Alternative Monetary Approaches to Interest Theory," *Review of Economic Statistics*, February 1941, XXIII, p. 44. Also, the supply and demand for money equation appears to have reference to a *flow* of transactions, rather than to the supply and demand for money to *hold*.

[127] Cf. W. Fellner and H. M. Somers, *loc. cit.*

[128] The following analysis is based on H. M. Somers, *op. cit.*

tion. For an individual, the marginal rate of return on securities is the rate of return which he can obtain by shifting additional resources into securities. The marginal rate of return on cash is measured by the rate of interest that a marginal increment of cash held might alternatively earn if it were to be invested, instead of utilized for cash-balances purposes. The marginal rate of return on production is the marginal efficiency of investment. The marginal rate of return on consumption is equal to the rate of time preference applicable to the marginal $100 of income that is consumed instead of saved.

Individuals have all four choices: to invest in securities, to hold cash, to invest in production, to consume. Firms have the first three choices, except that banks (other than the Federal Reserve Banks) have only the first two options. Neither the Federal Reserve nor the government acts on the marginal principle. Furthermore, it must be recognized that individuals and firms probably do not apply the marginal principle rigorously. Nevertheless, whether individuals and firms tend to equalize all of these marginal returns or not, their decisions in these four areas of choice impinge upon the rate of interest. The supply and demand for securities, liquidity preference, marginal productivity, and time preference all play their part, then, in determining the interest rate.

(c) Probably the most important contribution of the extended discussions stimulated by the Keynesian doctrine with respect to interest has been the gradual clarification of the implications of that doctrine and of the relation between it and other formulations of interest theory. Some important suggestions, however, have been made for the improvement of the doctrine itself. There is, first, Mr. Keynes' own suggestion, arising out of his debate with Ohlin, that requirements for cash balances include, in addition to those arising from the transactions, precautionary and speculative motives, those required in connection with current or prospective investment operations ("finance"). Although the original suggestion was rather confusing, it was gradually fitted into the structure of the liquidity preference theory and represents an improvement.[129] Hicks' somewhat broader statement that the present demand for money depends, in part, upon the volume of expenditure planned for the near future (including expenditure upon inputs and consumption, as well as upon securities) is a more satisfactory and inclusive statement of the amendment Mr. Keynes wished to make.[130]

---

[129] J. M. Keynes, "Alternative Theories of the Rate of Interest," *Economic Journal,* June 1937, XLVII, pp. 246–248. Cf. E. S. Shaw, "False Issues in the Interest-Theory Controversy," *Journal of Political Economy,* December 1938, XLVI, pp. 838–856; D. H. Robertson, *loc. cit.*

[130] J. R. Hicks, *Value and Capital,* pp. 241–242.

Other suggestions of considerable interest have been made by Fellner.[131] It is his position that the importance of the functional relation between the demand for cash balances for speculative purposes and the rate of interest has been exaggerated. It is not convincing, he believes, to argue that, in a period of depression, while other sorts of expectations are in general pessimistic and while the general movement of interest rates is downward, the expectation with respect to interest rates should nevertheless be that they are to rise. Hence he does not accept the Keynesian hypothesis that the schedule of liquidity preference is highly elastic, particularly at low rates of interest, but believes that, on the contrary, the schedule in question is probably quite inelastic.[132] It may even be positively inclined.

It follows that the *shape* of the schedule of liquidity preference (largely determined, in the Keynesian analysis, by the demand for speculative balances in relation to the rate of interest) possibly does not have much of a part to play in the explanation of the behavior of interest rates. Instead, Fellner stresses the part played by precautionary balances, the demand for which is conceived to shift considerably as a result of, but in the opposite direction to, shifts in the demand for funds for investment purposes. When expectations as to profits are good and the schedule of the marginal efficiency of capital shifts to the right, the demand schedule for funds for precautionary balances is likely to shift to the left, and *vice versa*. These shifts in the demand schedule for precautionary balances result in corresponding shifts in the schedule of liquidity preference, and thus affect the rate of interest. The latter is also affected, in the opposite way, by the change in investment.

Regardless of whether Fellner's position concerning speculative balances is accepted, it is quite evident that circumstances responsible for shifts in the schedule of liquidity preference are at least as important as the shape of the schedule of liquidity preference itself in the explanation of the behavior of interest rates. In other words, whether one adopts the loanable funds approach or the liquidity preference approach, the number of circumstances that have a bearing upon the determination of the interest rate structure is so great that a two-dimensional, partial equilibrium approach to the theory of interest must be regarded as far from satisfactory, except perhaps as a first approximation.

---

[131] W. Fellner, *Monetary Policies and Full Employment*, pp. 140–173.

[132] The fact that the cost of liquidity is lower at lower rates of interest is, Fellner suggests, partly or wholly offset by the fact that larger precautionary balances will be required at higher rates of interest because of the reduction in safety margins attributable to the higher cost of borrowing. *Ibid.*, p. 168.

THEORY OF RENT

The theory of rent has played a very small part indeed in recent theoretical discussions. The idea that rent constitutes a share in distribution functionally attributable to a peculiar factor, as interest is attributable to capital or wages to labor, is probably no longer very generally held. The old fires that burned so hotly have about died out.

There is to be noted a tendency to revert to the Paretian concept of rent, and to define it as the surplus return which an agent of production earns in a particular industry over and above its opportunity cost.[133] It is associated with the working of a dynamic economy, since it may result, for example, from an innovation, the initial effect of which is to increase profit for the enterprise responsible. In the course of time this profit becomes shared as "rents" with those agents of production in a position to bargain effectively for it.[134] Or it may result from the temporary profits that accompany the expansion of an industry under conditions of decreasing costs, or that accompany an increase in demand in the short period. Under pure competition, such rents are likely to be short-lived, but under monopoly, oligopoly, or monopolistic competition they are more likely to persist.

The concept of rent has, at least in one instance, been limited to the surplus return gained by an agent of production in a particular firm, over and above what this same agent could earn if it were employed by another firm in the same industry.[135] It would not appear likely, however, that rent so defined would be very common, and it is admittedly difficult to find illustrations that lend much importance to this version of the concept.

THEORY OF PROFITS

There are essentially two kinds of profit theory: (1) the type of theory which regards profits as a residual, the excess of price over cost; and (2) the theory which regards profit as the reward for a factor of production, enterprise, or the entrepreneur, in the same way that wages are regarded as the reward for labor, and interest for capital. Both types of

[133] Cf. R. Triffin, *Monopolistic Competition and General Equilibrium Theory*, pp. 173-177; K. E. Boulding, *Economic Analysis*, pp. 229-232, 442-444; G. J. Stigler, *The Theory of Competitive Price* (New York, 1942), p. 105; F. Machlup, "Competition, Pliopoly and Profit," *Economica*, February 1942, IX, pp. 20-21.
[134] R. Triffin, *loc. cit.*; B. S. Keirstead and D. H. Coore, "Dynamic Theory of Rents," *Canadian Journal of Economics and Political Science*, May 1946, XII, pp. 168-172.
[135] D. A. Worcester, Jr., "A Reconsideration of the Theory of Rent," *American Economic Review*, June 1946, XXXVI, pp. 269-277.

theory continue to exist side by side, and there is as yet no indication of agreement as to the approach which is the more appropriate.

(1) The theory which regards profits as a residual has been closely related, in recent times, to monopolistic competition theory. The existence of profit may be attributed to monopolistic restriction of output, or to a successful "innovation" with respect to which a particular firm gets a head start.[136] It may be the outcome of uncertainty, which has the effect of making entrepreneurs plan for wide safety margins, so that many firms are discouraged from entering the industry, while the more enterprising ones who do enter are rewarded with a profit.[137] Or it may arise from the fact that the industry is one in which indivisibility of important resources constitutes a serious obstacle to freedom of entry; a market area, for example, may provide the existing number of firms in a particular industry with more than the normal profit, but may not offer sufficient promise of profit to justify the establishment of an additional enterprise in the area.[138] In all of these cases, persistence of the profit depends upon a lack of freedom of entry. Also, in all of these cases the profit is likely in time to be resolved, wholly or partially, into rents attributable to one or another of the factors of production.[139]

(2) Proponents of the type of theory according to which profits are regarded as the reward for enterprise have equally stressed the relation between profits and dynamic change in the economy. The attempt has been made, however, to relate the return to the entrepreneur as a factor of production and to attribute profits to some function or functions performed by him. One of the difficulties which has continued to plague this approach is the difficulty of defining the entrepreneurial function and of locating it in the corporate form of enterprise. In fact, a considerable part of the attention devoted to the subject of profits in recent years has been focused on this problem.

Although the return to management as such is generally regarded as essentially a wage, functionally speaking, rather than an element in profits, the view is widely held that the making of those decisions as to policy which cannot be delegated is an entrepreneurial function. Considerable progress has been made in identifying the group within the corporation which is usually responsible for performance of this function.[140]

---

[136] R. Triffin, *op. cit.*, pp. 168–179.

[137] F. Machlup, "Competition, Pliopoly and Profit," *Economica*, February and May 1942, IX, pp. 15–17, 154–156.

[138] *Ibid.*, pp. 17–19, 167–170.

[139] Cf. above, p. 45.

[140] R. A. Gordon, *Business Leadership in the Large Corporation* (Washington, 1945), Ch. 4–11.

Although outside groups or important stockholders are sometimes involved and although every corporation is probably, strictly speaking, unique with respect to the location of the decision-making function, Gordon finds that "the main elements of business leadership are exercised by the executive group."[141] The reward for performance of this function is, however, not typically what the economist ordinarily thinks of as profits, but is more likely to be salary (possibly plus a bonus), combined perhaps with an opportunity to make capital gains by trading (with the benefit of inside information) in the stock of the company, and with, perhaps, a psychic element of prestige and a feeling of power. The executive group may nevertheless seek to maximize the net profit of the business, since their efficiency and their success as executives are likely to be measured by the criterion of profits. If, however, the making of those decisions which cannot be delegated to subordinates is one of the most important functions of entrepreneurship, those that perform this function in a large corporation are mainly rewarded by forms of remuneration other than profits.[142] One answer, not altogether satisfactory, is that the *firm* itself as a working organization should be regarded as the entrepreneur.[143] Another answer is that the compensation of certain executive officers should be regarded as part of the profit of the corporation, from the economist's point of view, and should therefore not be deducted from gross profit in arriving at net.[144]

There remains to be considered the reward for the function of bearing uncertainty. It has become increasingly clear, in the discussions of uncertainty that have occurred recently, that the analysis is best to be conducted in terms of successive time periods, since the problem is essentially a dynamic one. One technique which has received considerable use in this connection is to express expected net returns as a probability distribution.[145] Another technique is to conceive of each entrepreneur as de-

---

[141] *Ibid.*, p. 317.

[142] J. C. Baker, "Executive Compensation Payments by Large and Small Industrial Companies," *Quarterly Journal of Economics*, May 1939, LIII, pp. 404–434; R. A. Gordon, "Ownership and Compensation as Incentives to Corporation Executives," *ibid.*, May 1940, LIV, pp. 455–473; *idem*, *Business Leadership in the Large Corporation*, Ch. 14.

[143] J. H. Stauss, "The Entrepreneur: the Firm," *Journal of Political Economy*, June 1944, LII, pp. 112–127.

[144] W. L. Crum, "Corporate Earnings on Invested Capital," *Harvard Business Review*, Spring 1938, XVI, pp. 340–341; also in *Readings in the Theory of Income Distribution*, pp. 578–580.

[145] H. Makower and J. Marschak, "Assets, Prices and Monetary Theory," *Economica*, August 1938, V, pp. 271–282; A. G. Hart, "Risk, Uncertainty, and the Unprofitability of Compounding Probabilities," in *Studies in Mathematical Economics and Econometrics* (Chicago, 1942), pp. 110–118; also in *Readings in the Theory of Income Distribution*, pp. 547–557; K. E. Boulding, "The Theory of the Firm," *loc. cit.*, pp. 794–798.

termining his policy upon the basis of expectations as to receipts, less a risk premium, against which is balanced the anticipated cost of investment.[146] Entrepreneurs may be grouped according to the size of the risk premium they would feel it necessary to deduct from anticipated receipts in determining whether a particular venture would be worth undertaking. They also may be grouped according to their ability to bear uncertainty, which in turn depends upon the amount of their own capital and their ability to raise additional funds in an imperfect capital market. Thus the supply of entrepreneurial ability is limited, and there may be conceived to be a normal rate of profit that will compensate entrepreneurs for the assumption of uncertainty. When entry into an industry is contemplated, the anticipated rate of profit must be sufficient to cover not only the ordinary risk premium with respect to uncertainty as to future receipts and costs, but must also be sufficient to cover a risk premium against the possibility that other firms may simultaneously enter the industry. Similarly, in cases in which the development of an innovation is involved, the risk premium must be sufficient to cover the risk that other firms, unknown to the first, may simultaneously be developing a similar innovation.

In the case of the corporation, it appears then that the entrepreneurial function is divided between a group of the executive officers on the one hand, and the common stockholders (or other types of investors that assume a substantial burden of uncertainty as to future return) on the other. Whether there is any reason to expect, in a dynamic society, the profit which is the reward for the entrepreneurial function to tend toward any "normal" level is an open question.

---

[146] F. H. Hahn, "A Note on Profit and Uncertainty," *Economica*, August 1947, XIV, pp. 211–225. Cf. above, p. 46.

2

EMPLOYMENT THEORY AND BUSINESS CYCLES

William Fellner

DURING the last ten or fifteen years, the theory of employment has progressed significantly. It seems appropriate to characterize this advance as
a rapid further growth of ideas that had developed up to a certain point
in the framework of pre-Keynesian monetary and cycle theory. In the
recent period of development a systematic theory has emerged concerning
the relationship between certain basic functions, on the one hand, and
aggregate output and employment, on the other, on the assumption that
the basic functions (which, in reality, fluctuate during the cycle) are
"given." As compared with traditional cycle theory, this implies reduced
emphasis on fluctuations and a more intensive and more detailed treatment of the processes occurring at any one level through which the economy passes in the course of its fluctuations. Accomplishments along such
lines should be fitted into a broader framework in order to become generally applicable. In the first place, theories relating to "given" positions
and shapes of the basic functions must become better integrated with
theories of shifts in these functions, that is, with theories of economic
fluctuations. Secondly, recent analysis, in its concern with relationships
existing between aggregative concepts, has given little attention to the
indirect effect of relative price and cost changes on movements of broad
aggregates. This is another way of saying that the theory of employment
must become better integrated with value theory. The really interesting
open issues in the theory of employment bear closely on these two problems, namely, on the relationships existing between the theory of employment, on the one hand, and the theory of economic fluctuations and
value theory, on the other. We shall now turn to some of these issues.

I. THE ANALYTICAL FRAMEWORK: THE QUANTITY THEORIES vs.
VARIANTS OF THE SAVINGS-INVESTMENT APPROACH

(1) The "modern" theories of employment are rooted in monetary
theory. The monetary theories from which they were developed are savings-investment theories, rather than quantity theories. This is true both

of the "period analysis" versions and the "equilibrium analysis" versions of the contemporary theories of employment.[1] They both are usually expressed in terms of the savings-investment apparatus, rather than that of the quantity theories. Before contrasting the period analysis with the equilibrium analysis in the theory of employment, we shall raise the question concerning the difference in emphasis between the quantity theories, on the one hand, and the savings-investment framework, on the other.

(2) Theories of employment, when developed in terms of the savings-investment approach, typically argue in the following way. Alternative amounts of aggregate money income are associated with alternative amounts of consumption expenditure, on the one hand, and of savings, on the other, income being the most important of the variables on which consumption and savings depend. Furthermore, income, which by definition equals the value of the current output, is the sum of the value of consumption and of capital formation (provided government expenditures on currently produced goods and services are included in consump-

---

[1] Nothing short of bibliography filling many pages could cover the recent literature on these topics. We will limit ourselves at this point to the following brief references: J. M. Keynes, *The General Theory of Employment, Interest and Money* (London and New York, 1936); *idem*, "The Ex-ante Theory of Interest," *Economic Journal*, December 1937, XLVII, pp. 663–670; D. H. Robertson, *Banking Policy and the Price Level* (London, 1926); *idem*, "Saving and Hoarding," *Economic Journal*, September 1933, XLIII, pp. 399–413; *idem*, "Survey of Modern Monetary Controversy," reprinted from the 1938 volume of *The Manchester School* in *Readings in Business Cycle Theory* (Philadelphia and Toronto, 1944), pp. 311–329; Jacob Viner, "Mr. Keynes on the Causes of Unemployment," *Quarterly Journal of Economics*, November 1936, LI, pp. 147–167; Oscar Lange, "The Rate of Interest and the Optimum Propensity to Consume," reprinted from the 1938 volume of *Economica* in *Readings in Business Cycle Theory*, pp. 169–192; G. L. S. Shackle, *Expectations, Investment and Income* (London, 1938); M. Kalecki, *Essays in the Theory of Economic Fluctuations* (London, 1938); J. R. Hicks, *Value and Capital* (Oxford, 1938); Gunnar Myrdal, *Monetary Equilibrium* (London, 1939); Bertil Ohlin, "Some Notes on the Stockholm Theory of Saving and Investment," reprinted from the 1937 volume of *The Economic Journal* in *Readings in Business Cycle Theory*, pp. 87–129; J. E. Meade, "A Simplified Model of Mr. Keynes' System," *Review of Economic Studies*, February 1940, VII, pp. 123–126; James W. Angell, *Investment and Business Cycles* (New York and London, 1941); Arthur W. Marget, *The Theory of Prices* (New York, 1938–42); A. C. Pigou, *Employment and Equilibrium* (London, 1941); *idem, Lapses from Full Employment* (London, 1945); Gottfried Haberler, *Prosperity and Depression*, 3rd ed., (Geneva, 1941), Ch. 8 and 13; Alvin H. Hansen, *Fiscal Policy and Business Cycles* (New York, 1941); Mabel F. Timlin, *Keynesian Economics* (Toronto, 1942); Sir William Beveridge, *Full Employment in a Free Society* (London and New York, 1944–45); Oxford Institute of Statistics, *The Economics of Full Employment* (Oxford, 1944); David McCord Wright, *The Economics of Disturbance* (New York, 1946); Walter S. Salant, "The Demand for Money and the Concept of Income Velocity," *Journal of Political Economy*, June 1941, XLIX, pp. 395–422; Clark Warburton, "Monetary Expansion and the Inflationary Gap," *American Economic Review*, June 1944, XXXIV, pp. 303–327; John H. Williams, *Postwar Monetary Plans and Other Essays* (New York, 1944), Part II; R. F. Harrod, Alvin H. Hansen, Gottfried Haberler, and Joseph A. Schumpeter, "Keynes' Contribution to Economics: Four Views," *Review of Economic Statistics*, November 1946, XVIII, pp. 177–196; Lawrence R. Klein, *The Keynesian Revolution* (New York, 1947).

tion or in capital formation, which it is usual to do in the presentation of the theories themselves, although not in statistical practice).[2] Consequently, income is what it is *because* the consumption expenditure associated with that income level, *plus* the new capital formation, add up to that income. The consumption (and the saving) associated with each potential income level depends on the consumption function. The capital formation (or investment) of any period depends on profit expectations and on the terms on which funds are available for investment. Such a theory "determines" directly the amount of money income per period, and not the amount of real income or of employment. Certain further assumptions must be made concerning the behavior of wage rates and of prices before the conclusions relating to money income can be extended to physical output and employment. But the backbone of theories of this type consists of the savings-investment relationship. This, in turn, is dependent on the consumption function (indicating the aggregate consumption expenditures and savings forthcoming at alternative income levels), on some schedule expressing profit expectations for alternative amounts of investment,[3] and on the terms on which funds are available for alternative amounts of investment.[4] These functions and schedules are the "basic functions" on which the formal apparatus rests.

(3) Theories of money income based on the quantity theory approach typically argue from the supply of money to income. Income is what it is because a certain amount of money is available and because this money is being spent at a certain rate. Traditionally, the quantity equations have been used more widely in the discussion of price levels than in the analysis of the determinants of income. But the "price levels" in question are conceived of as being determined (1) by terms, such as M and V, or as M and the Marshallian K, which (if multiplied or divided by one another) express *money expenditures,* and (2) by terms, such as T, which express volumes of goods purchased. Consequently, the quantity theory approach—even if primarily concerned with price levels—implies a way

---

[2] In the presentation of the theory, it would, of course, be easy to allow for the government expenditure on goods and services as a separate item.

[3] In the Keynesian system proper, this is the schedule of the marginal efficiency of capital. A. P. Lerner calls this schedule the marginal efficiency of investment (i.e., of the investment flow) and distinguishes it from the marginal productivity of the capital stock. Cf. his *The Economics of Control* (New York, 1944).

[4] In the Keynesian system, these terms are subsumed under the concept of "the rate of interest," which, in turn, is determined by the liquidity preference schedule and the supply of money. Consequently, in the Keynesian formal system, in which money wage rates are assumed as "given," the amount of employment is determined by the following: the liquidity preference schedule (which expresses the demand for money for alternative rates of interest), the supply of money, the schedule of the marginal efficiency of capital, and the consumption function. All functions are expressed in terms of wage units, i.e., in terms of the money earnings of a labor unit.

of looking at the determination of the size of money flows, and the income concepts are concepts of money flows. More specifically, the quantity theories imply that the size of money flows is determined by the available supply of money and by some expression relating money stocks to money flows (i.e., by M concepts, and by V or K concepts, respectively). They imply that individuals and institutions aim at some relationship between their cash balances and their money expenditures, that is, at some rate of spending their cash balances.[5]

(4) The contemporary theories of employment have been developed mainly in terms of the savings-investment approach, rather than the quantity theory approach, because it is widely believed that the propensity to consume part of one's *income* is a truer (more "dependable") propensity than the propensity to hold some definite amount of *cash* in relation to one's expenditures. Obviously, any completed economic process can be expressed just as easily with the aid of the one as with the other apparatus. It always turns out that the public spent some fraction of its income on consumption and saved the other, just as it always turns out that the public was spending the available cash balances at a certain rate. Nobody can deny the logical validity of the quantity equations. But this is beside the point. If, for example, the public, at the end of each accounting period, was merely "left with" *ex post* cash-expenditure ratios, and if there existed no relationship between intentions or habits of the public, on the one hand, and these ratios, on the other, then the quantity theories would still not be logically fallacious, but they would be sterile. Similarly, if the propensity to consume, rather than velocity, could be indicted in this fashion, then the savings-investment approach would have to be regarded as sterile. Few economists would hold that cash-expenditure ratios (or velocities) actually are *mere* residuals in the foregoing sense. But many imply that they come close to being residuals, i.e., that they do not reflect dependable habits, while the propensity to consume (out of income) does. This is the reason why the savings-investment approach has gained ground rapidly in recent times. In the framework of the savings-investment approach, it must, of course, be added that output (income) consists of investment as well as of consumption and that the rate of investment, which is determined by profit expectations and the availability of funds, is obviously influenced by changes in the supply of money.

---

[5] Active balances are being spent at some rate, and, in addition, idle balances are being held. The latter (for which $V = 0$) diminish the average rate of spending of money as a whole but they constitute a distinct problem. Cf. Howard S. Ellis, "Some Fundamentals in the Theory of Velocity," *Quarterly Journal of Economics*, May 1938, LII, pp. 431–472.

(5) An earlier phase of development of the savings-investment analysis may be said to have begun with Wicksell's *Interest and Prices* (1898) and to have come to a close with the Fundamental Equations of Keynes' *Treatise* (1930). The further development and "modernization" of the approach during the nineteen-thirties should be attributed mainly to D. H. Robertson, to the neo-Wicksellians, and to the Keynes of the *General Theory* (1936). The most polemical presentation and advocacy of the approach is Keynes', and, at the same time, the Keynesian version has exerted the greatest influence on contemporary economic thought. Consequently, it has become easy to lose sight of the fact that the savings-investment approach can be integrated easily enough with the quantity theory approach. One may stress the significance of the main variables of the savings-investment approach and yet ask the question as to the direct influence of the supply of money on the propensity to consume (i.e., on the position of the consumption function) and on profit expectations.[6] In fact, while the emphasis of Keynesians, in the narrower sense, may be interpreted as an "anti-quantity theory" emphasis, the reasoning of the advocates of the savings-investment approach has not consistently been directed against the quantity theories. On the contrary, some economists who have made significant contributions to the development of the savings-investment analysis have also relied on the quantity equations, recognizing that importance may attach also to cash-expenditure ratios, as such, and thereby to velocities.[7] Yet the main emphasis has come to be placed increasingly upon savings-investment relationships, upon profit expectations, and upon the availability of funds. This trend of development has proved fruitful, and it will scarcely be reversed. The cleavage between this orientation and the quantity theories has recently been widened artificially. But this is now recognized by many economists, and it is unlikely that the cleavage will persist.

(6) The Keynesian version[8] differs from some of the competing versions of the savings-investment analysis not merely in that it presents a more intransigent front against the quantity theories, but in the further fact that the Keynesian version was developed in terms of simultaneous, realized magnitudes, while other versions were expressed in the framework of period analysis (sequence analysis). Economic models are established in such a way that they can create a presumption for dependable *ex post* relationships between simultaneous magnitudes only if either ex-

---

[6] In the Keynesian system proper, the supply of money affects directly merely the rate of interest.

[7] This is generally characteristic of Professor Robertson's work. Cf. also Pigou, *op. cit.*

[8] The version contained in the *General Theory*.

pectations are assumed to be correct or some definite assumption appears to be justified with respect to the nature of the errors. This is certainly true of the savings-investment approach. The approach, if expressed in terms of simultaneous, realized magnitudes, either merely states an accounting identity (in which case it possesses no significance *per se*), or it implies that the realized equal the expected magnitudes. A mere accounting identity is stated if we say that the income of any clock-time period multiplied by *what turns out to be the (ex post) "average propensity to consume"* is the value of consumption, to which it is necessary to add *what turns out to be the (ex post) capital formation (investment)* in order to arrive back at the income from which we started. What turns out to be the aggregate saving must always equal the value of what turns out to be the aggregate investment. The system must always be such as to satisfy the *ex post* identity of savings and investment.[9] This accounting identity appears to be the main thesis of the savings-investment approach, as expressed in terms of simultaneous, realized magnitudes. However, if we postulate that an equilibrium is established in which the *ex post* (realized) magnitudes equal the *ex ante* (expected or planned) magnitudes, then more is involved. In this event, the theory—even though it is expressed in *ex post* terms—maintains that the public decides to spend on consumption a definite part of its expected income and that the income of any planning period is what it is because the consumption so determined, plus the aggregate planned investment, add up to that income. So interpreted, the theory is concerned with the *determinants* of income, on the assumption that a condition becomes established in which the realized income equals the expected, the *ex post* "propensity" to consume equals the *ex ante* propensity to consume, and the realized equals the planned investment.

Aside from these assumptions concerning expectations, the characteristics of such a framework of the "Keynesian type" are those of the savings-investment framework in general. In other words, it stresses income-consumption and income-saving relationships, plus the determinants of investment (i. e., profit expectations and the costs of obtaining funds for investment). A theory of this kind *may* be integrated with the quantity theory approach by investigating the relationship between the supply of money and the consumption function, as well as the relationship existing between the supply of money and investment. At any rate, such a theory must be supplemented by an analysis of the behavior of costs (wage-price

---

[9] Because aggregate income minus *aggregate income times the ex post average propensity to consume* equals, by definition, the aggregate *ex post* savings. The same magnitude also equals the aggregate *ex post* investment, as was just shown.

behavior) in periods of expansion and contraction if it is to be a theory of real output and employment, rather than merely a theory of money income. All this is true of the savings-investment analysis in general and not merely of the particular version which runs in terms of simultaneous, realized magnitudes. The distinctive feature of this version is that it becomes a theory of income *determination* only on the postulate that an equilibrium is established in which the realized magnitudes of the system equal the expected magnitudes. Otherwise it is a definitional proposition of no significance.

(7) Of course, no economist suggests that, in the actual world, expectations are always fulfilled. To develop a theory on the assumption that they are, may serve one of two purposes. In the first place, it might be maintained that errors tend to cancel out in the long run. In other words, it might be maintained that while, for instance, the realized income of any single planning period is likely to be different from the income that was expected for that period, the deviations of *ex post* income from the *ex ante* (and therefore also the deviations of the *ex post* propensity to consume from the *ex ante*) may be disregarded in the interpretation of the *long-run* statistical relationship between income and consumption. It might be argued that, for the same reason, the deviations of realized investment from planned investment[10] may be disregarded in an analysis of long-run statistical relationships. This is one way of "justifying" *ex post* analysis. Secondly, it is possible to maintain that it is methodologically convenient to separate the problem of what would happen in the absence of erroneous forecasts from the problem of the consequences of errors. Theories in terms of simultaneous, realized magnitudes would then be interpreted as relating merely to a hypothetical condition with correct forecasts, and they would have to be supplemented by an analysis of the consequences of incorrect expectations. For the short run, this supplementary analysis becomes necessary even if we maintain that errors tend to cancel out in the long run. The inclination of economists to justify *ex post* analysis in some manner such as this is largely a consequence of the fact that statistical data are always *ex post,* and therefore the use of statistical data for analytical purposes always implies some method of rationalizing *ex post* analysis.

(8) This is not overlooked in the theories which were developed in terms of the period analysis (or sequence analysis). But in these theories, the equilibrium implied in the *"ex post* theories" appears merely as a

---

[10] These deviations express themselves in the involuntary (unplanned) accumulation or reduction of inventories, due to an excess or deficiency of actual demand as compared with expected demand.

special case, and the formal framework is made suitable also for the discussion of processes during which realized magnitudes are different from the expected. In the "Swedish"—neo-Wicksellian—version of the period analysis, the consumption of any planning period is conceived of as being determined by the expected income and by the *ex ante* (i.e., intended) propensity to consume.[11] Consumption—which is the product of expected income and the *ex ante* propensity to consume—and realized investment add up to realized income (value of output). Realized investment tends to differ from the planned (*ex ante*) investment whenever the realized (*ex post*) income differs from the expected (*ex ante*) income. In this event, the realized investment is affected by any unplanned accumulation or decrease in inventories which may occur as a consequence of the deficiency or the excess of demand as compared to the expected. The "Swedish" framework is suitable for the discussion of a dynamic model-process because the case in which the expected magnitudes equal the realized appears merely as a special case, which has been defined as monetary equilibrium. Only if realized income equals the expected, is realized saving equal to the expected and also realized investment equal to the expected. In such an equilibrium the planned (or expected) savings equal the planned (or expected) investment, since the realized savings are, by definition, always equal to the realized investment. In fact, such "monetary equilibrium," if it exists, may be said to be produced by the equality of planned savings with planned investment. Yet in the Swedish analysis this equilibrium is not postulated. Whenever planned savings do not equal planned investment, the realized magnitudes of the system will be different from the expected.

However, discrepancies between expected and realized magnitudes make it necessary to *explain* expectations—and the *realized* data to which they give rise—by past experience, that is, by the *realized* data of earlier periods. If this is done, and if expectations are treated merely implicitly as links between "past" and "present" realized data, instead of being made explicit in the formal apparatus, then models of the Robertsonian variety are obtained.

In the Robertsonian period analysis, the consumption of any period is conceived of as being determined by the income earned in the preceding period and by the propensity to consume out of that income. A period is defined in such a way that the income of any period is allocated to its use in the next period. Income remains unchanged if the consumption "out of" the income of the preceding period[12] *and* the aggregate investment of

---

[11] Which is a true *propensity* in the psychological sense.
[12] This consumption occurs in the present period.

the present period add up to a present income which is no different from the income of the preceding period. This condition is satisfied if that part of the previously earned income which "now" is *not* consumed (but is "saved" in the Robertsonian sense) equals the aggregate value which "now" is invested, so that the present consumption-plus-investment[13] equals the income of the preceding period. If, on the other hand, aggregate investment exceeds Robertsonian savings, then income rises from one period to the next, and if aggregate investment falls short of Robertsonian savings, then income declines. We have seen that, in the Swedish —neo-Wicksellian—version of the period analysis, the case in which realized magnitudes *equal the expected* appears as a special case (monetary equilibrium), and that the framework covers also the dynamic processes during which this condition is not satisfied. In the Robertsonian version, the case in which income—that is, the current value of output—*remains unchanged* is a special case. Neither the Robertsonian nor the Swedish period analysis implies correct expectations, although both are compatible with such an assumption.

(9) It clearly would be desirable to integrate the theories of income and employment with the theories of economic fluctuations. These theories do not really pertain to different types of factual observation. Monetary equilibrium is not observable at all. It is a helpful concept only to the extent to which it is useful to interpret observable phenomena as deviations from such a hypothetical condition. Therefore, it cannot be fruitful to treat the problem of income and employment in (hypothetical) *monetary equilibrium* as belonging in an area of analysis from which there exists no well-constructed bridge to the realistic subject of fluctuating levels of income and employment. Both the Robertsonian and the neo-Wicksellian period analyses contain these bridges. Analysis in terms of simultaneous, realized magnitudes, however, limits itself to one of the two areas, because it is meaningful only if monetary equilibrium is postulated. This is the real problem underlying the methodological discussion which for many years was apparently concerned with mere technicalities such as the savings-investment identity, alternative definitions of the multiplier, etc.

However, the advantages of the present forms of the period analysis are overstated if it is maintained that those abstaining from their use necessarily treat the economy as if it were constantly in monetary equilibrium. An economist may limit his *formal*—or quasi-mathematical—analysis to processes occurring "in monetary equilibrium," and he may prefer to treat the problem of deviations (i.e., the problem of incorrect expecta-

---

[13] That is, the present earned income.

tions) outside the formal framework, on a lower level of "generalization." In this event, the formal framework may be established in terms of simultaneous, realized magnitudes, but realistic conclusions cannot be derived before examining separately the question of the relationship between expected and realized magnitudes—and therefore of lags—for the period under consideration. The reason why such a procedure may seem preferable to some economists is that the standard varieties of the period analysis are highly schematic. The Robertsonian and the Swedish period analyses are directly applicable only to simplified model-processes. The functional periods with which they operate can scarcely be defined realistically. The notion of correct and incorrect expectations implies substantial oversimplification, because expectations do not typically relate to definite magnitudes, but to a range of probable magnitudes. Furthermore, the concept of expectations for the economy *as a whole* disregards the possible inconsistencies between the expectations of different individuals and also the inconsistencies between past and present expectations of one and the same individual for future dates. This specific difficulty does not arise in connection with the Robertsonian period analysis. The Robertsonian variety of the period analysis also possesses psychological implications, which express themselves in lags between "cause and effect," but the implied assumptions are comparatively simple. However, the assumed lag (between "today's" income and "tomorrow's" consumption) is highly schematic, that is, merely illustrative. Furthermore, the Robertsonian concept of monetary *equilibrium*[14] disregards the gradual growth in physical output which is attributable partly to the investment process itself and partly to exogenous factors of a rather "consistent" type (technological progress, etc.). A gradual increase in real output would, of course, have to be associated with an increase in the current value of output and of money income, unless a continuous fall in the price level is assumed. It is advisable to incorporate this gradual growth into the concept of dynamic equilibrium, and this requires supplementing the Robertsonian framework, to some extent, by further elements. Robertson recognizes this in his discussion of policies. It is possible to include these as well as further considerations in the Robertsonian *type* of period analysis.

Ultimately, the question is one of methodological preferences. Do we wish to use an analytical system of the "monetary equilibrium" variety (which can be defined in *ex post* terms)[15] and treat the problem of in-

---

[14] In which the value of output (income) remains unchanged by definition.
[15] That is, in terms of simultaneous, realized magnitudes, on the postulate that they equal the *ex ante* magnitudes.

stability[16] mainly on a less formal level, without the pretension of having developed a *generally* applicable apparatus (or "system") on this second level? Or do we prefer to have both levels covered by the formal apparatus, even though this coverage will merely "suggest" the type of approach to be followed in a realistic inquiry, rather than provide us with dependable tools for factual analysis?

(10) The writer's own position is influenced by the circumstance that economists employing the *ex post* systems (i.e., systems of the "monetary equilibrium" variety) frequently do not show sufficient awareness of the problems that are defined away from their technical framework. In recent years the role of several dynamic factors (capable of producing "cyclical" processes) was illustrated successfully with the aid of the Robertsonian *type* of period analysis.[17] It is true that in most cases the analysis of these processes implies substantially simplified relationships between lagged variables as well as a great many *ceteris paribus* assumptions, but such analysis has, nevertheless, proved revealing.

More complex and more complete "Robertsonian" systems (in an extended sense of the word) tend to become suitable for "econometric" purposes. The merits and limitations of econometric cycle models will be discussed elsewhere in this volume. In these models (of, e.g., the Tinbergen variety or Cowles Commission variety) the number of variables may become substantial and the time lags, instead of merely expressing schematic psychological assumptions, are chosen partly in view of the objective of obtaining realistic results. The ultimate question here would seem to be concerned with what we mean by "realistic." Systems which are realistic in the sense of being dependable for forecasting have not been invented. This is the reason why the stage at which we stop complicating the formal apparatus and start supplementing it with "judgment" has so far stayed a matter of methodological preferences. However, limiting the formal apparatus to monetary equilibrium analysis is an extreme procedure which easily becomes misleading.

II. TRENDS AND CYCLES

(1) Primary concern with the nature of the hypothetical equilibrium around which the economy is supposed to fluctuate is characteristic of a

---

[16] Instability could exist even in the monetary equilibrium of the Swedish school, because expectations could fluctuate even if they were always fulfilled. But the instability observed in the actual world is very largely a product of monetary disequilibrium.

[17] Cf., e.g., Paul A. Samuelson, "Interactions Between the Multiplier Analysis and the Principle of Acceleration," reprinted from the 1939 volume of the *Review of Economic Statistics* in *Readings in Business Cycle Theory* (Philadelphia and Toronto, 1944), pp. 261–269; Lloyd A. Metzler, "The Nature and Stability of Inventory Cycles," *Review of Economic Statistics*, August 1941, XXIII, pp. 113–129.

large portion of the recent literature in economic theory and policy. In a sense, one might say that theorizing in these terms takes the concept of monetary equilibrium at its face value. It is concerned with the development of the economy in monetary equilibrium, and it merely comments on the fact that the actual economic processes exhibit variations around the postulated equilibrium level. The characteristics of the assumed equilibrium-path are then treated as characteristics of the *trend*. Stagnationist hypotheses have mainly been developed on the basis of this type of reasoning.[18]

The link between the *ex post* ("monetary equilibrium") theories and the stagnation thesis may be described as follows. The assumption is made that in a certain kind of social and economic environment—in "mature" economies—the consumption function, the schedule of the marginal efficiency of capital,[19] and the interest rate stand in a relationship to one another which makes for a level of output that can be produced with a considerably smaller labor input than would be required for full employment of the available labor force. Hence underemployment equilibrium. The trend follows a path along which there is substantial unemployment. There will be fluctuations around the trend in the course of which higher and lower levels of output and employment will be realized than those corresponding to the normal (or true) values of these variables. But what really matters is the normal level, which, in the circumstances here assumed, is unsatisfactory.

The reason for this is that at satisfactory levels of activity the inducement to invest would be insufficient to absorb the substantial amount of savings which accrue at these levels. Income must be such that the consumption associated with that rate of income, plus the amount of investment forthcoming, should add up to that income. On "stagnationist" hypotheses we would have to assume that, in mature economies, the full employment level of income (output) typically does not satisfy this condition. The condition is typically satisfied at a level of considerable underemployment, at which a smaller amount of aggregate investment is required to fill the gap between the aggregate income in question and the aggregate consumption forthcoming at that rate of income. This means assuming that, in the social and economic environments here considered, the consumption function is too *low*, given the marginal effi-

---

[18] They were developed, aside from J. M. Keynes, *op. cit.*, mainly in Alvin H. Hansen, *Full Recovery or Stagnation* (New York, 1938); *idem, Fiscal Policy and Business Cycles*; also in J. M. Keynes, "Some Consequences of Declining Population Growth," *Eugenics Review*, April 1937, XXX.

[19] Expressing marginal profit expectations (including interest) for alternative amounts of investment.

ciency schedule and the rate of interest; or that the marginal efficiency schedule is too *low*, given the rate of interest and the consumption function; or that the rate of interest is too *high*, given the marginal efficiency schedule and the consumption function.[20] More precisely, the assumption means that these determinants of output are too low, or too high, *in relation to one another*.

The argument concerning the position of the basic determining functions in mature economies is considered convincing by some economists and unconvincing by others. The writer feels unconvinced, but such a statement is largely subjective, because the usual argument is too broad— it is not specific enough—to be proved or disproved with the aid of factual observation. The difficulties encountered in an attempt to test these hypotheses may be illustrated briefly with reference to a few propositions frequently advanced in this connection.

(2) The consumption function is considered "too low"[21] in mature economies because the full employment level of income has come to be associated with a high rate of physical output,[22] and because the amount of savings accruing at such a high rate of physical output would be too high to be absorbed by private investment. Since the time this view was first advanced, estimates have been published from which it is possible to derive certain conclusions concerning the historical behavior of the propensity to consume[23] during longer periods in which physical output increased significantly and in which employment trends were, on the whole, favorable.[24] These estimates suggest that, during the last seventy years, the average propensity to consume has not shown a decreasing trend for rising output. In the writer's opinion, this weakens one aspect of the stagnation thesis considerably, because it means that, if we should continue along the same "historical consumption function," investment would have to increase merely in the same proportion as that in which consumption rises, to fill the gap at satisfactory levels of employment. But it must be admitted that considerations such as these do not really *settle* the issue. The *absolute* amount of investment required for filling the gap is the greater, the higher the rate of output, and it is possible to base pessimistic forecasts on the expectation that the absolute amount of investment will not rise sufficiently for full production.

---

[20] "Too low" or "too high" as compared with the requirements of full employment.

[21] For full employment, given the position of the other basic functions.

[22] Due to the highly developed techniques employed in advanced economies.

[23] In the *ex post* sense, that is, of the *realized* income-consumption relations for closed periods.

[24] Simon Kuznets, *National Product Since 1869* (New York, 1946). These estimates relate to the United States. British data seem to indicate a rising tendency for the average propensity to consume.

In fact, the stagnation thesis is concerned more specifically with the inducement to invest than with the consumption function (although, fundamentally, it is, of course, concerned with these various determinants of output *in relation* to one another). It is maintained that, in the nineteenth-century population growth, territorial expansion and capital-using innovations were the main stimulants of investment activity. In mature economies, population growth has slowed down considerably, territorial expansion has ceased, and innovations are sometimes said to have lost their capital-using character. Looking at these arguments under a microscope, one again is apt to arrive at the conclusion that the facts do not lend them the support required for making a "strong case." But the argument is broad enough, and the facts are capable of being interpreted in a sufficient number of ways, to preclude settling the issue on such evidence. For instance, a strong case for the population growth argument of the stagnationists would, presumably, require that the historical marginal propensity to consume of a community in which the population is growing rapidly should be greater than the *per capita* marginal propensity to consume.[25] Recent estimates contradict this assumption, however, so far as the United States is concerned.[26] Historically, the *per capita* marginal propensity to consume does not appear to have been smaller than the marginal propensity to consume of the entire (rapidly growing) population. The representative family does not seem to have consumed a smaller proportion of its income-increments than the population as a whole (which has consisted of an ever-increasing number of families). If a constant population could expand economically along a historical consumption function which is no less favorable than that pertaining to a growing population, why should economic expansion materialize more readily in conditions characterized by rapid population growth? It is not easy to see why this should be the case. Yet it might perhaps be argued that the *composition* of the additional output (when the economy expands) is more predictable if the additional output is produced for additional persons with similar habits than if it is produced for a rising *per capita* consumption of a given population.[27] Expansion materializes more readily if *ceteris paribus* the uncertainty attaching to business expectation is smaller, that is, if conditions are more predictable.

Similar statements could be made with respect to the "territorial ex-

[25] That is, essentially, that the marginal propensity to consume of a growing population should exceed the marginal propensity to consume of a constant population.

[26] Cf. Simon Kuznets, *op. cit.*, Tables II 9, II 16 and II 17.

[27] However, this argument is weakened by the fact that, even in periods of significant population growth, the rise in aggregate consumption reflected itself, in a considerable measure, in rising *per capita* consumption.

pansion" argument of the stagnationists. If by "substantiating" we mean something in the nature of statistical testing, it would be difficult indeed to substantiate the hypothesis concerning an intimate connection between territorial expansion and a satisfactory level of employment, just as it is difficult to substantiate a relationship between the consumption function and population growth. Yet the existence of frontier conditions, in certain segments of an economy, or colonial expansion, might prevent or retard the growth of institutional rigidities, and these rigidities may, of course, produce stagnant trends. In this connection it should, however, not be overlooked that the unification of political control over large geographical areas may share many characteristics with territorial expansion in the narrower sense (i.e., with "conquest" in the crude sense). It might take another few decades before it will be possible to say whether the twentieth century will have brought less territorial expansion in the broader sense than the nineteenth. Finally, it should be pointed out that the "technological argument" of the stagnation thesis is also unconvincing if interpreted more or less literally. Innovation requiring less capital per unit of output need not for this reason provide a smaller stimulus to investment activity as a whole. But here, again, the growth of institutional rigidities may produce an environment in which the response to innovation is less favorable.

In summary, it may be said that, regardless of the merits and deficiencies of the stagnationist reasoning, the Keynes-Hansen school has raised several significant issues which, in many respects, must be regarded as open issues. This is true especially if, instead of interpreting the arguments of the stagnationists narrowly, we consider the possible causal nexus between the phenomena they emphasize, on the one hand, and the degree of uncertainty and institutional rigidities, on the other.

(3) However, at this point, we should direct our attention to the fact that the pessimism of the stagnationist outlook is not its only interesting property. It is characteristic of the reasoning that it relates primarily to "the trend," rather than to stages of actual dynamic development. To be specific, one might, for example, attempt to investigate the special circumstances (including Federal Reserve policies and fiscal policies) that prevented the incipient recovery of 1931 from materializing; one might analyze a great many other specific factors because of which the depression of 1929–33 turned out to be so exceptionally severe; and one might try to examine the after-effects of this depression on the dynamic development of the following decade. This certainly is one of the possible lines of approach, because it is obvious that during the Great Depression the measures which in present-day cycle theory are generally considered

appropriate to depressions were either not adopted at all or were adopted on an entirely insufficient scale. Such a line of approach would not regard the trend as a meaningful phenomenon *per se*, but merely as a convenient way of representing certain tendencies or drifts that can be "read from" completed dynamic processes (which alone are "real"!). It is characteristic of the stagnationist reasoning that it does not adopt such a line of approach. Instead, it argues its case primarily in terms of the trend itself, which is supposed to "exist" as such. It is not in specific phases of cyclical development that something went wrong, but the secular trend went wrong, and, consequently, *it* must be corrected more or less perennially by specific policies (mainly by public works, the redistribution of income, and credit policies) if a quasi-chronic state of depression is to be avoided. The duration and severity of the Great Depression and the incompleteness of the recovery during the nineteen-thirties are viewed as manifestations of the ailing secular trend.

It is not accidental that pessimistic rather than optimistic hypotheses were expressed in terms of such a "trend theory." An economist who believes that with a reasonable cycle policy the general drift of economic development is likely to be satisfactory, is more likely to emphasize the cycle problem and the difficulties arising from uncontrolled cycles. We shall see, however, that stagnationist assumptions can also be carried over into cycle models, although originally they were not so expressed.

(4) When adapted to the requirements of dynamic analysis, the savings-investment approach is essentially a general framework for "cycle theory." In fact, it was originally invented to serve this purpose (Wicksell), and, with a detour over the "equilibrium version," it is increasingly made to serve this purpose again. The detour was worth while because significant improvements were made on the equilibrium variety of the approach which can be carried over into its dynamic applications. Moreover, the concept of monetary equilibrium has proved useful by providing a standard with which reality may be compared. However, this tool also was originally invented for being used as a standard of comparison in dynamic theory in the framework of the savings-investment apparatus. Any reader of Haberler's *Prosperity and Depression*[28] can easily convince himself of the extent to which this apparatus has actually been used to develop hypotheses concerning the nature of economic fluctuations.

When that book was first published, it was possible to group most of the well-known business cycle theories in two main categories: the over-investment theories and the underconsumption theories. The theories belonging in the first of these two categories emphasized the fact that

---

[28] Gottfried Haberler, *Prosperity and Depression* (Geneva, 1937; 3rd ed., 1941).

specific scarcities may develop in the expansion phase of the business cycle, while other investment goods are overproduced. Investment turns down, in consequence of these scarcities, and, during the contraction phase of the cycle, it falls short of savings. One might view an overinvestment theory as a generalized "bottleneck" theory, where the bottleneck consists of the capital (or in real terms, of the *specific* capital goods) which would be required to carry the expansion further without a setback. The unavailability of this capital, or of these kinds of capital goods, is responsible for the ensuing contraction.[29] On the other hand, the underconsumption theories place the emphasis on disturbances that might develop from the failure of aggregate consumer demand to keep pace with the expansion of output, i.e., from the tendency of (Robertsonian) savings to outrun investment. It would, of course, always have been unreasonable to consider this type of theory (overinvestment *or* underconsumption theory) as anything but a simplified model or a standard pattern. When Haberler's book was first published, the two classes of theories just mentioned provided the best-known alternative standard patterns, although several important theories had already been developed which cut across these categories.

It is undeniable that certain difficulties have existed with these standard patterns, although their usefulness as conceptual aids is not destroyed. As for the overinvestment theories, downturns have occurred in periods which did not seem to be characterized by significant scarcities. However, certain phenomena *in the nature of* scarcities could probably be demonstrated for any upper turning point one might select for study.[30] Also, as Haberler argued, the economy may become gradually more sensitive to random disturbances as its resources become more fully utilized,[31] so that it is not necessary to make extreme assumptions with respect to the existing degree of scarcity in order to use a pattern resem-

---

[29] In other words, the available rate of voluntary saving becomes insufficient to continue the expansion at an unchanging rate, and other sources of credit supply cannot be relied upon indefinitely because this would result in runaway inflation. The specific capital goods which would be required to stabilize the rate of investment at a level corresponding to the rate of voluntary saving are not available in sufficient quantities.

[30] The 1937 upper turning point in the United States would hardly be used to illustrate the proposition that scarcities may put an end to cyclical expansion. Yet it could be argued that elements of scarcity—or "quasi-scarcities"—existed at that time. For example, while there existed considerable unemployment, the labor supply was restricted (the labor supply function had been shifted up) because of the organization of labor unions. Moreover, the Federal Reserve Board—in consequence of inflation fears—behaved precisely as the Central Bank is assumed to behave in the overinvestment theories prior to the upper turning point. During the year preceding the downturn, reserve requirements were raised on three occasions.

[31] Because the expansion of any one industry in relation to economic activity as a whole becomes increasingly dependent on preceding actual contraction in other fields of activity.

bling that of the overinvestment theories (in conjunction with other patterns). As for the basic pattern of the underconsumption theories, this raises important questions on the logical level which caused this type of theory to be considered an outcast in professional economics. Saving cannot produce contraction if it is offset by investment. Consequently, no underconsumption theory is logically consistent unless it provides an explanation of why the savings in which the "under"-consumption expresses itself should result in hoarding instead of being offset or absorbed by investment. The older underconsumption theories did not come to grips with this problem. It is questionable how well this difficulty is solved in the underconsumption theories which are in vogue at present.

(5) The pattern of the underconsumption theories can be made logically consistent, although, of course, it never will become more than one of the many patterns the economist should have at his disposal when attempting to interpret specific economic processes. It is true that, as long as resources are available for expansion, the average propensity to consume cannot be so low or the savings ratio so high that a consistent willingness on the part of investors to fill the gap[32] should fail to result in full production. It is also true—and this is usually overlooked even by the modern underconsumptionists—that such "willingness" on the part of the investors would justify itself from their point of view, regardless of how low the average propensity to consume is, provided this "willingness" remained consistent over time. In this event, the investment decisions of any period would justify themselves (in the aggregate, i.e., aside from partial overproduction and immobility)[33] because all output produced would consistently be absorbed either by the consumers or by the investors for whom it was produced, with no involuntary accumulation of inventories. A consistently high willingness to invest is bound to justify itself *ex post* (in the aggregate),[33] and the consumer too is bound to benefit from it, regardless of how low the average propensity to consume is, as long as the marginal propensity to consume is greater than zero. It certainly would be unrealistic to assume that investment opportunities ever were absent (or that in the predictable future they will be absent) in the fundamental sense of zero or negative marginal yields from investment, if by these "yields" we mean the returns that *would be* realized in a full production economy *in the absence of uncertainty*, i.e., in the event that (1) the magnitude and the composition

---

[32] That is, to undertake enough investment to offset, or absorb, the savings.

[33] That is, aside from specific disturbances which might "generalize" themselves in consequence of the incomplete mobility of resources. *The underconsumption theories are not theories of "generalized partial overproduction" in this sense.*

of consumer demand were known for each level of output, (2) investors assumed of one another that they will always be willing to absorb the remaining part of the available resources for investment, and (3) there were no technological uncertainty. Consequently, it is a fallacy to maintain that aggregate output *cannot* be high if the average propensity to consume is low. It can, provided investors, in spite of the existing uncertainty, are consistently willing to undertake a sufficient amount of investment of the kind which justifies itself *by subsequent further investment demand.*[34]

However, there exists a strong presumption that in an economy in which the average and marginal propensity to consume is low, the uncertainty attaching to business expectations is high. Consumer demand is a more stable (dependable, predictable) constituent of aggregate demand than is the demand for investment goods by which the gap must be filled. This is a consequence of the fact that consumer demand springs more nearly from "deep-rooted habits" of institutional (and partly, also, biological) character than does the demand for investment goods. Full production is the less likely to materialize, the higher the degree of uncertainty that attaches to business expectations. Even if the propensity to consume were very low, full production would be quite *conceivable.* But it would be *unlikely,* in consequence of the high degree of uncertainty existing in such circumstances.

The increased uncertainty stems partly from the fact that investors do not assume of one another that they will always be willing to fill a substantial gap by definite, predictable types of investment activity. Moreover, if they did so, and if the gap in question were substantial enough, then this would imply an ever increasing ratio of real capital to real output[35] and, therefore, it would imply constantly changing methods of production (possibly only in the sense of "movements along given production functions," but even these may be associated with a high degree of technological uncertainty). The writer believes that underconsumption theories can become logically consistent only if they are supple-

---

[34] It is generally true for expanding economies that part of the investment of any period justifies itself by subsequent further investment demand. This is merely another way of saying that the marginal propensity to consume is smaller than unity and that, therefore, the additional output of any period will not be completely absorbed by consumers. It must partly be absorbed by further net investment. *This is true of any sequence of periods.* It also is generally true that the investment for further investment is associated with investment for additional consumption. This is merely another way of saying that the marginal propensity to consume, while smaller than unity, is positive. Cf. p. 77, below.

[35] Cf. the present writer's *Monetary Policies and Full Employment* (Berkeley, 1946), pp. 43–46; E. D. Domar, "Expansion and Employment," *American Economic Review,* March 1947, XXXVII, pp. 34–55.

mented by an appropriate theory of uncertainty. Otherwise, these theories would either imply *zero* marginal efficiency—that is, lack of investment opportunities—in the "fundamental" sense ("net-of-uncertainty" sense) discussed on p. 66; or they would imply a *very low* marginal efficiency in this fundamental sense plus a floor to interest rates set by infinitely elastic liquidity preference. While Lord Keynes made the assumption (which seems implausible to the present writer) that these factors might become operative in the predictable future, it would be clearly unrealistic to assume that in the industrialized economies they *have been* operative because historically these economies have not experienced diminishing returns. *Cycle theories other than underconsumption theories do not have to overcome this conceptual difficulty because they typically argue from specific disturbances (partial overproduction) to general contraction, with reference to the incomplete mobility of resources.*[36] The underconsumption theories, however, are not theories of *generalized* overproduction in this sense. They argue directly in over-all terms, not via partial overproduction and immobility. Consequently, they have to explain why there should be an over-all deficiency of inducements to invest.

(6) Neither the older nor the contemporary versions of the underconsumption theory bring out these points clearly, but some of the contemporary versions can be translated into these terms. They then become logically consistent, which, of course, does not of itself settle the question of their contribution to the understanding of economic fluctuations. The "modern" versions of the underconsumption theory are essentially the dynamic versions of the stagnation thesis. They argue that, in the circumstances existing in "mature" economies, investment becomes insufficient to fill a very substantial gap. In consequence of the slowing down of extensive growth (population growth, territorial expansion),[37] the inducement to invest is too weak to accomplish this. Consequently, in the course of the expansion, a point is reached at which the gap between aggregate output and consumption becomes too great to be filled by the amount of investment which is forthcoming in the present social-economic environment. The economy cannot get beyond such a critical point, which may be one of substantial underutilization. This, however, does not answer the question of why the necessary amount of investment is not undertaken, even though (if it were undertaken consistently over

---

[36] Partial overproduction may give rise to a deflationary spiral and to generalized overproduction if resources cannot be shifted freely from the original fields of overproduction. Practically all cycle theories, other than the underconsumption theories, are ultimately based on this notion, provided they claim to be general cycle theories.

[37] Some would add: also in consequence of the changing character of technological innovations.

time) it would turn out to be profitable, regardless of population growth, territorial expansion, and the numerical value of the propensity to consume. Yet it may be possible to argue that, in the course of cyclical expansions, the uncertainty attaching to business expectations increases, due to the fact that the proportion of output absorbed by consumer demand falls and the proportion absorbed by investment activity rises. It may also be possible to argue that the slowing down of extensive growth has contributed to the development of institutional rigidities by which the uncertainty has been increased. Obviously the fact that a sufficient amount of investment (if it were undertaken consistently over time) would justify itself in the aggregate is compatible with *any* degree of uncertainty from the viewpoint of the individual investor.

(7) We may conclude that the standard patterns of the underconsumption theories and of the overinvestment theories can be made logically consistent, and that they continue to belong among the models the economist should have at his disposal when attempting to interpret dynamic processes. Other significant models cut across the distinction between the two older theories just discussed. During the last decade, some of these were developed further, and, on the whole, more emphasis has been placed on these patterns than on the two models so far considered. Even those writers who come nearest to "representing" modernized versions of one of the two traditional theories have combined these with elements taken from further patterns (e.g., Hansen).[38]

Of these further models, the innovation theory should be mentioned first. This conceives of dynamic development as being produced by waves of innovations (i.e., by waves of "setting up new production functions") and by the adaptation of the economic system to the new methods of production (Schumpeter).[39] Long waves of economic development—"Kondratieff" upgrades and downgrades—are interpreted as having been produced by waves of innovations, predominantly of a definite type (or of a limited number of types) by which the specific long wave in question is characterized. The Kondratieff wave (upgrade plus downgrade) stretching from the seventeen-eighties to 1842 is that of the industrial revolution; the next (1842–97) is that of steam and steel; the third (from equilibrium in 1898 through an upper turning point prior to the first war and a trough in the 'thirties, toward future equilibrium)

---

[38] Cf. mainly Alvin H. Hansen, *Full Recovery or Stagnation; idem, Economic Policy and Full Employment* (New York and London, 1947).

[39] Cf. mainly Joseph A. Schumpeter, *Business Cycles* (New York and London, 1939); for a brief outline of the theory, cf. *idem,* "The Analysis of Economic Change," reprinted from the 1935 volume of the *Review of Economic Statistics* in *Readings in Business Cycle Theory*, pp. 1–19.

is the long wave of electricity, chemistry, and motors. Shorter waves —Juglar cycles and Kitchin cycles—become superimposed upon these long waves, as innovations spread, and as they give rise to related innovations, gradually changing the character of the production processes throughout the economy. The Juglars appear to be one-sixth as long as the Kondratieffs and three times as long as the Kitchins.[40] The entire process is started by entrepreneurs (innovators) of exceptional talent, and it propagates itself through imitation by others. The scope of the innovation theory of economic development is sufficiently broad to have rendered it possible for its author to discuss modern business cycle history from the angle of a unique central hypothesis.

(8) Other important patterns, contributing to the explanation of dynamic processes, are more specific in the sense of relating to narrower aspects of these processes. This, perhaps, is the least true of the Acceleration Principle, which, while concerned with a specific aspect of dynamic development, nevertheless lends itself more readily to being extended in scope than do some of the other patterns. The most significant proposition involved in the Acceleration Principle is that a decreasing rate of growth during the expansion tends to lead indirectly to an *absolute decline* of business activity. The durable goods industries, and also the production activities resulting in goods "for inventories," are more nearly geared to some definite rate of growth than to some definite level of output. If, after a period of rapid growth, the economy tends to become temporarily stabilized at a higher level, then the output of the specific industries in question will *fall* to the mere replacement rate.[41] Therefore, the primary tendency of the economy toward stabilization (or toward a slower rate of expansion) might not *actually* result in stabilization (or in a slower rate of expansion) but might, instead, result in a significant contraction of output. Since the basic underlying forces—such as discoveries, population growth, etc.—would, of themselves, tend to produce growth at varying rates, it is possible to arrive at models of economic fluctuation, assuming that the response of the economy to these basic forces will be influenced by the Acceleration Principle.[42]

---

[40] For the three cycles thus resulting, cf. note 43, p. 71.

[41] Of the stock of durable goods and of inventories.

[42] Cf. J. M. Clark, *Strategic Factors in Business Cycles* (New York, 1935). It should be added that more recently the Multiplier theory and the Acceleration Principle have also been synthesized into cycle models (R. F. Harrod, *The Trade Cycle* [Oxford, 1936]; Paul A. Samuelson, *op. cit.*). The underlying idea here is that additions to investment give rise to subsequent additions to income at a decreasing rate, due to the multiplier, and that such a primary tendency toward change at decreasing rate may generate fluctuations via the Acceleration Principle. However, it should not be overlooked that the Multiplier-Acceleration process operates in the fashion described only if the original additions to investment result merely in subsequent *consumption* spending, except for

(9) Some of the further cycle patterns can only be mentioned briefly. The "cobweb" pattern was further developed, and also subjected to criticism, in the course of the last decade. The pattern describes fluctuations which, on rather specific assumptions of the theorem, are induced by a consistent tendency on the part of producers to shoot beyond the mark, i.e., by excessive increases in output when prices are high and by excessive curtailments of output when prices are low. Each individual producer is inclined to believe that prices will stay high (or low) until he completes his adjustment to the prices "now" prevailing, but since a great many producers act simultaneously, prices will have turned from high to low (or from low to high) by the time the individual producers have completed the expansion of their production, or its contraction, as the case may be. Certain cycles in agricultural production (corn-hog cycle) may be partly explained by this model.

Building cycles, which have a duration of between fifteen and twenty years, may also have something to do with processes of this kind, although their duration excludes placing the emphasis on the cobweb model alone. The reinvestment cycle model has also been used to explain waves in building activity and in the production of other durable assets. Here again the mere fact that durable assets must be replaced after some time does not explain the occurrence of cyclical fluctuations, because replacement dates are by no means uniquely determined by the physical condition of capital goods. But, since replacement is not indefinitely postponable, the reinvestment-cycle model may contribute to the understanding of fluctuations in the production of durable goods (such as houses), and it may contribute even to the explanation of economic instability in general.

The building cycle has been emphasized considerably in the recent literature on dynamic processes. The average duration of this cycle is much greater than that of the "business cycle" proper,[43] but building cycle turning points (especially the upper turning points) tend to show

such further investment as is induced by this additional consumption expenditure. If the original additions to investment result directly in additions to (or reductions in) *other kinds of investment activity*—aside from the investment induced by the consumption effect of the original investment—then the process becomes more complicated, and it should be approached in terms of the marginal propensity to spend (James W. Angell, *op. cit.*) rather than in terms of the marginal propensity to consume. Metzler's model of inventory cycles is also based on an ingenious blending of the Multiplier theory with what may be considered a variant of the Acceleration Principle (cf. Lloyd A. Metzler, *op. cit.*).

[43] In the United States, roughly five times as long, if by the business cycle we mean the *reference cycle* of the National Bureau of Economic Research. This cycle is defined as expressing fluctuations in aggregate economic activity, with a duration of more than 1 year but no more than 10-12 years, and not divisible into shorter cycles with amplitudes approximating their own. The average duration of these for longer periods is

a lead in comparison with the corresponding (i.e., nearest) business cycle turning points. Furthermore, the most seriously depressed periods of the last hundred years or more fall in downgrades of the building cycle.[44] They also fall in longer intervals marked by a downward trend in prices and interest rates, that is, they fall in the "Kondratieff downgrades" (long-wave downgrades) of Schumpeter's three-cycle model. The *direction* of causation can, of course, not be decided by statements such as these.

(10) The various theories surveyed express possible contributing causes and illustrate them with simplified models. They all may be said to fit into the doctrine of generalized partial overproduction,[45] except insofar as they have underconsumptionist implications. Ultimately, general contraction is explained *either* by partial overproduction plus immobility *or* by over-all underconsumption, although both basic types of explanation include many variants. Some specific theories (e.g., the overinvestment theories) are clearly variants of one of these two basic types. Others (e.g., the Acceleration Principle) may be fitted into either type. Which of these one wants to use—or to emphasize more than the alternative ones—in the discussion of a given period depends on the special characteristics of that period. This is not true of the savings-investment *framework*,[46] which is suitable for expressing *any* specific theory on the nature of dynamic processes. But the statement *is* true of the specific theories of which the body of "business cycle theory" mostly consists at present. Each of these expresses something in pure form that

---

slightly in excess of 40 months for the United States. The reference cycle corresponds roughly to the Kitchin cycle of Schumpeter's schema in that it relates to business in general (as all three cycles of the Schumpeter schema) and has an average duration of close to 40 months. The dating is different because the "Kitchin" is founded on the hypothesis that two longer cycles are superimposed upon it, while the National Bureau identifies the turning points of its reference cycle from the ups-and-downs of time series directly. Moreover, Schumpeter dates his cycles from "equilibrium neighborhood" through peak and trough to next equilibrium, while the National Bureau dates from trough to trough with no equilibrium implications. The three-cycle hypothesis relates to fluctuations in *aggregate* economic activity, although the Kondratieff wave is much better established for prices and interest rates than for physical time series. The building cycle discussed in the text relates directly to a *specific* kind of activity. For Kondratieff's findings, cf. Nikolai D. Kondratieff, "The Long Waves in Economic Life," reprinted from the 1935 volume of the *Review of Economic Statistics* in *Readings in Business Cycle Theory*, pp. 20–42. For criticism, cf. George Garvy, "Kondratieff's Theory of Long Cycles," *Review of Economic Statistics*, November 1943, XXV, pp. 203–220.

[44] The eighteen-seventies, the eighteen-nineties, and the Great Depression.

[45] Cf. p. 68, including note 36.

[46] That is, the framework based on the proposition that income rises if investment exceeds Robertsonian savings and that it falls if Robertsonian savings exceed investment; or on the proposition that expectations turn out to have been too cautious if investment *ex ante* exceeds savings *ex ante*, and that they turn out to have been insufficiently cautious if savings *ex ante* exceed investment *ex ante*.

in reality is found at best in highly impure form and, in certain periods, may not be found at all. Further progress depends, therefore, on the co-ordination of analytical thinking with empirical research.

(11) Empirical research has recently mainly proceeded along two lines. The first is characterized by the attempt to formulate systems of equations with a great many (dated) variables and to test how well the observed values of these variables fit alternative systems during some period of time. The problems raised by this method are mainly problems in statistical theory, and they will not be discussed here. An appraisal of the method would have to throw light on the question of what is proved by showing that good fits are obtained with certain systems.[47] However, it should not be overlooked that the much less sophisticated "garden variety" of "testing" hypotheses for plausibility (which means using few variables and not applying refined statistical tests) is subject to the same limitations, in addition to operating with obviously incomplete "systems." The question is essentially that of finding the appropriate limits to refining a method which, given the character of the available material, is incapable of contributing more than a certain amount to the understanding of a problem.

The other empirical line of approach is that followed by the National Bureau of Economic Research (Mitchell, Burns, Mills, and others).[48] This method rests on the observation of the behavior of a great many specific time series during their own "specific cycles" and during the "reference cycles." Specific cycle turning points are those of the specific time series in question, while reference cycle turning points are those of aggregate economic activity.[49] After the elimination of seasonal variations, the values assumed by each time series are plotted for nine stages of *each* specific cycle and for the nine corresponding stages of *each* corresponding reference cycle (in terms of index-numbers, with the average value of the time series *during the cycle in question* as the base). In this fashion, a specific cycle pattern and a reference cycle pattern is obtained *for each time series, for each cycle*. Subsequently, both the specific cycle and the reference cycle patterns are averaged for longer periods, that is,

---

[47] Considering the very substantial margins of error to which the observations are subject, and considering the sensitiveness of these systems to changes in their values, the question also arises as to what is disproved by showing that certain systems do not give good fits.

[48] Cf. Arthur F. Burns and Wesley C. Mitchell, *Measuring Business Cycles* (New York, 1946); Frederick C. Mills, *Price-Quantity Interactions in Business Cycles* (New York, 1946).

[49] In setting the reference cycle turning points, the National Bureau takes into account the information obtainable from Business Annals (Thorp) concerning the state of business in general, and also the clustering of specific cycle turning points around certain dates (cf. also note 43, p. 71).

the value found for each of the nine stages of the individual cycles is averaged over all cycles[50] which developed during the period. By this procedure, an "average" pattern is obtained and plotted for each time series, expressing its "average behavior" during its own specific cycle, on the one hand, and during the reference cycle, on the other.[51] The method lends itself to studying many significant problems, such as those relating to the duration and the amplitude of the cycles observed in the various time series; leads and lags of various time series as compared to others and as compared to business in general (i.e., to the reference cycle); the possible existence of higher cyclical units consisting of triplets of reference cycles[52] or of all reference cycles lying between certain particularly severe depressions; the relative intensity of price changes and changes of output in the various stages of the cycle, etc.

The National Bureau technique is different in several respects from the traditional techniques by which "cycles" have been found, i.e., the raw material for cycle research has been obtained. Materials so obtained have been used for many purposes, ranging from the mere graphic representation of the cyclical behavior of time series to the testing of the systems of equations previously mentioned. The following appear to be the most significant differences between the traditional techniques of decomposing time series and the National Bureau method. In the first place, customarily the secular trend has been eliminated prior to identifying the cycle. This means that the cycle expresses fluctuations around the trend. It follows from the description on p. 73 that the National Bureau first establishes the turning points of the cycle, and afterwards eliminates merely the inter-cycle portion of the trend (by defining *each* cycle as a movement around the average value *during the cycle itself*). The intra-cycle portion of the trend is not eliminated. Furthermore, traditionally merely "specific cycles" were found, although some of the time series for which they were established are of general significance as indicators of business conditions. Application of the concept of the reference cycle to specific time series is a characteristic feature of the National Bureau method. The writer regards both these new features as improvements. They express an outlook characterized by the postulate that the aggregate of the economic developments between any reference cycle trough and the successive trough constitutes a "real" or "meaningful" experience in the life of a social community. The averaging of the cycle patterns, for each time series over longer periods, which also is an original feature of

---

[50] Over the specific cycles, on the one hand, and the reference cycles, on the other.
[51] "Average behavior" during a longer period comprising many cycles.
[52] That is, Schumpeter's *Juglar cycle* (cf. note 43, p. 71).

the National Bureau method, expresses the idea that all these pieces of experience belong in a common family of experiences.

The main limitations of the method are connected with the use of averages as representative values. But, of course, some difficulty of this character must necessarily arise in any attempt at generalization. The National Bureau method makes it comparatively easy for the reader to gain an impression of *how* typical (or untypical, as the case may be) the average pattern of a time series was of its changing behavior during a longer interval of time.

III. RIGIDITIES AND THE PROBLEM OF UNCERTAINTY

(1) Bridging the gap between recent developments in the theory of employment, on the one hand, and value theory, on the other, will probably prove a difficult task. The modern theory of employment lives a disconcertingly independent life from value theory. The artificial separation of these two fields expresses itself most clearly in the fact that the modern theory of employment has little to say about the effects of changes in the cost-*structure* on aggregate output and employment. This gives the theory an essentially monetary character, even if the analysis appears to run in real terms. The "real" magnitudes are derived on drastic simplifying assumptions with respect to the price and wage level.

(2) One of these drastic assumptions is that a change in the general level of money wages does not affect the level of aggregate output and employment, *except through its repercussions via the interest rate* (i.e., except by changing the existing degree of liquidity in relation to the money requirements set by the volume of transactions). This latter qualification—with respect to repercussions *via* the interest rate—does not relate to any really distinctive effects of wage changes, because the effect *via* interest rates is precisely identical with that of changes in the supply of money, given all prices and wages.[53] The proposition concerning the neutrality of general wage changes[54] is derived from the assumption that prices tend to change in the same direction and in the same proportion as money wage rates. At present, this proposition is perhaps rarely maintained in quite the crude and definite form here presented. But it frequently is maintained in *approximately* this form.

The best way of understanding the limitations of the general-wage-

---

[53] In other words, the effect in question is a "purely monetary" effect. Lord Keynes tended to hold this view, although the view is qualified in Chapter 19 of the *General Theory*.

[54] Except for the "purely monetary" effect just mentioned.

level neutrality idea is that of inquiring into the conditions under which it *would* be true. This seems preferable to repeating the line of argument along which its justification is usually presented.[55] The proposition would be true if it could be taken for granted that, at each level of real output, a given rate of consumption per period of time tends to "justify"—and, therefore, to bring about—a definite rate of new investment per period.[56] If this were taken for granted, it actually would be inconsistent to argue that a change in money wage rates produces a change in real wage rates and, thereby, a change in real output. For, with the change in real wage rates, the amount of consumption would have to be different, at all levels of output, from the consumption that would have materialized prior to the wage change. For example, if we envisage a money wage reduction that results in reduced real wage rates, we must conclude that consumption at any level of output will tend to be smaller than would have been the case without the wage reduction.[57] Consequently, at any level of physical output, a different amount of investment (in the case of a wage *reduction*, a greater amount of investment)[58] would now be forthcoming per unit of simultaneous consumer demand. If it is postulated that this cannot be true—i.e., that at each level of output a given amount of consumption "justifies" no more and no less than a definite rate of new investment—then the change in money wage rates must not be assumed to shift the consumption function.[59] Hence, the change must not be assumed to result in changing real wages. Prices must be assumed to change in the same proportion.

Yet, if producers, under the influence of changing money wage rates, change the amount of net investment, per period of time, which is associated with a given amount of consumption (i.e., with a unit of simultaneous consumer demand), then the outcome is different. For example, if we postulate that a *decrease* in money wage rates induces businessmen to undertake *more* investment "per unit of consumer demand," then real wage rates will decrease.[60] In this event, total income (consumption plus

---

[55] This line of argument rests ultimately on the notion that in the very short run, wage costs are the only prime costs, and that, consequently, in the short run, prices adjust completely to the change in money wage rates. This means that reproduction costs also adjust, and that, consequently, there is no reason for a different outcome in the long run.

[56] Assuming that interest rates do not change, *aside* from the "purely monetary" effect (repercussions *via* the interest rate) considered in the preceding paragraph.

[57] Because the propensity to consume out of wage income is typically greater than out of non-wage income.

[58] In the event of wage increases: a smaller amount of investment.

[59] Because the ratio of consumption to investment must not be assumed to shift for any level of output.

[60] If we assume that *less* investment is undertaken in relation to consumers' demand, then real wage rates will rise.

investment) will become greater[61] in relation to consumer demand and, therefore, it will also tend to become greater in relation to the wage bill.[62] Non-wage income will become greater in relation to wage income, which is another way of saying that (given the man-hour output) real wage rates will decline. *Prices will fall in a smaller proportion than money wage rates because aggregate demand (consumption plus investment) will fall in a smaller proportion than consumer demand.* Postulating that investment increases per unit of consumer demand means postulating that a condition will establish itself in which the average propensity to consume is lower than was the case before. Such a condition will establish itself by a fall in real wage rates.

It seems, therefore, that the crucial question in this connection relates to the amount of investment which appears to be "justified" to producers *per unit of consumer demand.* There exists an underconsumptionist bias to the effect that this amount of investment tends to be a constant, aside from temporary fluctuations around a "normal" value. Or perhaps the implication is that the "normal" (and "justified") amount of investment is determined by the marginal propensity to consume—i.e., by the slope of the consumption function—because this determines the *increase* in consumer demand in which the investment and the attending rise in output results. In fact, as we have seen, the proposition that changes in the general level money wage rates produce no effect on output is justified only on the assumption that the ratio of new investment to consumption is a constant (or that it tends to be a constant, aside from erratic fluctuations around its "normal" value).

(3) There exists no such simple relationship between the "justified" amount of investment, on the one hand, and the simultaneous rate of consumption,[63] on the other. Widely different amounts of aggregate investment may prove to be justified *per unit* of simultaneous consumption, provided the willingness to invest stays high in the long run, so that, in each subsequent period, the justified amount of aggregate investment again is considered to be high, per unit of consumption. The additional output to which the new investment gives rise is subsequently always partly absorbed by consumers *and partly by further (subsequent) investors.* (This is always true if the marginal propensity to consume is smaller than unity.) If subsequent investors are consistently willing to absorb *enough* of the additional output to which previous investments gave rise,

---

[61] In the event of a wage increase: *smaller.*

[62] Considering that the propensity to consume out of wage income is greater than out of non-wage income.

[63] *Or* the marginal propensity to consume.

then the economy may go on expanding indefinitely, regardless of how low the propensity to consume is.[64] Of course, there always will be some rise in consumption, as well as in investment, as long as the marginal propensity to consume is greater than zero. No *logical* inconsistency is involved in visualizing an expanding full-employment economy in which output consists of consumption to the extent of 10 per cent and of investment to the extent of 90 per cent, just as there is no inconsistency in the more realistic assumption that consumption accounts for about 90 per cent and investment for about 10 per cent. In both economies, the additional output, which is attributable to the investment, is partly absorbed by subsequent consumption and partly by subsequent investment, *and this is true of any sequence of periods.* But in the first of these two economies, a much greater part is absorbed by subsequent further investment. This is a very significant difference, affecting importantly, among other things, the degree of uncertainty existing in the economy.[65] But within reasonable limits, the proportion of output which is absorbed by investment is *actually* variable (not merely "in principle," i.e., not merely if we disregard uncertainty). There is no reason to assume that the "justified" amount of investment should bear some simple relationship to the simultaneous rate of consumption or to the marginal propensity to consume.

It seems quite likely that a change in the general level of money wages would actually tend to change the ratio of investment to consumption per period of time; that is to say, it is quite likely that investment would not be changed in the same proportion as consumption. When we are concerned with consumption output, it may be reasonable to assume, in the first approximation, that the influence of wage changes is equally significant on cost, on the one hand, and on demand, on the other. With respect to investment, as a whole, such a premise does not seem equally plausible. For such investment activity as results in goods to be absorbed by subsequent, further investments,[66] wages are direct cost-factors, but they are not demand-influencing factors in any direct way. If it is assumed that general money wage increases *reduce* the ratio of new investment to consumption and that general money wage reductions *raise* the ratio of new investment to consumption, then money wage increases will tend to be associated with increased real wage rates and money wage reductions with reduced

---

[64] Unless the marginal efficiency of capital, in the "fundamental" or "classical" sense discussed on pp. 66–68, declines to zero or to the institutional floor level of interest rates.

[65] It affects uncertainty in more than one way. Cf. p. 67, above.

[66] Which, in turn, again result in goods to be absorbed by subsequent, further investment, etc.

real wage rates. In this event, *aggregate* demand adjusts incompletely to the wage changes, because investment demand adjusts incompletely. Therefore, prices also adjust incompletely. We are implying here that after the change in wage rates, wages are expected to stay at their new level.

There is much room for theoretical as well as empirical investigation on this subject. While, on the whole, there still exists a tendency to get around these problems with drastic simplifying assumptions, some work has been done on the relationship between changes in money wage rates, on the one hand, and changes in real wage rates, on the other (Dunlop, Tarshis).[67] It is likely that, in the future, we will witness a renewal of the effort to formulate a reasonably realistic theory of the relationship between money and real wages. It also seems likely that the effect of wage changes on aggregate output and employment will be investigated further.

(4) So far as the relationship between changes in real wage rates and employment is concerned, much of the theoretical thinking of recent times is either based on highly "orthodox" assumptions or on a simple reversal of these. To get the problem already discussed out of our way, let us assume that we are able to trace the effects of money wage changes on real wages, and that we are faced with a given change in money wage rates *and* with an attending change in the general level of real wage rates. Should it be taken for granted that aggregate output and employment will always move inversely to real wage rates? Or that it will move in the same direction, due to a favorable effect of wage increases on effective demand? Recent theory has had little to say on the subject, although common sense reasoning should show clearly enough that neither of these categoric views can possess general validity. If real wage rates rise beyond certain limits, the reward for bearing uncertainty must become insufficient to induce an adequate amount of investment activity. Moreover, there will develop a tendency to substitute capital for labor. If real wage rates decline to very low levels, the propensity to consume also declines very low, and production and employment could be high only if an unusually high proportion of output were allocated to further investment

---

[67] John T. Dunlop, "The Movement of Real and Money Wage Rates," *Economic Journal,* September 1938, XLVIII, pp. 413–434; Lorie Tarshis, "Changes in Real and Money Wages," reprinted from the 1939 volume of the *Economic Journal* in *Readings in the Theory of Income Distribution* (Philadelphia and Toronto, 1946), pp. 330–335; J. M. Keynes, "Relative Movements of Real Wages and Output," *Economic Journal,* March 1939, XLIX, pp. 34–52; cf. also John T. Dunlop, *Wage Determination under Trade Unions* (New York, 1947); Lloyd G. Reynolds, "Wage Differences in Local Labor Markets," *American Economic Review,* June 1946, XXXVI, pp. 366–375.

(rather than to consumption) in each subsequent period. As was pointed out before, such a condition is logically quite conceivable; most of the investment of each period could result in output for further investment in the subsequent period. If the willingness to invest should—in the long run—not slacken in these circumstances, the investments would prove profitable. Aggregate consumption would also be rising, provided the marginal propensity to consume was greater than zero (which, of course, should be assumed). But while such a condition is quite conceivable, it would create a very high degree of uncertainty because the system *could* cease to function satisfactorily whenever the willingness to invest for further investment declined. Owing to this uncertainty, the system would presumably never start functioning satisfactorily in conditions such as these. Consequently, "too high" real wage rates and "too low" real wage rates seem equally incompatible with full production. This raises the problem of an optimum, which so far has received insufficient attention.

(5) On the whole, the framework in which much of the recent analysis was developed is not particularly well suited for coping with tasks which involve the problem of uncertainty. Most analytical systems "get rid" of the uncertainty problem by a procedure which easily becomes misleading.[68] Marginal revenue is equated to marginal cost, or the marginal efficiency of capital is equated to the rate of interest! These, of course, are merely variations on the profit-maximization theme.[69] But what kind of "expectations" are expressed in these functions? For, surely, the producer should be said to equate the expected values of these functions. The implication of the conventional procedure is that the functions in question express something in the nature of mathematical expectations (or of most probable expectations) *discounted for uncertainty*. This, however, comes rather close to making the problem of uncertainty disappear completely.

It might be preferable to leave these "most probable" revenue and cost functions, and the marginal efficiency functions, undiscounted, and to take into account separately that producers do not typically aim at the simple objective of maximizing "most probable" profits (i.e., at equating the relevant marginal functions). They aim at some reasonable compromise between "most probable" profit-maximization and safety, *where "most probable," of course, merely stands for something in the nature of a "best guess."* Safety considerations alone would usually justify a *lower*

---

[68] However, for explicit discussion of these problems cf. G. L. S. Shackle, *op. cit.,* and his exchange of views with A. G. Hart in the October 1940 issue of the *Review of Economic Studies;* also A. G. Hart, *Anticipations, Uncertainty and Dynamic Planning* (Chicago, 1940). For further references cf. the present writer's *op. cit.*, p. 152.

[69] See also J. S. Bain, pp. 154–157, below.

rate of output[70] than that warranted by "most probable" profit-maximization, because the gap between "most probable" *average* revenue and "most probable" *average* cost (i.e., the gap between the AR and the AC function of value theory) typically is at a maximum for lower rates of output, and *this* is the gap—this is the "safety margin"—that counts for most safety considerations. *Safety margins here are meant to express the margins by which the actual outcome may fall short of the best guess without causing losses.*[71] Consequently, if uncertainty increases, and higher safety margins are required, those producers who stay in business will *ceteris paribus* reduce their output (in the direction of higher safety margins), and some producers will go out of business because the safety margins available to them are insufficient even for the "safest" rate of output. This, of course, is not the only way in which uncertainty can be taken into account. In fact, it is a crude way, but it may be adequate for certain purposes.

(6) The problem of interest-rate rigidities can also not be appraised adequately without a satisfactory analysis of uncertainty. The reduced emphasis on interest-rate adjustments is one of the characteristic features of recent theorizing on output and employment. Not much confidence is placed in the reduction of interest rates as a means of raising aggregate output, and, consequently, not much emphasis is placed on "too high" interest rates in the explanation of unemployment. In the Keynesian theory this lack of confidence is explained by the alleged infinite (or exceedingly high) elasticity of the liquidity preference function[72] at low net rates of interest, as a consequence of which it is said to be impossible to lower net rates sufficiently. Alternative explanations have not been explored thoroughly, and this is largely due to the circumstance that other explanations stress the uncertainty factor, for which no adequate allowance is made in the contemporary analytical systems. If we abstract from uncertainty by operating with "net" functions (discounted for risk), then sufficiently low net rates of interest should always produce a high rate of

---

[70] Assuming that the producer in question stays in business at all, in spite of the uncertainty.

[71] The output for which most probable *average* revenue minus most probable *average* cost is at a maximum gives the producer a higher safety margin than the output for which most probable marginal revenue equals most probable marginal cost, *provided* he feels that the unfavorable surprise (against which he is protecting himself) would express itself in lower demand and higher cost functions than those appearing most probable and *provided* that the shifts of the curves are approximately parallel shifts. Therefore, a compromise between the maximization of most probable profits and the maximization of safety margins should be expected to result in a rate of output lying *between* the output which equates most probable MR with most probable MC and the output which maximizes the excess of most probable AR over most probable AC.

[72] That is, of the demand for funds intended for new hoarding.

investment, unless the (net) marginal efficiency of capital declines to zero. Ineffectiveness of interest-rate policies could then be explained only on the assumption that net rates cannot be lowered sufficiently.[73] But this is no very plausible explanation. It seems far more likely that net rates could be lowered, practically, to any extent desired but that this, in itself, may fail to produce a high level of output. However, if this is maintained, then the emphasis must be placed on uncertainty.[74] In the first place, even with net rates in the neighborhood of zero, the actual terms of lending to business would still include the full premia for borrowers' uncertainty. Secondly, even if these were largely borne by some public agency[75] and, thus, gross rates of interest were also reduced to the neighborhood of the zero level, borrowing and investing would still require that the borrowers' safety margins should be sufficient in the face of the existing uncertainty. (It must be assumed that loan renewal depends on business results and is not guaranteed in advance indefinitely, because otherwise we would be discussing a policy of *unlimited subsidization* rather than a credit policy.) In other words, "most probable" yields (the "best guess" for yields) from real investment would still have to be in excess of the gross rates of interest by a sufficient margin, for a sufficient number of producers.

The main point here is that the limitations of interest-rate policies are connected with a much broader area than that which is visible to an investigator who discounts his functions for risk and then proceeds as though the resulting net profit expectations were maintained with certainty. Such an investigator cannot easily explain why a sufficient reduction of interest rates should not be the panacea for which the world is looking in periods of unemployment. Therefore, he will be inclined to

---

[73] Unless it is maintained that the marginal efficiency of capital had already declined to zero!

[74] In the Keynesian theory of speculative hoarding (which assumes a liquidity-preference floor to net rates of interest through the flattening out of the liquidity function), the emphasis also is placed on uncertainty of a specific kind, namely, on uncertainty *concerning future net rates of interest*. The public hoards because it believes that net rates are likely to rise (i.e., capital values are likely to fall) and that, therefore, it will pay to postpone security purchases. This is the only kind of uncertainty that is *not* defined away from the Keynesian system by "discounting for risk." All basic functions of the system are "discounted" and, therefore, they are "net of risk." Consequently, this specific kind of uncertainty has to bear the full burden of the Keynesian theory of hoarding. Our point is that if we do not get rid of other kinds of uncertainty in this fashion, then these other varieties—especially those attaching to profit expectations—can be made to share the burden. Hoarding which arises from this kind of uncertainty (precautionary hoarding) is not actually excluded from the Keynesian analysis, but it plays a subordinate and passive role because the phenomenon which gives rise to it is made to disappear in the formal system by "discounting for risk."

[75] Which, however, implies *subsidization* on a truly large scale. The feasibility of such a scheme is questionable.

argue that the difficulties arise merely from the impossibility of lowering net rates of interest sufficiently. An increasing number of economists feel that many crucial questions cannot even be *asked* in such a framework.

(7) Conditions are favorable to investment if, for a substantial number of firms, the existing relationship between gross[76] revenue expectations and gross[76] cost expectations (given the existing degree of uncertainty) is such as to make it appear unlikely that they will suffer losses on the investment projects which are open to them. The essence of the optimum problem raised in connection with wage theory (pp. 79–80) may now be restated in a few sentences. An increase in profit margins[77] *beyond certain limits* becomes self-defeating because uncertainty grows beyond all reasonable limits if the average propensity to consume falls to very low levels. Consequently, beyond a certain limit, the same factors which give rise to an increase in the safety margins produce an even greater increase in the degree of uncertainty, so that the relationship of these to one another becomes increasingly unfavorable. At the other end of the scale (i.e., for low profit margins), the opposite is true. Here, an increase in profit margins is favorable in spite of the lowering of the average propensity to consume, because a high average propensity to consume merely reduces but does not eliminate uncertainty, and, hence, it alone is insufficient to call forth an adequate rate of investment if profit margins fall below certain limits.

(8) In the present section, we considered so far two aspects of the problem of rigidities: the problem of wage rates and that of interest rates in relation to the requirements of full production. These problems appear as problems of "rigidity" if they are viewed in relation to full production because what matters, from this point of view, is the failure or the inability of these cost factors to "adjust" in such a way as to clear the market. The rigid behavior of cost factors is, of course, connected with monopoly power. Monopolistic tendencies have aggravated these rigidities considerably. However, rigidities in this sense are not exclusively a product of monopoly. In the preceding paragraphs it was argued that downward corrections of the wage level and of interest rates would not always create full production. Downward corrections of the wage level beyond certain limits may even exert an adverse influence; downward correction of interest rates seems always desirable in periods of unemployment, but such a measure—even if applied to gross rates—would still leave a limited number of investors with limited safety margins,[78] and,

---

[76] Gross, in the sense of "undiscounted for risk."
[77] And, thereby, in safety margins.
[78] Which depend on their expectations with respect to revenue and other costs.

therefore, it may fail to result in full production. Consequently, the absence of monopolistic rigidities would not automatically produce a cost behavior by which the market is always cleared. The absence of monopolistic rigidities *plus uncertainty* would,[79] but this is a different proposition. If by "rigidity" we mean failure to adjust in such a way as to clear the market, then rigidities are created partly by monopoly and partly by uncertainty, or rather by the interaction of these two elements. In this sense, the cost structure could show "rigidity" even if there were no monopoly. Uncertainty, in itself, may prevent gross interest rates from declining to the levels required for full production,[80] and wage adjustments beyond certain limits may not remedy such a situation.[81]

(9) The role of uncertainty should be stressed also in connection with rigidities in the commodity price structure, that is, in connection with rigid "relative prices." The views which have been expressed on this problem are partly contradictory. There seems to be good logic, as well as common sense, in the rather general contention that, in periods of underemployment, it would be beneficial to reduce the prices of specific commodities—or specific groups of commodities—for which the demand is elastic. Special emphasis may be placed on groups of complementary producers' goods (e.g., building materials), the demand for which might show an elastic response in the event of a joint and co-ordinated price reduction, while the demand for the single commodities of which the group consists might not be elastic. On the other hand, the view was also expressed that inelasticity might have advantages,[82] because if the prices of commodities are reduced for which the demand is inelastic,[83] the consumer spends less money on the commodity in question and, therefore, is left with more money for other purchases (in spite of buying an increased physical quantity of the commodity in question).

To the present writer this last view does not seem convincing. Let us assume at first that it actually is possible to increase the real output of a specific commodity by lowering its price.[84] In this event, the magnitude of the offsetting item (decreased physical demand for other goods) and, therefore, the net effect on real output depends on how elastic the de-

[79] In other words, Chamberlin's *perfect* (and not merely *pure*) competition would.

[80] The levels required for full production may in certain circumstances even be "negative levels," implying, of course, outright subsidization.

[81] Underemployment *equilibrium* is, of course, excluded if flexible wage rates are assumed. But underemployment is not excluded, especially if we assume that uncertainty grows with falling real wage rates.

[82] Cf. Donald H. Wallace, "Industrial Markets and Public Policy: Some Major Problems," in *Public Policy*, C. J. Friedrich and Edward S. Mason, eds. (Cambridge, Mass., 1940).

[83] In the sense of less than unitary elasticity.

[84] Owing to the fact that more is demanded at the lower price.

mand for the aggregate of the other commodities is in relation to the demand for the specific commodity under consideration. The other commodities are made more expensive in relation to the commodity in question. Therefore, there will be an adverse primary effect on the aggregate of the other markets. Disregarding at first the money income effect, we may conclude that the primary impact on real output will be favorable if the elasticity of the demand for the cheapened commodity is greater than the elasticity of the demand for the aggregate of the other commodities (i.e., *greater* than the *average* price-elasticity in the economy). In addition, there will be an expansionary money income effect (money expenditures will rise) if the elasticity of the demand for the cheapened commodity is *greater than unity*. Consequently, on these assumptions, a case can be established for the reduction of the "sticky" prices of commodities for which the demand possesses more-than-average *and* greater-than-unitary elasticity. More-than-average elasticity means that the primary adverse effect on the other markets is smaller than the favorable effect on the specific market in question; and more-than-unitary elasticity means that the repercussions via money income are also favorable. The question of whether the buyer is left with more money after completing the purchase of the cheapened commodity is not in itself decisive, because in this type of analysis it may not be taken for granted that, if "left with more money," the buyer will take more of the other commodities. Whether or not he will do so is "decided" by the assumptions we make with respect to the relative elasticities involved in the problem.

As was stated before, this kind of reasoning assumes that it is possible to increase the output of a commodity by reducing its prices. This is not necessarily true. In perfect competition, it would never be true (in the long run). But the problem should be considered in the context of imperfect competition, with a substantial area of monopolistic pricing. Whether monopoly output can or cannot be increased by administrative lowering of the price depends on the safety margin considerations to which reference was made in earlier parts of this section. In the first place, it is, of course, possible that the enterprise in question will give up producing the commodity (instantaneously, or in the long run), because, at the lower price, safety margins against unfavorable surprise are insufficient. Secondly, the enterprise may go on producing, but at a lower rate, because—given the price ceiling—safety margins[85] are considered adequate for a lower output, but not for the previous output, and even less

---

[85] E.g., in the sense of the gap between AR and AC, interpreted as "most probable" average revenue and "most probable" average cost (or the "best guess" for AR and AC, respectively; cf. p. 81, above, including footnote 71).

for the higher output which the authority hoped to call forth.[86] Thirdly, intervention of this sort may result in the desired increase in output, so far as the processes of production are concerned which are already carried on in the economy, and yet it may exert an adverse influence on the planning of new processes. This again is a matter of uncertainty. Only in cases in which these three qualifications may be ruled out as *practically* unimportant, should we expect a favorable "aggregate output effect" from the lowering of specific prices. In these cases, the elasticity considerations of the preceding paragraphs become relevant.

In conclusion, it should be repeated that the process of including problems of the cost-price structure in the theory of employment is still in its early stages. The theory of employment is frequently made to proceed on the assumption of a given cost-price structure, and it is then concerned almost exclusively with aggregate money flows, without investigating the relationship between these, on the one hand, and cost-price problems, on the other. At the same time, value theory typically proceeds on the assumption of a given aggregate output and employment, and it is concerned merely with the *relative* allocation of resources. It is to be expected that the links between the two will grow tighter and that significant interactions will be explored more fully.

IV. Policies

(1) In the recent discussion of full-employment policy, the emphasis has been placed increasingly on compensatory fiscal devices.[87] This accords well with the present state of the theory of employment, as interpreted in the preceding sections of this chapter.

Compensatory fiscal policies are, of course, *not* "cost-price policies";

[86] As my colleague, Professor Joe S. Bain, pointed out to me in discussion, these are cases in which the price reduction leads to rationing by the producer. The *demand* is always higher at the lower price. The existence of excess demand, of course, reduces the uncertainty but the safety margins must be sufficient to compensate for the remaining uncertainty as concerns shifts of the relevant functions.

[87] That is to say, on fiscal policies aimed at stimulating private expenditures and at supplementing them by public expenditures when increased aggregate expenditures seem desirable; and at reducing private as well as public expenditures in inflationary periods.

Full employment may be defined as a condition in which no person is unemployed who desires employment at the going money wage rates. In practice the closest conceivable approximation to full employment is a condition in which employment is "full," aside from a moderate amount of "frictional unemployment." Some degree of arbitrariness is involved in the concept of frictional unemployment because in many cases there exists no sharp distinction between the *inability* and the *unwillingness* to "move" (regionally or occupationally), and unwillingness to move cannot always be sharply distinguished from unwillingness to work at the going wage rates (i.e., from voluntary unemployment). There may exist any amount of *voluntary* unemployment in "full employment."

they do not aim at influencing the cost-price structure, although, indirectly, they may influence it. The theory of the relationship between cost-price problems and the level of employment is comparatively undeveloped and so is the corresponding policy discussion. The opposition to neglecting this aspect of the full-employment problem has gradually grown (cf. the work of Clark, Ellis, Haberler, and others),[88] but the main trend of thought has so far mostly proceeded along "monetary-fiscal" lines. This is not entirely accidental, nor does it merely reflect the unwillingness to invoke the resistance of power groups against interference with the cost-price structure. The problem of the effects of cost-price policies is inherently more complicated than that of the effects of tax increases and reductions, or of changing rates of public investment.

(2) The most obvious (although not the only) difficulty which arises if cost-price problems are disregarded in connection with compensatory fiscal policies relates to the inflation problem. To "compensate" deflation tendencies, with uncompromising consistency, means to guarantee the continued existence of a sellers' market without interruptions. In such circumstances, a continuous upward pressure on the general wage and price level would have to be expected. Furthermore, there would presumably develop a tendency toward quality deterioration, and pressure would be exerted to adjust the fiscal program to any existing maldistribution of resources. Inflationary tendencies would be generated by the concerted wage- and price-raising action of organized groups, because the economic penalty standing in the way of such action would be removed.[89] These tendencies would be reinforced by the dishoarding of idle balances (the maintenance of which would appear to be unjustified under such conditions). It is true that a group of producers which raises its selling prices would place itself at a competitive disadvantage in relation to other groups as long as these do not follow suit. But this would not check the inflationary tendency because—given the *de facto* guarantee of full employment—labor groups would always prefer higher money wage rates to the *status quo*, and, consequently, producers would usually be better off with higher prices, regardless of whether the other industries actually followed suit. Furthermore, it could be taken for granted that other industries, for the very same reasons, *would* follow suit.

It has been maintained that a national bargaining agency for the aggregate labor force would not behave in the manner here assumed be-

<hr>

[88] Cf., e.g., J. M. Clark, "Financing High Level Employment," in *Financing American Prosperity: A Symposium of Economists* (New York, 1945), pp. 71–125; Howard S. Ellis, "Economic Expansion Through Competitive Markets," *ibid.*, pp. 126–198; Gottfried Haberler, *op. cit.*

[89] Cf. A. C. Pigou, *op. cit.*

cause the wage increases envisaged above are obviously self-defeating for labor as a whole.[90] But this is more than questionable. Even an over-all bargaining agency for labor would consist of constituent groups, and the agency would usually find it more expedient to yield to each group in succession than to oppose all. Aside from this, the agency would always tend to maintain that the wage increases it is demanding *should* not result in price increases, while in reality they *would*.

(3) These are the main difficulties arising in connection with a *de facto* guarantee of full employment by means of fiscal policy. The range of attitudes that may be taken in an attempt to resolve these difficulties lies between two extremes. One extreme position would be that of advocating thoroughgoing and rigorous controls, extending to prices, wage rates, the quality of goods and services, and the regional and occupational composition of resources (including the labor force). Total economic controls could be handled effectively only by a government which itself is the only effective power group in the scene. The price is excessive.

At the other extreme, we have the *laisser faire* attitude in relation to cost-price problems. It is important to realize that a *laisser faire* attitude in this respect is compatible with a substantial amount of "compensatory fiscal policy." For example, it would be quite unconvincing to argue that during the Great Depression unregulated cost-price relationships prevented the government from adopting vigorous compensatory policies of a monetary-fiscal character. On the contrary, failure to adopt policies of this kind on a sufficient scale contributed greatly to the growth of cost-price maladjustments. But while *cost-price laisser faire* does not justify *monetary-fiscal laisser faire*, it does set limits to the effectiveness of compensatory fiscal policy. With unregulated cost-price relationships, fiscal policy must keep one eye on the full-employment problem and the other on the wage and price level. It cannot keep both eyes on the full-employment problem. Expansionary monetary-fiscal policies must be discontinued if they result in substantial cost-price maladjustments of the "inflationary" variety, and this *may* happen at levels considerably lower than that of full employment.

(4) Even though the United States does not at present have complete *cost-price laisser faire*, we are not far removed from this condition. Some existing measures (even aside from the temporary rent control) may be regarded as falling in the category of wage and price controls, but these are not major features of the present institutional setting. What degree of cost-price control will prove to be desirable and compatible with democratic political institutions is hard to foretell. As was pointed out

---

[90] Sir William Beveridge, *op. cit.*

before, this problem deserves more attention than it has received. However, it seems very likely that there exists a fundamental contradiction between truly thoroughgoing controls of this kind and democratic political institutions, although it also is very likely that more could be done to reduce the exploitation of man-made (or "institutional") scarcities. With a largely uncontrolled cost-price structure, monetary-fiscal policy will have to be oriented to "full-employment" objectives, on the one hand, and to "wage and price stability" objectives, on the other. It cannot be oriented to full-employment objectives alone. Such a policy can be successful only if moderate concessions at the expense of one set of objectives result in coming reasonably close to accomplishing the other. The problem is inherently one of balancing objectives. This is overlooked in much of the recent full-employment literature.

Despite these limitations, compensatory fiscal policy can go a long way toward eliminating periods of mass unemployment. It is to be hoped that the limitations so far discussed will mainly express themselves in an occasional dilemma at tolerably high levels of employment, where it will still be necessary, at times, to choose between some amount of cyclical unemployment and highly undesirable wage-price tendencies. It would be unwarranted to anticipate such a dilemma for thoroughly unsatisfactory levels of aggregate output and employment. Compensatory fiscal policy should be capable of going a long way toward preventing periods of mass unemployment, even if it is incapable of preventing business recessions. This, of course, would be a tremendous accomplishment. Most major depressions might not have developed beyond the stage of "tolerable" recessions if effective compensatory measures had been adopted six to twelve months after the downturn, and extended periods of stagnation (or of chronic depression) may be interpreted as aftermaths of violent and uncompensated cyclical contractions.

(5) It is conceivable that this high promise of monetary-fiscal policy induces many economists to underemphasize, or even to disregard, the limitations previously discussed. The fear is rather common that the public and the authorities will not realize the possibilities offered by the appropriate devices. Some degree of optimism may, however, not be unjustified in this respect. Looking at the other side of the medal, we see that compensatory—in this case anti-*inflationary*—fiscal policies were carried distinctly further during the Second World War than in previous major wars. These fiscal policies were far from adequate, but they were less inadequate than might have been expected on the basis of the experience of previous inflationary periods. On the whole, the history of the Second World War shows an increasing (but still inadequate) under-

standing of the issues involved in compensatory fiscal policy. Moreover, it should be taken into account that strategic power groups frequently have reason to believe that the inflationary distribution of a war burden will prove more favorable from their point of view than a strictly planned distribution. A major depression, however, is a disaster for all groups.

(6) What, in particular, are the fiscal devices most frequently advocated in recent literature? Flexible tax rates and the countercyclical timing of "noncompeting" public works[91] have received much attention, and rightly so. Insofar as the public works required for overcoming depression tendencies are useful *per se*—i.e., do not *merely* serve the purpose of generating a Multiplier Effect—the choice between reducing tax rates and stepping up the public works program becomes a matter of "opportunity costs," in a somewhat extended sense of the term. If, on the other hand, the public works in question are highly wasteful in any sense other than that of generating a Multiplier Effect, it seems preferable to accomplish the desired objective wholly by reduced taxation, and possibly by granting consumer subsidies (that is to say, by negative taxation). The urgency of certain "noncompeting" (or largely noncompeting) public works projects[92] is obvious at present. One might believe that for the next one or two decades the alternative method (reduced taxation) should be disregarded. However, the most urgent public works are not those which are most suitable for prompt adjustment to rapidly changing business conditions. Moreover, the response of the economy to the stimulus provided by public works is substantially reduced by high taxes. Consequently, it seems highly desirable to combine the two methods. It is recognized in the contemporary literature that further advance in the field of social security, and especially of unemployment insurance, would have the desirable by-product of lending more flexibility to the tax structure, because contributions are in the nature of taxes, and benefits in the nature of "consumer subsidies." But it also is necessary to lend tax rates substantially more flexibility.

The adjustment of tax rates to changing business conditions would presumably require (in addition to the pay-as-you-go system) some delegation of power on the part of Congress, because tax revision has proved a very time-consuming procedure. This also is recognized in the contemporary literature on the subject. The proposal has been made that Congress should delegate to the Administration the power of changing the

---

[91] That is, of public works which do not suppress a comparable amount of private investment, or, if possible, even stimulate private investment activity directly.

[92] Especially that of medical and educational projects, of slum clearance and low-cost housing, of projects aiming at the conservation of resources, road building, etc.

first-bracket individual income tax rate during the fiscal year.[93] Possibly, it might even be sufficient to have Congress delegate this power to a joint committee of its own.

(7) The fiscal policy proposals so far considered may be viewed as compensatory devices. This is not their only *raison d'être*, but, in addition to having other merits, they would perform the function of providing stimuli in periods of recession, and of checking inflationary tendencies. Other fiscal policy proposals widely discussed in the contemporary literature aim at strengthening the inducement to invest, aside from the problem of cyclical instability. The opinion is widely held that corporate taxes are less desirable instruments of fiscal policy than individual income taxes, not merely because individual income taxes are more equitable, but also because business management, in deciding about investment projects, is much more concerned with profits "after corporate taxes" than with dividends "after individual taxes."[94] However, if individual income taxes were to be substituted for the present type of corporate taxation, it would be necessary to find means by which undistributed profits become accessible to taxation. Otherwise, an unreasonable stimulus would be provided for accumulating undistributed profits. This would be adverse to the interests of stockholders, and it would have especially bad general economic effects in periods of business recession.

Yet the deterrent effect of individual taxes on the willingness of individuals to invest should also not be overlooked. This adverse effect—and, generally speaking, the deterrent effect of taxation—could be reduced by appropriate loss-deduction (or loss carry-over) provisions. The problem of "averaging devices" of this sort (i.e., of devices aiming at the averaging of income over longer periods, for tax purposes) has also received considerable attention in the recent literature.

(8) The impression should not be conveyed that the idea of compensatory fiscal policy is wholly the product of the last ten or fifteen years. It is more appropriate to say that the idea of compensatory credit policies (or "monetary" policies in the narrower sense), as well as that of compensatory fiscal policy, has a long history, but that recently the emphasis has been shifted increasingly from credit policies to fiscal policy. The limitations of credit policies—such as those of discount policy and of open-market policy—are generally assumed to be narrower than those of fiscal policy. The main reason for this is that additional central bank

---

[93] Cf. Committee for Economic Development, *Jobs and Markets* (New York and London, 1946).

[94] Cf. Harold M. Groves, *Production, Jobs and Taxes* (New York and London, 1944).

credit may, in certain circumstances, result in a comparatively large increase in hoarding and only in a small increase in investment, while it seems safe to assume that the additions to the income flow (rather than merely to the money stock) which are generated by expansionary fiscal policy[95] give rise at least to the "corresponding" increase in consumption expenditures, and probably also to induced investment.

Furthermore, if inflation rather than depression tendencies need be compensated, tax increases and budgetary savings can (jointly) always be made sufficient, while any increase in interest rates (plus credit restriction) may prove insufficient, provided the public owns enough idle balances. Also, governments can ill afford to bring about really significant increases in interest rates during inflationary periods, because the attending capital losses of bondholders would presumably make borrowing difficult in later periods in which this might again become desirable or necessary. Hence the shift in emphasis from "monetary" policy in the narrower sense to fiscal policy.

(9) There is some correspondence between this shift in emphasis, on the one hand, and the shift from the quantity theory approach to the savings-investment approach, on the other.[96] In the quantity-theory terminology, both the credit policies and the fiscal policies result in the creation or destruction of money stocks, and, consequently, the difference between the two types of policy is not emphasized "from the outset." In the savings-investment (or income-expenditure) terminology, fiscal policy changes the "strategic" variables (such as income itself) instantaneously, while credit policies do not directly or necessarily affect these magnitudes. However, any assumption concerning facts *can* be expressed in either conceptual framework. There obviously is no logical inconsistency in maintaining—in the framework of the quantity-theory approach—that the velocity of new money is different, depending on whether it enters through open market operations or through deficit financing.

Earlier in this chapter, the view was expressed that the shift in emphasis from the quantity theory approach to the savings-investment approach has proved fruitful, but that this shift may have been somewhat too complete. Substantial changes in the stock of money may well have an influence on the basic relationships (functions) of the savings-investment approach, and liquidity ratios need not be in the nature of mere residuals, even at low interest rates. A similar statement could be made of the shift in emphasis from "monetary" policies in the nar-

---

[95] E.g., the additional disposable income created by tax reductions or by public works.
[96] Cf. pp. 52–53, above.

rower sense[97] to fiscal policy. This shift in emphasis has also proved fruitful: fiscal policy is the more potent instrument, and the reasons, by and large, *are* those which were brought out in the literature of the last decade. But this shift in emphasis also tends to become unduly complete. It leads to overlooking the fact that in the past even the monetary policies (in the narrower sense) were not carried far enough and that nobody can tell what additional effects might have been obtained by carrying them further. The facts do not really *prove* that these policies are inherently inadequate, regardless of the scale on which they are undertaken. For example, during the Great Depression, open-market purchases were undertaken on an entirely insufficient scale. The stock of money was allowed to shrink violently, especially from the early part of 1931 on, which is all the more noteworthy because, at that time, signs of an incipient recovery were observable. Not only was the fiscal policy of the Great Depression inadequate, but the monetary policy was also. The same is true of inflationary periods.

(10) Opponents of the "modern tendencies" in this field usually emphasize the complications to which a large public debt may give rise, the "socialist" implications of public works projects, and the "superficial" character of monetary-fiscal remedies. None of these objections are *completely* unfounded, but it is likely that the appropriate compensatory policy could reduce the validity of these arguments to such an extent that the advantages of the policy would be entirely out of proportion to the valid elements of these objections.

(11) As for the public debt problem, this is a matter of internal transfers from taxpayers to the owners of government securities. In a full-production economy, this transfer burden is increasing, *relatively to income,* only in the event that the public debt rises more rapidly than productivity, and, thereby, more rapidly than aggregate real output.[98] On realistic assumptions, this seems unlikely. If, in the long run, periods with expansionary tendencies and periods with deflationary tendencies stand in a one-to-one ratio to each other (so far as average duration and vigor are concerned), compensatory fiscal policy does not lead to any long-run increase of the public debt. Such a one-to-one relationship must, of course, not be taken for granted. However, even a substantial

---

[97] I.e., from credit policies or interest-rate policies.

[98] Assuming a constant interest rate and a constant price level. Cf. Evsey D. Domar, "The 'Burden' of the Public Debt and National Income," *American Economic Review,* December 1944, XXXIV, pp. 798–827. When maintaining that a more rapid rise of the debt than of the tax base is highly improbable, we think of a rise in the debt such as is produced by compensatory fiscal policy. A national emergency would of course be a different matter (cf. footnote 101).

long-run excess of deflationary over expansionary tendencies may prove compatible with a rate of increase in the public debt[99] which *falls distinctly short* of the probable long-run increase in aggregate productivity and, *eo ipso*, of the long-run rise in the *yield of given tax rates*.[100] Furthermore, if the rise in the internal transfer burden, which is caused by the rise of the public debt in deflationary periods, should nevertheless threaten to grow to an alarming size,[101] it always should be possible to borrow directly *or indirectly* from the central bank.[102] This actually would change the internal transfer in question to a mere bookkeeping item, in addition to possessing other advantages.[103] Such operations become a variety of interest-free borrowing, provided the profits of the central bank, over and above a stated rate, are conducted back to the Treasury. The disadvantage of this solution may be that it forces the commercial banks to handle additional deposits without giving them additional earnings.[104] But there surely should be some way of overcoming this difficulty. To say that there is none, means to maintain that an economy is incapable of getting out of a depression because it is impossible to decide who should bear the costs of handling the additional deposits which must be created to offset the deflationary tendency!

(12) The opposition to compensatory fiscal policy rests only in part on the complications which might arise in connection with the debt. It is sometimes maintained—or at least the impression is conveyed—that large-scale public works projects do not accord with the principles of free enterprise. Yet in all countries (including the United States),

---

[99] Such as is produced by compensatory fiscal policy.

[100] *Eo ipso,* due to the progressive character of the federal tax structure.

[101] In a national emergency the debt would be rising much more rapidly than the tax base if the methods of financing should be such as in the past. An emergency would call for very severe taxation, and—to the extent to which inflationary borrowing is politically unavoidable—for interest-free borrowing from the central banks or for *very* cheap borrowing from the commercial banks. On realistic assumptions, compensatory fiscal policy (in contrast to a national emergency) is almost certain to be compatible with a gradual *reduction* of the debt burden in relation to national income and the tax base. This of course is partly a consequence of the high "initial" burden with which we start the postwar period.

[102] Indirect borrowing means, in this case, the coupling of government borrowing from the market with equal security purchases of the central bank on the market.

[103] Borrowing from the public or from the commercial banks *need not* result in the borrowing of idle money for government expenditures (as is intended in deflationary periods). Instead, it may result in the borrowing of money which would have been used by the public or by the bank for other purposes. The answer depends on the interest-elasticity of liquidity provisions. Direct or indirect borrowing from the central bank is not subject to this limitation.

[104] Because on these assumptions the commercial banks do not own the newly issued government securities. It is true that they own excess reserves, but it is implied that this, of itself, does not result in credit expansion. If it does, then we are faced with a milder deflationary tendency which can be handled by very much simpler methods, namely, by open market purchases or by the lowering of reserve requirements.

there exists at present a significant backlog of urgent public works which have nothing to do with "socialism," on any reasonable definition of this term. If, at some future date, we should run out of these projects, and the next items on the list should be either wasteful (except for the Multiplier Effect) *or* if they should suppress a comparable amount of private investment, then tax reductions become clearly superior means of combating depression tendencies. In such hypothetical conditions, if far-reaching tax reductions should not generate a sufficient expansionary effect, then consumer subsidies would have to be adopted. With the exception of adequate unemployment compensation, such subsidies might actually give rise to difficulties of a more fundamental character, because of the arbitrariness involved in distributing the funds, and because of the adverse influence which free gifts might exert on the supply of services. But at present these are remote worries, and, in all probability, they will remain remote for a long time to come.

(13) Compensatory fiscal policy does have socialist implications—and it probably is incompatible with the present type of political institutions—*if* it takes the form of a full-employment guarantee and if a rigorous and comprehensive system of direct controls is adopted to prevent the inflationary consequences which would otherwise result. But the policy cannot justly be said to have these implications *if it is geared to aggregate employment objectives, on the one hand, and to wage- and price-level objectives (price stability objectives), on the other.* In this event, comprehensive direct controls would not be required to forestall inflation and to prevent extreme maladjustments in the cost-price structure. This is a very substantial advantage, even though it is acquired at a cost.[105] The cost expresses itself in the fact that the policy can be successful only to the extent to which the high-employment objective is complementary to, or at least compatible with, the objective of a reasonably stable and reasonably free price level. But while, in these circumstances, compensatory policies are indeed subject to this limitation, they would probably prevent such developments as occurred during the last two or three years of the Great Depression and its aftermath.

(14) The objection that monetary and fiscal policy is "superficial" and that it does not penetrate to the roots of the maladjustments is somewhat vague but essentially correct. An approach which disregards the

---

[105] Cf. David McCord Wright, *The Economics of Disturbance* (New York and London, 1946). Professor Wright draws a contrast between social-economic systems characterized by rapidly changing methods of production, by economic fluctuations and by comparatively easy access to political power, and systems characterized by economic stability (including a tendency toward the "stationary") and by self-perpetuating power groups in the political scene.

interaction between cost-price problems, on the one hand, and aggregate output problems, on the other, is seriously incomplete on the theoretical level, and it leads to compromise solutions on the level of policy. The "cost-price" problems are mainly those arising from institutional scarcities (producers' monopoly power and unionism), from uncertainty, and from immobility, all of which mutually intensify each other. It would be highly desirable to explore more fully these interactions and their bearing on the problem of aggregate output and employment, and to examine more fully the types of policy that might have a favorable effect on cost-price behavior. For, while the Office of Price Administration and the War Labor Board would be unacceptable as peacetime agencies—and while, even if they were "acceptable," they would be run most ineffectively by a democratic government—it does not follow that nothing can be undertaken to prevent the full exploitation of institutional scarcities. All this points to areas of research which so far have remained comparatively undeveloped. But it does not justify the position that we should refrain from using the available weapons merely because our armory is incomplete.

The GNP Model: An Illustration

(1) It is usually possible to discern the progress achieved and also the difficulties not yet overcome at different periods in the development of fields of inquiry by examining the technical tools which are used contemporaneously. So far as the theory of employment is concerned, the GNP (Gross National Product) model provides an illustration. This model was developed during the period discussed in this volume. The technique suggested by the GNP models is as follows. The GNP may be viewed as the sum total of gross incomes, or, alternatively, as the aggregate gross[106] output of an accounting period. Let us first view it as aggregate gross *income*. From this gross income it is possible to derive (net) national income by certain adjustments, mainly by deducting depreciation and indirect business taxes. From national income, by further adjustments, we derive personal income, i.e., aggregate individual income payments.[107] If from these we deduct personal taxes, we

---

[106] "Gross" in the sense that depreciation of plant and equipment is *not* deducted. But the materials and services used up in the production of other items of current output *are* deducted.

[107] On the way from national income to individual income payments (personal income), the main items of deduction are corporate profit taxes, net corporate savings (i.e., undistributed profits), and social security contributions, while the main addition is for transfer payments (which are treated as "income" by the recipient but which do not constitute a compensation for a contribution to current output, such as veterans'

arrive at the disposable income of individuals. Part of the disposable income is spent on consumption, while the remainder is saved by individuals. By deducting the savings of individuals from the disposable income, we arrive at the value of one of the items of which the GNP consists when viewed as output rather than income, namely, at the value of the current output for ultimate consumption.[108] So from now on, we view the GNP as aggregate output. It consists of the "ultimate" consumption output just derived, plus private gross capital formation,[109] plus the government expenditures on goods and services produced during the period. Consequently, if we start from the GNP viewed as gross income, and move down, by the appropriate *deductions,* via disposable income to consumption expenditure, and then *add* private gross capital formation and government expenditures on currently produced goods and services, then *we must obtain once more the GNP figure from which we started.* The deductions (savings plus taxes) must always equal the additions (private investment plus government expenditures). The magnitudes included in the model are so defined that this instantaneous relationship must hold true. However, what does it mean to interpret the level of output of a period and its determinants, in these terms?

(2) Such an interpretation of aggregate output and its determinants is an application of the *ex post* variety of the savings-investment approach.[110] If no further assumptions are introduced, all valid statements which can be made in this framework are mere truisms, and it would be unreasonable to expect any degree of stability from the relationships existing between the magnitudes included in the model. Significance attaches to these relationships only if specific assumptions are introduced. For example, if we assume that income expectations are correct, or that errors tend to cancel out, then the relationship between disposable income and simultaneous consumption expresses a deliberate attitude, a true propensity (not merely an *ex post* ratio which is defined as a propensity). Relationships of this kind might show some degree of stability. Similarly,

---

benefits, unemployment benefits, etc.) and for interest payments by the government which are also interpreted as transfer payments but are distinguished from the others.

[108] If more than the current output is *consumed,* then this expresses itself in negative capital formation. Consequently, in computing aggregate output, we may treat the magnitude derived in the text as an item of current output. Aggregate output includes capital formation which may contain negative items.

[109] Consisting of construction (i.e., "plant" or buildings), producers' durable goods (i.e., equipment), the net increment in business inventories, and the net increment in claims against foreign countries. The concept is called "gross" because the depreciation of plant and equipment is not deducted.

[110] Cf. A. G. Hart, " 'Model Building' and Fiscal Policy," *American Economic Review,* September 1946, XXXV, pp. 531–558; Jacob Mosak, "National Budgets, and National Policy," *ibid.,* March 1946, XXXVI, pp. 20–43; also rejoinder and final reply, *ibid.,* September 1946, pp. 632–640.

if we assume that there is no unintentional accumulation or reduction of inventories, then capital formation may also be interpreted as expressing the results of investment plans. For the short run—and, therefore, with respect to the problem of business fluctuations—these assumptions would surely be unrealistic. With respect to long-run average relationships, they may be less unrealistic, but the long-run expectations themselves are significantly influenced by "short-run" disturbances, and so is the "secular trend." Also, the framework itself does not directly suggest relationships between cost-price behavior, or the supply of money, on the one hand, and the explicit variables of the GNP model, on the other.

Theorizing in terms of such models well illustrates the type of analysis applied in much of the contemporary literature in the theory of employment. We have, on the one hand, quantitative frameworks ("rigorous" within their own limits) which can be filled with empirical data. The GNP model is an example of such a framework. On the other hand, we have the somewhat abstract description of simplified model-processes[111] by which the "rigorous" systems must be supplemented to become suitable for the analysis of significant problems. As empirical data accumulate and analytical techniques are refined, some systematic framework may become applicable to phases of economic development which previously could only be characterized vaguely by "purely theoretical" model processes. Some of the contemporary econometric models go very much further in this direction than the comparatively simple GNP models just discussed. They include psychological, institutional, and technological lags, by which these analytical systems are made dynamic, i.e., monetary equilibrium implications are avoided. Lagged relationships may prove to be significant and reasonably stable, even if the future is not foreseen correctly. These complex models also include a great many more variables than those explicitly entering into the usual GNP models. However, no available formal model can claim to be considered a dependable instrument of projecting (forward and backward) and consequently we lack dependable criteria of superiority and inferiority. No available model is useful without being qualified and supplemented by less formal and often somewhat vague considerations and by "judgment." The degree of complexity of the models applied partly determines the nature of the appropriate supplementary considerations. The question of the optimum combination of these elements stays a matter of individual preferences. So far the results obtained with the most complex models have not been the best. But it certainly would be a mistake to turn to the opposite extreme.

---

[111] Such as the period analysis discussed in earlier sections.

3

MONOPOLY AND THE CONCENTRATION OF ECONOMIC POWER

J. K. Galbraith

EXCLUDING only the issues associated with fiscal policy and the level and stability of employment, no problem attracted more attention from economists during the 'thirties than that of monopoly. As usual, the sources of this interest are traceable in part to ideas and in part to circumstance. Several years before the depression started, certain long-held and vital assumptions concerning the structure of the typical market were undergoing re-examination. The results became apparent at a time when economists everywhere were looking for an interpretation of the current crisis in capitalist society. A retrospect on monopoly, in its theoretical and applied aspects, properly begins, therefore, with a review of the ideas which accounted for the original revival of interest. It is appropriately followed by a consideration of the effect of these ideas as they were carried into the world of policy and politics.

I

The first influential new step in the field of ideas was the publication in 1926 by Piero Sraffa of his now famous article, "The Laws of Returns under Competitive Conditions."[1] Subject to qualifications, the tendency at the time Mr. Sraffa's article appeared was to recognize the limiting case of monopoly, but to assume, in general, a rule of competition. Competition was not assumed to be perfect. Those already in the business might variously obstruct the entry of newcomers. Or entry might be rendered difficult by the prestige associated with trademarks and trade names. Imperfect knowledge of opportunities might interfere. Decreasing costs were deemed an especially serious handicap for the newcomer, who, because he was new, was likely to be small. If large scale and accompanying requirements in capital and organization brought substantial economies, the small newcomer was faced with an organic handicap. Nevertheless, these barriers, though widely recognized, were convention-

---

[1] *Economic Journal,* December 1926, XXXVI, pp. 535–550.

ally assumed to be of secondary effect. They were frictions that muddied and at times diverted but did not check the great underlying current which was toward a competitive equilibrium. Given that equilibrium, there was a presumption, again subject to many dissenting voices, that economic resources would be employed with maximum efficiency and the product so distributed as to maximize satisfactions. Sraffa attacked the assumption that the "frictions" were in fact a secondary and fugitive phenomenon. He argued they were stable and indeed cumulative and yielded a solution consistent not with a competitive, but a monopolistic equilibrium. He argued that monopoly, not free competition, was the more appropriate assumption in market theory.

In 1932–33 Mrs. Robinson and Professor Chamberlin produced the two books that were to become the texts for the revived interest in monopoly.[2] The first leaned heavily on Sraffa; the second had a more independent genesis. Both had a prompt and enthusiastic reception. This is not difficult to explain. For years there had been marked discontent with the accustomed assumptions and the standard analysis of competitive and monopolized markets. Discussion and teaching had too long centered on what, too obviously, were limiting cases. Even (or perhaps especially) students were reluctant to accept the results as descriptive of the real world. The new work had the great advantage, from the viewpoint of marketability, of adding something new to something old, and of adding almost precisely what the customers wanted. Both books were solidly in the tradition of Marshallian partial equilibrium analysis; and in the United States and the United Kingdom this had become not only an utterly respectable **but** an all but impregnable tradition in economic thought. The inhabitants of this citadel, although never too hospitable to strangers, were bound to accept old inhabitants armed with familiar weapons even though they used these weapons in a seemingly dangerous way. Both Professor Chamberlin and Mrs. Robinson offered an organized, intellectually palatable approach to the middle ground between monopoly and competition—an obvious antidote to the existing uneasiness. In this respect their contribution was sharply distinguished from that of Marshall, J. M. Clark, and others who had delved but briefly into this intermediate area, from that of teachers who had warned their students that the old categories were inadequate, and from that of Cournot, Edgeworth, and Bowley who, at most, had offered a smattering of mostly improbable solutions to mostly improbable situations.

In retrospect the most important contribution of Professor Chamberlin

---

[2] Joan Robinson, *Economics of Imperfect Competition* (London, 1933); Edward H. Chamberlin, *The Theory of Monopolistic Competition* (Cambridge, Mass., 1932).

and Mrs. Robinson was to emancipate the analysis of markets from the inadequate categories of competition (impaired by sundry frictions) and single-firm monopoly. Almost at once duopoly, oligopoly, and the purposeful differentiation of products became accredited and very useful categories in market analysis.

This liberalization of market categories was more important than the theory that explored them. Professor Chamberlin did make a notable refinement in the existing concept of competition. Where previously competition had often been loosely identified by the terms of rivalry in the market—conditions of entry, the energy and knowledge of participants, and the like—he in effect derived its character from the competitive equilibrium it was assumed to bring about. The concept of "pure" competition was thereby confined to markets where the demand for the product of the individual seller was infinitely elastic at the ruling price. This was a good deal more rigorous than existing definitions; it had, as I shall argue presently, important practical consequences.

Both Professor Chamberlin and Mrs. Robinson also made the marginal revenue curve a standard tool of market analysis and Professor Chamberlin's theory of monopolistic competition—of competition between numerous sellers differentiated by location, personality, or physical or psychic differences in their product—brought the vast phenomenon of merchandising and advertising within the scope of theoretical analysis. For the purposes of the present essay, however, it was the area of failure rather than achievement of the new work that is of prime significance. Without much doubt the dominant market of modern capitalism is not one made up of many sellers offering either uniform or differentiated products. Rather it is a market of few sellers, i.e., oligopoly. Apart from consumers' goods, the counterpart of few buyers associated with many or few sellers is also a common phenomenon. Where sellers are few the product is automatically identified with its vendor and hence there is always a measure of differentiation—the elasticity of substitution between products of a few sellers can never be quite perfect. But the ruling characteristic is the fewness of the sellers.

In dealing with small numbers or oligopoly, Professor Chamberlin, who went farthest with the problem on a general theoretical level, did little more than resurrect the engaging but largely irrelevant novelties of Cournot and Edgeworth. This was a failure of prime importance—one that economists were, on the whole, slow to recognize. The failure was inevitable. Success, by familiar standards, implied a determinate solution. One certain fact about oligopoly (and its counterpart on the buyer's side of the market) is that the entire market solution can be altered unilaterally by any single participant. This is at once the simplest and the most critical distinction between oligopoly and pure competition. It also means that the methodological device by which the competitive market has been analyzed, i.e., laying down general assumptions about the group response of numerous individuals to common stimuli, is inadmissible. Rather the assumptions must be sufficiently comprehensive to cover the behavior pattern of each participant in the market. Even though it is assumed that each participant seeks to maximize his return, the possible individual behavior patterns and resulting market solutions are almost infinitely numerous, and the assumption that all individuals will seek maximum pecuniary return (as distinct from non-pecuniary prestige, expression of individuality, etc.) is questionable. Edgeworth and Cournot and, in that tradition, Chamberlin, merely derived the market solution that followed from two or three out of a near infinity of possible behavior combinations. It follows that they were not offering a theory of duopoly or oligopoly but displaying a few samples. Little progress has been made to an analysis of oligopoly by this route and little could be expected.

The importance of oligopoly in the world as it exists was highlighted, almost simultaneously with the appearance of Professor Chamberlin's and Mrs. Robinson's books, by Berle and Means' mammoth study of the modern corporation.[3] This study was also launched well prior to the Great Depression; its inspiration, Professor Berle stated in the preface, was the Wall Street boom and the attendant pyramiding of "industrial oligarchies." But it was not Professor Berle's interesting and erudite study of the changing property rights of the individual security holder but Gardiner C. Means' statistics on the industrial predominance of the nation's 200 largest non-financial corporations that captured popular attention. These, he estimated, had combined assets at the beginning of 1930 of $81 billion, or about half of all assets owned by corporations. Although open to challenge as to detail, his calculations buttressed his contention that "the principles of duopoly have become more important than those of free competition."[4] The book had a popular as well as academic audience and the figure of "200" became a magic symbol in subsequent investigations of economic power.

The new market categories, plus the evidence of Berle and Means and of the scholar's own eyes as to the need for them, set the stage for the

---

[3] A. A. Berle and Gardiner C. Means, *The Modern Corporation and Private Property* (New York, 1934).

[4] *Ibid.*, p. 45. In particular it was pointed out against Means that his list of corporations included rail, power, and communications utilities where large scale was inevitable and also well recognized and where the area of private discretion had been circumscribed by the state.

revived interest in monopoly and its allied issues. One must also emphasize the *esprit* which Chamberlin's and Robinson's works gave to students of the field. Even though they substituted a new set of frustrations for the old ones, the new ones were welcome. It has been suggested that "the most revolutionary feature of the monopolistic competition theories [was] the unprecedented pace at which they conquered their audience."[5] Neither Chamberlin nor Robinson was destroyed and redestroyed as was Keynes a few years later. Their most effective critic, Professor Schumpeter, centered his attacks not on the validity of their analysis *per se* but more generally on the notion that it much affected the assessment of capitalist reality.[6] Rarely in economics have ideas had such an enthusiastic and uncritical welcome.[7]

II

The effect of the new market categories on empirical investigation and the search for policy was first evident in Arthur R. Burns' *The Decline of Competition*,[8] which appeared in 1936. Professor Burns began with the hypothesis that "elements of monopoly . . . can no longer be regarded as occasional and relatively unimportant aberrations from competition. They are such an organic part of the industrial system that it is useless to hope that they can be removed by law . . ."[9] He thereupon set himself the task of determining how "the resulting imperfectly or monopolistically competitive system"[10] works, the proper objectives of public policy concerning it and the means of achieving them. Professor Burns went some distance with the first part of his task, i.e., the description of markets and of the monopoly elements therein. His book is still an excel-

---

[5] Robert Triffin, *Monopolistic Competition and General Equilibrium Theory* (Cambridge, Mass., 1940), p. 17.

[6] *Business Cycles* (New York, 1939), p. 63 ff.; and in particular *Capitalism, Socialism and Democracy*, 2nd ed. (New York, 1946), p. 79 ff.

[7] Discussion of both the theory and theoretical developments following in its wake will be found elsewhere in this volume (pp. 6–9, 17, 20–22 above). It may be said, however, that both Chamberlin's and Robinson's books were, to a remarkable degree, less a beginning than a climax. Although the theory was the subject of exhaustive scrutiny and numerous refinements and corrections in detail, little was added in the way either of fundamental revision or noteworthy extension. This is not meant to detract in any way from the importance of such a contribution as Triffin's, just cited. This book provides an indispensable survey and *critique* of the whole development and has brought the work of Pareto and Stackelberg into focus with that of Chamberlin and Robinson. Triffin clarifies the notion of the industry by relating it to the system of external influences that bear on the equilibrium of the firm, but the basic theoretical system emerges largely intact.

[8] New York, 1936.

[9] *Ibid.*, p. 3.

[10] *Loc. cit.*

lent guide to techniques of trade-association control of prices, market sharing, price leadership, and the like. He was also among the first of many to discover that the assumptions of the new theory involved a series of traps for anyone who ventured recommendations on policy. In a tradition common to both bourgeois and socialist theorists (e.g., Enrico Barone and more recently Oscar Lange[11]) he accepted as ideal the level of employment and use of resources under conditions of pure competition. Monopoly or oligopoly, and the associated techniques of market control obviously inhibited such ideal use. But having rejected pure competition as an impractical goal, Professor Burns was brought face to face with the only apparent alternative to accepting things as they are, namely, to make the State the agency for planning or at least improving upon the allocation of resources. He accepted the alternative; but having grasped this nettle, he found himself faced with the further task of detailing the criteria and techniques for state control of resource use. On this he made little progress. The frustration proved to be a recurring one, for the norm of pure competition, however valuable as an intellectual design or model, provides few practical clues to action *vis-à-vis* markets where the possibility of such competition is rejected. This is a technical matter. There is the further question whether the State, in a capitalist society and especially in the United States, is a *deus ex machina* that can institute such comprehensive planning. Is the State, in a capitalist society, able, by a process of deliberate decision, to revise the basic constitution of the capitalist economy itself?

The new theory also had an influence on less cosmic lines of empirical study. Investigations of individual industries—the ubiquitous and useful "industry study"—were soon oriented toward the new market categories.[12] The way was also opened for a much more realistic analysis of the relation between competitive and monopolistic industries where the two are juxtaposed in the same market. This was particularly useful in dealing with the agricultural markets and deserves a special word.

So long as the standard dichotomy in market analysis was between competition and monopoly, it was obviously difficult to differentiate the purely competitive markets, in which most unprocessed farm products are normally sold, from the oligopolistic markets in which they are normally resold. So long as it was deemed inappropriate (as well as impolite) to characterize milk distributors or meat packers as monopolistic, they tended to be grouped with farmers as participants in a competitive

---

[11] See Oscar Lange and Fred M. Taylor, *On the Economic Theory of Socialism* (Minneapolis, 1938).
[12] See pp. 142–149 below [Bain].

market. However, in 1934 Professor J. M. Cassels distinguished between the behavior of the monopolistic and competitive firm in analyzing the responses of farmers to the class prices established by a monopolistic milk marketing co-operative.[13] Much more extensive use of this analysis has been made by Professor W. H. Nicholls, first in research bulletins of the Iowa Agricultural Experiment Station and in periodical articles, and later and more elaborately in his book *Imperfect Competition Within Agricultural Industries*.[14] The latter, though formally presented as an analysis of agricultural markets, is also a theoretical *tour de force* of formidable proportions. After formulating the conditions of demand (specifically of derived demand) for farm products, the author elaborates the market solutions to be expected under various combinations of few and many sellers, few and many buyers, and of bilateral monopoly, and with varying assumptions as to the degrees of interdependence recognized by market participants. The study ranks with Triffin's in the virtuosity with which theoretical tools are employed and it is a singularly useful guide to modern market literature. It is also, as Professor Nicholls himself is at some pains to make clear, a good example of the frustration which accompanies efforts to develop a "theory" of oligopoly along lines of the conventional approach to the competitive market. Professor Nicholls makes a limited selection from an endless number of equally plausible assumptions about individual behavior in the markets with which he is concerned.[15] He was eventually forced to conclude that the principal utility of such analysis in markets characterized by oligopoly or its counterparts is "to sharpen . . . thinking and tools of analysis in order to do a better job of empirical work."[16] It is not to be supposed, however, that this limited achievement is without importance. Even in the absence of a "theory" of the oligopolistic market, attention was usefully focused on the diverse behavior of the competitive and monopoloid sectors of the economy. This was of immediate assistance in explaining the different behavior of agricultural and industrial prices during the 'thirties and 'forties and it at least established a framework for appraisal of relative levels of resource employment in agriculture and industry. The latter lines of investigation rank with the most important of recent developments in agricultural economics.[17]

---

[13] *A Study of Fluid Milk Prices* (Cambridge, Mass., 1934).

[14] Ames, 1941.

[15] He quotes the apt observation of Professor Wassily Leontief that, when dealing with oligopoly, "the real issue is that of selecting an appropriate set of fundamental assumptions." *Journal of Political Economy*, August 1936, XLIV, p. 544.

[16] W. H. Nicholls, *op. cit.*, p. 165.

[17] They are most fully elaborated in T. W. Schultz, *Agriculture in an Unstable Economy* (New York, 1945).

III

The revival of interest in the theoretical aspects of monopoly and their application was paced, during the 'thirties, by a series of studies designed to measure the position of the large business unit in the economy. At least partly because of the extent and complexity of the statistical enterprise involved, much of this work was conducted under the auspices of the Federal Government. In scope and significance, it must be considered a landmark among government investigations.

The inspiration to much of this work was Berle and Means' earlier calculations of the industrial predominance of the 200 largest corporations. The most important of the further investigations was directed by Gardiner C. Means for the National Resources Planning Board. Making use of Bureau of Internal Revenue data, this study generally confirmed the pre-eminence of the large corporations.[18] Counting (subject to some possibilities of error) wholly controlled subsidiaries, the 200 largest non-financial corporations were credited for 1933 with control of between 19 and 21 per cent of aggregate national wealth, between 46 and 50 per cent of the nation's "industrial" wealth, and approximately 60 per cent of the physical assets of all non-financial corporations. The study presented consolidated income and asset accounts for the 200 corporations and examined their comparative predominance in different lines of economic activity.

The *rationale* of the study was an effort to discover the area of "administrative" as distinct from market co-ordination in the American economy. It was supplemented by an effort to establish the extent of the co-ordination between the 200 corporations (and an additional 50 financial corporations) by means of interlocking directorates and "interest groupings." Interesting new ground was broken in the investigation of the interest groups associated with such nuclei as J. P. Morgan-First National, Rockefeller, Kuhn-Loeb, Mellon, Du Pont, and the Chicago, Cleveland, and Boston financial communities.[19] While the identifying bond between the interest groups ranged from such subjective factors as known working relationships or interlocking directorates to firm financial control, in the case of the Rockefellers and Du Ponts, the study cast useful light on the agglomerative tendencies at work within the handful of pre-eminent corporations. Of the 200 largest non-financial corporations

---

[18] *The Structure of the American Economy*, Part I, *Basic Characteristics* (Washington, 1939), p. 99 ff.
[19] *Ibid.*, p. 306 ff. This study was made by Paul M. Sweezy.

and 50 largest financial corporations, 58 per cent of the industrial and utility assets, 82 per cent of the rails, and 51 per cent of the bank assets were aligned with one or another of the 8 interest groups mentioned above.

Finally, in what was to become one of the most quoted researches of the decade, Dr. Means' group examined the extent of concentration by markets. Census industrial classifications, 276 in all, were ranked in accordance with the proportion of the total output supplied by the largest four and largest eight firms. As a measure of market concentration, this exercise is crude. On occasion census classifications combine firms producing wholly unrelated products, while firms producing the same product may serve wholly distinct market areas.[20] Both defects, however, result in an understatement of market concentration, and the study was a convincing demonstration that oligopoly is the appropriate assumption in dealing with industrial markets in the United States. It went far toward establishing this assumption in American economic thought.

The 200 corporations received yet another examination at the end of the decade in a study sponsored by the Securities and Exchange Commission for the Temporary National Economic Committee. As its title— *The Distribution of Ownership in the 200 Largest Non-financial Corporations*—indicated, the focus was less on the economic power of the 200 corporations, which was largely assumed, than on their ownership. Throughout the 'thirties, partly as the result of W. Z. Ripley's earlier polemics,[21] partly because of the work of Berle and Means, partly, no doubt, as a continuation of a much older concern over the ethics and consequences of absentee ownership, the locus of control over the modern corporation was actively discussed. Much of this discussion is beyond the scope of this essay, but it is noteworthy that by the end of the decade it was commonly assumed that in most large-scale corporate enterprise, the divorce of ownership from control, either in an immediate or an ultimate sense, was complete. Because of its susceptibility to shrinkage in revenues, pyramided stock ownerships through holding companies, especially of rail and electric power utilities, captured popular attention during the depression. The drive for corrective legislation and attendant investigations made it clear to a large audience that the principal motive was extension of control without ownership. At the same time there was an increasing tendency to view management, even where its position was unsupported by legal reinforcements, as a self-appointed trust (or, less

---

[20] Raymond W. Goldsmith, Rexford G. Parmelee, et al., T.N.E.C. Monograph 29 (Washington, 1940).

[21] In particular his *Main Street and Wall Street* (Boston, 1939).

politely, as a self-perpetuating bureaucracy) with a negligible ownership stake. Goldsmith and Parmelee, working principally with data obtained directly from the 200 corporations, showed that the stake of officers and directors in ownership was indeed comparatively thin and the holdings of officers especially so. Only about 6 per cent of the common stock of the 200 corporations was owned by officers and directors; over half of all officers and directors had holdings that could be described as negligible. This could mean that corporate direction as exemplified by officers and boards had been largely professionalized but was still subject to control by principals. For at least a majority of the large corporations this might be the case, for the study showed the importance of family ownership either through direct stock ownership or, more especially, through estates, trusts, and family holding companies. The authors observed that "a small group of dominant security holders is not in evidence in only 30 per cent of the 200 large corporations."[22]

Although Berle and Means had classified only about one-third of their 200 corporations as "management controlled," the emphasis they gave to this type of control, together with that exercised through legal devices or extreme minority holdings, left the impression that control of the modern large corporation by owners was exceptional. There is no assurance that this impression is unjustified. A sizable but quiescent ownership interest may allow an active and aggressive management to exercise complete and final control, and the possibility is not an unlikely one. Moreover, as a subsequent investigator has pointed out,[23] certain of the ownership interests cited by Goldsmith and Parmelee are themselves owned by corporations, a fact which in turn raises the question of the control of these corporations. In other cases the ownership was split between two or more dominant family groups with at least a presumption in some of these cases that management provided the decisive influence.

Although the locus of ultimate power in the modern corporation remains, to a degree, conjectural, this element of conjecture might one day be removed for the two or three hundred larger corporations, by a detailed study of all of them. The issue is important and this would resolve it for business units responsible for the order of a third of all economic activity. One of the still unexploited opportunities offered by concentration of control is that of abandoning generalization in favor of a complete apprehension of the universe.

[22] Goldsmith, Parmelee, et al., *op. cit.*, p. xvi.

[23] R. A. Gordon, *Business Leadership in the Large Corporation* (Washington, 1945). Professor Gordon excluded twenty-four of the 200 corporations because a majority of the common stock was held by other corporations (in the case of three railroads) where there was control by lease by other corporations.

IV

It is now time to take the new ideas on monopoly into the world of affairs—to examine their nexus with depression and unemployment and the deeper questioning of capitalist institutions for which the depression provided a hospitable environment. At first glance, the new notions of generalized monopoly appeared to offer a ready explanation of contemporary distress. The classical solution of monopoly had always shown entrepreneurial returns maximized (or protected) at the expense of production. Under the label of imperfect competition, the monopoly solution could now be considered not the exception but the rule. It followed that restricted production and excess capacity were also the rule and their concomitant was unemployed resources. Not many accepted this vulgar formulation. Once outside the universities, however, the new theory was undoubtedly credited with diagnostic and even therapeutic values which it did not, in fact, possess.

At a more sophisticated level, the new work did strike a blow at the concept of inherent order in capitalist behavior: the doctrines of imperfect (and monopolistic) competition ran sharply counter to what Professor Roll has called the "optimal distribution of resources prejudice."[24]

Under some circumstances this might have been revolutionary. No idea is more deeply rooted in non-socialist economics than that of a rule of competition where the controlling *tendency* is for resources to be employed by firms and distributed between industries in such manner that they are combined with maximum efficiency into products that give maximum satisfaction. To be sure, for half a century economics has been a kind of trial of wits between those who sought to perfect this doctrine of ultimate harmony and those who—citing inequality and its perpetration by inheritance, external economies, immobility of resources, and other inhibiting forces—sought to limit it. But the doctrine was only completely vulnerable at one point and that was where monopoly entered—the defenders and attackers entirely agreed that monopoly (*cum* oligopoly) was deeply subversive of the competitive model. And, since oligopoly was stubbornly resistant to incorporation in a new system, at least by the old methods, it destroyed without leaving anything in its place.

One or two scholars have seen the development in the foregoing light. The late Heinrich von Stackelberg, whose book *Marktform und Gleichgewicht*[25] was published almost simultaneously with those of Chamberlin

---

[24] Eric Roll, *A History of Economic Thought* (New York, 1942).
[25] Vienna and Berlin, 1934.

and Robinson, and who dealt extensively with the problem of oligopoly, seems as a result of his analysis to have abandoned all hope for an economic order except as provided by the State. Many have considered it relevant that he was the most prominent German economist to identify himself whole-heartedly with National Socialism. Professor Eduard Heiman has also expressed alarm at the implications of the theory. He suggests that "it is time to recognize that the concept of a system of monopoly is self-contradictory and the very negation of everything economics stands for."[26] Oddly enough, Professor Heiman makes no effort to deny the existence of a system of monopoly *cum* oligopoly and consequently comes close to enjoining economists to avoid thinking of the world as it is.

Few American or British scholars drew any such nihilist conclusions. This was partly fortuitous. For many years prior to the revived interest in monopoly, work in the great tradition of Marshallian partial equilibrium analysis had been carried on with little regard to larger issues. Although in most American universities it still occupied the area that was honored with the label "economic theory," many if not most of its practitioners had narrowed their interests to questions of product price and factor cost determination. Investigators of such alien subjects as business cycles, money and banking, and international trade had appropriated the problems that are so painfully relevant to the real world.

More important, during the years of depression economic theory tended increasingly to polarize on two distinct though not unrelated norms. The first was the goal of an appropriate employment of resources, the alternative being idleness; the second was the goal of an appropriate employment of resources, the alternative being (in some sense) a socially less efficient employment of resources. In the first instance, the problem of monopoly bore upon the question of resource use when the opportunity cost was less efficient employment. The depression, obviously, was focusing attention on the seemingly far more urgent question of *any* employment vs. unemployment. This emphasis was enormously sharpened by the publication of Keynes' *General Theory*.[27] Although the assumption of imperfect competition is explicit in his analysis of the labor market and implicit in a good deal of his treatment of prices and of capital markets, Keynes was largely oblivious to either the old or the new market categories. Moreover he treated the problem of relative efficiencies of employment with something between neglect and contempt: "There is no reason to suppose that the existing system seriously misemploys the

---

[26] *History of Economic Doctrine* (New York, 1945), p. 219.
[27] *The General Theory of Employment, Interest and Money* (New York, 1936).

factors of production which are in use."[28] There is no need to emphasize the extent to which Keynes captured the attention of economists concerned with policy and herewith the interest that might otherwise have centered on the question of efficiency.

In one sense the new theory made it even more difficult than hitherto to establish a relationship between monopoly and economic distress. Under conditions of pure competition, *rigorously defined,* cyclical instability is conceptually possible. To monopoly and monopoloid forms, however, one can trace disparity in income and both a lower and a less stable consumption function than would be expected under pure competition. Imperfect competition, also, can be conceived as breaking the connection, through the interest rate, of the supply of savings and the demand for capital. It follows that imperfect competition or monopoloid forms are a necessary condition for consumption and investment fluctuation, and at least some types of inventory fluctuation. Thus imperfect competition or rather the absence of *absolutely* pure competition, including the labor market and the capital market, can be offered as a nearly comprehensive "cause" of cyclical fluctuations. But this is not to say very much. The appearance of oligopoly and its counterpart on the buyers' side of the market and monopolistic competition far antedated the theory that interpreted them. And a most portentous concomitant of the new theory was that in making it easy to assume that monopoloid forms were general in the economy, it made it difficult to recommend their elimination as a reform measure. A diagnosis that had related the stagnation of the 'thirties to monopoly in the old-fashioned sense would have made the life of any available monopolist miserable in the extreme. Once oligopoly and monopolistic competition entered the picture, to prescribe the elimination of monopoly became tantamount to demanding a wholesale revision of the economic order. Economists, some sections of the press oddly to the contrary, are not given to such violent prescriptions.[29] The highly restricted definition of pure competition, which the new theory brought into use, also helped make the competitive goal seem remote and impractical. In part, it should be added, this was the result of a too literal transference

---

[28] *Ibid.,* p. 379.

[29] It is intriguing that it is this revolutionary formula which Professor Hayek advances in its most uncompromising form. "The price system will fulfill [its] function only if competition prevails, that is, if the individual producer has to adapt himself to price changes and cannot control them." *The Road to Serfdom* (Chicago, 1944), p. 49. There is no nonsense here—the curve of the individual seller must be completely elastic at the ruling price.

To effect such a reorganization of the economy would, I suspect, take some of the most formidable planning (and one of the largest bureaucracies) of all time. Before it was completed both Professor Hayek and his book would have alienated some of their most devoted admirers.

of a scientific definition into the world of affairs. Without doubt there are many imperfect markets in which a "workable" competition yields the same effective solution, or has the same social effect, that the textbooks have associated with pure competition.[30] Apart from some not too consequential waste, I suggest that much of what is called monopolistic competition could be so classified.

The most important effort to build a bridge between the new market categories and the theory that dealt with them, on the one side, and the depression, on the other, was by way of price behavior. Given widespread oligopoly and hence a large area of entrepreneurial discretion in the setting of prices, attention was naturally directed toward the way in which the discretion was exercised—and the criteria of private and social benefit by which it *should* be exercised. In the latter half of the 'thirties, the problem of price policy assumed the stature of a new field of economic investigation. In its social aspects it was taken up somewhat gingerly. The notion that a private firm could be guided by considerations other than its own short- or long-run interest was not one that all economists embraced with appetite. To concede that a businessman should orient his price policy to social norms is to assert that the single-minded pursuit of profit is presumptively anti-social. It admits of a rule of private collectivism that accords important legislative functions to the private entrepreneur. Conservatives and liberals alike found the idea unappetizing. The implied alternative, namely that price behavior had become a fit area for state intervention, also had disagreeable overtones.

However, the debate over price policy had less to do with such broad philosophical issues than with the much more concrete problem of the different patterns of price behavior during the depression and their effect in accentuating deflation. The differences in frequency and amplitude of price change between different price series were one of the most thoroughly investigated phenomena of the 'thirties. (The reciprocal behavior has been equally apparent, though less thoroughly studied, during the postwar inflation.) Again the pioneer in these investigations was Gardiner Means.[31] He measured the frequency and amplitude of movement

---

[30] A persuasive argument along these lines is contained in the manuscript drafts of Professor Corwin D. Edwards' forthcoming book on policy for maintaining competition.

[31] In *The Structure of the American Economy,* p. 122 ff. Means' efforts to measure concentration of economic power and associated phenomena were clearly among the important research achievements of the 'thirties. It is not clear that either the studies or author have won the recognition they deserve. This may possibly be explained by the rather novel framework into which Means fitted his work. Instead of bringing statistical measures to bear on the conceptual framework used by other workers, he had a tendency to create his own. And because his framework was unfamiliar and at times, perhaps, somewhat artificial, his work had less influence than might otherwise have been the case.

of different series during the deflation phase and devised rough indexes of "depression sensitivity" for different commodities. He then related this sensitivity to concentration, type of product, and other characteristics of the industry. Both the conceptual and statistical aspects of the phenomenon of price flexibility and inflexibility were taken up by other students,[32] culminating in a detailed survey of the whole issue for the Temporary National Economic Committee.[33]

Although unchanging or infrequent price changes of small magnitude are not inevitably a concomitant of imperfect competition under conditions of changing demand—a formal point that has been made with some vigor by Professor Scitovszky[34]—they are a *possible* concomitant, as they are not of pure competition. For a variety of reasons, infrequent price changes are a likely price solution under oligopoly. To avoid change is by all odds the *simplest* way of maintaining the oligopolistic *entente* to which the seller is a party.[35]

A number who observed the phenomenon of inflexible prices took an uncomplicated view of its cyclical effect. Assuming a rule of pure competition, rigidly defined, the price dispersion associated with imperfect competition would not occur. Hence, whatever effect price dispersion might have in accentuating deflation was the result of imperfect competition. Hence the corollary: any steps that would diminish inflexibility would enhance cyclical stability. This primitive analysis of price inflexibility *cum* monopoly was extraordinarily influential in the making of actual policy during the 'thirties and it is not without influence today.

To say that a flexible competitive economy has greater cyclical stability than an inflexible and monopolistic one is to say little that is useful. The real question is whether, given a rule of monopoly or monopoloid forms, stability is enhanced by increasing the area of competitive and flexible prices. Here the conclusion is a good deal less certain. During the 'thirties,

---

[32] See, in particular, Edward S. Mason, "Price Inflexibility," *Review of Economic Statistics*, May 1938, XX, pp. 53–64; Donald H. Humphrey, "The Nature and Meaning of Rigid Prices, 1894–1933," *Journal of Political Economy*, October 1937, XLV, pp. 651–661; Donald H. Wallace, "Monopoly Prices and Depression," *Explorations in Economics* (Cambridge, Mass., 1936), p. 349 ff.; and my own paper "Monopoly Power and Price Rigidities," *Quarterly Journal of Economics*, May 1936, L, pp. 456–475.

[33] Saul Nelson and Walter G. Keim, T.N.E.C. Monograph 1 (Washington, 1941).

[34] Tibor de Scitovszky, "Prices Under Monopoly and Competition," *Journal of Political Economy*, October 1941, XLIX, pp. 663–686.

[35] Professor Oscar Lange observes in *Price Flexibility and Employment* (Bloomington, 1944), pp. 86–87, that "the formation of monopolistic and monopsonistic group behavior is not merely the result of 'greed for profit.' Rules of oligopolistic and oligopsonistic group behavior emerge because, without them, no firm would be able to predict the reaction of other firms to a change in its price." I would like to urge that the most elementary rule of behavior under oligopoly is to minimize the number of price changes and hence the number of times the understanding among oligopolists is put to a test.

the dominant tendency, without doubt, was to look upon price dispersion and the accompanying alteration in the terms of exchange between groups as an accentuating force in the downswing of the cycle. And the stable rather than the cyclically flexible prices tended to be regarded as the active or disturbing factor. (It is interesting that in the reverse situation of the 'forties, the flexible prices have been quite commonly viewed with alarm, the inflexible prices with some esteem.) The selection of the inflexible prices as the devil of the piece seems, however, to have been based more often on tradition than on analysis of demand and income effects. On the other hand there has been a strong post-Keynesian tendency to regard the cyclically inflexible prices as a stabilizing influence in the cycle. The most detailed argument has been advanced by Professor Hansen.[36] Associating cyclical fluctuations with changes in income resulting primarily from changes in investment activity, he argues that price dispersion is a symptom but not a cause of deflation and that "cyclical price flexibility all around . . . at the end of a boom, might well accelerate the downswing."[37] He does place emphasis on the importance of structural price flexibility—the adjustment of prices to changes in unit costs—a distinction which has been taken up by others. (It may be noted that to the extent that both cyclical and structural inflexibility are a concomitant of monopoly power, as they undoubtedly are, it may be difficult in practice to have one without getting the other.) Professor Hicks has also argued that stable prices, and by implication the imperfect competition with which they are associated, may act as a stabilizing influence in the economy.[38] A not dissimilar conclusion is reached by Professor Lange in his elaborate theoretical treatment of the relation of price behavior to economic activity.[39] He discards price flexibility as a norm for the modern oligopolistic economy—he does not deny that it may have served as a stabilizing influence in past periods—and argues that areas of rigid prices will minimize the amount of monetary management and public expenditure necessary to check the downswing of the cycle.

The relation of differential price behavior to the cycle or, more broadly, to the level and stability of resource employment is clearly unfinished

---

[36] Cf. *Fiscal Policy and Business Cycles* (New York, 1941), p. 313 ff., which closely follows his essay in *The Structure of the American Economy*, Part II, National Resources Planning Board (Washington, 1940).

[37] *Fiscal Policy and Business Cycles*, p. 322. Professor Hansen does not deny the usefulness of cost-price adjustments in other phases of the cycle, although he insists that they are of subsidiary importance.

[38] *Value and Capital* (Oxford, 1939), pp. 265–271. Hicks argues that rigid prices of factors are certain to be stabilizing where those not offered at the given price remain unemployed.

[39] *Op. cit.*, p. 87 ff.

business. Discussion remained active until war brought the overriding agreement that a high and highly organized output required stable prices and made the issue temporarily irrelevant.

In academic circles, price behavior and policy proved to be the most durable facet of the revived interest in monopoly. Well before the outbreak of the war, interest in academic circles in the theoretical issues associated with monopoly and competition was on the wane. At that time Professor Roll suggested, rather tentatively, that this lull occurred because the theoretical possibilities of the subject "are now exhausted" and the field was being abandoned to "descriptive" economists and those concerned with policy.[40] Be that as it may, the decline in interest in the universities was followed by a great burgeoning of interest in Washington. To that I now turn.

V

It has often been suggested that the "New Deal" lacked any defined economic "philosophy." Nearly the reverse is true—it had several of them. President Roosevelt, it now seems clear, *was* singularly uncommitted to any particular economic dogma within the broad framework of a liberal capitalist faith. This, however, made it possible to win his support for any persuasively argued idea. That opportunity was considerably exploited.

The first few years of the new New Deal were a Dutch pie that contained a small present for everyone—budget orthodoxy for the proponents of sound finance, currency and exchange manipulation for the monetary enthusiasts, price-fixing for those who were being punished too severely by deflation, a good deal of vague "planning" for those who had attended too many seminars in political science. Gradually two positions on economic policy began to dominate the others. One can sufficiently and not inaccurately be called the Keynesian view. The other had its citadel in the Department of Justice and its outposts in the Securities and Exchange Commission, the Federal Trade Commission, and, very importantly, in the Congress. It saw monopoly and the concentration and abuse of economic power as the principal problem. In general those who emphasized fiscal and monetary solutions were principally concerned with the immediate issues of income and employment; the anti-monopolists, on the other hand, regarded themselves as the architects of a permanent reform of capitalist institutions. Although this difference helped sustain a reasonably amiable coalition between the two groups, its importance

[40] Eric Roll, *op. cit.*, p. 523.

should not be exaggerated. For the enthusiasts, both were complete theologies wholly capable of answering the most urgent economic questions of the day.

Not since the time of Theodore Roosevelt—perhaps not even then—had there been so much interest in the anti-trust laws as in the late 'thirties, or such energetic efforts to enforce them. Although this activity was nourished by the contemporary academic interest in monopoly and imperfect competition, its most important roots were elsewhere. The principal entrepreneurs were lawyers. In their system of economic theory competition was good and performed indispensable regulatory functions. Monopoly was evil. So for many, who were in the Brandeis tradition, was size. The sophisticated problems which modern theory had associated with these concepts were not troublesome. For men who, in an honorable tradition of the American bar, were expiating a lifetime of service to American corporations by spending a few years harassing them, the suppression of formal collusion or deliberate conspiracy was, ordinarily, a sufficient goal in itself.

The anti-monopoly drive of the 'thirties drew strength from other sources. It was highly agreeable to progressives—including liberal congressmen—who, in a world of new and dubious formulas and amid charges and countercharges of sinister ideology, found comfort in the tried and tested radicalism of the Grangers and Populists. It even attracted a measure of support from businessmen and the conservative press. In a world where it was hard to defend the *status quo*, both were inclined to pay grudging lip service to what at least seemed like an effort to restore the *status quo ante*.

Most important of all, the anti-monopoly drive of the late 'thirties drew strength from the remarkable energy and personality of its leader, Thurman Arnold. Arnold was something of a convert. His *The Folklore of Capitalism*,[41] published in 1937, deprecated the anti-trust laws—he went so far as to assert that they were a façade which protected large corporations from more effective regulation. He suggested that "Theodore Roosevelt never accomplished anything with his trust busting. Of course he didn't. The crusade was not a practical one," and observed of past years that "whenever anyone demanded practical regulation, they [the anti-trust laws] formed an effective moral obstacle since all liberals would answer with a demand that the anti-trust laws be enforced."[42] On coming to Washington as head of the Anti-Trust Division of the Department of Justice, Arnold resolved his doubts. He launched a program not

---

[41] New Haven, 1937.
[42] *Ibid.*, pp. 211, 217.

only of vigorous enforcement of the laws but of equally vigorous claims on their behalf.

The "Arnold era" lasted, roughly, from 1938 to 1941. Arnold obtained substantial increases in the appropriations for anti-trust enforcement—from $435,000 in 1936 to $1,325,000 in 1941—and recruited an exceptionally able and spirited force of subordinates. His activities were characterized by both imagination and a well developed sense of drama. In addition to such conventional targets as oil companies, ALCOA, and the glass container industry, he reached out to such unsuspected (and unsuspecting) offenders as the American Medical Association and the Associated Press. A feature of his enforcement were the drives on entire industries, of which the most notable was that in 1940 on the building trades. For the first time anti-trust action was brought comprehensively to bear on a great number of local guild-monopolies which, previously, had enjoyed substantial immunity as the result of their small scale. This drive was also distinguished by the inclusion of the unions—once a favored target of the Sherman Law enforcement—although eventually (in the Hutchison Case) they were held to be substantially immune to such action.

During these years the anti-trust laws could perhaps be said to have had a fair trial. It was not an extended trial; it was subject to most of the numerous administrative and procedural handicaps that have always plagued anti-trust enforcement.[43] Yet, while one could reasonably ask for enforcement that was always as vigorous as during these years, it is doubtful, as laws are enforced in the United States, if one could ask for much more. What is to be concluded from this experiment?

It is easy—perhaps too easy—to say what the anti-trust laws cannot do. Certainly they cannot positively alter the basic structure of a capitalist economy. There is no evidence that the ownership and control of American industries was any less concentrated in 1940 than in 1935 or that it would have been more than marginally different by 1950 had the drive continued in the tempo of the late 'thirties. Nor is there any evidence that the drive contributed to recovery or any reason for supposing that it was capable of making the economy less subject to cyclical instability. In his requiem on the Arnold era[44] Thurman Arnold does make this case, but only by assertion. Further, it is now clear that anti-trust enforcement has, at best, only a tenuous connection with the factors which are significant in the monopoly or oligopoly equilibrium. As Professor Edward S.

---

[43] See Professor Walton Hamilton's colorful monograph for the T.N.E.C., *Anti-trust in Action*, T.N.E.C. Monograph 16 (Washington, 1941).

[44] *Bottlenecks of Business* (New York, 1940), p. 12 ff.

Mason[45] and others have observed, there is a notable gap between the legal and economic concepts of monopoly. The first tends to emphasize behavior in the market; the second is naturally concerned with the result or solution that is achieved. Anti-trust enforcement can, at best, make contact with only a few of the types of behavior—and not necessarily the most important ones—that are capable of yielding a monopolistic solution.[46]

The final problem of anti-trust policy, and the one which the theoretical work of the 'thirties made peculiarly evident, is its inability to make satisfactory contact with oligopoly. It is quite possible that imperfect knowledge, inertia, and the allowance that is made for public opinion all help make the market solution under oligopoly indistinguishable from that under monopoly. In any case there is, a priori, no reason for supposing that oligopoly has social consequence that is inherently more beneficent than single-firm monopoly. But oligopoly cannot be like competition. The oligopolist cannot escape from the circumstances that vest him with the power to influence the common market, and the formal solutions that represent him as ignoring the market effects of his actions are barren novelties. If this is granted, then it is just as important that the anti-trust laws come to grips with oligopoly as with monopoly. Or more so, since, from the statistics of concentration noted above, it is clear that oligopoly must be counted the ruling form in industrial markets in the United States. Oligopolistic price policies, even though they give results similar to those of pure monopoly, are presumably immune from anti-trust interference so long as no express or tacit collusion among sellers can be proved.

The problem would hardly be solved were the institution of oligopoly brought within the scope of anti-trust action either by legislation or judicial interpretation. In the past, the courts have shown themselves willing to punish those whose guilt has been established under the Sherman Act although the penalties have frequently been less than drastic. Especially

---

[45] "Monopoly in Law and Economics," *Yale Law Journal*, 1937, XLVII, p. 37.

[46] A recent writer, Professor Rostow, has taken considerable comfort from two recent decisions which, he holds, markedly narrow this gap between monopoly in law and in economics. In the case of the Aluminum Company, Judge Learned Hand held that market dominance, regardless of intent, forced ALCOA to behave as a monopolist; and the Supreme Court recently took cognizance of non-collusive oligopolistic behavior by the big tobacco companies. While these cases are not without importance, it can hardly be argued that they are more than a minor break with a tradition that is strongly behavioristic and which, in view of the difficulty of distinguishing ideal from unsatisfactory market solutions, is perhaps necessarily so. Cf. Eugene V. Rostow, *A National Policy for the Oil Industry* (New Haven, 1948), p. 123 ff. The decisions are those of Judge Learned Hand in the Aluminum Case (U.S. vs. Aluminum Company, Circuit Court of Appeals, 2d, 1945) and of the Supreme Court in American Tobacco Company vs. U.S. (328, U.S. 781, 1946).

under Arnold's leadership, the Anti-Trust Division had considerable success through consent procedure, in banning overt collusion in restraint of trade. These, and other remedies, all leave the basic market structure unchanged and the Courts have shown the utmost unwillingness to invoke remedies that do involve extensive structural changes.[47] Yet for oligopoly as for monopoly there is no other remedy that strikes at fundamentals. For monopoly, dissolution can indeed be regarded as a remedy, inasmuch as all customary definitions or concepts would confine it to a relatively limited number of firms. Such a remedy for oligopoly implies application to a large part of the economy. No one with a sense of history could suppose that the Courts would or could contemplate such a wholesale reorganization of the economy.

Nevertheless the anti-trust laws remain a useful instrument of social control and, quite possibly, the "Arnold era" showed how useful they can be. Although anti-trust action cannot produce important structural changes in the economy or even, in a negative sense, much retard basic trends toward corporate growth and concentration, it still may serve to "improve" the ruling equilibrium. The danger of anti-trust prosecution, or of public ill will leading to intervention by the Department of Justice is, without doubt, a fairly important consideration in corporate price policy. It is fair to assume, as a result, that prices are set closer to marginal costs —i.e., there is a lesser degree of monopoly in the economy—than would otherwise be the case. This, presumptively, means higher income and output and greater satisfactions than otherwise.[48] Without doubt Thurman Arnold was the ghost at more conferences on corporate price policy than either his predecessors or successors in office and, accordingly, the effect of the anti-trust laws on the oligopoly equilibrium was correspondingly more beneficial during his tenure.

Finally no one should underestimate the importance of the anti-trust laws in bringing business practice into accord with basic concepts of decency and equity or in preventing those with economic power from using it to combat innovation. It is not true that monopoly or oligopoly always breeds senescence and protection of the *status quo,* and the reverse may often be the case. The monopolistic or oligopolistic firm is likely to spend more money for research, if for no other reason than because it is

---

[47] The recent divorce of Pullman car operation from car manufacture is principally noteworthy as an exception to the rule. In the recent decision in the Aluminum Case, although the Court found that ALCOA had monopolized the ingot market and that, in writing the Sherman Act, the Congress "did not condone 'good trusts' and condemn 'bad' ones, but forbade all," it contented itself with postponing action until the effect of sale of government-owned war plants could be foreseen.

[48] Cf. Professor Hansen's plea (*op. cit.*) for "structural price flexibility," which comes to the same thing.

likely to have more to spend. In addition, because the firm is large in relation to the total industry, its share in the market for (say) a new product will remain considerable even though the innovation is appropriated by the industry at large and there is more than a chance that the benefits from cost reduction, though similarly generalized, will be perpetuated in the new oligopolistic equilibrium. None of these conditions hold under conditions approaching pure competition. It is interesting, not as proof but as illustration, to compare the rate of innovation in the oil industry with that in the bituminous coal industry. In the former, innovation has been richly financed and rapid. In the bituminous coal industry, which approximates conditions of pure competition, there is little research and little progress. It is also hard to see how any considerable research expenditure could be advantageous for most individual mine operators—even assuming that year in and year out, they could afford it. One should notice, also, the case of agriculture, where, as an aspect of pure competition, virtually all research is necessarily conducted by the government. But this is not a field for easy generalization. In supporting Group Health against the American Medical Association, Arnold showed that the anti-trust laws were both an important and effective weapon on the side of innovation. This was also shown in his attack on the restrictive covenants and conventions of local builders and building trades.

In placing the anti-trust laws in perspective, one has to conclude that they are not serviceable for many of the cosmic purposes that their ardent proponents hold sacred. But it would also be unfortunate if one were to seem to prove too much.

VI

The anti-monopoly crusade came to an end with the war. A number of business executives who came to Washington to help arm the republic felt that business would not be able to give war production its undivided attention until Thurman Arnold was safely leashed. With the help of the Services they devoted themselves unselfishly to that task. At a time when competition was being set aside and capitalism substantially adapted to planned production of war goods it was inevitable that they should succeed. Meanwhile, interest in Washington had partly shifted from Thurman Arnold's indictments to yet another manifestation of the revived interest in monopoly. This was the Temporary National Economic Committee.

The T.N.E.C. was billed as a catholic examination of modern capitalism; and its genesis, at least in part, was in the recession of 1937. However, in the main it was, as the public called it, a "monopoly" investigation; the stage for it was set by Arnold's spectacular drives, by the preoccupation of a keen group of legal scholars in the Securities and Exchange Commission and elsewhere with corporate size and the philosophy of regulation, and, more remotely, by the academic discussion of imperfect competition. More important, perhaps, as immediate background, were Gardiner Means' investigations of economic concentration and concomitant price behavior. These had been extensively discussed in Washington and were cited by the President in his message (April 29, 1938) requesting the investigation. The message also suggested that unemployment was the product of an inflexible price structure.

The T.N.E.C. was in a great Anglo-American tradition of conjoined lay and expert inquiry into economic questions. It was carefully planned. Funds were reasonably adequate. It had wide access to economic data at a time when these had reached a high order of excellence. It reached out to command a large amount of specialized talent. Yet by almost any standards the T.N.E.C. was an undistinguished and disappointing enterprise.

The Committee amassed a great deal of information about the American economy. Unfortunately, information that is not purposefully organized is a depreciated currency, and much of the T.N.E.C.'s contribution could be so described. Much of it lacked even novelty. The investigation of the steel industry went laboriously into the basing point system. It would seem incredible, at this stage in American history, were anything added to knowledge of this venerable institution, and nothing was. The investigation of the inflexibility of steel prices was more interesting, although it served to show that organized adversary debate between economists is poor scientific method. Elsewhere—on industrial insurance, the role of insurance companies in the concentration of economic power, the disenfranchisement of policy holders in mutual insurance companies, patent monopoly, and other subjects—the Committee broke into some new territory. But even on such subjects as insurance, where the findings were not without importance, they were rather by the way of confirming long-held opinions not only of economists but of the public at large.[49]

---

[49] As frequently with such enterprises, the usefulness of the T.N.E.C. findings is partly defeated by their sheer bulk—the printed record itself runs to some 17,000 pages. Mr. David Lynch, in *The Concentration of Economic Power* (New York, 1946), has performed the useful task of summarizing the principal findings. The book is marred, however, by the author's rather mechanical approach to economic judgments and by his tendency to interpose in his assessment of T.N.E.C. findings his own overdeveloped sense of business evil.

The work of the T.N.E.C. was somewhat retrieved by a series of useful monographs prepared under its sponsorship some of which have already been cited.[50] Mention should also be made of Professor Clair Wilcox's monograph, *Competition and Monopoly in American Industry*,[51] an ambitious and, on the whole, successful effort to classify a large sector of American industry in accordance with its market behavior. To do this Professor Wilcox established a certain number of definite categories of market control—simple monopoly, duopoly, monopoly through price leadership, through patent control, through market sharing, and so forth—and fitted (or on occasion crammed) industries into their appropriate categories. Under the direction of Willard L. Thorp and Walter F. Crowder, a further excursion was made into the statistics of concentration. In an attempt to measure trends in concentration, two indexes were constructed showing, on a 1914 base, the number of establishments accounting for half the wage earners in each Census industry and the proportion of all establishments needed to account for half of the workers. Although the effort was partly defeated by the relatively small number of years (eight in all) for which Census data were available, and by adventitious factors which warped the data in certain of these years, the study did show a perceptible though by no means powerful trend toward increased concentration—the present pattern of concentration was approximately achieved prior to World War I. The monograph also examined concentration in individual industries and products as well as certain characteristics of administration of large-scale enterprises.[52] Among other monographs deserving of at least passing mention were A. C. Hoffman's on large-scale organization in the food industries,[53] a study somewhat paralleling the work of Nicholls already mentioned[54]; the study by Helene Granby, Raymond Goldsmith, and Rexford Parmelee of security ownership in listed corporations[55]; and the work of Marshall E. Dimock and Howard K. Hyde on *Bureaucracy and Trusteeship in Large Corporations*.[56]

If, the monographs aside, the investigatory part of the Committee's work was disappointing, it stands as a superb achievement compared

---

[50] Cf. pp. 107, 113, 117 above.

[51] T.N.E.C. Monograph 21 (Washington, 1941).

[52] *The Structure of Industry*, T.N.E.C. Monograph 27 (Washington, 1941).

[53] *Large Scale Organization in the Food Industries*, T.N.E.C. Monograph 35 (Washington, 1941).

[54] Cf. p. 105 above.

[55] *Survey of Shareholdings in 1710 Corporations with Securities Listed on a National Exchange*, T.N.E.C. Monograph 30 (Washington, 1941).

[56] T.N.E.C. Monograph 11 (Washington, 1941).

with the Committee's interpretation of its findings and its recommendations. The latter will be read avidly but only by the connoisseur of
bromides. No serious effort was made to provide an appreciation or
rationale of large-scale enterprise and concentrated economic power as
facts of contemporary economic life. There was no effort to explain the
malbehavior of the economy during the whole of the preceding decade.
Indeed, there was no diagnosis of any kind. Rather, with a droll faith
in some occult process of democracy, it turned the task over to the American people. "The members of the Committee are not rash enough to
believe that they can lay down a program which will solve the great
problems that beset the world, but they are convinced that the information which this Committee has assembled . . . will enable the people
of America to know what must be done if human freedom is to be
preserved."[57]

The recommendations were as futile as the diagnosis. They called for
faith in free enterprise, vigorous enforcement of the anti-trust laws, compulsory licensing and some miscellaneous patent reforms, registration of
trade associations, an approach to federal charters for national corporations, more business research, and better food, housing, and health for
the underprivileged. Although no mention was made of the importance
of regular prayer, Representative Summers did remind the Committee
"that there is a living God whose laws control everywhere . . . as
distinguished from being governed by the theories of men."[58] In line,
presumably, with his faith in divine ordinance, he dissented from a
recommendation for the repeal of the Miller-Tydings Act.

The reasons for the failure of the T.N.E.C. are not simple. Perhaps
it would have done better had it had a more precise focus. Had it been
avowedly a committee on monopoly and the concentration of economic
power, it could hardly have avoided facing up to their implications for
modern capitalism. The broader charter, though in principle desirable,
allowed the Committee to sample too widely and too diffusely among
issues relevant to the overriding issue of underproduction and unemployment.

Also the T.N.E.C. came late in a liberal administration, at a time
when it was less important to display crusading fervor than to demonstrate comparative respectability. Hearings of the T.N.E.C. were marked

---

[57] *Final Report and Recommendations,* T.N.E.C. Document 35 (Washington, 1941).
[58] *Ibid.,* p. 50. Leon Henderson and Isador Lubin, the two economists most prominently associated with the work of the Committee in its final stages, declared the recommendations wholly inadequate. They cannot be criticized for failing to do more, for both
at the time were preoccupied with defense activities.

by none of the *élan* or sense of adventure of the Pecora investigations, for example. Witnesses and the public were assured, repeatedly, that it wasn't *that kind* of investigation. Unfortunately, there may be no other kind. Information that isn't in the public domain is usually being held out for a reason.

At times the Committee, in its desire to display its respectability, verged on Philistinism. In its final report it characterized the case for a secular decline in investment as "un-American." The merits of that case are not at issue here; the Committee could quite properly dissent from an argument that it did not find convincing. It must be condemned, however, for what was clearly an attempt to stigmatize an important and well-reasoned point of view.

There was a deeper reason for the failure of the T.N.E.C. The men who principally supplied its intellectual guidance were deeply committed to an ideal. That ideal was an economy in which the dynamic as well as the regulatory power was supplied by the competition of independent and comparatively small business units. But the Committee found itself exploring a world in which the typical industrial market is pre-empted by three, four, or half a dozen giant firms with, usually, a fringe of small hangers-on. There was no possibility of reconciling the ideal world with the real world. The Committee was too conscious of political reality to recommend (or even explore as a possibility) what would amount to a planned assault on the whole structure of modern corporate enterprise. And to replace giantism and oligopoly with modest-scale competitive enterprise would take nothing less. On the other hand the Committee was far too deeply committed to the small-scale, competitive ideal to admit of and prescribe for a monopolistic economy. Unable either to recommend what it wanted or to accept what it had, the Committee took the only available course. After declaring its faith in the anti-trust laws, an act of piety that never fails to sanctify the failure of a liberal's imagination, it submitted not a finding but an apologia, and quit.

VII

The war years were by no means barren of achievement, though little of it is of a sort that can be recorded in an essay of this kind. Economists assumed a commanding role in the design and administration of production, price, and distribution controls and in such diverse enterprises as wage stabilization, procurement, military intelligence, and international relations. Although there was a corresponding hiatus in scholarly production, it seems certain that the war experience will add realism and catholicity to economic research for many years to come. As a by-product of wartime economic planning there was also an important accretion of information on the American economy. Though, as noted, the problems of capitalism are not traceable to shortages of crude fact, the work of scholars will be both improved and made more difficult by the countless industry studies and market and wage analyses that were made by or on behalf of the war agencies. Even more important, the adaptation of the economy to war production threw unparalleled light on the mechanism that was being adapted. It will be unfortunate if the war experience is not carefully reviewed with this latter opportunity in mind.[59]

Two lines of inquiry relevant to this essay were stimulated by the war. The first concerned small business. For mobilizing economic resources a few large units are, without doubt, both more convenient and more effective than numerous smaller ones. During the war, capitalism was temporarily collectivized by the government. The great areas of private collectivism were brought within this system with comparative ease; numerous small units presented a far more serious problem. One result was that large concerns participated promptly and profitably in war orders; small concerns, on the other hand, were threatened with the loss of their labor or raw materials or of their markets. Because of incomplete mobilization and the compensating effects of increased income, the actual dangers to small business during the war were always more potential than real—the mortality rates for small enterprises were extraordinarily low. Nevertheless there were a succession of small business "crises" in Washington, and two congressional committees conducted semi-continuous investigations of the problems of small businessmen and of sundry wolves in small businessmen's clothing. As the war progressed to be vocally sympathetic with small business became one of the most popular manifestations of a social conscience. A probable result was that small plants received prime or subcontracts they otherwise would not have obtained and more attention than otherwise was given the small trader in the framing of price and rationing regulations. The chief harvest, however, was in oratory.

The war also focused attention on the large industrial combines of Germany and Japan and on the somewhat related question of international cartels. At the end of the war the Japanese combines were the subject of a special study by a staff headed by Professor Corwin Edwards

---

[59] I venture to refer to two papers of my own that were written with this end in view: "Reflections on Price Control," *Quarterly Journal of Economics*, August 1946, LX, pp. 475–489; and "The Disequilibrium System," *American Economic Review*, June 1947, XXXVII, pp. 287–302.

which, broadly speaking, recommended the retirement of the old families from both ownership and control, dissolution of the holding company structure, the elimination of banking control over industrial corporations, prohibition of control by single interest groups over unrelated activities, and protection of these reforms through enactment of an anti-trust statute. Special government machinery was outlined for the acquisition of securities from the family holding companies of the *Zaibatsu* with a view to resale to a more widely dispersed ownership. Subject to some modifications by the occupying authorities and a considerable lack of enthusiasm by the Japanese and some branches of the United States Government, the foregoing has become stated policy in Japan.

Policy in Germany has been confused by the fact of four-power occupation and by some marked extremes of American economic policy. The latter, at times, has amounted to arbitrary hostility to size *qua* size. The number of employees of a firm has been regularly advanced as a prime criterion of whether or not it should be split up; to divide any given firm into two or more parts has on occasion seemed a sufficient aim of policy. At times public ownership, in many cases a fairly obvious solution, has been resisted, not alone on usual conservative grounds, but because of a fear of "publicly owned cartels." Although the American "decartelization" program has been urged with crusading zeal, little has been accomplished. There was considerable passive resistance within Military Government. The British also argued vigorously against the oversimplification of the norm of free enterprise and competition implicit in the American proposals. The French have supported the American proposals, though apparently less on grounds of principle than from the conviction that they would make life unpleasant for the Germans. Initial support also came from the Russians, though the reasons would not be readily apparent from Marxian theory.

Much, though not all, of the war and postwar interest in cartels grew out of the anchor position of the German combines in numerous prewar cartel arrangements. Part of this discussion has been rather romantic. German cartel participants have variously been credited with maintaining expert espionage networks, arming Germany and disarming her potential enemies, and, at the appropriate time, calling the signals for war. Peace and prosperity have been seen as largely contingent on the destruction of cartels.[60] At an adequately restrained level, the discussion has resulted in a useful history of cartel arrangements in sugar, rubber,

---

[60] The Department of Justice has been the source of much of this colorful analysis. Cf. Joseph Borkin and Charles A. Welsh, *Germany's Master Plan* (New York, 1943); and Wendell Berge, *Cartels, Challenge to a Free World* (Washington, 1944).

nitrogen, steel, aluminum, and other products by Professor George W. Stocking and Dr. Myron W. Watkins[61] and a dispassionate survey of cartel and commodity agreement policy by Professor Edward S. Mason.[62]

VIII

The time has come for a brief word of summary. Quite clearly the last fifteen years have been marked by an active effort to resolve the problems presented by large-scale or monopolistic enterprise and to devise a public policy appropriate to their existence. It is apparent that, although the increment of knowledge has been considerable, both tasks have been attended by considerable frustration. The analytical task would appear to have failed because oligopoly, by all evidence the ruling market form in the modern economy, has not yielded to the kit of tools long employed for analysis of the competitive market. In the competitive market, the inability of the individual to affect the solution made it possible to eliminate the vagaries of individual behavior from among the market data. It was possible to proceed, therefore, with a relatively simple set of assumptions. It is of the essence of the oligopoly solution that any individual can affect the solution. The analysis, therefore, had to take on a wholly unmanageable burden of assumptions as to how each participant in the market would behave. The whole exercise, as a result, bogged down.

The dilemma in the field of policy is not unrelated. The problem of monopoly policy has long been intellectual property of men whose faith is in competition. A rule of oligopoly poses, for them, the unattractive alternatives either of recommending a wholesale dissolution of existing business units or of devising rules of behavior for a kind of society which none likes, which for some is a positive anathema, and to which conventional modes of analysis and thought are inapplicable.

Happily this is not the place where such riddles have to be solved. But a suggestion is in order. The dilemma may be more intellectual than real. We do live in an industrial community where oligopoly—or, more horrid word, private collectivism—is the rule. But, strangely, we do live. Our dissatisfaction with our world is less the result of having known

---

[61] *Cartels in Action* (New York, 1946).

[62] *Controlling World Trade* (New York, 1946). The study was sponsored by the Committee on Economic Development. A special virtue of Professor Mason's study is that he approaches his task with an excellent sense of the relation of cartels to the problem of equilibrium that arises when a small number of large sellers are juxtaposed in limited markets. It is this, rather than man's propensity for evil, that brings cartels into being.

any other than of having constructed a model of another economic society, the *rationale* of which we know and which is more companionable to our sense of elegance and order. We shall never find anything so agreeable in the world we have. But perhaps there will be compensation, once we have exchanged elegance for actuality, in a greater rate of progress in understanding what we have.

4

PRICE AND PRODUCTION POLICIES

Joe S. Bain

THE character and consequences of the price and output decisions of business firms in various industries have been studied for many years by American economists. Since the early 1930's, however, these matters have been the subject of a somewhat more intensive and systematic study, and a fairly well-defined field, bearing the label of "Price and Production Policies" or some equivalent, has come to be recognized. This field, in the tradition of some excellent earlier work antedating its emergence, has been primarily one of empirical research, offering opportunities for fact-finding and for inductive generalization. By now, a rather considerable effort has been expended in these directions. It is natural to inquire what, as the result of fifteen years of such effort, we have added to our knowledge.

The "price policy" field has been concerned in general with certain aspects of the manner in which business firms, singly and in groups, mobilize scarce resources to meet the effective demands for commodities. It naturally emphasizes description, explanation, and evaluation of the behavior of firms and industries in determining selling prices, outputs, and closely related matters, but it may appropriately encompass a good deal more. It has evidently taken its present form because of some shift in emphasis in investigating the affairs of business; as a new "field," it is essentially the result of a reorganization of one or more pre-existing fields, undertaken as a result of this altered emphasis. Since a part of the potential contribution of price policy research lies in its novel orientation, its antecedents may deserve some brief attention.

Business organization and behavior have been studied intensively in this country since the early "merger movement," and even the earliest treatments were in general concerned with all of what we currently regard as the primary issues: (1) the structure, organization, and ownership of business; (2) the competitive behavior and price policies of enterprise—including motives, strategy, and tactics; (3) the price, output, and associated results of this behavior; and (4) the public policy issues raised by such structure, behavior, and results. But the earlier work had a number of characteristics which were possible barriers to effective analysis. It was excessively compartmentalized—there was a "natural monopoly" utility field, a "trust problem" field, which encompassed industry which was not—but should be—"competitive," and special fields treating agricultural pricing, marketing institutions, and financial enterprise. Much of the work prior to 1930, moreover, featured simple description and superficial interpretation of financial organization, structural change, and competitive tactics, and in evaluating behavior emphasized the norms of law rather than those of economics. In it there was frequently a lack of close or extended analysis of price-output results, or of how observed market structure and competitive behavior affected the determination of prices and outputs. There were, of course, some notable exceptions, where the tools and criteria of the available economic theory were diligently applied, or where a largely *ad hoc* analysis of industrial behavior moved directly to essential economic phenomena. But the shortcomings noted in general reoccurred quite systematically.

These limitations were especially apparent in the trust problem and marketing fields. They arose primarily from a general lack of *rapport* with the corresponding field of "economic theory," and this in turn stemmed from the "institutionalist" bias of writers, from their frequent lack of theoretical training, and from the inadequacy of contemporary price theory. It was thus that industrial concentration and collusion could be viewed as aberrations from a competitive norm, the theoretical validity and precise content of which was seldom examined, and that the real significance of these aberrations for the general material welfare, presumably registered through alteration of price-output results, could be left without real analytical evaluation.

The emergence of the price policy field from these antecedents is traceable to several influences: (1) the experience of the Great Depression, which engendered a more critical attitude toward the operation of business institutions and the character of competition; (2) the N.R.A. episode, which exposed a large number of economists to the more intimate details of pricing and competition in American business; and (3) the reformulation of price theory to make it more congruent with actual business behavior. Chamberlin's work seems to have been by all odds the most important in the last regard. It related the theory of pricing specifically to the institutional framework and practice of the real economy—to concentration, product differentiation and its legal framework, collusive activities, trade practices, and barriers to entry; it predicted the probability of systematic and significant variations in competitive behavior and price- and output-results in response to variations in this framework; and it thus posed many new questions for empirical research. In fact it provided a major "revelation" to many, suggesting in a broad stroke a general theoretical interpretation of the economic significance of the developments of business institutions since the beginning of the merger movement.

Mrs. Robinson's work, although of a more formalistic character, was also influential; and such contributions as Zeuthen's *Economic Warfare*, though not widely read in this country, reveal a general tendency toward reformulation of price theory. The great formal contribution of Chamberlin, however, was in recognizing adequately the possible economic implications, with respect to price, output, product, and cost, of the governing institutional framework and of market structures, and in suggesting the necessity of an analysis employing several variables, several functional relationships, and several dimensions for the interpretation of actual price behavior. So interpreted, the doctrines of monopolistic and imperfect competition called for a new focus for empirical research in "institutional" fields. The relevance to ethical evaluation and public policy of this increased emphasis on patterns of price behavior (as opposed to institutional emphasis *per se*) was in turn quickly recognized by the expansion of general equilibrium and aggregative analysis to point up the impact of quasi-monopolistic pricing on various dimensions of the total material welfare.

The development of the price policy field then involved a certain reshaping of research emphasis. The study of matters of economic structure, business organization and ownership, corporate finance, and the like has been given a separate though related status. Price policy research has tended to be focused mainly on certain aspects of behavior in all types of enterprise not under government price regulation—"competitive" business as well as "trusts," marketing as well as manufacturing firms, international as well as intranational business arrangements. (The fields of regulated enterprise have been left largely compartmentalized, although this is not necessarily a good permanent arrangement.) The emphasis has been on the analysis of price-making and competitive behavior, its origins, and its results in output, price-cost relations, profits, selling costs, price flexibility, progressiveness in technique or product, and so forth. The terms and criteria of price analysis have been introduced into the empirical study of industry in pursuit of a precise knowledge of the economic consequences of institutional situations and practices, and to elevate this study from the level of casual description to that of systematic generalization and explanation.

The price policy field thus obviously transcends the narrower implications of its label. It is not confined to a study of choices of alternatives by business managements in setting prices, outputs, products, and selling costs, or to an examination of processes of price calculation and of co-operative activities with rivals. It embraces these things, but necessarily gives equal attention to the origins of observed behavior, to its results in terms of output and of price-cost and similar relationships, and to the evaluation of behavior and results from the standpoint of total welfare. In short, it is concerned in detail and on an empirical level with the range of problems with which price theory, broadly construed, deals. It need not be limited, of course, to the formulations and concepts of any particular version of *a priori* theory.[1]

For purposes of this review, we will not view the price policy field as embracing the general treatment of public regulatory policy toward business competition and pricing. The latter is certainly a closely related field, although it appropriately partakes as much of political as of economic science. Even excluding it *per se*, however, we must recognize that regulatory experience is one of the primary sources of data for price policy study, and conversely that it is this study which can identify and analyze what is to be regulated, and may indicate what the economic effect of various policy measures will be. Thus any basic account of developments in the price policy area must recognize the contribution of regulatory experience to research and analysis, and the effect of the latter on thought regarding public policy.

Research within a "price policy" area thus defined has been proceeding rather intensively since the earlier 1930's. We therefore address ourselves to the main question: What has been accomplished since then? What do we know about business price making, its origins, its results, and their significance, that was not known in 1933? Since the price policy field as defined is primarily one of empirical research (as opposed to abstract theorizing *per se*), this question should be taken to refer primarily to inductive and empirical knowledge, or to knowledge stemming from and extensively supported by empirical data. We need not limit ourselves, however, to conclusive and established findings. We will therefore inquire in turn into contributions in the form of:

(1) Additions to scientific knowledge—in the form of empirical generalizations, verification of hypotheses, or simply increments to information as yet not fully interpreted—concerning price making and competition, their origins, and their immediate results.

---

[1] Our view of the field as excluding *a priori* price theory proper is a provisional one, adopted in order to contain the present discussion within workable bounds.

(2) New hypotheses, issues, and directions for investigation into these matters.

(3) Developments of method of research.

(4) Developments of standards for the evaluation of price and related results from the standpoint of their effects on total economic welfare.

(5) Suggestions pertinent to public policy.

These headings should cover the main phases of work within the field defined.

Before we proceed to an appraisal of findings, however, an initial note of justifiable pessimism may be in order. Research in price policy has not yet found unity of direction; the field is still in the main a poorly charted area for exploration. Some forays have been made into its interior, but a large amount of effort has been expended at the borders in discussing the desirability of exploration, the equipment for the trip, the things to which the explorer might give attention, and the methodology of exploration in general. We are currently long on hypotheses and relatively short on discovery. Correspondingly the field has as yet no definitive work or works, nor has research as yet taken on such definite form that one can with impartiality construct a list of "important" (and thus of unimportant) contributions. Evaluations of particular items must be unusually subjective. Succeeding mentions of individual works are thus definitely not viewed as "academy awards" of merit, but are made as expedient in charting the main outlines of price policy research since 1933.

I. Empirical Findings

A field of empirical research is one in which students attempt to find out in fact what happens, in fact why it happens, and in fact what it leads to. The emphasis is on measured result, measured association, measured consequence. In approaching such research, however, there is no valid objection to referring to some *a priori* system of predicting behavior. In fact, such a system may be almost indispensable in suggesting directions for empirical work.

The theories of monopolistic and imperfect competition, which provided an initial orientation and stimulus for much price policy research, analyze pricing and production in three major steps. First, they point to certain significant aspects of the "structure" of markets—with emphasis on numbers of sellers and buyers, product differentiation, and ease of entry—which presumably influence competitive behavior and price results. Second, they deduce the price-calculating and competitive or collusive behavior associated with various sub-categories of markets, as classified on the basis of these characteristics. They do this largely by attributing certain explicit sellers' demand curves, cost curves, and demand-selling cost relations to various market situations, and by deducing the profit-maximizing adjustments to these "determinants" of behavior. Third, they thereby predict the results attributable to various market structures or situations.[2] These predictions, in the absence of more precise data for "assumptions" than are ordinarily available, are almost entirely qualitative in content.

Empirical price research has taken its approach in some part directly from the form of this theoretical analysis. One obvious opportunity has been to inspect various market structures in order to learn what theoretical "types" exist in fact, and thus to provide price theory with a more relevant set of assumptions. Another opportunity is to make statistical measurements of demand curves, supply curves, and other presumed determinants of firm and industry behavior, and to use them to analyze actual price determination; and a third is to ascertain price and output results in various industries. All of these steps may implement the application of price theory or help verify its predictions. Not all inductive analysis of price policies, of course, has been limited to so narrow a formula. Market structures may be analyzed in an endeavor to establish a broader environmental base with which to link competitive behavior, and the analysis of this behavior may not be restricted to the ascertainment of demand and supply functions, but may deal in a freehand and experimental fashion with the price-calculating and competitive action of firms. Explicit attention may be given to matters often only implicitly subsumed in *a priori* analysis, such as the influence of public opinion and of government attitude on price policies, and the relationship of wage policies and price policies. Finally, price research may attempt to find on an empirical level demonstrable connections among market structure, competitive and price-calculating behavior, and price results. Work along this line might ultimately verify the system of abstract theory, or elaborate it, or replace it with something else.

MARKET STRUCTURE

The narrower of the tasks mentioned have so far received much of the attention of students. A first major increment to our knowledge has been in the description and appraisal of American market structures, often

---

[2] We reserve for later consideration the accomplishment of general and aggregative analysis in relating immediate price-output results, predicted by particular equilibrium price theory or found in fact, to the total material welfare.

with especial reference to the formulations of price theory. In line with the growing emphasis on the significance in pricing of oligopoly (fewness of sellers within industries) and oligopsony (fewness of buyers), principal attention has been given to the number of sellers or buyers in various industries and to their proportionate control of output or sales, but emphasis has also been put on product differentiation among rival sellers. A number of surveys dealing with or touching on concentration and other characteristics of market structures for broad samples of American industry have appeared, including the Thorp[3] and Wilcox[4] monographs, the Means[5] study of structure, the Hoffman monograph on food processing and marketing,[6] and the Smaller War Plants study of concentration.[7] For particular industries, more detailed analyses of market structure have been made, emphasizing geographical, technological, legal, and other characteristics of structure, as well as concentration and product difference. The T.N.E.C. hearings and monographs, selected Federal Trade Commission material, and various other industry studies provide a fairly detailed appraisal of market structure in such industries as steel, aluminum, cement, petroleum, automobiles, rubber tires, building materials, electric appliances, liquor, cotton textiles, bituminous coal, motion pictures, and others. Further, recent studies of cartels have brought together considerable information upon the structure of international markets for a number of commodities and manufactured goods.

An obvious contribution of this descriptive work,[8] from the standpoint

---

[3] W. L. Thorp and W. F. Crowder, *The Structure of Industry*, T.N.E.C. Monograph 27 (Washington, 1940).

[4] Clair Wilcox, *Competition and Monopoly in American Industry*, T.N.E.C. Monograph 21 (Washington, 1940).

[5] National Resources Committee, *The Structure of the American Economy*, Part I (Washington, 1939), especially Ch. 7, App. 6.

[6] A. C. Hoffman, *Large Scale Organization in the Food Industries*, T.N.E.C. Monograph 35 (Washington, 1940).

[7] Smaller War Plants Corporation, *Economic Concentration and World War II*, Sen. Doc. 206, 79th Cong., 2nd Sess. (Washington, 1946).

[8] By taking census commodity categories, singly or in related groups, as the principal basis for defining the industry, the writers of such studies have in most cases implicitly sought some working adaptation of a Marshallian-Chamberlinian definition of an industry—a group of sellers with identical or close substitute outputs having access for the bulk of their sales to a common group of buyers. Although empirical application of this concept necessarily involves some arbitrary disregard of measurable cross-elasticity of demand as among sellers in different industries, such cross-elasticities as *must* be neglected are in practice ordinarily not so important as to reduce greatly the analytical validity and usefulness of the industry concept. In some cases, however, thoughtless handling of commodity classifications and neglect of geographical segmentation of the producers of related outputs into local industries have resulted in inaccurate implementation of the industry concept, and in these cases the published results require careful reinterpretation. The following comments rest upon such a reinterpretation of findings wherever this has been necessary in order to retain an analytically valid approximation to the concept of an industry.

of price and output study, is that it has provided a fairly comprehensive measure of market structures in those dimensions which appear theoretically to be most important in conditioning competitive behavior and price results. It shows how concentrated or unconcentrated various industries are and how differentiated their products are, and it supplies less complete information on relevant geographical and technical matters and conditions of entry. Referring directly to theoretical models, it suggests in what industries we have monopoly (one seller), monopsony (one buyer), oligopoly (a few sellers), monopolistic competition (a number of sellers with differentiated products), bilateral monopoly (one seller vs. one buyer), and bilateral oligopoly (a few sellers vs. a few buyers), and it furnishes a tentative basis for possibly desirable subdivisions and elaborations of the few simple categories of theory.

The principal general indications of studies of American market structure are (1) that concentration of output among relatively few sellers is the dominant pattern, (2) that fewness of buyers is common in producer goods markets, (3) that product differentiation is significant for practically all consumer goods and a number of producer goods, (4) that there are potentially many significant sub-varieties of "fewness" and concentration which would logically fall within the bounds of the oligopoly (or oligopsony) category,[9] and (5) that there are additional market characteristics, such as the durability of the output, the geographical pattern, the degree of imperfection in market organization, and several others upon the basis of which markets might be meaningfully distinguished. Such findings suggest that pure competition, many-small-seller monopolistic competition, and single-firm monopoly are in practice rather special cases, and that oligopoly, as the general case, may require elaboration and subdivision.[10]

These findings may thus suggest the elaboration of old or development of new theoretical models appropriate to particular cases, by feeding more precise or elaborate "market structure assumptions" into the deductive

---

[9] For example, very few sellers with equal shares (three, each with a third of the market); very few sellers with distinctly unequal shares (five, with the largest seller controlling two-thirds of the market); moderately few sellers (ten or fifteen) with various patterns of concentration; "quite a few" sellers (twenty to forty or more) with various patterns of concentration; the concentrated core with the competitive fringe (four sellers control 80 per cent of the market, and thirty small sellers divide the remainder); and so forth.

[10] These findings do not ordinarily reveal in which oligopolistic industries the sellers have explicit or tacit collusion on price or other matters, or the degree or effectiveness of the collusion. It is thus expedient, as well as theoretically scrupulous, to define oligopoly as occurring wherever there are a few firms (i.e., separate ownership interests) selling within an industry, regardless of the extent of collusion among them. The emergence of collusion is best viewed as a phenomenon of competitive behavior, apart from market structure.

mill. They may also tell us which models from developed price theory are applicable to given actual market situations, and they may allow us to predict (so far as the models are reliable) the general quality of price results forthcoming from these markets.

There is in fact a variety of applied price theory which involves little more empirical work than that already mentioned. The authors of a number of interesting studies have investigated particular market structures mainly in search of the appropriate assumptions for theory. Having found these, they have proceeded to construct the implied demand and supply situations and by deduction to predict (occasionally with hypothetical cost and price data) the price results attributable to the markets studied.[11] This is of course empirical research that is not very empirical, in that it leaves the substantial matters of competitive behavior and price results to hypothesis. It is an improvement over abstract theory which leaves its assumptions to guesswork or to excessively casual observation, but it is not a very reliable means of finding out what happens in the way of competition and pricing. The dominance of oligopolistic situations in actual markets implies in effect that reliable *a priori* predictions may not be available. Even if oligopolistic indeterminacy is disposed of, moreover, the interpretation or prediction of monopolistic prices which are charged through time and are dependent on a half-dozen variables, each of which is subject to uncertainty, evidently requires a much more complex formal theory than has yet been developed. Despite their merit as elaborations and adaptations of conventional theory, therefore, the last-mentioned studies have added to our empirical knowledge of price determination mainly by acquainting us with the setting of pricing action. Other studies which have stopped short of forays into hypothetical demand and cost curve construction have been almost as informative as those which have pushed on. Studies of market structures as a group have provided a knowledge useful in applying abstract price analysis to the real economy or as a basic starting point for further empirical investigation.

STATISTICAL STUDIES OF DEMAND AND COST

Beyond the basic market structures, the hypothetical determinants of pricing action are industry and individual-seller demand curves, cost curves, and other relationships between interdependent variables. A natural focus for price research has thus been on the quantitative determination of these relationships from statistics. Accurately determined,

---

[11] See, for example, W. H. Nicholls, *A Theoretical Analysis of Imperfect Competition with Special Application to the Agricultural Industries* (Ames, 1941) (a study containing some very interesting treatments of bilateral oligopoly); also H. B. Meek, "A Theory of Hotel Room Rates," *Hotel Administration*, June 1938, IX.

statistical demand, cost, and other functions might enable us to check the validity of abstract theoretical predictions (so far as these have objective content) and, if the theory is verified, to make objective and quantitative predictions of behavior. Several statistical studies of demand and cost with direct bearing on price policy matters have appeared, and their general content may deserve note.

Studies of demand might inquire into price-sales relationships either for individual sellers or for industries or related groups of sellers. In view of the theoretical and statistical problems involved, it is not surprising that there are practically no empirical studies of demand curves or similar relationships for individual sellers.[12] The *quaesitum* if conventional theory is to be implemented is the *ex ante* or anticipated demand curve for the seller's output. This might be sought either by attempting to find an objective *ex post* demand relation, which might be hopefully taken as a fair approximation to the seller's anticipated curve, or by inquiring into and attempting to quantify the seller's subjective impression of his future demand. Neither approach is very promising. In oligopolistic industries where there is no express or tacit collusion on price, the individual-seller demand curve is on realistic assumptions indeterminate and could not be uniquely ascertained by any means. In collusive oligopoly[13] or in non-oligopolistic industries the curves are hypothetically determinate, but the data from which such functions might be determined *ex post* are ordinarily unavailable or inaccessible, except where, in collusive oligopoly, the seller's demand curve might be determined as some share of the *ex post* industry demand, if the latter were known. Even should an *ex post* seller's demand curve be established, moreover, it might often be a rather poor approximation to its *ex ante* counterpart (if any) and further fail to reflect the fact that a range of alternative estimates may replace single-valued estimates in an uncertain world. Direct inquiry into sellers' subjective impressions of their future demand curves seems to this writer unlikely to yield reliable quantitative results useful in explaining price.[14] It may thus be legitimate to conclude that the individual-seller demand curves which hypothetically influence pricing will not ordinarily be reli-

---

[12] But see the interesting exploratory work of R. M. Whitman, "Demand Functions for Merchandise at Retail," *Studies in Mathematical Economics and Econometrics,* Henry Schultz Memorial Volume, Lange et al., eds. (Chicago, 1942), pp. 208-221.

[13] Collusive oligopoly here refers to all oligopolistic industries with agreements, practices, or formal or informal conventions whereby the several sellers obtain effectively concurrent and non-competitive action in setting and changing price, and possibly also in other matters. It thus embraces partial or imperfect collusion as well as full theoretical cartelization, and subsumes (in the view of this writer) most real oligopoly cases. "Fully recognized interdependence" ordinarily gives birth to collusion in this sense.

[14] Some of the reasons for this are discussed in the following section, pp. 154-155.

ably found or approximated on a quantitative level, unless as a collusive oligopolist's "share" of a known industry demand. Applied price analysis will ordinarily have to rely, if such reliance is justified, upon the statistically found *ex post* industry demand curve and upon an analysis of competitive and co-operative adjustments of rival sellers to this demand.

There are, of course, a number of studies of "industry" demands for products, measuring the combined demand for the outputs of several rival sellers on the implicit, and ordinarily supportable, assumption that they change their prices concurrently and by similar amounts. Leading examples of these in the industrial field are the General Motors study of automobile demand,[15] and the Yntema study of steel demand,[16] both prepared at the behest of leading producers in concentrated industries as they made ready to defend themselves against claims that they could reduce prices. A common difficulty with these studies has been that the basic quantity and other data occur in such form (often in annual aggregates) and behave and are interrelated in such fashion that they are not amenable to very meaningful treatment by the partial and multiple correlation techniques ordinarily employed. As a result no especial meaning can be attributed to most statistical industry demand curves which have been or could be forced out of available statistical data. The main positive contribution of such studies, in fact, has come from largely qualitative comment on and interpretation of particular industry demands. Thus the General Motors study illuminates very well the complicated behavior of the demand over time for an expensive durable good where there is a used-product market. The Yntema study develops a convincing case for the inelasticity of steel demand largely by qualitative analysis of the character of its uses. Experience in this field so far has suggested (1) that statistical measurements of industry demand curves will ordinarily be so unreliable (because of intercorrelations of variables, large probable errors, etc.) that they cannot be regarded as quantitative information usable in further analysis; (2) that an indirect and often qualitative approach to the evaluation of industry demands will often have to suffice; (3) that preponderant attention to net price-quantity relations, with comparative neglect of, or subordination of emphasis on, more complex relations, may often unnecessarily restrict applied analysis;[17] and (4) that the interpre-

---

[15] General Motors Corporation, *The Dynamics of Automobile Demand* (New York, 1939).

[16] United States Steel Corporation, *A Statistical Analysis of the Demand for Steel, 1919–1938,* T.N.E.C. Papers (New York, 1939). See also other T.N.E.C. Papers of U.S. Steel.

[17] The complex multi-variate relations, together with partial relations in addition to that between price and quantity, have frequently been calculated in statistical demand

tation of price policies should take explicit account of the uncertainties and complexities noted. Moreover, any statistical industry demand curve, no matter how reliable, will almost inevitably be determined *ex post,* and its correspondence to the industry demand anticipated by sellers may not be especially close. Finally, even possession of an industry demand curve which is regarded as a reliable approximation to the mean expectation upon which sellers acted would be only a beginning in the process of verifying the predictions of abstract analysis. For this, the competitive and co-operative adjustments of sellers to this demand must be analyzed; and on this level it may often be extremely difficult, with manifold uncertainty and with a multi-dimensional price-policy problem, to fill in the hypothetically determining relationships suggested by simplified theory.

Statistical studies of costs have also been made, particularly of the short-run net relation of production cost to output for the firms, as emphasized in conventional price theory. Much of the progress along this line has been made by Joel Dean, who in a number of monographs[18] has studied the short-run cost functions of firms in various industries, and has added considerably to factual knowledge of costs as well as to the refinement of applied statistical analysis. Statistical difficulties are encountered with costs as with demand—they loom large when analysis must depend upon a few annual observations, as it did in the Yntema study[19] of steel costs—but on the whole they are fewer, and the results obtained appear to be more reliable. One striking finding of such cost studies has been the apparent linearity, over wide ranges of output, of the short-run total production cost functions of observed firms, implying a constant short-run average variable and marginal cost except at extremely small or large outputs. This has in turn given rise to attacks on the validity of the finding, with some emphasis on the predisposition of statisticians to use linear regressions in correlation analysis, and on the tendency of accounting classifications and allocations of costs to bias the cost-output relation in the direction of linearity. Although there has been some merit in these criticisms as applied to certain studies, the better cost-curve analyses, like Dean's, have defended their findings rather well. Although the sample of firms studied is still extremely small, it would appear that for a large group of firms with multiple-unit plant equipment the propor-

---

studies, but have often been put aside and neglected as principal attention turned to the demand curve and its price elasticity.

[18] See Joel Dean, *Statistical Determination of Costs, with Special Reference to Marginal Costs* (Chicago, 1939), and a number of subsequent monographs developing statistical cost curves for different types of firms.

[19] United States Steel Corporation, *Steel Prices, Volume, and Costs,* T.N.E.C. Papers (New York, 1939).

tion of variable to fixed factors may be held relatively constant over a wide range of output, and that as a result short-run average variable and marginal costs may be approximately constant over a similar range. This finding, if further established, is relevant to price analysis. However, since the bulk of the firms in question operate in concentrated industries where the tendency to extend output is fully checked either by the decline of price with increasing output or by increasing marginal selling costs as more is sold at given prices, the finding is hardly revolutionary in its implications. The resistance offered to it suggests that some critics have been unduly enamored of the symmetrical U-shaped cost curves of conventional *a priori* analysis. As yet, the sample of firms and industries studied is very small. The data uncovered are interesting *per se,* have been useful in giving us a more accurate idea of the actual shapes of the functions emphasized in abstract theory, and have cast some added light on the phenomenon of price rigidity. They have not been put to more than casual use in the analysis of the determination and behavior of specific prices, and their potential utility in this regard remains to be exploited.

The "long-run" relation of cost to output, or to scale of plant or firm, has been studied in rough qualitative fashion in several industries, and with thoroughgoing statistical analysis in at least one instance.[20] More comprehensive studies made of this sort of relation—for example, the Federal Trade Commission study of size and efficiency—are fragmentary, based on unrefined data, and substantially worthless.[21] Engineering estimates of the cost-scale relationship, most of which are made for internal control purposes and remain unpublished, may constitute the best source of information on this subject.

Although beginnings have been made in the statistical ascertainment of cost and its relation to other variables, our knowledge so far is fragmentary and incomplete. A price committee of the National Bureau of Economic Research underlined this conclusion in an extensive survey[22] of our inadequate empirical knowledge of costs, and pointed to desirable directions for additional research effort in this field. A much more

---

[20] Joel Dean and R. W. James, "The Long-Run Behavior of Costs in a Chain of Shoe Stores—A Statistical Analysis," *Journal of Business, University of Chicago,* April 1942, XV.

[21] Federal Trade Commission, *Relative Efficiency of Large, Medium-Sized, and Small Business,* T.N.E.C. Monograph 13 (Washington, 1940). Some of the principal shortcomings of this work involve the use of insufficiently rectified accounting costs as basic data, and the non-recognition of differences other than those in scale of plant as the probable causes of the noted differences in average costs among plants of various sizes.

[22] Conference on Price Research, National Bureau of Economic Research, *Cost Behavior and Price Policy* (New York, 1941).

complete knowledge for many industries of cost-output relations, both short- and long-run, of the relation of cost to other variables, and of the composition of costs would indeed be useful. Substantially complete knowledge of such matters, however, would not lead at all easily or directly to an explanation of price behavior in terms of statistically found price-determining functions. Granted that *ex post* cost functions may represent workable approximation to the theoretically determining *ex ante* functions, comprehensive statistical testing of conventional theory requires also reliable industry and individual-seller demand curves, and as noted these have not been, and very well may not be, filled in. Unless they are, the processes of existing theoretical price analysis could certainly not be reproduced on an empirical level. Even if this barrier could be crossed, however, verification of simplified two-dimensional theory based on the assumption of given data should hardly be expected. Any applicable theory must be of a multi-variate, multi-dimensional character, including numerous functional relationships in addition to those between cost and output and between price and output, and quantitative verification of such elaborated models in an uncertain world may not, as we will note in a succeeding section, be at all feasible. (In developing and interpreting their findings, nevertheless, statisticians might be less influenced by the two-dimensional formulations of textbook theory, and might emphasize more the multi-variate relations with which they always necessarily deal in processing basic data.) Statistical cost studies promise to be most useful, for the time being at least, as general data in a type of applied analysis which from the standpoint of simplified theory appears to be of a catch-as-catch-can variety.

INDUSTRY STUDIES

A broader undertaking is the general empirical study of pricing and competition in the individual industry. Industry studies were made, of course, before 1933 and a number of them, including various Federal Trade Commission studies, were of very good quality. They were generally marked, however, by an extensive preoccupation with matters of finance and organization, by an interpretation of competition largely in legal terms, and by an attention to little else in the way of price results than profits. The later industry studies, in the "price policy" tradition, tend to accept the terms of Chamberlinian and post-Chamberlinian price theory at least as an orientation for investigation and sometimes as a specific formula for verification. Thus the "full-dress" industry study of recent years pays attention to the character and historical origins of market structure—including concentration, product differentiation, entry, technological and legal conditions, and geographical relationships—to the resultant conditions of demand and supply for the industry and for firms, to the character of price calculation and of rivalrous and collusive behavior, and to price results including profits, efficiency, selling costs, progressiveness, price rigidity, price discrimination, and so forth. And it often also examines at some length the interconnections of structure, behavior, and results—in effect, it moves in an empirical case study through most of the range of interests of the price policy field.

This acceptance of the terms of theoretical price analysis is a blessing and can be a curse. It is a blessing in that it provides a systematic orientation for the empirical study of industry behavior. It provides initially a reasonably pertinent set of precise questions, the answers to which will provide data for an evaluation of how, relative to its opportunities, the industry utilizes resources for production. It can be a curse if the investigator becomes preoccupied with an unduly narrow range of questions, as propounded by a simplified theory, or loses sight of the fundamental importance of the institutional conditions and arrangements which condition behavior, concentrating unduly on a maze of intersecting plane geometry which after all can only reflect the force of these fundamental determinants.

It is a tribute to the good sense of workers in this field that in all but a few studies they have been able to assimilate the essential import of modern price analysis without letting it obscure the significance of institutions or the fact that economics really deals with human beings and physical things rather than with mathematical symbols. The coverage of industries in empirical studies to date of course gives us only a small sample of the possible total. Book-length studies are available for such industries in the United States as aluminum,[23] steel,[24] newsprint paper,[25] petroleum,[26] butter and margarine,[27] motion pictures,[28] cigarettes,[29]

---

[23] D. H. Wallace, *Market Control in the Aluminum Industry* (Cambridge, Mass., 1937). See also, for more recent data, N. Engle et al., *Aluminum, An Industrial Marketing Appraisal* (Seattle, 1944); and C. F. Muller, *Light Metals Monopoly* (New York, 1946).

[24] C. R. Daugherty, M. G. de Chazeau, and S. S. Stratton, *The Economics of the Iron and Steel Industry*, 2 vols. (New York, 1937).

[25] J. A. Guthrie, *The Newsprint Paper Industry* (Cambridge, Mass., 1941); *idem*, "Price Regulation in the Paper Industry," *Quarterly Journal of Economics*, February 1946, LX, pp. 194–218.

[26] J. S. Bain, *The Economics of the Pacific Coast Petroleum Industry*, 3 vols. (Berkeley, 1944–47).

[27] W. R. Pabst, *Butter and Oleomargarine* (New York, 1937).

[28] M. D. Huettig, *Economic Control of the Motion Picture Industry* (Philadelphia, 1944).

[29] R. Cox, *Competition in the American Tobacco Industry, 1911–1932* (New York, 1933).

oranges,[30] automobiles,[31] and cotton textiles,[32] and briefer article-length surveys for such industries (or parts thereof) as electric lamps,[33] cranberries,[34] potash,[35] bakeries,[36] rubber tires,[37] electric appliances,[38] margarine,[39] barbering,[40] and farm machinery.[41] These are supplemented by a number of studies of international cartel organization and operation,[42] as well as by more fragmentary contributions of various sorts. In addition, several volumes have surveyed the character of competitive behavior and its results for a number of industries or firms. These include studies by Burns,[43] Hamilton,[44] and Nourse and Drury,[45] all of which, though necessarily cursory in empirical analysis of particular industries, have been influential in shaping thought and stimulating effort within the field. Finally, there has appeared a considerable amount of material which bears on competitive behavior and pricing but is in rather unorganized form, including T.N.E.C. industry materials not previously cited—in particular the hearings on the steel, petroleum, liquor, construction and other industries—and various publications of the war agencies during the past several years.

The number of items in this representative sample suggests the im-

[30] D. A. Revzan, *The Wholesale Price Structure for Oranges, with Special Reference to the Chicago Auction Market* (Chicago, 1944).

[31] Federal Trade Commission, *Report on the Motor Vehicle Industry* (Washington, 1939).

[32] S. J. Kennedy, *Profits and Losses in Textiles* (New York, 1936).

[33] A. R. Bright and W. R. Maclaurin, "Economic Factors Influencing the Development and Introduction of the Fluorescent Lamp," *Journal of Political Economy*, October 1943, LI, pp. 429–450.

[34] C. D. Hyson and F. H. Sanderson, "Monopolistic Discrimination in the Cranberry Industry," *Quarterly Journal of Economics*, May 1945, LIX, pp. 330–369.

[35] S. P. Hayes, "Potash Prices and Competition," *Quarterly Journal of Economics*, November 1942, LVII, pp. 31–68.

[36] L. G. Reynolds, "The Canadian Baking Industry; A Study of an Imperfect Market," *Quarterly Journal of Economics*, August 1938, LIII, pp. 659–678.

[37] *Idem*, "Competition in the Rubber Tire Industry," *American Economic Review*, September 1938, XXVIII, pp. 459–468.

[38] W. G. Keim and J. M. Blair, "The Electrical Equipment Industries," Chap. 4 (pp. 109–164) of *Price Behavior and Business Policy*, T.N.E.C. Monograph 1 (Washington, 1940).

[39] W. H. Nicholls, "Some Economic Aspects of the Margarine Industry," *Journal of Political Economy*, June 1946, LIV, pp. 221–242.

[40] W. F. Brown and R. Casady, "Guild Pricing in the Service Trades," *Quarterly Journal of Economics*, February 1947, LXI, pp. 311–338.

[41] J. T. Dunlop and E. M. Martin, "The International Harvester Company," Part II (pp. 63–137) of *Industrial Wage Rates, Labor Costs, and Price Policies*, T.N.E.C. Monograph 5 (Washington, 1940).

[42] See especially G. W. Stocking and M. W. Watkins, *Cartels in Action* (New York, 1946).

[43] A. R. Burns, *The Decline of Competition* (New York, 1936).

[44] W. Hamilton et al., *Price and Price Policies* (New York, 1938).

[45] E. G. Nourse and H. B. Drury, *Industrial Price Policies and Economic Progress* (Washington, 1938).

practicality of any item-by-item evaluation of industry studies. Such studies as a group, however, allowing for individual differences in quality, length, and scope, have resulted in a substantial accretion to our empirical knowledge of competition and pricing and of their origins and results. In a number of specific cases we can observe the significant characteristics of market structure, their effects on and reflections in conditions of demand and supply, the actual character of competitive and collusive action, and the statistical and qualitative measurements of the results which emerge. And we can appraise the apparent causal interconnections between structure, competitive behavior, and price results.

What is the net contribution to our general knowledge of business behavior which emerges from the industry studies now on hand? The verification and implementation of a priori price theory in its usual simplified form is not a primary nor a uniformly successful accomplishment. To be sure, it has been possible, on a strictly qualitative level, to support some of the broader hypotheses which theorists have advanced concerning the association of market structure with price making and its results. Distinct differences appear between price behavior in industries with atomistic structure and that in industries with a high concentration of sales in the hands of a few firms; the extent to which entry is blockaded seems actually important from the standpoint of profits; product differentiation and product variability are associated systematically with the behavior of selling and production costs; industries with few buyers have had price results different from those with many buyers; and so forth. But it has been ordinarily impossible to establish on a quantitative level the actual relationship of marginal costs to marginal receipts, or otherwise to implement the precise analytical constructions of a priori analysis. It has been possible to fill in tentatively certain blanks where a priori theory makes no unique predictions, especially in the ubiquitous category of oligopolistic industries. The bogey of potentially indeterminate behavior in this category has been at least in part removed by an identification of specific patterns of collusive and quasi-collusive behavior so common in such industries, by examining the content and workability of such collusion, and by pointing to reasonably systematic time patterns of price-output behavior as emerging from such industries. But the main accomplishments of empirical industry study are of more far-reaching character.

The first of these is in exploring in considerable detail the fundamental institutional, technological, and geographical conditions which lie behind "demand and supply" and affect enterprise behavior. Conventional a priori theory deals with the conditions of demand and cost for firms and industries largely as independent objective determinants of behavior. It goes behind the veil of demand and supply to the more fundamental determinants of behavior only in cursory fashion, referring briefly to such matters as the numbers of sellers and buyers, the degree of product differentiation, and the tendency to diminishing returns within the firm. Extended empirical research has pierced this veil much more thoroughly and with more careful observation, with the result that the general tendencies of price behavior are given a detailed explanation in terms not simply of demand and supply curves, but of the basic institutional, technological, and related conditions which shape and shift these determining functions. The optimum result might be characterized as a wedding of the theoretical and institutional approaches to economic behavior, or perhaps better as a theoretical interpretation of economic history. Thus in the study of the American aluminum industry,[46] the manner in which a monopolistic firm with certain costs adjusts its output to a given complex of demands is not the sole subject for investigation, and research is not confined to the statistical measurement of cost and demand functions. Attention is given in equal measure to the manner in which patent control, resource ownership, and international agreement combined to blockade entry and preserve monopoly; to the character and effect on demand of the substitute competition offered by copper and aluminum scrap; to the time trend of demand and its effects; and to the specific technological conditions which affect the relation of cost to scale and to integration. With the analysis placed on this foundation, the succeeding interpretation of behavior can trace the effect of technique, law, institutional device, and historical accident *through* demand and supply and *to* observed price-output results. The resulting accomplishment, noted in a number of industry studies, is to preserve the utility of technical analysis while avoiding the essential oversimplification and superficiality of its assumptions.

A related contribution of empirical industry study is to reveal the complexity of competitive behavior and of its determinants in actual situations, and thus to suggest reasons for wide divergences in the observed behavior of industries which would seem to fall within a single category in *a priori* theory. This contribution is significant because such theory overlooks strategic characteristics of market structure in its descriptive assumptions and recognizes too few variables and relationships to allow it to make certain very relevant distinctions among cases, and also because the usual static equilibrium formulation passes over essential process and sequence phenomena in price, cost, and output behavior and in the dynamics of product and technique. Thus for example in the analysis of

---

[46] D. H. Wallace, *op. cit.,* especially Parts II and III.

the automobile industry,[47] we find that very essential aspects of market structure and of competitive behavior have been touched on rather lightly in the theories of differentiated oligopoly. The problem of the determination of price, output, product, and selling cost is not simply one of oligopolistic interdependence at a price nexus, but is dominated throughout by the extreme durability of the product, its high unit cost and price, and its susceptibility to style change. The emphasis in analysis thus turns heavily on the pattern of shift through time of the demand for the new product in response to initial exploitation of a latent demand, to partial saturation of the demand, and to replacement cycles. It turns also on the manner in which the behavior of this demand can be influenced by sellers through product variation, introduction of instalment selling, organization and control of a used-product market, and integration or control of retail sales outlets. The essence of price policies in the automobile industry is found in the concurrent and the competitive adjustments of sellers to the shifting potential demand situation through time. A free-hand analysis of these policies reveals the emergence in the 1930's, by a process of progressive imitation, of a fairly regular pattern of competitive and of concurrent behavior possibly peculiar to a concentrated durable consumer-good oligopoly in maturity. Comparative analysis of oligopolistic behavior in such industries as those producing cigarettes, soap, rubber tires, and petroleum products reveals equivalent complexities in the setting and character of price policies and re-emphasizes the necessity of interpreting behavior through time. It also suggests that the oligopoly category may be logically divisible into several significant parts on the basis of differences with respect to conditions of entry, number of buyers, differentiation, variability, and durability of product, trend of demand through time, and other market characteristics. It is of course true that if a priori theory is overly general, theorizing based on empirical analysis can as easily become overly specific.

A third contribution of empirical industry study is of course in finding and measuring the significant results of competitive behavior in various industries. The ratio of profits to investment, of selling to production cost, of attained to optimum scale or utilization, and related results can be ascertained directly, and thus the strictly qualitative predictions of a priori theory can be replaced with a quantitative knowledge of the outcome of various patterns of competition within various market structures.

---

[47] See General Motors Corporation, op. cit.; W. Hamilton et al., op. cit., Sec. II (by M. Adams); Federal Trade Commission, Report on the Motor Vehicle Industry; H. B. Vanderblue, "Pricing Policies in the Automobile Industry," Harvard Business Review, Summer 1939, XVIII, pp. 385–401.

A considerable accumulation of such factual knowledge can be of the utmost importance to economics. It is much easier to measure such results, however, and to show their historical association with given situations, than to demonstrate a necessary and causative relation with chosen determinants.

An implication of the findings described is that it would be desirable in *a priori* theory to elaborate the basic assumptions by reaching further and in greater detail behind the veil of demand and supply into the technological, geographical, and institutional context of business action—to take account of the influence of more characteristics of market structure than has been customary. A related implication is that the formal apparatus of price theory should be further accommodated to the simultaneous treatment of numerous variables and their interaction through time. We will refer to this matter in the following section.

There appear to be definite limitations, however, on the progress of work within the field of industry studies. It is only in the extended studies—like the Wallace aluminum study, which clearly established a landmark in approach, method, and quality early in the development of this field—that a detailed measurement and evaluation of results, or any reasonably conclusive analysis of how one thing leads to another, can be undertaken. Yet each such study is time-consuming in the extreme, and the specific results of each become outdated rapidly if the industry in question is in the process of dynamic change. Shorter studies are perhaps better adapted to the time limitations of research workers and to the tempo of economic change; but in such studies the view of behavior is often excessively synoptic, and frequently little more can be done than to establish the general correspondence of a particular industry with some theoretical model, to carry through a rough and usually unsatisfactory statistical analysis of conditions of industry demand and cost, and to attempt a necessarily sketchy mensuration of significant results. Even a large amassing of studies of the latter scope will hardly provide the basis for any very extended scientific generalization.

Another difficulty concerns the availability of essential data. The great bulk of work in this field is perforce undertaken from the standpoint of the outsider, is based on published or other non-confidential materials, and proceeds by inferring as much as possible from this sort of data. The reluctance of businessmen to confide to economists their methods of price calculation and the character of their associations with rival firms—an attitude strongly encouraged in the United States by the anti-trust laws—has been a serious barrier to close investigation of price policy as seen by the price-maker. This attitude has very frequently been an obstacle to any conclusive empirical analysis of the processes of price and output determination.

A final limitation is evident if an optimistic view of potential accomplishment has been taken initially. It seems improbable that work in this field will ever approach the level of closely approximate quantitative explanation and prediction of prices, outputs, and associated magnitudes. The important determinants of any one quantity are nearly always several, and although each determinant may have a potentially objective magnitude, it is generally subject to manifest uncertainty and to subjective interpretation or estimate by decision-makers. The potential precision of explanation suggested by *a priori* price theory operating on the assumption of given data will thus probably never be approached. Empirical explanation must, moreover, early depart from the mold of static analysis of a single homogeneous time period and attempt to explain what happens in a situation evolving through a series of interrelated time periods, where the "given" does not remain given and where process is as important as equilibrium tendency. The accomplishment of empirical research into business pricing is thus likely to take the form of a *qualitative* interpretation of a historical process, and correspondingly of qualitative prediction. Conventional price theory will be useful for the interpretation of tendencies implicit in market situations, but perhaps not as a framework for detailed quantitative analyses.

OTHER FINDINGS

Not all of the significant empirical findings are contained in intensive studies of industries or firms which trace behavior through from its origins to its final consequences. The Burns study, for example, which early emphasized the unity between institutional fact and the theory of monopolistic competition, centered largely on a systematic view of practices of competition and collusion, and the Hamilton collection is a freehand description of business behavior in a number of selected cases. Of an essentially similar character is the Borden study of advertising, a broad but somewhat cursory survey of the probable effects of advertising on demand, cost, price, and so forth for a number of consumer goods.[48] Yet each was in its way penetrating and suggested a broadening and reorientation of inquiry into pricing and competition. Much essentially fragmentary and unorganized information on competitive behavior and tactics which has become available in the last decade and a half is also very suggestive of the character and complexities of competition. The digested results of the N.R.A. experience of course provided a mine of

[48] N. H. Borden, *The Economic Effects of Advertising* (Chicago, 1942).

fact which has been very enlightening to economists and which has been drawn upon heavily in later research. Much the same is true of the findings in various actions of the Federal Trade Commission, and also of its interpretation of the effect on pricing and competition of various regulatory measures.[49] The large number of anti-trust cases investigated or tried after the inception of the Arnold regime in the Anti-Trust Division of the Justice Department, and the connected writings of members of that regime,[50] emphasized the importance of collusive activities as a part of the price-determining process, and strongly suggested the necessity of accommodating "technical" analysis to admit this sort of fact. The same general suggestions are implicit in the wealth of recent materials on international cartel activities. It is time that theorists forsook their cautious adherence to the improbable assumption that interdependent oligopolists remain "independent" and rely on a guessing game as the road to satisfactory industry prices.

The experience of regulatory agencies during the war period—especially that of the O.P.A.—has of course provided a potentially valuable mine of information for future price policy study. Most of the published literature bearing on this experience so far, however, has been of a specialized character and is primarily concerned with an atypical regulatory problem. In the main it simply adds to the body of source material waiting to be tapped. Its considerable potentialities are emphasized by some retrospective surveys which have appeared recently.[51]

Any account of empirical price research must mention the extensive literature on commodity price rigidity. Originating with the Means pamphlet,[52] the controversy on price inflexibility was carried on in the journals and elsewhere for about a decade. As in the case of similar controversies, many of the arguments which were raised and finally settled or forgotten now seem relatively unimportant, and in retrospect it appears that the fashionable attention to this one aspect of price behavior resulted in some imbalance in emphasis within the field of price study. The principal issues included: (1) how inflexible industrial prices

---

[49] See, for example, *Report of the Federal Trade Commission on Resale Price Maintenance* (Washington, 1945) which casts considerable light on the character of competitive and co-operative activity in the distributive trades, and on the effect of state fair trade laws upon prices and margins. See also E. T. Grether, *Price Control Under Fair Trade Legislation* (New York, 1939).

[50] See especially Thurman Arnold, *Bottlenecks of Business* (New York, 1940).

[51] See, e.g., J. K. Galbraith, "Reflections on Price Control," *Quarterly Journal of Economics*, August 1946, LX, pp. 475–489; also Richard B. Heflebower, "Content and Research Uses of Price Control and Rationing Records," *American Economic Review*, May 1947, XXXVII, pp. 651–666.

[52] G. C. Means, *Industrial Prices and Their Relative Inflexibility*, Sen. Doc. 13, 74th Cong., 1st Sess. (Washington, 1933).

are, cyclically and secularly, and whether they have become more inflexible with the "decline of competition"; (2) why they are inflexible, in terms of the price-calculating operations and competitive relations of firms, and in terms of underlying market structures; and (3) what is the effect of industrial price rigidity on economic stability when agricultural prices are more flexible. The last question is not conclusively answered as yet, although a good many hypotheses, often based on hazy thinking or on misapplied partial equilibrium analysis, were tried and rejected. Adequate general analysis of income movements reveals the significance of such price inflexibility to be uncertain, or dependent on the relative weight of counterbalancing effects which are difficult to assess on a quantitative plane.[53] (One lesson to be learned from the controversy on this level is that the price theorist investigating prices will do well to suspect *ad hoc* norms in evaluating price results, and defer to genuine aggregative income analysis and to general equilibrium theory in this regard.) The discussion of the causes of price rigidity, beginning with Means' dichotomous distinction between administered and competitive prices, resulted in some needed elaborations of the theory of monopolistic and oligopolistic price determination, until it is at present possible to tabulate a whole array of rationalizations for firms' pursuing relatively rigid price policies. However, applied analysis in specific cases has not been carried far enough fully to rationalize observed results in particular industries. The statistical treatment of price inflexibility past and present has finally given us a fairly reliable measurement of the phenomenon, and an indication that inflexibility was not a sudden development of any particular decade.[54] The behavior of price over time should now assume a place commensurate to its moderate importance among the many significant results of industrial price policies.

The preceding pages survey the general character of the findings of various sorts of empirical studies in the price policy field since the publication of Chamberlin's work. In spite of the aggregate resultant contribution, our empirical knowledge of price-making, its origins, and its results, is still very fragmentary. We have accumulated a general knowledge of market structures; a few suggestive but inconclusive measures of demand and cost curves; a detailed analysis of pricing and competition in a few industries and a cursory survey of the same thing in

---

[53] See, for example, William Fellner, *Monetary Policies and Full Employment* (Berkeley, 1946), pp. 137–140.
[54] A good general study of price rigidity is found in T.N.E.C. Monograph 1, Part J Chap. 2 (S. Nelson, "Price Flexibility"). On p. 16 thereof, see a bibliography of literature on the subject,

a number of others; much undeveloped material on competitive behavior and tactics; a detailed analysis of price rigidity. Although the results of intensive individual studies are rich in suggestions, they are as yet too few, and their purposes are insufficiently unanimous, to permit much in the way of real comparative analysis, classification, or generalization.

There has not as yet been any general and conclusive test of the predictions of abstract price theory. A good many empirical results are consistent with such theory and suggest that its assumptions are in general valid and its predictions correspondingly useful. But theoretical analysis often overestimates the seller's knowledge of governing data and his ability and disposition to calculate. As a result, actual price-making probably constitutes at best a very rough and often indirect approximation, with a wide range of possible error, to the detailed predictions of geometrical analysis.[55] A further suggestion that may be elicited from empirical studies concerns the futility of attempting verification of over-simplified static theoretical models in a complex and dynamic real world.

Empirical measurement and analysis is still too scattered to permit much in the way of inductive generalization concerning price-making, its results, and its origins. Various observers have advanced general hypotheses on the basis of fragmentary and imperfect evidence, and indeed some very tentative classifications and generalizations are suggested by studies made so far. But any inductively derived explanatory systems are still definitely on the level of hypotheses tested only inconclusively and by small samples. They are best viewed as tentative theoretical suggestions, and as such they will be discussed below.

II. New Hypotheses, Issues, and Directions for Investigation

Creative empirical work in any field will take its direction from major hypotheses advanced by those with especial insight and ability to grasp the broad possibilities of system in a type of behavior. But as it progresses, empirical study should reshape and elaborate its objectives by additional hypotheses which it develops. Price policy research is strongly indebted to the initial insights of a few people, and a fair measure of its vitality is its ability as it proceeds to turn up significant new issues for investigation.

Probably the most important single stimulus to price policy work has come from the broad and connected set of hypotheses, amounting to a

---

[55] Cf. E. R. Hawkins, "Marketing and the Theory of Monopolistic Competition," *Journal of Marketing*, April 1940, IV, pp. 382–389.

new theoretical system, advanced by Chamberlin. Additional emphasis of this fact is hardly required at this date. It is also evident that the many writings on the theories of monopolistic and imperfect competition since 1933 have been a fruitful source of new hypotheses for empirical study.[56] Equal attention at least must be given to those who in a sense "pioneered" in this related field of empirical investigation—who emphasized the close relation between what had previously been an area of institutional study and the new theory, who formulated problems for empirical investigation, and who suggested the possibility of empirical generalizations which would do much more than test the simplified abstractions of *a priori* theory. In this regard major credit must be given to E. S. Mason of Harvard, who as much through the seminar room as through his writings[57] on price policy has influenced almost all workers in this field directly or indirectly. His ability to conceive the character and the exigencies of market analysis on the empirical level has been indeed striking. Especial importance may be attached to his suggestion that the explanation of price behavior be reduced to an objective level by going behind non-ascertainable demand curves to the observable characteristics of market structure, and by attempting to demonstrate the connection between market structure and price results. This suggestion has supplied a general basis for procedure in many industry studies. Other important influences on the development of a general attitude and approach to price policy research stemmed from A. R. Burns in his *Decline of Competition* and other writings, from Walton Hamilton, J. D. Black, and Donald Wallace. Their appreciation of the possibilities of research in this field, as much as their own empirical work, has been very important.

A number of new hypotheses and issues have emerged from empirical work on pricing, and these are important not only as they affect further research but also for the suggestions they make for possible revision of price theory. Two of the most prominent suggestions concern the character of the price-calculating processes of business firms and the question of whether the price-output results of various market situations are objectively determinate.

Conventional *a priori* theory apparently takes a rather unequivocal

---

[56] Especial importance may also be attributed to such theoretical works as A. G. Hart, *Anticipations, Uncertainty, and Dynamic Planning* (Chicago, 1940); J. R. Hicks, *Value and Capital* (Oxford, 1939); and M. Abramovitz, *Price Theory for a Changing Economy* (New York, 1939)—all bearing on the problem of dynamic adjustments.

[57] See, for example, "Industrial Concentration and the Decline of Competition," *Explorations in Economics* (New York, 1936); and "Price and Production Policies of Large-Scale Enterprise," *American Economic Review*, March 1939, Proceedings, XXIX, pp. 61-74.

stand on both issues. It suggests a definite process of calculating price, output, product, and selling cost, involving in general the finding of an optimum of maximizing positions where marginal cost is equal to marginal revenue. It also implies, at least in the Chamberlinian version, that price-output results are in general, barring non-collusive oligopoly, objectively determinate. That is, objective conditions of demand and cost govern behavior via the application of marginal calculation, and the subjective interpretations by sellers of these conditions are not so uncertain or random as to require abandonment of the assumption of uniquely and objectively given data.

The first point in itself has become the subject of much controversy. Many empirical studies suggest that business managers do take account of the demands for their own outputs, or, on the supposition of concurrent price policies by rivals, of their "industry" demands. It has also appeared that they are aware of their costs and of the manner in which these change with changes in output and product, and that they consider the relation of selling cost to demand. Such studies often also suggest, however, that the number of variables and functional relationships governing enterprise profit is great, especially when many of the variables are dated, and furthermore that the magnitudes of many relevant data are uncertain. And they suggest that all of this does result, at least in certain industries, in the employment of "crude" formulae or approximation methods of determining price, output, product, and selling costs, and that these may not result in precise equation of marginal cost to marginal revenue (or in whatever is equivalent to this as a means of maximizing profits in multi-variate models).

Controversy has flared when some have suggested that a marginal calculation is not followed at all, at least in oligopoly, and that pricing on the basis of full average cost plus a margin may constitute a more general rule.[58] In response to these insidious suggestions, "marginalism" has been avidly defended.[59]

In some perhaps uncommon cases, of course, for example in oligopoly with no express or tacit collusion, "full-cost" or kindred formula pricing may be the occasion of no legitimate controversy, since in the absence of a uniquely determined marginal revenue curve for the seller, employment of an arbitrary formula may involve no contradiction of theoretical predictions. In all other cases, use of genuinely arbitrary formulae might be surprising, although use of rough approximation should not be, just

---

[58] See, for example, R. L. Hall and C. J. Hitch, "Price Theory and Business Behavior," *Oxford Economic Papers*, No. 2, May 1939, pp. 12–45.

[59] See F. Machlup, "Marginal Analysis and Empirical Research," *American Economic Review*, September 1946, XXXVI, pp. 519–554.

as management should not be expected to conceive and solve a multi-dimensional problem in terms of an artificially simplified two-dimensional model occurring in economics textbooks. Empirical research, in any event, has not as yet established a major probability that any arbitrary formula is the key to price making in any market category. It has left open the possibility that flexible application of such formulae may give results roughly equivalent to marginal calculations, and it has suggested many apparent alternatives to straightforward "full cost" pricing. The facts here, and their interpretation, are still largely to be discovered.

What this research does suggest positively is the following (and this quite aside from any potential oligopolistic uncertainty): (1) The applicable theoretical models for profit maximization are much more complex, because of the number of variables, relationships, and time periods involved, than those ordinarily seen in textbooks. No simple verification of two-dimensional period-by-period balance of cost and marginal revenue should ordinarily be expected by the most doctrinaire proponent of "marginalism"; unless these two functions are implicitly redefined to reflect all forces bearing on the problem (and thus made intangible if not meaningless), profit maximization does not require that they be equated in every period. (2) If theory is taken in an applicable multidimensional version, the enterpriser's ability to carry out the implied profit-maximizing calculations can easily be overestimated. (3) The enterpriser's knowledge of governing data and functional relationships also tends to be overestimated in a priori theory which assumes given data. The range of uncertainty concerning many variables and relationships may be very great—in fact great enough to discourage precise handling. (4) In view of all this, we may question not only the ability but also the disposition of sellers to make highly complicated calculations with highly uncertain data, and may understand it as perfectly rational if they employ various simplified formulae and approximation methods in arriving at a desirable price and output.

So far as it intends to make objective predictions of behavior in objective situations, price theory must take some of these considerations into account. The task of empirical research would seem to be to find out in many more cases how prices are made, and to examine the price-making process to find if the results are highly systematic, or in fact rather arbitrary and capricious. It is not evident that the question of whether "profits are maximized" is really amenable to treatment.

All of this bears on the issue as to whether competitive behavior and price results are objectively determinate. There has been a thought-provoking exchange of views on this matter, principally between E. S.

Mason and E. G. Nourse. The essence of Mason's position is that there may be a determinate association between objectively ascertainable characteristics of market structure and price results. Accordingly he advanced the hypothesis that the objective market situation is primarily determining, in the sense that different individuals placed in the same situation would make price policy decisions in approximately the same way.[60] (It will be noted that this is the same sort of objective determinism which Chamberlin would suggest, except that it emphasizes as determinants ascertainable structural characteristics, such as the numbers of sellers and buyers, instead of the largely non-ascertainable individual-seller demand curves.) Nourse's position, as developed in two books[61] and other writings, is that with concentrated markets, large corporate firms, and the complex structure of modern entrepreneurship, competitive behavior is far from determinate. He holds that there is often a broad scope for creative decision-making by the business executive. In effect, different persons, each desiring to "maximize profit," might act in very different ways in the same objective situation, because they might interpret its possibilities differently, might see in different lights the feasibility of altering the market situation, or might be optimistic in different degrees. This is held to be especially true because of the wide range of discretion open to executives with regard to making innovations of technique or product, and because of the multiplication of uncertainty in situations which are dynamic in these dimensions.

The resulting issue has scarcely been resolved. Any hypothesis of objective determinism is in danger of overlooking the fact that human behavior and not simply equation-solving is involved, and of viewing business executives as possessed mainly of a sort of standard profit-maximizing reflex which automatically finds the correct implications of a given market setting. This view may be misleading if we recognize that the controlling variables are many, that some of their values are highly uncertain, that the ability and disposition of executives to solve highly complicated maximization problems employing guesswork data may be limited, and that in genuinely non-collusive oligopolistic situations the controlling data for the firm may not even be hypothetically determinate. In view of these considerations, significant differences in behavior might be expected to result from substituting different persons in given objective situations, and the fact that these situations are defined in empirically tangible and measurable terms in no wise alters this

---

[60] E. S. Mason, "Price and Production Policies of Large-Scale Enterprise," *loc. cit.*
[61] E. G. Nourse and H. B. Drury, *op. cit.;* also E. G. Nourse, *Price Making in a Democracy* (Washington, 1944).

probability. The question remains, however, whether behavior may not very frequently be determinate within a relatively narrow range, so that determinism is saved after all, and Mr. Nourse's creative executive is ordinarily confined to operations within narrow limits. The answer may lie in an extended comparative analysis of the uniformities of executive behavior in parallel situations. It will also be pertinent to observe, in the developing national policy situation, the extent to which business "profit maximization" becomes, through the recognition of all sorts of secondary and tertiary consequences of pricing action, an entirely plastic and indefinite concept. The writer suggests tentatively (1) that any given "static" market structure ordinarily confines executive discretion to a relatively narrow range (as long as, in oligopoly, he observes the usual tacit or explicit collusion on price), so that meaningful associations between quasi-static market structure and competitive behavior can often be established for moderate time intervals, but (2) that the executive has enough discretion at any one time that he may follow significantly different policies designed to *change* market structure through time, and (3) that the dynamic course of market structure (and hence behavior) over substantial time intervals may not be at all determinate.

Empirical research has also made a contribution to the general analysis of price in the area of geographical price policy and spatial price differentials. Detailed analyses of basing-point systems, of the sort developed by de Chazeau[62] in his work on steel, together with various controversial discussions of basing-point pricing,[63] have developed, in terms congruent with theories of oligopoly and monopolistic competition, an economic analysis of the origins of and alternatives to systems of geographical price discrimination. Strictly *a priori* analysis has of course shared the burden of this development. As a total result, we have a more adequate interpretation of geographical pricing phenomena.

An issue still worth attention was introduced, or revived in a new context, by the writing of those persons connected with the anti-trust law enforcement after 1937.[64] This concerns the character and importance of collusive activities in price and output determination in our

---

[62] C. R. Daugherty, M. G. de Chazeau, and S. S. Stratton, *op. cit.*, Ch. 12–14.

[63] Such as F. A. Fetter, "The New Plea for Basing Point Monopoly," *Journal of Political Economy*, October 1937, XLV, pp. 577–605; M. G. de Chazeau, "Reply to Professor Fetter," *ibid.*, August 1938, XLVI, pp. 537–566; A. Smithies, "Aspects of the Basing Point System," *American Economic Review*, December 1942, XXXII, pp. 705–726; V. A. Mund, "Monopolistic Competition Theory and Public Price Policy," *ibid.*, pp. 727–743; J. M. Clark, "Imperfect Competition Theory and Basing Point Pricing," *ibid.*, June 1943, XXXIII, pp. 283–300; and numerous others.

[64] See, for example, Thurman Arnold, *Bottlenecks of Business*; Corwin Edwards, "Can the Anti-Trust Laws Preserve Competition?" *American Economic Review*, March 1940, Proceedings, XXX, pp. 164–179.

predominantly oligopolistic economy. In the first flush of enchantment with the new price theory, and of reaction against the old "trust problem" study, there may have been some tendency to discount the importance of collusion. It may have been supposed that the theory of oligopoly pricing showed collusion to be unessential—"mutually recognized inter-dependence" taking its place or giving the same result—or that emphasis on the firm's demand curve eliminated the necessity of direct reference to crass institutional matters. Such an emphasis involves arid formalism and perhaps a flight from reality into the calculus. The suggestions of Arnold and Edwards were thus useful in reminding us: (1) that collusion in some sense often if not commonly plays a strategic role in the process of price formation; (2) that it is a very complex phenomenon, and can assume many significantly different forms; (3) that price behavior may vary with the sort of collusion adopted, and with the state of law and law enforcement affecting collusion. Such suggestions tend to undermine somewhat the notion that certain price results are inevitably associated with given market structures, unless indeed these market structures are defined to include in a given state all relevant aspects of the legal framework controlling or influencing competitive and collusive behavior. They imply that the theory of oligopoly price should put much more emphasis on collusive models,[65] and that empirical research should attempt to deal in some detail with the nature and effects of various types of collusive arrangements.

If empirical research has cast some light on the theoretical issues like those just described, it has made little definite progress as yet on a larger problem—that of establishing an objective classification of markets, each sub-category of which would contain industries with a uniform and distinctive type of competitive behavior. Such a classification is of course a goal of empirical generalization in the price policy field, if indeed such generalization is possible. Classifications so far developed appear to be substantially non-objective in character, or to be too general to allow separation of distinctive types of behavior, or, if more detailed, to represent imperfectly substantiated guesses requiring more extended empirical backing. "Degree of monopoly" classifications in the Robinsonian tradition, like those advanced by Lerner[66] and Rothschild,[67] rest upon practically non-ascertainable sellers' demand curves and can-

---

[65] Cf. D. Patinkin, "Multiple-Plant Firms, Cartels, and Imperfect Competition," *Quarterly Journal of Economics*, February 1947, LXI, pp. 173–205.

[66] A. P. Lerner, "The Concept of Monopoly Power," *Review of Economic Studies*, June 1934, I, pp. 157–175.

[67] K. W. Rothschild, "The Degree of Monopoly," *Economica*, February 1942, XXIV, pp. 24–39.

not be considered as objective or empirically applicable.[68] The Chamber-linian market classification, based simply upon a twofold classification of product difference and a threefold classification of number of sellers (one, a few, and many),[69] is objective but evidently too general. In particular, it leaves the oligopoly category, which in fact comprehends the great majority of actual cases, as a substantially undifferentiated and amorphous mass. The need is particularly evident for finding first whether other market characteristics, besides number of sellers and prod-uct differentiation, offer a basis for distinguishing (at least qualitatively) particular types of oligopolistic behavior, and second what the effect may be, within the general bounds of oligopoly, of differing degrees and patterns of concentration.

Empirical research, industry by industy or otherwise, simply has not proceeded far enough to give entirely reliable general suggestions on either of these points. There is really not enough accumulated infor-mation to permit the conclusive establishment of an explanatory classi-fication which will account even on a qualitative level for observed differences in oligopolistic behavior, or, conversely, to support the con-clusive rejection of the possibility of such a classification. And there are ample reasons for wondering if any such classification with demonstra-ble explanatory value can be developed in a world where the effects of dynamic change of and random uncertainty concerning the governing data may obliterate or obscure the virtual influence of basic environ-mental conditions. Nevertheless, various "scattered returns" have been drawn upon to formulate some tentative market classifications which go beyond those found in *a priori* theory. Even though these classifi-cations represent casually tested hypotheses rather than established findings, a mention of them may be deserved, in part because they have provided a basis for the experimental elaboration of the assumptions of *a priori* price theory.

J. M. Clark, in his notable article on workable competition,[70] has singled out as potentially important, in addition to number of sellers and product differentiation, such things as the size distribution of pro-ducers, the methods of price-making and selling, the perfection or im-perfection of market organization, and spatial relationships. Recognition

---

[68] The Triffin classification (Robert Triffin, *Monopolistic Competition and General Equilibrium Theory* [Cambridge, Mass., 1940]), resting on the cross-elasticities of sellers' demands, has a similar limitation.

[69] See F. Machlup, "Monopoly and Competition," *American Economic Review*, Sep-tember 1937, XXVII, pp. 445–451.

[70] "Toward a Concept of Workable Competition," *American Economic Review*, June 1940, XXX, pp. 241–256.

of these characteristics in classifying markets might give rise to a tentative classification (abbreviating Clark's own) of the following general form:

I. Pure competition—standard product, known (quoted or supply-governed) price, many sellers at any local market, free entry.
  A. Perfect competition (perfect factor mobility).
  B. Imperfect competition (imperfect factor mobility).
    1. Excess capacity (price less than average cost on average over time).
    2. No excess capacity.
II. Modified, intermediate, or hybrid competition.
  A. Standard products, *few sellers*, free entry but exit with loss.
    1. Quoted price, without significant spatial separation of producers.
      a. Open price.
      b. Imperfectly known price, chaotic discrimination.
      c. Open price with limited or occasional departures.
    2. Supply-governed price (open market).
    3. Quoted prices, with significant spatial separation of producers.
  B. Unstandardized products, *either many or few sellers*.
    1. Quoted prices.
    2. Supply-governed prices.

With the omission of numerous asides on the *assumed* shape of the individual seller's demand function in various sub-categories, this is the essence of Clark's classification so far as it runs in terms of ascertainable market characteristics. The state of current knowledge is reflected in the fact that although this classification may contain very pertinent suggestions, we cannot say with certainty whether or not Clark has hit upon the most essential characteristics distinguishing among markets within the oligopoly category or among markets generally. The writer would object strongly to lumping all differentiated-product industries in one category, regardless of number of sellers, and to neglecting the number of buyers, the durability of output, the difference between relatively easy and very difficult entry in oligopoly, and the time-trend of industry demand. And the extended distinctions among quoted and "supply-governed" prices in oligopoly seem to receive more emphasis than these actually tenuous distinctions may deserve. With Clark we would have automobiles, rubber tires, cigarettes, light bulbs, ladies' dresses, radio sets, optical goods, agricultural equipment, and electrical machinery nested incompatibly together in category II-B-1, although there are significant ascertainable and clearly explicable differences in competitive behavior and price results among these industries. But much more investigation would be required to evaluate Clark's classification conclusively.

The penchant of this writer, after the suggestions of Mason and

Wallace in their work at Harvard, would be to emphasize the following market characteristics as strategic in explaining observed differences in competitive and price behavior:[71] the number and size distribution of sellers, the number and size distribution of buyers, whether a producer or consumer good (linked to product differentiation), the conditions of entry, the durability of the product, the time-trend of industry demand. From this could develop an abbreviated classification in the following form:

I. Many sellers, free entry.
   A. Consumers' goods, differentiated products, many buyers.
     1. Durable and style-varied goods.
     2. Non-durable goods.
   B. Producers' goods, unimportant product differentiation (not distinguished on basis of durability).
     1. Many buyers.
     2. Few buyers.
     (Further distinction possible on the basis of time-trend of demand.)
II. Few sellers in general.
   A. Consumers' goods, differentiated products, many buyers.
     1. High concentration of output in hands of few sellers, very difficult entry.
       a. Durable goods, strong style elements.
       b. Non-durable goods.
     2. Moderate concentration, relatively easy entry (not distinguished on basis of durability).
   B. Producers' goods (not distinguished on basis of durability or product differentiation).
     1. High concentration, difficult entry.
       a. Many buyers.
       b. Few buyers.
     2. Moderate concentration, relatively easy entry.
       a. Many buyers.
       b. Few buyers.
   (Further distinction on the basis of time-trend of industry demand desirable.)

This classification, a revision of a basic model introduced by E. S. Mason about a decade ago, seems to the writer to establish sub-categories within each of which the available evidence (catalogued in the preceding section) points to significant uniformities of behavior and among which there are systematic and significant differences, with respect to such matters as profit rates, ratio of selling to production cost, price behavior over time, product behavior over time, and so forth. Discussion of these uniformities and differences would require more space than

[71] See J. S. Bain, "Market Classifications in Modern Price Theory," Quarterly Journal of Economics, August 1942, LVI, pp. 560-574.

here available, but in any event it must be emphasized that these are only very tentatively indicated and by no means conclusively established. The problem of explanatory classification thus remains open, and an explicit orientation of research toward its solution would be highly desirable. Experimentation with abstract price theory employing correspondingly elaborated assumptions, together with some realistic assumption concerning collusion, would also be desirable.[72]

These are some of the theoretical issues raised by recent price policy research. Although the stimulus to abstract analysis may be considerable, progress in the development of empirical generalities to resolve them is quite slow. The lagging pace of empirical discovery and generalization may be unavoidable, but it does raise primary questions concerning the *method* of research. What should research workers be doing and how should they be trying to do it? On these points there is much indecision, lack of direction, and difference of opinion. It may therefore be appropriate to consider the problem of method in this area of research.

III. Aim and Method in Price Policy Research

The variety of types of empirical price study reviewed earlier in this discussion suggests that there is as yet no settled agreement on specific objectives of research or on the method of analysis. At this stage, of course, there is no strong case for standardization of method; the field is new and much of the work necessarily involves exploration in methods. Some conscious recognition of alternatives in aim and method, and some weighing of their relative potentialities, may nevertheless be desirable.

There are several distinct but potentially allied aims of empirical research into pricing: (1) description and fact-finding, (2) interpretation and generalization, and (3) normative evaluation and critique. Several things may be emphasized about description and fact-finding. A considerable contribution to knowledge can result from comprehensive and detailed findings of the facts concerning market structures, competitive behavior, the processes of price formation, and the price, output, and allied results which emerge. The finding of facts, on any or all of these levels, is an indispensable part of effective empirical research, and con-

---

[72] As of the end of the period here surveyed, a well-developed and novel theoretical system has been put forth, which although it has not as yet obviously influenced price policy research, may eventually have some impact. This is the Neumann and Morgenstern work on the *Theory of Games and Economic Behavior* (Princeton, 1944), which suggests a new approach to the formation of business decisions under conditions of recognized interdependence. What influence it may have on the interpretation of price policies will be interesting to observe.

siderable debt is due to studies which in effect go no farther than this. But there is a question how much such facts *per se* contribute to our understanding of economic activity and its consequences. Even an indefinitely large compilation of facts, selected in accordance with some general criteria of relevance, may not lead at all automatically to effective generalization about or evaluation of the behavior in question. Fact-finding and measurement are in effect not desirably isolated from interpretation, explanation, and evaluation. Serious scientific generalization is the prime responsibility of any worker in this field; the production of systematic statistics and similar data contributes to, but is only a part of, this process. More important, adequate criteria of relevance cannot be maintained and adequate direction cannot be given processes of definition and measurement unless the person charged with organizing the facts is also well informed concerning the detailed problems of interpretation and evaluation. And we certainly should not confuse an unsystematized catalogue of facts with any real understanding of the pricing process.

Interpretation and explanation, proceeding from observed association in the specific case into empirical generalization comprehending many or all cases, is the appropriate central aim in price policy research. If our knowledge is to be operationally useful, we need to know what is systematically associated with what—for example, what the demonstrable association is among market structure, competitive behavior, and price results. Factual investigation should be oriented to the exigencies of generalization, and should be tested for its usefulness in this regard as rapidly as possible.

The attempt to develop empirical generalizations raises the question of method. Without attempting to exhaust the subject, we may note that there are two sets of choices with respect to method concerning which workers in the field seem to differ.

The first choice involves the degree of dependence upon the broad hypotheses and explanatory mechanisms of the existing *a priori* price theory. Three possible approaches are available here: (1) the attempt to verify (or disprove) the predictions of price theory in an explicit and quantitative sense, by measuring the presumably determining variables and functional relationships, and by checking their implications against measured results; (2) the attempt to establish, and possibly to elaborate and revise, the broad qualitative predictions of such theory, but without explicit dependence upon statistical ascertainment of determining functions; and (3) a strictly experimental attempt to find any sort of systematic associations, with little or no dependence upon conventional theory. There are examples of each approach. Joel Dean's statistical cost curve work seems related to the first; much of the general "industry study" approach espouses the second; Walton Hamilton is perhaps the most explicit exponent of the third.

If it is to do more than indicate the probable shapes of some of the determining functions employed in abstract analysis, the first approach labors under severe difficulties. Simplified textbook price theory does not ordinarily provide an adequate analytical framework for verification, and a sufficiently elaborated, multi-variate theory would require discouragingly complex statistical analysis. In numerous cases, the strategic individual-seller demand functions may not be susceptible of objective ascertainment, or if they are to be found, we must turn the subjective estimates of sellers into statistical data. The feasibility of this procedure may certainly be questioned, especially if sellers in complex and uncertain situations adopt short-cut formulae and do not deal explicitly with the theoretically controlling functions. Finally, the uncertainties of correlation analysis as employed in all these pursuits reduce the significance of the findings that emerge. For these reasons, effective empirical generalization on a quantitative level concerning the association of price results with determining variables seems unlikely to be attained. Perhaps it is better to regard price theory as an embarkation point and general guide, rather than as a fixed body of principles for detailed verification. A general commentary on and elaboration of conventional theory may have to be accepted as a sufficient accomplishment in this direction.

A somewhat less ambitious approach, following the general suggestion of price theory, attempts to establish systematic associations among easily ascertainable characteristics of market structure, patterns of competitive behavior and price policy, and observable price results.[73] This is indeed the general method common to a large number of empirical studies in the price policy field. It does not necessarily deny the implicit importance of governing functional relationships, but expediently chooses to adhere to what can be seen, measured, and exhibited, thus placing any generalizations which may emerge on a substantially objective level.

Studies following this pattern suggest that it has the advantage of flexibility while still recognizing some logical order. In particular, it need not be tied to the static reference implied in verification of conventional price analysis, and can deal directly with evolution as well as static equilibrium tendencies. Moreover, while able to admit as many ascertainable determinants as necessary, it is not committed to the defense of a fancifully complex maze of hypothetical governing relationships. But it has also very clear limitations. Such generalizations as the method develops have

---

[73] See E. S. Mason, "Price and Production Policies of Large-Scale Enterprise," *loc. cit.*

been and promise to be largely on a qualitative level. (The association between blockaded entry and large profits may be established, but hardly that between a certain "degree of blockading" of a certain percentage return on invested capital.) And simple associations are unlikely to be established—as between concentration and price rigidity—in a world where many dimensions of market structure bear on any single result. The demonstrable associations in each individual case may in fact be so complex that the scope of generalization is severely limited. Without the greatest perception and insight, research of this sort may lead only to analytical economic history for a catalogue of individual cases. This would be useful, but it would not reach the goal of generalization. It is therefore a very serious question whether price policy research can move with finality above the first level and gain a real foothold on the second.

A third approach recognizes no specific debt to the concepts and general hypotheses of price theory, and proceeds empirically to catalogue cases, perhaps in the hope of learning if regularities of any sort can be extracted. This attitude might presumably be justified by the supposition that the hypotheses of price theory are relatively useless or unduly restrictive, and that an honest and careful empirical study beginning from scratch will be at least as productive as any other. Unless the possibility and usefulness of generalization are also denied, the fruitfulness of such an approach will be tested by its demonstrated ability to arrive at any generalizations or explanations whatever. And, on the basis of current evidence, the validity of the more general hypotheses of conventional price theory does not seem so discredited as to recommend that they be abandoned indiscriminately.

So much for the general approach to interpretation and explanation of business behavior. A second choice in method concerns the appropriate scope of the individual investigation. Should we select the firm or industry as a focus for intensive investigation, or can meaningful results be extracted from a broad cross-section study of a large number of firms or industries?

If the student intends to verify or disprove the constructions of conventional price theory, the appropriate focus is first the firm—to be studied intensively and in detail—and second the industry. Really detailed analysis at this level should be required. Supposing that the defense or refutation of conventional theory or the development of a substitute is contemplated, the Oxford game of Twenty Questions, as played by Hall and Hitch and by Saxton[74] with a random sample of thirty or forty businessmen, is not a promising pursuit. Broad and superficial questionnaire

[74] C. Clive Saxton, *Economics of Price Determination* (Oxford, 1942).

investigations into pricing methods may raise many challenging questions, but they provide conclusive or reliable answers to practically none of them. Attempts to generalize from such casual findings are hardly to be taken seriously.

Is the conclusion different if the aim is to develop empirical generalizations of a qualitative sort, following the broad hypotheses of theory but not attempting to verify its reasoning in detail? Again the broad and relatively superficial studies, depending upon a limited range of information from each of a number of cases, have been disappointing. Suppose that we take 50 manufacturers in a variety of industries and market situations and ask them all, as Saxton[75] does, questions such as: "Do you find resistance to price changes from wholesaler, retailer, and/or consumer? . . . If demand increases sharply . . . would you increase selling prices (under various alternative cost conditions)?" And suppose we find that on the second question 29 answer "*no*," 6 "*yes*," and 15 "*maybe*" (depending on cost conditions). It is not apparent that by any number of such questions so administered we gain very much systematic knowledge of price policies, and it is certain that we learn little if anything at all about their origins or their consequences. Intensive investigation of fewer cases, not relying primarily on diffuse questionnaire data but probing at length into the basic environment of decision-making and into the objective consequences of these decisions, would seem to be a prime requisite for the development of meaningful or conclusive findings. In such studies, an appropriate employment of questionnaire and interview methods might assist considerably in gaining a knowledge of those managerial motivations and price-calculating processes which logically bridge the gap between observed environment and observed price and output results. The questionnaire technique *per se* has been disappointing in this field to date mainly because of the way in which it has been employed.

Related limitations have been encountered in attempts at generalization through studies involving broad correlations of published statistical data. Thorp's analysis of the (slight) relation between price rigidity and industrial concentration[76] was salutary in refuting some oversimplified hypotheses concerning this phenomenon. But its negative results suggested strongly that in a field of complex multi-variate relationships, the associations which can be tested from unrefined published data are few indeed. It is a bothersome fact that the bulk of relevant data for any firm or industry must be developed and refined by rather intensive investigation of that unit. The generally published data will not support much in

---

[75] *Ibid.*, pp. 182, 183.
[76] W. L. Thorp and W. F. Crowder, *op. cit.*

the way of meaningful correlation procedures, and there is no fast and easy shortcut to the information needed.

The most promising results we have to date—in the way of reasonably complete and defensible demonstration of possible causative associations, and of convincing appraisal of policies and their results—are found in the individual firm and industry studies, and principally in the more detailed and intensive ones. The method of the extensive case study, frequently repeated, seems the best yet discovered for this field. But each case study takes a long time, and many of them are required to permit effective generalizations. The prospect of getting general results in the near future is not promising.

IV. The Development of Norms of Price Behavior

Ideally, an integral part of research into price and production policies should be the evaluation, in terms of some sort of norms, of the price and related results to which these policies give rise. Description and interpretation of competition and its results are certainly desirable, but they find a justification beyond the simple pursuit of knowledge in the ultimate possibility of evaluating the efficiency with which the enterprise system utilizes resources. The more satisfying studies of price policy have in fact carried through from description and explanation of price policies and results to a critical evaluation of these results.[77]

Any account of developments in the price policy field should thus refer to progress in the development and application of norms of behavior. The process of normative evaluation of industrial behavior should generally involve three steps: identification of certain strategic dimensions of aggregate economic welfare which may be influenced by the price-output results of individual industries; establishment of causal interrelationships between specific price-output results and specific dimensions of the aggregate welfare; and definition of normative values for price-output results, either individually or as an interrelated complex. Thus we might identify the level of employment as strategic and a certain level as most desirable, establish a presumed relation between the ratio of profits to other income shares and the level of employment, and then attempt to define an ideal magnitude for profits in a given situation. Or we might define a hypothetically ideal allocation of resources, establish a connection between desirability of allocation and the price-marginal cost ratios or the selling cost-production cost ratios of industries, and attempt to define ideal ratios.

---

[77] It may be noted that normative standards can be meaningfully applied to any results which have been measured, even though their causes are imperfectly explained.

Similar sequences of reasoning might be developed to deal with cyclical stability, efficiency, progressiveness, and so forth.

The principal progress in the normative field during the period in question is found in the development of general economic analysis to the point where the existence of strategic relationships can at least be readily recognized and the idea of scientific material welfare norms of individual-industry price behavior introduced. Two developments deserve especial mention: first, the theory of general relative-price equilibrium and the underlying analysis of consumer choice and satisfaction have been extended to provide tentative norms of allocation in an economy of quasi-monopolistic firms (especially in work of Lerner and Kahn); and secondly, the Keynesian analysis of the determinants of employment has opened avenues for linking profit and price behavior with the level and stability of employment. With this fundamental beginning, a few writers have addressed themselves forthwith to the task of developing specific norms for price-cost relationships and similar individual-industry results in terms of their impact on employment, allocation, efficiency, progressiveness, stability, and the like.[78] The net resulting accomplishment to date is somewhat difficult to characterize. At a minimum, it has been demonstrated clearly that appropriate criteria for evaluating behavior can be drawn from an economic analysis which provides an explicit mechanism for tracing the impact of individual business actions on dimensions of the total welfare which commonly accepted value-judgments hold to be important. And it has thus been possible to envisage transcending a primary dependence either on the norms of law or on simple *ad hoc* judgments devised for the occasion. Beyond this, some very tentative norms have been advanced, at least for certain types of price result. But these norms so far have not been conclusive or even especially helpful in practice—at any rate not much more so than a good investigator's *ad hoc* evaluations.

The primary difficulties are found in the lagging development of "pure" economic analysis to supply the mechanism for developing norms. The Keynesian analysis, in its current state of development, places very uncertain limits, for example, on the desirable magnitude for profits. Interpretations of business cycles are sufficiently various and complex as to leave us without much guide on the desirable degree of price flexibility. Norms of allocation and income distribution derived basically from an analysis of purely competitive economies can be applied to an economy of

---

[78] D. H. Wallace, "Industrial Markets and Public Policy," in *Public Policy*, Harvard Graduate School of Public Administration (Cambridge, Mass., 1940), pp. 59–129; and J. M. Clark, "Toward a Concept of Workable Competition," *loc. cit.*

quasi-monopolistic markets only with adaptations which are as yet imperfectly developed. The evaluation of an economy in process of dynamic change in terms of norms drawn from the theory of stationary equilibrium is evidently unsatisfactory, as Professor Schumpeter has pointed out[79] (suggesting the rejection of much orthodoxy concerning static equilibrium norms for price behavior), but dynamic process analysis is as yet not sufficiently elaborated to give us an adequate substitute. And we have no adequate theoretical basis for developing norms of selling costs and non-price competition. This catalogue of obstacles may serve to emphasize one essential fact—the development of satisfactory norms of industry behavior is a task not of empirical investigation but of pure theory. No matter how adroit the student of price policy may be in applying received doctrine to the normative problem, he will be, until there are substantial advances in pure theory, in the position of shoveling down a mountain with a teaspoon.

This is to say that we neither have nor have in sight an adequate and dependable set of norms of satisfactory price-output results for individual industries. We are thus even farther from norms of satisfactory market structures. It is of course possible, while leaning heavily on undesirable *ceteris paribus* clauses, to make some general qualitative judgments concerning the relative desirability of certain results: obvious redundancy of plant is wasteful; huge competitive selling costs are questionable; very large profits gained without compensating advantage distort income distribution; and persistent suppression of product innovation is suspect. But in evaluating the general-equilibrium consequences of the particular-equilibrium behavior of an industry or group of industries, our theory permits us to make judgments mainly on the broadest and most obvious level, or, in effect, on a level which could be approximated fairly well with lay common sense.

In the industry studies reviewed earlier, the authors have been forced to rely for norms either on the rather inadequate theoretical models on hand or on makeshift substitutes. The element of improvisation is especially strong when they turn to the evaluation of selling costs, price inflexibility, or geographical price patterns; and blind faith seems to prevail when they turn to the problem of the allocation of resources. The allegiance to norms derived from an analysis of static equilibria is particularly apparent in a number of the studies mentioned. This is not said in disparagement of the work, as investigators have had to work with the tools at hand, and much of the improvisation has been of a high order. But

[79] J. A. Schumpeter, *Capitalism, Socialism, and Democracy* (New York, 1942), Part II.

there is a clear need for a general development of a basic theory and of norms both appropriate to a quasi-monopolistic economy in dynamic process, if evaluations of industrial price behavior are to have a certain and dependable reference.

V. The Influence of Price Policy Research on Attitudes Toward Public Policy

Chamberlinian and allied theory, and much of the price policy investigation related to it, have naturally influenced thinking on public policy toward competition and pricing. It would probably be too much to suggest that a new orthodox view of the proper ends and means of government regulation has emerged, since there is still much disagreement about both ends and means. Moreover, the bulk of "policy thought" over a considerable period has centered on fiscal and monetary matters, and has tended to neglect or regard as relatively impractical attempts to influence pricing and competition. Certain positive influences on policy thinking, however, are apparent.

The theory of monopolistic competition was salutary in focusing attention on the various specific price-output results potentially associated with various sorts of market structure. When extended by an adequate normative evaluation of such results, necessarily involving reference to general and aggregative analysis, this theory may ultimately assist us in suggesting explicit criteria as to (1) where government intervention is desirable, and (2) what the *ends* of this intervention should be. A much more explicit orientation for policy, or at any rate one more clearly linked to broad goals of welfare maximization, was thus introduced.

A second possible suggestion of the theory of monopolistic competition was that observed price-output behavior is relatively determinate by virtue of the independent action of sellers within the given market structures, and hence inevitable unless directly regulated. This is hardly a legitimate inference from the theory, but it was frequently drawn and has led to suggestions concerning the *a priori* futility of anti-trust prosecutions of collusion as a means of influencing behavior. It also led to proposals for direct price regulation as an alternative.[80] This was largely a transitional attitude, however. The arguments of Arnold and Edwards concerning the importance of collusion, and of Nourse concerning the potential variability of price policy, have shaken earlier convictions that price results

---

[80] See W. H. Nicholls, "Social Biases and Recent Theories of Competition," *Quarterly Journal of Economics,* November 1943, LVIII, pp. 1–26, for a related but much more extended discussion of this issue.

are strictly determinate regardless of collusion (or even with collusion) and that collusion and procedures directed against it are unimportant. At the present time the contributions of the new theory are mainly in facilitating the introduction of criteria of economic analysis more fully into considerations of regulatory policy, and in focusing attention on objective price-output results. Employing it, together with more general theory, we may be able to develop economic ends for policy, although in an unduly simplified form if the new theory refers primarily to static equilibrium situations. Since the new theory is primarily a description of unregulated behavior, it does not suggest much about the means for attaining these ends via regulation. Criteria of the appropriate means of policy emerge from a wide range of considerations somewhat broader than those ordinarily entertained in *a priori* economic analysis.

Empirical studies of pricing and competition, which are formally less restricted and can be more specific about the setting of observed behavior, have made contributions to the critique of past policy and the formulation of future regulative methods, at least as applied to specific industries. As represented in the more detailed industry studies, research of this sort permits a quantitative measurement of price-output results, whereas *a priori* predictions would give only general and perhaps very imprecise guides. Normative evaluation of these results is of course still necessary, and the equipment for this evaluation is quite imperfect. Given dependable evaluation, however, the detailed empirical studies may offer a reliable guide to the occasions for interference. They also offer specific insight in specific situations into the practicable alternatives to observed behavior, and into the character of possible policy means of attaining them. De Chazeau's appraisal of the basing-point problem in steel is a good example of the usefulness of this sort of research in shaping policy, and there are other instances of similarly good work. The most evident limitations are the large number of detailed analyses required to furnish a basis for comprehensive public policy, and the serious lag in the development of adequate norms for evaluating behavior. Nevertheless, recent general critical studies of regulatory policy, including a number of reinterpretations of American policy toward competition and concentration of industry, seem to reflect the beneficial influence of price policy studies.[81]

Special emphasis should be placed on two currents of policy thought

[81] Any general consideration of literature on regulation lies outside the intended scope of this paper. Illustrative of the trend mentioned, however, are Arthur R. Burns, "The Anti-Trust Laws and the Regulation of Competition," *Law and Contemporary Problems*, June 1937, IV, pp. 301–320; and Paul T. Homan, "Notes on the Anti-Trust Law Policy," *Quarterly Journal of Economics*, November 1939, LIV, pp. 73–102.

which have been engendered by empirical research into price policies: one stemming largely from the writings of E. G. Nourse, and the other from those associated with the Arnold administration of the anti-trust laws. Both tend to modify in some degree the rather negativistic policy suggestions early drawn from Chamberlin's analysis. As suggested above, the work of Nourse and Arnold has been useful on a theoretical level in reminding us that precise objective determinacy of price via independent action has not been demonstrated—that there is possibly a significant range of choice for the entrepreneur (Nourse), that market structures are not immutable, and that the price equilibria so precisely set forth in geometry may in practice not result from strictly independent action but may more often than not owe a great deal to good old-fashioned collusive activities (Arnold).

The positive policy thesis of Nourse, based on his general analysis and on historical studies of price policies and their makers, is that industrial price policies may be influenced significantly—particularly in the direction of "low" instead of "high" prices—by appropriate education and persuasion of price makers. This alteration of pricing is supposedly consistent with "maximum" profits, whatever those may be in a dynamic economy. This is not an idea to be rejected *a priori*, especially in an economy where "everyone is an economist," where secondary as well as primary effects of pricing actions are possibly taken into account, and where the "public relations" effect of pricing decisions may be viewed as significant. But the establishment in theory and in practice of a significant range of indeterminacy for the price-output decision does not guarantee the feasibility of Nourse's program.

The Arnold proposal for policy involved a very vigorous enforcement of the anti-trust laws against collusion (and this was indeed a novelty) together with amendment or repeal of laws favoring collusion or restraint of entry into various industries. The success of such a program as a means of securing generally desirable price-output results is of course not a foregone conclusion. But neither theory nor empirical study has yet demonstrated that a regime of concentrated industry leads to given and unalterable price output results regardless of collusion, nor shown the extent to which eliminable collusive activities have been strategic to the observed pattern of price behavior.

The present state of thought concerning public policy toward pricing and competition—if compared to that prevalent in 1930—serves to remind us of the subsequent accomplishments of price analysis and research in redefining problems and in increasing our general knowledge of the character of enterprise behavior. It also suggests the extremely inconclusive and fragmentary character of our solutions to these problems at present, and the nascent character of much of the needed research endeavor. A review of price policy research ten years hence may reveal the fruition of some of the early exploratory work.

5

FEDERAL BUDGETING AND FISCAL POLICY

Arthur Smithies

I. THE EVOLUTION OF FISCAL POLICY

UNDER the impact of depression and war, the theory of the relation of fiscal policy to the working of the national economy has made great strides. While important details remain to be worked out and formulations can be made more elegant, the theory is well advanced. Only twenty years ago fiscal policy—a policy under which the government uses its expenditure and revenue programs to produce desirable effects and avoid undesirable effects on the national income, production, and employment—was practically unknown. Except in times of war the policy of the United States during the nineteenth and early twentieth centuries was to hold government expenditures to a minimum, to pay the cost by taxation, and to retire the national debt as rapidly as feasible from the political point of view. This simple approach required very little in the way of a theory of government expenditures, while the theory of taxation was concerned primarily with the question of equity. Edgeworth, for instance, stated flatly that "the science of taxation comprises two subjects to which the character of pure theory may be ascribed: the laws of incidence, and the principle of equal sacrifice."[1]

One break with tradition had occurred in 1923 when the President's Conference on Unemployment recommended curtailment of public works in boom times and expansion in times of depression. While it was recognized that repercussions would spread to the production of materials for construction, there was no recognition of "multiplier effects" on consumers' demand.[2]

It was not until the Great Depression had descended on this country that the idea of a positive fiscal policy to promote recovery aroused real intellectual interest. It was only human suffering and political stress that compelled an economy-minded President to espouse it. In December 1933, Keynes was able to say, "You, Mr. President, having cast off such

[1] *Papers Relating to Political Economy* (London, 1925), Vol. II, p. 64.
[2] *Business Cycles and Unemployment*, Report and Recommendations of a Committee of the President's Conference on Unemployment (New York, 1923), p. xxviii.

fetters [of orthodox finance] are free to engage in the interests of peace and prosperity the technique which hitherto has only been allowed to serve the purposes of war and destruction."[3] Nevertheless, the theory of fiscal policy was to remain inchoate for some years and there is no sign that the President ever enjoyed his emancipation.

The theory of those early years was mainly of the "pump-priming" or "shot in the arm" variety. Government expenditures were expected to start the economy on its upward course. Recovery would permit emergency expenditures to be tapered off and higher revenue yields would produce a balanced budget. There was little thought of a systematic anti-cyclical policy, far less of the need to adapt fiscal policy to long-run economic objectives.[4]

The publication of the *General Theory* in 1936, the depression of 1938, and the work in this country under the leadership of Professor Hansen brought great advances. In 1938 the President avowed for the first time that he was striving for recovery through the effects of his fiscal policy on the national income. By the end of the decade Hansen had made a convincing case for anti-cyclical policy and had propounded his famous thesis that fiscal policy was required to offset secular stagnation.[5] Much can be said for and against the stagnation hypothesis and the argument will only be settled by events. For our present purposes, the important point is that the need for a positive long-run fiscal policy had become recognized.

The war gave a new impetus to thinking on fiscal policy—this time with the prevention of inflation as its main objective. Again Keynes was in the vanguard,[6] but was soon followed in the United States.[7] The President's budget messages urged higher taxes than had ever been imposed. Proposals for compulsory savings were advanced, but foundered on obdurate resistance within the administration. In the end, although taxes were raised higher than ever before, this country relied mainly on direct controls. This meant that we have as yet no answer to one main question of fiscal policy: is it possible to prevent inflation and achieve maximum production at the same time?

---

[3] Public letter to President Roosevelt, *New York Times*, December 31, 1933.

[4] It is difficult to document these statements. In this country most of the fiscal policy discussion took place within the government; the leading academic economists were neutral or hostile. The outstanding exposition of the pump-priming theory was Keynes' *The Means to Prosperity* (New York, 1933).

[5] See particularly his *Fiscal Policy and Business Cycles* (New York, 1941). See also Temporary National Economic Committee, *Hearings*, Part IX, for the views of many economists whom space prevents me from mentioning here.

[6] *How to Pay for the War* (London, 1940).

[7] See A. G. Hart et al., *Paying for Defense* (Philadelphia, 1941); W. L. Crum et al., *Fiscal Planning for Total War* (New York, 1942).

In the thinking about postwar fiscal policy, the emphasis naturally changed from curing depression to keeping the full employment that had been achieved under the impact of war. It was plainly evident in 1941 that full employment could be achieved through fiscal policy. Why could not the same thing be done, if necessary, in 1951? Consequently the idea of a government commitment to maintain full employment through fiscal policy became widely accepted. The British White Paper on Employment presented the interesting spectacle of the new economics wrestling with Treasury tradition. The Canadian and Australian documents were more forthright in their advocacy of fiscal policy. The Employment Act of 1946 in this country originated as a proposal to achieve full employment through fiscal policy alone.

The second important feature of postwar thinking is the prominence given to taxation. After the wartime pressure for increased taxes to prevent inflation, it was natural that tax reduction should come into prominence as a device to increase production and employment. During the 'thirties the major emphasis had been placed on higher expenditures, particularly government investment, and, while expenditures were increased to promote employment, taxes were raised to appease tradition. Today there is much more thought of higher expenditures and lower taxes as alternative routes to the desired national income. Also, during the 'thirties, it was widely held that steeply progressive taxes would not seriously retard production, since they would be paid largely out of income that would otherwise have been saved. Today there is a good deal more concern over the possible adverse effects of progressive taxation on the rate of investment and the rate of technical progress.[8]

Let me now turn to the major criticisms and qualifications that have been made to the argument for a positive fiscal policy:

(1) A government *commitment* to keep full employment through fiscal policy would leave the government at the mercy of monopolists of business or labor. If a monopolist were to raise the price of his product, the government would be called upon to spend more money to avoid the unemployment resulting from the monopolist's action. Consequently, to avoid inflation a government must be equipped with adequate monopoly controls. This point is clearly made in the *General Theory* and is, I believe, generally accepted.

(2) In a full employment situation, the government must be able to alter its course rapidly if there is a change of signals. We cannot fly too

---

[8] It is interesting to compare Professor Hansen's views in *Fiscal Policy and Business Cycles* with his more recent opinions in *Economic Policy and Full Employment* (New York, 1947).

close to the danger zone until we have better instruments and more knowledge.[9] Of course this criticism and the previous one are not arguments against a positive fiscal policy, but they are important qualifications on the extent to which it should be carried.

(3) Reliance on fiscal policy perpetuates maladjustments and may obscure the need for economic reforms. For instance, public investment in times of depression may prevent reduction of construction costs which should come down if private construction is to revive. Again, fiscal policy may be used to offset the ill effects of monopolistic action and consequently remove pressure to go to the source of the trouble.[10] Should some unemployment be permitted while the basic adjustments are made? If they are not made, will there be a day of reckoning that cannot be avoided? Objections such as these pose dilemmas which the politician rather than the economist must resolve since they require comparisons of present gain with possible future loss.

(4) Preoccupation with fiscal policy has diverted attention from other devices which should, along with fiscal policy, play an important part in a program for economic stability. In particular, it has been urged that monetary policy and debt management policy should be assigned more active roles.[11] This point of view has merit provided the scope of fiscal policy is not limited before it is known what contribution the other devices will make.

(5) It is frequently argued that fiscal policy should not be used to achieve high levels of national income if it involves the national debt increasing faster than the national income. Such a policy is held to lead to socialism, communism, or fascism. Even if this were true, the possible alternatives, including mass unemployment, might prove to be shorter and faster routes to damnation. The argument usually stops before the implications of eschewing fiscal policy are explored.

(6) Fiscal policy is objected to on the grounds that any departure from the rigid rule of annually balanced budgets would open the floodgates of government extravagance and should therefore be resisted. The National Association of Manufacturers, for instance, is uncompromisingly of this point of view.[12] A most effective answer to this argument has been presented by the Research Committee of the Committee for Economic De-

---

[9] Professor Albert Hart and other members of the C.E.D. research staff have done great service in emphasizing this point. See C.E.D. Research Staff, *Jobs and Markets* (New York, 1946).

[10] See the essays by J. M. Clark and Howard S. Ellis in *Financing American Prosperity*, Paul T. Homan and Fritz Machlup, eds. (New York, 1945).

[11] See C.E.D. Research Staff, *op. cit.*

[12] See *The American Individual Enterprise System*, The Economic Principles Commission of the N.A.M. (New York, 1946).

velopment.[13] It is pointed out that if the budget is to be balanced in depression, tax rates must be raised. In boom times, on the other hand, revenue is abundant, and if the budget is merely to be balanced there is ample room for extravagance. Thus, it is argued, both taxes and expenditures are likely to be higher under the balanced budget rule than if fiscal policy follows the rule of surpluses in boom times and deficits in depression. The C.E.D. is also rightly concerned with the question of extravagance, but attempts to combat it with reason rather than prejudice. Whether or not one agrees with the political philosophy of the N.A.M. or the C.E.D., one can readily agree that fiscal freedom cannot be permitted to undermine responsible government. One of the major purposes of this paper is to suggest ways in which freedom and responsibility can be reconciled.

Despite all qualifications and criticisms it is fair to say that, among academic and government economists, there is wide agreement that fiscal policy must form part of any program for economic stability.[14] There is also wide agreement that fiscal policy cannot be relied on exclusively. In particular, almost all economists would agree that it is essential to control or eliminate monopolistic practices.[15]

It is becoming more generally recognized that fiscal policy offers the best prospect of a conservative solution to the economic problem. Fiscal policy aims primarily at controlling aggregate demand and leaves to private enterprise its traditional field—the allocation of resources among alternative uses. It is therefore to be hoped that, through fiscal policy, economic objectives can be reached with less control by the State over the lives of its citizens than would be required by programs that called for the direct control of production and prices. The following quotation shows that at least one enlightened conservative is prepared to go somewhat further than I would. ". . . in view of its responsibility to maintain employment, the government must spend enough to close any gap between private (and business) spending and the total spending necessary to maintain full employment . . . However much the advocate of a liberal economy may hope for basic reforms which will eventually reduce the need for public spending, he cannot intelligently counsel economy and caution . . . Since reforms necessarily proceed slowly, private and

---

[13] *Taxes and the Budget: A Program for Prosperity in a Free Economy* (New York, 1947).

[14] See, for instance, *A Program for Sustaining Employment* (Washington, 1947), by the Committee on Economic Policy of the United States Chamber of Commerce.

[15] I refer the reader again to *Financing American Prosperity*. My statements here are confirmed by the measure of agreement that exists among Professors Clark, Ellis, Hansen, Slichter, and Williams.

government outlays must at any time add up to full use of resources. Naturally this offers no defense of purposeless or wasteful use of public funds."[16]

II. Fiscal Policy and Budgetary Principles

My own main criticism of the fiscal policy as worked out so far is that insufficient attention has been paid to its political and administrative aspects. For instance, the "Functional Finance"[17] approach gives one the impression that the sole objective of the fiscal operations of the government is to work miracles on the national income. Discussions of pyramid building and of digging up bottles of bank notes provide graphic illustrations of the economic theory, but arouse reasonable doubts in the mind of the practical statesman.

Unless the political issues can be satisfactorily resolved, fiscal policies cannot hope to succeed. I suspect that doubts on this question have furnished the basis for the Marxian theory of imperialism. In the opinion of neo-Marxians, it is politically feasible for a capitalistic country to embark on a course of foreign imperialism, but impracticable for it to expand investment within its own political boundaries. Tugan-Baronowski, in fact, agrees that pyramid building would do the trick, but he produces this example in order to ridicule the idea that adequate domestic policies will be undertaken, not to provide solace for the anti-Marxians.

Fiscal policy cannot be worked out on the assumption that government expenditures or taxes can be justified solely by their effects on the national income. If such a view became generally accepted, irresponsibility in government would be general. As Professor Schumpeter pointed out, Louis XV and Madame de Pompadour were extraordinarily efficient spenders; yet their spending did not bring prosperity to France. To make fiscal policy work, economists must contaminate themselves with political theory and public administration. That is where budgeting comes in.

The budgetary process in the United States is essentially one of program evaluation. As the functions of the government have grown more complicated, it has become essential to devise ways in which the relative merits of competing programs can be assessed, and in which the merits of the government's program as a whole can be compared with its cost. The result has been a budgetary process that is necessarily long and complicated, but has been increasingly successful in improving the efficiency of

---

[16] Howard S. Ellis, *op. cit.*, p. 137.
[17] See the celebrated article by Professor A. P. Lerner in *Social Research*, February 1943, X, pp. 38–51.

the government and in bringing essential issues before the President and the Congress for decision.

The most notable step forward was the Budget and Accounting Act of 1921. Before that act estimates were submitted by the individual departments to the Congress with no review by the President and with no regard to the requirements of the budget as a whole. Moreover, the requests of each department were sent to one of the eight separate and independent appropriations committees of the Congress, so that in the legislative branch of the government also there was no unified examination of the budget.

The Act of 1921 requires the President to prepare a complete budget of estimated revenues and expenditures for the government as a whole; and thus the budget goes to the Congress as the recommended program of the President. Soon afterwards the Congress overhauled its own machinery for receiving the budget. The eight independent committees were replaced by one appropriations committee in each House. These two committees are now responsible for the entire budget in Congress.

In 1946 a further important step was taken to improve congressional consideration of the budget as a whole. The Legislative Reorganization Act required that the appropriations and revenue committees of both Houses should meet jointly at the beginning of the session to prepare a "legislative budget" stating the objectives which the appropriations committees should strive to attain for the budget as a whole. If this procedure proves workable, there will be machinery not only for examining the whole expenditure side of the budget but also for considering expenditure policy in relation to revenue policy. The experience with the legislative budget in its first year has not been reassuring. Before the Joint Committee could agree on general targets the appropriations committees and the revenue committees had completed their work. The legislative budget never came out of conference. It is greatly to be hoped that the legislative budget procedure can be made to work, since, without it, Congress has no direct machinery for considering revenue and expenditure policies together.

The Budget and Accounting Act created the Budget Bureau and made it directly responsible to the President. On behalf of the President the Bureau examines the requests of the agencies and translates into specific terms the President's budget policy. The Bureau is organized to assess not only the intrinsic merits of particular programs but, more importantly, to appraise their relative merits and to achieve a proper balance within the limits of the budget as a whole.

In some quarters the Bureau has acquired an unenviable reputation of always saying "no." Occasionally it does say "yes." During the war, for instance, there could be no question of hindering war production with financial limitations. In general, however, it is the proper function of the Bureau of the Budget to cut departmental requests. The departments are principally concerned with their own programs and have a natural tendency to extend and improve the services they render to the public. The Bureau on behalf of the President has to take into account the political and economic limits on the budget as a whole. It must compare expenditures with the receipts that can be expected. The departments would probably not be doing their duty if they did not request more than the President allowed, and the Bureau would not be doing its duty if it did not in general reduce the requests of the departments.

The appropriations committees perform in the legislature somewhat the same functions as the Bureau of the Budget performs in the executive branch. It is their function to impose limits on the tendencies of subject-matter committees and of outside pressure groups to expand particular programs. It is also natural that the appropriations committees should have a somewhat more economical outlook on the budget than the President. After all, the Congress rather than the President has to finance the budget. It would be an indication that forces in the legislature were not properly balanced if the appropriations committees did not have a reputation for economy.

This brief description of the budgetary process indicates clearly that the requirements of good budgeting are by no means identical with the requirements for a positive fiscal policy. Of course the steps that have been taken to unify the budget are also indispensable for a coherent fiscal policy. But the process of program evaluation that is essential for good budgeting makes a flexible fiscal policy more difficult to achieve. It takes about six months to prepare the budget in the executive branch and about six months more for the Congress to consider it. Thus, budget plans must be begun about a year in advance of the time when they are to take effect. With our present limited foresight, fiscal policy may have to be adapted to changing economic conditions much more rapidly. How to do justice to both the program point of view and the fiscal policy point of view is one of the major problems yet to be faced.

I may have given the impression that the Budget Bureau is interested only in economy. Anyone who reads the President's budget messages will discover that in formulating the budget he is by no means forgetful of the requirements of fiscal policy. Yet it remains true that the main preoccupation of the Bureau is careful assessment and efficient execution of individual programs.

The Employment Act of 1946 should bring the fiscal policy point of view more to the foreground in the deliberations in both the legislative and executive branches of the government. Under this act, the President is required to report to the Congress on all policies of government that will contribute to the achievement of maximum production, employment, and purchasing power. The Congress is required to consider his report in a special joint committee. Fiscal policy certainly cannot escape consideration if the purposes of the act are to be achieved. The Council of Economic Advisers and the Bureau of the Budget must jointly work out for the President recommendations that will satisfy budgetary needs and also meet the requirements of fiscal policy. In the Congress, the fiscal views of the Joint Committee on the Economic Report must be fully taken into account in the recommendations of the appropriations committees and the revenue committees.

We now have the legislative and executive machinery required for budgetary and fiscal policy purposes. But machinery alone cannot do the job. There must be a much fuller understanding throughout the government of the national objectives. I have indicated that the proponents of fiscal policy have not fully appreciated the need for the rather tedious budget process, and that the budget process itself has been evolved with little regard for the need for a positive fiscal policy. Fiscal policy can be neither responsible nor acceptable without good budgeting. As was seen in the depths of the last depression, budgetary procedures can break down in the face of the very depressions that a proper fiscal policy seeks to avoid.

III. The Objectives of Policy

The function of the budget process[18] is to make a consistent whole of the entire policy of the government and to achieve balance among the various objectives of policy. Fiscal policy, on the other hand, is more directly related to the attainment of economic goals.

The main objectives of policy, in my opinion, are national security, social security, economic and social progress, and political stability. That some of these compete with each other, while others complement each other, is a proposition that we can easily illustrate.

---

[18] I say advisedly "budget process" and not Budget Bureau. As indicated above, the budget process continues until the budget is enacted by the Congress. In the executive branch, it is the responsibility of the President himself to carry out the budget process—a responsibility that he cannot delegate. The Bureau's function is to render the President assistance in the process and to see to it that the major policy issues are brought to him for decision.

It is sometimes thought that national security programs have a clear right-of-way in the budget. Nothing could be more erroneous. Any attempt to achieve complete security—if the term has any meaning—would require a budget very much larger than the present one. We are prepared to take national security risks for the sake of the other objectives of policy.

During the 'thirties, the preponderant view was that economic progress and social security went hand in hand, that every step toward greater social security also meant a more rapid rate of economic progress. An intransigent minority held that every measure to remove economic hazards retarded progress. Now it is more widely recognized, on the one hand, that progress and security may clash and, on the other, that greater security through public means may avoid private attempts to obtain security through restrictive practices.

Political stability, by which I mean no abrupt change in our political institutions or "the American way of life," is undoubtedly one of the dominant policy objectives of this country. Social and economic change is necessary for political stability, but too much change can destroy it. Both the reactionary and the radical are prepared to endanger political stability, the one by insistence on too little change, the other by insistence on too much. All the programs of government are subordinated to some extent to the objective of political stability. We are prepared to take risks with national security for the sake of political stability—a thoroughly rational course when one of the main objectives of national defense is to protect our political institutions.

These illustrations suffice to demonstrate the political character of the budgetary process. Various objectives of policy can be balanced and combined only through the interplay of political forces. In this paper, I am concerned mainly with the narrower field of economic objectives. Their attainment, however, must be considered as part of the budgetary process as a whole. And, as we shall see, the choice among economic objectives involves political decisions of the same character as the balancing of the economic with the non-economic.

The main economic goals to which fiscal policy can be directed are as follows:

(1) In line with the tradition of economics, the first goal that should be mentioned is that of maximum economic well-being. Despite the pitfalls in the concept of economic welfare, I fail to see how we can get along without the idea. Nothing that I shall say will depend on the thesis that welfare can be measured in any absolute sense. My only assumption will be that we can generally decide whether it has increased

or decreased. Of course, this is too general for many practical purposes, but we shall find it a useful starting point for our analysis.[19]

(2) A second goal, which has achieved wide national and international popularity, is "full employment," which means that all those willing and able to work should have an opportunity to work. It is still a matter of debate among its proponents whether "full employment" means that job vacancies should be more numerous or fewer than the number of the unemployed—in other words, whether labor should sell its services in a buyers' or a sellers' market. And if the latter, how much unemployment should be counted on as a regular thing from the point of view of avoiding inflation and keeping competition in the labor market?

As a general economic objective full employment is obviously incomplete. No mention is made of the rate of real wages and no question is raised about the rate of progress of real incomes in the future. Little is said of the distribution of incomes or of standards of economic welfare. The idea is that if full employment is won, all other blessings will automatically follow.

This approach can be attributed largely to the genius of Keynes for putting first things first. When the world was in a state of hopeless depression, it could easily be argued that if only employment could be increased by any means a democratic state could be persuaded to adopt, everything would be better. Total real wages, profits, saving and capital formation would all increase. The outlook for the future as well as the present would be improved. And who can contend that if the world had given its undivided attention to the attainment of full employment in the 'thirties, the outcome might not have been better than it was? Nevertheless, when we are trying to work out an approach to economic stability rather than to cure a deep depression, something more complex is required.

(3) A third approach would be to substitute real income for employment as a goal and to pay due regard to the effects of policy on the rate of accumulation of capital and the progress of technical knowledge. Tax policies in particular would be designed in part with a view to achieving an optimum, which is not necessarily a maximum, rate of capital accumulation. The effect of tax policies on the productivity of labor would be considered. Government expenditures would be distributed between de-

---

[19] I am fortified in this approach by finding that Professor Pigou uses it unhesitatingly; see his *A Study of Public Finance* (London, 1947). My own views, especially on long-term policy, have come mainly from practical experience with budgeting. I am gratified to find support for them in Pigou's book, which is strictly academic in origin. However, his discussion is limited in that he discusses the attainment of maximum satisfaction on the assumption that the operations of public finance do not affect the national income.

velopment and welfare programs by a comparison of the present and future real income needs of the country. It may turn out that there is some conflict between a real income objective and a full employment objective. A policy that maximizes employment of labor may not maximize real income and may not be consistent with the optimum rate of economic development.

(4) It may be desired to stress not total production and employment, but the contribution made to the total by private enterprise. Privately produced goods and services are preferred to those produced by the government, not because of any intrinsic superiority, but because there is political sentiment for leaving as much as possible of total production in private hands. To the extent that this objective is given weight, measures such as tax reduction and loans or guarantees to private enterprise would, on that account, be preferred to public welfare programs.

(5) In contrast to (4), we have what I may call the planned welfare approach. The best example of this is Beveridge's *Full Employment in a Free Society*. He urges that the nation must exterminate the giant evils of want, disease, ignorance, and squalor. The need for a frontal attack on these evils is so great that the government must take whatever action is necessary, regardless of private enterprise or vested interests. If the government takes its social obligations seriously, he argues, there will be no need to search for policies to increase production and employment. Beveridge believes that resources are so scarce that, to carry out these urgent social plans, government action must be extended to avoid waste. For instance, he believes that total investment should be subject to national planning. Beveridge is writing for postwar Britain. In the United States we can afford to indulge our whims more freely.

(6) A further economic goal is greater equality of incomes—as an end in itself rather than as a means to increase total production or to raise living standards at the lower end of the scale. We can agree that the greater equality of incomes that comes from the elimination of restrictive practices will also increase production and employment. Also greater equality will reduce saving and increase effective consumer demand. But it is quite possible that egalitarian policies may reduce both business and labor incentives and so retard economic development. In Australia, for instance, the margins for skilled labor over common labor allowed by the compulsory arbitration system are very much narrower than the margins in this country. I suspect that this emphasis on equality, rather than on the incentives to become skilled, may have something to do with the lower productivity and its lower rate of increase in Australia as compared with the United States. Other examples come readily to mind. A country

may have to choose between greater equality and greater productivity.

(7) The last economic objective I shall mention is stability of income and employment. It is easy to agree that if the total income over a period is given, economic well-being is greater if income is stable than if it fluctuates. Periods of unemployment are not compensated by periods of overemployment. But to state the case that way begs the question. The real issue is: Will real income increase more rapidly if it fluctuates than if it does not? If so, is a more rapid rate of increase worth the price of alternate booms and depressions?

In economic thinking about postwar policy, great stress has been put on the advantages of stability. With the benefit of hindsight, I am now inclined to think these advantages may have been overstressed. After making all allowances, countries that relaxed controls and allowed some inflation to occur seem to have increased production relatively more than those which did not. But the score can only be tallied after the "readjustment period," if any, has been undergone by the countries that experienced some inflation. Meanwhile, I do not think we should be too dogmatic in asserting the pre-eminent virtues of stability.

I do not propose to try here to formulate the economic objectives of the United States, although I suspect they partake of each of the goals I have mentioned. For present purposes, I need only assume that there is some objective of national policy. In the Employment Act of 1946 the Congress, by a large majority of both parties, undertook to define our economic objectives. The act states:

Sec. 2. The Congress hereby declares that it is the continuing policy and responsibility of the Federal Government to use all practicable means consistent with its needs and obligations and other essential considerations of national policy, with the assistance and cooperation of industry, agriculture, labor, and State and local governments, to coordinate and utilize all its plans, functions, and resources for the purpose of creating and maintaining, in a manner calculated to foster and promote free competitive enterprise and the general welfare, conditions under which there will be afforded useful employment opportunities, including self-employment, for those able, willing, and seeking to work, and to promote maximum employment, production, and purchasing power.

The passage of the Employment Act may turn out to be one of the most important events in the legislative history of the country. Or, at the worst, it may prove to be nothing but an empty gesture. This act can be significant only if all branches of the government become thoroughly indoctrinated with it, and if Presidents and Congressmen can be overthrown because they have failed to carry out its intent.

Of course the declaration of policy must be discussed and interpreted.

What precisely does "maximum employment, production, and purchasing power" mean? I believe it is one of the main functions of the Economic Report to clarify and explain the meaning of this act in the executive branch. It is one of the main functions of the Joint Committee to expose the objectives of the act to political debate and to convince the committees on special subjects that every program must be consistent with and, if possible, further the national policy objective. One of the great merits of the act is that it gives the President and the Congress an incentive to think on a plane of abstraction to which they have hitherto been unaccustomed. One can only hope that they will respond to this opportunity.

IV. The Mechanics of Fiscal Policy

To reach any of the economic objectives we have described, it is necessary that a certain level of national income be attained. In this section we shall discuss the relation of government expenditure and taxation to national income. We shall also see that a mere study of the mechanics of fiscal policy leaves undecided the question of what policy should in fact be pursued.

Government expenditures may consist either of payments for goods and services or of "transfer payments," such as veterans' benefits, unemployment compensation, or old-age pensions.

To simplify the argument, I shall assume that the government determines the total amount of tax to be collected, rather than the tax rates to be applied.

Let us assume to begin with that the process of taxation and government expenditure does not redistribute income either among profits, wages and other factor incomes, or among personal incomes of various sizes.

We shall also assume that the willingness of private enterprises and individuals to undertake expenditures depends on their incomes after taxes and also on circumstances independent of the government's policy. Then:

(1) An increase in government expenditure on goods and services with taxes unchanged will increase the national income by the value of the goods and services purchased by the government *plus* the induced effects on private consumption and investment, which I shall call the "repercussion effects."

(2) An increase in transfer payments with taxes unchanged will increase the national income by the repercussion effects only.

(3) A reduction in taxes with unchanged expenditures will produce the same result as an increase in transfer payments.

(4) It follows that an increase in government expenditures or an equal reduction of taxes will have the same effect on private income after taxes and on private expenditures.

(5) Equal increases of taxation and transfer payments will cancel each other out.

(6) Equal increases of government expenditure on goods and services and of taxes will increase the national income by the value of the goods and services. The repercussion effects will cancel each other out. Consequently, private income after taxes and private expenditures will remain unchanged.[20]

---

[20] These propositions can be proved algebraically as follows:

Let E = private expenditures on investment and consumption
G = government expenditures on goods and services
R = government transfer payments
T = Taxes
Y = national income

It is reasonable to suppose that E depends partly on national income after deducting taxes and adding transfer payments, and partly on other factors, denoted by B, which are independent of present national income. Assume therefore:

(1) $E = a (Y - T + R) + B$

We have also:

(2) $Y = E + G$

Thus substituting for E in (2)

(3) $Y (1 - a) = B + G - a (T - R)$

Then

(4) $\Delta Y = \Delta G + \dfrac{a \, \Delta G}{1 - a}$ (proposition 1)
          (T and R constant)

(5) $\Delta Y = \dfrac{a \, \Delta R}{1 - a}$ (proposition 2)
          (G and T constant)

(6) $\Delta Y = \dfrac{-a \, \Delta T}{1 - a}$ (proposition 3)
          (G and R constant)

The term on the right of each of these expressions denotes the "repercussion effects." The increase in private income is $\Delta Y - \Delta G$. Thus if $\Delta G = \Delta R = - \Delta T$, in (4), (5), and (6) respectively, the increases in private income and, from (1), the increases in private expenditure are equal (proposition 4).

If T and R both increase and $\Delta T = \Delta R$, it is clear from (3) that Y is unchanged (proposition 5).

If G and T both increase and $\Delta G = \Delta T$, we have from (3)

$\Delta Y = \Delta G$ (proposition 6)

If the objective of fiscal policy is to achieve a given income goal, Y_A, we have from (3),

(7) $G - a (T - R) = Y_A (1 - a) - B$

It is obvious that an indefinite number of combinations of G, T, and R can be selected to give the required result.

How far must these conclusions be modified when we consider the effects of fiscal policy on income distribution? There can be little question that the federal budget redistributes income in the direction of equality. The tax system as a whole is progressive.[21] But government expenditures are probably more equally distributed than all incomes. Government procurement and construction programs may be assumed to be distributed among income classes in much the same way as the incomes of the whole employed population. On the other hand veterans' benefit payments, unemployment compensation, old-age pensions, and welfare expenditures in general go mainly to the lower end of the income scale.

During the past twenty-five years there have been great changes in the size and composition of the federal budget, and its redistributive effects have been considerable. Yet for all this, the relation of consumers' expenditure to disposable income seems to have been affected little, if at all. The statisticians, despite their disagreements on the subject, all seem prepared to relate aggregate consumption to aggregate income without taking into account changes in income distribution. While total saving varies greatly between incomes of various sizes, the saving out of increments of income varies very much less—and that is the relevant factor here.

So far as repercussions on consumption expenditure are concerned, therefore, there seems to be little to choose between *general* increase in expenditure and *general* reductions in taxes. Of course, it is easy to think of particular cases, such as a tax on the very rich to pay bounties to the very poor, where the effect is considerable; but so far there has not been enough political latitude for such devices to make them practically important.

The redistributive effects of the budget may well have much more important consequences on private investment. Although it is difficult to verify statistically, profits after taxes have an important independent effect, I believe, on the rate of private investment. A general increase in taxation accompanied by a corresponding general increase in government expenditures, is likely to reduce profits and to slow down the rate of private investment. In other words, a tax reduction may be assumed to have more favorable repercussions on private investment than an equal increase in government expenditures.

We assumed that private expenditures do not depend directly on government expenditures. This may not be true. Free medical services would reduce private medical expenditures and this might increase saving rather than other kinds of consumers' expenditure. Old-age insurance

[21] See Helen Tarasov, *Who Does Pay the Taxes?* (New York, 1942).

may tend to reduce saving. But the same statistical argument we used above indicates that these effects have not been important so far.

Government investment expenditures may encourage or deter private investment. Regional development, for instance, opens up new fields for private enterprise, and the expansion of the automobile industry would not have been possible without the national highway program. On the other hand, the government can compete directly with private investment and so reduce its rate.

Government expenditure programs may encourage private investment by providing a relatively assured market for the products of private enterprise. I feel sure the aircraft industry considers the government a less volatile customer than the commercial air lines.

All these factors must be taken into account when we attempt to assess the repercussions of an increase in government expenditures.[22]

We have discussed so far the effect of government expenditures and taxes on money national income and expenditures, while the prime objective of fiscal policy is to achieve satisfactory rates of production and employment. By now all economists will agree that when resources are unemployed an increase in money national income will also increase real income. But there is also general agreement that the smaller the increase in money income required to evoke the desired increase in real income, the better.

Expenditure and tax reduction policies may have different price effects. Expenditure programs can be and usually must be selective in their impact on industries or regions. The effects of tax reduction are more evenly spread over the economy. To restore production to a depressed industry or a depressed region through tax reduction may require so much tax reduction as to bring price inflation to the rest of the economy. On the other hand, to increase expenditures for goods and services may not be the most efficient way to cure a general slump. Production and prices might go up in some areas while others would remain depressed.

Little has been said in this country of the possible effects of the budget on the productivity of labor. For a given real income, the higher government expenditures and taxes, the lower will be the probable rate of real wages—assuming that wage-earners do not count the services of government as part of their real wages. It is possible that high taxes lower willingness to work. This may not be important in the United States, but it is possible that heavy taxation in other countries has lowered the productivity of labor.

I have tried to outline, in a very cursory way, the mechanics of fiscal

---

[22] See, for instance, Hansen, *Fiscal Policy and Business Cycles*, Ch. XII.

policy. Despite the foregoing qualifications, the propositions we have stated above furnish a guide to the directions policy might take. I want to emphasize that, from the point of view of their influence on national income, taxation and expenditure adjustment must be regarded as alternatives. The choice of alternatives depends on what else the government wants to do besides achieve the desired income goal.

It follows from what we have said that, within wide limits, a given national income can be reached in an indefinite number of ways. A study of fiscal mechanics alone cannot tell us what fiscal policy should be followed. The main purpose of this essay is to insist that the right fiscal policy cannot be determined until we also have a basis for deciding the relative merits of alternative programs.

To simplify the discussion and to isolate the area of controversy, let us distinguish between long-run fiscal policy and short-run, or compensatory, policy. From the long-run point of view, there can be little doubt that the government's taxing and spending operations must be planned with full regard for their economic impact. To what extent and in what manner short-run economic fluctuations should be compensated is more debatable.

The distinction between long and short run corresponds to the distinction that is made in modern business-cycle analysis between the equilibrium value of national income (or any other central variable) and its actual value.

The equilibrium value of income at any time depends on the growth of population, of technical knowledge, and of the stock of capital, and on the long-run propensities to invest and consume. It also depends on the programs and policies of the government. Public expenditure and taxation policies may hasten or hinder the course of economic development, and will affect the normal rate of employment of economic resources.

At any time the actual level of national income may and probably will diverge from its equilibrium value. The economy will be thrown out of equilibrium by external shocks such as war, famine, or revolutionary changes in industry; and these shocks will result in alternate periods of prosperity and depression. The destruction and shortages of a war normally give rise to a postwar boom followed by a postwar depression. Here again the government's fiscal policy can exacerbate or offset fluctuations in private business. The normal tendency is for government to embark on new projects when income is high and revenue plentiful. Economic stability requires that this tendency be reversed.

A long-run fiscal policy designed to keep the equilibrium national income at a satisfactorily high level would change little from year to year. The normal trends that should prevail in major expenditure programs, such as public works and social welfare, and in taxation, would be known. As we shall see later, such a policy would require no radical departure from established tradition and would permit full justice to be done to the requirements of good budgeting.

Legitimate controversy begins when compensatory action is considered. As we have already seen, some of the main objections to fiscal policy are related to the questions of whether the government should guarantee a certain level of employment and whether fiscal policy should cover up maladjustments. These objections raise doubts as to how far compensatory action should be taken. They are irrelevant to the question of long-run policy.

V. Long-Run Fiscal Policy

We have seen that an indefinite number of fiscal policies could be consistent with a given national income, and if national income were the only objective our problem would be indeterminate. As it is, it is necessary to find the fiscal policy that will help most effectively attain all or most of the country's objectives. That policy can only be found through the budget process of program evaluation.

I can describe this process best by starting with a highly simplified situation. Suppose the sole function of government is to provide consumers' goods and services to the public and the sole purpose of taxation is to contract private spending in order to make way for public spending. For present purposes, transfer payments can be considered as negative taxes. I assume further that the objective of government is to adopt policies that will maximize well-being for the community as a whole and at the same time achieve the desired level of national income.

Suppose the country is in a state in which its fiscal policy is preventing it from attaining its national income goal and that new measures are being considered. Then, from what we have said in Part IV, it follows that a given increase in national income can be achieved either by increasing expenditure or by reducing taxation. If expenditures are increased the country gets more "government goods." If taxes are reduced, it gets more "private goods."

If the social utility of additional government goods is greater than that of additional private goods, the appropriate policy will be to increase expenditures. Otherwise, taxes should be reduced. This process of comparing utilities should be carried on until the income goal is reached.

If our starting point had been one of potential inflation, the alternatives would be to reduce expenditures, to increase taxation, or to make some combination of the two. The utility comparison again furnishes the guide.

Suppose the national income is at the prescribed level: the government's program may still be out of gear on utility grounds. Expenditure programs already under way may have a low utility while taxation is "oppressive," that is, its disutility is high. In that event expenditures and taxes should both be reduced until the marginal utility of expenditure is equal to the marginal disutility of taxation and the income objective is reached with a lower budget.

On the other hand, the right income might be attained, but the marginal utility of the last increment of the prospective expenditure program might be greater than the marginal disutility of taxation. Then more expenditures and more taxes would be called for. Or the government could allow some price inflation to take place. In that event the consequences of the inflation should be judged in the same way as an increase in taxation. If the government is to obtain resources for its program, a levy must be made on someone.[23]

To complete the picture, both the expenditure and the taxation side of the budget should conform to the utility rule. As ultimate objectives, the marginal utility of all expenditure programs should be equal and the marginal disutility of taxation should be the same for every taxed group.

This approach lets the chips fall where they may so far as budget balance and the national debt are concerned. If the need for a large government program were urgent—if, for instance, the whole nation had to go underground to avoid the atomic bomb—a budget surplus would probably be required if inflation were to be avoided by fiscal policy alone.[24] If, on the other hand, the need for government goods were low and there were a strong preference for private goods, it might be necessary to budget for deficits to attain the desired level of income. If the national debt did not increase any faster than the national income, a deficit policy could be continued indefinitely without ill effects. If it did increase faster,

---

[23] Let us assume the existence of a welfare function (cf. P. A. Samuelson, *Foundations of Economics*), $W = W (Y, G, aT)$, which relates welfare to the national income, government expenditure on goods and services, and the goods and services aT, of which the private economy is deprived through taxation. This function increases with Y and G and decreases with T. The objective of the economy is then to maximize welfare subject to equation (7) above. For this it is necessary that $\dfrac{\partial W}{\partial G} = -\dfrac{\partial W}{\partial T}$.

[24] I am not suggesting that such a policy should be pursued. As in the war, inflation would and probably should be controlled in part through direct controls.

interest payments would occupy an increasing share of the expenditure side of the budget, or taxes would have to be raised to avoid inflation. It is interesting to note that, in a well-ordered economy, deficit financing should be associated with a limited view of the functions of government, while to finance a more "radical" program, surpluses may be required.

If it is required that budget balance or some other budgetary condition should be the rule, either the income goal or the utility condition must be abandoned. If our analysis required a deficit to reach the income goal, the achievement of the same goal with a balanced budget would require expenditures of low social utility and taxes of high disutility.

We have so far tacitly assumed that the money and the real income goals are fixed. It should not be overlooked that with continuing technological progress the goal will increase from year to year. If prices are to be kept stable the money income goal and the real income goal will increase by the same proportion. With an increase in real income, the social disutility of a given amount of taxation will decrease. Thus, there would be room to consider the adoption of expenditure programs of lower priority. Depending on the usefulness of such programs, tax rates should be held the same or reduced.

The utility of expenditures depends on political and social attitudes toward the function of government and the services it should perform. The long-run trend in this country appears to be in the direction of increasing the functions of government. This change in attitudes may preclude any downward tendency in the appropriate tax rates.

The long-run policy would determine tax yields and expenditures at high levels of employment and income when no compensating action is required to offset deflationary or inflationary influences in the private sector of the economy.

This policy would be subject only to gradual change. It might require a surplus or a deficit or balance in the budget every year. There is nothing but tradition that would make such a formula more difficult to apply than one that required budget balance every year.

It will be seen that my solution for long-run policy corresponds formally with the "stabilizing budget" advocated by Mr. Beardsley Ruml and the C.E.D. But there is an important difference in substance. The C.E.D. maintains that the cash budget of the Federal Government should yield a surplus of $3 billion at high levels of income. It reaches this conclusion largely by deciding in advance the amount of debt reduction that should be undertaken. Expenditures and taxation must be consistent with that objective. In my scheme, expenditures and taxes are considered on their merits, and the behavior of the national debt is the resultant. Both schemes are equally feasible from the point of view of practical operation, but I feel that mine puts first things first.[25]

We shall next try to bring the argument closer to reality by considering some of the major questions connected with the receipts and expenditure sides of the budget. Of course, in an article of this length, it is possible only to offer some discursive remarks on some of the major questions of public finance.

VI. Long–Run Policy: Receipts

(1) Taxation. The principle of equal marginal disutility that we have used above means that the tax system is designed to raise given amounts of revenue with the least possible sacrifice to the taxpayer. If the notion of maximum satisfaction or well-being has any validity, the principle of least sacrifice has much more validity than the principle of equal sacrifice. I suspect, however, that our present tax system corresponds more closely to the latter principle.

The principle of least sacrifice, if fully applied, would presumably mean that all incomes of taxpayers would eventually be reduced to equality, and that the marginal utility of the income left to each taxpayer would be lower than that of any non-taxpayer. If the principle of maximum well-being were applied fully to the budget as a whole, it would be necessary to go further. Transfer payments would be made to non-taxpayers until the marginal utilities of all incomes were equal. Transfer payments very much of this type do occur in the family endowment schemes of Canada and Australia, but have won little support in the United States. In this country, transfer payments are usually made either to benefit special groups—e.g., veterans or unemployed—who have special claims, or to further specific social objectives—e.g., better nutrition.

There are strong arguments why least sacrifice cannot be completely accepted even as an ultimate objective. For example:

(a) There is a solid basis for the view that paying taxes makes for political responsibility, and consequently some taxes should be paid by the bulk of income recipients.

(b) Experience with wartime tax systems has shown that high taxes

[25] It is beyond the scope of this paper to consider the question of autonomous wage pressure on the price level, but I should indicate my opinion of the relation of this kind of pressure to fiscal policy. The possibilities of autonomous wage increases have a bearing on how much employment should be regarded as "full" and therefore on fiscal policy. But once a wage increase has occurred, fiscal policy should be adapted to the situation; it should not be used in an attempt to lower wages. Such an attempt could only lead to unemployment and loss of production. The main answer to the wage question must be found in the labor market itself.

can lead to social waste and extravagance. It is doubtful whether tax enforcement could ever eradicate dubious expense items when the "government pays 90 percent," although this objection might apply less forcefully to the individual than to the corporation income tax.

(c) The degree of income equality after taxes that least sacrifice implies might prove inconsistent with the desired rate of capital accumulation and economic progress. The principle of least sacrifice should be applied to both the present and the future.

In general, tax systems based on relative degrees of sacrifice do not pay enough attention to the effect of taxation on incentives and productivity. Of course, manifest inequities can undoubtedly impair productivity, but there is no reason to believe that the tax system that achieves the greatest equity will also provide the most effective stimulus to productive effort. Unfortunately we have no empirical evidence that is in any way conclusive of the effects of taxation on incentives, and the prospect of getting any is not bright. I doubt whether time-series analysis will settle the question; and the method of direct inquiry obviously can only produce biased results. Tax policy will probably continue to be an arena for political as much as economic argument.

We can conclude, however, that the principles of least and equal sacrifice provide the limits to an acceptable tax system. For the reasons indicated, it is not desirable to go as far in the direction of progressiveness as least sacrifice would require. On the other hand, it would probably be politically impossible to adopt a tax system that imposed less sacrifice on high incomes than on low incomes even though economic arguments were found for it.

We have seen that all forms of taxation involve a transfer of private savings to the government. Are there any grounds for modifying our conclusions on the argument that taxation of saving diminishes the supply of funds for private investment? If the money market were homogeneous, there would seem to be no validity in this argument. Assume, to begin with, that the taxation leaves the rate of private investment unaffected. Then it follows that the national debt will be reduced by the amount of the savings transferred below what it would have been had there been no transfer of savings to the government. This means that funds equal to the savings transferred will be available for private investment. Thus our original assumption that the rate of investment is unaffected by the taxation can be retained so far as the supply of funds is concerned. To illustrate: Suppose the government plans to spend an extra $1 million. To avoid inflation it imposes new taxes of $1.2 million. As a result private consumption is cut by $1 million, offsetting the inflationary effects of the new expenditures, and savings are reduced by $200,000. The government will use the $200,000 to buy government securities from private holders, who will then be able to increase their holdings of private securities by the same amount. Thus while the taxation diminishes the rate of increase of assets in private hands, it does not diminish the flow of new funds into private investment.

With a non-homogeneous money market, our conclusion must be modified. It is possible that the taxation of saving may dry up sources of funds that normally go into risky ventures, while the funds released by the government seek a safe resting place. To the extent that this is true, our argument on utility grounds must be modified. The government would then have to consider whether a less equitable tax system and payment of services on a higher national debt were justified by the added stimulus to private investment.

My last observation on taxation relates to Mr. Colin Clark's brilliantly suggestive generalization, based on inductive evidence, that no democratic state will tolerate, on a permanent basis, taxes in excess of 25 per cent of its national income.[26] In my terminology this means that the marginal disutility function of taxation becomes inelastic when taxes approach this limit. If inflation is to be avoided, a limit is thus placed on expenditures. Or, if expenditures are increased beyond that limit, inflation must be met by direct controls. Direct controls may be regarded as imposing for a limited period less disutility than taxation, since, with them, the public is permitted to accumulate savings which compensate present deprivations with a claim on future production. Tax yields in the United States are today not far below Mr. Clark's limit, and I have seen nothing in our recent political history to prove that he is wrong. His generalization may turn out to be as hard to believe in and as hard to refute as the Paretian alpha.[27]

(2) SOCIAL SECURITY. Ever since the Federal Social Security System was inaugurated there has been keen controversy on how it should be financed:

(a) Should it be based on the contributory principle, that is, should it be financed chiefly by taxes which fall most heavily on the sector of the community that derives the greatest benefit?

---

[26] "Public Finance and Changes in the Value of Money," *Economic Journal*, December 1945, LV, p. 371.

[27] One of my critics has questioned my whole discussion of the disutility of taxation on the grounds that so little is known of the laws of incidence. I can only say in reply that, whatever the laws of incidence, taxes are borne by the economy as a whole, and political judgments are made as to whether the general level of taxation is too low or too high. I therefore believe that attempts to generalize about taxes as a whole are useful undertakings.

(b) Should reserves be accumulated now to avoid raising taxes in the future when old-age payments increase as the population grows older?

In terms of our analysis so far, the answer to the first question is that the social security system should not be considered in isolation. It should be treated as part of the total government program and the extent to which it is contributory will depend on the general weighing of advantages and sacrifices.

To the second question our analysis gives an unqualified negative. The accumulation of a cash reserve is in itself deflationary. To offset it, either government expenditures must be increased or other taxes must be lowered. The disbursement of the reserve would in itself be inflationary. To avoid the inflation taxes would then have to be increased or expenditures reduced. In fact, the budgetary situation would be the same as it would have been if the reserve had never been accumulated. Thus, there is no justification for distorting the budget in order to make possible the accumulation of the reserve in the first place.[28]

As far as economics goes, social security should be financed on a pay-as-you-go basis, and the contributory principle should not necessarily be adhered to. But there is more than economics involved. Opponents of social security feel they can limit its extent by keeping to the contributory idea. And many of its supporters believe that the program is rendered immune from political cuts and interference if the analogy with private insurance is maintained. They are even prepared to accept lower benefits in exchange for the greater political security and social dignity of the contributory system. In addition, there is still a vigorous reluctance in this country to support programs which allegedly provide something for nothing. Thus, while it is still open to debate how far the contributory principle will be carried, there is virtually unanimous agreement that it should not be abolished.

(3) SALE OF GOVERNMENT SERVICES. While the government finances most of its program by taxation or borrowing, it habitually sells some services, such as postal services. Why should not the services of the post office be provided on the same basis as the services of the army or the police force? The answer is that the government undertakes to supply as much postal service as is required, and the demand for it is elastic. If it were provided "free" the demand would expand until it was used to satisfy needs of very low priority, and the program would not be justified on the basis of the tax criterion. The need to charge fees could

---

[28] This is from the long-run point of view. We shall see later that from the short-run viewpoint accumulation and decumulation of reserves furnish a useful element of built-in flexibility.

be avoided if the total supply could be controlled by the government and rationed among consumers. This is feasible with policemen, but would obviously create unwarranted inconvenience and administrative difficulty if applied to the post office. The general rule is that where demand is sufficiently elastic, fees must be charged. But there are exceptions. It may be that the demand at zero price is not too large from a public policy point of view. The demand for policemen is probably elastic, but if fees for them were charged, we should almost certainly have too few police. Again, I feel that many government documents, now distributed free in the interests of general enlightenment, might be found to have very elastic demands if fees were charged. The demand for highway services is probably elastic, but the toll system was abolished —presumably on the grounds that the cost of free roads to the government was justified by the encouragement they gave to economic development.

If the demand is inelastic, whether or not fees should be charged should depend on who benefits from the services. If the services benefit all sections of the community, there is no objection in principle to providing them free. If they are designed to benefit a particular group, fees as a rule should be charged. It is argued, for instance, that charges should be made for the use of the airways on the grounds that free airways give the airlines a competitive position in relation to land and water carriers that is unduly favorable. But this criterion should be applied with care. Any given recreational facility provided by the government will benefit most those who live closest to it, and that would suggest that fees should be charged. However, it may be reasonable to assume that one way or another, the government provides recreation equally for all parts of the economy. In that event there would be no objection to providing all recreational services gratis, assuming the demand is sufficiently inelastic.

If fees are charged they should, I believe, cover the full costs of the services to the government. This is at variance with a prominent school of thought which holds that the rule should be marginal costs.[29] I have no satisfactory proof that full costs is the correct rule, but I do believe that the marginal cost principle would do injustice to the programs for which fees are not charged. The difference between average and marginal costs of the services must be financed through the budget, and would compete with other services. Can it be proved that to allow the postal deficit to

---

[29] See Harold Hotelling, "The General Welfare in Relation to Problems of Taxation and of Railway and Utility Rates," *Econometrica*, July 1938, XVI, pp. 242–269; and A. P. Lerner, *The Economics of Control* (New York, 1944). For an interesting alternative solution, see R. H. Coase, "The Marginal Cost Controversy," *Economica*, August 1946, New Series XIII, pp. 169–182.

compete with the national defense program would be preferable to raising postal rates sufficiently to eliminate the deficit?

To charge fees based on cost does correspond generally with our tax criterion for other types of expenditure, but the need to operate on a fee basis prevents those operations from being financed in a way that will help to produce the desired level of national income. Instead, a criterion of annually balanced budgets must be retained for this part of the government's program.

VII. Long–Run Policy: Expenditures

(1) General Program Evaluation. Our earlier assumption that the government acts as a kind of collective economic brain is of course a drastic simplification. Over two-thirds of the budget at the present time is directed to non-economic objectives. The economic objectives we have set forth may conflict with each other. Full employment may not mean maximum real income. Maximum production by private enterprise may not mean maximum satisfaction. The term marginal utility should be replaced by some more general term, such as marginal net advantage, to give the impression that the government is seeking to do justice to a complex of objectives.

As I have said above, the budgetary process is essentially political. The economist has no method of deciding whether money should be spent for public health or public education, or, above all, how the needs of national security should be balanced against those of social security. Nor can he balance the advantages of expenditures against the burdens of taxation. Nevertheless, economic analysis is essential if good political decisions are to be made. And in many cases economic analysis can be decisive. Economic analysis figures much more prominently in the political documents of today than in those of the 'twenties and the 'thirties.

The process of deciding on the relative merits of programs necessarily begins in the executive branch of the government. It is not feasible or desirable for the President to attempt to leave all political decisions, especially those requiring economic judgments, to the Congress. If constructive leadership is to be exercised by the government as a whole, the President must take the lead. His communications to the Congress must take the form of positive recommendations—on both general objectives and specific programs. Moreover, the executive branch is better organized than the legislative to consider the complicated interrelations among the parts of the government program. Our discussion has demonstrated the importance of the single executive budget. We can hope that, as the years pass, the Congress will devote an increasing amount of its attention to the broader policy aspects of the budget and less to matters of administrative detail.

To achieve the best division of labor between the executive and legislature, it is essential that the President submit his recommendations in a way that makes clear the decisions underlying them. This has been done to an increasing extent in the messages transmitting the budget. Last year a significant improvement was made when it became possible to discuss the program of the government in terms of its major functions.

The question of classification of expenditures may seem a humdrum and trivial matter, but that is by no means correct. Traditionally, the budget has been prepared in terms of organization units and in many cases there is no close correspondence between organizations and functions. For instance, the conservation and development of natural resources is a function performed by the Interior, War, and Agriculture Departments. The general function of transportation comes under the Interstate Commerce Commission, the Maritime Commission, the Civil Aeronautics Board, the Civil Aeronautics Administration, the Federal Works Agency, the Post Office and other agencies. If the budgets of all these agencies were presented independently of each other, they would give little indication of the government's policy in any field.

Now that the budget is classified under thirteen major functions and more detailed sub-functions, it becomes more feasible for the government's program to be presented in the way recommended in this paper. When the Congress comes to debate the budget in terms of functions, a great step forward will have been made.

The success of the political process depends very largely on the Civil Service. In my judgment, the Civil Service should avoid, as far as practicable, making decisions which in their nature are political. It is its function to crystallize political issues and to present them for decision at the political level. If the Civil Service is to enjoy the confidence of successive Presidents and Congresses, it must not encroach on their fields. On the other hand, it is difficult for the Congress or the President to perform their functions properly unless they do have confidence in the Civil Service. Otherwise too much of their attention will be diverted from the policy questions that are their main concern.

I have said enough to indicate that good ideas are not enough to make the budgetary process work as it should. Effective organization is almost equally important. As we saw early in this paper, great improvements have been made, especially in the last decade, but in its ordinary operations, with which we are here concerned, the government of this country rarely attains the sureness and decisiveness that it displays in times of crisis.

(2) PUBLIC INVESTMENT. Suppose our economic objective calls for an increase of taxation to finance a new dam or a bridge. How can we decide whether the increase of real income that the investment will bring in the future will justify the present sacrifice by the taxpayers? To estimate the returns from private investment in a limited field is notoriously difficult. In the case of T.V.A., for instance, one would have to forecast the future industrial history of a large region. Who in 1933 forecast the use of T.V.A. power in the war; and who in 1948 can forecast the effects of the use of atomic energy on the need for hydroelectric power? These things cannot be done, and yet no one could reasonably suggest that we should not have a public investment program merely because we cannot estimate its benefits.

One way toward a partial solution would be to consider first the investment needs of the country, public and private. There appears to be some ascertainable relation between the rate of increase of real income and the rate of increase of the stock of real capital. By comparing future benefits with present costs, it may be possible to work out a national investment policy. It would then be necessary to decide how much of the total could be contributed by private investment. The balance would be what is required from the public investment program. I am inclined to believe that an approach on these lines would give a better indication of the proper size of the public investment program as a whole than an estimate obtained by summing the costs of individual "meritorious" projects. If we had such a check on the total, rough and ready methods could be more readily accepted in distributing that total among claimants.

I am not suggesting that future *national* income should be the sole criterion of public investment policy. It is a responsibility of the Federal Government to help to remove income disparities among regions. People in one region have a legitimate claim to protection against floods caused by the agricultural practices in another. Many other examples could be given.

It has frequently been suggested that, because of their investment character, public works should be financed by borrowing rather than through taxation. Our analysis does not support this point of view. We have argued that every expenditure program should be preferable to a reduction of taxation or should justify an increase—as the case may be—since taxation is the device for diverting resources from private to public use. Further, it should be impossible to say whether any particular program is financed "out of taxation" or "out of borrowing"—since all programs should satisfy the tax criterion. Consequently, attempts to separate the finance of public construction from that of current expenses is likely to impair the process of program evaluation.[30]

There may be, however, one valid element in the argument. Suppose our economic objective requires budget deficits. Then it is important that interest should not become an increasing proportion of the national income. This consideration may require more emphasis on programs that tend to increase national income, and this may commend public works. But is this necessarily the case? Is it not possible that better education may do more to increase future production than investments in steel and concrete? This is one of the instances where principles that are admittedly good for private business might lead the government astray.

(3) SUBSIDIES TO PRODUCERS. Our principles provide a *prima facie* case against subsidies to private production. In general, it is not justifiable to restrict through taxation purchases of the things people want in order to induce them to buy something else at an artificially low price. Nevertheless there are important exceptions to this general rule. For example:

Subsidies to private investment may be justified on the ground that its social net product is greater than its private net product. A railroad that opens up new territory increases the national income by more than it increases the income of the railroad. Thus, from the public point of view, we can justify investment that would be unprofitable to the railroad if it undertook the whole cost.

It has long been recognized that economic well-being can be increased by subsidizing industries with decreasing costs induced by external economies, on the assumption that when the infant has grown up it will be self-supporting. The argument has the same validity and the same limitations as the infant-industries argument for tariffs.

Agricultural subsidies are a general practice in industrialized countries. It is the function of the agricultural sector to help replenish the populations of the cities. Under *laissez-faire* conditions, this is brought about by agricultural incomes falling below industrial incomes. It is not consistent with the principles of economic welfare to allow this income disparity to persist. However, a subsidy program that achieved income parity could

---

[30] This section has been written from the point of view of the United States at the present time. To apply it to a country in its early stages of development further explanation is required. In the first place, borrowing from abroad need not satisfy our tax criterion except for the service charges on the borrowing. The foreign borrowing itself increases the supply of goods and services to the borrowing country. There is therefore no need to release them from private use by taxation. The same reasoning would apply to public investment of domestic funds that produced a rapid increase of final output.

check this desirable population flow to the cities. The perpetual dilemma of agricultural policy is to encourage necessary readjustments, and at the same time do justice to the farmers.

When compared with other expenditure programs, subsidies become more acceptable to the extent that the private enterprise objective is considered important. For instance, in this country subsidies to private housing are eminently respectable. Public housing except for the lowest income groups is viewed with alarm.

(4) LOANS TO BUSINESS. A loan by the government to business at a lower rate than the private money market will offer—or a government guarantee of a private loan—is in effect a subsidy to the extent that the cost of borrowing is lowered, and should be judged on the same basis as a subsidy. It is frequently argued that there is no need to apply the tax criterion to a loan, since it will eventually be repaid to the Treasury. This is incorrect according to our principles. If the income goal has been reached, new loan expenditures should be offset by increased taxation or reduced expenditures in other directions. The repayment of the loan, however, is in the nature of a tax on the earnings of the enterprise financed by the loan. During the repayment period, other forms of taxation can be reduced correspondingly or government expenditures can be increased according to social needs.

I have assumed in this argument that loans are made only to selected industries or businesses. If the government succeeds in making credit generally cheaper, we cannot say that there is a *prima facie* case against it. Whether it is good or bad will depend on whether or not it is desirable to increase the rate of capital formation. Here again, if the income goal has been reached, the expansionary effects of the cheaper credit should be offset with increased taxation. In policy discussions, it is usually taken as axiomatic that the objective of policy, in the long run at least, should always be to make credit cheaper. In certain circumstances, a case could be made for raising interest rates and lowering taxes.[31] One of the luxuries of the present period of full employment is that it provides a respite from thinking only of how to cure a chronic depression.

VIII. COMPENSATORY POLICY

We now come to our last question. How is long-run policy to be adjusted from time to time to offset fluctuations in private economic activ-

---

[31] I would remind the reader that I am here considering long-run policy, not countercyclical policy. There too a rise in interest rates might be regarded as an alternative to a tax increase; but it is improbable that an increase of interest rates and a tax reduction would be desirable at the same time.

ity? My discussion here will be brief, since the subject has been treated at length elsewhere in this volume.

One simple answer that has obvious appeal is that the entire long-run policy should be adjusted. In the event of a depression the entire expenditure side of the budget should be speeded up and taxes reduced. In short, the same principle that we have worked out for the long-run should also be applied to the short-run. Instead of making plans that will remain fairly stable from year to year, the budget should be made to fit the economic needs of each particular year.

Such a policy commends itself from the point of view of economic theory, but it could not be carried out without serious impairment of the budgetary process. As we have seen, that process is necessarily lengthy, and programs may have to be adjusted quickly to meet changing economic conditions. It is preferable therefore to consider short-run policy as a supplement to long-run policy, and it should be designed to interrupt as little as possible the application of budgetary principles to the long-run program.

We can consider compensatory devices according to whether they are (1) "built-in," (2) administrative, or (3) legislative.

(1) "Built-in" Devices. Built-in flexibility of the budget is achieved when certain programs fluctuate by law in a way that will offset private economic fluctuations. If our long-run policy is consistently carried out, the behavior of the budget will automatically tend to offset ups and downs in the private sector.

With a progressive income tax, for instance, a larger proportion of the national income is taxed when national income is high than when it is low. It therefore operates automatically to check booms and depressions. The social security system accumulates funds at high levels of income when tax receipts exceed benefits, and it decumulates at low levels when tax receipts fall off and claims for benefits rise. The agricultural price-support program automatically expands and contracts as farm prices rise and fall.

These examples indicate that there is already some built-in flexibility in the federal budget. Any scheme for extending Social Security benefits will bring more such flexibility. It may become feasible to tie tax *rates* to some economic indicator, but at present we do not have sufficiently precise knowledge of economic interrelationships to make this feasible.

Built-in devices commend themselves highly on budgetary grounds. Their automatic operation means that they come into operation without the need for hasty political or administrative decisions. Long-run policy can be preserved intact.

However, these arrangements cannot be relied on exclusively if we want full compensatory action. For a considerable amount of inflation, or unemployment, as the case may be, must take place before they come into effect with any force. They can mitigate but cannot prevent inflation or deflation.

(2) ADMINISTRATIVE DEVICES. It has often been suggested that the executive should be granted discretionary power by the Congress to vary the rate at which programs are carried out or the rates at which taxes are collected.

The Congress does habitually make appropriations for more than one year for long-run construction or procurement programs, and the executive does have the legal authority to control rates of expenditure from year to year. But these programs prove in practice exceedingly difficult to adapt to changing economic conditions. In many cases it takes one or two years for programs to become fully reflected in construction activity. Once a program has been enlarged, it is difficult to contract it without waste, to say nothing of resolute opposition from all interested parties.

In the past, government corporations, such as the Reconstruction Finance Corporation, have provided the administration with a flexible instrument of policy. However, by the Corporation Control Act of 1945, the Congress asserted its determination to exercise greater control over government corporations; and the tendency now is to bring the corporations under stricter budgetary control rather than to exempt them from it. Here there is a conflict between the long- and short-run points of view. From the long-run point of view, there can be no question that the programs of the corporations should be subject to regular Congressional approval; but if that is done the executive is deprived of a useful counter-cyclical weapon.

It seems very doubtful that Congress would agree to give the President discretionary power to alter tax rates. It also seems to me doubtful that the President, from a political point of view, would want it.

On the whole, therefore, I believe that the practical possibilities of administrative devices are strictly limited.

(3) LEGISLATIVE DEVICES. I conclude that apart from built-in flexibility, we must rely for compensatory action on measures that are passed by the Congress. In fact that seems to be in line with the intention of the Employment Act, which makes the President and the Congress partners in their responsibility for economic stability.

Anti-depression action will, I believe, require special requests by the President for appropriations to carry out special projects such as roads or housing, or to provide relief in the case of distress. It should also require special action to reduce taxes on a temporary basis. This seems all very similar—painfully similar, some will say—to what was done in the 'thirties. But there can be a difference. The 'thirties were a highly experimental period. Many things that were tried had to be rejected. Some that were retained were badly executed, and some were misdirected. The difference can be achieved by advance preparation. We shall probably never have a blueprint on the statute book. But it is possible that the Congress could pass a tax law in advance—to be put into force by a joint resolution. And the Executive can, and, under the Employment Act, presumably will, get its plans ready. So long as the imaginative vigor of the 'thirties is not lost, a much better job can be done next time we are confronted with depression.

What should be the objective of compensatory policy? Should it be to iron out all fluctuations, or should it allow mild ups and downs in business? Our discussion in the last paragraph has answered the question to some extent. If Congressional action must be relied upon, it is doubtful that action will be taken before some signs of depression have appeared. And in the present state of our forecasting knowledge, it is doubtful whether it should.

Even if forecasting were good and action could be taken in time, it is not certain that complete stability should be the objective. It still remains true that trouble can be caused by price and wage maladjustments, which, if they are not to be perpetuated, should be allowed to correct themselves. There will continue to be shifts between industries and regions. It should not be national policy to prevent these changes, but they do involve depressions in some segments of the economy.

There is no reason, however, why these changes which should be allowed to occur should have secondary depressing effects. There are no grounds for the belief that a general depression does anyone any good. The best way to avoid secondary effects is to reduce tax rates. I conclude, therefore, that tax reduction should always be part of anti-depression policy.

One further point: foreign investment policies should not be undertaken as compensatory devices. It is essential from the point of view of good international relations, that lending policy be designed to help carry out foreign policy and not domestic policy. There is the strongest political temptation to export unemployment. But in the interests both of domestic stability and international harmony, it should be resisted.

It is much easier to propose a feasible legislative program of fiscal policy to offset deflation than to propose one to prevent inflation. While strong political forces can be mustered to relieve a depression, innumerable obstacles and pressures appear when any attempt is made to cut inflation. My conclusion therefore is that fiscal control of inflation must depend on prompt abandonment of anti-depression measures and the anti-inflationary safeguards that are built into the long-run program.

In the field of compensatory action, I believe fiscal policy must shoulder most of the load. Its chief rival, monetary policy, seems to be disqualified on institutional grounds. This country appears to be committed to something like the present low level of interest rates on a long-term basis. There is not much room for reductions to alleviate depressions, and it seems generally agreed that, with the national debt at its present size, any appreciable increases in rates would cause serious financial disorders. No one has been prepared to suggest an increase in long-term rates to check the present inflation.

Other methods of adjustment, such as anti-monopoly policy, belong clearly to long-run rather than to compensatory policy. While many economists have recommended elimination of monopolies in times of depression, few, if any, have been willing to urge an increase in monopoly to check a boom.

I have some hopes that in the area of administered prices big business may come to practice private compensatory fiscal policies. The practice of accumulating reserves in prosperous times and disbursing them as dividends when current profits are low is all in the right direction. A stable dividend policy could be supplemented and strengthened by a fluctuating price policy. It can be argued that the present inflation of food prices would be less if managed industrial prices were higher, and that these higher prices would be justified if there were assurance of sharp price cuts in the event of a depression. Attempts by government to enlist the aid of business management have not been successful in the past. They are not likely to be in the future so long as government retains its ambivalent attitude toward the question of monopoly control.

Although this discussion has not been optimistic, the least that can be hoped for is that more government action will be taken to mitigate depressions in the future than was taken in the past. Built-in flexibility is now more potent; it is unlikely that tax rates will ever again be raised with the onset of depression; and the political demands for government action will be more insistent. Finally, the long-run budget will be a much higher proportion of the national income than it was before the war. With a budget of between $30 billion and $40 billion, it would be impossible for the national income to fall to anything comparable with that of 1932 or 1933.

The type of policy suggested here would require the use of an extraordinary budget in addition to the regular budget. In my view, the regular budget would represent the long-run program on the expenditure sides. It would, however, reflect the effects of built-in flexibility. Of course if the total program were designed to achieve full employment in the ensuing year, there would be no such effects. The extraordinary budget, on the other hand, would show the effects of the special revenue and expenditure measures proposed by the President. Depending on the time when action was required, it might not even be submitted at the same time as the regular budget.

I know that extraordinary budgets are anathema to many authorities whose objectives are the same as mine—to improve the budgetary process. But I can see no other way to do justice to the requirements of good budgeting and an effective and well-timed fiscal policy.[32] The use of an extraordinary budget would permit separation of that part of the budget which can be the subject of long-run planning from the programs that must be adopted in response to immediate needs. With the extraordinary budget, compensatory measures could be dropped more easily after the need for them had passed than if they had become part of the regular budget.

The economist will doubtless be irritated with the intrusion of public administration into this paper, and the public administrator, if he reads it, with the economic jargon. The political theorists will consider it naïve. However, someone must try to bring together the fruits of political, economic, and administrative theory if we are to have a successful fiscal policy.[33]

---

[32] I am happy to find that Mr. Gerhard Colm came to the same conclusion. See his article, "Comment on Extraordinary Budgets," *Social Research*, May 1938, V, pp. 168–181.

[33] After I had exhausted all the space available for this paper, I found there were many things left unsaid or unnoticed. Despite the advice of my helpful critics, there is still no discussion of national debt management. Against my own inclinations, I have had no space to consider the international aspects of domestic fiscal policies. I have not been able to give enough attention to the other measures which should complement fiscal policy.

The paper may appear to be more an exposition of my own ideas than a review of economic thought. To that I would reply that it is a review of the spoken as well as the written word—much of what I have written is an attempt to systematize what has been discussed in government circles, and especially in the Bureau of the Budget, over a number of years.

6

THE THEORY OF INTERNATIONAL TRADE

Lloyd A. Metzler

I. Introduction

The interwar period was a period of extraordinary and perhaps unprecedented developments in the field of international trade. The gold standard, which had been abandoned during the First World War, was never re-established on a firm basis, and exchange rates of many countries underwent substantial fluctuations. The Great Depression of the 'thirties, which sharply reduced the level of output and employment in many countries, had a drastic effect upon international trade. Neither the timing nor the severity of the depression was uniform as between countries, and the consequence was a serious lack of balance in the international payments and receipts of many countries. Partly to offset these discrepancies, and partly to guard the dwindling markets for goods, country after country imposed additional barriers to international commerce.

Even after the general economic recovery of the late 'thirties had begun, the trade restrictions and special trading arrangements were for the most part retained. The Second World War was of course the occasion for much more comprehensive and complete governmental controls of international trade, but even if the war had not occurred we should have inherited an enormously complex system of trade regulations as our legacy from the unstable 'thirties. During the war years, it became increasingly apparent that such a complicated system would not automatically revert to a system of unregulated multilateral trade, and that any attempt to restore the old system would require constant international supervision and co-operation. This was the genesis of such organizations as the International Monetary Fund, the International Bank for Reconstruction and Development, and the proposed International Trade Organization. Whether these agencies will succeed in their avowed purpose of assisting in the establishment of a stable and relatively free international economic order remains to be seen. The difficulties encountered in postwar recovery and the general trend toward state intervention in economic activity have seriously complicated the problems of the new organizations.

In any event, it is not the purpose of this paper to discuss the future prospects for international trade or the future development of commercial policy. Nor do I intend to describe further the interesting history of international trade during the interwar years. This empirical enquiry has already been performed in a number of admirable studies, and it seems neither necessary nor useful to summarize the work of these able economists.[1] This paper is primarily a review or a summary of recent changes in the theory of international trade. The empirical developments are mentioned largely because of the profound influence which they have had upon economic theory. If the interwar period was a period of disturbed conditions in international trade, it was also a period of rapid change in the theory of international economics. The changes were so numerous, in fact, that it is quite impossible to summarize all of them. Nevertheless, it seems to me that the most significant of the recent developments can be classified under four main heads as follows: (1) the balance of payments and the theory of employment; (2) fluctuating exchange rates; (3) price theory and international trade; (4) commercial policy and the theory of international trade. Although the discussion below is by no means exhaustive, an attempt has been made to evaluate the principal contributions in each of these four branches of international economics.

II. The Theory of Employment and the Balance of Payments

The revolution in economic theory which occurred in the nineteen-thirties had a profound influence upon almost all branches of economics, and this was no less true of international trade than of other specialized fields. Since the new approach to economics was primarily a reconsideration of traditional ideas regarding money, interest rates, and prices, it was natural that the most important changes in international economics should have been in the monetary aspects of the subject. The revolution actually extended considerably beyond the monetary theory, however, as a later discussion of commercial policy will show.

Prior to the publication of Keynes' *General Theory*, the monetary theory of international trade had been one of the most widely accepted of economic doctrines. For more than a century and a half, English econo-

---

[1] Perhaps the most interesting of these empirical studies are Seymour E. Harris, *Exchange Depreciation* (Cambridge, Mass., 1936); Margaret S. Gordon, *Barriers to World Trade* (New York, 1941); Howard S. Ellis, *Exchange Control in Central Europe* (Cambridge, Mass., 1941); U.S. Dept. of Commerce, *The United States in the World Economy* (Washington, 1942); League of Nations, *International Currency Experience: Lessons of the Inter-war Period* (Princeton, 1944).

mists and others in the English tradition had believed that the monetary system operates in such a way that a country's balance of payments tends automatically toward a state of equilibrium. If one country had a deficit in its balance of payments with another, for example, it was recognized that part of its payments abroad would have to be made in gold, and it was believed that the gold movement would bring about certain price changes which eventually would restore an even balance of payments. As a result of the increased supply of money in the surplus country, and the reduced supply in the deficit country, prices and costs would rise in the former and fall in the latter. The deficit country would then become a relatively cheap market in which to buy goods, and its exports would rise while its imports declined. This process would continue, according to the classical view, until a balance between payments and receipts was again established.[2] The classical explanation of the balancing process was eventually modified to consider the influence of interest rates on capital movements, to allow for a fractional reserve banking system, to recognize the similarity between gold movements and changes in foreign balances, and in other respects as well, but in substance the theory remained essentially as it was originally developed by the early English economists.

The important feature of the classical mechanism, for the purpose of the present review, is the central role which it attributes to the monetary system. The classical theory contains an explicit acceptance of the Quantity Theory of Money as well as an implied assumption that output and employment are unaffected by international monetary disturbances.[3] In other words, the classical doctrine assumes that an increase or decrease in the quantity of money leads to an increase or decrease in the aggregate money demand for goods and services, and that a change in money demand affects prices and costs rather than output and employment. The Keynesian revolution cast doubt upon both of these crucial assumptions. Say's Law of Markets, which had been the bulwark of both the Quantity Theory of Money and the classical theory of the balance of payments, was rejected, and the possibility of general overproduction or general unemployment was finally acknowledged. In the course of this revolution, the monetary system, regarded as a director of economic activity, was relegated to a somewhat secondary position, and economists increasingly emphasized the effects of saving and spending habits upon the circular flow of income.

After the foundations of the classical theory had crumbled, it was only

---

[2] See, e.g., John Stuart Mill, *Principles of Political Economy*, Ashley ed. (London, 1909), Ch. XXI, Sec. 4.

[3] Cf. James W. Angell, *The Theory of International Prices* (Cambridge, Mass., 1926), Ch. III–VI.

a short time until a new explanation of the balancing process in international trade emerged. Although the new theory of the balance of payments was a direct outgrowth of the *General Theory*, Keynes himself had little to do with it; the first contributions were made by Mrs. Robinson[4] and R. F. Harrod.[5] Some of the practical as well as the theoretical implications of the new doctrine were later investigated by Haberler,[6] Salant,[7] Kindleberger,[8] Metzler,[9] Machlup,[10] and others. The essence of the new theory is that an external event which increases a country's exports will also increase imports *even without price changes*, since the change in exports affects the level of output and hence the demand for all goods. In other words, movements of output and employment play much the same role in the new doctrine that price movements played in the old. Before discussing the relation of employment to the balance of payments in detail, however, a brief account should be given of a number of empirical studies of the adjustment process which were published during the inter-war years, for these studies, although carried out along classical lines, had a profound effect upon later developments in international trade theory.

EMPIRICAL STUDIES AND THE CLASSICAL THEORY

At the suggestion of Taussig, several economists made detailed investigations of the balancing process under conditions of both fixed and fluctuating exchange rates.[11] In each of these studies a period of time was selected in which a particular country's balance of payments had been subjected to a disturbing influence, and the manner in which the balance of payments had adjusted itself to this disturbance was then examined. The general conclusion of most of the empirical investigations was that the balancing process had occurred largely as envisaged in the classical theory; i.e., the price movements and gold movements had agreed with classical expectations. Taussig himself later made additional studies

[4] Joan Robinson, *Essays in the Theory of Employment* (New York, 1937), Part III, Ch. I.

[5] R. F. Harrod, *International Economics*, revised ed. (London, 1939), Ch. V.

[6] Gottfried Haberler, *Prosperity and Depression* (Geneva, 1940), Ch. XII.

[7] William A. Salant, "Foreign Trade Policy in the Business Cycle," *Public Policy*, Vol. II (Cambridge, Mass., 1941), pp. 208–231.

[8] Charles P. Kindleberger, "International Monetary Stabilization," in *Postwar Economic Problems*, S. E. Harris, ed. (New York, 1943), pp. 375–395.

[9] Lloyd A. Metzler, "Underemployment Equilibrium in International Trade," *Econometrica*, April 1942, X, pp. 97–112.

[10] Fritz Machlup, *International Trade and the National Income Multiplier* (Philadelphia, 1943), *passim*.

[11] The best known of these studies are: J. H. Williams, *Argentine International Trade under Inconvertible Paper Money, 1880–1900* (Cambridge, Mass., 1920); Jacob Viner, *Canada's Balance of International Indebtedness, 1900–1913* (Cambridge, Mass., 1924); Harry D. White, *The French International Accounts, 1880–1913* (Cambridge, Mass., 1933).

which gave further support to this view.[12] At the same time, however, some of the evidence which Taussig accumulated led him to doubt the adequacy of the classical theory. It was not that the balance of trade and the level of prices failed to conform to disturbing influences in the manner envisaged by the classical theory. Quite the contrary, they appeared to conform too well and too quickly. When Great Britain increased her capital exports, for example, Taussig observed that the British balance on current account adjusted itself with amazing rapidity to the new capital position, even though both gold movements and changes in prices appeared to be relatively small.

. . . The actual merchandise movements seem to have been adjusted to the shifting balance of payments with surprising exactness and speed. The process which our theory contemplates—the initial flow of specie when there is a burst of loans; the fall in prices in the lending country, rise in the borrowing country, the eventual increased movement of merchandise out of one and into the other—all this can hardly be expected to take place smoothly and quickly. Yet no signs of disturbance are to be observed such as the theoretic analysis previses . . .[13]

The smoothness and speed with which many countries' balances of payments seemed to adapt themselves to changing circumstances in the years before the First World War led Taussig to surmise that the classical theory might be an incomplete explanation of the adjusting mechanism. "It must be confessed," he said, "that here we have phenomena not fully understood. In part our information is insufficient; in part our understanding of other connected topics is also inadequate."[14] Even before the theory of employment was developed, historical studies thus indicated that the balancing of international payments and receipts might be attributable to economic forces not considered in the classical theory. Despite his misgivings, Taussig never abandoned the classical theory, for he could find no other explanation of the balancing process.

Meanwhile, other empirical studies were being made along entirely different lines, and these cast further doubt on the effectiveness of the price adjustments envisaged by the classical doctrine. The interwar period was a period in which extensive studies were made of the elasticity of demand for individual products, and the studies showed, almost without exception, that quantities sold were much less responsive to changes in prices than had formerly been suspected.[15] The elasticities proved in most cases

---

[12] F. W. Taussig, *International Trade* (New York, 1928), Ch. XX–XXV.

[13] *Ibid.*, p. 239.

[14] *Ibid.*

[15] The pioneer work in this field was of course that of H. L. Moore and Henry Schultz. See particularly the latter's book, *The Theory and Measurement of Demand* (Chicago, 1937).

to be less than unity, and in some instances they were so small as to be almost negligible. Studies of demand elasticities for imports as a whole were not made until a later date, but when they were made they confirmed the supposition which the earlier studies of individual commodities had raised that the physical volume of imports might not be responsive to changes in prices. Hinshaw,[16] for example, estimated an elasticity of demand for imports in the United States of about .5, while a study of British imports[17] showed a price elasticity of approximately .64.

If these elasticities are representative of price elasticities in general, it is apparent that the operation of the classical mechanism is even more difficult to explain than Taussig had supposed. Not only did the trade balances move with surprising rapidity, but they moved in the expected direction despite the fact that the physical volume of imports is normally responsive only in a slight degree to changes in relative prices. In order to attribute the observed adjustments to changes in relative prices, it would in many instances be necessary to assume that demand elasticities are much higher than those which have actually been measured.

INCOME AND THE BALANCE OF PAYMENTS

Although the empirical evidence accumulated during the interwar period had clearly indicated the need for a reconsideration of the balance-of-payments mechanism, no substantial revisions of the accepted theory were made until Keynes published his *General Theory*. Thereafter, the missing link in the classical theory became almost self-evident: the rapid adjustment of a country's balance of payments which Taussig had observed, and which seemed to occur without the assistance of price changes or changes in central bank policy, was found to be largely the result of induced movements of income and employment. Suppose, for example, that Country A increases its imports from B, and that a deficit thus arises in A's balance of payments. The deficit may initially be financed by gold shipments or by a movement of short-term balances, but regardless of the method of financing, a more or less automatic mechanism will soon offset at least part of the initial disturbance. Income and employment will expand in the export industries of B; the demand for home goods will therefore rise in that country, and the expansion will spread from the export industries to the entire economy. As output and employment increase, Country B will increase its imports from A, thereby offsetting a part, or perhaps all, of the initial rise of exports to A.

---

[16] Randall Hinshaw, "American Prosperity and the British Balance-of-Payments Problem," *Review of Economic Statistics*, February 1945, XXVII, p. 4.
[17] Tse-Chung Chang, "The British Demand for Imports in the Inter-War Period," *Economic Journal*, June 1946, LVI, p. 197.

This, in brief outline, is the revised theory of the balance of payments which grew out of the theory of employment. Although the new theory, in complete form, was first presented by Mrs. Robinson and by Harrod in works previously cited, its main features can be found as early as 1936 in a remarkable article by Paish.[18]

Perhaps the most important single feature of the new concept is its comparative independence from banking policy. The cumulative movements of output and employment which account for a large part of the adjustment of the balance of payments will normally be influenced only to a small extent by central bank action; to a much greater extent such income movements are a direct consequence of changes in the demand for goods and services. In the preceding illustration, for instance, if the initial surplus in Country B were offset by a gold inflow into that country, the central bank might attempt to neutralize or sterilize the gold. In other words, the banking authorities might prevent the gold inflow from increasing either the reserve ratios of the banks or the amount of money in circulation. This they could easily do by selling securities. Unless domestic investment were highly sensitive to a change in interest rates, however, such action would not stop the rise of employment which was initiated in the export trades, and the adjusting process would accordingly proceed as before. The divorcing of the modern balancing mechanism from bank policy explains why a balancing tendency between foreign payments and receipts is sometimes apparent even when banks at home and abroad are carrying out neutralizing operations. Bank policy, apart from its influence on capital movements, can affect the balance of payments only through the circular flow of income, and the relation of bank policy to the circular flow is at best tenuous and uncertain. In the words of P. B. Whale:

Since gold movements (or more generally, changes in reserves) and discount rate adjustments are displaced from their central position in the process of international price adjustment, the question of "observing the rules of the game", as this is ordinarily understood, loses much of its importance.[19]

In short, a central bank which attempts to stabilize by offsetting rising exports with a sale of securities is not really interfering much with the "natural" balancing mechanism. But neither is it achieving much stability.

---

[18] F. W. Paish, "Banking Policy and the Balance of International Payments," *Economica*, November 1936, New Series III, pp. 404–422.

[19] P. B. Whale, "The Working of the Pre-War Gold Standard," *Economica*, February 1937, New Series IV, p. 31; cf. also League of Nations, *op. cit.*, Ch. IV.

ANTECEDENTS OF THE MODERN THEORY

In the foregoing account of the balancing mechanism, the adjustment of international payments and receipts through changes in real income and employment has been referred to repeatedly as the "new" or "revised" or "modern" theory. Although this theory undoubtedly contains significant elements of innovation which justify calling it a new or modern theory, it also has, like other scientific innovations, important antecedents. Indeed, after the publication of Viner's comprehensive studies[20] it is now clear that even many of the English economists who are commonly regarded as members of the classical school subscribed to a theory of adjustment which differed considerably from the classical theory, and had much in common with the modern view. Ricardo, for example, believed that some disturbances to the international balance, such as an increase of agricultural imports resulting from a crop failure at home, could be rectified without gold movements and corresponding price changes. Although his reasoning on this point was somewhat obscure, Wheatley, as Viner shows,[21] gave an account of the same type of adjustment which indicated clearly how the international accounts *might* be balanced without gold movements and price changes. Wheatley argued that if England increased her agricultural imports because of a crop failure, this in itself would increase the incomes of exporters to England, and that the ability of such exporters to purchase English goods would therefore be greater than before, even without price changes. To some extent, in other words, the balance of payments tended to adjust itself by means of changes in purchasing power at home and abroad. A similar view was presented later (1840) by Longfield,[22] and still later (1889) by Bastable,[23] who applied this purchasing power theory to the disturbance resulting from the payment of a loan. Bastable argued that a payment from Country A to Country B would automatically increase the purchasing power of the receiving country and reduce the purchasing power of the paying country. Imports of A would therefore fall while imports of B would rise, even without price changes, and Bastable believed that the paying country could thereby achieve an export surplus equal to the annual payments, without gold movements. During the interwar period, ideas similar to Bastable's appeared in the well-known theory of Ohlin[24]

[20] Jacob Viner, *Studies in the Theory of International Trade* (New York, 1937), especially Ch. VI and VII.

[21] *Ibid.*, pp. 295–297.

[22] *Ibid.*, p. 297.

[23] *Ibid.*, pp. 302–303.

[24] Bertil Ohlin, "Transfer Difficulties, Real and Imagined," *Economic Journal*, June 1929, XXXIX, pp. 172–178.

and other Scandinavian economists that reparations and similar transfers can be carried out by means of shifts in purchasing power, and that no price movements need occur.

All of these purchasing power arguments sound surprisingly like the theory discussed earlier in the present review. What, then, is the justification for calling the adjustment through changes in income a new or modern theory? Wherein does it differ from the theories of Wheatley, Ricardo, Bastable, Ohlin, and others? The difference, in my opinion, is primarily that the earlier expositions lacked a theory of employment or income, and were therefore unable to explain just how far the adjusting process could go. Some of the earlier explanations were vague and ambiguous as to the extent of income movements, while the later ones were frequently erroneous. There was a strong tendency in the later discussions, for example, to cling to the assumption that full employment prevails at all times, and to assume, therefore, that in the case of a money transfer, purchasing power is increased in the receiving country and reduced in the paying by exactly the amount of the transfer. In the words of Iversen, ". . . the total amount of buying power in the two countries together is unchanged; only its distribution between them is changed."[25] In the light of the modern theory of employment, it is obvious that this doctrine of the conservation of purchasing power, which was an integral part of a number of the pre-Keynesian discussions, cannot be supported. When secondary as well as primary changes in income have been taken into account, it is clear that something more than a mere shift in purchasing power has occurred; in addition, there may be a net change in output and employment both at home and abroad. It is the ability to set limits to these changes in purchasing power, or at any rate to determine the conditions on which the changes depend, which distinguishes the new theory from the older shifts-of-purchasing-power doctrine. From this point of view, the theory of Bastable and Ohlin is a stepping stone to the new theory, but is not in itself a complete explanation of how balances of payments are affected by changes in income.

LIMITS TO THE ADJUSTING PROCESS

If the modern theory establishes more definite limits than its predecessors to the balancing influence of income movements, what are these limits? In particular, is the theory of employment a complete explanation of the balancing process or is it only a partial explanation? In order to give complete answers to these questions, it would be necessary to con-

[25] Carl Iversen, *Aspects of the Theory of International Capital Movements* (London, 1936), p. 232.

sider the components of national income in considerable detail. The following remarks will therefore be limited to a summary of general conclusions and to a statement of the opinions of a number of economists.

The balancing process is closely related to what might be called "the fundamental income identity for an open economy." This identity states simply that, for any individual country, savings are the sum of two components: (1) net domestic investment; (2) the balance of payments on current account. Although this is an identity, being simply a definition of savings over any past accounting period, it may also be regarded as a condition of equilibrium, provided all the components are interpreted as intended savings, intended investment, etc. Let us see, now, how the income identity can be applied to our earlier discussion of the balance of payments between Countries A and B, when this balance is disturbed by an increased demand in A for the products of B. Consider the situation in B, the country which initially has an increase in exports. Since income rises in B, we may take it for granted that savings, interpreted in the *intended* sense, will also rise. From the savings-investment relation it follows that the sum of domestic investment plus the balance on current account must also be higher than before. Thus, net domestic investment must be higher than in the initial position, or the balance on current account must be more favorable to B, or some combination of these two must occur. Which outcome is most likely? In the earlier discussions of the balancing process by Mrs. Robinson and R. F. Harrod, there was a tendency to take the level of investment as given, and to consider only the influence of saving and consumption on the balance of payments. Under these assumptions, the balancing process is obviously incomplete. Unless domestic investment increases in B, for example, savings can remain above the previous level only to the extent that the balance on current account remains more favorable to that country. The induced rise of income in B will thus offset a part, but not all, of that country's surplus on current account.

Later discussions modified this view somewhat by showing that investment, in the short run at any rate, may depend upon the level of income, and that induced cumulative movements of income may accordingly be large enough to offset a balance-of-payments disturbance completely.[26] While some differences of opinion still exist concerning the role of induced investment, the conclusion of most economists seems to be that,

---

[26] See, e.g., Lloyd A. Metzler, "Underemployment Equilibrium in International Trade," *loc. cit., passim;* League of Nations, *op. cit.,* Ch. IV, Sec. 5; Ragnar Nurkse, "Domestic and International Equilibrium," in Chapter XXI of *The New Economics,* Seymour E. Harris, ed. (New York, 1947).

except under unusual conditions, the adjustment of a country's balance of payments by means of income movements is likely to be incomplete.

PAST AND FUTURE

Like the classical theory of the balance of payments, the theory which has emerged in the last ten years envisages a more or less automatic balancing mechanism. Unlike the classical theory, however, the new explanation, as we have seen, normally accounts for only a part of the adjustment and thus constitutes a theory of disequilibrium as well as a theory of equilibrium. Moreover, the cumulative movement of income at home and abroad which is the essence of the modern theory will not occur unless the disturbing influence affects the circular flow of income as well as the balance of payments. The adjustment of a country's balance of payments to speculative capital transfers or other disturbances which have no *direct* effect upon the circular flow of income is thus likely to be slow and insignificant. On the other hand, if the initial disturbance is an increase or decrease of direct investments abroad or any other event which alters the flow of income, the secondary adaptation of the balance of payments to the new conditions will probably be substantial. In this respect, as in others, the new theory differs from the classical, for the adjustment envisaged by the classical theory was much the same regardless of the nature of the initial disturbance.

Perhaps the most important difference, however, is in the nature of the adjustment itself. In the modern view, a country with a deficit in its balance of payments is likely to eliminate this deficit, in part at least, through a low level of income and employment. The conflict between domestic stability and international equilibrium, which has long been a familiar part of classical monetary theory, is thus shown to be much more important than had formerly been supposed. In an unstable world, the choice confronting an individual country is not merely between price stability and international equilibrium, as envisaged by the classical theory, but between stability of employment and international equilibrium. In recent years there has been a growing recognition of this conflict and the difficulties of resolving it. The necessity for international cooperation to ensure a balanced and stable rate of economic growth throughout the world has thus become increasingly apparent.

It cannot be said that much has yet been accomplished in reaching this objective. Nevertheless, a tremendous change is evident almost everywhere in the attitude of individual countries toward control of the rate of economic activity. If international planning for stability is not yet popular, many countries at least are making plans of their own for stabilizing their economies and using their resources fully. It remains to be seen how successful the new programs will be, once the prolonged period of transition from war to peace has been passed. It is my own judgment, however, that most of them, while not perhaps eliminating all fluctuations of economic activity, will probably eliminate the large movements of employment which we associate with major business cycles. If so, the conditions under which international trade is carried on in the future will be entirely different from the conditions of the interwar period, and probably somewhat different also from the conditions before the First World War. Fluctuations of demand arising from movements of income will be relatively small, and resources will be largely employed, as postulated by the classical theory of the balance of payments. This means, among other things, that induced movements of output and employment, such as those which have explained a part of the balancing of international accounts in the past, will probably not be permitted in the future. We have thus reached the somewhat paradoxical result that the more successful Keynesian remedies prove to be in solving problems of domestic stability the less need we shall have for Keynesian economics in describing international affairs.[27]

What, then, will be the mechanism of adjustment in the future? If induced changes in employment are prevented or greatly reduced, virtually the only method of balancing international accounts without resort to direct controls will be through changes in the terms of trade, i.e., through the price system. This does not mean, however, that the classical mechanism of price adjustments will experience a renaissance, for countries which adopt policies to stabilize output will no doubt be equally interested in stabilizing the general level of prices and costs. It is therefore not to be expected that general price movements will supplant movements of output as regulators of the balance of payments. Although the classical theory, in the strict sense, will thus be as outmoded as the modern theory, the method of adjustment which finally evolves will probably be more nearly akin to the classical mechanism than to the modern. Even without general price and cost changes, the essential means of adjustment contemplated by the classical theory—a change in the terms of trade —can be accomplished through changes in exchange rates, and if the present trend toward widespread state control of trade is to be halted the international monetary system will have to move increasingly toward such an arrangement. Indeed, in a world of high and stable employ-

---

[27] It is perhaps unfair to describe the modern theory of adjustment of the balance of payments as "Keynesian economics," since Keynes himself had little to do with it. The new theory is Keynesian only in the sense that it is a direct outgrowth of the theory of employment.

ment, movements of exchange rates are virtually the only more or less automatic means of influencing international trade without resorting to direct controls. For this reason, it seems appropriate to review, in the section which follows, the developments during the interwar period in the theory of fluctuating exchange rates.

III. FLUCTUATING EXCHANGE RATES

ECONOMIC EVENTS AND ECONOMIC THEORY

During the First World War, the gold standard was suspended throughout the world, and although most countries eventually returned either to the gold standard or to the gold exchange standard after the war had ended, the resumption of gold payments was a long and protracted process. Throughout most of the decade of the 'twenties there were accordingly substantial fluctuations in the external values of many currencies. Moreover, the process of stabilization had hardly been completed when a large part of the world once more abandoned the gold standard as a consequence of the Great Depression in the early 'thirties. Later, during one period in the middle 'thirties, currency values were relatively stable without a formal return to the gold standard, but this stability was again disrupted, this time by the United States depression of 1937–38 and by the abnormal capital movements which preceded the outbreak of the Second World War. The interwar period was thus a period of fluctuating exchange rates; only a few years during the entire period were characterized by exchange-rate stability.[28]

It was natural, under such conditions, that economists should have devoted considerable attention to the effects of exchange fluctuations and that permanent contributions should have been made, in consequence, to this particular branch of the theory of international trade. The theoretical development, however, did not proceed at a uniform rate throughout the interwar years. The underlying causes of exchange fluctuations in the 'twenties were quite different from the causes of the later exchange movements, and the theories developed in the two periods were likewise different. Movements of exchange rates in the early 'twenties were largely an aftermath of the war. Postwar inflation had brought about marked disparities in the internal price levels of different countries, and the exchange-rate movements of this period were principally a reflection of

---

[28] One of the best descriptions of exchange-rate movements during the interwar period as a whole is in the League of Nations study previously cited. (*International Currency Experience: Lessons of the Interwar Period*, Ch. V). For an excellent account of the exchange situation in the early 'thirties, see Seymour E. Harris, *op. cit., passim.*

these price movements. Indeed, inflation and the resulting price differences played such a dominant part in the determination of exchange rates during this period that a distorted theory of exchange rates enjoyed wide popularity. This was the theory of purchasing power parity, which attributed changes in exchange rates entirely to relative movements of internal purchasing power.[29] Even at the height of its popularity, however, the parity theory was a target of severe criticism, and eventually it was almost completely discredited as an explanation of exchange rates.[30] There is no need, in a review such as this, to discuss the criticisms in detail. The inability of the parity theory to allow for shifts in international demand, for capital movements, for technological changes, or for any other events altering the terms of trade soon made it apparent that the theory was not a *general* explanation of exchange rates, but was applicable only under special conditions.[31] There were also other criticisms of a more technical nature, such as the difficulty of selecting an appropriate index of prices or costs, but these need not concern us here.

The movement away from the parity theory was accelerated in the early 'thirties, when the Great Depression forced most countries off the gold standard once more, and when exchange rates were subjected to influences which clearly could not be explained by price movements alone.[32] The balance-of-payments difficulties of the depression years were principally attributable to the fact that the depression did not affect the demand for all countries' exports uniformly. Although induced movements of real income tended, to some extent, to redress the balance, as described in the preceding section, these income movements did not effect a complete adjustment.

From the point of view of economic analysis, one of the most important results of the experience with fluctuating exchange rates during the 'thirties was a profound skepticism concerning the effectiveness of exchange-rate adjustments in rectifying a balance-of-payments discrepancy. This skepticism was partly a consequence of certain special conditions of the 'thirties which are not likely to be repeated in the future, but it was

---

[29] See Gustav Cassel, *Money and Foreign Exchange after 1914* (New York, 1922), pp. 137–186.

[30] One of the definitive accounts is that of C. Bresciani-Turroni, "The Purchasing Power Parity Doctrine," *L'Egypte Contemporaine*, 1934, pp. 433–464.

[31] Cf. Jacob Viner, *Studies in the Theory of International Trade*, pp. 379–387. In my opinion, the criticism of the parity doctrine went too far, and the theory was rejected even for situations in which it was valid. During the 'twenties, for example, disparities in price movements between countries were clearly the most important influences on exchange rates, and purchasing power parity was therefore a useful doctrine. See Lloyd A. Metzler, "Exchange Rates and the International Monetary Fund," in *Postwar Studies No. 8*, Board of Governors of the Federal Reserve System (Washington, 1947).

[32] See Seymour E. Harris, *op. cit., passim*, but especially Ch. IV.

also a consequence, as we shall see, of more fundamental difficulties with the balance-of-payments mechanism. Consider first the special conditions of the 'thirties.

The adjustment of exchange rates in the 'thirties was complicated both by large-scale speculative capital movements, which added to the instability of exchange rates, and by competitive devaluation, which reduced the effectiveness of depreciation for the deficit countries. Although these complications created serious doubts regarding the benefits of flexible exchange rates, neither of them presents an insurmountable obstacle to a flexible exchange system. Moreover, there are good reasons for supposing that such disturbing events, in the future, will be entirely prevented or at any rate greatly reduced. Under the Articles of Agreement of the International Monetary Fund the member countries have committed themselves, in effect, to submit the question of exchange-rate adjustments to international collaboration. Changes in the par value of a currency are to be made only when necessary to correct a fundamental disequilibrium,[33] and this presumably means that a member of the Fund will not be able to devalue its currency unless it has a persistent deficit in its balance of payments.[34]

If devaluation is limited to deficit countries, the degree of such devaluation will likewise be limited largely to the amounts needed to restore equilibrium, and will not be affected, to the extent that it has been in the past, by speculative capital transfers. During the war, and even before, comprehensive exchange controls were adopted throughout the world, and up to the present time most of these controls have been retained. While controls of foreign exchange received on current account will eventually be removed, under the Fund agreement, there is no commitment to remove controls of capital movements, and it is generally believed that such capital controls will continue in force. Indeed, under certain conditions the Fund itself may require a member country to adopt controls of capital exports.[35] It will be impossible, of course, to control or prevent every undesirable capital transfer, since some transfers can be disguised as export transactions. Nevertheless, the bootleg trans-

---

[33] Articles of Agreement of the International Monetary Fund, Article IV.

[34] See Ragnar Nurkse, *Conditions of International Monetary Equilibrium*, Princeton University, Essays in International Finance, No. 4 (Princeton, 1945); see also Gottfried Haberler, "Currency Depreciation and the International Monetary Fund," *Review of Economic Statistics*, November 1944, XXVI, pp. 178–181; and Alvin H. Hansen, "A Brief Note on 'Fundamental Disequilibrium,'" *ibid.*, November 1944, XXVI, pp. 182–184.

[35] Article VI, Section 1(a) of the Article of Agreement provides that "a member may not make net use of the Fund's resources to meet a large or sustained outflow of capital, and the Fund may request a member to exercise controls to prevent such use of the resources of the Fund."

fers which manage to evade control will clearly be much smaller and less disruptive than were the speculative capital transactions of the 'thirties.

THE STABILITY OF EXCHANGE MARKETS

Although some of the most troublesome features of the fluctuating exchange rates during the 'thirties can thus probably be prevented in the future, one fundamental problem remains to be discussed before concluding that exchange-rate adjustments are an effective way of balancing international payments and receipts. Even in the absence of speculative transactions there is some doubt as to whether currency depreciation, in the short run at least, can eliminate or reduce a deficit in a country's balance of payments. Exchange-rate movements affect the principal items in a country's balance of payments—exports and imports—primarily by altering the ratio of domestic to foreign prices, and if elasticities of demand are small, such relative price movements may be ineffective or may even affect the balance of payments adversely. In other words, the questions which were asked in an earlier section concerning the operation of the classical gold-standard mechanism under conditions of inelastic demand must be asked again with regard to fluctuating exchange rates.

In classical and neo-classical economics the possibility of exchange fluctuations having a perverse effect was seldom if ever discussed, but during the interwar period the question assumed increasing importance. Empirical investigations, on the one hand, revealed that price elasticities of demand were much smaller than had usually been assumed; and on the other hand, the experience of certain countries with depreciation, particularly producers of primary products, led these countries to doubt the effectiveness of this method of increasing the value of exports. The possibility that flexible exchange rates might be inherently unstable, a fall in the price of a currency increasing rather than reducing that country's deficit, was thus widely discussed, and an important contribution to the theory of exchange stability was gradually developed. Before considering the part played by individual economists in this development, however, a brief account will be given of the present status of the theory itself.

Stability of market exchange rates, like the stability of any price system, requires that a fall in the price of a particular currency shall reduce the excess supply of that country's currency on the foreign exchange markets, or that a rise in price shall reduce excess demand. A theory of exchange stability, based upon this principle, was developed during the interwar years, but the theory remains in a relatively elementary state. It is customary, and indeed necessary in the incomplete state of our knowledge, to discuss the effects of depreciation for the simplified case of two countries trading in only two commodities. Even with this simplification the theory of exchange stability, as it was worked out during the interwar period, remains somewhat complicated. Since most of the basic conclusions are simple, however, it seems better to state these conclusions in the form of a few categorical remarks than to present the cumbersome algebra. In what follows, the terms "exports" and "imports" will be understood to include all of the items in a country's foreign receipts and payments on current account.

If the demand for both exports and imports is inelastic, depreciation normally reduces a country's foreign-exchange receipts as well as its disbursements. The physical volume of exports is increased, of course, but the increase in volume does not compensate for the decline in foreign price, and the foreign-exchange value of exports accordingly declines. With respect to imports, both the physical volume and the foreign price decline to some extent, and depreciation thus reduces expenditures of foreign currency no matter how small the elasticity of import demand may be. The final effect upon a country's balance of payments therefore depends upon the magnitude of the decline in the foreign value of exports compared with the decline in the value of imports. The balance of payments will not be improved unless the value of imports falls more than the value of exports. While it is conceivable that this may occur even when the demand for both exports and imports is inelastic, it is not likely to occur if such elasticities are exceedingly small.

Most economists who have considered the problem of exchange stability have presented what might be called an "elasticity of the balance of payments." Consider only two countries, Y_1 and Y_2, and let η_1 and η_2 be the elasticities of demand for imports in the two countries. Similarly, let e_1 and e_2 be the elasticities of supply of exports. If the discrepancy between exports and imports is small, relative to the total value of foreign trade, it can easily be shown that a devaluation of the currency of either country in the proportion K will bring about a change, positive or negative, in that country's balance of payments on current account, which has the following value, relative to the value of exports:

$$K\left\{\frac{\eta_1\eta_2\left(1 + e_1 + e_2\right) + e_1e_2\left(\eta_1 + \eta_2 - 1\right)}{\left(\eta_1 + e_2\right)\left(\eta_2 + e_1\right)}\right\}$$

The foreign exchange market is obviously unstable unless the expression in brackets is positive, for exchange stability requires that depreciation must increase a country's net supply of foreign exchange. If the supply schedules of exports are positively sloped while the demand schedules for imports are negative, all of the elasticities of supply and demand in the above expression will be positive.[36] From this it follows that the elasticity of the trade balance cannot be negative unless $\eta_1 + \eta_2 - 1$ is negative and large. A sufficient condition for stability is thus that the sum of the two demand elasticities shall be greater than unity. Even if this sum is smaller than unity, the elasticity of the trade balance may still be positive if the supply elasticities, e_1 and e_2, are sufficiently small.

Since stability depends upon supply elasticities as well as demand elasticities, it may be useful to consider two limiting cases. First, if exports are produced under constant supply prices, as they are for many manufactured products, both e_1 and e_2 are infinite, and the elasticity of the balance of payment becomes $\eta_1 + \eta_2 - 1$. The minimum requirement for stability in this case is thus that the sum of the two demand elasticities shall exceed unity. At the other extreme, where the supply of exports is completely inelastic, as it is in the short run for certain agricultural products, the elasticity of the balance of payments is always positive and has a value of unity, regardless of the demand elasticities. Under such conditions, depreciation always improves a country's balance of payments no matter how inelastic the demands for imports may be.

The foregoing conclusions are the principal technical results of the interwar discussion of exchange stability. When we attempt to apply these results to actual problems and to form a judgment as to the effects of exchange-rate movements, we are confronted, unfortunately, with a serious lack of empirical evidence. Almost no information is available concerning supply elasticities, and estimates of demand elasticities are available only for a few countries. Nevertheless, such information as we do have indicates rather small demand elasticities—estimates of .5 for the United States and .64 for the United Kingdom have already been mentioned. If such elasticities are typical, we are forced to conclude, I believe, that fluctuations of exchange rates are not likely, in the short run at least, to bring about an appreciable improvement in a country's balance of payments. But perhaps this is too pessimistic. It is no doubt true that the demand for imports is frequently inelastic, but in the short run the same is true of the supply of exports, particularly of agricultural exports, and the theory of exchange stability discussed above has shown that inelastic export supplies may conceivably com-

---

[36] Demand elasticities are here defined, in the Marshallian manner, as $-\dfrac{dx}{dp} \cdot \dfrac{p}{x}$ whereas supply elasticities are defined as $\dfrac{dx}{dp} \cdot \dfrac{p}{x}$, without the change in sign.

pensate for the unfavorable effects of inelastic demand. Even if the reaction of the balance of payments is favorable to the depreciating country, however, it is likely to be small in magnitude. If the demand for imports is highly inelastic, as it normally is in the short run, the elasticity of the balance of payments will likewise be inelastic, unless the supply of exports is completely unresponsive to changes in price. A small change in the balance of payments, relative to the value of exports, may therefore require a very large proportionate change in exchange rates.

If we consider the problem over a longer period of time, the prospects for exchange depreciation are more promising. In the short run the demand for imports is inelastic primarily because both producers and consumers cannot rapidly adapt their purchasing habits or methods of production to a change in relative prices. In the long run, however, the possibilities of substitution between domestic and foreign products or raw materials is considerably greater. It seems probable, therefore, that the long-run elasticity of demand for imports in most countries is larger than the statistical evidence, based upon short-run conditions, would indicate. If a country with a balance-of-payments deficit depreciates its currency, a considerable improvement in its balance of payments may eventually occur, even though the immediate effects are small. During the interwar years, the long-run influences were for the most part nullified by competitive devaluation; hardly any of the deficit countries had an opportunity to test the effects of cheaper currency over a protracted period of time. The interwar experience therefore gave a somewhat distorted view of the effects of depreciation.

HISTORY OF THE STABILITY DISCUSSION

The foregoing account of exchange fluctuations and the balance of payments has been presented without any reference to the economists who were responsible for this line of thought. Actually, the conditions of exchange stability discussed above were discovered independently during the interwar period by three different economists. So far as I am aware, the correct conditions of exchange stability appeared first in the *Economic Journal* of 1920, in a brief and unfortunately neglected note by C. F. Bickerdike.[37] At the time the note was published, the pound sterling was an inconvertible currency. Currency controls which had been introduced during the war were removed in the early part of 1919, and as a result the dollar price of the pound sterling declined sharply,

---

[37] C. F. Bickerdike, "The Instability of Foreign Exchange," *Economic Journal*, March 1920, XXX, pp. 118–122.

from $4.76 in February of that year to $3.81 in December. A large part of this depreciation was attributable to the abnormal British demand for imports at the end of the war, and to the discrepancy which had developed during the war between the British and American price levels.[38] Nevertheless, the violence of the decline in the price of sterling led to a considerable amount of discussion in the United Kingdom as to whether free exchange markets for inconvertible currencies were not inherently unstable. In other words, the British began to doubt that currency depreciation would reduce the deficit in their balance of payments, and suspected, on the contrary, that such depreciation might only make the situation worse. Bickerdike's note was, to my knowledge, the first scientific expression of these doubts. Bickerdike derived a formula for the relation between depreciation and the balance of payments which was essentially the same as the one given above, and he then gave a pessimistic interpretation to his results:

With the prospect of inconvertible paper money in many countries for a considerable time, it is important to recognize that a high degree of instability of exchange rates is almost inevitable, and is not solely due to the continual increase of such money to which Governments have been obliged to resort. The question may be looked at from the point of view of very short periods, such as day to day, or rather short periods, such as a year, or over considerable periods of years. In each case a consideration of the circumstances leads to the conclusion that a high degree of instability is to be expected with inconvertible paper currencies.[39]

Bickerdike pointed out, as we have shown above, that in the short run the foreign and domestic elasticities of demand are likely to be small, and that modest balance-of-payments deficits may therefore produce violent changes in exchange rates. It is perhaps arguable, in this regard, that he did not attach sufficient importance to the stabilizing influence of inelastic short-run export supply. In any event, his work was largely forgotten after the postwar period of exchange fluctuations had ended, and the subject was not revived again until the 'thirties.

The second presentation of the theory of exchange stability was in Mrs. Robinson's well-known essay on the foreign exchanges, published in 1937 at the end of another period of fluctuating exchange rates.[40] Although Mrs. Robinson's method of presentation was somewhat different, her analytical results were the same as Bickerdike's, and she reached

---

[38] In 1919, the British wholesale price index stood at 242 (1913 = 100), compared with an index of 206 for the United States. (League of Nations, *Statistical Yearbook*.)
[39] C. F. Bickerdike, *op. cit.*, p. 118.
[40] Joan Robinson, "The Foreign Exchanges," in her *Essays in the Theory of Employment*, pp. 188–201.

similar conclusions. She placed more emphasis than had Bickerdike, however, on the stabilizing effects of low supply elasticities. She pointed out, for example, that the inelasticity of the Australian wool supply was an important factor in the benefit which that country derived from depreciation in 1931.

The third treatment of the subject of exchange stability was by A. J. Brown.[41] Except for a complication introduced by the presence of imported raw materials in exports,[42] Brown's analytical results were the same as those of Bickerdike and Mrs. Robinson. His interpretation of the results, however, was more optimistic. He argued, in particular, that the foreign elasticity of demand for British exports is likely to be high, since Britain is competing with other countries in these foreign markets, and depreciation would enable her to take customers away from her rivals. This is a question of considerable importance for the theory of exchange rates, and it is a question which, in my judgment, has not been satisfactorily answered. It is frequently said, by analogy with the theory of perfect competition, that a country which is small, or a country whose exports constitute a small part of the world market, can improve its balance of payments by means of depreciation, since the demand for this single country's products will normally be highly elastic.[43] From this it is then sometimes concluded that discussions of exchange stability which consider only two countries involve a pessimistic bias, and that if a world economy consisting of many countries were taken into account the probability of exchange stability would be appreciably greater.

Graham raised the same point in a slightly different way in two articles in the *Quarterly Journal of Economics.*[44] Although he did not state whether he was considering a system of flexible exchange rates or the classical gold-standard mechanism, his argument is applicable to either case, since he dealt with the barter or reciprocal-demand diagrams of neo-classical economics. He argued that the classical analysis in terms of two commodities and two countries exaggerated the instability of the terms of trade. With a wide variety of exports, or with several countries participating in trade, Graham believed that the terms of trade, or the exchange rates, would be confined within rather narrow

---

[41] A. J. Brown, "Trade Balances and Exchange Stability," *Oxford Economic Papers,* April 1942, No. 6, pp. 57–76.

[42] His treatment of raw materials contained an error. He argued that a high proportion of foreign raw materials in exports is a stabilizing factor. Although space does not permit a demonstration here, it can be shown that this is incorrect, and that the contrary is true.

[43] See, e.g., Seymour E. Harris, *op. cit.,* pp. 62–66.

[44] Frank D. Graham, "The Theory of International Values Re-examined," *Quarterly Journal of Economics,* November 1923, XXXVIII, pp. 54–86; *idem,* "The Theory of International Values," *ibid.,* August 1932, XLVI, pp. 581–616.

limits, through the substitution of the products of one country for those of another. In his own words, ". . . any alteration in the rate of interchange will affect the margin of comparative advantage of some country in the production of some one of the commodities concerned, will bring that country in as an exporter where formerly it was an importer, or as an importer where formerly it was an exporter, according as the terms of trade move one way or the other . . ."[45]

While these substitution effects on the supply side undoubtedly exert a stabilizing influence, it seems to me that Graham has overstated his case. The mere existence of a large number of trading countries or a large number of commodities will not stabilize the exchange markets unless there is a wide variation in cost conditions among the different countries. In other words, competition, by itself, is no guarantee of stability. Suppose, for example, that three countries, B, C, and D, were in close competition in the import market of A. The world demand for the products of any one of these countries would then be highly elastic; if B depreciated, for instance, she could thereby increase her exports to A at the expense of C and D. But this would involve a deterioration in the balances of payments of C and D which, in turn, would normally lead to exchange adjustments in these latter countries, and when all such secondary adjustments have been taken into account it is by no means clear that the initial depreciation by B would have reduced the deficit in that country's balance of payments. In order that substitution between products shall stabilize the exchange markets, it is not only necessary that B, C, and D shall be in close competition in A, but also that A shall be in close competition with at least one of these countries in the markets of a third country.

Graham was well aware of this fact, but he believed that the type of "linked" competition which he postulated in his numerical examples was fairly common in the actual world. In other words, he felt that a number of countries would always change from exporters to importers of particular commodities with slight movements in the terms of trade. With the world divided as it has been in the past between exporters of raw materials and exporters of manufactures, Graham's supposition of continuous variation seems to me too optimistic. Indeed, our experience during the Great Depression has shown that enormous deterioration can occur in the terms of trade of an agricultural country without materially altering the character of that country's exports or imports. The substitution effects which Graham discusses are thus slow to occur and frequently do not take place rapidly enough to offset the adverse effects of low

---

[45] *Idem*, "The Theory of International Values Re-examined," *loc. cit.*, p. 86.

elasticities of demand.[46] In the short run therefore, and perhaps even over periods of time as long as five to ten years, low elasticities of demand may be a serious source of instability in foreign-exchange markets, even with a large number of countries competing in world markets.

ADJUSTMENT OF EXCHANGE RATES IN THE FUTURE

Both the interwar experience with fluctuating exchange rates and the theory of exchange stability which emerged during the interwar years have clearly shown that adjustments of exchange rates are not likely, in the short run, to be an efficient or effective means of eliminating a deficit or a surplus from a country's balance of payments. If the demand for imports is inelastic, as it appears to be in many countries, currency depreciation may have an insignificant or even a perverse effect upon a country's balance of payments. Considering the low price elasticities which have been found in most empirical studies of demand, it seems probable that depreciation, in the short run, cannot improve a country's trade balance unless the inelastic demand for imports is matched by a correspondingly inelastic supply of exports. Even in this case the elasticity of the trade balance will probably be small, and a substantial movement of exchange rates may therefore be required to eliminate rather modest deficits. In other words, over comparatively short periods of time, movements of exchange rates are not an efficient means of allocating resources between foreign and domestic use.

This fact became increasingly apparent in both theory and practice during the interwar years, and it has now been explicitly recognized in the plans and institutions which have been developed for international trade in the future. Under the Articles of Agreement of the International Monetary Fund, exchange rates are stabilized, and exchange adjustments are to be made only occasionally in response to a fundamental disequilibrium in a country's balance of payments. In the short run, deficits are to be met by the use of foreign balances or, under the proposed International Trade Organization,[47] by the direct control of imports. While this procedure is clearly more realistic than some of the earlier proposals for a flexible exchange system, there is a danger that in recognizing the limitations of exchange adjustments we shall overlook their benefits. In the long run, when time has been allowed for the sub-

---

[46] In his second article, Graham recognized this possibility and conceded that the classical reciprocal demand equations, for the short run, might have considerable validity.

[47] Havana Charter for an International Trade Organization, United Nations Conference on Trade and Employment, held at Havana, Cuba, November 21, 1947 to March 24, 1948. *Final Act and Related Documents* (Havana, 1948), Articles 13, 14, 15, and 23.

stitution of one method of production for another, and when consumers have had an opportunity to adjust their spending to a change in relative prices at home and abroad, demand elasticities for imports will obviously be considerably greater than the elasticities computed for the interwar period. Movements of exchange rates are therefore likely to have a significant ultimate effect upon a country's balance of payments even though the immediate effects are small. The problem which confronts us today is how to preserve the long-run position of exchange adjustments while frankly recognizing the short-run limitations. To solve this problem, we must prevent the direct controls, which may be necessary in the short run, from becoming frozen into a permanent system of trade regulations.

IV. Price Theory and International Trade

Among economists, the interwar period will no doubt be remembered most vividly as the period of the Great Depression and the closely related revolution in the theory of employment. Even without the Keynesian revolution, however, the period would have been one of extraordinary growth in economics, particularly in the field of general price theory; several important discoveries were made, during the interwar years, in such diverse subjects as the theory of consumer's choice, the theory of production, and the theory of monopoly and competition. Since price theory, or the theory of value, has always been intimately associated with international economics, it was not surprising that many of the innovations in price theory were eventually applied to the special problems of international trade. The classical theory of the international price system was thus somewhat modified and modernized. Despite these modifications, however, many of the conclusions which the English economists had reached with more antiquated equipment remained essentially unchanged. Because of space limitations, it is impossible to consider all of the recent changes in the theory of international prices. The following discussion is therefore limited to the innovations in three broad fields, the theory of demand, the theory of production, and the theory of general equilibrium.

THE THEORY OF DEMAND AND THE GAINS
FROM INTERNATIONAL TRADE

The theory of demand, or the theory of consumer's choice, enters into international economics primarily in the discussion of the gains from international trade. In the classical theory, the benefit which a country derived from specialization and trade was measured by the difference between the international rate of exchange of commodities and the rate which would have prevailed in the absence of international trade.[48] In other words, the gain from trade was an objective quantity, indicating the saving in resources from specializing and trading rather than producing all commodities at home. One of Mill's great achievements, of course, was to show how the gain from trade, thus measured, is determined by conditions of demand both at home and abroad.[49] Although Mill did not go beyond this conception, and did not attempt to relate his demand schedules to underlying utilities, he was nevertheless able to reach conclusions with respect to commercial policy which require very little modification even today. It remained for Marshall to apply the utility concept to international demand, and to measure the gain from trade by means of his well-known theory of producer's and consumer's surpluses.[50] This refinement, however, was not revolutionary, for Marshall's conclusions tended, in the main, to confirm those of Mill. Subsequent developments with regard to demand theory consisted principally of discarding the concept of measurable utility and substituting ratios of marginal utilities. With this innovation, attempts to measure the total gains from trade by means of Marshall's consumer's and producer's surpluses were discarded, but once more the fundamental principles remained largely intact. Prior to the interwar period, the principal modifications of the classical concept of "gains from trade" thus consisted primarily in changes in the theory of demand. On the side of production, the labor theory of value, although largely discredited in general price theory, continued to be employed in the theory of international trade.[51]

Although Bastable had earlier altered the classical theory of production to some extent by introducing diminishing returns into his theory of international trade,[52] perhaps the principal innovation in this regard was made by Haberler, who employed a production substitution curve to indicate the possible combinations of quantities of two goods which could be produced with given quantities of the factors of production. This curve was defined in such a way that its slope at any given point represented the

---

[48] See David Ricardo, The Principles of Political Economy and Taxation, Gonner, ed. (London, 1891), Ch. VII.

[49] John Stuart Mill, Essays on Some Unsettled Questions of Political Economy, 3rd ed. (London, 1877), pp. 1-21.

[50] Alfred Marshall, Money, Credit and Commerce (London, 1923), Appendix J.

[51] See, e.g., F. Y. Edgeworth, Papers Relating to Political Economy, Vol. II (London, 1925), pp. 42-45; also F. W. Taussig, International Economics (New York, 1928), Part I.

[52] C. F. Bastable, The Theory of International Trade, 4th ed. (London, 1903), pp. 29-30,

ratio of the marginal costs of the two products.[53] Haberler then demonstrated that the gains from international trade could be indicated, if not measured, by means of his production substitution curves. Leontief later made this idea more precise by combining the production substitution curve with a system of indifference curves.[54]

The principal advantages of the new approach, as Haberler pointed out, were, first, that it dispensed with the labor cost or real cost theory of value and, second, that it enabled one to consider a number of different factors of production simultaneously. Viner, however, argued that these advantages were illusory, and that the substitution curve concealed a number of important problems. In particular, he attacked the assumption of a fixed quantity of factors of production which is implied in the substitution curve. He insisted that the substitution curve could not be accepted as a fixed curve, determined by technological conditions, because the amount of each of the factors of production was not fixed but depended upon its price. The latter, in turn, was influenced by international trade.[55] In short, Viner argued that if the supply of the factors of production can be varied, the "real cost" of supplying such services must be taken into account along with the utility of commodities, in measuring the gains from trade. A similar objection was raised with regard to the use of indifference curves, but this is an older argument and is perhaps a less distinctive contribution of Viner than his discussion of real costs. The essence of the argument is that indifference curves for a country as a whole depend not only upon the amounts of the commodities but upon their distribution between different individuals, and since international trade affects the distribution of income it also produces a shift in the community indifference curves.

Considering these logical flaws in the theory of international trade, it is natural to inquire what remains of the concept of gains from international trade. If the assumption of fixed quantities of resources is rejected, and if it is impossible to derive meaningful indifference curves for a country as a whole, in what sense can we say that international trade contributes to welfare? Answers to these questions were given in 1939 by Samuelson, who demonstrated that even without the restrictive classical and neo-classical assumptions international trade involves a potential, if not an actual, economic gain to all participating countries.[56] Samuel-

[53] Gottfried Haberler, *The Theory of International Trade* (New York, 1936), pp. 175–182.

[54] W. W. Leontief, "The Use of Indifference Curves in the Analysis of Foreign Trade," *Quarterly Journal of Economics*, May 1933, XLVII, pp. 493–503.

[55] Jacob Viner, *Studies in the Theory of International Trade*, pp. 516–526.

[56] Paul A. Samuelson, "The Gains from International Trade," *The Canadian Journal of Economics and Political Science*, May 1939, V, pp. 195–205.

son's argument consisted essentially in proving that, if trade is opened between countries, each country, if it chooses to do so, can obtain more of every commodity while performing less of every productive service. Although no objective measure can be given for the total gain, in this case, it is nevertheless clear that an increase of the quantity of every commodity and a decrease in the amount of every type of work performed represents an improvement of welfare. In this sense, international trade involves a gain for all countries. Samuelson was careful to point out that his demonstration did not imply that completely unrestricted trade is the optimum position for all countries. His argument, on the contrary, was restricted to the proposition that some degree of trade, *however restricted or unrestricted it may be,* is necessarily better for all countries than no trade at all.[57] The modern conception of the gains from trade thus provides no answer to the problem of free trade vs. protection. It simply shows that protection, if carried to the point where all trade is eliminated, will reduce welfare, compared with any intermediate position.

INTERNATIONAL TRADE AND THE DISTRIBUTION
OF INCOME

We have argued above that new developments in price theory have refined but have not fundamentally altered the classical concept of the gains from international trade. In one respect, however, the application of innovations in price theory to the special problems of international trade has been more revolutionary. Although the classical theory gave a good explanation of the gains which international trade brings to a country as a whole, the traditional theory was never able to explain adequately how these gains are distributed between different factors of production or between different industrial groups. In other words, the classical theory could not explain the relation of international trade to the distribution of income. The clarification of this relation during the interwar period was therefore a major achievement in international economics.

It can hardly be said that the classical economists were entirely unaware of the influence which foreign trade can exert upon the distribution of a country's income. The later development of the classical theory itself was to a considerable extent an outgrowth of the controversy in England over the Corn Laws, and one of the principal issues in this controversy was the conflict of interests between owners of agricultural

---

[57] In a reflective and perhaps nostalgic mood, an economist once remarked that the argument over whether some trade is necessarily better than no trade at all reminded him of a favorite cliché of his college days: "Prohibition is better than no liquor at all."

land and industrialists. With the help of the Ricardian theory of rent, the English economists of the nineteenth century were able to show clearly that tariff reductions in a country (such as England) importing agricultural products could reduce the landowners' share of the national income.[58] But despite their insight into this particular problem, they never succeeded in integrating their international economics with a general theory of distribution. This is hardly surprising, for until Clark, Marshall, Wicksteed and others had generalized the Ricardian law of diminishing returns into a law of variable proportions for all factors of production, no completely general theory of distribution was available.[59] Even after the theory of distribution had been discovered there was a considerable lag in applying it to international problems, and the theory of distribution did not become a systematic part of international economics until the interwar period of the present century.[60]

The pioneer work was a Swedish essay of 1919 by Heckscher.[61] Because of language difficulties, this essay was generally neglected by English and American economists, but it is now recognized as one of the first contributions to an important development in international economics. Heckscher's contribution consists essentially in explaining the flow of international trade in terms of the relative scarcity or abundance of different factors of production. The classical economists had explained the flow of trade by means of their law of comparative advantage, but the fact of comparative advantage itself had been accepted more or less without explanation. By using the generalized theory of production—the doctrine of marginal productivity—Heckscher was able to show that in many instances the advantage which a country enjoys in the production of a particular commodity is attributable to a large supply, relative to other countries, of the factor or factors of production which are most important in that commodity. In other words, if Country A has more land per laborer than Country B, rents, relative to wages, will be lower in the former country than in the latter. Country A will therefore have a

---

[58] J. S. Mill, *Principles of Political Economy*, Book V, Ch. IV, Sec. 5.

[59] George J. Stigler, *Production and Distribution Theories* (New York, 1941), *passim*, but especially Ch. I.

[60] In his *Theory of International Trade* (Dublin, 1887), C. F. Bastable had included a chapter on "The Influence of Foreign Trade on the Internal Distribution of Wealth," but his discussion did not go much beyond that of the classical economists. Cf. also Simon N. Patten, *The Economic Basis of Protection* (Philadelphia, 1890), Ch. V.

[61] Eli F. Heckscher, "Utrikhandelns verkan på inkomstfördelningen," *Ekonomisk Tidskrift*, 1919, Del II, pp. 1–32. Among English-speaking economists, this work has been known largely through the writings of Bertil Ohlin. Fortunately, we are soon to have an English version of Heckscher's paper, translated from the Swedish by Professor and Mrs. Svend Laursen, in *Readings in the Theory of International Trade*, to be published under the auspices of the American Economic Association.

comparative advantage in wheat and other products requiring much land and little labor, while Country B has a comparative advantage in manufactures. Although this proposition may now seem self-evident, it nevertheless represented a major improvement in the theory of international trade, for it opened the door to a systematic treatment of the relation between international trade and the distribution of income within a single country. Thus, by demonstrating how international trade increases the demand for the factors of production which a country has in relative abundance, while reducing the demand for its relatively scarce factors, Heckscher also showed that international trade has a tendency to equalize the *relative* returns to land, labor, and capital, throughout the world. The full significance of this conclusion will become apparent in our later discussion of the theory of tariffs.

Heckscher's analysis concerning the relation of comparative advantage to relative quantities of the factors of production, and his conclusion that international trade has an equalizing tendency upon relative factor prices, later became the basis for the well-known treatise of Ohlin.[62] Ohlin modified and refined the Heckscher theories in several respects. Among other things, he considered the possibility that a change in relative factor prices, brought about by international trade, might eventually alter the available supply of some of these factors.[63] He also took account of the complications which arise when more than two factors of production are considered, and when relations of complementarity exist among some of the factors.[64] Apart from such complications, however, Ohlin's conclusions were in substantial agreement with those of Heckscher.

GENERAL EQUILIBRIUM

To complete our discussion of price theory and international trade, a word should be said about two studies in the field of general equilibrium. The classical theory, in its rigorous form, dealt only with the problem of two countries trading in two commodities, and subsequent revisions or refinements of the classical theory have seldom gone beyond this simple framework. Even the work of Ohlin, which is sometimes considered as a more general approach, is best understood in the classical context; i.e., the Heckscher-Ohlin conclusions can be most clearly stated and most rigorously demonstrated if the theoretical scheme is limited to two countries, two commodities, and two factors of production. The only rigorous attempts, so far as I am aware, to develop a completely gen-

[62] Bertil Ohlin, *Interregional and International Trade* (Cambridge, Mass., 1933).
[63] *Ibid.*, Ch. VII.
[64] *Ibid.*, pp. 97–99.

eral approach to international economics, are the studies by Yntema[65] and Mosak.[66] Yntema's work appeared in 1932, and the work of Mosak, which the latter regards as a sequel to Yntema's book, was published twelve years later.

Except for their greater degree of generality, both of these books adopted a distinctly classical point of view, and in the main their conclusions confirmed the classical reasoning. Like the classical economists, Yntema and Mosak were interested primarily in the effects of international disturbances, such as tariffs and indemnity payments, upon relative prices at home and abroad. Apart from a final chapter in Mosak's book, little attention was paid in either book to the influence of international trade on the level of output. In at least one respect, however, both books have gone considerably beyond the classical theory: both authors have shown that a study of dynamic economics, of stable and unstable market systems, can be extremely useful in the field of international trade, particularly in complex problems involving a large number of countries and a large number of commodities.

Yntema's study of dynamic problems was necessarily elementary, since he was writing at a time when little was known about the stability of market systems. Nevertheless, he carried the discussion of stable and unstable international markets beyond the pioneer stage at which Marshall had left it,[67] and in Chapter V of his book he adopted a method which was surprisingly similar to the dynamic approach which Hicks later presented in *Value and Capital*. He argued, for example, that a money payment from Country 2 to Country 1 would normally increase money prices and costs in the latter and reduce them in the former, essentially through the operation of the quantity theory of money. In studying the static equations of supply and demand, he therefore suggested that any shapes of these functions, such as extremely inelastic demands, which indicated that a money payment would *reduce* prices in the receiving country and raise them in the paying country could be rejected as fundamentally unstable.[68] Here, in a book published in 1931, is the germ of the Hicksian concept of imperfect stability. Elementary and incomplete as it was, Yntema's conception of the relation between dynamics and statics was nevertheless prophetic of the work to be done later in the field of general price theory.

[65] Theodore O. Yntema, *A Mathematical Reformulation of the General Theory of International Trade* (Chicago, 1932).

[66] Jacob L. Mosak, *General-Equilibrium Theory in International Trade* (Bloomington, 1944).

[67] Cf. Alfred Marshall, *op. cit.*, Appendix J.

[68] Theodore O. Yntema, *op. cit.*, p. 80.

Mosak began his study of general equilibrium where Yntema had ended, and in several respects he advanced the theory of international trade beyond the stage at which Yntema had left it. Perhaps most important, Mosak took account of the effects of shifts in purchasing power, such as those associated with indemnity payments, on the demand for internationally traded goods. Yntema had neglected such income effects, and in this respect his system was even more classical than that of many of the classical economists. Except for Chapter IX of his book, Mosak dealt with a system in which incomes were entirely expended on commodities, either foreign or domestic. For this reason, the "balance-of-payments problem," as such, did not enter explicitly into most of his work; equality between supply and demand in all commodity markets in Mosak's system, implies equilibrium in the foreign exchange markets. He made a sweeping application of Hicks' concepts of perfect and imperfect stability to the special problems of international trade, but his conclusions in this regard are vitiated to some extent by the fact that the Hicks conditions are not true stability conditions except under special circumstances.[69]

It is extremely difficult, in a review such as this, to evaluate the position or importance of the two general-equilibrium studies in the body of international economics as a whole. Unlike the classical theory, the more general approaches to international economics have not had a profound influence upon economic policy. To some extent this is probably attributable to their complexity—to the fact that the general solutions admit many different possible consequences of a given policy. To some extent, also, it may be a result of the fact that the more general theories have not, on the whole, revealed any serious flaws in the classical position. Both Yntema and Mosak discuss the classical theories as special cases of their more general theories, and their results tend largely to confirm the classical reasoning.[70]

V. The Theory of Tariffs

The preceding account of the relations between price theory and international economics has considered only the logical development of the theory, and no attempt has been made to relate this development to problems of economic policy. For this reason, the discussion above probably has an unrealistic and abstract quality which belies the true nature of the

---

[69] See Paul A. Samuelson, "The Stability of Equilibrium: Comparative Statics and Dynamics," *Econometrica*, April 1941, IX, pp. 97-120; and Lloyd A. Metzler, "Stability of Multiple Markets: the Hicks Conditions," *ibid.*, October 1945, XIII, pp. 277-292.

[70] Theodore O. Yntema, *op. cit.*, pp. 80-87; Jacob L. Mosak, *op. cit.*, Ch. IV.

classical tradition. In the actual course of its growth, the accepted theory of international trade was intimately connected with highly controversial questions of policy. Indeed, almost all of the major contributions to the theory of international trade were a direct outgrowth of practical economic issues. During the nineteenth century, foreign trade policy was for the most part synonymous with tariff policy, and the theory of tariffs accordingly occupies a prominent place in the classical economics. Even during the interwar period of the twentieth century, when other methods of trade control such as import quotas, exchange controls, etc., were widely adopted, tariffs continued to occupy an important place in the commercial policies of many countries. It seems appropriate, therefore, to conclude this review with a brief discussion of some recent changes in the theory of tariffs.

The tariff literature is perhaps as voluminous as that of any branch of applied economics, but fortunately it will not be necessary to make a detailed study of all the books, articles, and pamphlets dealing with this subject. Much of the writing about tariffs is concerned with problems of politics, ethics, or administration, and all of these questions, however important they may be, are outside the scope of the present review. With regard to the purely economic issues, recent developments in the theory of tariffs may be grouped under three main heads: (1) tariffs and the terms of trade; (2) tariffs and the distribution of income; (3) commercial policy and the revival of mercantilism. Each of these will be considered in turn.

TARIFFS AND THE TERMS OF TRADE

Events of the interwar period led to a notable revival of interest in tariffs regarded as bargaining weapons. The Reciprocal Trade Agreements program in the United States, the new tariff policy of the United Kingdom, and tariff increases in other countries all emphasized once more the monopolistic character of tariff restrictions, and the effects of tariffs on the terms of trade. A number of economists dealt with these problems, but perhaps the outstanding contributions were those of Samuelson,[71] Kaldor,[72] Benham,[73] and Scitovszky.[74] The outcome of the discussion was to demonstrate, anew, the shaky foundation of some of the arguments for free trade. Samuelson, for example, pointed out that tariffs

---

[71] Paul A. Samuelson, "Welfare Economics and International Trade," *American Economic Review*, June 1938, XXVIII, pp. 261–266.

[72] Nicholas Kaldor, "A Note on Tariffs and the Terms of Trade," *Economica*, November 1940, New Series VII, pp. 377–380.

[73] Frederic Benham, "The Terms of Trade," *ibid.*, pp. 360–376.

[74] Tibor de Scitovszky, "A Reconsideration of the Theory of Tariffs," *Review of Economic Studies*, Summer 1942, IX, pp. 89–110.

or other trade restrictions, if they improve the terms of trade and increase the welfare of the country imposing them, will do so by worsening the position of some other country. Since the gains of one country cannot be measured against the losses to another, there is no presumption that trade restrictions always reduce welfare for the world as a whole. Scitovszky carried this point of view further by showing that a tariff in one country increases the probability that retaliation will prove profitable to other countries. He thus developed a theory of tariff retaliation which depicted each country as raising tariffs in a rational manner in order to secure for itself a more favorable position in world markets. Although each country separately might gain, in Scitovszky's view, by a moderate increase in tariffs, the effect of all countries following the same policy would be to reduce the welfare of each of them. In the end, therefore, Scitovszky believed tariff retaliation would lead either to bilateral barter deals or to some form of tariff bargaining. Since each country may have a rational interest in higher tariffs, quite apart from the pressure of special groups within the country, Scitovszky emphasized that a free-trade system, like a cartel, has a natural tendency to disintegrate, and must be enforced by some kind of international convention.

The general effect of the work by Samuelson, Scitovszky, and others was to call attention to the similarity between the theory of tariffs and the theory of monopoly. An individual country, under certain conditions, can gain by limiting trade with other countries, just as a monopolist can gain by restricting the supply of the monopolized product. The rational argument against tariffs is not, as free-traders sometimes suppose, that tariffs harm all countries, but that, like monopoly restrictions, they impose a loss on some countries which is greater than the gain to the country imposing them. In modern terminology, we would say, following Lerner, that tariffs result in an inefficient allocation of resources, since the price ratios between commodities differ from one country to another.[75]

TARIFFS AND THE TERMS OF TRADE: THE CLASSICAL VIEW

What relation does this recent work have to the general literature on the theory of tariffs? Perhaps most important, the new contributions to tariff theory correct a misconception which has long been common among advocates of free trade. In popular discussions, and even among some professional economists, the classical theory of comparative advantage has frequently been presented as a proof that all countries gain, individually, by a policy of unrestricted commerce. When the monopolistic character of tariffs and other impediments to trade is considered, however, it

[75] Abba P. Lerner, *The Economics of Control* (New York, 1944), pp. 356–362.

is obvious that this popular view is incorrect. Tariffs do not always involve a decline in the welfare of all countries, but may involve a loss in some countries and a gain in others. The importance of this misconception regarding tariffs, and the tendency to disregard the influence of tariffs on the terms of trade, are well illustrated by the following quotations from a report on tariffs prepared in 1930 by a distinguished committee of British economists:

As a matter of history, the assertion that the advantages of Free Trade depend upon its being mutual, has always been made by people who were attacking Free Trade. It has never been made by any of the principal advocates of Free Trade. For this there is a simple reason. It represents complete misunderstanding of the nature of international trade and the working of tariffs.

International trade is never free of all obstacles. The argument of the Free Traders has been directed to making the obstacles as few as possible. The gain through removing one obstacle depends in no way at all upon the removal of all the other obstacles or any of them.

. . . For other countries to tax our exports to them is an injury to us and an obstacle to trade. For us to tax their exports to us is not a correction of that injury; it is just a separate additional obstacle to trade.[76]

In the light of recent tariff discussions, statements such as these obviously need to be made more cautiously and with more reservations. As a practical matter it may well be true that actual tariffs have been so high as to inflict injury upon all parties, but there is no presumption, from the law of comparative advantage, that this will always be true. The arguments for retaliation are stronger than the literature on free trade would lead one to suppose.

Although the recent contributions to the theory of tariffs have made an important correction in free trade arguments such as those above, it would be a mistake to suppose that the modern view represents a pronounced divergence from the classical theory. The English economists of the nineteenth century, while they did not perhaps give the point sufficient emphasis, were fully aware of the favorable effects which a tariff may have upon a country's terms of trade.[77] Indeed, one of the primary purposes of Mill's profound work in international trade was to show how tariffs and other obstacles to trade affect the ratio of interchange between exports and imports. As Taussig has shown,[78] Mill probably drew too sharp a distinction between revenue duties and protective duties, but

---

[76] Sir William Beveridge et al., *Tariffs: The Case Examined* (London, 1931), pp. 108–110.
[77] Cf. Marion C. Samuelson, "The Australian Case for Protection Reexamined," *Quarterly Journal of Economics*, November 1939, LIV, pp. 147–148.
[78] F. W. Taussig, *International Trade*, p. 146.

with regard to revenue duties he, Mill, never had any misconceptions about the benefits which a single country could derive, at the expense of its neighbors, from imposing such duties. The following quotation, if any is necessary, should make this obvious:

A country cannot be expected to renounce the power of taxing foreigners, unless foreigners will in return practice toward itself [sic] the same forbearance. The only mode in which a country can save itself from being a loser by the duties imposed by other countries on its commodities, is to impose corresponding duties on theirs.[79]

Marshall,[80] Edgeworth,[81] and Taussig[82] were likewise untouched by the error of the free-traders. All of these economists recognized the possible gains which a country may achieve by means of tariffs. Marshall, however, felt that as a practical matter the terms-of-trade argument for tariffs was not of great importance. In the first place, he doubted whether any single country in the modern industrial world was of sufficient importance to have an appreciable effect on the terms of trade. Second, his observations, particularly in the United States, led him to the conclusion that the pressure of special interests usually forces tariff rates far above the optimal level, so that the country imposing such tariffs, as well as the rest of the world, is likely to lose.[83]

Space limitations forbid any further elaboration of this theme. The point to be emphasized is the continuity between the classical theory and the recent discussions of the relation of tariff to the gains from trade. By utilizing modern price theory, contemporary economists have given a more precise statement of the possible gains and losses from tariffs, and they have indicated, perhaps more accurately than before, the limits to a rational tariff policy; but they have not altered the fundamental principles as developed by Mill, Marshall, Edgeworth, and Taussig. Further elaboration was needed, not because the classical view was incorrect, but because it was not given sufficient emphasis, and, as a consequence, was later misinterpreted by advocates of free trade.

TARIFFS AND THE DISTRIBUTION OF INCOME

The preceding discussion has been concerned primarily with the effects of tariffs on the distribution of world income between countries.

---

[79] John Stuart Mill, *Essays on Some Unsettled Questions of Political Economy*, p. 29.
[80] Alfred Marshall, *Money, Credit and Commerce*, Appendix J and Ch. VIII–X.
[81] F. Y. Edgeworth, *op. cit.*, Vol. II, Sec. IV.
[82] F. W. Taussig, *International Trade*, Ch. XIII.
[83] It is interesting to note, also, the similar remark of Edgeworth on this point: ". . . protection might procure economic advantage in certain cases, if there was a Government wise enough to discriminate those cases, and strong enough to confine itself to them; but this condition is very unlikely to be fulfilled." Edgeworth, *op. cit.*, Vol. II, p. 18.

An equally important problem, and one which was never satisfactorily solved by the classical economists, concerns the effects of tariffs upon the distribution of income within a single country. Even though a country has no monopolistic position in world markets and cannot gain a larger share of the world's income by restricting trade, it may nevertheless be true that a particular class or group within the country would be benefited by a tariff. This question of income distribution has been a central issue in almost all tariff controversies. In the United States, it took the form of an assertion that tariffs on manufactures protect or raise the real wages of workers. In the United Kingdom the issue appeared in the familiar conflict between landlords and manufacturers over the effects of the Corn Laws on agricultural rents and real wages. More recently, the question arose again in a report on the Australian tariff which was prepared in 1929 by a distinguished group of Australian economists.[84] The outstanding feature of this report was that it gave qualified support to the tariff as a permanent part of Australia's commercial policy. Although the terms-of-trade argument played some part in the conclusion of the Australian economists, their principal reason for favoring protection was the belief that tariffs maintained a better distribution of income between landlords and workers than would otherwise have been possible. A tariff reduction, according to the report, would reduce the Australian output of manufactured goods and increase the output of the principal export goods, wool and wheat. And since wages are normally a much greater proportion of the value of manufactures than of the value of agricultural products, the effects of this shift in the composition of Australian production would be to increase the demand for land and reduce the demand for labor. Workers would accordingly receive a smaller proportion of the national income than under protection, even if labor were perfectly mobile between agriculture and industry.[85]

The Australian report, as well as the tariff controversies in the United States, the United Kingdom, and other countries, have all emphasized the influence of tariffs on the distribution of income. In this particular branch of economic policy, however, economic theory, until recently, has had little to contribute. As noted earlier, the classical economists, with their over-simplified theory of production, were unable to cope with the

[84] *The Australian Tariff, an Economic Enquiry*, a report prepared for the Commonwealth Government by J. B. Brigden, D. B. Copland, E. C. Dyason, L. F. Giblin, and C. H. Wickens (Melbourne, 1929).

[85] Thus, on p. 5 the report states: "The tariff has had the effect of pooling the national income to a greater extent than would have been practicable if assistance to industry were derived solely through the more obvious method of taxation. Employment has been subsidized at the expense of land values, enabling the standard of living to be maintained with a rapidly increasing population."

problem.[86] They realized, of course, that protection benefits the producers of particular commodities, and that factors of production which are specific to these protected industries will likewise gain from tariffs. But if labor and capital are mobile, and the standard wage rate tends to equality in all industries, the traditional theory of international economics cannot show how tariffs affect the distribution of income between such broad categories as "labor," "capital," and "land." In the absence of a theory of production which recognized the substitution of one factor for another, there was a tendency to assume that the reward of each of the factors depended upon the productivity of the entire economy, and to conclude that foreign trade, which increases the effectiveness of the economy as a whole, must also increase the rewards to each of the factors separately.[87]

Although widely held, this view was by no means universal even among followers of the classical tradition. As early as 1906, for example, Pigou had pointed out that a tariff increases the output of one industry, A, at the expense of another industry, B, and that if one factor of production plays a more important part in A than in B, the change in the composition of the national income will increase the proportion of the total product accruing to that factor.[88] Moreover, even if the tariff reduces the national real income as a whole, Pigou argued that the absolute position of the favored factor might be improved. "The increase per cent in the share of the dividend obtained by the favored factor might exceed the shrinkage per cent of the dividend itself."[89] Viner and Ohlin later expressed similar views, although the latter regarded it as unlikely that the *absolute* as well as the *relative* returns to the favored factor would be increased by protection.[90] Thus during the interwar years there seems to have been agreement that tariffs tend to increase the relative share of the national income accruing to certain factors of production, but there were doubts as to whether the *absolute* returns to the favored factors are also increased. If protection went so far as to reduce real income as a whole, it was believed that the absolute returns to the favored factors might conceivably be reduced even though their relative share in total income was increased. In other words, economists were still uncertain about the effects of protection upon the real income of certain factors, even though

[86] This is perhaps a slight exaggeration, for the classical economists had a great deal to say about the effects of the Corn Laws on agricultural rents. See, e.g., three letters of Colonel Robert Torrens to the Marquis of Chandos (London, 1839).

[87] See, e.g., F. W. Taussig, "How the Tariff Affects Wages," in *Free Trade, the Tariff and Reciprocity* (New York, 1920), p. 59.

[88] A. C. Pigou, *Protective and Preferential Import Duties* (London, 1906), p. 58.

[89] *Ibid.*, p. 59.

[90] Jacob Viner, *Studies in the Theory of International Trade*, pp. 533–534; Bertil Ohlin, *Interregional and International Trade*, p. 44.

they were agreed that such protection would probably increase the *proportion* of the national income accruing to the favored factors of production.

Much of this uncertainty was eliminated in 1941 in a paper by Stolper and Samuelson which presented a remarkable application of the Heckscher-Ohlin system to the special problem of tariffs.[91] The paper demonstrated that, regardless of its effects on the term of trade and real income as a whole, protection, unless followed by retaliation, always increases the real return as well as the relative share in the total product of the factor of production which is relatively most important in the protected industries. Suppose, for example, that a country has two industries, clothing and food, and two factors of production, labor and capital. Suppose further that labor is more important in the production of clothing than in the food industry, and that the country is an importer of clothing. A tariff on clothing will then increase production in that industry and shift both capital and labor from agriculture to manufacturing. According to the Stolper-Samuelson argument, this shift of resources will necessarily reduce the proportion of labor to capital in both industries. In other words, the food industry, where a comparatively small amount of labor is employed, cannot supply enough labor to maintain the old labor-capital ratio in the clothing industry without creating a disparity between the marginal productivities, and consequently the wage rates, in the two industries. Now if the ratio of labor to capital is reduced in both industries, it follows from the law of variable proportions that the marginal product of labor, and hence the real wage rate, must be higher than before, regardless of whether real wages are measured in terms of the protected commodity, clothing, or the unsheltered commodity, food. Thus if protection increases the money price of clothing, it must increase the money wage rate even more. The real return to the second factor, capital, is *reduced,* compared with the free-trade position, for the shift in the composition of output brought about by the tariff makes capital a more abundant factor in both industries. And since the quantities of the factors are assumed to be unaffected by the tariff, it is clear that the tariff has increased the relative as well as the absolute returns to labor, and has reduced both the relative and absolute returns to capital. This conclusion, which Stolper and Samuelson reached in their paper, does not depend upon any monopolistic or other restrictions to the movement of factors of production. On the contrary, it assumes that labor and capital receive the same return in all industries. Neither does the result depend upon a gain

---

[91] Wolfgang F. Stolper and Paul A. Samuelson, "Protection and Real Wages," *Review of Economic Studies*, November 1941, IX, pp. 58–73.

in real income for the country as a whole, such as that which might arise from a favorable movement in the terms of trade. Even when protection leaves the external prices of exports and imports unchanged, and when the national real income as a whole is accordingly reduced, it remains true that the real income of the factor most important in the protected industries is increased by the tariff.

When we attempt to make practical applications of the Stolper-Samuelson tariff argument, a number of complications arise. Perhaps the most important of these is the large number of factors of production. The conclusion summarized above concerning the effects of tariffs on the distribution of income can be rigorously proved only for the simplified case of two factors of production; when more than two factors are involved, the terms "relatively scarce factors" and "relatively abundant factors" lose some of their precise meaning. Moreover, if some of the factors are complementary it is no longer possible to say that the marginal product of a particular factor depends exclusively upon its amount, relative to some other factor.[92] Despite this complication, however, it seems reasonable, as Stolper and Samuelson have suggested,[93] to propose a number of tentative conclusions. In the United States during the early nineteenth century, for example, our comparative advantage in agriculture was clearly governed by the large amount of land per worker. Under these circumstances, the tariffs which were imposed upon manufactured imports may well have improved the standard of living of the working class as a whole, since labor is a more important factor in manufactures than in agriculture. The same argument is applicable to the present position of Australia. In other words, the Stolper-Samuelson theorem provides a scientific foundation for the conclusion of the Australian committee that the tariff has helped to maintain the living standard of the working class.

Recent discussions of tariffs and the distribution of income thus give limited support to the "pauper labor" argument for tariffs. We would no doubt agree today with Taussig that "no economist of standing would maintain that a protective tariff is the one decisive factor in making a country's rate of wages high," but it is doubtful whether we would also agree that "no economist, . . . would sanction the pauper-labor argument for tariffs." On the other hand, as Viner has pointed out, the favorable effect on the distribution of income from the point of view of one factor of production is not, *ipso facto*, a valid argument for tariffs from the point of view of the country as a whole. If repercussions on the terms of trade can be neglected, tariffs always reduce the total quantity of com-

---

[92] See *ibid.*, pp. 72–73.
[93] *Ibid.*, p. 73.

modities available to the country as a whole, and the gain to one factor of production is therefore more than offset by losses to others.[94]

COMMERCIAL POLICY AND THE REVIVAL OF MERCANTILISM

Having touched upon two aspects of the theory of tariffs, it seems appropriate to conclude this section with a few remarks concerning commercial policy as a whole. Although this subject is much broader than the theory of tariffs, the tariff question has been at the center of so many of the historical conflicts in commercial policy that it seems best to consider the broader subject here.

The basic conflicts in the field of commercial policy are well illustrated by the familiar differences of opinion between the mercantilists and the classical economists. To the mercantilists, the primary functions of foreign trade were to provide an outlet for a country's surplus production and to acquire a large stock of the monetary metals.[95] In order to achieve these ends, they advocated tariffs, export subsidies, and other measures designed to assure a country a steady and substantial export surplus. The classical system of economic theory was developed, in part, as a refutation of these mercantilist doctrines, and although the classical theory has been misinterpreted and misused by the advocates of free trade, it remains nevertheless as a bulwark against protectionism and other commercial restrictions. The fundamental tenet of the classical theory was that the purpose of all economic activity is not to find markets for surplus production or to increase mercantile profits but to satisfy human wants. Foreign trade, like other economic activity, was to be evaluated according to its contribution to this want-satisfying function. The classical economists accepted Say's Law and therefore believed that general over-production was impossible. From this it followed that the primary problem in economics was not how to find employment for unused capital, labor, and land, but how to use these resources in the most effective manner.

In the field of international trade, this meant a shift in emphasis from exports to imports. The usefulness of exports was to be judged not by their contribution to output and employment but by the value of the imports obtained in exchange. To the mercantilist argument that export subsidies were desirable because they created an outlet for surplus production, the classical economists replied that no such outlet was needed, and that an increase of exports, in itself, meant a smaller amount of goods available for domestic consumption.[96] In other words, exports were con-

---

[94] Jacob Viner, *Studies in the Theory of International Trade*, pp. 533–534.
[95] Cf. James W. Angell, *The Theory of International Prices*, Ch. II.
[96] Cf. John Stuart Mill, *Principles of Political Economy*, Book V, Ch. X, Sec. 1.

sidered to be desirable only if the additional imports which could thereby be obtained were worth more to consumers than the home consumption which had to be sacrificed. From this it followed that an export surplus, financed by imports of the precious metals, was not a desirable long-run policy, since monetary stocks of metal have no intrinsic ability to satisfy wants. It would be better, according to the classical view, to export only enough to pay for imports and to use the additional resources to produce for home consumption. In any event, the classical system envisaged an automatic tendency toward a balancing of exports and imports through the effects of gold movements on the level of prices. Attempts to maintain an export surplus were therefore regarded as self-defeating: tariffs and other impediments to trade, instead of increasing employment at home, would simply transfer resources from export industries to domestic-goods industries, thereby reducing the effectiveness of labor and other factors in satisfying wants.

Among economists in England, this classical system rapidly supplanted the mercantilist doctrines, and it was by far the most widely accepted system throughout the nineteenth century. Among businessmen and statesmen, on the other hand, the mercantilist doctrines continued to have much influence. Time and again, the argument that tariffs increase employment appeared in popular discussions, and just as regularly these arguments were refuted—sometimes impatiently—by economists.[97] Apart from the appeal to special interests which is no doubt the dominant factor in almost all tariff legislation, the genuine economic reasons for the persistence of the mercantilist arguments did not become apparent until the decade of the nineteen-thirties when the Keynesian revolution led to a reconsideration of the classical position. It was Keynes himself who pointed out the grain of truth in the mercantilist system, and except for the fact that this review is supposed to cover the whole field of international economics it would perhaps be best simply to refer the reader to Keynes' discussion.[98] The classical argument against an export surplus as a permanent policy stands or falls with the acceptance or rejection of the idea that the economic system tends automatically toward a state of full employment, and since Keynes had rejected this idea he was bound to reject also the idea that encouragement of exports through subsidies or reduction of imports through tariffs will have no influence on employment. If a country starts from a position in which it has unemployed resources, it is no longer true, as the classical economists assumed, that an

---

[97] See, e.g., F. W. Taussig, presidential address before the American Economic Association, 1904, reprinted in *Free Trade, the Tariff and Reciprocity*, p. 29.

[98] J. M. Keynes, *General Theory of Employment, Interest and Money* (New York, 1936), Ch. XXIII.

increase of exports means a reduction of goods available for domestic consumption. On the contrary, if we consider the repercussions of higher income earned in the export trades on the demand for goods and services, it is probable that an increase of exports means also an increased demand for and an increased output of domestic goods. An export surplus financed by an inflow of gold may therefore be a direct cause of increased income and a higher standard of living in the exporting country. Thus the mercantilists may have been justified, in certain circumstances, when they advocated an export surplus as an outlet for excess production. The theoretical foundations of the classical view, as Keynes shows, were weaker than had been suspected.

One problem still remains, however: How can the promotion of an export surplus as a permanent policy be reconciled with the classical argument that imports tend automatically to balance exports? If a country reduces its imports by means of tariffs, will not the increased employment in the protected industries soon be offset by a corresponding reduction of exports? In order to answer these questions, we must refer again to what was said in Section II concerning the balancing mechanism. It must be conceded that the imposition of a tariff or the granting of a subsidy *will* set up a balancing process, although the mechanism is somewhat different from that envisaged by the classical economists. If the initial disturbance is a tariff, imports will eventually rise, despite the tariff, as a result of higher income and employment at home, while exports will decline as a result of lower income abroad. It was argued in Section II, however, that this balancing process is likely to be incomplete. The modern theory of the balance of payments thus suggests that a country may have an export surplus over a considerable period of time without any pronounced automatic tendency toward a complete equalization of exports and imports.

A large export surplus cannot be maintained indefinitely, however, for eventually the rest of the world will be drained of all its monetary gold. Even before this occurs, other countries will probably be provoked to retaliation, particularly if unemployment prevails in the rest of the world. The most any individual country can hope to do is to maintain an export surplus which will ensure it a reasonable proportion of the world's new production of gold. If this policy succeeds, and retaliation is avoided, the export surplus, as Keynes shows, is doubly beneficial to the exporting country. On the one hand, it increases income and employment directly, and on the other hand, the increase of gold stocks, by reducing the rate of interest, tends to increase domestic investment. Both of these favorable effects would have been denied by the classical economists, who saw no need for a stimulation of employment and who had a somewhat exaggerated idea of the effectiveness of the balancing process.

While all of this clearly indicates that the economic grounds for mercantilism were stronger than economists have generally recognized, the revival of the theory of mercantilism is not necessarily a reason for its advocacy as a practical policy. On questions of policy, the primary problem, of course, is the reconciling of divergent national interests. The classical economists minimized this problem, for they believed that, within limits, national self-interest coincides with the welfare of the world economy as a whole. The revival of mercantilism demonstrates, unfortunately, that such harmony of interests cannot be taken for granted. The practical conduct of international trade is thus much more a problem of negotiation and compromise than the classical economists believed. If unemployment prevails through the world, as it did in the decade of the 'thirties, a mercantilist policy clearly benefits some countries at the expense of others. And this easily leads to retaliation which deprives all countries of the benefits of international specialization without increasing employment in any of them. But on these political questions, I can perhaps not do better than to quote a passage from Keynes' discussion of mercantilism:

. . . There are strong presumptions of a general character against trade restrictions unless they can be justified on special grounds. The advantages of the international division of labour are real and substantial, even though the classical school greatly overstressed them. The fact that the advantage which our own country gains from a favourable balance is liable to involve an equal disadvantage to some other country (a point to which the mercantilists were fully alive) means not only that great moderation is necessary, so that a country secures for itself no larger a share of the stock of precious metals than is fair and reasonable, but also that an immoderate policy may lead to a senseless international competition for a favourable balance which injures all alike. And finally, a policy of trade restrictions is a treacherous instrument even for the attainment of its ostensible object, since private interest, administrative incompetence, and the intrinsic difficulty of the task may divert it into producing results directly opposite to those intended.[99]

VI. Conclusions

The review presented above of international economics during the interwar years has covered a wide variety of subjects. In the monetary part of the field, it has attempted to describe recent developments in the theory of the balance of payments under conditions of both fixed and flexible exchange rates. And in the so-called "pure" theory of interna-

---

[99] *Ibid.*, pp. 338–339.

tional trade it has presented an account of the adaptation of new discoveries in price theory to the special problems of international trade. Finally, the recent changes in the theory of international trade have been related to selected problems in tariff policy.

Considering the diversity of subjects discussed, it is perhaps useful to inquire, in conclusion, whether the recent innovations and discoveries in all the various branches of international economics have anything in common. Is there, for example, any unifying principle or any basic philosophy which unites the modern theories of the balance of payments with the revised theory of tariffs? Or has each of the new discoveries in each of the separate branches been a more or less isolated phenomenon? A cursory glance at the preceding pages may suggest that the latter has been true. I believe, however, that a more careful study will convince the reader that the new theories have not been as disconnected and isolated as seems at first to be the case. The connecting idea, however, is essentially negative. Historically, the interwar period will probably be remembered as a period of retreat from the price system, when all sorts of temporary or provisional measures were adopted to regulate economic activity. The market mechanism had broken down and no one seemed to know quite why or just what to do about it. This was perhaps even more true of the international mechanism than of domestic markets, and to a very great extent the theoretical developments reflected the empirical. Where the classical economists had discussed the broad operation of the price system, twentieth-century economists described the exceptions and qualifications, or the special circumstances in which the international price mechanism would not work. Thus, for example, the balance of payments mechanism under the gold standard was found to be less effective and more disruptive than the classical economists had believed. And even with flexible exchange rates, it was realized during the interwar years that a balancing of foreign receipts and expenditures cannot be taken for granted. Doubts concerning the price system were by no means limited to the monetary aspects of international economics. In the field of price theory, too, there was a movement away from traditional ideas. Increasing emphasis was placed upon the fact that an unimpeded working of the free market system is not necessarily in the interest of each individual country. The classical conception of a harmony of interest between countries, which even the classical theory did not entirely support, was called further in question. Much importance—perhaps too much— was attached to the benefits which individual countries could derive by the regulation of exports and imports.

Part of this general retreat from the price system in international economic theory was no doubt beneficial, for it contributed to a more realistic appraisal of international trade than we had inherited from the classical economists. It seems likely, however, that the pendulum has now swung too far in the anti-classical direction. The interwar years give a distorted picture of the normal working of an international market system—indeed, it is more of a caricature than a picture—and economic theory has shared in this distortion. If in the past we have expected the price system to accomplish too much, there is a danger that in the future we shall expect it to do less than it is capable of doing.

Our major error in the past, and the error which contributed perhaps more than anything else to discrediting of the price system, consisted in expecting the price mechanism to solve the problem of economic stability. On this point we were immensely enlightened during the interwar years, and it is now generally recognized that economic stability requires constant supervision and planning. To the extent that the world succeeds in solving the problem of stability by measures supplementary to the price system, the equally important problem of the allocation of resources, both domestic and international, might reasonably be left to the market mechanism. In the absence of severe depressions, there is reason to believe that the balances of payments of most countries could be kept in reasonable equilibrium by means of moderate adjustments in exchange rates. The trade restrictions and trade controls which grew so rapidly in the interwar years would therefore be unnecessary. Moreover, in a stable and expanding world economy, individual countries would have less incentive to adopt trade controls in order to safeguard their domestic markets. World economic stability would thus greatly reduce the force of the two most important incentives for controlling international trade in the past. Whether this would be sufficient to counteract the present trend toward increasing state intervention can hardly be foretold. But at any rate it is clear that our hopes for a revival of the market mechanism, however weak they may be, are greatly dependent upon a world stability which must be achieved, for the most part, by conscious planning and direction.

7

ECONOMICS OF LABOR

Lloyd G. Reynolds

LABOR economics, like other parts of economics, consists of two principal kinds of work—the development of general propositions about the role of labor in the economy, and the testing of these propositions through factual studies. Many of the central issues are not economic in the technical sense of being amenable to the categories of economic theory. A successful attack on them requires the diverse techniques of psychology, sociology, politics, law, and administration. The student of labor who wishes to grasp the phenomena of his field *in toto* must turn himself into a multiple-social-scientist by acquiring the rudiments of the several relevant disciplines. On the other hand, those who wish to remain within the confines of economic analysis must cut their studies to the limitations of their method. Tendencies in both directions are observable among economists working in the labor field, and the results of their work will eventually be more persuasive than abstract argument about the relative desirability of the two approaches.

The heterogeneity of the field raises difficult problems concerning the proper scope of the present essay. I have deliberately concentrated attention on problems which can be related to the general body of economic theory. Areas of study which cannot be approached *via* economic theory have been treated somewhat more briefly. I want to be very clear that this allocation of space is not intended as a judgment of relative importance. The political and social consequences of trade unionism are probably more important than its strictly economic effects. In stressing economic problems, I have been somewhat influenced by the fact that this volume is addressed to people with a background of economic analysis, and that one of its main purposes is to illustrate the interrelations of various fields of economic study. There is the further consideration that application of political, psychological, and other non-economic types of analysis to labor problems is still in its infancy, and one can do little more at present than to indicate some of the more important unresolved issues.

A different kind of problem is presented by the very great volume of writing on labor matters. In order to hold the essay within reasonable bounds, it has been necessary to concentrate almost entirely on work done in the United States within approximately the past fifteen years. Even within this area, no attempt will be made to review all of the published material. The literature of trade unionism and collective bargaining alone is so extensive that even to prepare a bibliography of it would be a formidable task. Fortunately or unfortunately, the scientifically relevant literature is a relatively small portion of the whole. The general policy followed here is to omit mention of writings by unionists, management officials, political leaders, and popular writers generally. I have also had to omit any detailed reference to the periodical literature, though much relevant material has appeared in this form. Among books, I have slighted specialized studies in favor of more general works, and have given preference to books with some analytical framework over purely descriptive writings.

I. WAGES IN THE ECONOMY

Interest in wages has been stimulated recently by the longest and sharpest increase of money wage rates in American economic history. Average hourly earnings in manufacturing, which stood at $0.437 per hour in October 1932, had increased to $1.227 per hour by June 1947. The rise of wages was almost continuous over this fifteen-year period, being interrupted only for a short time during 1938. Particularly sharp increases in the general wage level occurred during 1933–34, 1937, 1941–42, and 1946–47. The economic consequences of these increases were debated almost continuously in both political and academic circles.

During this period also the wage structure of such basic industries as steel, automobiles, electrical products, textiles, rubber, and petroleum products began to be determined primarily by collective bargaining. This led naturally to active discussion of the probable effects of a bargained wage structure. Another significant development was the marked increase in the quantity of wage data available. The wage studies of the Bureau of Labor Statistics were considerably enlarged, first as a consequence of the N.I.R.A. and other recovery programs of the 'thirties, and again during the wage stabilization program of World War II. In spite of recent reductions in B.L.S. activities, we have today an unprecedented amount of information about the details of the national wage structure.[1]

Under collective bargaining it does not seem very useful to regard

---

[1] The material collected by the Bureau of Labor Statistics is the leading source, but by no means the only source of wage information. For a fuller discussion of wage data, and also for material pertinent to later sections of this chapter, see L. G. Reynolds, "Research in Wages," Social Science Research Council Memorandum No. 4, 1947.

wage rates as market prices. They are administered prices, i.e., they are held constant for considerable periods while other things are adjusted to the given wage. They may also in a sense be termed "legislated" prices, though the legislation is enacted by private agencies with relatively little public control.

Contemplation of a system in which more and more wage rates are determined by collective bargaining suggests at least four types of issue. First, what are the objectives of unions and employers in wage bargaining? The objectives of unions are especially important, since the union normally appears as the aggressor—at least during periods of stable or rising employment. What are the pressures which influence the union's initial wage demands and the amount for which it will actually settle in a particular case?

Second, how has the national wage structure evolved in recent years under the stress of collective bargaining and of government wage regulation? What has happened to wage differences between industries, between different firms in the same industry, between low-skilled and high-skilled occupations, and between different regions of the country? Can one say that the wage structure has been distorted as compared with some hypothetical competitive pattern of wage rates because of the differing strength of unionism in different sectors of the economy?

Third, how does the economy adapt itself to the kinds of change in money wage rates which occur under collective bargaining? How does a general change in wage rates throughout the economy affect the general level of prices, output, and employment? How do particular industries adapt themselves to a rate of wage change greater or less than that occurring in the system as a whole? The problem of how a wage change confined to one firm will affect output and employment in that firm is perhaps less important, since under collective bargaining one may expect most wage movements to be at least industry-wide. This question has considerable analytic interest, however, and a satisfactory way of handling it would be highly desirable.

Fourth, there is the problem of developing normative rules concerning the desirable movement of wages over time under conditions of shifting demand and changing technology. Such rules are necessary to guide public policy concerning wages, or even to determine whether any public policy is required. It may be that the wage movements which occur spontaneously under collective bargaining produce reasonably satisfactory results. But we need some way of determining how satisfactory they are and, if public regulation seems desirable, of appraising the direction which such regulation should take.

Discussion of recent work on wages in the United States may usefully be organized around these four groups of problems, which we may refer to briefly as wage determination, wage behavior, economic adaptation to wage changes, and criteria of wage adjustment.

With respect to wage determination, particular importance attaches to an understanding of union wage demands and the pressures influencing them. Much useful work has already been done on this matter and much more is in process.[2] Slichter's volume on the economic policies of unions, though oriented mainly toward non-wage policies, explores the attitudes of unions toward various systems of wage payment, and the problem of cost differentials between union and non-union plants. Further, many of the non-wage policies which he analyzes have as direct an impact on unit labor cost as the wage level itself. Dunlop has constructed a systematic statement of the economic issues which a union confronts in developing its wage program, and assembled information on the choices which particular union groups have made on these issues. Ross has explored the way in which unions formulate their wage demands, and has emphasized the extent to which wage settlements are influenced by the union leader's necessity of maintaining the union and his leadership of it against rival cliques, other unions, and the employer. His political model of the union as a wage-setting institution forms an interesting and useful contrast to the economic models of Dunlop and others. Lester has explored the conditions under which regional or national collective bargaining may produce wage standardization of one sort or another. A forthcoming book by Lindblom attempts a comprehensive analysis of union wage objectives and tactics. One should mention also Palmer's incisive analysis of the effect of non-union competition on union wage tactics, and Kennedy's recent study of union attitudes toward incentive wage systems.

These studies have perhaps raised more questions than they have answered. It appears, for example, that wage demands are usually formulated by the chief officers of the union, with the membership playing a permissive or ratifying role. Yet the leaders presumably put forward demands which they believe will arouse the enthusiasm or at least the approval of the rank and file. What are the channels through which

[2] John T. Dunlop, *Wage Determination Under Trade Unions* (New York, 1944); Van Dusen Kennedy, *Union Policy and Incentive Wage Methods* (New York, 1945); Richard A. Lester and Edward A. Robie, *Wages under National and Regional Collective Bargaining: Experience in Seven Industries*, Industrial Relations Section, Princeton University (Princeton, 1946); Gladys Palmer, *Union Tactics and Economic Change* (Philadelphia, 1932); Arthur M. Ross, "Trade Unions as Wage-Fixing Institutions," *The American Economic Review*, September 1947, XXXVII, pp. 566–588; Sumner H. Slichter, *Union Policies and Industrial Management* (Washington, 1941).

membership sentiment is transmitted to the leaders? How do the leaders decide that ten cents an hour this year will keep the members in line whereas five cents an hour would leave them discontented? How do they judge the feasibility of selling non-wage gains to the membership in lieu of wage gains? Again, while there is little indication that union presidents listen to their research directors or make explicit use of economic analysis in formulating their wage demands, it is difficult to believe that the economic situation of the industry at the time has no effect on their deliberations. Is it not possible that, while union leaders make no calculation of demand elasticities and so on, the economic situation may influence their thinking in other ways—for example, their estimates of how large a wage increase the employers will concede without a fight?

There is a clear tendency for certain "key bargains" to have an influence far beyond the workers immediately affected. Such are the bargains between the Steelworkers and the United States Steel Corporation, the Automobile Workers and General Motors, the Mine Workers and the coal operators' associations, the Rubber Workers and the "big four" rubber companies. The terms of settlement reached in these key bargains spread through the imposition of identical demands on other companies in the same industry, imitation of these demands by unions in other industries, and wage increases by non-union employers in an effort to keep pace with the union scale. While some of these focal points—notably wage changes announced by United States Steel—existed in pre-union days, it seems likely that widespread unionization has increased both the speed and the uniformity with which wage changes are transmitted throughout the economy. It would be interesting to test this hypothesis by a detailed comparison of wage changes during 1946–48 with other periods of general wage change during the 'twenties and 'thirties which were less influenced by collective bargaining.

Management opinion concerning the proper level and structure of wages, while clearly less important than it was in pre-union days, still has a significant influence on the course of events. A few managements have a direct hand in shaping the key bargains which become patterns for the remainder of the economy; and managements outside the key group may be able to deviate a good deal from the general movement. Indeed, use of the term "pattern" suggests much more uniformity than actually exists in economy-wide wage changes. A statistical study of the 1946 movement, for example, indicates that even in manufacturing the increases varied from zero to more than thirty cents per hour, while the average increase was considerably below the nominal pattern of eighteen and one-half cents. This raggedness of general wage movements must be caused partly

by the differing resistances of different managements to union wage demands, and partly by differences in the judgment of non-union firms as
to how far they dare lag behind the general advance.

Some work on management wage policies—largely unpublished as yet
—has been done at Princeton, Yale, Massachusetts Institute of Technology, and a number of other centers. The main limitation of these studies
is that, for practical reasons, they have been based largely on interviews
with company officials. Information obtained in this way is bound to contain a high percentage of rationalization, since the past decisions being
investigated were arrived at through discussions which cannot readily be
reconstructed after the event, and were probably affected by circumstances of the moment which were never recorded and have now been
forgotten.

Moreover, wages are only one of the many things with which the principal officers of a company have to deal. The crucial decisions may relate
to pricing, sales strategy, production and inventory policy, and investment planning; wage questions, particularly where wages form a small
percentage of production costs, may be settled in a relatively offhand
manner. An understanding of wage policy, therefore, requires that it be
regarded as only one (and perhaps a minor) aspect of the general strategy
of the firm. What is required, in other words, is an inclusive study of the
economics of the enterprise. A specialized study limited to wage-setting
will miss so many central problems of the business that it can yield only
dubious results. The only published study which approaches the necessary breadth of treatment is the monograph prepared in the late 'thirties
for the Temporary National Economic Committee.[3]

Most studies of management wage policies relate to general or "across-
the-board" changes in the plant wage level. It should be remembered,
however, that management—alone, or through negotiation with the
union—is continually adjusting the rates paid for particular jobs within
the plant. Moreover, under incentive systems, earnings may vary over a
wide range with no change at all in job rates as a result of variations in
worker effort, changes in production methods, management's strictness or
laxity in revising piece rates, and so on. Economists have tended to regard
the detailed determination of job rates and earnings as minutiae, and
have left discussion of them largely to the industrial engineers. This attitude is unwarranted; the rules of procedure which the engineers have
evolved actually pose some very interesting theoretical problems. For ex-

---

[3] Douglass V. Brown, John T. Dunlop, Edwin M. Martin, Charles A. Myers, and John
A. Brownell, *Industrial Wage Rates, Labor Costs and Price Policies,* T.N.E.C. Monograph 5 (Washington, 1940).

ample, the principles used by engineers in evaluating the relative worth of various jobs take little if any account of the principles which economists from Adam Smith on have proclaimed as the natural or competitive determinants of wage differences between occupations. Yet these apparently arbitrary and non-competitive rules seem to work reasonably well in practice. What is the explanation? Is any set of occupational rates feasible provided it is consistently applied? Even more interesting questions are suggested by the structure of incentive wage systems. Pioneer work in this area has been done by Dickinson, who has tried to apply the techniques of the economist, the psychologist, and the industrial engineer to the problems of wage rate determination.[4]

The second main area for investigation is the actual behavior of bargained wage rates over the course of time. Union objectives are one thing; accomplishment is another. It is quite conceivable that the various unions, despite their efforts to outstrip each other in wage increases, have succeeded only in maintaining about the same relative position. It is even possible, though not very likely, that the earnings of unorganized workers in the economy have risen as rapidly as those of organized workers during the past fifteen years. It is quite another thing if the effect of collective bargaining has been to set up widely differing rates of wage increase in the various unionized industries, leading presumably to distortion of the wage-price structure and misallocation of resources. In this connection the statistician is faced with a nice problem: How is one to measure or even detect wage distortion in the absence of the norms of proper wage relationships which would be provided by a perfectly competitive labor market? The absence of such norms makes it difficult to be at all certain whether collective bargaining is forcing the wage structure closer to or farther away from the "competitive pattern." We may quite possibly be approximating competitive norms more closely in some respects (for example, intra-plant occupational differentials) and departing more widely from them in other respects (for example, inter-industry differences in wage levels).

In addition to such conceptual difficulties there are serious deficiencies in the statistical data with which we have to work. The most satisfactory data would probably be base rates of pay (and, for incentive jobs, actual hourly earnings as well) for certain key occupations, collected once a year or so from a sample of identical establishments selected to represent the major industries and major industrial areas of the nation. Even this information would be far from perfect because of unavoidable variations

---

[4] Z. C. Dickinson, *Compensating Industrial Effort* (New York, 1937); *idem, Collective Wage Determination* (New York, 1941).

from plant to plant in the content of jobs with identical titles, and also because of variations in the quality of the workers employed. The unfortunate fact, however, is that occupational wage data of any sort are very rare—so rare that it is difficult to trace even the broad outlines of the national wage structure over the course of time.[5] The familiar series of average hourly earnings and average weekly earnings in particular industries, while useful in forming rough conclusions about long-run trends in workers' real income and general welfare, cannot be said to measure the price of labor with any precision because they are influenced by so many factors other than changes in base rates of pay.

In spite of these difficulties, one can point to considerable progress in studying the behavior of wages. During the past few years there has been much useful exploration of just what is meant by "wages" or "the price of labor." It has been pointed out that earnings may be computed over different periods of time, that unit labor cost to the employer will behave differently from earnings, that both earnings and labor costs are influenced by various types of fringe payment and working rules as well as by base rates, and so on.[6] This recognition of a plurality of wage concepts is very important for clear analysis, and reflection on it suggests a number of further problems. The question arises, for example, whether the most common type of published wage statistics—average hourly earnings for a plant or an industry—really measures anything which is either statistically precise or theoretically interesting. Again, the fact that the wage concept which interests workers and is therefore relevant to labor supply differs from the wage concept which is important to employers throws some doubt on the appropriateness of constructing labor supply and demand curves on the same diagram, i.e., using identical units on the wage axis.[7] Moreover, most of the theoretical literature on wages seems to

---

[6] The main bodies of data are: (a) the common labor rates published by the National Industrial Conference Board since about 1920, and by the Bureau of Labor Statistics from 1926 to 1942; (b) occupational wage rates in those industries—building construction, printing, and baking—for which local union scales have been compiled annually by the B.L.S. over a long period of time, plus a few industries such as cotton textiles which have been surveyed by the Bureau at irregular but frequent intervals; (c) the occupational rates gathered on a large scale by the B.L.S. for the National War Labor Board during the years 1943–45, and the data on occupational rates in major industries gathered through the B.L.S. program of industry wage surveys from 1945 to 1947. This material for the period 1942–47 begins to approach in completeness what is needed; but there is little in earlier years with which one can compare it, and it is likely that budgetary limitations will prevent similarly comprehensive studies from being made at all frequently in the future.

[6] See particularly Sumner H. Slichter, *Basic Criteria Used in Wage Determination*, Chicago Association of Commerce and Industry (Chicago, 1947), Appendix; and John T. Dunlop, *op. cit.*, Ch. 2.

[7] It is not meant to suggest that this is not *formally* permissible. It clearly is, since the worker's scale of units (say, weekly take-home pay) is convertible at will into the employ-

assume that wages are paid entirely on a time basis. What kinds of conceptual adjustment are necessary to handle wage payments on an output or incentive basis?

There have also been several ground-clearing studies of what the national wage structure looks like and how it changes over the course of time. Douglas' volume on the history of wages in the United States was a pioneer effort in this field.[8] More recently, Lester has made a careful analysis of the "north-south" wage differential, the extent to which it can be accounted for on productivity grounds, and the changes in its size during recent decades.[9] He has also summarized the evidence revealed by wartime studies of the Bureau of Labor Statistics concerning the extent of wage differences for allegedly comparable work in particular localities.[10] This material is both more voluminous and more carefully prepared than any previous information on the subject.

A large amount of work on the behavior of wages and related variables has been published by the National Bureau of Economic Research, and more work of this sort is in process. One should mention particularly Wolman's work on the history of wages in the United States, Fabricant's studies of productivity, Kuznets' national income studies, and a projected series of reports on wages and employment changes in particular industries (of which two have already appeared).[11] At the Brookings Institution, Bell has endeavored to relate the trend of wages in various industries

---

er's scale (say, unit direct labor cost). The point is that, since "wages" in the worker's sense can change without any change in "wages" to the employer, the supply and demand curves become quite unstable, and this raises some doubt as to their usefulness.

[8] Paul H. Douglas, *Real Wages in the United States* (Boston, 1930).

[9] Richard A. Lester, "Trends in Southern Wage Differentials since 1890," *The Southern Economic Journal*, April 1945, XI, pp. 317–344; *idem*, "Southern Wage Differentials: Developments, Analysis, and Implications," *ibid.*, April 1947, XIII, pp. 386–394; *idem*, "Diversity in North-South Wage Differentials and in Wage Rates within the South," *ibid.*, January 1946, XII, pp. 238–262; *idem*, "Effectiveness of Factory Labor: South-North Comparisons," *The Journal of Political Economy*, February 1946, LIV, pp. 60–75.

[10] *Idem*, "Wage Diversity and Its Theoretical Implications," *The Review of Economic Statistics*, August 1946, XXVIII, pp. 152–159.

[11] Leo Wolman, *Hours of Work in American Industry*, National Bureau of Economic Research, Bulletin 71 (New York, 1938); Solomon Fabricant, *Employment in Manufacturing, 1899–1939*, National Bureau of Economic Research (New York, 1942); *idem*, *Labor Savings in American Industry, 1899–1939*, National Bureau of Economic Research, Occasional Paper 23: November 1945 (New York, 1945); Simon Kuznets, *National Income—A Summary of Findings*, National Bureau of Economic Research (New York, 1946); *idem*, *National Income—A Summary of Findings*, National Bureau of Economic Research (New York, 1945); *idem*, *National Product Since 1869*, National Bureau of Economic Research (New York, 1946); *idem*, *National Product in Wartime*, National Bureau of Economic Research (New York, 1945); George J. Stigler, *Domestic Servants in the United States, 1900–1940*, National Bureau of Economic Research, Occasional Paper 24: April 1946 (New York, 1946); *idem*, *Trends in Output and Employment* (New York, 1947).

during the 'twenties and 'thirties to changes in productivity, prices, and output in those industries.[12]

Dunlop has done a large amount of work on the behavior of wages and on the theoretical significance of this behavior. The subjects which he has investigated include the cyclical behavior of money and real wages in the United States and the United Kingdom; the timing and amplitude of wage changes in various industries during the 1929–37 cycle in this country, and their relation to price and employment changes in each industry; the behavior of man-hour output and unit labor costs during this same period; the definition and measurement of "labor's share" of national income; and the cyclical and secular behavior of various types of wage differential—occupational differences within an industry, inter-industry differences, geographical differences, differences between union and non-union rates, and so on—in the United States.[13] These studies provide an unusually clear focusing of statistical material on theoretical issues, and suggest a large number of hypotheses for future study.

The problem of how the economy adapts itself to changes in the level and structure of money wage rates is really a complex bundle of problems which must be separated out for analysis. As a minimum, one must distinguish a wage change confined to a single firm, a wage change applied uniformly throughout an industry, and a wage change extending throughout the economy. Under each of these headings one could set up numerous sub-cases, depending on whether the change in question is an increase or a decrease, whether it is large or small, whether it is expected or unexpected, whether it occurs at a time of rising, falling, or stable demand, and so on. If we had adequate methods for analyzing these three types of wage change, we should be well on the way toward an understanding of actual wage movements such as occurred in the spring of 1946 and 1947. For any such movement can be broken down analytically into an average rate of wage change for the economy, deviations of particular industries from this rate, and deviations of individual firms from the average rate of change for their industries.

The reactions of the individual firm to wage changes are not handled

[12] Spurgeon Bell, *Productivity, Wages, and National Income*, The Brookings Institution (Washington, 1940).

[13] See particularly the following writings: John T. Dunlop, *op. cit.; idem,* "Trends in the Rigidity of English Wage Rates," *The Review of Economic Studies,* June 1939, VI, pp. 189–199; *idem,* "The Movement of Real and Money Wage Rates," *The Economic Journal,* September 1938, XLVIII, pp. 413–424; *idem,* "The Economics of Wage Dispute Settlement," *Law and Contemporary Problems,* Spring 1947, XII, pp. 281–296; *idem,* "Wage-Price Relations at High Level Employment," *The American Economic Review,* May 1947, Proceedings XXXVII, pp. 243–253.

very satisfactorily by the existing theory of the firm. This is explained mainly by the fact that theorists have concentrated on defining equilibrium positions under static or quasi-static conditions, and usually also under "long-run" assumptions about the mobility and transformability of capital. Hicks, Hart, and others have sketched out the beginnings of a theory of business planning under conditions of change and uncertainty. Much more work will be necessary, however, to develop this theory to the point of practical usefulness.[14]

There has been very little investigation of the reactions of particular firms to changes in wage levels. The T.N.E.C. monograph already referred to, Lester's recent investigations, and some unpublished investigations by the writer in New Haven, are the only studies which come to mind. It is interesting that these studies show little trace of the effects which existing theories of the firm would lead one to think a wage increase must have on production methods, investment, and employment.[15] The explanation may be partly that the field studies have been superficial and have not extended over a sufficiently long period of time. A more fundamental explanation is probably that the theoretical models ordinarily used to deduce the effects of wage change are static models, whereas actual wage changes occur under dynamic conditions. Wage increases, for example, normally occur at a time when the firm's revenues are also rising, and the problem of how to finance the increase is not so acute as it would be under static conditions. If it were possible to investigate thoroughly a sufficient number of cases over a sufficiently long period, it would doubtless appear that the effects of a wage change are extremely variable, depending among other things on the stage of the cycle, the size of the change, the ratio of labor to total cost, and the nature of the product market.

The magnitude of the effects would also be expected to increase with the period of time taken into account. If one is interested mainly in questions of resource allocation, these delayed effects of a wage change are undoubtedly of real importance. But for many purposes, notably

---

[14] For a fuller discussion of this point see my article, "Toward a Short-Run Theory of Wages," *The American Economic Review*, June 1948.

[15] For a discussion of the significance, or lack of significance, of this fact see Richard A. Lester, "Shortcomings of Marginal Analysis for Wage-Employment Problems," *The American Economic Review*, March 1946, XXXVI, pp. 63–82; Fritz Machlup, "Marginal Analysis and Empirical Research," *ibid.*, September 1946, XXXVI, pp. 519–554; *idem*, "Rejoinder to an Anti-Marginalist," *ibid.*, March 1947, XXXVII, pp. 148–154; Richard A. Lester, "Marginalism, Minimum Wages and Labor Markets," *ibid.*, March 1947, XXXVII, pp. 135–148; George Stigler, "The Economics of Minimum Wages," *ibid.*, June 1946, XXXVI, pp. 358–365; *idem*, "Professor Lester and the Marginalists," *ibid.*, March 1947, XXXVII, pp. 154–157.

questions of cycle theory, it is the effects within the first six to twelve months that really matter. These effects are probably much smaller than might be inferred from the existing theory of the firm.

The defects in the theory of the firm hamper us also in analyzing the effects of change occurring throughout an industry; for despite efforts to improve on Marshall, present theories of industry adjustment lean very heavily on the presumed adjustments of an average or typical firm. Further difficulties arise from the fact that under oligopoly the inter-action of cost and price changes becomes very complex and it is probably impossible to make any mechanical prediction of causal sequences.[16] On the research side, there has been scarcely any attempt to trace out the consequences of changes in the wage level of an industry. Statistical correlation of wage changes in particular industries with changes in prices, productivity, and employment in those industries do not seem to yield very significant results. What is probably required is industry case-studies in which thorough familiarity with the history and structure of the industry would enable one to read meaning into the statistical series.[17]

Most important and most elusive is the problem of how an economy-wide wage change affects the general level of prices, output, and employment. The difficulty of analyzing these effects is part of the larger difficulty of securing an agreed framework for cycle analysis—whether to use equilibrium or sequence analysis, what assumptions may reasonably be made about reactions within the system, and so on. To discuss these matters here would mean retracing the ground covered in Chapter 2 of the present volume; the reader is referred to that chapter, and particularly to the section of it which deals with cost-price relations.

Most of the work which has been done on wage-employment relations in the economy—for example, by Bergson, Douglas, Keynes, Lerner, and Slichter[18]—uses an equilibrium approach. I am inclined to think that sequence analysis probably affords a more useful approach to this kind

---

[16] For a few remarks on this problem see my article, "Relations between Wage Rates, Costs, and Prices," *The American Economic Review*, March 1942, Proceedings XXXII, pp. 275–289; reprinted in *Readings in the Theory of Income Distribution* (Philadelphia, 1946), pp. 294–313.

[17] Waldo E. Fisher, *Wage Rates and Working Time in the Bituminous Coal Industry, 1912–1922* (Philadelphia, 1932).

[18] A. Bergson, "Prices, Wages, and Income Theory," *Econometrica*, July–October 1942, X, pp. 275–289; Paul H. Douglas, "Wage Theory and Wage Policy," *International Labor Review*, March 1939, XXXIX, pp. 319–359; J. M. Keynes, *The General Theory of Employment, Interest, and Money* (London, 1936); A. P. Lerner, "The Relation of Wage Policies and Price Policies," *The American Economic Review*, March 1939, Proceedings XXIX, pp. 158–169; Sumner H. Slichter, "Wage-Price Policy and Employment," *ibid.*, May 1946, XXXVI, pp. 304–318; *idem*, "The Changing Character of American Industrial Relations," *ibid.*, March 1939, Proceedings XXIX, pp. 121–137.

of problem. The only authors (to my knowledge) who have applied sequence analysis to the effects of general wage changes are Bissell, Johannesen, and Lundberg.[19] Sequence analysis has its own type of abstraction, and it may well be argued that manageable models will be too simplified for any practical use, or even that the "period" concept itself is hopelessly artificial. Nevertheless, further experiments in this direction should be welcomed.

In the meantime, the consequences of general wage change remain among the most controversial and least understood subjects in economics. The issue is clearly of great practical importance. In a highly unionized economy, any approach to full employment seems likely to generate a rate of wage increase which will lead to some increase in the general price level. The question then arises of how rapid and protracted a price inflation the economy can tolerate as the price of reasonably full employment. There are also interesting questions as to the monetary prerequisites for a continuing rise of wages and prices, and as to whether such a movement can be stable over any extended period or whether it must involve frequent relapses.

The fourth type of problem suggested above was the development of norms of desirable wage behavior over time. Stated most broadly, the problem is what kind of wage structure and what patterns of change in this structure will be most conducive to full employment of economic resources and the most efficient allocation of these resources among competing uses. The following are only a few of the questions which arise under this heading. Over a period of several decades, should the general wage level rise at a rate which just absorbs the gains of technical change and leaves the general price level unchanged? Or should the wage level rise more rapidly or less rapidly than this? Should the general wage level respond to cyclical fluctuations in the level of employment, and if so, how? What pattern of wage differentials will promote the most efficient adjustment of resources to any given pattern of demand and technology—for example, is it desirable that wage rates for a particular occupation be completely equalized as among firms, industries, and geographical areas? Should changes in wage differentials be used as a means of transferring labor and other resources from declining areas, industries, or occupations into expanding sectors of the economy? Should the wage structure be used as a means for achieving

---

[19] Richard Bissell, "Price and Wage Policies and the Theory of Employment," *Econometrica*, July 1940, VIII, pp. 199–239.

None of Johannesen's work is available in English, but a brief summary of his method will be found in Lundberg's book.

E. Lundberg, *Studies in the Theory of Economic Expansion* (London, 1937).

a desirable distribution of personal incomes, or should this problem be handled entirely through the tax and outlay structure?

Answers to these questions will require the best analytical tools which can be developed, a great deal of practical judgment, and perhaps the addition of political norms of equity in income distribution, the desirable balance between security and progress, and so on. It will probably be very difficult to get agreement on rules of the game even among economists, let alone public and private officials. Yet unless this can be done, there is no basis for appraising the desirability of the wage structure which is developing under collective bargaining, or for attempting to influence private wage bargains in one direction or another. There is already a good deal of public intervention in these nominally private wage negotiations, and a secular increase in such intervention seems almost certain. The problem is to ensure that increased public intervention means the application of considered principles of wage settlement rather than the mere transfer of a power struggle from conference rooms in Pittsburgh to conference rooms in Washington. One may even hope that, if workable standards of public interest can be developed in this field, they may in time have a direct influence on union and management behavior.

II. Labor Supply and Labor Mobility

The movement of workers from one employer, occupation, or area to another has usually been treated as an aspect of wage determination. From certain assumptions about worker behavior there are derived supply curves of labor which are used to explain the level of wages and employment in a firm, industry, or area. Under collective bargaining the usefulness of this approach is very much reduced. It is still true that potential mobility determines the lowest wage which an employer can pay and retain his labor force. The *effective* lower limit to wages, however, is the rate which the union can be persuaded to accept. This will normally be higher, and often very much higher, than the limit set by mobility alone. In this case mobility has no direct bearing on the wage level. It retains at most some usefulness in explaining management wage decisions under non-union conditions.

The characteristics of labor mobility are very important, however, in connection with what may be termed "labor market engineering"— the effort to ensure that the detailed articulation of specialized labor demands and labor supplies will go on with a minimum of personal hardship and economic waste. Included under this heading are such programs as decasualization of irregular occupations, reduction of seasonal fluctuations of employment, organization of public employment service offices, transfer of workers from depressed to prosperous industries or areas, transfer of the chronic surplus of farm population into urban employments, and the provision of adequate vocational training and guidance for young people. A realistic understanding of how workers actually choose jobs is necessary in order to estimate how far manipulation of wage differentials may be effective in redistributing labor supplies, and what supplementary measures will be most useful. It will be worth while, therefore, to discuss briefly a few of the more important aspects of labor mobility: movement into and out of the labor force, into and out of employment, between geographical areas, between employers in the same area, and between occupational levels.[20]

THE BEHAVIOR OF AGGREGATE LABOR SUPPLY

It is not possible here to go into the various possible ways of defining employment, unemployment, and the labor force. It should be noted, however, that the problem is of practical importance as well as theoretical interest; a shift of definitions can easily make a difference of several million in the number counted as unemployed at a particular time.[21] It is worth noting also that efforts at precise measurement of employment and unemployment have been intensified considerably since about 1930.[22] These measures have dealt with numbers of individuals rather than with man-hours or efficiency units, and have tended to assume that a single figure could be meaningful for all purposes. Most of them have also tended, in varying degrees, to understate the amount of unemployment at a particular time (especially with respect to the definitions

---

[20] For a more detailed statement of research problems and hypotheses in the field of labor mobility, see Gladys Palmer, "Research Planning Memorandum on Labor Mobility," Social Science Research Council Pamphlet No. 2, 1947.

[21] On this whole range of problems see the following writings by Clarence D. Long: "The Concept of Unemployment," *Quarterly Journal of Economics*, November 1942, LVII, pp. 1–30; *The Labor Force in Wartime America*, National Bureau of Economic Research, Occasional Paper 14 (New York, 1944); *The Size of the Labor Force under Changing Incomes and Employment* (unpublished manuscript prepared for the Conference on Research in Income and Wealth, National Bureau of Economic Research, 1946).

[22] Louis J. Ducoff and Margaret J. Hagood, *Labor Force Definition and Measurement*, Social Science Research Council (New York, 1947); Aryness Joy, "Meaning of Unemployment Statistics," *Journal of the American Statistical Association*, June 1941, XXXVI, pp. 167–174; Russell Nixon and Paul Samuelson, "Estimates of Unemployment in the U.S.," *The Review of Economic Statistics*, August 1940, XXII, pp. 101–111; Arthur Reede, "Adequacy of Employment Statistics," *Journal of the American Statistical Association*, March 1941, XXXVI, pp. 71–80; W. S. Woytinsky, "Controversial Aspects of Unemployment Estimates in the United States," *The Review of Economic Statistics*, February 1941, XXIII, pp. 68–77.

most relevant to "full employment"), and to understate the amount of cyclical variability in employment and the labor force over the course of time.

With respect to the size and composition of the aggregate labor force, Long's studies indicate that the proportion of people in each age- and sex-group who were in the labor force remained relatively stable in the United States between 1890 and 1940. The proportion of the total population in the labor force fell very slightly, a somewhat larger percentage of work seekers among adult women being more than offset by smaller percentages for boys and girls and for older men. As between different cities in the United States at the same time, the studies of both Long and Douglas indicate a clear inverse relation between income levels and the percentage of the population in the labor force.[23]

There is relatively little evidence on the shape of the (instantaneous) supply curve for labor in the country as a whole. The issue is whether this curve is positively or negatively elastic with respect to money or real wage changes, and whether the curve as a whole shifts in response to variations in employment opportunities, and if so, in what direction. Wage changes do not seem to have any appreciable short-run effect on the proportion of the population seeking employment. There is some reason to think that wage increases produce a slight decrease in the number of hours which people desire to work, particularly in the case of married women with family responsibilities. On the whole, however, the supply curve of labor with respect to wages can probably be taken as substantially vertical over short periods.

The question whether labor supply fluctuates sympathetically with changes in employment opportunities is probably of greater practical importance, but the evidence on it is not at all clear. Woytinsky has asserted that deep depression increases the labor force by compelling wives and children of unemployed workers to enter the market in larger numbers, but the statistical calculations advanced in support of this proposition have been challenged by other writers. Long concludes that the relation is slight and is probably in the opposite direction, i.e., a general decline in employment is likely to produce a slight decline in the proportion of the population in the labor force as some of the unemployed abandon the search for work which there seems little hope of finding.[24]

[23] Paul H. Douglas, *The Theory of Wages* (New York, 1934); *idem* and Erika Schoenberg, "Studies in the Supply Curve of Labor: The Relation in 1929 Between Average Earnings in American Cities and the Proportions Seeking Employment," *The Journal of Political Economy*, February 1937, XLV, pp. 45–79; Clarence Long, *The Size of the Labor Force under Changing Incomes and Employment.*

[24] D. D. Humphrey, "Alleged 'Additional Workers' in the Measurement of Unemploy-

If one could measure labor supply in the sense of available man-hours of standard efficiency, this measure would probably be found to fluctuate in the same direction as the level of employment. During a cyclical upswing, the number of individuals available for employment probably increases, both because some people will accept work who would not actively seek it and because employers lower their hiring standards to take in workers previously regarded as unemployable. It seems likely also that the work week will be lengthened somewhat and perhaps approach more closely that which would be freely chosen by employees, and that disguised unemployment in its various forms will be reduced. Opposite tendencies will be set in motion during a cyclical downswing. If this hypothesis is correct, the gap between actual and "full" employment may be considerably larger during a depression than is indicated by the statistics of "visible" or "superficial" unemployment, and the lower the level of employment the greater this discrepancy will be. During an upswing, the goal of full employment will recede as it is approached—though of course not indefinitely—and the number of additional jobs required will be considerably larger than it appeared to be at the bottom of the depression.[25]

MOVEMENT BETWEEN EMPLOYMENT AND UNEMPLOYMENT

The characteristics of this type of movement are now rather well known as a result of the intensive studies of unemployment in this and other countries during the 'thirties.[26] One tends to think of "the unemployed" as a stable group of individuals occupying the same status year

---

ment," *The Journal of Political Economy*, June 1940, XLVIII, pp. 412–419; Clarence Long, *The Size of the Labor Force under Changing Incomes and Employment*; W. S. Woytinsky, *Additional Workers and the Volume of Unemployment in the Depression*, Committee on Social Security of the Social Science Research Council (Washington, 1940).

[25] In support of this, I would be inclined to argue that the surprisingly large wartime increase in the visible labor force—from 53.5 million in December 1940 to 63.2 million in December 1944—was due to the fact that the 1940 Census, taken at a time of relatively low employment, seriously understated what might be termed the "full-employment" labor force, and consequently the true volume of unemployment. Long, however, who has done more work than anyone else on these matters, is of the opinion that the wartime increase was due mainly to special and temporary circumstances—military mobilization and the Selective Service system—rather than to the increased demand for labor. See Clarence Long, *The Labor Force in Wartime America*, pp. 50–55; and *idem*, *The Size of the Labor Force under Changing Incomes and Employment*, Sec. 4, pp. 4–5.

[26] Ewan Clague, Walter J. Couper, and E. Wight Bakke, *After the Shutdown—* (New Haven, 1934); Daniel Creamer and Charles W. Coulter, *Labor and the Shut-Down of the Amoskeag Textile Mills*, W.P.A. National Research Project, Report No. L-5 (November 1939); Edward J. Fitzgerald, *Selective Factors in an Expanding Labor Market: Lancaster, Pa.*, W.P.A. National Research Project No. L-4 (June 1939); L. C. Marsh, *Canadians in and out of Work* (Toronto, 1940); Gladys L. Palmer and Constance Williams, *Reemployment of Philadelphia Hosiery Workers after Shut-downs in 1933–34*, W.P.A. National Research Project in Cooperation with University of

after year. Actually, during times of high employment, there is rapid turnover among the unemployed, and a cross-section analysis at any time will show relatively few who have been out of work for more than a few months. "The unemployed" resemble the changing occupants of a subway train rather than water in a stagnant pool.

A general decline in employment obviously increases the number entering the unemployed group and reduces the chances of leaving it. But the really significant thing is that the incidence of both layoffs and new hirings is very uneven. Layoffs are most numerous among workers in heavy industry, workers with relatively little trade skill, those with low seniority, the less employable, the very old, and the very young. New hirings are confined largely to workers of high employability, in the prime of life, with good work experience, and so on. These preferred types of workers continue to turn over in much the usual way, and even in deep depression there are still many short-term unemployed. In addition, however, there accumulates an increasing number of less employable people, who have been unemployed for relatively long periods, and whose chances of re-employment diminish with the passage of time.

This hard core of unemployment is not immediately affected by economic recovery. The first effect of recovery is that fewer people lose jobs, rather than that more are absorbed from the unemployed. The next effect is likely to be that new entrants to the market and the short-term unemployed are able to find jobs more readily. Recovery must be well under way before the longer-term unemployed are called on. It must be remembered, too, that the unemployed at the bottom of a deep depression are a very atypical group as regards geographical location, occupational skill, and industrial attachment, as well as personal traits. Unless the configuration of demand which develops during the recovery is very similar to that which existed during the previous expansion, or unless the long-term unemployed are highly mobile, their reabsorption may prove very difficult. It is this which makes long-standing unemployment a peculiarly intractable problem, treatment of which requires more than the creation of an adequate overall demand for labor.

MOVEMENT BETWEEN GEOGRAPHICAL AREAS

This matter has also been studied considerably in recent years, and it is possible here to mention only a few of the apparent conclusions

Pennsylvania, Industrial Research Department, Report No. P–6 (January 1939); H. W. Singer, "The Process of Unemployment in the Depressed Areas," *The Review of Economic Studies*, June 1939, VI, pp. 177–188; *idem*, "Regional Labor Markets and the Process of Unemployment," *ibid.*, October 1939, VII, pp. 42–58.

from this work.[27] Geographical movement of workers occurs mainly during periods of rising employment; and the main economic stimulus to movement seems to be inter-area differences in the number of job opportunities available. This may mean either that job openings are particularly abundant in the new area or that the outlook is particularly unfavorable in the old. Those who leave agriculture for urban employments, for example, seem to be mainly young people who have no hope of becoming farm operators, or older people forced off the land for one reason or another. Those well established in agriculture seem willing to remain there even at incomes much below those which they might earn in the city. The Oxford Economic Institute's studies of migration between certain counties in England found that the greater the difference in the unemployment ratios of two counties, the greater, other things being equal, was the likelihood of migration between them. Moreover, the lag between the occurrence of a discrepancy in unemployment ratios between two areas and an increase in migration between them seemed to be only about six months.[28]

The relation between geographical wage differentials and labor mobility is difficult to evaluate, since wage differences usually occur along with differences in job opportunities and other factors. A few things, however, can perhaps be said. First, high wages in an area do not seem to have very great attractive power *unless* accompanied by job openings; and while we might expect the two to occur together, this will not always be the case. Second, most people who have jobs are sufficiently attached to their home communities so that they have little interest in jobs elsewhere, even at considerably higher wages. Interest in opportunities elsewhere is usually awakened by the loss of employment at home or by some personal or family disturbance. Third, even when the person is predisposed toward movement for one reason or another, his movement is about as likely to follow lines of personal contact[29] as it is to follow wage contour lines.

[27] The bibliography of this subject is very large. The following are only a few key references: Carter Goodrich et al., *Migration and Economic Opportunity* (Philadelphia, 1936); Clark Kerr, "Migration to the Seattle Labor Market Area, 1940–1942," University of Washington Publications in the Social Sciences, August 1942, II, No. 3, pp. 129–188; Bureau of the Census, *Civilian Migration in the United States: December 1941 to March 1945*, September 1945, Series P-S, No. 5; idem, *Internal Migration in the United States, 1935–1940*, April 1944, Series P-44, No. 10; Francis M. Vreeland and Edward J. Fitzgerald, *Farm-City Migration and Industry's Labor Reserve*, W.P.A. National Research Project, Report No. L-7 (August 1939).

[28] H. Makower, J. Marschak, and H. W. Robinson, "Studies in Mobility of Labor: Analysis for Great Britain," *Oxford Economic Papers*, May 1939, No. 2, pp. 70–79; September 1940, No. 4, pp. 39–62.

[29] It is well known that international migration is largely a group rather than an individual matter. The first to move to the new land send back for their relatives and friends,

It should be noted also that geographical mobility is quite selective with respect to personal and occupational characteristics. Mobility is highest among the young, single, and unattached; it is reduced by age, family responsibilities, and home ownership. Among occupational groups, professional people are much more mobile than any others, followed by executives and other white-collar workers. Skilled manual workers appear to be somewhat more mobile than the semi-skilled and unskilled. The labor force is not a homogeneous mass, all parts of which are equally responsive to wage differences or other economic stimuli.

MOVEMENT AMONG EMPLOYERS

This sort of movement has always been of particular interest to economists because of its presumed influence on wage determination. Yet there has been surprisingly little investigation of workers' decisions about taking and leaving jobs. In recent years one can think only of Palmer's studies in Philadelphia, Yoder's studies of the Minneapolis-St. Paul area, Davidson and Anderson's study of a California community, Maclaurin and Myers' study of a New England factory city, and the investigation of the New Haven labor market now being carried on at Yale.[30]

The results of these investigations cannot be described in any detail here, but we may note a few of the hypotheses which seem to be emerging. First, only a small percentage of the workers in an area—the unemployed, the new entrants, and those strongly dissatisfied with their present jobs —can really be regarded as in the labor market at any time. Most workers already have jobs with which they are reasonably well satisfied. These people do not behave like participants in a market; they are members of an organization with which they hope and expect to remain indefinitely. There is an economic basis for this, since both income and security tend to be increasing functions of length of service with a particular firm. Probably even more important in binding the worker to the plant, however, are his established relations with workers and

---

and thus whole groups are transferred from a particular community in the old country to a particular community in the new. Although similar studies have not been made with respect to internal migration, it would probably be found to follow the same general pattern.

[30] P. E. Davidson and H. Dewey Anderson, *Occupational Mobility in an American Community* (Stanford University, California, 1937); Helen Hermann, *Ten Years of Work Experience of Philadelphia Machinists*, W.P.A. National Research Project in Co-operation with University of Pennsylvania, Report No. P-5 (September 1938); W. R. Maclaurin and C. Myers, *The Movement of Factory Labor* (Cambridge, Mass., 1943); Gladys L. Palmer, "The Mobility of Weavers in Three Textile Centers," *Quarterly Journal of Economics*, May 1941, LV, pp. 460–487; L. G. Reynolds and Joseph Shister, *Job Satisfaction and Labor Mobility* (New Haven, 1948).

supervisors, and a preference for an accustomed routine over the perils of novelty and experimentation.

Second, wages are only one of five or six major factors affecting the worker's satisfaction with his job. At least equally important are the physical nature of the job, the degree of independence and participation in deciding how the job is to be done, equitable or inequitable treatment in work assignments and promotions, and regularity and security of employment. Moreover, his satisfaction with his wage rate need not be based on inter-plant comparisons; rate comparisons with other jobs in the same plant, and the adequacy of the worker's income to maintain his family at its accustomed standard of living, appear to be the commonest determinants of the worker's satisfaction with his wages. It is quite unrealistic to assume that the worker's willingness to leave his job depends mainly on the wage level of his plant relative to other plants, as is implied in the usual labor supply curves.

Third, workers who are in the market because of unemployment or dissatisfaction with their present jobs seek work primarily through relatives, acquaintances, former employers, union officials, and other personal contacts. The choice of a new job is usually based on a very limited comparison of alternative opportunities, and in many cases the worker takes the first job he hears about. This is due partly to a widespread feeling among workers that jobs are scarce and that one should seize the bird in the hand, which apparently persists even during the present period of high employment. It is due mainly, however, to the fact that the nature of the market makes job shopping very difficult. There is no central point at which workers can learn about the full range of job openings in the city, employers' use of the local office of the state employment service usually being insufficient to accomplish this end. Moreover, many of the most important things about a job—treatment by supervisors and fellow-workers, the detailed content of the job, the pace of work, the actual personnel practices of the company—cannot be learned until one has worked on the job. The only way in which a worker can really shop the market is to try out one job and then, if necessary, quit it and try again. While this process may well lead the worker from poorer to better jobs, there is no reason why it should lead him to the best job open at a particular time.

Fourth, the job choices of young people entering the labor market seem on the whole to be less systematic and well informed than the choices made in later life. There is little calculation of long-run advantage, and often no comparison even of the immediate advantage of alternative jobs. A large proportion of the first jobs turn out to be blind alleys, and many youngsters must experiment again and again before settling into permanent employment. There is no assurance that this process will secure the allocation of labor supplies which would have resulted from informed foresight.

These brief and over-simplified remarks are perhaps sufficient to raise some doubts concerning such concepts as the supply curve of labor to the firm, the labor market, a competitive wage structure, and so on. Economists have tended to regard rational behavior by workers as synonymous with complete responsiveness to wage differentials. This is too limited a view. Given their preference scales and their conception of the alternatives actually open to them, most workers make a rational job adjustment. But their conception of their situation is quite different from that which might be held by an omniscient observer, and their preference systems embrace a great many things besides hourly rates of pay. The fact that workers do not jump constantly from job to job in pursuit of maximum earnings proves nothing about their rationality, though it may prove something about the rationality of economists who expect them to do so.

MOVEMENT AMONG OCCUPATIONAL LEVELS

Under this heading arise two different but related problems. Of major long-run importance is the question how freely children of parents in one occupational stratum are able to enter other occupational strata on the basis of individual aptitude and preference. How firm are the barriers between non-competing groups and social classes, and are these barriers tending to increase or decrease in importance? Considerable interest attaches also to those shorter-range occupational movements which can be achieved within the working life of the individual. What are the chances that a person launched into a particular occupational level in early life will be able to move to some other level? What are the channels of vertical mobility and what are the principal obstacles? How closely is vertical mobility related to occupational wage differentials, either as cause or consequence?

The question of long-range occupational movement has been studied but little in recent years. The principal works have been Taussig and Joslyn's study of the origins of American business leaders, the study by Davidson and Anderson already referred to, and the Lynds' qualitative analysis of social mobility in an Indiana factory city.[31] More

---

[31] P. E. Davidson and H. Dewey Anderson, *op. cit.;* Robert and Helen M. Lynd, *Middletown* (London, 1929); *idem, Middletown in Transition* (New York, 1937); P. A. Sorokin, *Social Mobility* (New York and London, 1927); F. W. Taussig and C. S. Joslyn, *American Business Leaders* (New York, 1932).

thorough investigation, which is much to be desired, would probably reveal conflicting tendencies at work. One might find, for example, that it is becoming easier for the children of manual workers to enter the lower grades of white-collared work, and that this is partly responsible for the relative decline of clerical salaries relative to wages for manual labor. At the same time, entrance to the higher levels of business and professional employment may be growing more difficult as a result of rising educational requirements and educational costs. Taussig's study revealed a marked and growing tendency for business proprietors and officials to be recruited from the children of business families. He was careful to point out, however, that this can be ascribed to interclass differences of opportunity only on the assumption that differences in inherited characteristics are not significant—a matter on which there is still no general agreement.

There has also been little investigation of the shorter-range currents of occupational movement,[32] and significant work might be done on this subject. Taking into account only the manual occupations, it is likely that the skilled trades are tending to become a closed group and that the chances of movement from semi-skilled to skilled work are declining. The field of unskilled and semi-skilled work contains, of course, an enormous range of jobs, varying widely in wage levels and in total attractiveness. Movement of workers among these jobs is probably affected by a wide range of factors, including individual abilities and preferences, training, length of service, union rules, personal contacts, and the accident of being around when a vacancy occurs. A significant fact is that most specialized factory jobs are learned by doing them. New men are trained only as vacancies occur, and it is therefore not possible for surpluses of trained workers to develop and "beat down" the wage level of the job as is sometimes assumed in theoretical arguments.

For the economy as a whole, therefore, the upper limit of occupational wage differentials is largely a matter of custom or regulation, though for an individual employer it may be a matter of enforced conformity with practice in other plants. The situation will be equally stable whether machinists are paid 50 per cent more than laborers, 100 per cent more, or 200 per cent more; and which of these things will happen is not determined by competitive forces. There is doubtless a lower limit which is in part competitively determined.[33] A reduction of the differential be-

---

[32] P. E. Davidson and H. Dewey Anderson, *op. cit.*; W. S. Woytinsky, *Labor in the United States* (Washington, 1938); *idem, Three Aspects of Labor Dynamics* (Washington, 1942).

[33] For an illuminating discussion of this matter see A. Bergson, *The Structure of Soviet Wages* (Cambridge, Mass., 1944).

tween laborers and machinists to 10 per cent might make recruitment of machinists difficult, at least until such time as people came to regard the new situation as normal.[34] It seems probable, however, that occupational differentials in the United States are still somewhat wider than is necessary on grounds of recruitment, for one rarely hears of any difficulty in inducing workers to move up from less skilled to more skilled jobs.

III. Trade Unionism and Labor Relations

The past fifteen years have seen an unprecedented growth of union membership in the United States. The number of union members has increased from some three million in 1932 to about fifteen million at the present time. About half of the wage and salary earners eligible for union membership are now in unions, and it seems likely that this proportion will increase further in the future. Already collective bargaining has a dominant influence on wages and other terms of employment not only in the unionized sector of the economy but in the non-union sector as well.

The implications of this development are so important that adequate discussion of them would require a separate chapter. It is possible here to mention only a few of the key issues in this field. The warning issued at the beginning of the chapter should perhaps be repeated at this point: brevity of treatment is not meant to indicate that the matters treated are unimportant. It represents primarily limitations of space plus the fact that on some very important subjects relatively little work has yet been done.

TRADE UNION STRUCTURE, OBJECTIVES, AND TACTICS

Studies of unionism *per se* may be divided into two broad categories: first, efforts to trace the development of a particular union over the course of time; second, attempts to generalize about some aspect of unionism from the experience of a number of unions. The first type of study has thus far been commoner than the second, possibly because a single union affords a more clear-cut and manageable area of work, and also because such studies are or should be a prerequisite to generalizing studies.

---

[34] If wages served the function imputed to them by Adam Smith (and most subsequent economists) of equalizing the total attractiveness of different jobs, the machinist's wage should clearly be *less* than that of the laborer. The perverse behavior of occupational wage differences—i.e., the fact that the jobs which are paid more highly are also more attractive in most other ways—is probably to be explained on the ground that wage rates do not and are not meant to serve an equalizing purpose. High wages are rather a prestige index attached to jobs which have come to be regarded as "superior" through a consensus of management opinion, influenced somewhat by opinions of workers and (increasingly) trade union officials.

The union histories which have been written vary greatly in thoroughness, objectivity, organization, and general quality. Many of them lack a clear conceptual framework and thus do not really provide raw material for generalizations about unionism as a whole. They remain discrete assortments of facts instead of cumulating into a developing body of knowledge. Exceptions occur sufficiently often, however, to justify hope for the future. One might mention as examples McCabe's volume on the pottery industry, Haber's study of the building trades, Seidman's history of the needle trades, Hill's study of the teamsters, Lahne's book on the cotton mill workers, Jensen's study of the lumber industry, and Loft's volume on the printing trades.[35] More such studies, which relate the union to the structure of its industry and which attempt to explain historical developments instead of merely recounting them, are much to be desired.

Comparative or generalizing studies may be divided broadly into studies of trade union government, trade union objectives and policies, and the collective bargaining and political tactics of unions. Each of these areas, of course, embraces a large number of subordinate problems. Thus the first area includes numerous problems which arise in the government of a single union—securing efficient administrative organization, maintaining a proper balance between the authority of national and local officials, ensuring an adequate voice for the membership in the development of union policies, protecting individual members against arbitrary expulsion or other forms of discipline, and so on. There are also numerous problems of inter-union relations, including jurisdictional disputes, the controversy over craft vs. industrial organization, and the relation of individual international unions to the top federations.

Among works on trade union structure and government one should note particularly the studies by Galenson and Seidman, and the somewhat older volumes by Saposs and Hardman.[36] A major study of representative government in trade unions is now in process under Leiserson's direction, and the results should greatly advance our knowledge on this subject. The internal politics and administration of unions have also

---

[35] David McCabe, *National Collective Bargaining in the Pottery Industry* (Baltimore, 1932); W. H. McPherson, *Labor Relations in the Automobile Industry* (Washington, 1940); William Haber, *Industrial Relations in the Building Industry* (Cambridge, Mass., 1930); S. E. Hill, *Teamsters and Transportation* (Washington, 1942); H. Lahne, *The Cotton Mill Workers* (New York and Toronto, 1944); Joel Seidman, *The Needle Trades* (New York, 1942); Vernon Jensen, *Lumber and Labor* (New York, 1945); Jacob Loft, *The Printing Trades* (New York, 1944).

[36] Walter Galenson, *Rival Unionism* (New York, 1940); Joel Seidman, *Union Rights and Union Duties* (New York, 1943); David Saposs, *Left-Wing Unionism* (New York, 1926); J. B. Hardman, ed., *American Labor Dynamics* (New York, 1928).

been discussed considerably in the periodical literature, and something like a political science of union operations is in process of development.[37] There has not yet been a definitive analysis of the major structural change in the American labor movement during the past fifteen years, i.e., the great increase in the number and membership of industrial unions both within the CIO and the AFL.[38] Most prewar writing on the subject tended to highlight the more dramatic incidents in the CIO-AFL cleavage and, in greater or lesser measure, to choose sides in the controversy. The time has perhaps come for a more dispassionate treatment which would view this controversy as incidental to a major structural shift similar to that which occurred much earlier in the British, Swedish, and many other foreign labor movements.

One major category of union objectives, those having to do with wages, was discussed in Section A. With respect to non-wage objectives, Slichter's comprehensive study is the most important to appear in recent years.[39] A number of more specialized studies have appeared as doctoral dissertations, and the previously cited volume by Millis and Montgomery provides an excellent review of the literature on this as well as on other aspects of unionism. There is still room for much study of union objectives and policies, particularly those of the newer industrial unions. Casual observation suggests that some types of union rule which have been highly valued by many craft groups and which have played a prominent role in the literature—for example, limitations on number of apprentices and restrictions on technological change—are of much less interest to industrial unions. A careful documentation of differences in objectives between the older and newer unions, and of the apparent reasons for these differences, would be very valuable.

The problem of union objectives in the broader sense of reform of the existing industrial order vs. drastic alteration of the existing order, and the related problem of union reliance on collective bargaining vs. reliance on legislation, have been relatively little studied since the appearance of Perlman's *Theory of the Labor Movement* and the latter volumes of the

---

[37] Philip Taft, "Understanding Union Administration," *Harvard Business Review*, 1946, XXIV, pp. 245–457; *idem*, "Opposition to Union Officers in Elections," *Quarterly Journal of Economics*, February 1944, XVIII, pp. 246–264; *idem*, "Democracy in Trade Unions," *The American Economic Review*, May 1946, XXXVI, pp. 359–369; Theresa Wolfson, "Union Finances and Elections," *Annals of the American Academy of Political and Social Science*, November 1946, CCXLVIII, pp. 31–36.

[38] See, however, the discussion in H. A. Millis and R. E. Montgomery, *Organized Labor*, Vol. 3 of *Economics of Labor* (New York and London, 1945); Herbert Harris, *Labor's Civil War* (New York, 1940); and Everett M. Kassolow, "New Patterns of Collective Bargaining," in *Insights into Labor Issues*, R. Lester and J. Shister, eds. (New York, 1947).

[39] Sumner H. Slichter, *Union Policies and Industrial Management.*

Commons history. The most suggestive work which has appeared relates to European labor movements, though it is not without relevance for the United States.[40] In a forthcoming revision of his *Theory*, Perlman will examine the question of whether recent events in the United States and elsewhere require any modification of his original thesis. The growth of organized labor as an interest group fully comparable in strength to industry and agriculture, and the choice which labor makes between pursuing its objectives through the agencies of government and pursuing some of the same objectives through private collective bargaining, will obviously have great influence on the future development of our governmental institutions. Careful analysis of the political objectives and tactics of organized labor in this country, and comparisons with other countries in which these tactics have been much more highly developed, provides one of the most interesting avenues of labor study.

UNION–MANAGEMENT RELATIONS, COLLECTIVE BARGAINING, AND THE ROLE OF GOVERNMENT

Even more intriguing than analyses of unionism *per se* are the problems arising out of the collective bargaining relationship. Here one encounters socio-psychological questions of conflict between basic attitudes of union and management officials, administrative problems of collective bargaining procedure, legal and political issues of how the relative rights and duties of unions and managements should be defined, and of how government may best contribute to the prevention or adjustment of industrial conflict.[41] Active study of these matters is under way at a number of university centers. Only a few of the more extensive investigations now in process can be mentioned here.[42]

Kerr and others at California have in process a series of studies in collective bargaining, with particular reference to the patterns of bargaining which have developed on the Pacific Coast. Harbison and his associates at Chicago are exploring a variety of situations in particular companies in an effort to detect the basic factors influencing the course of union-management relations. At Yale, Bakke has investigated the objec-

---

[40] Adolf Sturmthal, *The Tragedy of European Labor, 1918–1939* (New York, 1943).

[41] To anyone with a flair for observing and dealing with human beings under curious and ever-changing circumstances, this complex of issues will probably always remain the heart of "the labor problem." It is not without significance that many of the ablest labor scholars have become deeply involved in these matters *via* arbitration work and service on governmental tribunals. Unfortunately, some of those who have done most in this way have written least about their experiences.

[42] A more complete listing of studies under way on this and other labor matters will be found in the compilation prepared annually by the Labor Market Research Committee of the Social Science Research Council. The most recent report, entitled "University Research Programs in the Field of Labor," was issued in February 1947.

tives and attitudes of union and management officials and analyzed the possibility of reconciling these objectives; Chamberlain, in addition to an earlier volume on collective bargaining procedures, has studied the issue of alleged union encroachment on "managerial prerogatives" in a number of basic industries; and Lindblom has completed a monograph on the question of how far bargained wage structures interfere with the adjustments necessary in a competitive and changing economy. Other studies in this general area which deserve mention include Pierson's discussion of collective bargaining systems, Teller's quasi-legal analysis of management functions under collective bargaining, the Twentieth Century Fund volume on recent collective bargaining developments in particular industries, edited by Millis, and Selekman's recent study of union-management relations.[43]

Several studies of collective bargaining have been focused primarily on "union-management co-operation," though this phrase seems to mean somewhat different things to different people and stands in need of sharper definition. Nyman's study of the Naumkeag Steam Cotton Company, and Smith and Nyman's study of numerous other cotton mills, dealt with union policy toward and union participation in revision of work loads and incentive rates.[44] Slichter's study of union policies dealt at length with union participation in the development of improved production methods which was initiated on several railroad systems, in the men's and women's clothing industries, and in a number of other places during the nineteen-twenties.[45] The National Planning Association is at present investigating some ten or twelve instances of unusually harmonious industrial relations in an effort to determine the main factors responsible for the absence of conflict in these cases, and to discover whether

[43] E. Wight Bakke, *Mutual Survival* (New Haven, 1946); Neil Chamberlain, *Collective Bargaining Procedures* (Washington, 1944); idem, *The Unions' Challenge to Management* (New York, 1948); idem, "Grievance Proceedings and Collective Bargaining," in *Insights into Labor Issues*; F. H. Harbison, "Some Reflections on a Theory of Labor-Management Relations," *Journal of Political Economy*, February 1946, LIV, pp. 1–16; idem, "A Plan for Fundamental Research in Labor Relations," *The American Economic Review*, May 1947, XXXII, pp. 375–383; idem, *Patterns of Union-Management Relations* (Chicago, 1947); Clark Kerr, "Collective Bargaining on the Pacific Coast," *Monthly Labor Review*, April 1947, LXIV, pp. 650–674; idem, Robert K. Burns, and Robert Dubin, "Toward a Theory of Labor-Management Relations," in *Insights into Labor Issues*; idem and Lloyd Fisher, "Multiple-Employer Bargaining: The San Francisco Experience," in *ibid.*; H. A. Millis, ed., *How Collective Bargaining Works* (New York, 1942); F. C. Pierson, *Collective Bargaining Systems* (Washington, 1942); Benjamin M. Selekman, *Labor Relations and Human Relations* (New York and London, 1947); L. Teller, *The Law Governing Labor Disputes and Collective Bargaining* (New York, 1940); idem, *A Labor Policy for America* (New York, 1945); idem, *Management Functions under Collective Bargaining* (New York, 1947).

[44] R. C. Nyman and E. D. Smith, *Union-Management Cooperation in the Stretch-Out* (New Haven, 1934); idem, *Technology and Labor* (New Haven, 1939).

[45] Sumner H. Slichter, *Union Policies and Industrial Management.*

these factors are peculiar to the situations in question or whether they have transfer value to other situations.

Much work remains to be done even on the strictly economic consequences of collective bargaining.[46] Collective bargaining affects the cost-price-output structure of industry not only through wage determinations but also through rules governing the selection and promotion of workers, speed and methods of work, introduction of changes in technology and job conditions, and so on. These rules tend in general to impose additional costs on the employer in order to protect certain non-wage interests of the worker, but the relation between costs and benefits is rather variable. Some types of rule—for example, grievance procedures and protection against arbitrary discharge—may confer great benefits on the worker with little cost to the employer or possibly even a reduction in costs. Other types of rule may impose considerable costs on the employer with relatively little benefit to the worker. It is probably true that under non-union conditions the interests of workers were unduly sacrificed to those of enterprise owners and consumers. The question is whether collective bargaining is currently producing a proper balancing of the interests of these groups, or whether the interests of workers are now being unduly advanced to the detriment of consumers.[47]

Exploration of this question will probably require case studies of the effect of contractual rules and informal union policies on productivity and labor costs in particular plants and industries. It is dangerous to conclude too much from the rules themselves. Some of the most important practices may not be written into the contract, the contractual terms may be administered in ways quite different from what a literal reading of them would suggest, and some of them may not be enforced at all in practice. Intimate observation of the day-to-day administration of a plant is necessary in order to judge the actual impact of unionism on productivity and cost levels.

Discussion of public policy toward collective bargaining centered from 1937 to 1947 on the operation of the National Labor Relations Act and on the recurring proposals for its amendment. Enactment of the Labor-Management Relations Act of 1947 opened a new chapter in this discus-

---

[46] Some of the central issues are presented very succinctly in *idem, The Challenge of Industrial Relations* (Ithaca, 1947); see especially Ch. 2, "The Effect of Trade Unions on the Management of Business Enterprises." Slichter's earlier volume referred to above is also very relevant in this connection.

[47] The answer to this question will always be a matter of judgment rather than of precise measurement. How can one determine precisely how fast workers *should* work on a particular operation? How can one say just how much more consumers should pay for a product in order that workers may have pleasanter surroundings in the plant, free recreational facilities, rest periods, paid vacations, and other types of benefit?

sion, which will probably proceed with fresh vigor as the provisions of the new law are clarified by administrative action and court decision, and as proposals for further legal changes are debated in the political arena. The books of Bowman and Rosenfarb[48] provide good summaries of the operation of the N.L.R.A. from its passage up to their respective dates of publication. Among the more recent discussions of public policy should be mentioned the volumes by Slichter and Gregory.[49]

Despite the extensive literature on public policy in labor matters, the field bristles with unresolved issues both of general principle and of administrative technique. Three examples only need be cited. First, in what respects should the individual worker's freedom of action be protected against authority wielded by union officials? Where individual freedom conflicts with the requirements for strong and stable unionism, which should be given preference? Second, in what sectors of the economy is it important that work stoppages be prevented, and what types of governmental action are likely to be most effective to that end? If one is interested in equity as well as peace, the problem of stopping strikes turns out to be extremely intricate, and one cannot say that effective measures have even been devised, much less given practical application. A third kind of issue, raised by Simons, Lindblom, and others, has to do with the consequences of industrial peace rather than the prevention of industrial strife. Is peace in some cases too dearly bought? Are the collective bargaining settlements arrived at by the parties, particularly the wage settlements, so disruptive to the economy's operation as to call for some public control over their terms? This issue will become increasingly important as union organization increases in strength, and might become very acute in the event of a vigorous effort to maintain full employment through fiscal policy.

It should be noted that, in addition to federal regulation of labor relations, there has been a great extension of state legislation on this subject during the past ten years and a very large number of court decisions in labor cases. There has been no recent effort to integrate all this material and to present a unified picture of the current state of labor law. The last comprehensive treatise on the subject was published by Witte in 1932.[50] Considerable portions of this excellent work have now become out of date, and a thoroughgoing review of labor law is very much needed.

---

[48] Dean O. Bowman, *Public Control of Labor Relations* (New York, 1942); Joseph Rosenfarb, *The National Labor Policy and How It Works* (New York and London, 1940).

[49] Sumner H. Slichter, *The Challenge of Industrial Relations*; Charles O. Gregory, *Labor and the Law* (New York, 1946).

[50] E. E. Witte, *The Government in Labor Disputes* (New York and London, 1932).

HUMAN RELATIONS IN INDUSTRY

This currently popular phrase is in some ways a very good title for the work now to be discussed, since its generality allows it to embrace the variety of problems which have interested psychologists, sociologists, anthropologists, and others. The problems range over the whole field of labor and industrial relations, including such things as the motivation of the individual worker (and, for that matter, the business manager and the trade union official); the relation between the behavior of these people in the plant and outside the plant; the social structure of the factory—the formal and informal lines of communication, hierarchy of authority, organization of work groups, and so on; worker response to various structures of incentives and to various personal and social situations, as indicated by output, absenteeism, turnover, and the like; and the possible ways of integrating the various groups in the enterprise into a more harmonious work team.

The subject matter, in other words, is identical with that used by economists and other students of labor questions. The phrase "human relations in industry" connotes, not a separate subject-matter specialty, but a different point of view and method of approach. Those adopting this approach have in common a distrust of the economist's simple assumptions about human motivations, as well as his tendency to personify such complex entities as the union and the business firm and to reason about group behavior on individualistic lines. They are highly conscious of the complexity of human motivation, the extent to which the individual's actions are conditioned by his personal history and by the social structure within which he acts, and the large area of industrial behavior which cannot be explained at all by economic analysis.

Sharing this critical attitude toward economic methods, they are much less agreed on what alternative conceptual systems can usefully be applied to industrial situations. No one has yet succeeded in developing a conceptual framework which fully satisfies his co-workers,[51] and rival systems of concepts will probably remain in competition for a long time to come. This lack of a settled method of analysis, while somewhat frustrat-

---

[51] This is explained partly by the fact that the different members of this group have started from different disciplinary backgrounds, as is indicated by such varied titles as psychologists, social psychologists, industrial psychologists, anthropologists, social anthropologists, sociologists, and industrial sociologists. It will probably be realized increasingly that, regardless of starting points, the problems on which all these people are converging are identical problems. Moreover, these central problems of behavior will probably yield only to some synthesis of psychological and sociological methods of attack. It is even possible that economics may play a modest role in the final synthesis of knowledge on these matters.

ing to the systematic mind, at the same time provides a challenge to the exploration of fresh scientific territory.

The first substantial impetus to this type of study came from investigations of the behavior of small groups of factory workers carried on co-operatively by the Western Electric Company and a group of research workers from the Harvard Business School during the late 'twenties and early 'thirties. These studies, which have been exhaustively reported,[52] suggested that non-economic elements in worker behavior were much more important than had been generally realized. During the late 'thirties and early 'forties work along somewhat similar lines was pursued by Chapple and Warner. Chapple attempted to develop a quantitative analysis of interpersonal relationships in the factory on the basis of frequency, regularity, and duration of personal contacts between any two individuals, the person taking the initiative in making the contact, the responsiveness of each person to the other during the conversation, etc., and developed some interesting mechanical devices for recording and analyzing conversations.[53] Warner, applying an anthropological approach to the study of a New England factory city, attempted to describe the broader community framework within which the processes of industrial relations go on, and to trace the way in which this framework influenced the course of strikes and other key events occurring during the period studied.[54]

Investigation along psycho-sociological lines is now proceeding most actively at Yale, Chicago, and the Massachusetts Institute of Technology. Bakke, who during the 'thirties made pioneer studies of workers' motivation and the social consequences of unemployment, has since extended his studies to other fields. A study of attitudes toward unionism by workers, employers, and the public is substantially completed, and there is now under way an intensive case study of human relations in a large business organization at all levels from the company president to the lowest labor classification. Bakke has also developed a systematic theory of human behavior for use in the analysis of industrial situations.[55]

Gardner, Whyte, and others at Chicago have, either completed or in process, a variety of in-plant studies on such subjects as systematic output

---

[52] Elton Mayo, *The Human Problems of an Industrial Civilization* (New York, 1933); F. J. Roethlisberger, *Management and Morale* (Cambridge, Mass., 1946); *idem* and W. J. Dixon, *Management and the Worker* (Cambridge, Mass., 1941); T. N. Whitehead, *Leadership in a Free Society* (Cambridge, Mass., 1936).

[53] Eliot D. Chapple and Conrad Arensberg, *Measuring Human Relations* (Provincetown, 1940).

[54] See his *Yankee City* series, Vols. 1–4 (New Haven, 1941–47).

[55] E. Wight Bakke, *Principles of Adaptive Human Behavior* (New Haven, 1946); *idem, Why Workers Join Unions* (New York, 1945); *idem, The Unemployed Worker* (New Haven, 1940); *idem, The Unemployed Man* (London, 1933); *idem, Citizens Without Work* (New Haven, 1940).

restriction among factory workers, the relation between variations in individual output under an incentive wage system and various social characteristics of the workers, the characteristics of the workers joining the union in a newly organized plant as compared with those who do not join, problems in the relationship of workers and first-line supervisors, and problems of customer-worker relationships in stores and restaurants. Gardner's recent book provides perhaps the best general exposition of the human relations point of view to be found in any single source.[56] McGregor and others at the Massachusetts Institute of Technology use a clinical approach to industrial relations situations in particular plants, and are working also on a general theory of behavior into which particular observations can be fitted. There are no doubt numerous other studies of this type which might be mentioned. Published work is somewhat difficult to locate because it may appear in any of a large number of social science journals.

It may be desirable in conclusion to emphasize again one or two of the points made in earlier sections. The study of the phenomena of industrial employment calls for a wide variety of analytic techniques. Few problems can be handled primarily by economic analysis, and in most parts of the field the role of economics is quite limited. Where a problem is amenable to economic methods, however, there is no reason for not using the best theoretic tools available, while at the same time trying to refashion these tools into more realistic and useful forms. This seems to be increasingly recognized, and among the younger men entering the labor field the gap between theorists and research workers appears to be narrowing. It is probably more true today than it was a generation ago that the people most highly trained in deductive analysis are among those best informed on factual questions and most active in empirical investigation.

The problems not susceptible to economic analysis are being studied increasingly by the use of other social science disciplines, and a serious effort is being made to fashion new analytic systems suited to these problems. Most of the work on these matters is still necessarily on the prescientific level of careful observation and description. The outlines of the phenomena have to be sketched in before we can say what are the key questions to be answered. There is good reason to hope, however, that description will be followed before too long by analysis and generalization.

---

[56] Burleigh B. Gardner, *Human Relations in Industry* (Chicago, 1945); William F. Whyte, ed., *Industry and Society* (New York and London, 1946).

8

DEVELOPMENT AND USE OF NATIONAL INCOME DATA

Carl S. Shoup

THE present time happens to be particularly appropriate for reviewing the developments of a decade in the field of national income. Ten years ago the first of the "Studies in Income and Wealth" was published, containing the papers and discussions at the initial sessions of the Conference on Research in National Income and Wealth, held in 1936. It was in 1937 also that there appeared the first of the series of volumes on national income by Simon Kuznets under the auspices of the National Bureau of Economic Research. A debate was under way in the scholarly journals over the implications of defining saving and investment, as Keynes had done the year before in his *General Theory*, so that they are equal in amount.

Ten years later, Kuznets had completed his work with the publication of a summary volume, late in 1946. The Department of Commerce, in July 1947, had issued its revised series of estimates of national income for the period 1929–46. The new series reflects some major changes in concepts as well as improvements in the data. In Great Britain the annual White Paper on national income had become an established institution, the seventh one appearing in 1947. In 1946 a mimeographed report (to be available soon as a United Nations publication) was submitted by the Sub-Committee on National Income Statistics of the League of Nations' Committee of Statistical Experts. The report presented a 100-page memorandum by Richard Stone, "Definition and Measurement of the National Income and Related Totals." In 1947 the United Nations had under way a project for reconciling inter-country differences of concept, to enhance the comparability of the national income series of the several nations. In the autumn of that year, workers in the national income field from many countries attended the International Statistical Association and Econometric Society meetings, and organized an International Association for Research in Income and Wealth. By 1947, a few courses in national income were being offered in American universities, and extensive use was being made of J. R. Hicks and Albert Gailord Hart's volume,

The Social Framework of the American Economy, an adaptation of a similar volume by Hicks published earlier in England. A general treatise on national income by the present writer, *Principles of National Income Analysis,* designed in part to meet the needs of students specializing in national income, was published in 1947. Although the coming decade will probably show an increase, not a slackening, in the amount of time and effort spent on national income analysis in almost every country, including the United States, it cannot quite duplicate the excitement and the hazards of the pioneering period just concluded.

I. THE ORGANIZATIONS CONCERNED

As the experience of this decade has shown, the study of national income has reached a stage where substantial advances in assembly and interpretation of the data usually require resources on a scale so large that some organization—foundation, research bureau, or government—must participate. The same is true to a considerable degree even in the refinement of conceptual issues; criticism, rejoinder, and further exploration have flourished through the medium of conferences, held at more or less regular intervals, that bring together the geographically scattered workers in this field. Consequently, a résumé of developments during the past ten years may start with an account of organizational activity in national income research.

The Income Conference, first held in 1936, as noted above, was originated and has been maintained by the National Bureau of Economic Research. Membership in the Conference has been by invitation, extended to persons who have been actively interested in national income research. Each member is entitled to vote at meetings and elections of the Conference, to receive reports and publications of the Conference (subject in some cases to charges), and to be reimbursed for his expenses in traveling to and from and in attending the Conference, if arrangements cannot be made to have these outlays met by the agency or organization with which he is connected. In 1947, owing to the growing number of members, it was decided that only the expenses of actively participating members (authors and discussants) could be thus defrayed, in the future. Membership has not been static; new members have been added, and invitations have been discontinued to those whose interest has shifted away from national income research. The annual conferences have also been attended by non-members upon invitation.

Although this restriction of the annual conferences to those receiving invitations gives rise to certain dangers of exclusiveness and inbreeding, it has probably been an essential element for the degree of 'success that has been achieved. Progress in a highly technical field of research, in its formative period, could easily be hampered rather than helped by time- and energy-consuming conferences where the technician and non-technician spent most of the day trying to understand one another. Even the selected group of research workers engaged in the same field found it difficult enough to understand each other when the Conference was initiated. The development of a common technical vocabulary has been one of the major achievements of the Conference.

The other phase of the National Bureau's support of national income study has been reflected in the series of volumes by Simon Kuznets and his associates at the Bureau. In these volumes the national income data for 1919–38 have been assembled and interpreted (some data are presented for the period since 1869).

The Federal Government entered the field of national income research in the early 1930's as a result of a Senate resolution directing the Department of Commerce to prepare estimates of national income. A large amount of data and interpretative material has been published: in special reports and bulletins in the 1930's, and in articles in the *Survey of Current Business* in the 1940's. The 54-page Supplement to the July 1947 *Survey* represents more than five years of intensive work by Milton Gilbert, director of the National Income Division of the Bureau of Foreign and Domestic Commerce, and his associates, particularly Edward F. Denison, George Jaszi, and Charles F. Schwartz.

The National Industrial Conference Board and the Brookings Institution have also carried on research in national income, though not on the extensive and continuing scale of the National Bureau and the Department of Commerce.

In Great Britain it has been a government department, the Central Statistical Office, that has played the chief role in developing national income data during the past decade, under the guidance of Richard Stone. The data, together with a rather limited amount of conceptual explanation, have appeared in the White Papers noted above; the conceptual issues have been discussed at greater length by Stone and others in articles in the scholarly quarterlies, especially the *Economic Journal*. In the past few years two privately supported research groups have embarked on work in the national income field, also under the supervision of Stone: the National Institute of Economic and Social Research in London, and the Department of Applied Economics at Cambridge. But so far there have been no regular series of conferences, in Great Britain or elsewhere, like those in the United States.

In the Netherlands the Central Bureau of Statistics has been active in national income computations and analysis. Government departments in Australia, Canada, and Eire have recently published estimates of national income for their respective countries. The Scandinavian countries are represented by the two-volume work of Lindahl, Dahlgren, and Kock, on the national income of Sweden, published in 1937, for the period 1861–1930, and by a recently published official series for Denmark. A substantial amount of activity is under way in Norway. In other countries, too, the collection of national income data has already started, but the work is apparently not yet very far advanced. Generally speaking, all of this activity is taking place under government auspices.

II. Advances in National Income Theory in the Past Decade

National income theory, in the sense understood here, is concerned primarily with conceptual problems, as distinguished from a study of the measurement and explanation of the reasons for business fluctuations, the implications of the existing distribution of income, and similar topics that are referred to below under the heading of "Uses Made of National Income Data." There is first of all the basic problem of specifying what it is that is being measured when a total of national income is cast up, so that changes in the total from one period to another, or one place to another, can be interpreted correctly. Different totals may of course be constructed, each measuring a different thing; but the thing that each total measures needs to be described clearly, and that is not so simple a task as might at first appear. Moreover, to avoid misunderstanding, it is desirable either to attach the term "national income" to but one of these totals, devising other terms for the others, or to specify what species of national income is being reckoned: for example, national income at factor cost, national income at market prices, gross national income.

Once the basic definitions have been constructed, at least provisionally, there must be examined a large number of sub-problems relating to the inclusion or exclusion of this or that item, in order to avoid double counting, or to avoid gaps, or to assure consistency with the deflating technique (product-price index) that is to be applied to the year-by-year or nation-by-nation series of totals, or to maximize the usefulness of the series for economic policy decisions.

THE MEANING OF THE TOTALS

Great progress has been made in the past ten years in developing uniform and distinctive labels for various totals, especially through the efforts of the government research staffs in the United States and the British Commonwealth. The progress in making quite clear all the implications of each of the totals has been somewhat less satisfying. Much of the advance in this area has come in the course of discussing issues raised by the various constituent items—a natural enough procedure, but one which, as indicated further below, has left the analysis of the total concepts in a somewhat more fragmentary and disorganized state than might have been hoped for. And it may be argued that progress on many of the sub-problems raised by the constituent items would have been more rapid if, concurrently, more attention had been paid to what the changes in the total or totals were supposed to measure: for example, changes in total output, or total input; changes in welfare (however defined), or changes in economic power. Similarly, much of the discussion of whether part or all or none of government services should be included in national income would have been more fruitful if the discussants had first reached a more precise agreement, or agreement to disagree, on the attributes of a final product (as contrasted with an intermediate product), since national income is the sum of the final products turned out during the period. Likewise, some of the argument over the treatment of taxes in computing factor payments would have produced more light than it did, if it had been accompanied or preceded by more thought on the type of price index needed to make periods and countries comparable. This point of view may not be shared, however, by many of those who have made the most outstanding contributions to the solution of the issues raised by the various constituent items. Instead, it appears that in government research circles, particularly, whether in the United States or abroad, attempts at precise description and analysis of what each of the totals is supposed to measure are considered as rather less urgent tasks than the careful and orderly presentation of constituent elements in a way that allows the reader to construct any one of several totals himself, and, especially, allows him to use the relationships between the constituent items in the study of problems of current economic policy. Thus the League of Nations' sub-committee points out that "where national income studies are used in connection with the formulation of economic policy, . . . it is the interrelationship of transactions that is important rather than individual totals, such as the national income, or gross national product." The totals are obtained by "a suitable combination of these constituent transactions."[1] Richard Stone, in his accompanying memorandum, says that

---

[1] League of Nations, Report of the Sub-Committee on National Income Statistics, *Measurement of National Income and the Construction of Social Accounts*, mimeographed, p. 1.

"modern inquiries which had their origin in an attempt to measure certain broad totals have changed their emphasis and now concentrate more on the structure of the constituent transactions and on the mutual interdependence of these transactions."[2] The question at issue, consequently, is whether the formulation of standards for the "suitable combinations" has been given adequate attention.

The discussions on the meaning of the totals that have marked the past decade resist ready summarization. Several debates on this issue can be found in the proceedings of the Conference on Income and Wealth, and Kuznets has devoted chapters to it in his volumes on national income and national product, but there is still room for a more thoroughgoing, unified analysis. It is not even clear, in some discussions, whether changes in the totals are to be taken as measuring changes in output or changes in input; if the latter can be measured, it presumably requires the use of an index of factor prices, not product prices. And if a change in output is being measured as an indication of change in consumers' welfare, the theoretical requirements for being able to ascertain whether such a change has occurred need to be developed more than they have been in the American literature. On this point, fortunately, the British analysts have given substantial aid, especially J. R. Hicks in his article in *Economica* for May 1940. There he distinguished between a welfare total and a productivity total. Both of them are output, not input, concepts, but they differ in that the welfare total does include, and the productivity total does not include, indirect taxes and other payments that, not being considered a part of factor payments, simply drive a wedge between the market value of the product and the total of factor payments. These two measures can, and ordinarily will, give different quantitative results when the two periods or two countries that are being compared with respect to total national income show movements in product prices and in amounts consumed that are not the same, product for product, in the two periods or countries. More analysis would seem to be needed, however, before it becomes indisputably clear what it is that the productivity index measures.

As the remarks above imply, the interpretation of the total for national income is in large part a problem in the construction of index numbers. The total, standing by itself, means nothing; it is compared with its constituent parts, or it is expressed on a per-person basis and compared with prevailing prices, or it is compared with totals for other periods or other regions. In this last case, deflation by an index number of product prices is essential. The theoretical groundwork for the construction of such an

---

[2] *Ibid.*, Appendix, p. 23.

index has been advanced in the past decade by explorations into the theory of consumer choice and consumer welfare, particularly in Great Britain. This theory, as presented by Kaldor and Hicks, shows that an unambiguous answer as to whether the consumer is better off or worse off, after prices and his money income have changed, requires that, in addition to an assumption that his wants have remained unchanged, there be changes in prices and money income of a nature that allows him to make a choice between the two assortments of goods—the assortment that he purchases in the first period and the assortment that he purchases in the second. This choice must of course be present only in one of the two periods (otherwise he would not in fact buy different assortments in the two periods). The assortment that he prefers is the one he buys when he has the chance to buy either. This reasoning is then extended to a group of consumers, without making interpersonal comparisons of utility, by ascertaining whether it would be possible, by a redistribution of the goods, to leave each person better off than in the earlier period; if so, national income in the sense of consumer goods and services is said to have increased.

In the United States, the Department of Commerce has well under way the construction of index numbers for deflating various parts of its product series. Kuznets, in his *National Product Since 1869*, has made use of price indexes that are more suitable because more comprehensive than those that were available when his earlier estimates were made. Finally, the puzzling problems of deflation raised by the shift from peacetime goods to wartime goods after 1940 provoked a lively discussion in the American field which, while it hardly settled all the issues (and some of them seem capable of resisting settlement indefinitely), cleared some ground.

One aspect of attempting to ascertain just what the totals imply is seen in the computation of the total for a period shorter than a year. Such a computation as that made by Barger, and published in 1942, serves to sharpen some of the conceptual problems; so, too, presumably, would a computation using a period longer than a year as the time unit.

Perhaps the most significant change that has occurred during the past decade with respect to the concept of a total has been the growing use of several types of totals: national income, gross national product, net national product, for example. Not all of them were primarily inventions of the past decade; the gross national product concept was developed before then, but even the gross national product, as it is defined today, has no exact counterpart in the earlier literature.

The two most widely used total concepts are: national income, computed as the sum of factor payments, themselves computed after the subtraction of indirect taxes but before subtracting direct or personal taxes, which are deemed by Kuznets, economists in the Department of Commerce, and the British White Paper to be paid out of the factor payments; and gross national product, computed as the sum of net foreign investment, net change in inventory, goods and services flowing to consumers (consumer outlay), goods and services utilized by government (government purchases), construction, and production of other fixed tangible capital assets for business. The "gross" element arises from the fact that the last two items are computed without subtracting an amount representing the depreciation or obsolescence of buildings, machinery, and equipment. Moreover, the gross national product (except as defined by Kuznets), unlike the national income total, nowhere subtracts indirect taxes. Since the market value of the finished products listed immediately above includes the amounts that flow to government as indirect taxes, the gross national product includes an amount equal to such taxes. This inclusion, however, is best regarded not as a "gross" element but as a method of stating the value of the finished product at a higher price level (market prices) than that used in stating the sum of factor payments. Opinion on the degree of usefulness of the gross national product concept is not unanimous; for example, whether it is a better index of activity than is national income. In any event, the extended discussions of the gross national product concept over the past decade have helped provoke a realization of the issues involved in attempts to "gross up" the national income total.

An intermediate total that may well prove more useful for certain purposes than either gross national product or national income is net national product, as defined by the Department of Commerce. This, with minor qualifications, is equal to national income plus indirect taxes; it is the sum of final products expressed at market prices (hence including indirect taxes) but with construction and plant and equipment data on a net basis, that is, after depreciation and whatever obsolescence the data reveal.

Still a fourth total has recently been devised by the British White Paper: gross national product at factor cost, which is, in effect, gross national product minus indirect taxes, or, alternatively, national income as the sum of factor payments, before deducting depreciation and obsolescence in computing the factor payment, profits.

The problem of which total to use is especially important when it is desired to express each of the components on the product side as a per cent of the total. If each of these components is to be expressed as a per cent of national income, which does not include indirect taxes, each one must be purified by subtracting the amount of indirect-tax loading that goes into the market price of each. This is, of course, a formidable task, which has so far been essayed only by the British computers. This difficulty emphasizes one reason for using a net national product concept rather than national income, as those terms are defined above.

Among the totals, that for personal income has been developed and refined during the past decade to a considerable extent. This series, formerly known as income payments to individuals (in Department of Commerce terminology), has been expanded in the revision published in 1947 to include net imputed rent of owner-occupied dwellings and income in kind paid to the armed forces (value of food, etc., supplied to the armed forces). It also now includes an adjustment to remove, from the data showing change in inventories held by unincorporated concerns, that part of the change reflecting change in price levels. These alterations in the personal income series exemplify more the increase in available data than an alteration in standard concept. In general, there has been perhaps less discussion of what the concept, personal income, should include than might have been expected.

ADVANCES IN DEALING WITH CONSTITUENT PARTS OF THE TOTALS

It was indicated above that more substantial advances in national income theory had been made during the past ten years with respect to particular constituent items than in interpreting the totals themselves. The greatest advance of all has been in segregating the major sectors of the economy that differ notably in the kind of accounts they keep and the functions they perform, and, by a system of double-entry bookkeeping, connecting the sectors by an internally consistent system of accounts.

With respect to individual items where considerable advances have been made during the past ten years, those noted in the following summary must be taken as samples rather than a complete listing, which is impracticable within the scope of this essay.

The Government Sector

The treatment that should be accorded government items in the national income accounts has been discussed repeatedly during the past decade. Whether substantial progress has been made in this part of the field, as a result of discussions is pretty much a matter of opinion, for, despite the amount of time and effort spent in exploring the conceptual aspects of this problem, there is still no general agreement among national income analysts. The problem falls into two subdivisions: the treatment of government outlays when computing national income as the sum of final products, and the treatment of taxes and subsidies when computing national income as the sum of factor payments.

Under the product approach, three schools of thought can be distinguished. The Department of Commerce and the Central Statistical Office, along with government statisticians in other countries, consider that all government outlays are outlays for final products, not intermediate products, and hence should all be counted in the total. The only exceptions are outlays that are transfer payments, that is, payments not for current goods or services, and hence not for either final or intermediate products. Interest on the public debt, or at least the central government debt, is so considered. But police services, fire-fighting services, education, and national defense or national aggression, to name a few of the major items, are all considered to be final products.

The second school of thought, upheld by a few individual students in the field, including the present writer, and represented also in the pre-war German and the Swedish computations of national income, maintains that government services must be divided into two parts: one part consists of final goods, either as consumer goods or as additions to the country's stock of capital equipment, while the other part consists of intermediate goods which are used up, or utilized, by government itself or by private business, in turning out final products. The distinction is based on the particular definition of final product which any one proponent of this method has presumably developed, explicitly or implicitly.

The third point of view is represented by the practice adopted by the National Bureau of Economic Research in the early 1920's and carried on by Kuznets. It assumes that the nature of the government's product is best determined, or at least determined with the minimum amount of arbitrariness, by noting how much is paid in personal taxes, and how much in business taxes. An amount of government product equal to the amount of personal taxes paid is considered to be consumer goods. On the product side of the national income accounts this item appears, not as government product, but as a part of the total consumers' outlay, or flow of goods and services to consumers. An amount of government product equal to the amount of business taxes paid is assumed to be intermediate product, hence not included in the national income. Government construction is considered to be a final product. If the total of government outlay is greater than the sum of these three amounts, that is, if there is a deficit on current account, this excess, or deficit, is presumed to represent expenditures that resulted in no product at all.

Some reconciliation between these strongly divergent points of view may be expected, or at least hoped for, but only if more attention is devoted to what is meant by "final product" in general, and if the proponents of the three methods specify more clearly than they have so far how much of their respective prescriptions reflect conceptual differences, and how much they reflect differing estimates of the difficulty of separating government outlays into the two classes of final and intermediate product on the basis of the data available.

The other subdivision of the government-sector problem, the treatment of taxes and subsidies, has likewise been discussed at length during the past decade, and here too disagreement has persisted. But it is perhaps less clear than with respect to the product approach how far the disagreement is real, and how much of it would disappear if the parties to the controversy tried first to reach agreement on how the total of national income, computed from the factor-payment side, should be defined and adjusted by index numbers for year-to-year and place-to-place comparisons. Both Kuznets and the Commerce-White Paper computations subtract business taxes ("indirect taxes" in White Paper terminology) but not personal taxes. Others, including the present writer, are disposed to make no distinction between business taxes and personal taxes in computing the national income total on the grounds that use of product-price indexes to make the totals comparable from year to year or place to place will adjust for any change in prices caused by a shift from one type of tax to another. To this the other group replies that a comparison of the component parts of the national income for any one year—wages compared with profits, for example—cannot be made unless a decision is first reached as to what taxes come out of factor payments and what taxes are simply something added to, but not a part of, factor payments. And to this in turn the reply may be that such a comparison is one of relative inputs, not output, and so of course requires different rules, or additional information. This highly condensed version of the disagreement is intended merely to suggest, rather than define sharply, the nature of the dispute. Here again, as with the product side of the government sector, it seems likely that a much better understanding would result if some stipulations were first made on the broader conceptual issues: whether it is changes in (or relative amounts of) input or output that are being measured; if output, what concept of final product is being employed; and what type of price index is to be used in ascertaining the real, as opposed to money, changes or relative amounts. There is a widespread reluctance to open up once more the discussion on how to treat the government items in national income computations; the subject seems to have been worn threadbare by repeated papers, discussions, and comments. But it is not very satisfactory to leave the problems suspended in their present state of semi-solution.

Saving and Investment

If the national income analysis and estimates prior to 1937 did not explicitly assume that the total of saving could differ from the total of investment, neither did they face the issue explicitly and draw, for the reader's benefit, the implications that would follow. Keynes' decision, in his *General Theory*, to define saving and investment so that they are equal in amount for any past period, forced the pace of analysis in this part of the national income field. The structure of the British White Papers on national income has obviously been built largely around this saving-investment concept. The Department of Commerce has made increasing use of the identity, and in its revised data published in 1947 it presents for the first time an annual series from 1929 showing total gross private saving, government surplus or deficit (saving or dissaving), and total gross investment, the sum of the first two items equaling the third item. In Kuznets' series, too, total saving equals total investment, although less emphasis is placed upon this equality—or perhaps it should be said that the equality is more taken for granted—than in the other two series. For national income analysis, the chief significance of utilizing the Keynesian definitions is probably the stimulus given to "model-building" in estimating inflationary and deflationary pressures, or in testing business forecasts for internal consistency (these points are noted in Section IV below). And one of the indisputable benefits is that no one can now talk loosely of saving and investment in national income data in a way that implies, even aside from statistical discrepancies, the one may differ from the other, without being suspected of economic illiteracy (excepting, of course, the cases where the analyst makes explicit use of the Robertsonian definitions, or some other particular set of definitions that he is able and willing to specify). A great deal of potential misunderstanding has thus been avoided.

Inventory Valuations

The usual method of valuing inventories on the books of business firms has been to count them at cost, or, if the market cost of replacing them is lower, at that lower value. When prices in general rise, after the firm has accumulated an inventory at lower price levels, the firm's sales at the new high price level are likely to show a substantial profit. But most of this profit must be kept in the business; the money is needed to restock the inventory, which must now be done at the new high price level.

National income analysts have sought ways to avoid including this profit, which they do not regard as real, in the total of national income, and they likewise wish to avoid writing down the national income in periods of falling prices when large nominal losses are recorded under this traditional method of inventory accounting.

On this point, great progress has been made in the United States in the past decade, owing largely to the pioneering work of Kuznets and his associates, and to the later work of the Department of Commerce. The British have been unable to get far with this problem, since they lack adequate data on capital formation in general, and inventory changes in particular. The method used by Kuznets cannot readily be summarized here, but the effect is to obtain a measure of the changes in inventory holdings during a given year valued at the price level of that year, hence uninfluenced by the particular cost level that happened to obtain when the inventory was accumulated. Of course, there still remains the problem of making this year's figure comparable with that of another year when a different current price level obtained, but this is part of the general problem of adjusting the national income total for year-to-year and place-to-place comparisons.

Progress has also been made by Kuznets, using Fabricant's computations, in adjusting depreciation charges to the price level of the year for which the charges are made.

Financial Intermediaries

When a financial intermediary, like a commercial bank, renders services free of direct charge, or at a service charge set below cost, there arises the possibility that a part of the economy's total of final goods and services will be understated through the omission of part or all of these services. The financial institution counts on covering part of its expenses by its receipt of income from investments that are made with funds belonging not to it but to its customers. Although the treatment of financial intermediaries had been discussed for some time, the analysis had been chiefly in terms of these intermediaries as aggregations of individuals, and it remained for Yntema, of the Department of Commerce, to discover and point out clearly the problem of imputed income that was involved. As a result, the revised Commerce series marks a notable advance in the treatment of the income of financial intermediaries. To the depositors of the bank there is imputed an amount of interest equal to the difference between the amount the bank receives as interest and dividends and what it pays the depositors as interest. The imputed interest is allocated among business firms, governmental units, and individuals. Each of these is then considered as spending this imputed interest in purchasing services from the bank.

III. Advances in the Compilation and Publication of National Income Data

The advances made during the past ten years in the compilation and publication of national income data have been very great indeed. Data are now at hand in some degree for several countries for which virtually nothing was available a decade ago. And in those countries that were already publishing substantial amounts of data in 1937, notably the United States and Great Britain, the improvement in range, precision, and tabular presentation of the data has been remarkable.

The countries for which little or no data were available ten years ago may be grouped into three classes—those for which that condition still obtains; those for which there have been computed some rough estimates of total, with occasionally some of the sub-totals specified; and those which have published fairly detailed series covering a period of several years. The present essay cannot give a complete statement of progress for each country with respect to the national income data that are in preparation or that have been completed, but a few major examples will illustrate the varying degrees in which progress has been made.

Canada, Australia, Eire, and the Netherlands have recently published detailed series for several years. The Canadian data, for example, include the period 1938–46. They are published as "National Accounts: Income and Expenditure," compiled by the National Income Unit of the Dominion Bureau of Statistics. The factor-payment side of the compilation is not so detailed as in the British and United States estimates; rent, interest, and corporate profits are lumped in the item "investment income." On the product side, domestic investment is divided between plant and equipment, and inventories (a division which the British White Paper has not yet achieved), but the data on consumer outlay are not divided between durable goods, semi-durable goods, and services, as in the United States series. The Canadian figures also include a series on personal income. There is no statement of the saving-investment equality. Totals are given for both national income (at factor cost) and gross national product.

For France, the *Commissariat Général du Plan de Modernisation et d'Équipement* has published estimates of national income in considerable detail, but the data cover only the two years 1938 and 1946 (with some totals for 1929, and projections for 1947 and 1950).

In Germany it appears that little or no progress has been made, either by the economics staffs of the occupying forces or by the Germans themselves, in developing current national income data that would match in scope and detail the German series of the prewar years.

The progress made in the United States during the past ten years may be noted by comparing the Department of Commerce booklet of November 1938, *Income in the United States, 1929–37,* with its revised series in the July 1947 Supplement to the *Survey of Current Business,* "National Income and Product Statistics of the United States, 1929–46." The most striking improvement is, of course, the computation of the national income (or, rather, the gross national product) from the product side. The earlier publication contained no information on how the national income, viewed as a flow of final goods and services, is divided among consumers' goods and services, private domestic investment in buildings, plant, equipment, and additions to inventory, net foreign investment, and government goods and services. The product computation is made from statistical sources different from those used in reaching the factor-payment total, and thus the two totals serve as a partial check on each other. Reconciliation of the two requires a small item of "statistical discrepancy." The current series presents not only the totals for each of these items for each of the years 1929–46 (and in Kuznets' series the data are carried back to 1919 on an annual basis), but also the sub-totals for durable goods, non-durable goods, and services to consumers; and sub-totals for federal war, federal non-war, and state and local purchases of goods and services. In the same category of improvement in data may be placed the Commerce tables showing the relation of the product total, when defined as gross national product, to the national income total as the sum of factor payments.

A second major improvement is the compilation of data on saving, and the relation of those totals to the total of investment (see the sub-section above on "Saving and Investment"). These data are brought together, on a gross basis, in a table of "Gross Savings and Investment Account." At this point attention should be called to the work done by the Securities and Exchange Commission in estimating liquid savings of individuals. This series is especially significant for comparison with the Commerce data, since it is compiled from different sources. Conceptual differences in coverage make precise comparison difficult, but the July Supplement presents the summary results of such an inquiry.

Another major advance over the 1938 compilation is the construction of double-entry tables for each of five sectors in the economy, covering both the factor-payment and the product items. The total of wages and salaries of employees of private business concerns, for example, is entered on the left-hand side of a "consolidated business income and product account," and on the right-hand side of a "personal income and expenditure account." The other three accounts are: "consolidated government receipts and expenditures account," a "gross savings and investment account," and a "rest of the world account." These double-entry accounts as presented in the July Supplement cover the year 1939. A highly condensed double-entry table entitled "The Nation's Budget" was published in the 1946 and the 1947 Budget Messages of the President, and appears currently in the President's Economic Report.

A fourth important achievement of the Department of Commerce is the speed with which it makes available its national income and product data following the close of the year, and the issuance of quarterly estimates, soon after the close of each quarter, of national income totals at annual rates adjusted for seasonal variation.

Equally notable progress in the assembly and publication of national income data in the United States has been shown in the series compiled by Kuznets and his associates at the National Bureau of Economic Research. While the Department of Commerce has taken over the task of maintaining an annual current series, and has limited its data to 1929 and the following years, Kuznets has been engaged in refining his annual series covering 1919–38, and pushing the product data as far back as 1869, in terms of averages for a decade for the earlier period. One result of this activity is the publication of by far the most detailed series on national income that has yet been made public for any country (excepting only the Swedish estimates noted earlier in this article): *National Income and Its Composition, 1919–38*. This volume sets a standard for explicit statement of the sources utilized, the reasons for decisions taken in combining the underlying data in one way rather than another, and the publication of the many industry-by-industry sub-series.

The British White Papers on national income represent an advance over the earlier pioneering work of Stamp, Bowley, and Colin Clark chiefly in the systematic presentation of the material in the light of recent developments in economic theory, especially with regard to the relations of the government accounts to the rest of the economy, and the saving-investment equality. There has also, of course, been a growth in the amount of data available. The successive White Papers have varied considerably in the amount and type of data they have presented, as well as in the amount of explanatory material accompanying the data, and some of the most useful or interesting arrangements and explanations of an earlier issue have not been repeated in a later one. Taken as a whole, the series represents great progress in the compilation and presentation of national income data, but the student specializing in national income will want to be sure that he has inspected all the issues, not merely the most recent one.

With respect to the availability of data suitable for compilation in national income estimates, the decade has seen both advances and reverses. In the United States, salary and wage data from the Federal Bureau of Old-Age and Survivors' Insurance, the state unemployment compensation agencies, and the Federal Railroad Retirement Board became available just in time (1940) to help offset the handicap imposed by the fact that during the defense and war periods the biennial Census of Manufactures was discontinued. The first Census of Manufactures since that for 1939 will be taken in 1948, covering the year 1947. The data compiled from income tax returns and published annually in *Statistics of Income,* by the Federal Treasury, are presented in more detail and with less time lag than a decade ago. On the other hand, Congress has shown itself unreceptive, in recent years, to pleas for funds for various types of census in addition to that for manufactures, for studies of the distribution of consumer income, and for similar data. The economy wave in the appropriations passed in 1947 struck the Census and other fact-gathering agencies severe blows, and the effect will be felt for some time to come in less adequate national income data than had been hoped for. The present writer has the impression that the outlook is not much better abroad. The British data on capital formation are inadequate, but the government, although obviously interested in planning, seems unwilling to push forward with censuses; many income tax data are not made available, in summary form, even where they are known to exist, and the Board of Inland Revenue so far shows little indication of changing its policy of withholding much of such information. In more than one Western European country the government has ordered the production of national income estimates without providing for the necessary basic censuses. It almost seems that the very ingenuity of the national income estimators in constructing bricks with very little straw may prove self-defeating; government legislators, if not government officials, like to believe that a national income estimate is something that can be produced without much expense. They may even come to believe that it is not an estimate but a recorded fact.

The distribution of families and single persons by size of income is one of the sectors of the national income field in which notable progress has been made in the United States during the past decade. The great survey, under the auspices of the National Resources Committee, of income for the twelve-month period ending June 30, 1936, which included personal interviews with 300,000 families, was published in 1938. The one other similar study covering the United States was that for the calendar year 1941 and the first quarter of 1942, published in 1945. The decade also saw the completion and the appearance of the first volumes of three state-wide studies of income distribution, for Delaware, Minnesota, and Wisconsin. The subject has been explored in some particular phases in two of the volumes in the National Bureau's "Studies in Income and Wealth" series. Sample surveys of distribution by income size have been obtained from time to time in connection with the monthly Labor Force surveys of the Census Bureau and the liquid-asset surveys made under the auspices of the Federal Reserve Board. A considerable amount of information was obtained in the last decennial census of population.

There is nothing available for any other country to compare with these surveys, even though one of their major effects is to stimulate an appetite for more and to lead to a realization of how much we should like to know and cannot know until adequate continuing financial support for such projects becomes available. Similar comments apply to the accompanying studies on the use consumers make of their incomes.

Other areas in the United States in which substantial improvements have been made in the basic data include rents received by individuals, where the Department of Commerce has been able to utilize data from *Statistics of Income* to a greater degree than before; income from professional activities, which has been thoroughly studied by Milton Friedman and Simon Kuznets, and which Commerce has made the subject of extended inquiry by questionnaires; and consumer outlay, which, instead of being estimated as a residual, by subtraction of all other kinds of product from the total of products (itself derived from the total reached by adding the factor payments), is now estimated with the aid of data on output at the manufacturing level, with allowance for wholesale and retail mark-ups, etc. This is not a complete list, but it indicates the diversity of fields in which it has been found possible to improve the data despite the relative lack of support from Congress.

IV. Uses Made of National Income Data

A summary of the uses made of national income data during the past decade must be kept within fairly narrow bounds if it is not to become a summary of activities in fields of economic analysis that are covered in other monographs in this volume. The concepts and data of national income are tools, and they have been found useful in several sectors.

Here, only a brief indication can be given of what these sectors are and how the tools have been employed.

With respect to government finance, the inflationary or deflationary pressures in existence at the moment have been described in recent years in terms of inflationary or deflationary "gaps." These gaps are simply inconsistencies of certain sub-totals within the national income or gross national product totals as assumed in the first stage of the analysis. A preliminary assumption of an unchanged price level, for instance, is made, and the amount that consumers would want to spend, out of the assumed total income, is compared with the amount of consumer goods that would be available in view of the total amount of production and the total amount of capital-goods production, exports, and government purchases, that are being assumed. Or the amount that could be expected to be saved is compared with the expected total of investment. The inconsistencies are then removed by altering the basic assumptions about the price level or the total amount to be produced or the amount of production that is to be in the form of non-consumer goods.

This technique is at least useful in exposing hidden inconsistencies in any forecast. Fiscal policy prescriptions can be tested for the presence of quantitative absurdities by casting them in terms of this national income analysis. This is not to say that the mechanism can be guaranteed to detect all major errors in the forecast, or that it can in some way lead positively to the correct forecast. The failure of more than one forecast in recent years, based on this analytical framework, is evidence that, at the moment, the technique has more value in eliminating from discussion a number of erroneous conclusions than it has in pointing directly to the right one. But even this is a great advance in the analysis of government finance. A comparison of the kind of information and analysis, or rather the lack of it, that was available for formulating federal financial policy in World War I, and in the great deflation of the early 1930's, with that which was available, and published (in Congressional Hearings) in World War II sufficiently demonstrates the point.

The topic covered in the immediately preceding paragraph is of course but part of a much larger one, namely, the attempt to forecast the level of business activity for months or years ahead, not with particular regard to fiscal policy, but in general. In this attempt, as well as in the narrower one of estimating the pressures that would be exerted by changes in fiscal policy, a considerable amount of research has been done in constructing probable relationships between various sub-totals of the national income. For example, the amount that consumers may be expected to try to spend out of an assumed disposable income (personal income after taxes) is estimated on the basis of past relationships of these two amounts. The records are of too short duration, and the years they cover are too extraordinary (especially the first half of the 1930's, and the war years), to inspire a great deal of confidence in the resulting ratios as predictors, but again, they may at least dispel erroneous ideas that would otherwise get into the analysis. Moreover, their value may well turn out to be greater than the tone of the present comment would suggest. The techniques used in developing these ratios and adapting them for predictive purposes fall outside the scope of this paper. But in general it seems that the work is emerging from an early stage, into a more sophisticated period. In the early years of pioneering enthusiasm, every bit of national income data was eagerly seized upon for use in constructing a predictive mechanism, sometimes without due regard to the degree of error in the historical sub-totals (which, after all, are only estimates themselves, for the most part) or even without a full understanding of the conceptual content of some of the sub-totals. That pioneering enthusiasm, somewhat uncritical but probably indispensable to an opening up of this new and difficult territory, is being supplemented by a more methodical, if slower, approach, from which it seems reasonable to expect important developments. The revised data issued in 1947 by the Department of Commerce for the period 1929–46 will aid greatly in the refinement of this analysis.

The annual totals of national income, or gross national product, have been used to establish trends in other annual data. For example, the number of non-agricultural and non-professional business firms in operation in the American economy in 1929–40 has been correlated with the gross national product (excluding government and agriculture), and the postwar data on number of firms is observed to show a close return to the prewar relationship, after the large decrease in number of firms caused by the war.[3]

The national income data have been especially useful in giving a correct sense of proportion about the structure of the economy, entirely apart from any attempts at prediction. The amount, and proportion, of the nation's output that is going into capital equipment and foreign investment, and hence is not available for immediate use by consumers or government, is indicated by the national income data; and estimates by Kuznets as far back as 1869 give at least a rough impression of changes that have occurred in this proportion over the decades. As a result of the compilations published during the past ten years much more is known about the proportion of output that takes the form of investment, and of the proportions in which this sub-total is divided among plant and equip-

---

[3] *Survey of Current Business*, July 1947, XXVII, p. 15.

ment expenditures, construction, increases in inventory, and foreign investment, and, in some series, government capital outlay. The interpretation of these findings has progressed rapidly in certain directions, notably, as already indicated above, in illustrating and extending Keynesian theory. At the same time, it appears that much, if not the main amount, of interpretation of the data on amount of investment is yet to come. Not as much progress has been made as might have been expected in comparing and contrasting the amounts of capital formation of different types, or in drawing inferences from the absolute and percentage amounts of total investment.

The national income data are also now the common mode of expressing the size of the economic role that government plays in the economy: the ratio of taxes to national income, or of government expenditures to net or gross national product. These ratios indicate the importance of the government in its role of dispenser of goods and services. Some of this product, however, has been produced in private business establishments, not in government departments. The cost of fire protection dispensed free of charge by the government is made up, in part, of the firemen's salaries, and, in part, of the cost of the fire trucks, hose, etc. The firemen's salaries represent production directly by the government; the trucks and hose are produced by private business firms. The role of the government as a producer is shown by comparing the total of factor payments made by the government with the total of factor payments in the economy.

Some important decisions on the definition of goods and services purchased by government, and on factor payments made by government, have been taken recently without as much discussion in the journals or proceedings of conferences as could be justified. The decision of the Department of Commerce to omit from national income all interest payments by government is a case in point. The decision was not hastily made; long discussions preceded it; but relatively little of the debate has appeared in print where it could be analyzed by others. In this respect the advance in the use or at least in the understanding of government data in the national income has not been as great as could have been wished for. A similar comment may apply to the recent decision of the Department of Commerce to define, as a factor payment, corporate profits before deducting corporation income tax rather than corporate profits after deducting that tax, as had been the practice theretofore. The treatment of the corporation income tax in defining the factor payment of profits raises some fundamental and difficult problems of the definition of a factor payment and, indeed, the whole idea of a system of distribution of economic rewards. Traditional economic theory has not adequately re-analyzed the concept of a factor payment in the light of the existence of income and other taxes, and a discussion linking up national income theory and economic theory at this point seems somewhat overdue. Again and again the reader in the national income field encounters these cases where the decisions made in the compilations of the data have to some extent outrun the relevant abstract analysis available in published form. This remark is not a criticism of the compilers; they have had to make the decisions, if the data were to appear at all, and in their oral discussions and office memoranda much abstract analysis has doubtless been used in reaching the decision. Moreover, the Department of Commerce staff has made an effort to obtain the benefits of theoretical criticisms from others. The implication intended here is that, in one way or another, the national income specialist and the student of economic theory need to be drawn together more, and to take more interest in each other's problems.

In war time the study of the product components of national income becomes particularly important. A "maximum" war effort is, of course, a relative concept, but even a relative maximum cannot be aimed for very well unless data are at hand on the total past output of the economy, the total possible output under assumed wartime conditions respecting the labor force, capital equipment, etc., and the minimum amount that must be allowed for continued production of consumer goods and non-war capital formation (perhaps negative) and non-war government services. The maximum output minus this minimum sub-total gives at least a goal to aim for in the production of war goods and services. In the absence of such data it seems likely that the aim will be set below rather than above this maximum. The data on consumer goods and services produced during 1941–45 indicate that the United States fell considerably short of a maximum practicable war effort; yet, would the President have dared to set the sights on war production as high as he did if data on national income and its components had not been available?

And in aiming at the maximum, the national income sub-totals on the factor-payment side indicate what kind of behavior is expected of consumers with respect to departure from established habits of spending and saving; the proportion of personal disposable income that must be saved if inflation is to be avoided can be computed, approximately, and this figure in turn gives some indication of the extent and severity of direct controls, like rationing, that must be employed in view of the amount of taxation assumed (which is the chief element in determining how much of the consumers' income will be disposable income).

It must not be inferred that these wartime uses of the national income data always reached a high degree of precision. For some purposes the figures could come out a few billions one way or another without appreciably changing the conclusions that would be drawn from them. But the sub-totals, or most of them, were so magnified under the pressure of the war economy that it was helpful, indeed essential, to have even an answer that might be several billions in error.

The past decade witnessed the first use, as far as the present writer is aware, of national income data as determinants of the amount of aid that should be extended by a government to its political subdivisions; moreover, national income data were used in determining how an international financial burden should be apportioned.

Federal aid to the states is determined in part by the per capita incomes of the several states, in grants under the Hospital Survey and Construction Act of 1946, and in the School Lunch Act of the same year. The data utilized are the Department of Commerce series on income payments to individuals, and hence do not include undistributed corporate profits. This omission needs to be kept in mind in deciding how much weight to give to the state income-payments data as determinants in the distribution of federal aid, as does also the unavoidable incompleteness in the computations of dividend and other property income on the basis of the state in which the recipient resides.

The international use of national income data was in the allocation of the costs of the United Nations Relief and Rehabilitation Administration. A requisition was made of each nation equal, with important exceptions, to 1 per cent of the national income. In view of the rudimentary nature of the estimates of national income for most of the countries, this first attempt does not supply much useful experience for future calculations of the same kind, but the fact that national income was considered to be a possible international "tax" base is another indication of the interest that national income analysis will have for students of public finance.

The data on individual income, arranged by size classes, and its allocation between saving, spending, and tax payments, have been the subject of considerable analysis during the past few years. For the most part, the analysis has been concerned with discovering and stating clearly some of the more interesting or puzzling relationships revealed by the data rather than with searching for the reasons for those relationships. The large amount of data at hand (inadequate though it still is for many purposes) from studies differing in time, scope, and geographic coverage have made it necessary to spend much time and effort on this preliminary surveying of the material, including attempts to reconcile data from different studies; no doubt the coming decade will see somewhat more of interpretation of the relationships.

Two of the most interesting uses of national income data are those made by Wassily W. Leontief and Morris A. Copeland. Leontief, depending largely on Census of Manufactures data, has computed the quantitative input and output relationships of each major sector of the economy (automobiles, petroleum and natural gas, yarn and cloth, agriculture, etc.) with each of the other sectors. Copeland is at present engaged in compiling data on the money flows within the economy, a project which of course extends beyond the boundaries of national income analysis.

Since changes in *per capita* national income, as distinguished from any one of its constituent items, are a partial indicator of changes in the material welfare of the group of persons making up the nation, it might be supposed that one of the most prominent uses made of the national income figures would be the drawing of inferences regarding the advance or decline in material welfare over a period of years, or, as among different nations, differences in welfare at any one time.

Such use has in fact been made of the data, but not perhaps to as great a degree as might have been expected. Moreover, the inferences drawn have been for those kinds of time-span that might have been thought most difficult to analyze: decades in the past, including the latter half of the nineteenth century, and decades projecting into the future. There has been relatively little year-to-year comparison for the recent past. Totals have indeed been deflated by product-price indexes, and the reader is thus enabled to draw his own conclusions about the fluctuating totals in the 1930's, for instance; nor have the implications of these fluctuations passed entirely unnoticed. But there has not been much intensive analysis or extensive debate over whether 1932, for example, was a year of less material welfare than 1933. It may seem self-evident that so refined an analysis cannot or should not be undertaken, but in any event the relative emphasis on long periods in the past and in the future is another indication of how the theory of national income totals, including the theory of deflating for price changes, has suffered a relative lag.

NATIONAL WEALTH

Very little has been accomplished during the decade in examining and refining the conceptual problems of national wealth. Perhaps this is because continuing data have been at hand for constructing national income estimates, whereas little has been done in recent years to collect data for the purpose of computing national wealth. Still it might be thought that the discussion of concepts would not be so entirely dependent for stimulation upon the existence of current data. The question is probably not so much one of stimulation in an absolute sense, as it is one of relative stimulation. The task of constructing national income estimates has seemed so urgent and at the same time so practicable that it has easily absorbed all the energy available from those working in the field of income and wealth.

In the process of refining the concepts useful for income analysis, there has, of course, been considerable implicit or fragmentary progress in the same task in the field of national wealth; this will be clearly apparent when that latter task is explicitly approached in a comprehensive study. Inventory valuations, depreciation charges, the distinction between consumer outlay and investment—these and many other subjects on which progress has been made in the past ten years would have had to be worked up also in any study of national wealth.

BIBLIOGRAPHY

The foregoing essay has purposely refrained from citing particular works or articles, except as reference is made to them in the text of the discussion; the attempt has been to give a general view of the broad advances in national income theory and compilation. The following suggestions are offered in the hope that they may be useful to those who, while not specializing in this field, would like to study some of the more recent comprehensive works. In addition to the particular works cited here, the reader is referred to the series of volumes of proceedings (Studies) of the Conference on Research in National Income and Wealth.

Barger, Harold, "Outlay and Income in the United States, 1921–1938," *Studies in Income and Wealth,* IV (New York, 1942), pp. xxvii + 391.

Clark, Colin, *The Conditions of Economic Progress* (London, 1940), pp. xii + 504.

Derksen, J. P. D., *A System of National Book-keeping; Illustrated by the Experience of the Netherlands Economy.* National Institute of Economic and Social Research. Occasional Papers, X (Cambridge, England, 1946), pp. 31.

Fabricant, Solomon, *Capital Consumption and Adjustment* (New York, 1938), pp. xx + 271.

Friedman, Milton, and Kuznets, Simon, *Income from Independent Professional Practice* (New York, 1945), pp. xxxiii + 599.

Gilbert, Milton, and Jaszi, George, "National Product and Income Statistics as an Aid in Economic Problems," reprinted in William Fellner and Bernard F. Haley, eds., *Readings in the Theory of Income Distribution* (Philadelphia, 1946), pp. 44–57.

Hicks, J. R., and Hart, A. G., *The Social Framework of the American Economy: An Introduction to Economics* (New York, 1945), pp. xvi + 261.

Kuznets, Simon, *National Income: A Summary of Findings* (New York, 1946), pp. 144.

——, *National Income and Its Composition, 1919–1938*, 2 vols. (New York, 1941), pp. xxx + 929.

——, *National Product Since 1869* (New York, 1946), pp. xvi + 239.

Perroux, François, Uri, Pierre, and Marczewski, Jan, *Le Revenu National* (Paris, 1947), pp. 310.

Shoup, Carl S., *Principles of National Income Analysis* (Boston, 1947), pp. xv + 400.

Stone, Richard, *Definition and Measurement of the National Income and Related Totals.* Memorandum Submitted to Sub-Committee on National Income Statistics of the Committee of Statistical Experts, League of Nations (Princeton, June 1946), pp. 23–128 of mimeographed report of the sub-committee.

GOVERNMENT PUBLICATIONS AND DOCUMENTS

United States: Department of Commerce, National Income Division, "National Income and Product Statistics of the United States, 1929–46." Supplement to *Survey of Current Business*, July 1947, XXVII, pp. 54.

United States: National Resources Committee, *Consumer Expenditures in the United States: Estimates for 1935–36* (Washington, 1939), pp. ix + 195.

——: *Consumer Incomes in the United States: Their Distribution in 1935–36* (Washington, 1938), pp. viii + 104.

Great Britain: Financial Secretary to the Treasury, *National Income and Expenditure of the United Kingdom, 1938 to 1946.* Cmd. 7099 (London, 1947), pp. 60.

PERIODICALS

Hicks, J. R., "The Valuation of the Social Income," *Economica*, May 1940, New Series VII, pp. 105–24.

Hoffenberg, Marvin, with assistance from Mabel S. Lewis, under the direction of John H. G. Pierson, "Estimates of National Output, Distributed Income, Consumer Spending, Saving, and Capital Formation," *Review of Economic Statistics*, May 1943, XXV, pp. 101–174.

MacGregor, D. C., "Recent Studies on National Income," *Canadian Journal of Economics and Political Science*, February 1945, XI, pp. 115–129; and May 1945, XI, pp. 270–280.

Schwartz, Charles F., and Graham, Robert E., Jr., "State Income Payments in 1946," *Survey of Current Business*, August 1947, XXVII, pp. 9–24.

Stone, Richard, "The Measurement of National Income and Expenditure: A Review of the Official Estimates of Five Countries," *Economic Journal*, September 1947, LVII, pp. 272–298.

9

MONETARY THEORY

Henry H. Villard

I. Introduction

In the social sciences our accumulated knowledge is so small and the unexplored areas so vast that of necessity we measure progress by the understanding we obtain of particular and pressing problems. Thus Adam Smith did not write primarily as a scholar but rather as a social surgeon to remove from the body politic the surviving malignant remnant of Mercantilism, while the emphasis of Ricardo and Mill on diminishing returns and the rent of land directly reflected their interest in the ultimately successful campaign of the rising business classes to end the impediment to further industrialization represented by the Corn Laws.

In the same way recent monetary theory directly reflects the unprecedented depression which rocked the industrialized world during the nineteen-thirties; in the United States, perhaps worse hit than any other country, the increase in productive capital, which had averaged 6 per cent a year for the first three decades of the century, over the 'thirties as a whole was negligible in amount. As a result the center of interest has in general shifted from the factors determining the quantity of money and its effect on the general level of prices to those determining the level of output and employment. In addition, the purely monetary devices for control, on which great store had been laid, were found to be broadly ineffective, taken by themselves, in bringing about recovery from the Great Depression. And finally, as a result of the way in which the war was financed, it seems quite likely that it will prove impossible to use such devices for the effective control of a future boom. The general change in emphasis is well indicated by the altered character of university courses: in 1930 an outstanding elementary text devoted 144 of its 1250 pages to Money and Banking and 16 to the Business Cycle; in 1947 a new elementary text devoted 205 of its 700 pages to National Income and Employment and 55 to Money and the Interest Rate! The implications of this decreased emphasis need to be made quite clear. Basically it reflects a reduced interest in the factors influencing the quantity of the available means of payment and an increased interest in the factors influencing the level of spending. Apart from unguarded statements monetary theorists have of course generally been aware that money had not only to be created but also spent if it was to have any effect on the economy. But up until relatively recently the economy abhorred any large amount of idle balances. Thus the emphasis of monetary theorists was on changes in the quantity of money, accompanied by the sometimes stated and sometimes implied assumption that balances, once created, would not long stay idle. It is with monetary theory in this narrow sense that this paper will be mainly concerned.

This narrow construction of monetary theory perhaps requires defense. There can be no question that the fields covered by monetary theory, the theory of compensatory fiscal action, and business cycle theory are at least closely related if not actually overlapping. Further, business cycle theory to a major extent, and fiscal theory to a lesser extent, evolved out of monetary theory; as a result courses and economists have often in recent years been labeled "monetary" when in fact they were dealing with employment, output, and income. But a broad use of monetary theory would not only make it a synonym for business cycle theory but also would make it impossible to describe separately work dealing predominantly with the factors influencing the quantity of money. In other words, it has seemed desirable to separate monetary from fiscal and cyclical theory in such a way as to minimize the overlapping between the fields. I sincerely hope that those who have been accustomed to define monetary theory more broadly will not take offense at the relatively limited meaning which is used in what follows, and will remember that it is monetary theory in the narrow sense which is described as having declined considerably in importance in recent years. It should hardly be necessary to point out that the depression greatly increased the importance of monetary, fiscal, and cycle theory taken together.

This paper will start with a description of some of the recent changes in environment, both to summarize the contribution of those who have worked on the statistical side of monetary problems and at the same time to explain why the changes involved have been so largely responsible for our decreased interest in the quantity equation in recent years. A second section will be devoted to the concepts of monetary equilibrium which were developed as alternatives to the quantity equation, while a third will cover changes in the explanation of the determination of the rate of interest. Two final sections will deal with the financing of the war and the heritage that the war has left us.

Any summary of developments during such a dynamic period in monetary thought cannot fail to be impressionistic. In a literal sense, therefore, the summary will inevitably be wrong; but in a broader sense it is only the surviving impact of thought which is important. The obscure and forgotten passage or the uses to which discarded tools of analysis *might* have been put are not what matter, however much they may delight the historian and prove that there is nothing new under the sun. It is, then, to the broad view that this essay will be devoted; he who seeks details will have to look elsewhere.

II. The Changing Monetary Environment and the Decline of the Quantity Equation

Few analytical devices in economics have been as useful over as long a period as the quantity equation of exchange. By the start of the 1930's there was considerable agreement that the equation was perfectly valid when properly—i.e., tautologically—defined.[1] As first propounded by Professor Fisher, T included "all things sold for money" during any period, so that V became all uses of money to buy "things" and P a hybrid price level applying to all sales of "things" for money. The implications of this usage were not made clearer by a general tendency to refer to T in this sense as "trade" and to P as the "general" price level. Even if there can be no analytical objection to this formulation, when an attempt is made to derive statistical values, especially from figures for bank debits, many problems arise. Even today little is known regarding the extent to which bank debits reflect "money to money" transactions, such as transfers of funds from one account to another of the same economic unit; while the inclusion of sales of not only current output but also such diverse things as stocks and bonds, urban and agricultural land, and second-hand cars and antique furniture—to mention only a few examples—makes it difficult either to calculate an appropriate price index for P or to attach any significance to the resulting level of T.

Although somewhat less easy to understand and therefore less generally known, the "cash balance" version of the quantity equation (especially as it was used at Cambridge University) and other examples of the income approach were more in line with recent developments.[2] This does not result from the cash balance equation itself—most simply written as M equals kPT where k equals $1/V$—as the formulation is subject to the same problems and criticisms as the Fisher equation if the various terms

---

[1] If V is the use of M to buy T, T specific items sold for M, and P prices of T when sold for M, then the equation is valid because it is a truism. The charge that the equation was not valid arose because in some earlier presentations use had been made of such approximations as existing price indexes, which rendered the equation formally incorrect.

[2] For the derivations of these approaches, see A. W. Marget, *The Theory of Prices* (New York, 1938), pp. 302-343 and 414-458.

are given the same meaning. But the *emphasis* was on *k* defined as the relationship between people's money balances and their *incomes*, so that PT referred, not to the total value of monetary transactions, but to the total value of transactions in current output—in other words, the national income. This relationship seems clearly more significant for business cycle problems than Fisher's V.[3]

It was a combination of this shift in theoretical interest from the "transactions" to the more fruitful "income" version of the quantity equation and the availability of national income estimates that made substantial statistical progress possible during the 1930's, while the statistical work itself stimulated further analysis of the variables involved. Thus relatively full information regarding the behavior of the terms of the quantity equation did not become available until the controversy over the "quantity theory" as an explanation of prices had largely died down.[4]

Perhaps the best place to start a description of the statistical progress which took place is with the clarification—largely by Currie and Angell—of the concept of "money," which has come increasingly to mean currency outside the banking system (in the hands of the public) and demand deposits (deposits subject to check), including all government deposits but excluding all interbank deposits. Currie uses this meaning exclusively, while Angell also computes values for "total" money (including time and saving deposits) but lays greatest emphasis on money in the first sense, which he calls "circulating" money. Although the term may of course be applied to any of a number of concepts, it seems clear that this definition is most useful when our interest centers upon the primary function of money as a *means of payment* or upon the most "liquid" form that assets can take. The emergence, moreover, of large holdings by individuals of U. S. Savings Bonds, which are payable in a specific number of dollars on demand, has eliminated the claim of time and saving deposits to special consideration. This development, plus the general acceptance of the narrower meaning of money, has led to the development of a new concept of "liquid assets" to include money, time and saving deposits, and U. S. Bonds, although there is of course no sharp line between assets which are or are not "liquid" but rather an infinite series of gradations.[5]

---

[3] This point is discussed further on pp. 323–324 below.

[4] The volumes which contributed most to our understanding of the statistical magnitudes involved were L. Currie, *The Supply and Control of Money in the United States* (Cambridge, Mass., 1934); J. W. Angell, *The Behavior of Money* (New York, 1936); and *idem*, *Investment and Business Cycles* (New York, 1941). Much interesting work has also been done by the Board of Governors of the Federal Reserve System and the Federal Deposit Insurance Corporation, particularly through the periodic surveys of deposit ownership which are published in the *Federal Reserve Bulletin*.

[5] Estimates of the distribution among various holders of "liquid assets" in this sense have been published periodically in the *Federal Reserve Bulletin* since 1945.

Probably the most striking fact to emerge from recent statistical studies is the constancy of income velocity before 1929 and the size of the apparently permanent decline since that date. Between 1899 and 1929 income velocity—the national income divided by money as defined above—ranged from 2.72 to 3.35, a variation of less than 25 per cent; yet during the same period income and money increased more than fivefold.[6]

INCOME VELOCITY AFTER 1929

Year	Money*	National Income†	Income Velocity
1929	27.33	87.4	3.20
1930	26.32	75.0	2.85
1931	24.44	58.9	2.41
1932	21.03	41.7	1.98
1933	20.53	39.6	1.93
1934	23.56	48.6	2.06
1935	26.88	56.8	2.11
1936	31.10	66.9	2.15
1937	31.75	73.6	2.32
1938	31.50	67.4	2.14
1939	35.05	72.5	2.07
1940	39.49	81.3	2.06
1941	46.27	103.8	2.24
1942	54.64	136.5	2.50
1943	79.90	168.3	2.11
1944	100.45	182.3	1.81
1945	118.53	182.8	1.54
1946	119.41	178.2	1.49
1947	109.80	202.6	1.85

* In billions. Through 1939 the estimates are from Angell, *loc. cit.* Thereafter the total used is the sum of "Currency outside banks," "Demand deposits adjusted," and "United States Government deposits" for the end of June as reported in the *Federal Reserve Bulletin.*

† In billions. All estimates are the revised national income series of the Department of Commerce.

After 1929 velocity declined rapidly to about 60 per cent of its predepression level; thereafter, except for the boom year of 1937, it did not exceed 70 per cent of its previous level until the war. During the war velocity first rose to 2.50 during the relatively tight credit conditions which marked the start of large-scale war finance in 1942—a level higher than in any year since 1930—and then declined to 1.50 as the money supply expanded during the later years of the war.[7] Figures for the period since 1929 are given in the table above.

[6] J. W. Angell, *Investment and Business Cycles*, pp. 337–338.

[7] During 1947 a decrease of 8 per cent in the supply of money (as a result of the reduction in Government balances to very low levels) brought about a rapid rise in velocity to a level close to that of the 'thirties. It will be interesting to see how long this increase continues.

In addition to demonstrating the extent to which income velocity has declined, recent studies have clarified the factors influencing the maximum level of income velocity.[8] Of basic importance are the intervals between successive payments during the circular flow of money from income recipients to producers and back to income recipients, the degree of overlapping of payment schedules (whether income received Friday is used to pay bills Saturday or vice versa), and the degree of business integration; the amount of friction in the payment-transfer mechanism also plays a role in the result. Because it is impossible to eliminate "financial" transactions adequately, it is possible to determine only approximately how many exchanges take place in the course of the circuit flow of an average dollar from income recipient to producer and back again, but it appears that, as we are presently organized, roughly ten dollars' worth of "unfinished" output is exchanged for every dollar's worth bought by income recipients.[9]

The significance of these studies lies not so much in the actual numerical estimates made as in their conclusion that at least minimum balances and maximum levels of income velocity are determined by relatively constant factors unlikely to change rapidly except under the impact of runaway inflations or drastic changes in payment practices or in the degree of business integration. It is true that at present and probably in the future actual balances will substantially exceed such *minimum* balances, which reduces the practical importance of this information. But the understanding of the monetary process that has been achieved is considerable, as can be seen by comparison with formulations in which the level of actual balances is taken as being determined by the quantity of "ready purchasing power" which people find it desirable "to keep by them."[10] For such a quantity would appear to be capable of rapid variation in any direction, when in fact a reduction in balances below the minimum level is likely to be difficult to achieve except under unusual circumstances.

Finally, these statistical studies have made clear that stock market speculation can have a major effect on the level of exchange velocity without reducing the amount of money available for purchasing current output. Thus our broadest measure of exchange velocity indicates an in-

---

[8] Most of the credit again belongs to Professor Angell; see especially his article on "The Components of Circular Velocity of Money," *Quarterly Journal of Economics,* February 1937, LI, pp. 224–272.

[9] *Idem, The Behavior of Money,* p. 191. This includes "normal" financial transactions in which money is shifted between balances before being spent, but excludes transactions connected with the stock market and the like. Additional discussion will be found in H. H. Villard, *Deficit Spending and the National Income* (New York, 1941), p. 37, note.

[10] See Alfred Marshall, *Money, Credit and Commerce* (London, 1923), p. 43 ff.

crease of 85 per cent from 1922 to 1929 at a time when income velocity was virtually constant. It was the distorting influence of changes of this sort—plus the difficulty of obtaining appropriate measures of the price level involved—which made the transactions version of the quantity equation so difficult to interpret.

To a major extent recent developments in monetary theory reflect the implications of these findings—especially the decline in income velocity. For up to 1930 the relative constancy of the relationship between money and income justified concentration on the factors determining the quantity of money—on monetary theory in the narrow sense which we employ. When changes in the quantity of money could be expected to have a broadly proportionate ultimate influence on incomes in either an upward or downward direction—despite year to year variations resulting from minor changes in velocity—it was natural to stress the importance of monetary changes, which appeared to be both strategic and controllable. Actually there probably still exists an upper limit to the expansion of the national money income that is possible with a given quantity of money; but, even if the limit is now somewhat lower than it was in the past, it seems highly probable that ever since 1929 the quantity of money in existence could have supported a level of income substantially higher than that which actually prevailed. Hence it is the factors determining the *use* of a stock of money more than adequate to meet current or prospective requirements that have become of primary importance in recent years.

Furthermore, right up to the war, our production was less than that permitted by our labor force and plant facilities. In other words, the quantity of current output offered for sale, instead of increasing slowly along a secular trend line, was subject to wide fluctuations from one year to the next—sometimes with little or no variation in prices. Hence theoretical analysis has increasingly concentrated on setting forth both the determinants of the flow of spending and the effect of the resulting spending on output and employment, rather than the changes which the quantity of money could be expected to have on the level of prices under conditions in which it could be assumed that income velocity would be relatively constant and output at about the highest level permitted by our labor force and plant facilities.

It should be made quite clear that the quantity equations are no less true for a period in which income velocity and output vary widely than for a period in which they are relatively constant; they are merely less useful. Although rarely if ever put forward in an unqualified form, the essence of the "quantity theory" was that a change in money could be expected to have a proportionate effect on prices, which is only true when there are no changes in either velocity or output. For the quantity equations to be most useful, the conditions underlying the quantity theory must prevail. What is here suggested is that such conditions did in fact generally prevail before 1929—perhaps to a greater degree than was realized at the time. But when income velocity started to vary widely after 1929, so that the quantity approach could only state that income would be equal to the money supply multiplied by a variable of unknown magnitude, other tools were developed to determine the level of incomes, although the quantity equations of course remained not only formally valid but useful for various purposes, especially elementary instruction. In the same way, the fluctuations in output that have taken place in recent years have made it far more difficult to determine the effect of changes in spending on prices; but here, in contrast to the previous case, relatively little has been done in the way of developing alternative tools of analysis.

Keynes' *A Treatise on Money*[11] is especially interesting in this connection because it represents a transition from the monetary theory of the quantity equations to the modern theory of income, output, and employment. In view of the emphasis on saving and investment contained in the *Treatise*, it is easy to forget that its "Fundamental Equations" summarized the factors determining the *price levels* of consumption goods and output as a whole. Keynes started by distinguishing between the normal income of entrepreneurs—that "which, if they were open to make new bargains with all the factors of production at the currently prevailing rates of earnings, would leave them under no motive either to increase or to decrease their scale of operations"[12]—and their "windfall profits"—the difference between their actual receipts and their normal income. Defined in this fashion, windfall profits (positive or negative) become the difference between the actual level of the national income and that level which would be just sufficient to continue the current level of output at the current level of factor costs—which may appropriately be called the "equilibrium" level.

The broader and more important of the two Fundamental Equations, that determining the price level of output as a whole, was formulated by Keynes in the following fashion:

$$\Pi = \frac{E}{O} + \frac{I-S}{O}$$

[11] London, 1930.
[12] *Ibid.*, Vol. 1, p. 125.

where Π was the price level of output as a whole, E normal income excluding windfall profits, O the volume of output, I the value of the current production of investment goods, and S saving out of normal income. Further, the *Treatise* makes clear that, under these definitions, windfall profits are equal to $I - S$.[13] Hence, as normal income plus windfall profits equals actual income, this equation in fact tells us that actual income divided by the volume of current output will give the price level of such output; or alternatively that the actual price level will differ from the "equilibrium" level by the excess of actual over "equilibrium" income divided by current output.

To state that the price level of current output is determined by the actual expenditure on such output (i.e., the actual national income) divided by the volume of such output clearly does not represent an improvement of the quantity equations; hence the *Treatise* equations in reality must (and will below) be judged in terms of their contribution to concepts of monetary equilibrium. In other words, the analysis of the *Treatise*, although cast in the form of quantity equations, in a broad way marks the end of the equations as tools of new theoretical analysis in both Great Britain and the United States. This of course does not mean that the quantity equations were never heard of after 1930. Analytical and statistical work like that already summarized was largely inspired by the equations, while their place in elementary texts remained relatively secure, because of the ease with which they imparted a preliminary understanding of monetary processes. But it seems fair to say that almost all new analytical work designed to explain the problems of the 'thirties represented a break from, rather than an evolution of, the quantity equation approach, and made little use of quantity equation concepts.

To this generalization there is a notable and outstanding exception. Professor Marget in his two-volume *The Theory of Prices*[14] has sought both to defend the equations against the aspersions cast on them by advocates of the newer approach (particularly Keynes) and also to renovate the equations as tools of theoretical analysis, particularly the transactions equation in the form originally propounded by Professor Fisher. There can be no question of Marget's contribution to the history of doctrine or of the extent to which he has demonstrated the falsity of many Keynesian generalizations, even when the generalizations remain suggestive.[15] But his contribution is considerably more than this; his painstaking discussion

---

[13] *Ibid.*, p. 138.
[14] New York, 1938 and 1942.
[15] Keynes' suggestion that monetary and value theory have been inadequately integrated, for example, for me remains suggestive even after Marget has demonstrated that every economist since Aristotle applied the same methods of analysis to both fields.

of the equations themselves has added insight into problems that must be faced in any careful formulation of the terms involved. To give but one example, his analysis of possible discrepancies between "current output" and "goods sold" is undoubtedly definitive.[16]

Marget's plea for a return to the transactions type of equation, however, is less likely to be accepted. The fundamental issue is a perennial one in economics: workability vs. completeness. It is Marget's position that any formulation that does not include all possible types of money and all possible uses is less than complete. Hence he objects to income velocity on the ground that it is a "hybrid" concept; for income velocity is actually an *average* relationship between *all* balances and the national income, most balances being in fact held against the purchase of "unfinished" output rather than against the purchase of the "finished" goods and services whose value adds up to the national income. Any such average he rejects because it involves more than a simple relationship between cash balances and the specific outlay against which they are held, which is the only sort of relationship sufficiently definitive to be acceptable to him. Thus he would meet the criticism that the transaction version of the quantity equation has been relatively barren because it lumped various things together, the economic significance of which was quite diverse, by arguing for expansion of the formulation until each diverse item was treated separately.

Whatever the ultimate appeal of such a program, it seems to me that, in the present state of economics and probably also in the foreseeable future, all workable relationships and analyses are bound to be both incomplete and "hybrid" in the sense that they summarize complicated variables. The important thing is that the relationship chosen should be "strategic" and, if possible, relatively constant, in order to eliminate immediate need for the more complete analysis which we are not yet in a position to undertake. In fact, the very reason that the quantity equation was originally so analytically useful and has continued as such an important teaching aid is that it summarized all the manifold forces influencing prices into exactly three variables.[17] Hence Marget's plea is not so much for what has been achieved by the transactions form of the quantity equation as it has been used, but for what might be achieved in the future if it were possible to break down the summary averages of the original

---

[16] *Op. cit.,* Vol. I, p. 538 ff.

[17] While progress in understanding our complex economic environment will undoubtedly require increasingly complicated analysis, most recent progress has taken the form of developing more "strategic" groupings of a quite small number of variables. This is true not only of the shift from the transactions to the income version of the quantity equation, but also of the evolution of Keynes' ideas from the *Treatise* to the *General Theory.*

equation into all the components necessary to deal with all separable price levels. One can, I believe, with all sincerity wish such an undertaking well and at the same time doubt both its probable achievements and the impact that it is likely to have on monetary theory in the immediate future.

The importance of not only monetary theory but also monetary policy declined in the latter half of the 1930's. For once a "reflation" such as was achieved by 1935 has been brought about, further increases in the money supply by Central Bank action alone are likely to lead to broadly compensating decreases in income velocity—at least over the range of increases which are possible without arousing insuperable political opposition; hence at such times monetary control devices are not likely to be of much aid in combating a depression. From the point of view of control, therefore, their main use would have been to prevent a boom from getting out of hand after the existing supply of excess or idle balances had been exhausted. Our failure to recover fully before the outbreak of the war meant that they did not have a chance to undertake this modest role, and now even this role is likely to have been reduced, if not largely eliminated, as a result of the repercussions which the use of such controls would entail on the debt structure which we have inherited from the war. As a result we face an urgent need at the present time to develop alternative methods of control; this problem will be more fully considered when our postwar heritage is discussed below.

III. Monetary Equilibrium, Period Analysis, and the *General Theory*

As the extent to which the banking system could vary the money supply became clear, efforts had been made on the Continent, and especially in the Swedish literature, to formulate what would have occurred "naturally" or "normally" in the absence of monetary "disturbances." Keynes' *Treatise* was primarily responsible for drawing attention, in Great Britain and the United States, to the resulting concept of an "equilibrium" in which money would be "neutral" in its effects on the economy. Changes in money were thought of as being brought about by the rate of interest, which was either so low as to cause banks to create additional funds to be added to those in existence or so high as to induce people to pay off bank loans and in this way reduce the money supply. Wicksell's pioneer formulation ran in terms of discrepancies between the "market" or actual rate of interest and the "natural" rate, which he defined as that rate which would keep prices constant, as he was working at a time when the major emphasis was on price stability.[18] This meant that an increase in the money supply equal to the increase not only in population but also in productivity would be "natural" under the definition used. On the other hand, Hayek, following the Austrian tradition of studying the effects of the imposition of money on a completely "non-monetary" economy, defined the "natural" rate as that which would keep the effective quantity of money (money times velocity) constant, so that it would be "natural" for the price level of output to fall during periods of technological progress or when the supply of the productive factors was increasing. In other words, Hayek's definition meant that when there was no divergence between the two rates of interest, the level of the national money income would be constant. Finally, Keynes in the *Treatise*, as we have seen, defined "normal" income as that which provided just enough entrepreneurial income to maintain the present level of employment and output at present factor prices.

The fundamental common problem faced by all these analyses was to define "equilibrium"; in the main it was the difficulty of giving meaning to this concept that caused the whole approach to be abandoned. This is true even when the emotional connotations of "natural," "normal," or "neutral" are discarded and the problem is stated in terms of "equilibrium" without normative significance; and it also applies whether the mechanism of change is stated in terms of discrepancies between saving and investment or "market" and "natural" rates of interest.

For example, as the role of payment practices and the degree of business integration in determining income velocity became clearer, even a theoretical definition of a "natural" rate which would eliminate "monetary" disturbances when there were changes in these factors became increasingly difficult.[19] For the distinction between "real" and "monetary" factors is a tenuous one at best. It was often argued that a release of money as a result of the reduction in money payments that follows from increased business integration should be offset if money was to remain "neutral"; but would not integration reduce exchange value even in a barter economy and therefore constitute a "real" rather than a "monetary" factor? Or should the release of money resulting from integration be offset only to the extent that it exceeded the decrease of exchange value that would have taken place in a barter regime?

It was the *Treatise* more than any other volume that brought the problem of equilibrium to a head and represented a crossroads in the develop-

---

[18] Constant prices in this formulation also made saving equal to investment. For a summary of some of the other meanings given the "natural" rate by Wicksell, see A. W. Marget, *op. cit.*, Vol. I, pp. 201-204.

[19] Cf. G. Haberler, *Prosperity and Depression*, 3rd ed. (Geneva, 1941), pp. 61-62.

ment of monetary theory.[20] For the fundamental distinction that Keynes made in the *Treatise* between "normal" income and "profits" premised the existence of a lag in the adjustment of factor contracts, entrepreneurial commitments, or both: if entrepreneurs revised their commitments or labor reopened its contracts just as soon as there was a change in income, then there could be no difference between "normal" income and "profits." In the *Treatise* Keynes showed little interest in this problem, except to argue that a sufficient lag did exist to make his distinction between actual and "normal" income worth while. As a result the *Treatise* was criticized both because of the ambiguity of its discussion of the lag involved and for the extent to which the time period in question could be expected to vary over the course of the business cycle. Against these criticisms there were two possible lines of defense: either the various factors influencing the revision of contracts could be examined, and explicit assumptions could be made regarding the time period in question; or a "timeless" analysis could be developed and the problem avoided in this fashion. In the first of these directions lies modern period analysis, with its explicit assumptions regarding lags and leads, the fixity of contracts, and similar factors; in the other, the instantaneous analysis of Keynes' *General Theory of Employment, Interest and Money*.[21]

It is too early to attempt any definitive appraisal of the relative fruitfulness of the two approaches, but it seems fair to say that round one has gone to the instantaneous approach. I should make clear that in judging "fruitfulness" I am laying major weight on the impact on public policy that has been or seems likely to be achieved before the economic system under study changes so drastically as to move the whole matter into the field of the economic historian. For however much the careful step-by-step procedure of period analysis commends itself as the only way to attain *complete* knowledge of the operation of our economic system, to date most examples can best be described as methodological explorations rather than positive contributions.[22] The difficulties to be faced are formidable. Least important, perhaps, is the criticism leveled against the *Treatise* to the effect that entrepreneurs are always out of adjustment

---

[20] Chronologically Hayek follows the *Treatise*, but his methodological approach really belongs with the analyses of the preceding period.

[21] London, 1936.

[22] The best example of D. H. Robertson's work is his article in the *Economic Journal* (September 1933, XLIII) and the best summary of the Stockholm School is that of Bertil Ohlin, also in the *Economic Journal* (March and June 1937, XLVII). A possible exception to the generalization in the text and the outstanding example of sustained work along period analysis lines is J. R. Hicks' *Value and Capital* (Oxford, 1939), although, as the title suggested, the author is not mainly concerned with problems in the field of monetary and business cycle theory.

during a period of expansion or contraction.[23] Once the emphasis shifts away from "equilibrium" to period analysis, it becomes clear that lack of adjustment is to be expected. For it is the purpose of such analysis to show why the economy is out of balance, what is done about it, and what the consequences are.

Far more important is the fact that no satisfactory bridge has been built between a mechanical analysis in which income received in one period is disposed in the next and an expectational analysis in which emphasis is placed on the extent to which the expectations held at the start of the period are in fact realized during the period. The mechanical approach puts major emphasis on such things as the flow of funds through the economic system from producer to income recipient and back again and the expansion or contraction of output through successive intervals of time. It has the advantage of showing how various changes take place within the institutional framework of the particular economy; but, because it does not deal with expectations, it gives little light on many of the factors responsible for the changes involved. The expectational approach, on the other hand, just because it does not demonstrate in step-by-step fashion the way in which funds move through an economy or output changes, often finds itself dealing with expectations which are inevitably doomed to disappointment from the start, as they involve a change of output or a movement of funds faster than the institutional arrangements of the system permit.[24] As with Professor Marget, who in fact advocates a form of period analysis, one can wish period analysis every success and yet remain skeptical as to whether it will prove fruitful within the immediate future even for problems which the Keynesian approach has been least successful in handling.[25]

In contrast to the complexities of period analysis, the approach of the *General Theory* attempts to explain changes in the level of economic activity by means of a handful of variables: the *quantity of money* and *liquidity preference* determine the rate of interest; the rate of interest and

[23] R. F. Harrod, *The Trade Cycle* (Oxford, 1936), p. 66.

[24] Hicks' analysis (*op. cit.*) again comes closest to meeting this problem, but the degree of simplification involved seems to me larger than can ultimately be accepted for monetary and business cycle theory. For income recipients at least, Robertson's analysis falls mainly in the first class, while most of the Swedish work falls in the second, although the line between the two approaches is not always sharp.

[25] Haberler in the course of an extended discussion of period analysis (*op. cit.*, pp. 177–195) suggests that the mechanical and expectational approaches are likely to come together because the concept of expectations regarding uses of future income raises so many difficulties that the time period at issue may be shortened until the expectations are related to income actually realized in some past period—in other words, to Robertson's "disposable" income. If this in fact is to be the bridge between the two approaches, then the doubts expressed regarding fruitfulness seem confirmed, because so short a period would eliminate much of the content of the expectational approach.

the *marginal efficiency of capital* determine the level of investment; and the level of investment and the *marginal propensity to consume* determine income, output, and employment. In his enthusiasm for explaining "dynamic" changes in the simplest possible terms Keynes is sometimes reminiscent of the quantity theorist in believing that his analysis explains rather more than it actually does. In the marginal propensity to consume and the multiplier, for example, Keynes wanted and thought he had a largely constant factor which would permit us to say that "when there *is* an increment of aggregate investment, income *will* increase by an amount which is [the multiplier] times the increment of investment"[26]—just as a quantity theorist would say that, when there is an increase in money, income will increase by an amount which is income velocity times the increase in money.

If it were true that the propensity to consume were relatively constant, Keynes would of course be correct in taking investment as the major variable, just as the quantity theorist took money when changes in income velocity were small. In the *General Theory* considerable space was devoted to arguing that the propensity reflected a stable psychological law which applied over wide ranges of income and broad periods of time.[27] But the stability of the propensity has been widely questioned in theoretical discussion.[28] Moreover, the statistical attempts to verify the stability of the consumption function have run into serious difficulties; the main source of error in the predictions of postwar income and employment made toward the end of the war was apparently the result of inadequate estimates of the possible level of consumption, which in turn appear to have been caused by overestimates of the stability of the consumption function.[29]

---

[26] *General Theory*, p. 115. My italics. The multiplier is equal to one divided by one minus the propensity to consume.

[27] The notation of Keynes reflects his belief in the constancy of the "marginal" propensity to consume by making it equal to what I would think should be described as the "average" propensity to consume. Thus he writes $\Delta Y_w = k \Delta I_w$, where $1 - \frac{1}{k} = \frac{dC_w}{dY_w}$ (*General Theory*, p. 115); but this can only be true if $\frac{\Delta C_w}{\Delta Y_w} = \frac{dC_w}{dY_w}$. Hence if $\frac{\Delta C_w}{\Delta Y_w}$ represents the "average" propensity to consume for the change in income ΔY_w, Keynes is in fact assuming that the "marginal" and "average" propensity are the same—or alternatively that the "marginal" propensity is constant—over the range of income ΔY_w.

[28] B. Ohlin, "Some Notes on the Stockholm Theory of Savings and Investment," *Economic Journal*, June 1937, XLVII, pp. 221–240; D. Robertson, "A Survey of Modern Monetary Controversy," *The Manchester School*, 1938, pp. 133–153; and G. Haberler, *op. cit.*, pp. 222–232, are among the critics of the alleged stability. For further references, see below, p. 329, note 30.

[29] See W. Woytinsky, "What Was Wrong in Forecasts of Postwar Depression," *Journal of Political Economy*, April 1947, LV, pp. 142–151, and references there cited.

Certainly much of the appeal of the Keynesian approach lay in the stability of the multiplier which Keynes premised. For the idea that, once investment was given, saving, income, and employment would all fall into line through the operation of a (more or less) uniquely determined multiplier gave a certain grandeur to the analysis, which made it appear capable of explaining a wide variety of situations and therefore quite "dynamic" in character. When it is realized that the marginal multiplier (for small changes in investment), the average multiplier (for appreciable changes), and the total multiplier (for investment as a whole) may have substantially different values, the analysis comes to be seen as considerably more limited and pedestrian in its scope and therefore more "static" in character. But the set of relationships which Keynes set forth—even if some of the components are less constant than he cared to admit—will certainly have a continuing impact on economic thinking because the variables he related to one another are of fundamental importance to any understanding of the problems with which he was concerned.

Any more complete attempt to appraise the full impact of the Keynesian approach, even if it were as yet possible to do so, would take us beyond the confines of this paper. But it is perhaps worth while to conclude by pointing out that all that has been said regarding the alternative approaches can be rephrased in terms of the saving-investment controversy. For it was the failure to keep factor contracts and entrepreneurial commitments up to date which was responsible for the difference in the *Treatise* between actual and "normal" income and therefore between saving and investment. Saving was confined to the income involved in the contracts and commitments made at the start of the "period," while investment was related to the income actually realized at the end of the "period," which could, of course, be more or less than that involved at the start. As a result a major factor determining the size of the discrepancy between saving and investment was the speed with which contracts and commitments were revised—the slower the revision the larger the discrepancy. Had the "period analysis" character of the difference between saving and investment in the *Treatise* been more fully recognized, it is possible that the advent of the *General Theory* would not have been marked by the extended and largely fruitless controversy as to whether saving and investment are equal or unequal.[30]

What the *General Theory* did in effect was to stress that *during any period* saving was equal to *spending on investment*. (This follows because saving was defined as income less consumption, and income is

---

[30] Sixteen of the major articles on this subject are cited in H. H. Villard, *op. cit.*, p. 28, note.

equal to spending on total output and consumption to spending on consumption; hence by subtraction saving is equal to spending on investment.) The main reason that this caused so much difficulty was that most economists have instinctively thought as consumers, who received income in the present period and then elected whether or not to spend it in a future period.[31] Hence most economists have typically—and frequently unconsciously—meant by saving the difference between the income of the present period and the consumption of a future period—a difference which might either be held idle or invested in the future period. In contrast, Keynes emphasized relationships *within a single period*, stressing that the income of any given period would not have been received unless an identical amount of spending on consumption and investment had taken place.[32] What caused so much misunderstanding and difficulty was the mental adjustment involved in not pursuing the usual more or less instinctive time sequence but instead identifying saving with the *simultaneous* spending on investment which gave rise to the income of the present period, rather than with the spending which might or might not take place *in a future period*.

What Keynes succeeded in doing was to make clear that discrepancies between saving and investment, at least in the *ex post* meanings given the terms before the *General Theory*, depended on implicit or explicit period analysis. For when saving was thought of as income which was "hoarded" rather than spent on consumption, what must have been referred to was income of a period different from that in which the "hoarding" was thought of as taking place; for if the money involved has been "hoarded" in the sense of not being spent on output in the present period, then it would not have been part of present income.[33] That it was desirable to make clear the "period analysis" character of all *ex post* differences between saving and investment is obvious. Yet in appraising the over-all effect of the way in which this matter was pre-

---

[31] The definition given by Keynes added to the confusion. For he defined saving as "the excess of income over consumption" (*General Theory*, p. 62). While actually the "excess" in any period—for the economy as a whole but not necessarily for every individual within the economy—is always identical with spending on investment during the period, the casual reader is likely to think of it as a sum which could be "hoarded."

[32] This does not deny that what happened in one period may influence what happens in a subsequent period, nor does it imply that the amount spent during a given period must "come out of" the income of that period, as this depends on the *length* of the period. If the period is so short that there is no time for any money to be spent more than once, then *all* the spending of the period will "come out of" previously unused cash balances and total income will be less than cash balances; if, however, the period is long enough, money may be spent often enough for total income to be a multiple of average cash balances.

[33] This is, of course, true only for the economy as a whole, as the "hoarding" of one individual may be offset by the "dishoarding" of another.

sented in the *General Theory*, I think it fair to say that it greatly impeded progress in economic thinking—and this despite the fact that the *General Theory* as a whole certainly made the greatest contribution to our ultimate understanding of economic fluctuations of any volume published in the decade of the 'thirties. For it was a paradox of Keynes' greatness that he treated what was a minor clarification of concept as a great new discovery, thereby completely confounding his less nimble-witted colleagues—though it is only fair to admit that Keynes' disciples were frequently *plus royalistes que le roi*. The resulting years of controversy were only ended by the war; their effect was not only to divert much effort of economists into "translating" Keynes into more conventional terms but also to present to the layman the spectacle of a science deeply divided. It is perhaps the ultimate irony of his career that Keynes, with his intense interest in practical programs to reduce business fluctuations, should have contributed so much to the failure of American economists as a group either to develop an agreed program for mitigating the business cycle or to carry any appreciable weight in public decisions on matters of economic policy.

IV. Liquidity Preference and Interest

During recent years Keynes' *General Theory* represents the outstanding development in interest theory, so that it is appropriate to start with a consideration of that volume. It is the contention of the *General Theory* that the rate of interest is entirely determined by two factors: the supply of money and liquidity preference; in other words, liquidity preference is a function which relates the demand for money to the rate of interest. Keynes argues that people have three reasons for desiring "liquidity": the transactions-motive, the precautionary-motive, and the speculative-motive. The first of these is the familiar concept of balances needed to bridge the gap, for both business and income-recipients, between receipts and expenditures connected with current output;[34] the second is "to provide for contingencies requiring sudden expenditure and for unforeseen opportunities of advantageous purchases" and is thought of as varying with the level of income;[35] and the third is to secure "profit from

---

[34] To the more usual formulation Keynes added the need for funds "due to the time-lag between the inception and the execution of the entrepreneurs' decisions," which he called the demand for "finance." See "Mr. Keynes and Finance: Comment," *Economic Journal*, June 1938, XLVIII, p. 319. The fundamental structure of the Keynesian analysis is unaffected by this addition, which is simply another factor adding to the demand for transaction (and probably also precautionary) balances.

[35] *General Theory*, p. 196. The distinction between precautionary and speculative balances has always seemed to me finely drawn.

knowing better than the market what the future will bring forth"—in other words, from the expectation that money will decline in value less than other assets.[36] In short, as Keynes uses them, transaction and precautionary balances are "active" balances held in connection with the production of current income and speculative balances are "idle" balances held on capital account. Note that it is all these balances which are related to the interest rate by liquidity preference; hence "liquidity preference," as Keynes uses the term, covers considerably more than a speculative desire to hold assets in liquid form because it is thought that illiquid assets are likely to depreciate in value.[37]

As with so much of Keynes' work, an appreciable part of the novelty of his treatment of interest arises from either terminological innovations or unusual assumptions. Take, for example, the fact that in Keynes' formulation changes in the desire to save appear not to have any effect on the interest rate. Keynes tells us that economists have generally assumed "that, *ceteris paribus,* a decrease in spending will tend to lower the rate of interest and an increase in investment to raise it. But if what these two quantities determine is, not the rate of interest, but the aggregate volume of employment, then our outlook on the mechanism of the economic system will be profoundly changed. A decreased readiness to spend will be looked on in a quite different light if, instead of being regarded as a factor which will, *ceteris paribus,* increase investment, it is seen as a factor which will, *ceteris paribus,* diminish employment."[38] To what extent is this a real and not merely an apparent contrast with the usual formulation, in which changes in the "readiness to spend"— or in saving in a non-Keynesian sense—are thought of as having an important influence on the rate of interest?

Actually Keynes' startling conclusion that "a decreased readiness to spend" will diminish employment rather than increase investment follows directly from the fact that he *includes* liquidity preference within the *ceteris paribus* assumption; in other words, he assumes that liquidity preference is unaltered despite a "decreased readiness to spend." But this is another way of saying that the individual wishes to hold idle the money he was previously ready to spend; for if the quantity of money and liquidity preference (and therefore the rate of interest) are unchanged, then a decrease in spending can only mean that the funds involved have been shifted from transaction and precautionary balances

---

[36] *Ibid.,* p. 170.

[37] Haberler suggests that the relationship between speculative balances and the rate of interest be called "liquidity preference proper" to distinguish it from the relationship between all balances and the rate of interest (*op. cit.,* p. 210).

[38] *General Theory,* p. 185.

to speculative balances.[39] Under these circumstances investment need not increase and employment as a result will fall. But there is no reason why liquidity preference must remain unchanged, and when it is removed from *ceteris paribus*, quite different results from those which Keynes indicates are possible. For the money freed by the "decreased readiness to spend" may well decrease the individual's liquidity preference, which in turn can be expected to reduce the rate of interest and increase investment, exactly as in the more conventional formulations.[40] Had Keynes said that when an individual saves in order to "hoard," the social effects are quite different than when an individual saves in order to invest, his meaning would have been clearer but his statement less startling.

Of course, the concept of "hoarding" is not a part of the Keynesian system. This is understandable because the instantaneous approach of the *General Theory* avoids so far as possible specific reference to time periods, while "hoarding" in its usual meaning must have a time dimension. For "hoarding" which is timeless becomes identical with holding money; accordingly, as all money must be held by someone at all times if it is to be counted as money, it becomes correct to say that all money is "hoarded" and that changes in "hoarding" from one period to the next are the same thing as changes in the quantity of money. From this it follows that "it is impossible for the actual amount of hoarding to change as a result of decisions on the part of the public, so long as we mean by 'hoarding' the actual holding of cash. For the amount of hoarding must be equal to the quantity of money . . . ; and the quantity of money is not determined by the public."[41] Here again is a startling result based on an unusual meaning for a common term; but in this case the usage on which the result depended was reasonably clear.

What have these changes and innovations contributed to interest theory? The pervading emphasis which Keynes has laid on the dependence of saving and interest on the level of income has been of great importance. The "classical" theory of saving and interest had been most concerned with long-run problems in which it seemed appropriate to take the level of income as more or less fixed and to investigate the forces determining the amount of such income which would be saved and

---

[39] Following Haberler's suggestion, the situation is one in which "liquidity preference proper" has increased sufficiently to absorb the money freed by the "decreased readiness to spend."

[40] Again following Haberler, if there is no change in the individual's "liquidity preference proper," the money freed by the "decreased desire to spend" can be expected to act on the rate of interest and the level of investment in the same way as any decrease in over-all liquidity preference.

[41] *General Theory*, p. 174.

invested. Keynes was by no means the first person to indicate that saving and interest were influenced by the level of income and much of his criticism of "classical" theory, if it was meant to apply to all the work of all his predecessors and not to those "real capital" theorists who were primarily concerned with long-run equilibrium, can only be characterized as overly exuberant. In fact, Keynes himself came to agree that he was "shying at a composite Aunt Sally of uncertain age."[42] But exuberance aside, Keynes clearly deserves credit for emphasizing the extent to which an increase in investment, working through an increase in income, could be expected to provide an offsetting quantity of saving. In part this emphasis was the result of the definitional identity between saving and investment; but back of this lay the real fact that large changes in saving and investment were possible with little change in the level of interest if accompanied by large changes in income. In fact it is quite possible that the start of an upturn will bring such a release of speculative (idle) balances that at least the early periods of recovery may be accompanied by a lower rate of interest than that which had previously prevailed.

In addition to his emphasis on changes in income, Keynes' most important contribution has been the insight which he has given us on the behavior of speculative balances, both in general and especially as a result of changing anticipations regarding the rate of interest. Applied to perpetual bonds, which present the simplest as well as the most extreme case, Keynes points out that it is impossible for the rate anticipated a year hence to exceed the current rate by more than the square of the current rate.[43] For otherwise it would be more profitable to hold money than bonds, as the reduction in the capital value of such securities during the year as a result of the rise in the interest rate would be greater than the sum received as interest. Of course most bonds are not perpetual, so that rate increases in excess of the square of the current rate can be anticipated without causing a complete shift into idle balances. But clearly whenever appreciable rate increases are anticipated the effectiveness of monetary policy is greatly reduced, and recovery is likely to be slow even if vigorous action is taken by the monetary authorities. For when the recession phase has come to an end and prices of securities are high and yields low as a result of a reflationary "cheap money" policy, a time may come when any further expansion of the money supply will flow overwhelmingly into idle (speculative) balances because investors

---

[42] "The 'Ex-Ante' Theory of the Rate of Interest," *Economic Journal*, December 1937, XLVII, p. 663.

[43] *General Theory*, p. 202. If the current rate is 3 per cent, the anticipated rate cannot be more than 3.09 per cent.

generally believe that the present low level of the interest rate will not be maintained.[44]

In appraising the probable importance in actual practice of such a situation, Keynes himself has repudiated the extreme possibility that *all* additional funds will flow into idle balances, stating that while this "might become practically important in future, I know of no example of it hitherto. Indeed, owing to the unwillingness of most monetary authorities to deal boldly in debts of long term, there has not been much opportunity for a test."[45] Yet it is by assuming implicitly or explicitly what is in effect an "absolute liquidity preference" under which the demand for idle (speculative) balances is insatiable, that Keynes achieves his most striking differences from other theorists. In appraising his contribution one has again to weigh the real insight that he has given us against the confusion that has resulted from his perennial inclination to treat an unusual, and therefore startling, situation as if it applied generally—in short, to make a "general theory" of a special case.

Much of the credit for clarifying the issues raised by liquidity preference belongs to J. R. Hicks, whose *Value and Capital*, appearing just before the war turned economists' minds to other things, marked the end in Great Britain of the controversies raised by the *General Theory*. Hicks agrees with Keynes and most other modern interest theorists that the determination of the rate of interest is not adequately explained by "real capital" theories relating to "real" economies. But, while stressing in the Walrasian tradition that the interest rate can only be determined in relation to other prices, he finds it a matter of convenience whether the rate is treated as "determined" by the demand and supply of loan funds or of money.[46] The first treatment he suggests is most useful when attention is to be focused on the difficulties which result from the fact that "the" rate of interest is in fact a complex of rates, while the second serves to stress the closeness of the connection between the demand for money and interest rates—a matter stressed not only by Keynes but also by Hicks himself.[47]

Hicks' contribution, of course, is far broader than a clarification of

---

[44] Of course, if the expectation of rising rates is not realized, it will in time give way; hence Keynes' analysis applies fundamentally to cyclical problems. It also implies sizable rationality on the part of those holding balances, which is hardly completely correct. Thus during the war period individual holdings of *currency* increased faster than their holdings of deposits and much faster than the money holdings of business as a whole. Those holding actual cash—for the quite complicated reasons that they do hold cash—are obviously acting from different motives than those which Keynes has indicated.

[45] *General Theory*, p. 207.

[46] *Op. cit.*, Ch. XII, especially pp. 160–162.

[47] *Ibid.*, pp. 237–239.

controversy, representing an outstanding reformulation of theory. In the case of interest, he suggests that the fundamental explanation grows out of the fact that money has "general acceptability" while other securities (in the broadest possible sense) do not; in other words, money is the most perfect type of security and interest a measure of the imperfect "moneyness" of other securities. "The nature of money and the nature of interest are therefore very nearly the same problem. When we have decided what it is which makes people give more for those securities which are reckoned as money than for those securities which are not, we shall have discovered also why interest is paid."[48] In the *General Theory*, besides the obvious risk of default, we have seen that Keynes placed great stress on the risk of future changes in interest rates. Hicks believes that this is an incomplete formulation and that interest cannot be explained by risk-premiums alone. For even if there is no risk of default or of changes in interest rates, there would remain: (1) the cost of converting money into securities (i.e., investment costs); and (2) the cost of "rediscounting" the security if money comes to be desired before the security matures (i.e., possible disinvestment costs). Hence the interest rate in equilibrium must be high enough to cover these costs for the marginal lender, as well as risks of rate changes and default.[49]

As to relative interest rates, Hicks feels that no serious problems arise; for the actual span of rates from long to short can either be explained "in terms of expectations about the future course of the short rate" or alternatively "in terms of expectations about the future course of the long rate."[50] While this may be adequate for the relatively rational inhabitants of the simplified models with which Hicks is dealing, it is not of much aid in explaining the complexities of the actual behavior of the numerous interest rates found in the real world. By far the greatest amount of factual information on actual rate behavior over a long period of time is contained in Frederick R. Macaulay's study for the National Bureau.[51] Series starting before the Civil War are presented for call money and commercial paper rates, for railroad bond yields, and for railroad stock prices, as well as much information on such related financial series as bank clearings and commodity prices. Despite the wealth of material presented, however, the study, as its title indicates, is fundamentally concerned with the problems which arise when an attempt is made to

[48] *Ibid.*, p. 163.
[49] *Ibid.*, Ch. XIII.
[50] *Ibid.*, p. 152.
[51] *Some Theoretical Problems Suggested by the Movements of Interest Rates, Bond Yields and Stock Prices in the United States Since 1856* (New York, 1938). See also David Durand, *Basic Yields of Corporate Bonds, 1900–1942* (New York, 1942).

find some order in the array of rates. Macaulay concludes that "statistical examination reveals that the relations (between long- and short-term rates) as they actually occur show a definite tendency to run *counter* to these theoretical rationalistic expectations" based on "complete knowledge of the pertinent facts and logical use of such knowledge."[52] In what is perhaps his most interesting contribution, he explains this result by the extent of irrationality in the real world, the chief cause of which "is the inability of human beings to foresee the future, let alone adjust the present to it."[53] Certainly the facts that are presented and the difficulties in interpreting them that Macaulay poses make it clear that the behavior of relative interest rates is still to be fully explained.

V. WAR FINANCE

By far the most difficult period in which to appraise fairly the role of monetary economics is during the war. First of all, many economists were in the government service, where their contributions were buried in unpublished memoranda; hence it should be remembered that the somewhat critical remarks which follow are made on the basis of the work of those who remained able to publish. Secondly, my basis of judgment is not confined to monetary matters narrowly conceived, but I know of no way of appraising policy in regard to the numerous monetary problems raised by a modern war except in terms of the contribution that is made to winning the war. In short, I propose to appraise, with the qualifications indicated and the benefits of hindsight, the contributions of monetary economics to the war mobilization. My conclusion is that the record is not one of which economists can be proud. The remainder of this section sets forth the reasons for this judgment.

Total war requires the largest possible expansion of the labor force (including those in the armed services), the greatest possible increase in hours worked, and the quickest possible transfer of labor from peacetime to wartime production. In the United States, from early in 1940 to the wartime peak, hours worked in all manufacturing industry increased 20 per cent, the total labor force increased 25 per cent (of which perhaps a quarter was the result of the normal growth of the population), and employment (excluding relief but including the armed forces) increased 45 per cent. Hence, if the hours worked elsewhere rose as much as in the manufacturing industry, at the peak we expanded our employed labor resources (including the armed forces) by almost 75 per

---

[52] *Op. cit.*, p. 3; italics in original; parenthesis supplied.
[53] *Ibid.*, p. 20.

cent of the prewar level. Even the labor force increase appears to have surpassed that of Germany and equaled that of Great Britain, as the percentage of our population in the labor force by the end of the war was comparable to the similar British figure throughout the year, and actually exceeded it during our seasonal peaks of employment.[54] But both Germany and Britain relied heavily upon labor compulsion in comparison with our overwhelming use of monetary incentives; yet the use of monetary incentives did not cost us excessively in comparison with Britain, as the British cost of living between 1939 and 1945 rose almost exactly the same amount as ours.

This mobilization of our resources was accomplished by arrangements which J. K. Galbraith has called the "disequilibrium system."[55] In essence this system brings about a divergence between income and "spending" in the sense of expenditure on consumption, which is another way of saying that it brings about a large volume of saving. The purpose of this saving is to supplement—by an amount highly important at the margin— the monetary incentives which would be provided by income alone if income were restricted to permissible expenditure on consumption plus voluntary saving. The system must of course be operated in such a way as to preserve the public's faith in the future value of money, in order to make sure that the large volume of saving continues to have an incentive value. As long as it is operated in this way, it seems clear that it will provide considerably more monetary incentives than either an "equilibrium" system or an uncontrolled inflation.[56] The only alternative would seem to be greater reliance on non-monetary incentives, which must in the main involve compulsion.

In the United States the divergence between income and spending was, to a major extent, the result of adequately effective price control. There are of course other possibilities; either some variant of the Kalecki plan, involving control over total spending, or some type of forced saving could have been used. But I suspect that the incentive to earn additional income was greater under price control than under either alternative. For the Kalecki plan would have placed a legal limitation

---

[54] Both the growth in the American population and the sharp seasonal fluctuations in the labor force make comparisons difficult; the estimates presented in the text make no allowance for seasonal changes and should therefore not be compared directly with those for other countries.

[55] "The Disequilibrium System," *American Economic Review*, June 1947, XXXVII, pp. 287–302.

[56] Galbraith suggested (*ibid.*, p. 293, note) that the system he described might be called a "forced equilibrium" but prefers "disequilibrium" as shorter and more suggestive. I think "controlled disequilibrium" is more descriptive, in order to give us a phrase—"uncontrolled disequilibrium"—to characterize an unrestrained inflation.

on the dollars that could be spent and a forced saving plan would have compelled workers to take part of their earnings in bonds redeemable only after the war. Under price control, on the other hand, the failure to spend was entirely *voluntary*—the result of the goods people wanted not being available. Hence I believe that workers would in all probability work harder under price control, if only because they knew that they *could*, if they wanted to, "blow" their earnings *at once* on something. Moreover, as some price control and rationing of especially scarce goods was inevitable, the greater administrative ease with which price control could be extended until it became widespread was a point in its favor compared with control of spending or forced saving, which must be on a broad basis from the start.

In the United States the operation of the economy in such a way as to preserve the public's faith in the future value of money (and therefore of savings fixed in terms of money) appears to me to have involved only a postwar problem. For the large increase in money during the war *did not in fact* undermine people's confidence in their savings *during the war itself*.[57] Just what weight should be given to the postwar effects of different methods of war finance in a total war is not easy to determine. Obviously most people would prefer victory with a postwar financial problem to defeat; but it is equally obvious that the large holdings of liquid assets which accumulate under a "disequilibrium system" make it undesirable to scrap controls and raise wages substantially immediately after the end of the war. That this need not be done is amply demonstrated by Great Britain, whose cost of living was in 1947 at about the same level as at the end of the war. Moreover, it should be remembered that a smaller increase of money during the war would have had little effect in holding down postwar spending unless stabilization of the wartime pattern of interest rates on government bonds was abandoned after the war.[58] But the reader should be warned that economists who discount the extent to which maximum incentives were needed during the war, who feel that practical politics will bring about a quick abandonment of wartime controls after the war, and above all who be-

---

[57] Put more technically, this amounts to saying that the wartime "margin of tolerance" was not exceeded. Maximization of the effectiveness of a "disequilibrium system" would involve, among other things, a comparison of the incentive to further expansion of the labor force provided by higher unspent incomes with the resulting pressure on current and postwar prices. The fact that the labor force was expanding (allowing for seasonal factors) right up to V-E Day without undue pressure on *current* prices seems to me to indicate that whether the system was carried too far depends on the effects on *postwar* prices that can be attributed to it. Whether it was not carried far enough need not be considered.

[58] This point is elaborated in the final section on our postwar heritage.

lieve in the importance of rehabilitating monetary controls, will be critical of the "disequilibrium system" because of the postwar problems created by the large holdings of liquid assets to which such a system gives rise.

If this analysis of the system which permitted our effective war mobilization has been broadly correct, it seems to me appropriate to judge the publications of economists during the period in which the system was being constructed by their contribution to its erection.[59] Broadly, I think it is fair to say that much of the advice given hindered completion of the system and therefore our mobilization for war. Economic literature at the start was overwhelmingly concerned with the prevention of inflation, so that it was not until relatively late in the war that the difficulties and limitations of an all-out anti-inflationary program began to be considered. In the main this concentration on inflation apparently resulted partly from an unawareness of the magnitude of the potential expansion of our labor resources or of the required shifts within the labor force and partly from general doubt regarding the efficacy of price controls, especially in the absence of widespread rationing.

The general literature is largely devoid of attempts to determine the probable expansion of the labor force and employment during the war—to say nothing of output, which presented a much more difficult problem because of its changing composition.[60] It is true, of course, that estimates of future income underlay all estimates of the "inflationary gap"; but those using the "gap" immediately focused on the effect of spending the estimated income on the diminishing supply of consumption goods, rather than on the real factors involved. Thus we find that J. P. Wernette, writing in September 1941 "as though the country were actually engaged in a serious war," urged that, if perfection was impossible, the "government should lean toward over use of non-expansionist financial methods," as "everyone agrees that taxes should be heavy enough to avoid inflation."[61] Again William Fellner, writing in early 1942, believed that a tax program to bridge the gap would mean an effective rate of 30 per cent on the income of those with incomes of $3,000, 40 per cent of $4,000 incomes, 50 per cent of $5,000 incomes, and 90 per cent of $20,000 incomes, which could be expected to eliminate individual savings; yet there is no discus-

[59] I am acutely aware of the problem of criticism based on hindsight; but if the prescriptions of economists were wrong even for reasons which seemed excellent at the time, we must face the fact that the economic advice given was undesirable.

[60] What one would have liked would have been something, however crude, comparable to E. E. Hagen and N. B. Kirkpatrick's "The National Output at Full Employment in 1950," *American Economic Review*, September 1944, XXXIV, pp. 472–500.

[61] "Financing the Defense Program," *American Economic Review*, December 1941, XXXI, pp. 755, 761, 763.

sion of the effects on production of this level of taxation.[62] When one adds
the work of the Iowa State group led by A. G. Hart,[63] the estimates of
Shoup, Friedman, and Mack,[64] and the general interest in the "inflationary gap," as well as the discussion of the spending tax—to cite but a few
outstanding examples—it seems clear that the emphasis was heavily on
"stabilization."

Certainly the "inflationary gap" was the most important analytical tool
developed during the period, if judged only by the number of alternative
meanings that were spawned. Perhaps its most generally accepted meaning was what has been called the "consumer expenditure gap"—the
difference between what consumers would like to spend on consumption
and the value, at a specified price level, of the goods and services estimated to be available. But the "total expenditure gap," the "disposable
consumer income gap," and the "tax gap" were also distinguished, as
well as whether the "gap" was "total" or "primary."[65] In general, interest
in the gap diminished before any general agreement on definitions was
reached; certainly there was little statistical contribution in the published literature, as events moved too rapidly.[66] Looking back on the
history of the concept, I venture to predict that far more work in clarifying the meaning of the "gap"—especially in relating the required taxes
(or deficits) to the desired effect on the national income—will have to
be done before the high hopes of future usefulness held at the time will
be justified.

The failure to relate monetary policy to the possible expansion of the
labor force was matched by a lack of interest in the required shifts
within the labor force; yet these shifts raised serious implications for
any stabilization program. For the use of monetary incentives necessarily

---

[62] "War Finance and Inflation," *American Economic Review*, June 1942, XXXII, pp.
246, 248, 251.

[63] *Paying for Defense* (Philadelphia, 1941).

[64] *Taxing to Prevent Inflation: Techniques for Estimating Revenue Requirements*
(New York, 1943).

[65] See W. A. Salant, "The Inflationary Gap," and M. Friedman, "Discussion of the
Inflationary Gap," *American Economic Review*, June 1942, XXXII, pp. 308–320.

[66] The important volume of Shoup, Friedman, and Mack did not appear until the summer of 1943, though its estimates were for the amount of taxes needed in June 1942.
This book is probably the most important to emerge from the discussion of the "gap,"
though its concepts are somewhat different from the more widely used estimates of the
Office of Price Administration. Clark Warburton's "Monetary Expansion and the Inflationary Gap," *American Economic Review*, June 1944, XXXIV, pp. 303–327, appeared
even later and involved a new meaning of the "gap" which made it equal to the change
in money holdings of individuals and business enterprises. Most "gaps" are *ex ante* in
character, as *ex post* we identify what consumers wanted to spend during any period
with actual value of goods and services purchased during the period; but Warburton's
"gap" of course has both an *ex ante* and an *ex post* aspect, and may be negative as well
as positive.

involves an increase in average incomes, unless one is prepared to set up differentials in favor of war industries by *cutting* wages in existing employment—which seems sufficiently detrimental to morale to be unacceptable during a major war even assuming it to be administratively feasible. To take an arbitrary example, if a third of the working force were to be shifted and it was felt that a 50 per cent average differential (including overtime and the like) was necessary, an average increase in labor incomes of 17 per cent would result. Yet one of the earliest pleas for stabilization of prices states that "monetary stabilization must be supplemented by a labor policy which assures that particular wages *will not rise* while there exists an 'excess supply' of that grade of labor, and that wages *will rise* when a 'shortage' of that grade of labor exists."[67] There was apparently no recognition that this sort of wage policy, if the shifts involved were of any size, would be inconsistent with the program of price stabilization that was advocated.

It was not until early in 1943 that a careful analysis was presented by Friedman of the continuing importance of the role of income in organizing resources during wartime and of the desirability, in contrast to peacetime, of divorcing spending on consumption from the receipt of income.[68] Such a divorce could be achieved by taxation of incomes, forced savings, or a tax on spending—the last being the alternative chosen by Friedman. At the same time Shoup discussed at length the effect of various types of taxation (particularly the income tax) on the supply of effort and therefore the volume of output.[69] The net effect of these contributions was to favor the use of the spendings tax as part of the fiscal program, as a result of explicit recognition of the limitations of income taxation because of its effect on incentives.

The spendings tax was an American version of the Kalecki plan.[70] Kalecki had proposed that everyone be issued a quantity of coupons for purchases in retail stores, but in this form the plan involved both administrative difficulties and problems of equity. The spendings tax represented an alternative method of controlling total spending and in this way preserving the flexibility of the price system.[71] Whatever its

[67] G. L. Bach, "Rearmament, Recovery, and Monetary Policy," *American Economic Review*, March 1941, XXXI, p. 32. My italics.

[68] "The Spendings Tax as a Wartime Fiscal Measure," *American Economic Review*, March 1943, XXXIII, pp. 50–62.

[69] "Problems in War Finance," *American Economic Review*, March 1943, XXXIII, pp. 74–97.

[70] *General Rationing*, Bull., Institute of Statistics (Oxford, England), January 11, 1941, Vol. 3, No. 1.

[71] The standard arguments for the superior economy of a price system were usually offered; but such arguments really apply to long-run adjustments and wartime problems are short-run in character. As economic theory tells us little about the process of adjust-

theoretical merits—and I believe that the importance and extent of economic flexibility can easily be overstated in wartime[72]—there can be no doubt that the spendings tax would itself have raised serious problems of equity and administration. Perhaps the most serious of the former would have been the treatment of housing expenditure—the home owner vs. the rich renter whose contractual rent is in excess of his entire permissible spending. Even K. E. Poole, though he concludes that the plan is administratively workable, admits that "the administration of the spendings tax would apparently have to be substantially better than that of an income-capital gains tax of approximately equal efficiency."[73] Hence it is understandable that Congress did not show much enthusiasm for the proposal.

Advocates of the spending tax did not feel that any extended evaluation of price control and rationing as an alternative method of limiting spending was necessary. Wallis stated simply that "specific controls, such as price ceilings and rationing . . . cannot control inflation,"[74] and Fellner argued that "price control and rationing are inadequate substitutes for anti-inflationary fiscal policies. Direct controls can be expected to forestall inflation only if the pressure against which they have to operate is held within rather narrow limits."[75] This is not surprising, as those in charge of price control themselves had grave doubts as to the potency of the weapon they were using; the Statement of Considerations accompanying the General Maximum Price Regulation, according to Galbraith, "carried a heart-felt warning that it would not work unless strong steps were taken to restore and maintain equilibrium at the then ruling

---

ment, it also has little to say regarding the short-run wastes involved in reaching adjustment. Hence the applicability of the usual arguments to wartime problems is not clear. A similar point in criticism of the Kalecki plan was made by R. E. Holben, "General Expenditure Rationing with Particular Reference to the Kalecki Plan," *American Economic Review*, September 1942, XXXII, pp. 513–523, who also opposed closing the gap "during the present transition stage" (p. 522) of the war economy.

[72] Thus W. A. Wallis, an early advocate of the spendings tax, argued that the "possibilities of substitution quickly convert what would otherwise be an acute specific shortage into a mild general shortage" in "How to Ration Consumers' Goods and Control Their Prices," *American Economic Review*, September 1942, XXXII, p. 511. It seems to me that "quickly" refers to periods longer than the war itself!

[73] "Problems of Administration and Equity under a Spending Tax," *American Economic Review*, March 1943, XXXIII, pp. 63–73. As proposed, it would have been necessary for those with capital to show that all assets sold were balanced by assets purchased. It seems to me that the possibilities for evasion on the part of those possessing capital, and especially those engaged in small businesses, would be sufficient to make the tax politically unacceptable, especially when it was known that it would almost certainly be in effect for too short a time for efficient administration to develop and when Poole admits that hoarded cash and anticipatory buying would inevitably make the tax inequitable for "the first year or two" (p. 67).

[74] *Op. cit.*, p. 502.

[75] *Op. cit.*, p. 235.

prices."[76] Yet, despite the widespread doubts of economists and most of the standard texts, price control, *even without extensive formal rationing*, proved unexpectedly effective as a device for limiting spending. But as price control alone takes a relatively small administrative staff, the program was less wasteful of manpower than had been feared. Further, for a short period and with a large second-hand market, the inequity of "bare-shelf rationing" (resulting from goods not being available) also turned out to be bearable.[77] Hence the method of limiting spending so as to control inflation which economists, by and large, would have been the last to recommend was not only the one used, but was used with outstanding success.

Compared with previous wars, perhaps the most remarkable thing about the recent war was the lack of interest in, or discussion of, methods of raising the money to meet war expenses. This is because the technical problem of ensuring that the government had the dollars it needed when it needed them presented no difficulty. We understood how to provide smoothly, through an expansion of bank deposits (and therefore currency), the sums which were not raised by taxation or voluntary saving and we did not delude ourselves into believing that individual borrowing secured by government bonds was less inflationary than an equivalent credit extension by outright purchase.

There are, of course, many who feel that the banks should not have been allowed to absorb as much of the increase in the debt as they actually did, or that the "pattern of rates" on government securities should not have been stabilized at the levels actually selected. But it is not clear that a change in the amount taken by the banks or the pattern of rates used would have had any appreciable effect on our ability to wage war. Hence these matters raise in the main the important question of the controls to be used in the postwar period, which will be discussed in the following section. The only probable objection to this generalization is likely to be that a higher rate of interest during the war might have decreased spending and increased voluntary saving.[78] But the Savings Bond program generally and the Savings Bonds themselves

---

[76] *Op. cit.*, p. 290, note.

[77] As impersonal (highly competitive) markets are the exception rather than the rule, business usually distributed short supplies of goods reasonably equitably to maintain distributive channels and trade relations. In fact, it is likely that many of the advantages of a spendings tax would be lost because business would not have allocated goods where demand was greatest (even at the expense of maximum wartime profits) for fear of the "inequitable" treatment of its distributors that would be involved!

[78] Whether people could have been induced to hold more government bonds and less bank deposits is again a postwar problem; for during the war the holders of the balances were induced over all to keep them idle, and an idle balance has no more effect than an equal amount of government bonds.

represented relatively generous treatment for most saving likely to have resulted from a voluntary reduction in spending. Until we know more about the effect of interest on savings, I doubt whether there is much more that can be said in appraisal of the program actually pursued.[79]

VI. The Postwar Heritage

By the end of the 1930's it had become quite clear that monetary policy (in the sense here used) could not by itself promote recovery. But I think it would have been fairly generally agreed that there remained for monetary policy an important role in setting the scene for recovery and in ensuring that the subsequent prosperity did not become inflationary. The government debt which we inherited from the war, however, has drastically restricted the ability of the Federal Reserve System to move against inflation.[80] Of the present gross federal debt totaling $260 billion roughly $100 billion, or 40 per cent, is held by commercial banks and the Federal Reserve System. The normal statement of the problem facing the Federal Reserve System is that, so long as the banks continue to hold such a large amount of securities, they will be able to obtain whatever reserves they wish by selling securities to the Reserve banks, thus causing a multiple expansion of the money supply. I think this statement obscures the fundamental issue. Even if the banking system held no federal bonds whatsoever so that all open-market purchases or sales were from the general public, attempts to control the general credit situation, either by open-market operations or changes in reserve ratios, would inevitably lead to unacceptable repercussions on the government bond market; in other words, the problem would be the same as it now is. Hence the essence of the situation is that control has been taken from the Reserve System, not by the bond holdings of the banks, but by the decision to stabilize the price of government bonds and therefore the general structure of interest rates.

Before discussing the desirability of this decision it is worth making clear that the banking system could be shielded relatively easily from the effects of changes in the rate of interest—or, if one prefers it the other way round, the Reserve System could be shielded from the effects of bank holdings of government bonds. A rash of proposals has been put forward

---

[79] Cf. Seymour E. Harris, "A One Per Cent War?" *American Economic Review*, September 1945, XXXV, pp. 667–671.

[80] The debt inherited from the war has also restricted to a lesser extent the ability of the System to bring about easier credit conditions, because of the resulting capital gains on government bonds.

to achieve this end;[81] but the simplest to understand, as well as in all probability the most effective, would involve giving the Reserve System the power: (1) to raise member bank reserve requirements to any level; (2) to pay interest on member bank reserve balances; and (3) to lower as much as is necessary its own Gold Certificate reserve requirements against Federal Reserve notes and deposits.[82] With these powers the Reserve System would be able to acquire most bonds now held by the banks by extensive open-market operations offset by increased reserve requirements to levels between 60 and 75 per cent; the loss of earnings on government bonds could be offset, to whatever extent desirable, by the interest paid on the reserve balances which the banks would have acquired. In this way the banking system would be rendered almost completely impervious to changes in the price of government securities, and the ratio of capital to assets other than reserve balances raised to a higher level than it has been in decades.[83]

While these changes could be made relatively easily,[84] they are almost

---

[81] Originally proposed by L. H. Seltzer to deal with the prewar problem of excess reserves, the idea has recently been advocated not only by Seltzer, "A Uniform Treasury Certificate as Bank Reserve," Commercial and Financial Chronicle, February 28, 1946, pp. 1087, 1116–1117, but also by the Committee for Economic Development, Jobs and Markets (New York, 1946); S. E. Leland, "The Government, the Banks and the National Debt," Commercial and Financial Chronicle, January 17, 1946, pp. 242, 281–284; and R. I. Robinson, "Monetary Aspects of Public Debt Policy," Postwar Economic Studies, No. 3, Board of Governors of the Federal Reserve System (Washington, 1946). As originally proposed, the banks would have been required to hold some sort of special government security; but the possible variations are almost endless. All security reserve proposals involve serious administrative complexities because two types of reserves would have to be adjusted every time deposits shifted between banks. After considerable study I am convinced that the proposal summarized in the text is simpler to understand, as well as more effective, than any alternative. For this reason I have concentrated on it rather than undertake an extended discussion of a somewhat specialized subject.

[82] If it was proposed to save the Treasury money—i.e., pay less interest on reserve balances than was received on government securities purchased—arrangements would have to be made, to the extent that the matter is not already covered in the recent Reserve-Treasury agreement regarding excess earnings, for the Reserve System to return whatever difference there was to the Treasury.

[83] Two problems would remain: the plan could not be applied as outlined above to non-member banks and transitional arrangements would have to be made for the few surviving banks—largely concentrated in the Dallas District of the Reserve System—which still have the major portion of their assets in forms other than government securities.

[84] Judging from the economic, not the political point of view. The fact that this variant would give the Reserve System the power to determine the interest to be paid on reserve balances—and therefore the general level of bank earnings—insures widespread bank opposition; it might be necessary to guarantee a fixed return on reserve balances by giving banks a "certificate of deposit" bearing a rate of interest fixed contractually for a term of years. Doubt regarding the chances of political action has also been expressed in strong terms by Allan Sproul, President of the New York Reserve Bank, "Monetary Management and Credit Control," American Economic Review, June 1947, XXXVII, p. 346. It is also worth noting that freeing of interest rates would require a modification of various government loan and loan-insurance plans, such as those applying to residential mortgages.

certainly not worth making unless it is planned to use changes in interest rates as a control device.[85] Apart from variations in interest rates it is true that the reserve proposal outlined would aid in checking the multiple expansion of deposits which results when banks "play the pattern of rates" by selling short-term securities to the Reserve System in order to buy long-term issues from the market. During the war we undertook to stabilize a "pattern of rates" which was based on and adjusted to the prewar degree of rate instability; hence this pattern can continue without support only so long as banks think it will not continue. If they become increasingly convinced of its permanence, the low end of the pattern will increasingly require support at a time when securities at the high end may be above par. In other words, when a particular pattern is chosen, support (and therefore expansion) is called for whenever *any portion* of the pattern starts to fall below par, not the pattern *as a whole*. If most short-term securities were transferred from the banks to the Reserve System in line with the reserve balance proposal outlined above, in effect the System could adjust its holdings in such a way as to conform with the pattern that it was committed to maintain, so that intervention would only be necessary when the pattern as a whole required support. But the importance of such a change would depend upon the extent of the divergence between the market pattern and the pattern chosen for stabilization, as weakness at the low end would have to be balanced by strength at the high end if the pattern as a whole was not to require support. At present, however, the high end is exhibiting so little strength that almost nothing would be achieved from not being obliged to support the low end *if* it were necessary to support the pattern as a whole. Hence the interest-bearing reserve plan, or any other variant of the security reserve proposals, does not seem worth the candle unless interest rate changes are to be resurrected as a control device.

Should this be done? Despite the great theoretical interest in the rate of interest up to the war there has been increasing doubt as to whether the practical importance of interest changes was commensurate with its place in theory. Just before the war a group of Oxford economists interviewed business men regarding the effect of the interest rate on their business decisions and concluded: "The majority deny that their activities have been, or are likely to be, directly affected in any way by changes in interest rates. Of those who take the view that they might sometimes be affected, few suggest that the influence is an important one."[86] The same

---

[85] Use of interest rates as a control device of course involves not only changes in rediscount rates but also open market operations and the like, which change rates by changing the availability of credit.

[86] H. D. Henderson, "The Significance of the Rate of Interest," *Oxford Economic Papers*, No. 1, October 1938, p. 9.

problem has been examined by Professor F. A. Lutz; he concludes that changes "will not affect" decisions regarding inventories, are "not likely to influence investment decisions in manufacturing industry," under certain circumstances "may affect investment decisions in the area of public utilities (including railroads) and residential construction," and under certain circumstances would also affect "the readiness of financial institutions to grant credit or to float bonds and stocks, so that the interest rate may influence the volume of investment even without changing the profit calculations of entrepreneurs."[87] While the last two categories are of major importance in capital formation, the limited circumstances in which they are influenced by interest rate changes make it clear that the weapon is a less powerful one than we had thought in the past. But should we nonetheless seek to use it, even if we know that it is likely to turn out to be a weak reed?

From the factual point of view we are really asking whether the tail should be allowed to wag the dog. For total private debt is only perhaps one-third of all debt. This means that any permanent rise in the rate of interest will ultimately increase the cost of perhaps 80 per cent of all debt—with the resulting adverse effects on income distribution—in order to affect decisions involving 20 per cent. It is true that during certain phases of the business cycle the percentage of the annual changes in the debt (and therefore of the current offsets to saving) influenced by changes in the rate of interest may be considerably greater than 20 per cent; the extent to which this is likely to be the case will of course depend on the future fiscal policy of the Federal Government. But the ultimate cost in adverse effects on income distribution is obviously far greater than when the Federal Government was a minor debtor, adjusting itself to policy determined with other considerations in mind. Further, there is also an increasing belief that the amount saved out of current income (in Keynesian terminology, the marginal propensity to consume) is quite insensitive to changes in the rate of interest, so that consumer spending can far better be influenced by direct control over instalment credit and the like rather than through general changes in the level of interest rates. Even the extent to which people utilize their existing liquid asset holdings is not likely to be much influenced by interest rate changes.

Nor are the secondary effects of interest rate changes likely to be large.[88] The actual pattern of bond holdings casts doubt on whether small

[87] "The Interest Rate and Investment in a Dynamic Economy," *American Economic Review*, December 1945, XXXV, p. 830.

[88] By far the most comprehensive discussion of this problem is that of L. H. Seltzer, "Is a Rise in Interest Rates Desirable or Inevitable?" *American Economic Review*, December 1945, XXXV, pp. 831–850, who suggested most of the points made in the text.

increases would prevent holders from selling their securities to the banks (and thus hold down bank expansion); and there is not much more reason to believe that such increases would "mop up" idle balances, or that such balances would remain "mopped up" even if a temporary shift was brought about. On the other hand, large increases in the rate of interest might well be dangerous. Not only would there be the possibility that the decline in the price of government securities would be interpreted as a breakdown in government credit, but in the short run bank capital would be endangered and in the long run bank earnings would be unacceptably large—unless in both cases some variant of the interest-bearing reserve balances plan had previously been put into effect.

Perhaps the best argument for reinstating monetary controls is that we have so few others. Seltzer, after rejecting interest rate changes, could only name budgetary policy, Savings Bond campaigns, and control over margin and consumer credit, concluding that the problem of control over inflation was still unsolved.[89] Since then control over consumer credit has been dropped; only "jawbone control" by the Council of Economic Advisers has been added. Of course this situation holds no terror for the confirmed believer in secular stagnation. As monetary controls since the middle of the 1930's have, in any event, been merely potentially important in checking a boom, their loss will not disturb anyone convinced that booms have disappeared.

Nor does this terrify the advocate of "functional finance," who is quite willing to rely almost exclusively on budgetary policy.[90] After the level of government expenditure had been decided by balancing the social utility of additional government expenditure against additional private expenditure at roughly the full employment level of income, the extent of taxation would be entirely determined by the need to contract or expand the national income so as to keep it at the level required for full employment—let the debt fall where it may. Theoretically there is much to be said for this approach; certainly it has helped to clarify our understanding of the underlying issues. But its terminology is well calculated to scare the daylights out of Congressmen, who must be prevailed upon to put it into effect!

Even conservative use of budget policy, unadorned by the trapping of "functional finance," has made little progress. There is no inclination to delegate even limited control over taxation to the executive; yet without some such delegation—unless similar power be given to a Congressional committee—rapid action cannot be expected. On the expenditure side—

[89] Ibid., pp. 846–847.
[90] A. P. Lerner, Economics of Control (New York, 1944).

assuming that increased expenditure would be part of conservative budget policy—there is also little that has been done in the way of advanced planning. Perhaps most fundamental of all, there is meager general understanding of the probability of a major business cycle or of the magnitudes that would be involved with our present level of national income. True, the inauguration of the Council of Economic Advisers may in time help notably. But it seems fair to say that the present period is woefully lacking in devices for control of the level of economic activity. It is on the ground that any weapon is better than none when the arsenal is almost empty that the advocate of the re-establishment of the use of monetary controls can base his case at the present time.

The weakness of the case for a reinstatement of monetary controls involves a further decline in the importance of monetary theory in general and interest rates as a control device in particular. This in turn has stimulated work on other aspects of the interest rate as well as different types of controls.[91] One aspect much in need of further investigation is what *does* determine where investment is undertaken, and therefore the way in which capital is allocated. The extent of the tendency of business men to confine new investment to lines similar to those in which they are already engaged particularly needs investigation. Another important problem is the role played by the risk element. The difficulties that small business experiences in obtaining long-term capital may result from a reluctance on the part of the lender to appear to "gouge" the borrower by charging a rate sufficient to cover the actual risks involved, while the borrower may be unwilling to pay, not because the rate would be burdensome, but because it would reflect on his credit standing! It has long been pointed out that part of the control over credit exercised by commercial banks was through changes in the freedom with which funds were made available at constant rates of interest. A similar situation probably prevails among other lenders as well. It is probable that much future research will deal with the organization and functioning of particular credit markets, and especially with the non-price elements involved. Already such markets as those for consumer credit, residential mortgages, and stock market funds have been singled out for special stimulation or control, and the trend is likely to continue.

Another area where further research is needed is in regard to the management of the present volume of government debt. While much has appeared regarding the debt, it has usually been from the point of view

---

[91] See H. C. Wallich, "The Changing Significance of the Interest Rate," *American Economic Review*, December 1946, XXXVI, pp. 761–787; and *idem*, "Debt Management as an Instrument of Economic Policy," *ibid.*, June 1946, XXXVI, pp. 292–310.

of the restraints exercised by the debt on monetary or fiscal policy. What we need to know is how to manage the structure and composition of the debt in such a way as to reinforce monetary and fiscal policy; particularly what we do not want is to have debt management determined predominantly by technical considerations—to be "for the sake of the debt." Although developed to combat inflation during the war, the Savings Bond program probably represents the most outstanding innovation in our debt structure. With close to one-fifth of the total federal debt in this form, an important stabilizing influence on economic activity is likely to emerge if, as seems likely, people expand their holdings during periods of prosperity and redeem their securities to maintain their consumption during periods of depression. The general precedent set in connection with Savings Bonds—and also in the opposite direction in regard to eligibility for bank purchase—might be extended to other separable groups. The argument that present levels of interest unduly burden institutions such as savings banks, insurance companies, and corporations not operating for profit has recently been met by the issuance of special securities limited to such investors. When knowledge has been accumulated about the effects of these and similar changes, it should be possible to design a policy of debt management which would give maximum aid to both economic stabilization and the achievement of other objectives of economic policy.

10

DYNAMIC PROCESS ANALYSIS

Paul A. Samuelson

I. INTRODUCTION

THE geometric progressions of the Malthus population theories and the concern of the classical economists with the approach toward a stationary state remind us that dynamic analysis is not new in economics. Nevertheless, it is fair to say that not until the second quarter of this century has there been great progress in working out the specific quantitative development of dynamic processes.

In a literary and intuitive way, the economist of a score of years ago was acquainted with such dynamic models as J. M. Clark's "principle of acceleration," or with the Aftalion theory of business oscillations resulting from the lagged over-response of output to previous capital formation —a process which its formulator compared to the successive over- and under-heating of a room that results when the fuel we add to the fire at one moment gives rise to heat at a later time.

Numerous other instances of rudimentary dynamics prior to, say, 1925 could be given in the related field of economic price theory. Marshallian and Walrasian notions of stable and unstable demand-supply intersections provide a class of examples. However, if we look for pre-1925 examples of dynamic processes in the third great area of their present-day prominence—i.e., in the field of "income analysis" rather than business cycle or price theory—we shall not fare so well; since, with the honorable exception of Knut Wicksell, economists had scarcely come to recognize this as a problem distinct from that of business fluctuations.

In the last two decades, progress in dynamics erupted on many fronts. Frisch, Roos, Tinbergen, Kalecki, and many others[1] began to formulate mathematical models that give rise to cycles of varying periodicity and amplitude.

[1] See the valuable summary of much of this discussion in J. Tinbergen, "Annual Survey: Quantitative Business Cycle Theory," *Econometrica*, July 1935, III, pp. 241-308; R. Frisch, "Propagation Problems and Impulse Problems in Dynamic Economics," *Economic Essays in Honour of Gustav Cassel* (London, 1933), pp. 171-206; M. Kalecki, "A Macrodynamic Theory of Business Cycles," *Econometrica*, July 1935, III, pp. 327-344; C. F. Roos, "A Mathematical Theory of Price and Production Fluctuations and Economic Crises," *Journal of Political Economy*, October 1930, XXXVIII, pp. 501-522.

In the general field of income analysis, Robertson, Keynes, Haberler, Kahn, Harrod, Marschak, Hansen, and Machlup were among the many writers in English who placed stress on dynamic processes; on the Continent the whole of the "neo-Wicksellian" school, particularly the Swedish economists Myrdal, Ohlin, Lindahl, and Lundberg, stressed this mode of thinking.[2]

And in more recent years, Metzler, Goodwin, Smithies, Haavelmo, Koopmans, Klein, Hicks, Lange, Tintner, Domar, the present writer, and many others[3] have elaborated upon further dynamic models which study the stability and fluctuating deviations around any defined equilibrium and which straddle the three fields of cycles, price theory, and income determination.

II. Nature of Dynamics

Since almost any problem in economics has been, or can be, treated dynamically, it is clear that the only thing that different dynamic studies have in common is their *method*. And since the formal methods involved in dynamics are usually numerical and mathematical, the ordinary student of economics frequently finds himself shut out from an understand-

---

[2] D. H. Robertson, *Essays in Monetary Theory* (London, 1946), Ch. IV, "Saving and Hoarding," reprinted from the 1933 *Economic Journal;* J. M. Keynes, *The General Theory of Employment, Interest and Money* (New York, 1936); G. Haberler, *Prosperity and Depression* (New York, 1946); R. F. Kahn, "The Relation of Home Investment to Unemployment," *Economic Journal,* June 1931, XLI, pp. 173–198; R. F. Harrod, *The Trade Cycle: An Essay* (Oxford, 1936); A. H. Hansen, *Fiscal Policy and Business Cycles* (New York, 1941); F. Machlup, *International Trade and the National Income Multiplier* (Philadelphia, 1943); J. Marschak, "Identity and Stability in Economics: A Survey," *Econometrica,* January 1942, X, pp. 61–74; Bertil Ohlin, "Some Notes on the Stockholm Theory of Saving and Investment," reprinted from the 1937 *Economic Journal* in *Readings in Business Cycle Theory* (Philadelphia, 1944), pp. 87–130; G. Myrdal, *Monetary Equilibrium* (London, 1939); E. Lundberg, *Studies in the Theory of Economic Expansion* (London, 1937); E. Lindahl, *Studies in the Theory of Money and Capital* (New York, 1939).

[3] L. A. Metzler, "Underemployment Equilibrium in International Trade," *Econometrica,* April 1942, X, pp. 97–112; *idem,* "The Transfer Problem Reconsidered," *Journal of Political Economy,* June 1942, L, pp. 397–414; R. M. Goodwin, "Innovations and the Irregularity of Economic Cycles," *Review of Economic Statistics,* May 1946, XXVIII, pp. 95–104; A. Smithies, "Process Analysis and Equilibrium Analysis," *Econometrica,* January 1942, X, pp. 26–38; T. Haavelmo, *The Probability Approach in Econometrics,* supplement to *Econometrica,* July 1944, XII; T. Koopmans, "The Logic of Economic Business Cycle Research," *Journal of Political Economy,* April 1941, XLIX, pp. 157–181; L. R. Klein, *Economic Fluctuations in the United States, 1921–41,* 2nd draft (Chicago, 1947; Cowles Commission); J. R. Hicks, *Value and Capital* (Oxford, 1939); O. Lange, *Price Flexibility and Employment* (Bloomington, 1944); G. Tintner, "A 'Simple' Theory of Business Fluctuations," *Econometrica,* July–October 1942, X, pp. 317–320; E. Domar, "Capital Expansion, Rate of Growth, and Employment," *ibid.,* April 1946, XIV, pp. 137–148; P. A. Samuelson, *Foundations of Economic Analysis* (Cambridge, Mass., 1947), Part II.

ing of much of the modern discussions—unless he is willing to put in a fair amount of concentrated effort in mastering the rudiments of the dynamic method.

Statics and dynamics differ in many ways, so that the investigator must develop new ways of looking at things in a dynamic world. For instance, consider such a classic illustration of logical fallacy as: "I'm glad I don't like olives, because if I liked them I'd eat them—and I hate them." Statically, this is nonsensical, a complete fallacy. But from a dynamical viewpoint, this same argument can be modified to explain why a person at times eats olives and at others does not.[4]

Statics concerns itself with the simultaneous and instantaneous or timeless determination of economic variables by mutually interdependent relations. Even a historically changing world may be treated statically, each of its changing positions being treated as successive states of static equilibrium. A "still" cameraman could capture in a cross-cut photo all that was relevant to such a world; and the printed picture would be the same whether the previous or subsequent positions of the system were subject to rapid or to negligible change.

It is the essence of dynamics that *economic variables at different points of time are functionally related;* or what is the same thing, that *there are functional relationships between economic variables and their rates of change, their "velocities," "accelerations,"* or higher *"derivatives of derivatives."* It is important to note that each such dynamic system generates its own behavior over time, either as an autonomous response to a set of "initial conditions," or as a response to some changing external conditions. This feature of self-generating development over time is the crux of every dynamic process.[5]

Most dynamic economic processes fall into one of two categories: (a) discrete processes, treated in "period analysis," and (b) continuous processes involving flows, treated in "rate analysis." In mathematical terms, period analysis falls under the category of "difference equations," while rate analysis involves "differential equations."[6] The choice between period

---

[4] Similarly, there is the beautiful example of static economic fallacy presented in D. H. Henderson's *Supply and Demand,* in which the novice economist is tempted to argue that a tax will cause price to rise, but at the higher price demand will fall off so that price will fall, . . . etc. But from a dynamic viewpoint, one must admit the possibility of cobweb oscillation not so very different from those just described.

[5] See the author's *Foundations of Economic Analysis.*

[6] By a differential equation, mathematicians mean a relationship holding between the value of a function and its various derivatives; for example,

$$\frac{d^3 y(t)}{dt^3} = f\left[y(t), \frac{dy(t)}{dt}, \frac{d^2 y(t)}{dt^2} \right]$$

is a differential equation—of the sort called third order, involving as it does derivatives up to the third derivative. If we add to this differential equation the "initial values" of

or rate analysis is usually one of convenience, since by taking periods of short enough duration we can approximate to rates and can neglect the interrelations within the period.

Period analysis lends itself to exposition in terms of simple arithmetic examples rather than the more complex mathematics of differential equations. But really to understand these numerical examples, one must still study the elements of "difference equations," which are closely analogous to differential equations. Period analysis has the disadvantage that in speaking of investment or income of a period, one often loses sight of the "per unit time" dimensionality of these concepts; rate or flow analysis, on the other hand, is not so likely to suppress the time dimensionality.[7]

III. Outline of the Discussion

The nature of dynamic processes can best be appreciated from a study of concrete examples. Moreover, if one agrees that the common core of dynamic process analysis consists of its formal *method*, and recognizes the intrinsic technical difficulties of that method, then the advantages of a case treatment of the subject are reinforced.

For these reasons, I have confined my survey to an elucidation of half a dozen different general models or cases, each illustrating some important economic problem. Cases I and II, dealing with compound-interest exponential growth at discrete and continuous stages respectively, are presented for the insight they give into the simple mathematics of the problem. Case III, dealing with some relationships between the stock of capital and the flows of investment and income, provides insight into "rate" as distinct from "period" analysis. Case IV is concerned with the familiar dynamic multiplier response of income to a continued stream of new investment. Case V illustrates in a quantitative way the well-known qualitative properties of the cobweb cycle. In conclusion, there follows a

---

the function and its first two derivatives, we have a well-determined differential equation system which will generate its own behavior over all subsequent time.

By a difference equation, mathematicians mean a relationship holding between the value of a function at a number of different time points; for example,

$$y(t + 3) = f [y(t), y(t + 1), y(t + 2)]$$

is a difference equation of the third order. If we prescribe the initial values $y(0)$, $y(1)$, and $y(2)$, the system generates its own subsequent behavior. The name "difference equation" comes from the fact that "different" time periods are involved and also from the fact that such relations may be rewritten in an alternative—but equivalent—form involving "finite differences" of the form

$$\Delta y(t) = y(t + 1) - y(t), \quad \Delta^2 y(t) = \Delta [\Delta y(t)], \text{ etc.}$$

[7] Nevertheless, it would be a mistake to think that all flow analysis is necessarily dynamic. In a static Marshallian wheat-market equilibrium, the quantities sold are stationary flows per unit time, but the system may still be regarded as static.

brief summary of the significance of past accomplishments in this field for future developments of economic science.

In order to free the bulk of the discussion from mathematics of any complexity, I have confined to the Appendix a brief treatment of dynamic processes involving more than one period.

CASE I. COMPOUND INTEREST AT DISCRETE INTERVALS

Perhaps the oldest dynamic process that economists have handled rigorously involves the growth of an initial sum of money invested and reinvested at compound interest. The value at the end of t periods—called $V(t)$—of an initial principal, V_0, is given by[8]

$$V(t) = (1 + i)^t V_0 \qquad (1)$$

where i is the rate of interest per period of compounding. This familiar solution is an instance of a "geometric progression or exponential term multiplied by a scale factor"—and is of the general form $M^t K$.

Now the essential thing about a sum invested at compound interest is the fact that its *value at one period is always proportional to its value at a previous period*. In mathematical terms, this is described by saying that $V(t)$ satisfies a simple "difference equation"; namely

$$\begin{cases} V(t+1) = (1+i)\,V(t) \\ V(0) = V_0 \end{cases} \qquad (2)$$

In other words, the sequence generates its own growth, once we give it the "initial condition," V_0, to start it off—as is shown in detail in the following table:

t	0	1	2	. . .	t	t + 1	. . .	∞
$V(t)$	V_0	$(1+i)V_0$	$(1+i)^2 V_0$	. . .	$(1+i)^t V_0$	$(1+i)V(t)$	. . .	∞

This self-generating property is characteristic of all dynamic processes. Let us therefore summarize and generalize what we have learned:

(1) The simplest dynamic process for any variable, $X(t)$, is that generated by a difference equation system of the general form

$$\begin{cases} X(t+1) = a\,X(t) \\ X(0) = X_0 \end{cases}$$

[8] Throughout this paper the notation for any variable, X, at time 0, 1, . . ., t, t + 1, . . . is given by $X(0)$, $X(1)$, . . ., $X(t)$, $X(t + 1)$, ... The initial values of an economic variable when regarded as constants are denoted with subscripts

(2) We suspect that its solution over all subsequent time is given by a geometric progression or exponential expression of the form

$$X(t) = M^t K$$

We also suspect that the constant, K, depends only on the initial condition, X_0; and that the constant, M, depends only on the constant, a, in the difference equation.

(3) These suspicions are verified once we experimentally try $M^t K$ wherever $X(t)$ appears in the difference equation. This gives us

$$M^{t+1} K = a M^t K$$
$$M^0 K = X_0$$

Cancelling the $M^t K$ from both sides of the first equation, we find

$$M = a$$
$$K = X_0$$

(4) Therefore, the solution to the difference equation

$$X(t + 1) = a X(t)$$
$$X(0) = X_0 \qquad\qquad (3)$$

is always given by

$$X(t) = a^t X_0 \qquad\qquad (4)$$

In the compound-interest case, a = 1 + i, and the solution grows at a very rapid rate. If the interest rate were a negative fraction, then the value of our principal would ultimately decay away to nothing, after the fashion of a disintegrating radioactive material. This is because *a* would then be a fraction less than one, and any fraction when raised to higher and higher powers becomes smaller and smaller and ultimately approaches zero.

Already our simple mathematical analysis reveals one possibility that goes beyond the compound interest example. What if *a* itself is negative? Then obviously we get an oscillation, with every other year being alternately negative and positive. For example, when a = —2 and X_0 = 10, our sequence becomes an "explosive oscillation": +10, —20, +40, —80, +160, —320, . . ., or $(-2)^t$ 10. But if a = —½, we get a decaying oscillation of the form: +10, —5, +2.5, —1.25, +.625, . . . ,

---

as follows: $X(0) = X_0$, $X(1) = X_1$, etc. Structural coefficients such as the marginal propensity to consume or the "relation coefficient" in the Acceleration Principle are represented respectively by such letters as a and β. Small a's are often used for structural coefficients in the general case.

or $(-\frac{1}{2})^t$ 10. This every-other-period oscillation will later be seen to be important in connection with the cobweb cycle.

Later, in Case IV we shall study the case of a repeated stream of investment which causes income to grow to a new "multiplied" level. But already we have seen how the simpler case of a single non-repeated impulse of investment is to be handled.

Let us make the conventional assumption that "today's" extra consumption, $C(t)$, is always some fixed fraction—say $\frac{3}{4}$—of yesterday's extra disposable income, $Y(t-1)$. Then, in the initial period of a single impulse of investment of spending, extra consumption is still zero and extra income is equal to the single pulse of investment spending, I_0. In subsequent periods after investment has disappeared, income is equal to consumption, which in turn is a fixed fraction of previous income. Thus, we have the difference equation system

$$\begin{cases} Y(t) = C(t) + 0 = \frac{3}{4}\, Y(t-1), \text{ or } Y(t+1) = \frac{3}{4}\, Y(t) \\ Y(0) = 0 + I_0 \end{cases} \quad (5)$$

Obviously, therefore, the resulting pattern of income is the decaying geometrical progression

t	0	1	2	. . .	t	$t+1$	. . .	∞
$Y(t)$	I_0	$\frac{3}{4} I_0$	$(\frac{3}{4})^2 I_0$	. . .	$(\frac{3}{4})^t I_0$	$\frac{3}{4} Y(t)$	. . .	0

Another example illustrates the rate of price increase as a result of a wartime inflationary gap. Suppose the government is willing to release only k_1 per cent of full-employment production for civilian use; and suppose that families and businesses insist upon spending on civilian goods $k_2 > k_1$ per cent of their full-employment real income. Let us define our time units so that there is a lag of one period between receipt of civilian income and its expenditure. Then the impasse can only be circumvented by having prices bid up in each period by just enough to ration out the goods released for civilian use. The excess spending of "yesterday's" income is handled by letting prices rise enough to induce "forced saving." The growth rate of prices can be shown[9] to be proportional to $\left(\dfrac{k_2}{k_1}\right)^t$.

This says that the rate of price inflation is increased by a shortened expenditure lag and by large government use of resources relative to voluntary saving.

[9] T. Koopmans, "The Dynamics of Inflation," Review of Economic Statistics, May 1942, XXIV, pp. 53–65. See also J. M. Keynes, How to Pay for the War (London, 1940), and the later "inflationary gap" discussions.

CASE II. CONTINUOUS COMPOUNDING AND DIFFERENTIAL
EQUATION RATE ANALYSIS

So far we have been concerned with "period analysis" over discrete time. In contradistinction, rate analysis concerns itself with flows, with instantaneous rates of change, with speeds, or in calculus terms, with derivatives. These "differential equation" procedures are closely related to the "difference equation" procedures of period analysis.

To see this, let us return to the compound interest example. Suppose the rate of interest were 100 per cent per annum so that $1 + i = 1 + 1 = 2$. Then the value of an asset would double every year, or grow like the progression 2^t.

What if a bank now offered us 50 per cent interest compounded every 6 months? or $33\frac{1}{3}$ per cent compounded every 4 months? or $1/100$ per cent compounded every $1/n$ of a year? Because of interest earned on interest within the year, we should obviously find ourselves successively better off. But no matter how indefinitely small the period of compounding becomes, we shall never find ourselves better off by more than an important limiting value. It will be found that 100 per cent interest *compounded instantaneously* causes a principal to grow at the rate of $(2.71828 . .)^t$ or $(1 + 1.71828 . .)^t$—or in words, at the same rate as $171.828 . .$ per cent compounded only once a year.

The important number $2.71828 . .$ is called by mathematicians e (after Euler, and because it is the basic "exponential" number).[10] It bridges the

---

[10] Mathematically,

$$e = \lim_{n \to \infty} \left(1 + \frac{1}{n} \right)^n = 1 + \frac{(1)}{1} + \frac{(1)^2}{1 \cdot 2} + \frac{(1)^3}{1 \cdot 2 \cdot 3} + \ . \ . \ . \ + \frac{(1)^s}{1 \cdot 2 \cdot 3 \cdots s} + \ . \ . \ .$$

and also we have the "magic series"

$$e^t = 1 + \frac{(t)}{1} + \frac{(t)^2}{1 \cdot 2} + \ . \ . \ . \ + \frac{(t)^s}{1 \cdot 2 \cdots s} + \ . \ . \ .$$

Using the simplest rules for differentiating a power, the reader can easily deduce from this series the remarkable fact that e^t is its own first derivative. Also that the proportional rate of change of e^{mt} is m. Even without expressing e^t as a series, we can see that it is the only function of t that has a derivative equal to itself. More generally, let us ask for the function whose derivative is proportional to itself, or which satisfies the differential equation.

$$\frac{dx(t)}{dt} = m\,x(t)$$
$$x(o) = x_0$$

where m is any constant.

We may rewrite this as

$$\frac{dx}{x} = m\,dt$$

or, since percentage and logarithmic changes are the same thing, as

$$d \log_e x = m\,dt;$$

gap between discrete difference equation analysis and continuous differential equation analysis.

Let us now summarize our conclusions:

(1) Any process which grows continuously at a constant instantaneous percentage rate, m—i.e., which satisfies the differential equation

$$\frac{1}{y(t)}\frac{dy(t)}{dt} = m \quad \text{or} \quad \frac{dy(t)}{dt} = m\,y(t) \tag{6}$$

—has for its solution the exponential expression

$$y(t) = (2.71828\ldots)^{mt}\,y_0 = e^{mt}y_0$$

where y_0 is the initial value of the process.

(2) An interest rate of i per year compounded once a year grows like $(1+i)^t$. But when compounded instantaneously, a percentage rate of i per year gives rise to the faster growth rate of e^{it} or $[(2.718\ldots)^i]^t$. When i is very near to zero, the expressions for instantaneous and discrete compounding are not very far apart.[11]

(3) Thus, just as $X(t) = M^t\,X_0$ is the solution of the simplest *difference* equation, so is $x(t) = e^{mt}\,x_0$ the corresponding solution of the simplest *differential* equation of continuous growth. And just as $-1 < M < 1$ leads to a decaying, settling-down solution, so does $m < 0$ lead to a stable solution. When m is negative the rapidly growing exponential term is thrown into the denominator, and the solution decays away to the stable

---

and, taking the indefinite integral of both sides (which is just the opposite of differentiation), we have

$$d \log_e x = mdt,$$
$$\int \log_e x = \int mt + K$$

Taking anti-logs of both sides, we get

$$x = e^{mt}\,e^K = e^{mt}\,K'$$

We may easily determine the constant K' from the initial condition

$$x(0) = K'\,e^0 = x_0$$

or

$$K' = x_0 \quad \text{and}$$
$$x(t) = e^{mt}\,x_0$$

is our solution.

[11] There is also some *instantaneous* rate of interest, called ?, which will give the same growth rate as will i compounded *once per annum*. This is defined by the equation

$$e^? = (1+i)$$

But, in mathematical language, the power to which e must be raised to equal $(1+i)$ is called the "natural logarithm of $(1+i)$" and therefore we can write

$$? = \log_e (1+i)$$

because, by definition

$$e^? = e^{\log_e (1+i)} = (1+i)$$

The exponentials and logarithms are like man and wife; they are opposites in the same sense that P and Q are opposites along a demand curve. If we run up to the curve $y = e^t$ vertically from the horizontal axis and read off the vertical ordinate, we have the exponential function $y = e^t$. If we pick a y value and run horizontally over the curve and read off the corresponding t value, we have the natural logarithm of y, or $t = \log_e y$.

equilibrium level. Likewise $|M| > 1$ and $m > 0$ lead to explosive instability, or to growth at an exponential rate.

CASE III. CAPITAL FORMATION, CAPITAL, AND INCOME[12]

Let us illustrate the case of continuous growth by a number of examples. If we write the stock of capital as $K(t)$, then net investment, $I(t)$, is nothing but the derivative or rate of increase of $K(t)$, $\dfrac{dK(t)}{dt}$. Under what conditions will investment be always proportional to the stock of capital? The answer is simple:

$$\frac{dK(t)}{dt} = mK(t) \tag{8}$$

only when $K(t) = e^{mt} K_0$ and when

$$\frac{dK(t)}{dt} = e^{mt}(mK_0) \tag{9}$$
$$= e^{mt} I_0$$

Only in the case of steady exponential growth can the proportion between a stock and a flow be maintained.

Similarly, as Domar has shown, the public debt and its rate of change, the deficit, will remain proportional to income if, and only if, all three magnitudes are growing or decaying at a compound-interest or exponential rate. Or, as numerous writers have shown, births and deaths and the relative number of people in different age groups can only remain invariant if population is rising or falling at an exponential rate.

A more complicated problem has been posed by Harrod and Domar. What are the conditions of economic expansion which will cause (a) capital, $K(t)$, and income, $Y(t)$, to grow *proportionally* and at such a rate that (b) investment, $I(t)$ or $\dfrac{dK(t)}{dt}$, will be equal to the exact fraction of income, a, that people try to save at full employment? Writers on the acceleration principle often use the letter β to denote the ratio between the capital stock and flow of income.

In symbols

$$K(t) = \beta Y(t)$$
$$I(t) = \frac{dK(t)}{dt} = aY(t) \tag{10}$$

---

[12] E. D. Domar, *op. cit.*; also *idem*, "The 'Burden of the Debt' and National Income," *American Economic Review*, December 1944, XXXIV, pp. 798–827; and R. F. Harrod, "An Essay in Dynamic Theory," *Economic Journal*, March 1939, XLIX, pp. 14–33.

Hence

$$\frac{dK(t)}{dt} = \left(\frac{a}{\beta}\right) K(t)$$

implying that

$$K(t) = e^{\frac{\alpha}{\beta}t} K_0$$

$$I(t) = \frac{dK(t)}{dt} = \left(\frac{a}{\beta}\right) e^{\frac{\alpha}{\beta}t} K_0 = e^{\frac{\alpha}{\beta}t} I_0 \qquad (11)$$

$$Y(t) = e^{\frac{\alpha}{\beta}t} Y_0$$

In words, the smaller is the ratio of capital to income, β, and the greater is the fraction of income saved, a, the faster must the economic top keep spinning if full employment is to be maintained from growth factors alone. The following table shows, for different values of a and β, the indicated necessary rate of dynamic growth if full employment is to be self-maintained.

"Needed" Rate of Growth Under Various Conditions
(in % per year)

Saving Proportion, a	"Relation" of Capital to Annual Income, β			
	½	1	4	10
0%	0	0	0	0
10%	20	10	2½	1
20%	40	20	5	2

So far, our flow analysis of investment and capital has yielded only exponential growth trends. However, it is easy to illustrate a decay toward a stationary position of equilibrium. We have only to suppose that the level of investment, $I(t)$, becomes positive whenever the level of capital, $K(t)$, is below a crucial equilibrium level, $\overline{K}$; and investment is negative whenever capital exceeds that equilibrium level. (The level of $\overline{K}$, we may assume, depends on the interest rate, income, and the state of technology.)

In simplest terms, let I be proportional to $[\overline{K} - K(t)]$, called $- [k(t)]$ or

$$I(t) = -m [K(t) - \overline{K}] = -m\, k(t)$$

But since

$$\frac{dK(t)}{dt} = \frac{d[K(t) - \overline{K}]}{dt} = \frac{dk(t)}{dt} - o = I(t)$$

we have

$$\frac{dk(t)}{dt} = -m\,k(t) \qquad\qquad (12)$$

and

$$k(t) = e^{-mt}\,k_0 \qquad\qquad (13)$$

so that the deviation, $k(t)$, approaches zero, and $K(t)$ approaches in the long run to $\overline{K}$.

Cyclical oscillations will occur if an excess of capital, rather than leading to negative investment, instead leads to a "deceleration" of the algebraic rate of investment. In this case

$$\frac{dI}{dt} = -m\,k(t) \qquad\qquad (14)$$

or

$$\frac{d}{dt}\left[\frac{dk(t)}{dt}\right] = \frac{d^2k(t)}{dt^2} = -m\,k(t) \qquad\qquad (15)$$

Thus, the rate of investment will decrease algebraically in proportion to the amount of excess capital.

As is shown in the Appendix, such a system gives rise to sinusoidal oscillations around the equilibrium—oscillations which are exactly like those of a pendulum. Intuitively, we can glimpse this as follows: Suppose capital is growing, and it pushes through its equilibrium level. Its inertia causes it to overshoot the mark, because the positive level of investment is only gradually tapering off. But after capital has grown to a critical peak, its decelerating effects finally cause investment to become negative. Capital is now returning toward its equilibrium level at an increasing rate. It passes through the equilibrium level with negative investment at its peak rate. Now there is a downward over-shoot, which lasts until the gradual acceleration of investment, due to capital shortage, causes investment to become positive—at which point capital has reached its trough and has begun to revive. And so forth.

CASE IV. THE MULTIPLICATION OF A STREAM OF INVESTMENT

R. F. Kahn, J. M. Clark, J. M. Keynes, Fritz Machlup, and others have analyzed the case whereby a new plateau of income will—after a spending lag—lead to a new higher plateau of investment.[13] Instead of the single impulse of investment discussed earlier, we now have a constant stream of new impulses, and after we have superimposed their effects, we finally build up to a new steady state. This takes time because extra consumption at time t, $C(t)$, is supposed to be a fraction, a, of extra disposable income at time $t - 1$, $Y(t - 1)$.

Mathematically, we always have the income identity

$$Y(t + 1) = C(t + 1) + I(t + 1)$$

and now after the new steady level of investment spending begins at time $t = 0$, $I(t) = \bar{I}$, so that

$$Y(t + 1) = C(t + 1) + \bar{I} = aY(t) + \bar{I} \qquad (16)$$
$$Y(0) = \bar{I}$$

This is a difference equation which generates its own solution. But something new has been added; the constant investment term, $\bar{I}$, means that the solution will not be a geometric progression decaying away to zero, as in the case of the response to a single pulse of spending. Instead, the system will grow so as to "decay away" to a new equilibrium plateau of income. Our solution can be thought of as consisting of two parts: a "new equilibrium component" and a temporary transient; or

$$Y(t) = \bar{Y} - M^t K$$

where $\bar{Y}$ is the new stationary equilibrium level of (extra) income, and where $M^t K$ is called a "transient" because it will finally disappear as a subtraction from the new income level.

After some experimentation, one will find it wise to work with deviations from the new equilibrium income level, $\bar{Y}$. That is, we define $y(t) = Y(t) - \bar{Y}$, even though we don't know yet what $\bar{Y}$ is—except that if we put $\bar{Y}$ into our system it must repeat itself. Therefore

$$\text{Let } Y(t) = \bar{Y}$$
$$Y(t + 1) = \bar{Y}$$

[13] R. F. Kahn, op. cit.; J. M. Clark, The Economics of Planning Public Works (Washington, 1935); J. M. Keynes, The Means to Prosperity (New York, 1933); F. Machlup,

and

$$Y(t + 1) = aY(t) + \overline{I} \text{ becomes } \overline{Y} = a\overline{Y} + \overline{I} \qquad (17)$$

or

$$\overline{Y} = \frac{1}{1 - a}\overline{I}$$

Obviously, $1/(1 - a)$ is the ultimate "multiplier," and it can always be solved for statically by forgetting the time subscripts on the Y's, and solving our dynamic equations for a timeless or stationary income level.

What happens now if we put $Y(t) - \overline{Y} = Y(t) - \frac{1}{1 - a}\overline{I} = y(t)$ in our basic dynamic equation? The stationary income level terms will then just cancel out the stationary level of new spending, and we will be left with

$$[Y(t) - \overline{Y}] = a[Y(t - 1) - \overline{Y}]$$
$$Y(0) - \overline{Y} = \overline{I} - \frac{1}{1 - a}\overline{I} = -\frac{a}{1 - a}\overline{I}$$

or with

$$y(t + 1) = ay(t)$$
$$y(0) = \frac{-a}{1 - a}\overline{I}$$

But this is a simple difference equation with the simple geometric progression solution:

$$y(t) = -a^t\left(\frac{a}{1 - a}\overline{I}\right)$$

so that our final solution for $Y(t)$ becomes

$$Y(t) = \frac{1}{1 - a}\overline{I} - a^t\left(\frac{a}{1 - a}\overline{I}\right)$$

Therefore, if $0 < a < 1$, Y will climb from $\overline{I}$ dollars up indefinitely close to $\overline{I}/(1 - a)$ dollars. The following table provides a quick summary of the results reached thus far in the analysis of a constant stream of investment.

"Period Analysis and Multiplier Theory," reprinted from the 1939 *Quarterly Journal of Economics* in *Readings in Business Cycle Theory*, pp. 203-234.

t	0	1	2	$\cdots$	t	$t+1$	$\cdots$	∞
$Y(t)$	$(1)\bar{I}$	$(1+a)\bar{I}$	$(1+a+a^2)\bar{I}$	$\cdots$	$(1+a+a^2+\cdots+a^t)\bar{I}$ $= \dfrac{1-a^{t+1}}{1-a}\bar{I}$	$aY(t)+\bar{I}$	$\cdots$	$\dfrac{1}{1-a}\bar{I}$
$Y(t)-Y(\infty)$	$(1)\bar{I} - \dfrac{1}{1-a}\bar{I}$	$(1+a)\bar{I} - \dfrac{1}{1-a}\bar{I}$		$\cdots$	$= \dfrac{1}{1-a}\bar{I} - a^t\left(\dfrac{a}{1-a}\right)\bar{I}$		$\cdots$	
$= y(t)$	$= -1\left(\dfrac{a}{1-a}\right)\bar{I} = -1\left(\dfrac{a}{1-a}\right)\bar{I}$	$= -a\left(\dfrac{a}{1-a}\right)\bar{I}$	$-a^2\left(\dfrac{a}{1-a}\right)\bar{I}$	$\cdots$	$-a^t\left(\dfrac{a}{1-a}\right)\bar{I}$	$ay(t)+0$	$\cdots$	0

We may summarize the general mathematical case as follows: Suppose that instead of a simple difference equation of the form

$$X(t + 1) = a X(t)$$
$$X(0) = X_0$$

we have a constant term as well, or

$$X(t + 1) = a X(t) + A$$
$$X(0) = X_0 \tag{18}$$

Then our solution consists of two terms: a "steady state" solution, $\overline{X}$, plus a "transient" of the form $M^t K$; or,

$$X(t) = \overline{X} + M^t K$$

where $\overline{X}$ is found by substituting X with no time subscripts in both sides of the equation and then solving statically to get

$$\overline{X} = \frac{1}{1 - a} A \tag{19}$$

and where $M^t K$ depicts the deviations from equilibrium

$$x(t) = X(t) - \overline{X} = X(t) - \frac{1}{1 - a} A$$

satisfying the simple difference equation

$$x(t + 1) = a x(t)$$
$$x(0) = X_0 - \frac{1}{1 - a} A \tag{20}$$

Hence, our full final solution[14] becomes

$$X(t) = \frac{1}{1 - a} A + a^t \left(X_0 - \frac{A}{1 - a} \right) \tag{21}$$

It may be remarked that X_0 will often equal A, if previously the system has been in equilibrium at zero.

If a is less than one in absolute value, and only then, will the solution settle down to a new equilibrium level. Otherwise it will explode.

---

[14] In the special "resonant" case where $a = 1$, no stationary solution exists. In this case the solution grows steadily according to the law $X(t) = X_0 + At$, as can be verified by taking the limit as $a \to 1$ of the general expression (21).

CASE V. COBWEB CYCLES[15]

An example that throws light on the nature of business cycles as well as on the requirements for a stable equilibrium is that of the familiar cobweb phenomenon. This is a beautiful case because its formal difficulties are so slight, and yet at the same time it illuminates the basic problems so clearly.

We make the usual assumption that the demand curve relates this period's price, $P(t)$, to this period's quantity, $Q(t)$. But this period's

Table 1

	Demand Relationship	Supply Relationship
$Q(t)$	$P(t)$	$P(t-1)$
0	200	50
30	170	65
50	150	75
60	140	80
70	130	85
80	120	90
90	110	95
100†	100†	100†
110	90	105
120	80	110
121	79	118
122	78	126
123	77	134
124	76	142
125	75	150
126	74	158
127	73	166
128	72	174
129	71	182
130	70	190

† Equilibrium level.

---

[15] For references, see M. Ezekiel, "The Cobweb Theorem," reprinted from the 1938 *Quarterly Journal of Economics* in *Readings in Business Cycle Theory*, pp. 422–442. The definitive treatment of non-linearity is that of W. Leontief, "Verzögerte Angebotsanpassung und Partielles Gleichgewicht," *Zeitschrift für Nationalökonomie*, 1934, V, pp. 670–676.

quantity supplied, Q(t), is assumed to be a determinate function of last period's market price, P(t — 1). The length of our time period is that between seasons of a crop, or between the starting of the productive process and the pouring of goods onto the market.

For simplicity, let us suppose that $\overline{P} = 100$ and $\overline{Q} = 100$ represents the unique point of intersection of the assumed supply and demand relations. Obviously, this is the only equilibrium level which will be self-maintaining through time if once established. But is it a stable equilibrium in the sense that a disturbance—such as might be caused by bad weather—will be followed by a return to equilibrium level? Or will P and Q depart ever further from equilibrium if once disturbed? In any case, what are the laws of motion of the system when out of equilibrium?

To make matters simple, let us assume a linear demand relation of the sort that each one-unit increase in quantity is followed by a one-unit decrease in the price for which it will sell. If Q(t) goes from 100 to 100 + h, then P(t) will go from 100 down to 100 — h.

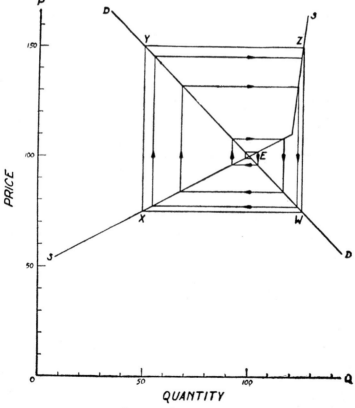

FIG. 1. Cobweb cycles.

Our assumption about supply will be a little more interesting. First, let us suppose that each one-unit increase in P(t) will be followed in the next year by a two-unit change in quantity supplied, Q(t + 1). But to add variety to the problem, let us suppose that this 2Q for 1P relation holds only for price changes between $50 and $110, and that at all higher prices there is so much cost resistance to further expansion of output that there is only 1/8 of a unit change in Q(t + 1) for each unit change in P(t).

Figure 1 depicts our demand-supply relations, D-D and S-S. Table 1 illustrates the same numerically for selected numbers, between which the reader can linearly interpolate.

Because the supply curve consists of two straight lines intersecting in a corner, we have a curvilinear rather than a linear system. And, as we shall see, this introduces new richness into the problem that will make possible something that is important for the study of business cycles—namely, a theory of the unique amplitude of *cyclical* fluctuations.

Let us now experiment with our model. If we start out with Q(0) = 100, obviously P(0) = 100, Q(1) = 100, P(1) = 100, ... and so forth. This equilibrium state is depicted for Q in Figure 2 by the horizontal line $\overline{Q}$.

But suppose that for some reason we started out with Q one unit above the equilibrium, so that Q(0) = 101. Then from our demand curve, P(0) = 99; but next year's supply will subsequently fall short of 100 by 2 units, or Q(1) = 98, and P(1) = 102. It is easy to show—as in columns 2 and 3 of Table 2—that our Q's and P's begin to depart ever further from the equilibrium level in an explosively oscillatory way according to the formula.

$$Q(t) = 100 + (-2)^t [Q(0) - \overline{Q}]$$
$$P(t) = 100 - (-2)^t [Q(0) - \overline{Q}] = 100 + (-2)^t [P(0) - \overline{P}] \quad (22)$$

The geometric rate of oscillatory explosion is $(-2)^t$ because the numerical slope of the supply curve is twice as flat as that of the demand curve. If the condition were reversed, the solution would spiral in toward the stable equilibrium level at the rate of $(-\frac{1}{2})^t$. If the slopes were exactly equal in absolute value, then we would have a sort of "neutral equilibrium," with motion around it in closed boxes whose dimensions depend only on the size of the initial disturbance. With no further disturbances, the cycles would not be changing in amplitude, but there would still be no possibility of a theory of a unique amplitude.

But let us not forget the curvilinearity of our system. All the above holds only so long as P remains below $110. Above this figure, our

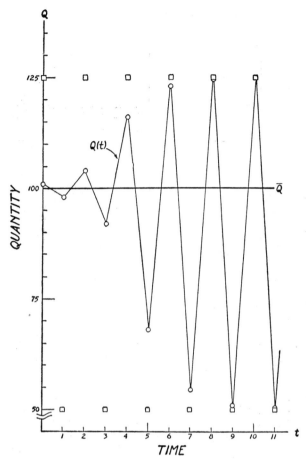

Fig. 2. Cobweb cycles over time.

simple geometric progressions no longer hold. This is shown in Table 2, beyond the time, t = 5.

Because of non-linearity, the simple pattern of our sonnet is ruptured, but there remains rhyme and reason in our verse. First, it is clear from the figures that the oscillation of price and quantity continues, but no longer at such an explosive rate. Indeed, Figure 1 shows that the oscillation is growing until it approaches the "box" YZWX. For if Q ever reached 125 or fell to 50, it would subsequently go round and round the box forever. If ever Q exceeded this range, it would spiral back toward the YZWX box. In actuality, without a new disturbance, Q and P can never quite reach the promised land of the box, but will approach indefinitely close toward it.

We may conclude that in a non-linear system, there may occur certain special periodic motions. These cycles with definite amplitudes can be

Table 2

COBWEB CYCLE AWAY FROM EQUILIBRIUM AND TOWARD A STABLE PERIODIC BOX MOTION

Time t	Quantity Q	Price P	New Era Time $t'=t-6$	Periodic Box Motions Q^*	P^*	$Q-Q^*$ q	$P-P^*$ p
0	101	99					
1	98	102					
2	104	96					
3	92	108					
4	116	84					
5	68	132					
6	$122\frac{3}{4}$	$77\frac{1}{4}$	0	125	75	$-2\frac{1}{4}=-\frac{9}{4}$	$+2\frac{1}{4}$
7	$54\frac{1}{2}$	$145\frac{1}{2}$	1	50	150	$+4\frac{1}{2}=\frac{9}{2}$	$-4\frac{1}{2}$
8	$124\frac{7}{16}$	$75\frac{9}{16}$	2	125	75	$-\frac{9}{16}=-(\frac{1}{4})\frac{9}{4}$	$+\frac{9}{16}$
9	$51\frac{1}{8}$	$148\frac{7}{8}$	3	50	150	$1\frac{1}{8}=(\frac{1}{4})\frac{9}{2}$	$-1\frac{1}{8}$
10	$124\frac{55}{64}$	$75\frac{9}{64}$	4	125	75	$-\frac{9}{64}=-(\frac{1}{4})^2\frac{9}{4}$	$+\frac{9}{64}$
11	$50\frac{9}{32}$	$149\frac{23}{32}$	5	50	150	$\frac{9}{32}=(\frac{1}{4})^2\frac{9}{2}$	$-\frac{9}{32}$
$\ldots$							
$2t-12$	$125+q(t)$	$75+p(t)$	$2t'$	125	75	$-\frac{1}{8}q(2t'-1)=-(\frac{1}{4})^{t'}\frac{9}{4}$	$-q(2t')$
$2t-11$	$50+q(t)$	$150+p(t)$	$2t'+1$	50	150	$-2q(2t')=(\frac{1}{4})^{t'}\frac{9}{2}$	$-q(2t'+1)$
$\ldots$							
∞	125	75	∞	125	75	0	0
$\infty+1$	50	150	$\infty+1$	50	150	0	0

thought of as "generalized equilibrium states," which may be stable or unstable. As Leontief has shown in the cited article, there may even be boxes within boxes, alternately stable and unstable.

Let us take a further step. What are the quantitative laws of approach to the periodic box motion YZWX, or to $[Q^*(t), P^*(t)] = [50,150]$; $[125,75]$; $[50,150]$; $[125,75]$; etc.?[16]
Previously when we were interested in the behavior of our system around the equilibrium point $(\overline{Q}, \overline{P}) = (100, 100)$, our crucial variables were the deviations $[Q(t) - \overline{Q}]$ and $[P(t) - \overline{P}]$. Similarly, now we are interested in the deviations around the periodic box motions $[Q^*(t), P^*(t)]$. It is convenient, therefore, to work from now on with the new deviations

$$q(t) = Q(t) - Q^*(t)$$
$$p(t) = P(t) - P^*(t) \tag{23}$$

Also, like Mussolini, Lenin, Napoleon, and the Church, we find it convenient to begin to count our time periods from the date of intro-duction of the revolutionary non-linearity—so that our new t' will be o when the old t was 6. Columns 4–8 have been added to Table 2 to show the new era data.

If we look at our table, it becomes clear that the deviations from the box are approaching zero. It is less obvious, but careful attention will show that the numerical value of each odd-year quantity deviation is going downhill in a geometric progression, and the same is true of each even-year quantity deviation. But the two rates of decay are quite differ-ent, that of the even years being like $- \frac{3}{4}, ., -(\frac{1}{4})\frac{3}{4}, ., -(\frac{1}{4})^2 \frac{3}{4}, .;$ the odd years being like $\frac{1}{2}, ., (\frac{1}{4})\frac{1}{2}, ., (\frac{1}{4})^2 \frac{1}{2},....$

It is exactly as if our deviations satisfied the difference equation system

$$q(t' + 1) = M q(t')$$
$$q(o) = -\frac{3}{4} \tag{24}$$

but where the M coefficient is a periodic function of time, being -2 when t is odd and $-\frac{1}{8}$ when t is even.[17]

---

[16] It may be noted that we can write this special periodic motion in the trick way

$$Q^\cdot(t) = 50 \frac{(1)^t + (-1)^t}{2} + 125 \frac{(1)^t - (-1)^t}{2}$$

$$P^\cdot(t) = 150 \frac{(1)^t + (-1)^t}{2} + 75 \frac{(1)^t - (-1)^t}{2} = 200 - Q^*(t)$$

where $(1)^t$ and $(-1)^t$ cancel each other out in the proper way depending upon whether t is even or odd.
[17] Generally, we find the M coefficients alternate, in one case being the ratio of the supply and demand curves' flatness on the left side of the YZWX box, and in the other

Mathematically, this introduction of coefficients which are periodic functions of time turns out to be the general case when the stability of a periodic motion is to be tested. But where in the region of non-linear dynamics Henri Poincaré, G. D. Birkhoff, van der Pol, and other mathematicians tread warily, we shall venture no further. However, the reader should verify that when Q starts out at any value greater than 150, the resulting motion spirals in toward the box in even-odd geometric progressions.

The above cases provide an introduction to the economics of dynamic processes. But as soon as we encounter models involving several periods of time or higher derivatives, the exact quantitative treatment becomes somewhat more complex—although still within the scope of elementary college mathematics.

(Thus, in the simplest model where the Acceleration Principle and the multiplier interact, we will encounter for $\alpha = \frac{1}{2}$ and $\beta = 2$, the difference equation

$$y(t+2) = 1.5\,y(t+1) - y(t) \qquad (25)$$

and instead of its having for its solution simple exponential terms of the form M^t, we find that the answer leads to a pure sine wave of about 9 years' duration. If $\alpha\beta < 1$, we get a sine wave which is multiplied by a dampening exponential factor; and if $\alpha\beta > 1$, we get explosive oscillations.)

The Appendix provides a bird's eye survey of some aspects of the more complex analysis necessary if the economist is to follow closely recent work in business cycle, income, and value theory.

IV. CONCLUSION

The significance of dynamic analysis for economics may be briefly sketched, along with some indications of possible future trends in the field.

In the first place, the economist has no choice but to study dynamics; for otherwise there is little possibility of presenting a reasonably realistic description of such phenomena as speculation, cyclical fluctuations, and secular growth. In addition, dynamic process analysis is an enormously flexible mode of thought, both for pinning down the implications of various hypotheses and for investigating new possibilities.

---

case the corresponding ratio on the right-hand side of the box. So long as the geometric mean of the supply slopes is less than the geometric mean of the absolute demand slopes, the periodic motion will be stable.

Actually, it is so flexible a method that there are dangers involved in its use: the number of conceivable models is literally infinite and a lifetime may be spent in exploring possibilities; furthermore, by supplying the proper stage directions at the proper time, we can specify any sort of a sequence development desired and may find that there is almost no empirical content in the theory being expounded.[18]

Nonetheless, despite these possible pitfalls, dynamic analysis has produced many useful results. In the field of pure theory, the important problem of the *stability of equilibrium* is wholly a question of dynamics. For it involves the question of how a system behaves after it has been disturbed into a disequilibrium state.

As an example, let us consider the case of an agricultural or labor market characterized by a so-called "backward rising" supply curve. The higher the price, the smaller is the amount supplied. It used to be thought that this necessarily led to cumulative price instability because "a reduction in demand will reduce price, which will increase quantity, which will reduce price, and so forth indefinitely." This reasoning is quite wrong. If the supply curve is steeper than the demand curve, the market will be stable with the above-described tortoise-hare sequence being a convergent one.

The relevance of dynamics for the problem of stability of equilibrium will come as no surprise to anyone who thinks seriously about the matter. Less expected is the fact that knowledge about dynamic stability leads to information about the "comparative statical" behavior of a system. Thus, we can rule out the hypothesis that the marginal propensity to consume is constantly greater than one if we reject the assumption of instability of income determination. This alone tells us that the multiplier—a comparative-statics concept—is positive rather than negative.[19] This relation between comparative statics and dynamics I have elsewhere called the "correspondence principle."[20]

But it is probably in the field of business cycles proper that dynamic analysis has proved itself most indispensable. Implicit theoretical concepts have been sharpened by translation into dynamic terms, and useful distinctions have been made between exogenous, endogenous, and mixed cyclical theories.

Thus dynamic analysis is able to show that innovations may cause quasi-periodic oscillations even if they are not themselves distributed in

---

[18] An example of this is provided by the notion of a "self-generating" business cycle, during which "costs overtake revenues" and "dictate a downturn," etc.

[19] From dynamics we set up the hypothesis that $|a| < 1$, which implies $\frac{1}{1-a} > 0$,

[20] *Foundations of Economic Analysis*, Ch. IX, X.

a smooth oscillation. Even irregular random shocks may keep a cycle alive if the economic system's structure is not heavily "damped."

At the other extreme, dynamics can clear up a false difficulty that has been raised in connection with a self-generating cycle theory. It used to be thought that such a theory begged the question, by assuming the presence of the cycle whose existence was to be proved. But actually, a non-cyclical disturbance can be shown to be capable of starting off a repeating, self-perpetuating oscillation. And if indeed the system can be shown to perpetuate a cycle once started, it is only too easy to envisage, throughout the course of all history, disturbances sufficient to explain why the "first" cycles should have gotten started.

Dynamic process analysis also liberates economists from the necessity of having separate theories of the "turning-points" in addition to theories of cumulative upward and downward swings. Even a simple theory of inventory cycles, or acceleration-multipliers, can explain all four phases of an idealized cycle.[21]

At its best, dynamic analysis can enrich our understanding of possibilities without leading to credulity in new, over-narrow, monistic dogmas concerning the cyclical process. In the hands of an eclectic economist whose judgment stems from an immersion in history and statistics, dynamic analysis could lead to the hypothesis that the weighting of exogenous and endogenous factors is quite different for the so-called 50-year-long (Kondratieff) waves than it is for the "major cycles" which average slightly less than a decade in length, or for the shorter inventory-credit cycles, or for the cycles of the American construction industry.

But to explore further developments in this field would carry us over into the fields of econometrics and theory, and out of the present into the future.

---

[21] A fact which is overlooked by chastened prophets who, after every short-term downturn, utter plaintively, "But inventories did not seem high relative to sales."

APPENDIX

PROCESSES INVOLVING SEVERAL PERIODS

As soon as we leave the simpler cases, where today's variable depends only upon its value at one previous time period, the situation becomes a little more complicated. For example, if one combines the Acceleration Principle with the multiplier, or if one works out a theory of inventory cycle, or if one works with many countries in international trade—in all of these cases[22] national income turns out to depend on its own value at more than one previous period. In short, we end up with something like, say,

$$Y(t + 2) = 5Y(t + 1) - 6Y(t) + A \qquad (26)$$

instead of just

$$Y(t + 2) = 5Y(t + 1) + A$$

As before, we have a "steady-state" part, $\overline{Y}$, in addition to a "transient." This "steady-state" can be found statically by putting $\overline{Y}$ on both sides of the equation:

$$\overline{Y} = 5\overline{Y} - 6\overline{Y} + A$$

or

$$Y = \frac{1}{1 - 5 + 6} A = \frac{1}{2} A \qquad (27)$$

As before, the transient can be found by working with deviations from $\overline{Y}$, i.e., with $y(t) = Y(t) - \overline{Y}$; and as before we end up with a "reduced" or "homogeneous" difference equation possessing no constant term, A:

$$y(t + 2) = 5y(t + 1) - 6y(t) + 0 \qquad (28)$$

---

[22] L. A. Metzler, *op. cit.; idem,* "Nature and Stability of Inventory Cycles," *Review of Economic Studies,* August 1941, XXIII, pp. 113–129; F. Machlup, *International Trade and the National Income Multiplier* (Philadelphia, 1943); P. A. Samuelson, "Interactions between the Multiplier Analysis and the Principle of Acceleration," reprinted from the 1939 *Review of Economic Statistics* in *Readings in Business Cycle Theory,* pp. 261–269. For a fuller mathematical treatment of difference and differential equations, see P. A. Samuelson, *Foundations of Economic Analysis,* Mathematical Appendix B, and references cited there.

Of course, now it takes two starting or initial values to get the sequence going. But clearly if we know $Y(0)$ and $Y(1)$, we can also calculate $y(0)$ and $y(1)$. Our system can therefore be written in the form

$$\begin{cases} y(t+2) - 5y(t+1) + 6y(t) = 0 \\ y(0) = y_0 \\ y(1) = y_1 \end{cases} \qquad (29)$$

Can we now expect the solution to this many-period equation to be of the simple geometric progression form $M^t K$? The answer is "not quite." Our system now will have *two* fundamental exponential responses, in much the way that striking a key on the piano will sound higher overtones as well as the key's own fundamental pitch. The quality of the final note depends upon the superposition of these different exponential sequences.

If three past periods were involved in our process, we could expect "three fundamental geometric progression responses"; and if our difference equation were of the nth order, we would have n geometric progression responses.

t	0	1	2	3	4	. . .	t	$t+1$	$t+2$	∞
$y_1(t)$	1	3	9	27	3^4	. . .	3^t	3^{t+1}	$3^t 3^2$	∞
$y_2(t)$	1	2	4	8	2^4	. . .	2^t	2^{t+1}	$2^t 2^2$	∞
$y_3(t)$	1	4	14	46	$3^4(2)-2^4$	. . .	$3^t 2-2^t$	$3^{t+1}2-2^{t+1}$	$+5y_3(t+1)-6y_3(t)$	∞

Perhaps the above numerical example will help make this clear. Consider

$$y(t+2) - 5y(t+1) + 6y(t) = 0$$
$$y(0) = 1$$
$$y(1) = 3$$

Then we have the sequence shown in the first row of the above table. Obviously, $y_1(t) = 3^t(1)$ is a solution.

But consider

$$y(t+2) - 5y(t+1) + 6y(t) = 0$$
$$y(0) = 1$$
$$y(1) = 2$$

Its solution turns out to be as given in the second row of the table.

Therefore, $2^t(1)$ is a solution to the difference equation as well as

$3^t(1)$. In fact if we start out in the third row with the initial conditions, $y(0) = 1$, $y(1) = 4$, it is not hard to show that the combined progressions

$$y(t) = 3^t(2) - 2^t(1)$$

also form a solution to (29).

How did we guess the fundamental exponential responses 2^t and 3^t? Why not 4^t? Why should there always be as many different fundamental responses as the number of periods in the difference equation? Why not either more or less?

To answer these questions, let us try a response of the form $y(t) = M^t K$, where K and M can be anything at all. Substituting, we find

$$M^{t+2} K - 5M^{t+1} K + 6M^t K = 0$$

or

$$M^t K [M^2 - 5M + 6] = 0 \qquad (30)$$

Now this equation can be satisfied only if the expression in brackets is zero, once we rule out the uninteresting case where K itself is zero. But the expression in brackets is a polynomial of the second degree in the unknown M. Such a polynomial or quadratic equation has two different roots or solutions, M_1 and M_2.

In this cooked-up case, it is easy to see that

$$M^2 - 5M + 6 = (M - 2)(M - 3) = 0$$

which can be equal to zero for the two cases

$$M_1 = 2$$
$$M_2 = 3$$

Therefore, either

$$M_1^t K_1 \text{ or } M_2^t K_2$$

is a solution. In fact, their sum

$$y(t) = M_1^t K_1 + M_2^t K_2$$

is also a solution of the difference equation, no matter what our choice of the two K's. This is very lucky, since we have two different initial conditions which have to be satisfied by an appropriate choice of K's. Specifically

$$y(0) = K_1 + K_2 = y_0$$
$$y(1) = M_1 K_1 + M_2 K_2 = y_1$$

so that

$$K_2 = y_0 - K_1$$

and

$$M_1 K_1 + M_2 y_0 - M_2 K_1 = y_1$$

or

$$K_1 = \frac{1}{M_1 - M_2} y_1 - \frac{M_2}{M_1 - M_2} y_0$$

$$K_2 = \frac{1}{M_2 - M_1} y_1 - \frac{M_1}{M_2 - M_1} y_0$$

To summarize:

(1) When given the difference equation

$$Y(t+2) + a_1 Y(t+1) + a_2 Y(t) = A$$
$$Y(0) = Y_0, \qquad Y(1) = Y_1 \qquad\qquad (31)$$

we solve for the stationary part by setting $Y(t) = Y(t+1) = Y(t+2) = \overline{Y}$ to get

$$\overline{Y} = \frac{1}{1 + a_1 + a_2} A \qquad\qquad (32)$$

(2) To this we add the "transient solution"

$$y(t) = Y(t) - \overline{Y} = M_1{}' K_1 + M_2{}' K_2 \qquad\qquad (33)$$

where $y(t)$ satisfies the difference equation

$$y(t+2) + a_1 y(t+1) + a_2 y(t) = 0$$
$$y(0) = y_0 = Y_0 - \overline{Y} \qquad\qquad (34)$$
$$y(1) = y_1 = Y_1 - \overline{Y}$$

and where M_1 and M_2 are roots of the quadratic equation in M

$$M^2 + a_1 M + a_2 = 0, \qquad\qquad (35)$$

or

$$M_1 = \frac{-a_1 + \sqrt{a_1{}^2 - 4a_2}}{2}, \qquad\qquad (36)$$

$$M_2 = \frac{-a_1 - \sqrt{a_1{}^2 - 4a_2}}{2},$$

and where the K's are defined in terms of the initial conditions, y_0 and y_1, as follows:[23]

$$K_1 = \frac{y_1 - M_2 y_0}{M_1 - M_2}$$

$$K_2 = \frac{y_1 - M_1 y_0}{M_2 - M_1}$$

(37)

Fortunately, in most economic problems we need only know the value of the biggest M, because eventually that will dominate the final solution. Thus,

$$2^t(100) + 3^t(.01)$$

eventually differs by a negligible percentage from $3^t(.01)$.

Hence, regardless of the K's, we need usually only be sure that the largest root M is less than one in absolute value. That being the case, the equilibrium level must be stable and the transient terms must eventually die down.

It does not require much imagination to guess how the general case of n periods is to be handled. Given

$$Y(t+n) + a_1 Y(t+n-1) + \ldots + a_{n-1} Y(t+1) + a_n Y(t) = A$$

(38)

we easily get the solution

$$Y(t) = \frac{1}{1 + a_1 + \ldots + a_n} A + \left[M_1{}^t K_1 + M_2{}^t K_2 + \ldots M_n{}^t K_n \right]$$

(39)

where the M's are the n roots of the nth degree polynomial

$$M^n + a_1 M^{n-1} + \ldots + a_{n-1} M + a_n = (M - M_1)(M - M_2) \ldots$$
$$\ldots (M - M_n) = 0 \quad (40)$$

and where the K's depend only on the initial condition.

If, and only if, the largest M is less than one in absolute value, the equilibrium will be stable and the disturbed system will always move back toward it.[24]

---

[23] The reader should verify that in the special case where $y(t+2) = y(t)$, our solution can be written

$$y(t) = \frac{(1)^t + (-1)^t}{2} y_0 + \frac{(1)^t - (-1)^t}{2} y_1$$

which looks similar to footnote 16.

[24] If two or more roots of the polynomial coincide—so that it contains repeated factors of the form $(M - M_1)^{1+s}$—our solutions of the form $M^t K$ will be too few. But the clue

THE MYSTERIOUS COMPLEX ROOTS

However, there is still a mathematical difficulty to be overcome. So simple a sequence as

$$x(t+2) = -x(t)$$
$$x(0) = x_0 \qquad\qquad (41)$$
$$x(1) = x_1$$

when we try the substitution $M^t K$, leads to the quadratic equation
$$M^2 = -1 \qquad\qquad (42)$$
which has no real roots at all. Or to put the matter differently, any geometric progression that begins with 1 and M will give the positive number M^2 for the next term, while our difference equation insists that the next term be negative.

Of course, the mathematician will say that $M^2 = -1$ has two "complex" or "imaginary" roots, $M = + \sqrt{-1}$ and $M = - \sqrt{-1}$, so that $M^2 = \sqrt{(-1)(-1)} = -1$. But as economists interested in the real world, what are imaginary numbers to us? The answer is that, like Voltaire's God, if they did not exist we would still find it convenient to invent them. And, like Mutt and Jeff, they always occur in pairs, with a plus and a minus term involving $\sqrt{-1}$. In pairs which can always be *combined* to form the real numbers that we require as practical men.

As a matter of fact, since $\sqrt{-1}$ raised to any even power is a real number, we may—by the use of the trick shown in note 24—write the solution to the above equation as

$$x(t) = x_0 \left\{ \frac{(1)^t + (-1)^t}{2} \right\} \left\{ \sqrt{-1} \right\}^t + x_1 \left\{ \frac{(1)^t - (-1)^t}{2} \right\} \left\{ -\sqrt{-1} \right\}^{t-1}$$
$$(43)$$

---

to the proper treatment is provided by watching what happens as M_2 gets closer and closer to M_1. Then in addition to $M_1^t K_1$, $\dfrac{M_2^t - M_1^t}{M_2 - M_1} K_3$ is also a solution. But as $M_2 \rightarrow M_1$, the latter expression becomes $t M_1^{t-1} = \dfrac{\partial}{\partial M} [M^t]_{M\,=\,M_1}$.

Therefore, in the general case of $s + 1$ repeated roots, we always make up for the s missing exponential terms by using expressions of the form

$$M_1^t, t M_1^{t-1}, t(t-1)M_1^{t-2}, \ldots, t(t-1) \ldots (t-s+1)M_1^{t-s} = \frac{\partial^s}{\partial M^s} [M^t]_{M\,=\,M_1}$$

or if more convenient,
$$M_1^t, t M_1^t, t^2 M_1^t, \ldots \ t^s M_1^t$$

Note that so long as $|M| < 1$, the powers of t will not affect the stability of the solution, since M^t will dominate.

For even t's, i.e., $t = 2T$, the second term is zero and the first term is $x_0 (-1)^T$; for odd t's, $t = 2T + 1$, the first term is zero, and the second term is $x_1 (-1)^T$. But combining the terms in brackets, we see that we can write

$$x(t) = (\sqrt{-1})^t \, K_1 + (-\sqrt{-1})^t \, K_2 \qquad (44)$$

where the K's are complex numbers of the form

$$K_1 = \tfrac{1}{2}(x_0 - \sqrt{-1} \, x_1)$$
$$K_2 = \tfrac{1}{2}(x_0 + \sqrt{-1} \, x_1) \qquad (45)$$

Note that K_1 and K_2 are Mutt and Jeff complex numbers, with $\sqrt{-1}$ having opposite signs—or as the mathematician would say, they are "conjugate complex numbers."

But there is still another way that our solution to (41) can be written, using the sine and cosine trigonometric functions. Let us try as a solution

$$x(t) = C_1 \cos 90°t + C_2 \sin 90°t \qquad (46)$$

Then

$$x(t + 2) = C_1 \cos (90°t + 180°) + C_2 \sin (90°t + 180°)$$

But adding $180°$ will always reverse the sign of the cosine and sine functions. Therefore, this satisfies our difference equation, once C_1 and C_2 have been determined so as to fit the initial conditions:

$$C_1 = x_0, \, C_2 = x_1$$

We have two expressions for the same solution:

$$x(t) = x_0 \cos 90°t + x_1 \sin 90°t \qquad (47)$$
$$= x_0 \frac{(1)^t + (-1)^t}{2} (\sqrt{-1})^t + x_1 \frac{(1)^t - (-1)^t}{2} (-\sqrt{-1})^{t-1}$$

This suggests that complex numbers are to be identified in a special way with the simple trigonometric functions. The sine and cosine functions provide a smooth way for having $(-1)^t$ go from $+1$ to -1 as t goes from o to 1. When $t = \frac{1}{2}$ or any fraction, imaginary numbers are involved—but always in pairs which combine to form real number solutions.

More precisely, wherever we have complex roots

$$M_1{}^t = (u + \sqrt{-1}\, v)^t$$
$$M_2{}^t = (u - \sqrt{-1}\, v)^t \tag{48}$$

we can write these as

$$(\sqrt{u^2 + v^2})^t\,(\cos \theta t \pm \sqrt{-1}\sin \theta t) \tag{49}$$

where

$$\cos \theta = \frac{u}{\sqrt{u^2 + v^2}}$$
$$\sin \theta = \frac{v}{\sqrt{u^2 + v^2}} \tag{50}$$

The K's will come in pairs so that all terms involving $\sqrt{-1}$ can cancel, and we finally end up with

$$(\sqrt{u^2 + v^2})^t\,(C_1 \cos \theta t + C_2 \sin \theta t) \tag{51}$$

For stability $|M| = \sqrt{u^2 + v^2}$, the "absolute value" or "modulus" of the complex roots, must be less than one. The relation between complex exponentials and the sine and cosine functions is further explored in the next section.

THE GENERAL THEORY OF DIFFERENTIAL EQUATIONS
WITH CONSTANT COEFFICIENTS

Whatever is true for difference equations holds perfectly well for differential equations, so long as we use e^{mt} instead of M^t, and use

$$\left[y(t), \frac{dy(t)}{dt}, \frac{d^2y(t)}{dt^2}, \ldots, \frac{d^ny(t)}{dt^n} \right]$$

wherever

$$[y(t), y(t+1), y(t+2), \ldots, y(t+n)]$$

appear.

Thus we saw earlier that

$$y(t+2) - 5y(t+1) + 6y(t) = 0$$
$$y(0) = 1$$
$$y(1) = 4$$

has the solution

$$y(t) = 3^t(2) - 2^t(1)$$

It follows, therefore, that

$$\frac{d^2y(t)}{dt^2} - 5\frac{dy(t)}{dt^2} + 6y(t) = 0$$

$$y(0) = 1$$

$$y'(0) = \left[\frac{d}{dt}y(t)\right]_{t=0} = 4$$

must have for its solution

$$y(t) = e^{3t}(2) - e^{2t}(1)$$

as the reader can verify.

Indeed, we always solve the general differential equation

$$\frac{d^nY(t)}{dt^n} + a_1\frac{d^{n-1}Y(t)}{dt^{n-1}} + \ldots + a_{n-1}\frac{dY(t)}{dt} + a_nY(t) = A$$

$$Y(0) = b_0$$

$$Y'(0) = b_1$$

$$\cdot \quad \cdot \quad \cdot \quad \cdot \quad \cdot$$

$$Y^{(n-1)}(0) = b_{n-1} \tag{52}$$

as follows:

First, we determine the stationary state level, by setting $Y(t) = \overline{Y}$, $\frac{d}{dt}\overline{Y} = 0 = \ldots = \frac{d^n}{dt^n}\overline{Y}$, to get

$$\overline{Y} = \frac{1}{a_n}A \tag{53}$$

Then we work with deviations from the equilibrium level, $y(t) = Y(t) - \overline{Y}$. These transient terms which must be added to $\overline{Y}$ satisfy the "reduced" differential equation:

$$\frac{d^ny(t)}{dt^n} + a_1\frac{d^{n-1}y(t)}{dt^{n-1}} + \ldots + a_{n-1}\frac{dy(t)}{dt} + a_ny(t) = 0$$

$$y(0) = Y(0) - \overline{Y} = b_0 - \frac{A}{a_n}$$

$$y'(0) = Y'(0) = b_1 \tag{54}$$

$$\cdot \quad \cdot \quad \cdot \quad \cdot \quad \cdot \quad \cdot \quad \cdot \quad \cdot$$

$$y^{(n-1)}(0) = Y^{(n-1)}(0) = b_{n-1}$$

Its solution is of the form

$$y(t) = e^{m_1 t}K_1 + e^{m_2 t}K_2 + \ldots + e^{m_n t}K_n \tag{55}$$

where the substitution of $e^{mt} K$ into the differential equation shows that $(m_1, m_2, \ldots m_n)$ are to be the roots of the polynomial,

$$m^n + a_1 m^{n-1} + \ldots + a_{n-1} m + a_n = 0 \qquad (56)$$

The K's are determined by the initial conditions

$$
\begin{aligned}
K_1 + K_2 + \ldots + K_n &= y(0) \\
m_1 K_1 + m_2 K_2 + \ldots + m_n K_n &= y'(0) \\
m_1^2 K_1 + m_2^2 K_2 + \ldots + m_n^2 K_n &= y''(0)
\end{aligned} \qquad (57)
$$

$\cdots\cdots\cdots\cdots \qquad \cdots\cdots\cdots$

etc.

If all the roots are real and negative, the system is stable and the transient dies away. If some of the roots are repeated, the missing e^{mt} terms will be replaced by terms of the form te^{mt}, $t^2 e^{mt}$, $\ldots$, $t^i e^{mt} = \dfrac{\partial^i}{\partial m^i} e^{mt}$, $\ldots$ and higher powers of t. These powers of t will not affect the stability of the system if $m < 0$.

But again, not all roots have to be real. Earlier we saw in equation (15) the case where the acceleration of capital depended inversely upon its own level and gave rise to pendulum-like oscillations rather than to exponential growth or decay. This was a relation of the type

$$\frac{d^2 y(t)}{dt^2} = -y(t) \qquad (58)$$

where the appropriate time units have been used to get rid of any numerical constants.

Obviously, neither e^t nor e^{-t} will do as a solution, since when differentiated twice, each of these gives rise to itself multiplied by $(1)^2$ or $(-1)^2 = 1$. What we need is some kind of a periodic or repeating function of time.[25]

A bold man would try $e^{\pm\sqrt{-1}\,t}$, since

$$\frac{d}{dt} e^{\pm\sqrt{-1}\,t} = \pm\sqrt{-1}\, e^{\pm\sqrt{-1}\,t}$$

$$\frac{d^2}{dt^2} e^{\pm\sqrt{-1}\,t} = \frac{d}{dt}\frac{d}{dt} e^{\pm\sqrt{-1}\,t} = +\sqrt{-1}\,\sqrt{-1}\, e^{\pm\sqrt{-1}\,t} = -e^{\pm\sqrt{-1}\,t}.$$

But what in the real world is the meaning of e raised to an imaginary number? Let us take the magic series for e^t, given in footnote 10, and

---

[25] This follows from the earlier demonstration that capital will oscillate. We can further show the constancy of amplitude of these oscillations by the fact that

$y''(t) = -y(t)$ implies $\dfrac{d}{dt}\left[\dfrac{y'^2 + y^2}{2}\right] = [y'(t) y''(t) + y'(t) y(t)] = 0$ or

$y(t)^2 + y'(t)^2 = $ constant, and the oscillations can neither explode nor decay.

drop every other term, and then change the sign of every other term of what is left. This will give us two new functions, $f_1(t)$ and $f_2(t)$:

$$f_1(t) = 1 - \frac{t^2}{1 \cdot 2} + \frac{t^4}{4!} - \frac{t^6}{6!} + \ldots$$

$$f_2(t) = \frac{t}{1} - \frac{t^3}{3!} + \frac{t^5}{5!} - \frac{t^7}{7!} + \ldots \tag{59}$$

where n! stands for "n factorial" or $n(n-1) \ldots (3)(2)(1)$, and, so to speak,

$$e^{\pm\sqrt{-1}t} = f_1(t) \pm \sqrt{-1}\, f_2(t) \tag{60}$$

Obviously, differentiating either of these new functions twice will give us itself back again but with algebraic sign reversed. The reader should verify this and also that

$$\frac{d}{dt} f_2(t) = f_1(t), \quad \frac{d}{dt} f_1(t) = -f_2(t)$$

$$\begin{aligned} f_1(0) &= 1, & f_2(0) &= 0 \\ f_1'(0) &= 0, & f_2'(0) &= 1 \end{aligned} \tag{61}$$

It follows that

$$y(t) = f_2(t)\, y(0) + f_1(t)\, y'(0)$$

is the solution to our system (58).

But from trigonometry, we know that the periodic function cos t has the same properties as $f_1(t)$, t being measured in terms of "radians"—i.e., in units equal to $360°/2\pi = 57.29°$. And sin t has the properties of $f_2(t)$. It can be shown that no other functions can have these properties.

This suggested to Euler one of the most "beautiful" relations in all mathematics:

$$e^{\pm\sqrt{-1}t} = \cos t \pm \sqrt{-1} \sin t \tag{62}$$

The patient reader can use this to verify that the complex numbers, m_1, m_2, K_1, and K_2, in the differential equation solution expressed in the form

$$y(t) = e^{(u+\sqrt{-1}v)t} (\alpha + \sqrt{-1}\,\beta) + e^{(u-\sqrt{-1}v)t} (\alpha - \sqrt{-1}\beta) + \ldots \tag{63}$$

can always be grouped in pairs to give the real expression

$$y(t) = e^{ut} (C_1 \cos vt + C_2 \sin vt) \tag{64}$$

where $u < 0$ is the condition for stability, where the C's depend on the initial conditions, and where the period of oscillation is given by $2\pi/v$.

11

ECONOMETRICS*

Wassily Leontief

I

THE combination of theoretical and statistical analysis is relatively new in economics. Traditionally, economic theory was developed as a deductive discipline. The typical argument of economic theory starts from a set of fundamental observations on the nature of consumers' choice, the operation of the profit motive, and a description of the basic technological and institutional framework within which the system is supposed to operate, such as the prevalence or absence of competitive pricing, the basic characteristic of the monetary institutions, etc. From there on, pure logical reasoning takes over and leads to a set of interrelated, general conclusions concerning the properties of the resulting economic mechanism. Thus one arrives at theories of prices and of distribution, explanation of cyclical fluctuations or, say, theory of international trade.

Each one of these theories has an empirical basis in so far as the fundamental assumptions which stand at the beginning of the particular chain of reasoning are supposed to describe certain factual relationships. However, these assumptions and consequently also the conclusions are couched, as a rule, in very general terms. The use of the mathematical mode of expression which has for some time found increasing favor among theoretical economists, helps only to emphasize the very general

* The widest possible interpretation of its title would have required us to cover in this essay all the various fields of quantitative economic analysis. On the one hand, following the precedent established by Harold T. Davis in *The Theory of Econometrics* (Bloomington, 1941), it should have included a discussion of the mathematically formulated pure economic theory. On the other, heeding the suggestion of one of the two official reporters assigned to review this essay, it should also have concerned itself with descriptive statistical studies of National Income or, say, compilations of balances of Foreign Trade.

The author has deliberately chosen the middle course, that of interpreting "Econometrics" as a special type of economic analysis in which the general theoretical approach —often formulated in explicitly mathematical terms—is combined—frequently through the medium of intricate statistical procedures—with empirical measurement of economic phenomena.

Without embarking upon a thankless terminological controversy one can defend this particular selection of material on the ground that a wider definition of our subject matter would bring together a large number of barely related subjects, while a more restricted one would lead to separation of closely connected problems.

character of both assumptions and conclusions. Although dealing in quantities, the mathematical economist eschews the use of actual numbers. In using algebra rather than arithmetic he is able to derive and to state propositions which will apply to a great range of specific factual situations. He can prove, for example, that in a regime of cost minimization with fixed output, the effect of an increase of the price of any factor of production X upon the quantity of another factor Y used in the same process will necessarily be equal to the effect of the change in the price of Y on the quantity of X. This proposition follows from the general principle of cost minimization and thus applies to any two cost factors in any and every industry. To give another example from the theory of international trade, one might quote the proposition according to which a free-trade country can always profit from the introduction of a small import duty, provided the others do not retaliate. Here again a very general proposition has been derived from quite general factual assumptions. A large part of traditional economic theory as it is used in explaining the operation of the economic system consists of such propositions derived from a set of equally general basic postulates. In selecting these factual assumptions the theorist has been and still is prone to lean rather heavily on what he considers to be common sense or a matter of common knowledge. Naturally he lays himself open to serious criticism on the part of other social scientists who urge on him the revision of these fundamental assumptions in the light of modern experimental psychology, sociology, or even unprejudiced simple direct observation.

The empirical element, however, enters economic analysis not only on the higher level of primary assumptions. Even a most realistic description of fundamental modes of economic behavior and basic types of economic organization cannot reach down to the individual, the particular aspects of concrete economic processes. Even a very elaborate theory of saving derived from the most up-to-date psychology of consumers' behavior cannot deduce the specific fact that American families with an annual income of $3,000 tend to spend on the average $2,600 on current consumption and save the rest. No theory of international trade can possibly produce the numerical estimate of, say, the elasticity of American demand for English exports. At the same time many economic processes can be explained only in terms of the actual magnitudes of consumers' propensities to save, elasticities of demand for foreign imports, and other factual relationships of a similar kind. Unable to arrive at the crucial figures by general reasoning, the theorist resorted to what might be called conditional formulation. Instead of describing the effects of one million dollars' worth of additional investment, he states only that, if the propensity to consume is such and such, national income will react in such and such a way. Mathematical formulation facilitates establishment of conditional propositions of this kind. The relevant elasticities, propensities, and other similar constants can conveniently be represented by symbolic letters, say, a, η or A throughout the whole argument and also in the final conclusions. Intricate relationships can thus be set up and studied without any reference to the actual magnitude of the many unknown constants involved in each one of them.

The further the deductive theorist entered into the analysis of special situations, the more he found it necessary to resort to conditional formulations. His writing became replete with abstract models containing algebraic symbols representing quantities of unknown magnitudes. Economic theory unmistakably began to lose its contact with reality as soon as it made an attempt to penetrate beyond the limit of conclusions which could be derived from what is often referred to as its *a priori* assumptions but could better be described as its general empirical postulates. A new contact with reality had to be established on the much lower level of special and, in so far as it pertained to measurable facts, quantitative information.

One of the first elaborate attempts to fill the empty boxes of abstract, theoretical argument with actual statistical data was undertaken by Irving Fisher in his *The Purchasing Power of Money*.[1] Concurrently Henry L. Moore[2] used the least square method of curve fitting to determine, from empirical data, the shape of the demand curve for labor. The late 'twenties and early 'thirties are marked by a number of bold and determined advances into the new territory. Paul H. Douglas and C. W. Cobb in their original paper on the "Theory of Production,"[3] followed by Douglas' *Theory of Wages*[4] and a long series of subsequent articles, undertook the difficult task of empirical application and verification of the marginal theories of production and distribution. The name of Henry Schultz is associated with statistical analysis of consumers' demand. His progress, from the early article on the demand for beef[5] to the more elaborate *Statistical Laws of Demand and Supply with Special Application to Sugar*[6] and finally the monumental *Theory and Measurement of De-*

---

[1] New York, 1911.

[2] Henry L. Moore, *Laws of Wages, an Essay in Statistical Economics* (New York, 1911).

[3] "A Theory of Production," *American Economic Review*, Proceedings, 1928, XVIII.

[4] New York, 1934.

[5] "The Statistical Measurement of the Elasticity of Demand for Beef," *Journal of Farm Economics*, July 1924, VI.

[6] Chicago, 1928.

mand,[7] marks the general development of this particular field of studies. Ragnar Frisch's *New Methods of Measuring Marginal Utility*[8] introduces statistical approach into the range of the conceptually most refined type of analytical problems. Charles F. Roos' analyses of the automobile and the residential building markets[9] and J. Tinbergen's original statistical work on business cycles[10] belong to the same early "Sturm und Drang" period in the continuing development of the new type of economic analysis.

The Econometric Society was organized in 1930 and the first issue of *Econometrica* appeared in January 1933. The following paragraph from the opening editorial written by Professor Frisch deserves to be quoted in full:

But there are several aspects of the quantitative approach to economics, and no single one of these aspects, taken by itself, should be confounded with econometrics. Thus, econometrics is by no means the same as economic statistics. Nor is it identical with what we call general economic theory although a considerable portion of this theory has a definitely quantitative character. Nor should econometrics be taken as synonymous with the application of mathematics to economics. Experience has shown that each of these three viewpoints, that of statistics, economic theory, and mathematics, is a necessary, but not by itself sufficient, condition for a real understanding of the quantitative relations in modern economic life. It is the *unification* of all three that is powerful. And it is this unification that constitutes econometrics.

Reviewing the ever broadening stream of writing on the general subject of statistical implementation of economic theory which has appeared since that time, one cannot help noticing that a very large part of it has been devoted to methodological problems, to questions of ways and means rather than to actual analysis, and that, even in those instances when concrete factual problems have been taken up, the interest of the author was very often centered mainly on certain methodological aspects of his task. This situation is typical of what might be called the second, reflective stage in the development of a new field of inquiry, a natural reaction to the first stage during which preoccupation with the new ends detracts the attention of the investigator from critical examination of the available means.

---

[7] Chicago, 1938.

[8] Tübingen, 1932.

[9] Charles F. Roos, *Dynamic Economics, Theoretical and Statistical Studies of Demand, Production and Prices* (Bloomington, 1934).

[10] *Statistical Test of Business-Cycle Theories, I. A Method and Its Application to Investment Activities; II. Business Cycles in the United States of America, 1919–1932,* League of Nations Economic Intelligence Service (Geneva, 1939).

II

The function of statistical analysis in application to econometric research is that of an intermediary between a general theoretical hypothesis and the directly observable facts. In the explanation of the price developments on the American wheat market the theory conceives of each individual price-quantity combination as a point of intersection between a positively inclined supply curve and a negatively sloped demand curve. The determination of the shapes of the particular curves, which—in accordance with the above hypothesis—would fit the actually observed price-quantity data, is the specific function of the statistician. The relation between the three tasks, that of the observer, the theorist, and the analytical statistician, and in particular the establishment of the proper line of demarcation between the competencies of the latter two, is anything but simple. In the example above the theorist may include in his general prefabricated model the assumption that both the demand and supply curve are, say, straight lines, and leave to the statistician only the determination of their actual slopes and the corresponding shifts. Or he can allow the statistician to make the choice between different possible shapes of the curves (exponential function, second-degree parabola, and so on) to be fitted to the given data, such choice being made then on the basis of certain statistical tests. Yielding additional ground, the theorist might let the statistician decide which variables are to be included and which excluded from a particular explanatory relationship. J. Tinbergen in *Business Cycles in the United States of America, 1919–1932* offers a good example of acceptance and rejection of explanatory variables, on the basis of high or low coefficients of correlation, respectively.

Why should one not go further in the same direction and limit the theorist to the simple task of stating the purely formal properties of any complete and consistent explanatory hypothesis—such, for example, as the requirement that it contain a number of independent relationships equal to the number of the unknowns? Why not let all the particulars such as the composition—in terms of the variables involved—and the general form and actual shape of the individual equations be determined by the statistician on the basis of given numerical observations and with the help of advanced testing procedure?

The statistician will be the first to refuse to shoulder such responsibility, and to point out the basic weakness of the preceding argument. It is precisely the modern theory of statistical inference which makes the econometrician particularly wary of any attempt to usurp the prerogatives of the theorist.

Twenty years ago the statistical economist was prone to pride himself on the fact that he was approaching his task without any "preconceived notions," i.e., without any theoretical propositions based on evidence other than that contained in the statistical data on which he was about to perform his numerical analysis. Now he knows that a considerable amount of outside information is necessary to justify the application even of such familiar statistical devices as, for example, the least squares method of curve fitting.

Statistical testing of hypotheses, of which curve fitting is a special case, is a procedure of choosing between two or more specified alternatives. Its outcome in any particular instance depends upon (a) the nature of admissible alternatives and (b) the criteria on the basis of which the choice is being made. Insofar as the determination of a basic set of *all possible* alternatives lies outside of the competence of the statistical testing procedure itself, no analysis of real phenomena can possibly be reduced to an automatic sequence of statistical tests.

Anticipating some of the conclusions reached at the end of the following survey, one could say that in its present conditions the further progress of quantitative economic analysis will depend upon successful, essentially non-statistical search for promising analytical insights, as much as upon the final statistical sifting of the empirical "pay dust."

III

Considerable progress has been achieved in recent years toward the understanding of proper and improper application of statistical procedures to economic analysis. Much of this methodological research was done abroad, particularly in Norway, Sweden, and Holland, where it has been associated with the names of Ragnar Frisch, Herman Wold, and Tjalling Koopmans. In the United States the Cowles Commission at the University of Chicago is the most conspicuous center of advancement and vigorous promotion of this new type of empirical quantitative analysis in economics. (Some members of the present Chicago group belong at the same time to the European circle.) Its general credo is formulated and systematically presented by Trygve Haavelmo in a volume entitled *The Probability Approach to Econometrics*,[11] published as a special Supplement to *Econometrica*, first issued in hectographed form at Harvard in 1941.

[11] *Econometrica* (Supplement), 1944, XII. See also: Tjalling Koopmans, "Statistical Estimation of Simultaneous Economic Relations," *Journal of the American Statistical Association*, December 1945, XL; and M. A. Girshick and Trygve Haavelmo, "Statistical Analysis of the Demand for Food," *Econometrica*, April 1947, XV.

The basic orientation of the new approach to econometrics is succinctly formulated in the opening sentences of this monograph: "This study . . . represents an attempt to supply a theoretical foundation for the analysis of interrelations between economic variables. It is based upon modern theory of probability and statistical inference."[12]

If the general philosophical foundation of the new methodology is derived directly from the modern theory of statistical inference, its concrete elaboration in application to economic analysis carries the unmistakable mark of a lineage leading directly back to the earliest attempts to derive statistical demand and supply curves from market data. It is essentially a systematic attempt to develop a method to bridge the commonly recognized gap between abstract theory and the actually observed facts which it is supposed to explain. Let it be stated at the outset that a great part of this analysis cannot be made intelligible without the use of rather involved mathematics. The most that the following non-technical discussion can aim at is to indicate what kind of questions are being raised by the new school of econometricians and what type of reasoning is employed in its work toward the solution of these questions.

The familiar problem of statistical derivation of empirical market supply and demand curves, which has already been referred to as the prototype of much of present-day econometric analysis, can serve as a convenient point of departure for such a presentation.

The Marshallian partial equilibrium theory interprets every price-quantity combination in any particular market as a point of intersection between a market supply and a corresponding market demand curve. Faced with the problem of explaining a set of different price-quantity combinations observed over a period of time in the same market, the statistical economists utilized and elaborated the idea of shifting supply and demand curves. The essential feature of this scheme is the distinction between the constant elements of the underlying causal relationships on the one hand and their changing elements on the other. The first are represented by the slopes of the hypothetical supply and demand curves which are assumed to be invariant throughout the whole period of observation, the second by their levels, which shift from one price-quantity combination to another.

Furthermore, the changing elements can occasionally be split into a systematic part dependent, within the framework of the particular explanatory scheme, upon the action of some specific and observable outside factors, and a random component representing the influence of all other, unknown outside variables.

---

[12] *Op. cit.*, p. iii.

Let p_t represent the price and q_t the quantity of some commodity purchased at that price at the time t. Let also y_t represent the consumers' income assumed to be a *known* outside factor influencing the quantities purchased at any particular price. The effects of all the other *unspecified* outside factors responsible for the otherwise unexplained parts of the demand and supply shift must be represented by two separate variables, say u_t and v_t.

Assuming, finally, the simplest, that is additive, relationship between all the variables, the following two linear equations describe the market situation at any particular point of time, t:

(1) $$q_t = a_1 p_t + \beta y_t + u_t$$
(2) $$q_t = a_2 p_t \qquad + v_t$$

The constants a_1 and a_2 (the former usually expected to be negative) are the invariant slopes of the demand and the supply curve respectively. $\beta y_t + u_t$ describes the "level" of demand and v_t the level of supply. The constant β measures the influence of income on the quantity demanded so that βy_t represents the systematic component of the total demand "shift."

Given a_1, a_2, and β, the theory set down in these two equations would make it possible to explain, i.e., to compute, the price p_t and quantity q_t prevailing at the time t provided the income y_t and the size of the catch-all shifts u_t and v_t were known: solving equations (1) and (2) for p_t and q_t we have

(3) $$p_t = \frac{\beta}{a_2 - a_1} y_t + \frac{u_t - v_t}{a_2 - a_1}$$

(4) $$q_t = \frac{\beta a_2}{a_2 - a_1} y_t + \frac{u_t a_2 - v_t a_1}{a_2 - a_1}$$

This new system is often referred to as the "reduced form" of the original "structural" equations (1) and (2). Each separate structural equation is supposed to represent an autonomous relationship; autonomous in the sense that the factors determining its form are assumed to be independent of the factors determining the form of any other relationship belonging to the same theoretical model.

The demand function (1) and the supply function (2) can be recognized as being autonomous with respect to each other from the fact that they do not contain any common structural parameters (p_t, q_t, y_t, u_t, and v_t are variables, the magnitudes of which do not constitute a part of the structural characteristic of this particular theoretical system). If the shape of one of them, say of (1), were affected through the change in a_1, β or both, the structure of the other could still remain the same as before. And, even if a_2 in (2) had actually changed at the same time, the theory as stated in the two equations does not suggest any possible connection between the two changes.

In contrast to the basic relationships (1) and (2), the reduced equations (3) and (4) are structurally interdependent. They contain common structural constants a_1, a_2, and β which could not vary without necessarily affecting both (3) and (4), simultaneously. In short, the essential distinction between the original structural and the derived "reduced" system is that in the former the separate equations contain the same "unknown" variables (p_t and q_t) but have different structural constants (a_1, a_2, and β) while in the latter they have some common structural constants but contain each a different dependent variable. Thus each of the equations of the reduced system can be directly used to derive the value of one of the unknowns of our problem from the fixed magnitude of the constants a_1, a_2, and β and the values of the exogenously determined variables, y_t, u_t, and v_t.

Income, y_t, is an independently defined variable. It can be identified and, in principle at least, measured without reference to the particular theoretical context in which it appears in the above equations; not so the residual shifts u_t and v_t. Representing the impact of "all other factors," these magnitudes are actually defined through equations (1) and (2); and they can be measured only by reference to the other terms in these relationships. Thus:

$$(5) \qquad u_t = q_t - a_1\, p_t - \beta y_t$$
$$(6) \qquad v_t = q_t - a_2\, p_t$$

At this stage of the argument the "stochastic" element comes in. A combined effect of many unknown causal factors can often be advantageously described in terms of a probability distribution. Even if the magnitude of a particular shift u_t or v_t at the time t seems to be unexplainable and unpredictable it might be still possible to make an empirically significant statement about the probability with which shifts of various magnitudes are likely to occur, a statement analogous to that which defines, for example, the chance of drawing a red ball from an urn containing two red and eight white balls as being one in five, i.e., $1/5$.

Introduction of random or "error" elements into description of economic relationships is certainly not new. The realization of the necessity to describe explicitly the nature of the probability distribution of such variables and the insistence on the fact that such specifications have to be considered an integral part of the analytical scheme as much as any other theoretical relationships is, however, typical of the modern stochastic approach.

The assumptions concerning the probability distribution of random variables can of course—as any other kind of theoretical assumption—be stated with various degrees of generality. In the particular instance discussed above, u_t and v_t can be defined, for example, as normally distributed variables without any further specification. In detail this means that the probability of the actual simultaneous occurrence of shifts u_t and v_t of any particular magnitudes is described by the well-known normal error function. This function contains five constants—the averages, i.e., the most probable values of u_t and v_t, their respective "standard deviations," and finally another coefficient describing the degree of interdependence between the magnitudes of the two types of shifts. A more specific, less general assumption could state that u_t and v_t are distributed independently of each other, i.e., that the probability of occurrence of a demand shift, u_t, of any particular magnitude is independent of the size of the supply shift, v_t, which happens to be associated with it. Such an assumption implies that the last of the five coefficients of the normal distribution function mentioned above equals zero. The constants of the distribution functions included in any particular theoretical system must, in principle at least, be treated at par with the other structural constants such as a_1, a_2, or β in the equations above.

Since u_t and v_t are *defined* by equations (5) and (6), the assumption that they represent random variables implies that the independent variables p_t and q_t which appear on the other side of these relationships are also random. Moreover with a_1, a_2, β, and y_t considered as given, the probability of "drawing" at the time t a price p_t *and* quantity q_t of any particular magnitude, i.e., the joint distribution function of these two variables, is uniquely determined by the joint distribution function of the random shifts u_t and v_t.

In terms of such stochastic theory, to explain the prices and quantities observed on a given market means, in the particular case under consideration, to derive their joint probability distribution from the known probability distributions of the supply and demand shifts u_t and v_t and the known income variations y_t, on the basis of the structural relationships (1) and (2). As equations (3) and (4) clearly show, the distribution of prices as well as that of quantities depends in this particular instance simultaneously upon both the supply and the demand shifts. In some cases one might be interested not in deriving the complete probability distribution functions of p_t and q_t but only in determining their mean, i.e., most probable, values. In the example used here this would require only the knowledge of the corresponding mean values of u_t and v_t; in general, however, explicit assumptions concerning the shape of the entire distribution function of the latter variables would be necessary.

One way of determining the unknown empirical magnitudes of such theoretical constants as a_1, a_2, and β in our system of the demand and supply equations is that of direct observation or controlled experimentation. The slope of the supply curve, a_2, could for example be obtained from a detailed study of the cost function of all the individual enterprises supplying the particular market. The effect of income variation on consumers' demand, measured by β, could be determined through detailed study of consumers' budgets or even by means of direct questionnaires. The Cowles Commission econometricians are inclined to minimize the practical significance of this type of empirical study. If mentioned at all, it is referred to mainly by way of contrast with the other, in their view much more important, source of empirical information: observation of the behavior of economic variables as they change under the influence of the free, uncontrolled forces of the market mechanism. In so far as these forces are assumed to operate according to rules laid down by some specified stochastic relationships, the proper statistical procedure for determination of the unknown magnitudes of the relevant structural constants must obviously be developed within the tenets of the same theoretical model. In the particular instance of supply and demand analysis discussed above, the estimation of β, a_1, a_2, and of the theoretical constants of the assumed joint probability distribution function of the random shifts u_t and v_t has to be made with the price-quantity data as its empirical basis and equations (1) and (2) as its theoretical background.

First let the case be considered in which the only specification of the distributions of the random variables u_t and v_t is that they are normal. Since the difference of two normally distributed variables is, according to the well-known proposition of probability calculus, also normally distributed, the second right-hand terms of equations (3) and (4) can be considered as representing normally distributed random variables. Equation (3) can thus be interpreted as describing a linear relationship between the independent variable y_t and the dependent variable p_t, subject to a normally distributed "error" $\dfrac{u_t - v_t}{a_2 - a_1}$. If both the incomes ($y_t$) and the corresponding prices (p_t) are known for a number of different points of time, the unknown coefficient, $\dfrac{\beta}{a_2 - a_1}$, can in this case be determined through application of the conventional "least squares" method. Applying, accordingly, the same formula which is used to compute the slope of a linear price trend (only in this instance the prices are plotted not against "time" but against income), we have

$$(7) \qquad \frac{\beta}{a_2 - a_1} = \frac{\Sigma p_t' y_t'}{\Sigma (y_t')^2}$$

p_t' and y_t' represent the deviations of price p_t and income y_t from their respective averages computed from all the price and income figures under consideration. The summation sign, Σ, extends over all the separately observed points of time.

The same "least squares" method applied to equation (4) gives

$$(8) \qquad \frac{\beta a_2}{a_2 - a_1} = \frac{\Sigma q_t' y_t'}{\Sigma (y_t')^2}$$

This is the "slope" of the regression line of the quantities (or rather of the deviations, q_t', of the observed quantities from their respective means) against income.

These two equations are obviously insufficient to determine the magnitudes of a_1, a_2, and β. The particular combination in which these constants happen to appear in the above formulae makes it possible however to compute the value of a_2. The empirical slope of the supply curve can be obtained by dividing the left- and the right-hand terms of equation (8) by the corresponding terms of equation (7):

$$(9) \qquad a_2 = \frac{\Sigma q_t' y_t'}{\Sigma p_t' y_t'}$$

Furthermore a substitution of the thus determined value of a_2 into equation (7) or (8) establishes the following relationship between the two remaining unknown coefficients, a_1 and β:

$$(10) \qquad \beta = \frac{\Sigma p_t' y_t'}{\Sigma (y_t')^2} a_1 + \frac{\Sigma q_t' y_t'}{\Sigma (y_t')^2}$$

This equation could be used to compute the unknown slope, a_1, of the demand curve, provided it were possible to evaluate the income effect, β, on the basis of some outside information. On the other hand β could be computed if a_1 were given. Without additional sources of information, however, the observed price-quantity combinations are not sufficient to derive, on the basis of the given theoretical model, the empirical magnitude of the structural constants a_1 and β; in the language of recent writing on this subject, a_1 and β remain "unidentified."

In connection with the possible use of "outside" information it is important to note that on occasion it might turn out to be in conflict with some of the probabilistic assumptions of the originally accepted theoretical model. Had, for example, the slope of the supply curve, a_2, been known, the original assumption concerning the form of the theoretical probability distribution would obviously have had to be given up. With q_t, p_t, and a_2 known, the magnitudes of the individual supply shifts v_t can be determined directly from equation (6); v_t can no longer be considered to represent a random variable. It has now to be treated like y_t, as a given independent variable. But the demand shift, u_t, can still be considered a normally distributed random variable. Equation (3) must now be interpreted as showing a linear relationship between two independent variables, y_t and v_t, and the dependent variable, p_t, subject to a normally distributed "error," $\dfrac{-v_t}{a_2 - a_1}$:

$$(11) \qquad p_t = \frac{\beta}{a_2 - a_1} y_t + \frac{1}{a_2 - a_1} u_t - \frac{v_t}{a_2 - a_1}$$

The unknown coefficients $\dfrac{\beta}{a_2 - a_1}$ and $\dfrac{1}{a_2 - a_1}$ of the two independent variables y_t and u_t can be again computed on the basis of the conventional least squares formulae. The ratio of the two determines β and a substitution of the known magnitude of a_2 into $\dfrac{1}{a_2 - a_1}$ gives a_1.

The carrying power of the statistical procedure can, however, also be increased without additional information through introduction of stronger assumptions, in particular through a more detailed specification of the probabilistic foundations of the basic theoretical model.

Instead of making the only assumption that the random supply and demand shifts u_t and v_t are distributed normally, one can assume for example that they are distributed not only normally but also independently from each other, i.e., that no correlation exists between the supply and the demand shifts. In the mathematical language of the joint distribution formula of u_t and v_t this additional assumption means that

$$(12) \qquad \Sigma u_t' v_t' = 0$$

i.e., that the sum total of the "cross product" of the deviations of the u_t and v_t from their respective means equals zero.[13]

---

[13] Strictly speaking, this assumption implies only that the expected value of that expression equals zero.

Equations (5) and (6) make it possible to translate this new condition into the terms of the observed prices, quantities, and the unknown structural constants. Multiplying the left- and the right-hand sides of the two equations and then summing up over all the price-quantity combinations, we have

$$(13) \qquad \Sigma u_t' v_t' = \Sigma q_t'^2 - a_1(\Sigma p_t' q_t' - a_2 \Sigma p_t'^2) - a_2 \Sigma p_t' q_t' = 0$$

This new condition, in conjunction with the previously derived relationships (9) and (10), constitutes a system of three equations just sufficient to compute the unknown magnitudes of the three empirical constants a_1, a_2, and β. A substitution of the value of a_2 as defined by (9) into (12) gives

$$(14) \qquad a_1 = \frac{\Sigma p_t' y_t' \, \Sigma (q_t')^2 - \Sigma q_t' y_t' \, \Sigma p_t' q_t'}{\Sigma p_t' q_t' \, \Sigma p_t' y_t' - \Sigma q_t' y_t' \, \Sigma (p_t')^2}$$

and this substituted in its turn into (10), determines the magnitude of β,

$$(15) \qquad \beta = \frac{(\Sigma p_t' y_t')^2 \Sigma (q_t')^2 - (\Sigma q_t' y_t') \Sigma p_t' q_t'}{\Sigma (y_t')^2 (\Sigma p_t' q_t' \, \Sigma p_t' y_t' - \Sigma q_t' y_t' \, \Sigma p_t')}$$

The theory of supply and demand underlying the above analysis is static; that is to say, the values of both unknowns q_t and p_t as entered into the two structural equations (1) and (2) belong to the same point of time, t. The general approach to the problem of statistical estimation remains unchanged even if the theoretical scheme is made dynamic. Let, for example, the structural demand equation (1) be modified by a substitution of the last year's price, p_{t-1}, for this year's income, y_t:

$$(16) \qquad q_t = a_1 p_t + \beta p_{t-1} + u_t$$

A corresponding substitution of p_t for y_t must then also be made in equations (3) and (4) of the reduced system. For purposes of estimation of the unknown theoretical constants, the relevant probabilistic properties of these two equations remain, however, the same as before. Considered at the point of time, t, the price p_{t-1} which prevailed in the previous point of time, $t-1$, is a fixed magnitude that cannot possibly be influenced by the random supply and demand shifts u_t and v_t which occur only at the later time, t. Thus all the statistical formulae derived from the original set of structural equations remain in force, provided the price p_{t-1} is substituted everywhere for the income y_t.

This elementary exercise in methodology of empirical supply and demand analysis brings out the two characteristic aspects of the new probabilistic reformulation of statistical analysis as applied to economics: the emphasis on what might be called the general equilibrium approach to the estimation of every individual constant and the predilection for stochastic models in which the error elements are associated with separate structural equations rather than with individual economic variables.

The first is an important recognition of a fundamental consistency requirement. So long as the econometrician's inductive procedure represents no more and no less than a mirrored image of his explanatory theory, he must in his capacity as statistician grapple simultaneously with as many structural relationships as are contained in his theoretical model. This means in particular that every modification in the basic theoretical model—a change, for instance, in only one of, say, twenty structural relationships—requires, except in some special cases, an entirely new set of statistical estimates of all the coefficients in all equations.

Having thus clearly formulated the internal logic of that particular approach to empirical analysis, Haavelmo and his school have forcefully brought out one of its principal practical limitations. The greater the complexity of the observed phenomena and the corresponding intricacy of the theoretical model required for their adequate explanation, the less reliance can be placed on indirect induction and the more emphasis will have to be put on direct observation and controlled experiment.

The simultaneous equation method of statistical estimation is fortunately well adapted to incorporation of the magnitudes of constants known through other sources of information. Thus it always can be used as a last resort for estimating empirical coefficients which cannot yet be evaluated on the basis of some less indirect and more reliable inductive procedures.

The traditional method of probabilizing a "pure" theoretical model is that of splitting all or at least some of the observed variables into two parts: their "true" values and the random errors of observation. Although not neglecting such inaccuracies of measurement as a possible source of disagreement between observed and theoretical relationships, Haavelmo and his school put much greater emphasis on another explanation of this discrepancy—the disturbances caused by the presence of some active variables not accounted for in the approximate or incomplete mathematical formulation of the true structural relationships. It is the same kind of discrepancy which occurs whenever an important independent variable has been neglected in multiple correlation analysis. Rather than stressing the problem of reducing the size of such unexplained residuals through systematic modification of the basic theoretical model, the proponents of the probabilistic approach to econometrics emphasize the necessity of first explicitly specifying and then consistently treating the joint distribution of all the random variables occurring in any complete set of structural relationships. While in application to proper errors of measurement the assumption of normal distribution seems to be quite justifiable, a similar assumption—as it is usually made—also in respect to random shifts ascribed to missing variables can be defended mainly—if not solely—on the grounds of convenience of computation.

IV

Econometric research with its basic orientation toward theoretically grounded statistical inquiry has a natural tendency to reflect the prevalent trends of general economic thought. In recent years the two principal influences were the Keynesian type of general equilibrium analysis and the dynamic business cycle theories.

The aggregative character of the Keynesian system, its actual or apparent ability to cut through the maze of individual facts and figures and reduce the description of the basic economic reality to a small number of structural relationships involving only a few strategic variables, makes it particularly suitable for statistical application. The characteristic vagueness of its original formulation provides room for many different interpretations and thus makes possible the choice of a particular theoretical model to suit the available store of primary statistical information.

Dynamic relationships provide a solid logical basis for quantitative prognostication. Combinations of structural equations containing lagged relationships between the values of independent variables lead naturally to formal solutions which make it possible to explain, i.e., to predict, their future changes.

Both the general equilibrium approach and the use of dynamic relationships—it must be stated at the outset—were introduced into econometric analysis a long time ago by Tinbergen. None of the similar studies published after his *Business Cycles in the United States*[14] can vie with it either in conceptual breadth or in scope of factual statistical coverage.[15]

The statistical study of the consumption function—i.e., of the income-expenditure and the corresponding income-saving relationship—has pro-

---

[14] See exact reference in note 10, p. 391.
[15] In this connection it should be mentioned that Keynes in a lengthy review of Tinbergen's volumes revealed a decidedly skeptical attitude not only toward Tinbergen's findings in particular but also this type of econometric research in general.
J. M. Keynes, "Official Papers: The Statistical Testing of Business Cycle Theories," *Economic Journal*, September 1939, XLIX, pp. 558–569. See also J. Tinbergen, "One Method of Statistical Research: A Reply," *ibid.*, March 1940, L, pp. 141–154.

ceeded, for example, in recent years along the same two parallel lines as before.

One approach relates the aggregate disposable consumers' income to total expenditures. A linear least square regression relationship is usually fitted to a set of annual national-income-expenditure figures.[16] Frequently corrections are introduced for changes in costs of living, population growth or even for variations in general business conditions.[17]

The other is the budget studies approach. Conceptually it goes one step behind the national totals and breaks up both the income and the expenditure figures by income levels of the individual recipients.

A statistical relationship is first established between the income and the expenditure (or saving) variations from income class to income class. Weighed in accordance with the total number of recipients belonging to each income class, this function gives the corresponding total of national expenditures.[18]

The two other major structural relationships of Keynes' general theory —the investment, or, as it was originally called, the marginal efficiency of capital schedule, and the liquidity preference function—have still received relatively little special attention among the econometricians. Mordecai Ezekiel's attempt to derive a statistical investment schedule led to an interesting methodological controversy with Lawrence R. Klein.[19]

Turning to the recent work aimed at construction of empirical general equilibrium systems, we find it convenient to make a distinction between so-called National Budget models and general equilibrium models proper.

The former represent an outgrowth of national income statistics which, through successive steps of progressive refinement and differentiation, were developed into more or less intricate systems of national bookkeeping.[20] Although cast occasionally in formal mathematical terms, these schemes—as any other accounting systems—involve primarily a consistent

---

[16] See, for example, Jacob L. Mosak, "Forecasting Postwar Demand," *Econometrica*, January 1945, XIII.

[17] Arthur Smithies, "Forecasting Postwar Demand," *Econometrica*, January 1945, XIII; W. S. Woytinsky, "Relationship Between Consumers' Income, Savings, and Disposable Income," *Review of Economic Statistics*, November 1946, XXVIII; Louis H. Bean, "Relationship of Disposable Income and the Business-cycle Analysis," *ibid*.

[18] See, for example, Jerome Cornfield, W. Duane Evans, and Marvin Hoffenberg, "Full Employment Patterns, 1950," *Monthly Labor Review*, February and March 1947, LX, pp. 163–191, 420–433.

[19] Mordecai Ezekiel, "Statistical Investigation of Saving, Consumption and Investment," *American Economic Review*, March 1942, XXXII; Lawrence R. Klein, "Pitfalls in Statistical Determination of Investment Schedule," *Econometrica*, July–October 1943, XI.

[20] See, for example, *National Budgets for Full Employment*, National Planning Association (Washington, 1945); "Forecasting Postwar Demand," papers by Arthur Smithies, S. Morris Livingston and Jacob L. Mosak, *Econometrica*, January 1945, XIII; also a survey article by Albert G. Hart, "Model-Building and Fiscal Policy," *American Economic Review*, September 1945, XXXV.

use of definitional propositions ("Net National Income = Gross National Product — Federal Corporate Income Tax — Federal Excise Tax — State and Local Business Taxes — Depreciation and Depletion") not subject to empirical testing. Besides conventional projections of past time trends, each such budget model includes, however, at least one causal relationship between separate accounting items. The one which is always present is some sort of an empirical consumption or saving function.

The National Budget models usually contain many more dependent variables than they have equations and are used mainly as an *ex ante* device to check the internal consistency of various alternative assumptions concerning the possible future magnitudes of these variables.[21]

Much more ambitious and, from the point of view of potential scientific development, more promising are the dynamic general equilibrium systems conceived along the lines of Tinbergen's original empirical work. Klein's models,[22] published a short time ago, are good examples of the current state of this type of econometric analysis, much of it centering now in the Cowles Commission for Research in Economics at the University of Chicago. The general approach is essentially the same as that described in some detail in the second part of the present survey. The basic structural equations are of two kinds, the "economic behavior" equations and the definitional. The first describe causal interrelationships between variables and each of them contains a different random error term analogous to the supply and demand shift discussed above. The definitional equations simply explain the terminology; they do not contain, for obvious reasons, any error terms. The system is complete; that is, the number of independent structural equations is just sufficient to determine the magnitudes of all the unknown variables. Completeness, it should be noticed, can always be achieved by shifting any surplus variables from the category of unknowns into that of "given" or, as they are often called, "exogenous" magnitudes. Introduction of additional structural equations is associated on the other hand with transfer of exogenous variables into the category of "endogenous." Some of the behavior equations are dynamic, i.e., they describe relationships between variables belonging to different points of time. All equations are linear.

The factual information used for estimation of unknown theoretical constants consists of statistical data describing the observed changes in

---

[21] In this respect the budget model technique bears considerable resemblance to the so-called method of balances used by Russian economic planners, which consists in matching the prospective supply of particular commodities against the sum total of various types of expected demand.

[22] Lawrence R. Klein, "The Use of Econometric Models as a Guide to Economic Policy," *Econometrica*, April 1947, XV.

the magnitudes of all the "endogenous" and "exogenous" variables. The method of estimation is that of least squares applied to equations of the reduced system (see Section III above).

The unknown magnitude of an endogenous variable for any year, t, can be computed by inserting in the appropriate equation of the reduced system the given (i.e., observed or assumed) values of the exogenous variables and the values of the unknown for the previous periods, $t - 1, t - 2$, etc.

Whenever possible the final numerical results are stated within the limits of a certain probable error of estimate. These errors are stated on the assumption that the basic theory, as described by the original system of structural equations, is correct.

Klein presents three different computations based on three alternative sets of structural equations: "The reader is free to choose among the models, all of which rest on different hypotheses. . . . On the basis of a limited number of observations available for testing different economic models . . . it is not yet possible to select a unique model."[23]

Gerhard Tintner[24] makes the next logical step in the direction indicated by the above quotations. He starts with a set of statistical data describing simultaneous changes in a group of economic variables, makes certain probabilistic assumptions concerning the errors of observation, and then proceeds to determine by formal statistical reasoning how many and what significant independent linear relationships can be found to exist between the variables involved. The problem of identification of the individual equations thus found with some kind of preconceived structural relationships is then tackled separately on the basis of common sense considerations. Its solution is somewhat facilitated by a preliminary decision to allow some of the unknown empirical relationships to include only certain particular variables and not others. In principle an analytical procedure which lets a large group of heterogeneous but simultaneously observed facts "speak for themselves" inevitably confronts the investigator with the subsequent task of giving meaningful interpretation to whatever these facts might be saying.

The modern school of econometricians certainly does not entirely ignore the presence of that serious methodological problem. The very title of Tjalling C. Koopmans' long review[25] of the recently published monumental volume, *Measuring Business Cycles* by Arthur F. Burns and

---

[23] *Ibid.*, p. 113.

[24] Gerhard Tintner, "Multiple Regression for Systems of Equations," *Econometrica*, January 1946, XIV.

[25] Tjalling C. Koopmans, "Measurement without Theory," *Review of Economic Statistics*, August 1947, XXIX.

Wesley C. Mitchell,[26] testifies to the existence of such awareness. Following the well-established tradition of the National Bureau of Economic Research, the authors approach their task in a thoroughly empiristic spirit. Rather than aim at statistical application or empirical verification of complete or partial business cycle theories, they present a series of systematically conceived measurements of various aspects of cyclical movements as it is displayed in a long array of different economic time series. Koopmans' emphatic criticism is directed mainly against the absence in the background of a definite, complete, and stochastically formulated structural model. On the basis of Klein's experience one might add that even the use of modern methods of statistical inference would, in the present state of economic knowledge, hardly make possible any decisive choice between two or more alternative and significantly different theoretical hypotheses.

The difference between the direct empiricism of the Mitchell-Burns reference cycle technique and the sophisticated statistical positivism of the Cowles Commission school should not be overemphasized. Both, although recognizing the importance of using "outside" information, derive their explanatory schemes mainly from observations of the very same data which they are trying to explain.

A different approach to empirical general equilibrium analysis has been developed by the present writer.[27] Its theoretical orientation has greater kinship with classical Walrasian than with the aggregative Keynesian type of approach. For determination of the actual magnitudes of the relevant empirical constants it relies on direct observation rather than on indirect methods of probabilistic inference such as were described above.

A large statistical "input-output" table describing the qualitative interrelationships between all the various branches of production, transportation, distribution, and consumption for one particular year constituted the factual basis of subsequent analytical procedures. The entries in this table are arranged in a checkerboard fashion, each row and the corresponding column of figures bearing the name of a separate industry—Grain Farming, Steel Works and Rolling Mills, Railroads, and so on. The entries along any one row show the distribution of the total output of the particular industry among all the other branches of the national economy. Thus the figures entered in the "Steel Works and Rolling Mills" row represent the amounts of the product of this industry directly

---

[26] National Bureau of Economic Research (New York, 1946).

[27] Wassily W. Leontief, *The Structure of American Economy, 1919–1929* (Cambridge, 1941); also articles in the following issues of the *Quarterly Journal of Economics*: February 1944, February 1946, and November 1946, Vols. XLVIII, L, and LI.

absorbed by, say, Grain Farming, by the Railroads, by the Automobile Industry, etc.

The last entry in each row shows the total output of the industry (in this particular example this would be the total output of Steel Works and Rolling Mills), i.e., it represents the sum total of all the other entries along the same row. Government, Households, and Foreign Countries are treated as separate industries, that is, as separate branches of the economy. If read by columns the same figures show the quantities of the various kinds of inputs absorbed by each individual industry. The Steel Works and Rolling Mills column shows the amount of coal obtained by this industry from Coal Mining, the amount of Transportation received from Railroads, and so on down the column to the amount of labor (labor hours) obtained from the Households, which are also treated as a separate "Industry."

Detailed input-output tables describing the inter-industrial relationships within the industries have been constructed for the years 1919, 1929, and 1939, the latter compiled by a special Inter-industrial Relationships Unit in the Bureau of Labor Statistics.

The amounts of the products of each one of the other sections of the economy absorbed by any particular industry (i.e., the magnitudes of the entries in one particular column of the input-output table) depend, first, upon the total level of its own output and, second, upon the quantity of each kind of input absorbed per unit of that output. The subsequent theoretical analysis is based on the fundamental assumption that the latter relationships are technologically determined and thus can be treated as structural constants. Given the actual magnitudes of these "technical coefficients," a system of linear equations can be set up describing the interdependence between the outputs of all the separate branches of the national economy. This system makes it possible to compute, for example, the direct and indirect dependence of the output (and the corresponding labor requirements) of any one industry upon the final (i.e., consumer or investment) demand for the product of any other industry.

The same set of technical input-coefficients determines also the price or rather the price-wage-profits structure of the national economy. It can be described in terms of a system of simultaneous value-equations—one for each industry. The price of any one kind of output equals its unit costs of production augmented by the unit profits. The *unit* costs are nothing but the sum total of the technical input coefficients of the particular industry, each multiplied by the price of the respective cost factor. Solved for the price of any one commodity, this system of equations makes it possible, for example, to determine the direct and indirect dependence of one particular price on the wage and profit rates prevailing in all the different branches of the economy.

The apparent difficulty of handling very large numbers of simultaneous equations—until recently the most widely cited obstacle to construction of (relatively) non-aggregative empirical general equilibrium systems—has been easily overcome through the use of modern large-scale computing machinery.

In treating technical input coefficients as independent structural parameters, this approach assumes them to be independent of the prices of the respective cost factors and thus eliminates from this particular general equilibrium model the "substitution effect" of the marginal productivity theory. This can be considered to be its fundamental weakness.

Since, as mentioned above, much of the present-day quantitative analysis is being conducted in terms of summary series such as the Net National Income, Total Output, or the Average Price and Wage Level, etc., one of the special issues of econometric analysis to elicit a considerable amount of discussion in the last few years is the question of aggregation. To be sure, under the name of the index number problem, it has been known for a very long time; Keynes' *General Theory* and the subsequent attempts (some of which were discussed above) to construct empirical general equilibrium systems made it a subject of critical importance.

The fundamental argument of modern economic theory runs in terms of individual households, separate enterprises, and a third element—which can no longer be neglected—the government. Much of the statistical data to the interpretation of which the theoretical economic models are supposed to be applied are available, however, only in the form of large totals and broad averages. It is only natural that in some of the pioneering studies in the field of econometric analysis theoretical relationships which were meant to hold within an individual enterprise or a separate household were directly applied to large statistical aggregates. Paul Douglas, for example, in his *Theory of Wages* and the series of subsequent studies, applied the marginal productivity model directly to industry as a whole. He obviously transferred the theory of income division between capital and labor within an enterprise to the analysis of the total shares of the same two factors on the national scale. A series of critical papers, the first of which appeared in 1943,[28] have shown that the mar-

---

[28] M. W. Reder, "An Alternative Interpretation of the Cobb-Douglas Function," *Econometrica*, July–October 1943, XI; see also: M. Bronfenbrenner, "Production Function, Cobb-Douglas, Interfirm, Intrafirm," *ibid.*, January 1944, XII; Marschak and Andrews, "Random Simultaneous Equations and the Theory of Production," *ibid.*, July–October 1944, XII. A general survey of all of the work done by Douglas and his followers on aggregative statistical production functions is given in his Presidential

ginal productivity theory cannot by reason of simple analogy be applied directly to aggregate totals, of even similar and physically homogeneous factors of production.

By the time this discussion of Douglas' production function was drawing to its conclusion, the aggregative character of the Keynesian theories used as a basis of various statistical general equilibrium models was recognized as an issue of considerable immediate importance. A number of methodological articles on the subject were soon published in quick succession.[29] The theoretical conditions for admissible aggregation thus far derived are so stringent that their consistent application would have put under ban most of the simple statistical general equilibrium models. The entire question is, however, still wide open. Introduction of probabilistic considerations is likely to result in a more favorable final verdict. Marschak and Andrews, for example, assume some of the basic structural technological constants to be the same for all individual enterprises and take the inter-firm difference to be the result of random causes.

A general survey of the main new developments in the field of econometrics must of necessity leave out a large amount of significant work accomplished in this country during the recent years in all the principal fields of quantitative empirical analysis. Questions of foreign trade and of industrial costs, highly technical issues which come up in the study of income distribution and explanation of the location of industries, old problems of demand analysis and new problems arising in connection with current issues of economic policies have been approached and their solution has been advanced through combined application of the tools of modern theoretical and statistical analysis. Much of that work has been done by government economists in response to the needs of public administration and by business economists in the service of private enterprise. Much and very likely most of it never will be made public, partly because it was deemed to be routine and partly because it was considered to be of too great immediate importance. Both reasons are evidence of the

---

Address before the American Economic Association: Paul H. Douglas, "Are There Laws of Production?" *American Economic Review*, March 1948, XXXVIII, pp. 1–42.

[29] Lawrence R. Klein, "Macroeconomics and the Theory of Rational Behavior," *Econometrica*, April 1946, XIV; *idem*, "Remarks on the Theory of Aggregation," *ibid.*, October 1946, XIV; Kenneth May, "The Aggregation Problem for a One Industry Model," *ibid.*, October 1946, XIV; Shou Shan Pu, "A Note on Macroeconomics," *ibid.*, October 1946, XIV; Kenneth May, "Technological Change and Aggregation," *ibid.*, January 1947, XV; W. W. Leontief, "Introduction to a Theory of the Internal Structure of Functional Relationships," *ibid.*, October 1947, XV.

The problem of aggregative variables was clearly posed in a much earlier paper by Francis W. Dresch, "Index Numbers and the General Economic Equilibrium," *Bulletin of the American Mathematical Society*, February 1938, XL.

fundamental recognition of the econometric approach as an indispensable device of practical economic analysis.

In the first, introductory part of this survey it was observed that the outstanding developments of the last years lie primarily in the realm of methodology rather than in the direction of factual analysis. Certain signs seem to indicate that this phase is now drawing to its close and that the years immediately ahead will witness new accomplishments in many fields of applied studies.

The predominantly descriptive statistical publications of the National Bureau of Economic Research and various other private and governmental agencies fall outside the scope of this survey. One cannot overemphasize, however, the dependence of the analytical and admittedly more speculative kind of research described above on the carefully sifted and critically presented factual information contained in such exemplary studies as Simon Kuznets' *National Product in Wartime*,[30] Solomon Fabricant's *Employment in Manufacturing, 1899–1939, An Analysis of Its Relation to the Volume of Production*,[31] or *Income from Independent Professional Practice*[32] by Milton Friedman and Simon Kuznets. The latter monograph significantly contains a chapter on "Demand and Supply Curves for Professional Services."

The hope described shortly before his death by Irving Fisher, the founder and Grand Old Man of the Econometric Society, as "one of the great ambitions" of his life seems to be nearing its fulfillment as quantitative empirical research contributes its ever-mounting share toward "making economics into a genuine science."[33]

---

[30] National Bureau of Economic Research (New York, 1945).
[31] National Bureau of Economic Research (New York, 1942).
[32] National Bureau of Economic Research (New York, 1945).
[33] "Irving Fisher at Eighty," *Econometrica*, April 1947, XV. Professor Fisher died on April 29, 1947.

12

SOCIALIST ECONOMICS

Abram Bergson

In this survey, attention is focused on recent theoretic studies of the economic problems of socialism and, insofar as they bear on these problems, on recent inquiries in the cognate field of welfare economics. From one point of view, these writings, which are notably abstract, might be considered as providing a theoretic basis for the work of a Central Planning Board seeking to rationalize the planning system of a socialist state. Reference is of course to a socialist state which has not yet reached the era of unlimited abundance; in other words, one which still faces, like its capitalist predecessor, the fundamental problem of allocating scarce resources among alternative uses. In the light of whatever ends the Board serves, its task is to assure as far as practicable that the available resources are utilized to the optimum advantage. Our chief aim here is to appraise in summary fashion the contributions which have been made to the solution of the Board's task.

Among the studies to be considered, of course, are the recent contributions to the debate, provoked originally by the famous article of Mises,[1] as to whether socialism can work at all, and how well. By now it seems generally agreed that the argument on these questions advanced by Mises himself, at least according to one interpretation, is without much force. We shall try here to arrive at an understanding as to just what has been settled and just what remains unsettled in this debate.

Unfortunately, it does not seem possible to refer also to recent contributions to the discussion of the other basic issue in the larger controversy over socialism, that concerning planning and freedom. In view of the special circumstances in which the Russian Revolution has unfolded, the experience of that country perhaps is not so conclusive on the question of planning and freedom as is sometimes supposed. It must be conceded too that the emphasis that critics of socialism have lately placed on this issue sometimes has the appearance of a tactical maneuver, to bolster a cause

---

[1] "Die Wirtschaftsrechnung im sozialistischen Gemeinwesen," *Archiv für Sozialwissenschaften*, April 1920, XLVII, pp. 86–121. A translation, to which references are made in this survey, has been published in F. A. Hayek, ed., *Collectivist Economic Planning* (London, 1935).

which Mises' theories have been found inadequate to sustain. But certainly arguments revolving around the question of planning and freedom must be given the most serious consideration; without reference to them, one obviously is in no position to strike a balance for socialism.

I. The Ends

Of the writings surveyed here, a considerable number are concerned with one large problem: to define (in a sense that will become clear) the allocation of resources that would be an optimum. On this problem, the basic works were all published some years ago. Mention is to be made particularly of the writings of Pareto[2] and Barone[3] in the field of socialist economics and of Marshall[4] and Pigou[5] in the field of welfare economics. These studies provide all the essentials of a solution to the question just posed. In more recent studies, however, much has been done to clarify and elaborate the analysis.

Marshall, Pigou, Pareto, and Barone on "Ends." The definition of the optimum allocation involves, for one thing, the formulation of a scale of values, on the basis of which the alternative uses of resources are to be evaluated. In the present context, this scale of values might be considered as representing the ends which the Central Planning Board serves. In order to describe the recent doctrinal developments relating to this aspect of the analysis, it is necessary to refer briefly to the formulations in the basic works just mentioned.

In the case of Marshall and Pigou, the needed scale of values is given immediately in their proverbial conception of "welfare" as the sum of the utilities of the individual households in the community.[6] It is supposed that for different persons of equal sensitivity the marginal utility of income is the same when incomes are equal. The optimum allocation of resources, then, is one which maximizes welfare in this sense. One condi-

---

[2] V. Pareto, *Cours d'Économie Politique*, Vol. II (Lausanne, 1897), pp. 90 ff., 364 ff.

[3] E. Barone, "Il ministerio della produzione nello stato colletivista," *Giornale degli Economisti e Rivista di Statistica*, September and October 1908, Serie 2a, XXXVII, pp. 267-293, 391-414. A translation has been published under the title "The Ministry of Production in the Collectivist State," in F. A. Hayek, *op. cit.* References made to this paper are to the translation.

[4] A. Marshall, *Principles of Economics,* 1st ed. (London, 1890); 8th ed. (London, 1920).

[5] A. C. Pigou, *Economics of Welfare,* 1st ed. (London, 1920); 4th ed. (London, 1934).

[6] For references to the pertinent passages in the works of Marshall and Pigou, see A. Bergson, "A Reformulation of Certain Aspects of Welfare Economics," *Quarterly Journal of Economics,* February 1938, LII, pp. 310-334.

tion for the attainment of the optimum is immediately apparent: incomes must be equal.

In the case of Pareto and Barone, the criterion for an optimum allocation of resources is somewhat more complex: it must be impossible by any reallocation of resources to enhance the welfare of one household without reducing that of another.[7] If a reallocation which would lead to this result were possible, it is reasoned, the resources of the community could be used to better advantage by making it; in the optimum such opportunities already must have been completely exploited.

For Pareto, this formulation had one outstanding virtue: it is possible to define the optimum allocation of resources without assuming (as Marshall did) that welfare is the sum of the utilities of individual households. This assumption Pareto considered objectionable, on the ground that the utilities are incommensurate:

nous ne pouvons ni comparer ni sommer celles-ci, car nous ignorons le rapport des unités en lesquelles elles sont exprimées.

As Pareto and Barone recognized, however, their formulation provides a necessary but not sufficient criterion for the definition of the optimum allocation. The question remains, how to decide between different allocations which make some households better off and others worse off, i.e., where there is a redistribution of income. This matter Pareto disposes of simply by assuming that incomes are distributed "suivant la regle qu'il plaira d'adopter." Similarly, Barone supposes that the distribution of incomes is on the basis of some "ethical criterion."

ALTERNATIVE ENDS. One of the recent doctrinal developments concerning ends involves the introduction into the analysis of variants of the scales of values of Marshall and Pigou and Pareto and Barone. All these writers, evidently, consider the case where alternative uses of resources are evaluated on the basis of the preferences of individual households— the preferences of the households, as they see them, are to count. If such a scale of values is in operation, consumers are "sovereign." Interest has focused recently on the variants of this case that arise where the Board itself undertakes to determine, to a greater or less extent, what is good for consumers and allocates resources on this basis.

An important precedent for the consideration of this variant is found in the well known argument of Pigou that consumers do not correctly weight their own interests in decisions on savings; that, as a result of a

---

[7] See *ibid.* This is the verbal equivalent of a mathematical criterion which Pareto introduced. As the writer points out in the article just cited, Pareto himself misinterpreted his criterion; the correct interpretation given here is due to Barone.

telescopic faculty, they tend to undervalue future as compared with equivalent present satisfactions. From this it follows at once that if consumers are sovereign in respect of questions of saving and investment, the aggregate saving will be less than is socially desirable. There is a case for disregarding consumers' preferences in this sphere.

This particular argument has recently been extended to socialist economics. Thus Dobb[8] now argues that the socialist Board must disregard consumers' preferences on the question of savings and observe instead the principle that future satisfactions be valued equally with equivalent present satisfactions. Lange[9] introduces the same postulate.

Under this assumption, as we understand it, the Board would value equally a marginal "dollar" of present and future income, provided that income is constant. To the extent that income is expected to rise as a result of the investments undertaken, presumably the marginal dollar in the future still would be valued less than in the present. This would result from the operation of the law of diminishing utility within each income period and has nothing to do with the telescopic faculty referred to by Pigou. Thus, in deciding on the amount of investment the Board presumably would strike a balance between two opposing considerations: on the one hand, the fact just mentioned that with a rising level of income the marginal dollar in the future would be worth less than in the present; on the other hand, the fact that by investing a marginal dollar now an agio might be earned as a result of the supposedly greater productivity of roundabout processes.

Dobb[10] envisages that under socialism there will be many other exceptions to the principle of consumers' sovereignty. He considers that consumers are to a greater or less extent irrational in many decisions other than that on saving; and furthermore, that in many cases (e.g., education, health care), even if the consumer chooses rationally from his own point of view, his decision may not be in accord with the social interest. Dobb refers also in this same connection to goods (e.g., police protection) which by their very nature cannot possibly be allocated among households in accord with their individual preferences.[11]

---

[8] M. Dobb, *Political Economy and Capitalism* (New York, 1940), pp. 298–299, 311–312.

[9] "On the Economic Theory of Socialism," in B. Lippincott, ed., *On the Economic Theory of Socialism* (Minneapolis, Minnesota, 1938), p. 90 ff. This is a revision of two articles which were published originally in the *Review of Economic Studies*, October 1936 and February 1937, IV, pp. 53–71, 123–142. Unless otherwise indicated references are to the revision.

[10] *Op. cit.*, p. 309 ff. See also *idem*, "Economic Theory and the Problems of a Socialist Economy," *Economic Journal*, December, 1933, XLIII, pp. 588–598.

[11] One other case to which Dobb refers as indicating the need for a departure from consumers' sovereignty requires special comment. This is the case where the individual

If a free market prevailed for consumers' goods generally, the implication is that commodities such as are covered by the foregoing considerations should be distributed communally in the form of "social services." The question of the types of goods that should be distributed in this fashion also is discussed by Dickinson.[12]

THE WELFARE FUNCTION. Another recent development, for which the present writer is largely responsible,[13] has been to clarify the question of the number and nature of the decisions on ends required to formulate the needed scale of values. This important question is left in doubt by the various writings, both old and new, that have been cited.

From the formulation of Marshall and Pigou, and of recent writers who follow them in using the utility calculus, one might gain the impression that in reality only one such decision is involved, that is the decision to maximize "welfare." Once this decision is taken it would seem that all else is determined, i.e., it remains only to settle, presumably by empirical investigation, whether consumers do or do not value future satisfactions "accurately," whether or not they are "rational" in one or another kind of choice, whether they are indeed equally "sensitive" or if not just how their "sensitivity" varies, and so on.

Evidently, however, these implications are rather startling, and it is not

---

consumer's desire for a thing depends on the fact of others possessing or not possessing it. "Conspicuous consumption" is the familiar example of this sort of situation.

As Paul Samuelson observes (*Foundations of Economic Analysis,* [Cambridge, Mass., 1947], p. 224), the welfare analysis as it usually is formulated assumes that the individual's preferences depend only on the amounts of goods he consumes and not on the amounts consumed by others. In the case of "conspicuous consumption," one must restate the principle of consumers' sovereignty so that the utility of any household depends not only on the amounts of goods it consumes but also on the amounts consumed by others.

The Board might consider, however, as Dobb implies, that because of their "conventional" character consumers' preferences in this case should be overruled. If the Board did so, there would indeed be a departure from the principle of consumers' sovereignty.

But of more interest perhaps is the fact, which Dobb does not bring out, that even if the Board determines to adhere to the principle of consumers' sovereignty in this case (where the tastes of different households are interdependent), there would be very real difficulties in implementing it in practice. It can be shown that in a free market where consumers take prices as parameters (see in Section II, below, the discussion of the distinction between consumers' sovereignty and freedom of choice), the allocation of goods as between consumers could never be an optimum one. If an effective barter market could be arranged, where consumers could trade among themselves, however, it would seem that in theory the optimum might be attained. The individual household in the former case (the free market) would disregard and in the latter case (barter) take into account the effects on its welfare of changes in the consumption pattern of other households which might be induced by its own choices.

The work of Samuelson, referred to above, unfortunately reached us too late to be taken fully into account in this essay. On a number of points, Samuelson presents a more exact formulation of the welfare analysis than hitherto has been available.

[12] H. D. Dickinson, *Economics of Socialism* (Oxford, 1939), p. 51 ff.

[13] Abram Bergson, *op. cit.* See also O. Lange, "Foundations of Welfare Economics," *Econometrica,* July–October, 1942, X, pp. 215–228.

very surprising that followers of Marshall and Pigou are in doubt as to their validity. This I take it is what Dobb[14] and Kahn[15] after him wish to convey when they express the suspicion that the welfare that is being maximized may be entirely "subjective" after all (like "a black cat in a dark room").

Pareto and Barone, as has been mentioned, are explicit that the question of income distribution must be the subject of a decision on ends. In view of their silence on the question of consumers' sovereignty, however, one inevitably is led to wonder how *this* question is settled. Uncertainty on this score is only enhanced by recent efforts, such as that by Hicks,[16] to establish by use of the Pareto-Barone formulation welfare principles that are in some sense "positive" or "scientific." By implication, such principles would require no decisions on ends for their derivation.

In dealing with this whole question, the present writer has found it useful to introduce into the analysis a welfare function, W, the value of which is understood to depend on all the variables that might be considered as affecting welfare: the amounts of each and every kind of good consumed by and service performed by each and every household, the amount of each and every kind of capital investment undertaken, and so on. The welfare function is understood initially to be entirely general in character; its shape is determined by the specific decisions on ends that are introduced into the analysis. Given the decisions on ends, the welfare function is transformed into a scale of values for the evaluation of alternative uses of resources.

On this basis, it has been argued, decisions on the following questions on ends are involved in the welfare formulations that have been outlined:

(a) CONSUMERS' SOVEREIGNTY. The question of whether and to what extent consumers will be sovereign, as the writer sees it, involves one such decision or a complex of such decisions. If one understands "welfare" to *mean* that consumers are sovereign, of course, the question is already decided when it is determined to maximize welfare; but obviously nothing in substance is gained by this type of implicit theorizing, in which many economists seem to engage. Whether by definition or otherwise a decision on ends must be introduced. It seems clear, furthermore, that differences in opinion as to consumers' "rationality," the accuracy of their evaluation of future satisfactions, etc., will often turn on divergences in ethics; the extent to which such divergences might be resolved by empirical investi-

---

[14] "Economic Theory and the Problems of a Socialist Economy," *loc. cit.*, p. 594.
[15] R. F. Kahn, "Some Notes on Ideal Output," *Economic Journal*, March 1935, XLV, pp. 1–35.
[16] J. R. Hicks, "Foundations of Welfare Economics," *Economic Journal*, December 1939, XLIX, pp. 696–712.

gation is a question on which the philosophers themselves seem to differ.

If the decision is in favor of consumers' sovereignty, the welfare function may be expressed in the form,

$$(1) \quad W = F (U^1, U^2, U^3, \ldots \ldots).$$

Here U^1, U^2, U^3, etc., represent the utilities of the individual households as they see them and W, the welfare of the community, is understood to be an increasing function of these utilities. The welfare of the community, then, is constant, increases or decreases, according to whether the utilities of the individual households are constant, increase or decrease. If the decision is against consumers' sovereignty, the welfare function must be expressed by a formula in which the Board's own preference scales are substituted for the utility functions of the individual households.

Evidently, the formula in (1) is nothing more nor less than a generalization of the Marshall-Pigou formulation; according to the latter W is the *sum* of the utilities U^1, U^2, U^3, etc. Evidently, also, to maximize W would satisfy the criterion of Pareto and Barone. Indeed, this function might be considered as an explicit formulation of the scale of values implicit in their criterion.

(b) INCOME DISTRIBUTION. The writer follows Pareto in thinking that utilities are incommensurable,[17] and agrees with Robbins[18] that because of this, principles of income distribution cannot be deduced from the utility calculus either by the rules of logic or by empirical demonstration. The familiar appeal (in which Lerner[19] and Lange[20] now join) that we must "assume" the comparability of utilities in order to establish a basis for normative precepts does not seem to us to meet the issue.

But all of this says nothing more than that here too a decision on ends is involved. As the writer sees it, ends are essentially principles for the evaluation of alternatives that otherwise are incommensurable. That is why an *evaluation* is needed. Once an evaluation is made, the alternatives are indeed commensurable. Given the ethical principle according to which incomes are to be distributed, the marginal welfare per "dollar" for different households necessarily is the same *in the light of this principle* when the distribution is realized.

---

[17] Their incommensurability is reflected in the appearance of a dimensional constant in empirical measures of utility.

[18] L. H. Robbins, *Nature and Significance of Economic Science*, 2nd ed. (London, 1935), Ch. VI; *idem*, "Inter-personal Comparison of Utility," *Economic Journal*, December 1938, XLVIII, pp. 635–641. The latter article replies to R. F. Harrod, "Scope and Method of Economics," *ibid.*, September 1938, XLVIII, pp. 383–412.

[19] A. P. Lerner, *Economics of Control* (New York, 1944), pp. 24–25.

[20] *On the Economic Theory of Socialism*, p. 100, note 54.

(c) INTERRELATIONS IN THE WELFARE OF DIFFERENT HOUSEHOLDS. Insofar as Marshall and Pigou conceive of welfare as the sum of the utilities of different households, their formulation involves an additional decision on ends, namely, one to the effect that the interrelations in the utilities of the different households have a zero social value. The magnitude of the change in the community's welfare resulting from a change in the budget position of any one family does not depend at all on the living standards enjoyed by other households.

For purposes of analyzing the optimum allocation, however, it is unnecessary to refer to this special and obviously very dubious case; it has been shown that all propositions of interest can be deduced from the more general function in the formula given above. The demonstration of this point would seem to be one of the more interesting doctrinal gains resulting from the introduction of the welfare function into the analysis.

Pareto's criticism of the Marshall-Pigou formulation, then, misses the point. From a purely formal point of view the objection to the Marshall-Pigou formulation is not (as Pareto implied) that incommensurate utilities are added, but that their aggregation involves a redundant and indeed dubious assumption.[21]

In the writings under review, the principle of consumers' sovereignty usually is interpreted as referring to the household's preferences not only as between consumers' goods but also as between jobs. Hence, the utility functions in the formula should be considered as representing for the different households the balance of utilities from consumption and of disutilities from work done.

It has been found convenient, following Pareto and Barone, to distinguish between the "wage" which a household earns, and its "income" which differs from the wage by the amount of a social "dividend" or "tax," as the case may be. On balance the aggregate amount of the dividends and taxes for all households equals the aggregate amount of "profits" (including "interest" and "rent," if charged) available to the community after provision is made for capital accumulation and communal consumption. Given the wages of the different households, a decision on the dividend or tax is, in effect, a decision as to the optimum

---

[21] As Samuelson makes clear (op. cit., pp. 224–226), the assumption of the independence of the contribution of each household to total welfare is distinct from and additional to the assumption, referred to above, p. 415, note 11, regarding the independence of the *structure of tastes* of the different households. All that independence in the latter sense implies is that each household's marginal rates of substitution depend only on the quantities of goods it consumes and not at all on the quantities consumed by other households; quite conceivably this condition might obtain at the same time that the household felt its total utility affected by general changes in living standards of other households.

distribution of income, i.e., the distribution for which the marginal welfare per "dollar" is the same for different households.

For purposes of analyzing the distribution of income in terms of these two income categories ("wages" and the "dividend" or "tax"), our impression is that it is necessary to introduce into the analysis one further assumption on ends, which is not entirely clear in the writings under review. The assumption is that the comparative marginal welfare per "dollar" for different households would not be changed by any change in the composition of their budgets (including changes in work done) for which their own total utilities are unchanged.[22] This requirement, a fundamental one, assures that the decision on the distribution of income is consistent with the principle of consumers' sovereignty. As we shall see, it means in effect that differences in disutilities must be taken into account in the distribution of income.

II. Optimum Conditions

Given the scale of values, the definition of the optimum allocation is formulated in these terms. In accord with familiar theoretic procedures, technical knowledge and tastes are taken as given, i.e., it is assumed that they are not affected by the changes under consideration; also the question of the resources to be allocated to research is left out of account. On this basis it is possible to derive from the given ends a series of conditions ("equations") which must be satisfied if the optimum allocation is to be achieved. The optimum conditions are sufficient in number to determine the amounts of each and every sort of goods and services allocated to each and every use (the "unknowns"). Thus, if the scale of values implied by the ends were known in complete detail (that is, if all the utility functions were known), and detailed information were available on techniques and on the stocks of resources on hand, it would be possible at least theoretically to solve this system of equations for the concrete values of all the unknowns.[23]

In respect of this aspect of the analysis, recent writings have been concerned chiefly to formulate explicitly the optimum conditions (which are not in every case clearly stated in the works of Marshall, Pigou, Pareto, and Barone) and to develop the analysis to deal with various complexities. In this connection it is necessary to make a blanket acknowledgment

---

[22] See below, p. 422.

[23] As far as we know, Barone is the only writer in the field of socialist or welfare economics who has counted up and matched equations and unknowns. Much the same ground has been covered many times, however, in discussions of the determinacy of competitive equilibrium.

to the studies of several writers, especially Lerner,[24] to whom I refer also on specific points.

For convenience, we present below a brief inventory of the more interesting optimum conditions as they have come to be formulated. That the conditions listed are indeed requirements for an optimum, the uninitiated reader should be able to satisfy himself without too much difficulty. Our brief comments are intended only to be suggestive on this score. Except as indicated, the conditions listed are either stated or implied in one or another of the basic works to which reference already has been made.

The main conditions, then, are as follows:

(a) *The ratio of the marginal utilities (the marginal rate of substitution) for each pair of consumers' goods must be the same for all households.* If this is not the case there is always the possibility of an exchange of goods between a pair of households which would increase the utility of both, and accordingly, assuming consumers' sovereignty, would increase welfare.

(b) *In every industry factors must be combined in a technologically optimum manner,* in the sense that it is not possible technologically to dispense with any amount of any factor without a reduction in output.

(c) *The marginal value productivity of each factor must be the same in every industry.* The "prices" at which marginal productivities are valued are understood, for the time being, to represent not market prices but merely indexes of the comparative social values of alternatives. In the case of consumers' goods, the "prices" are proportional to the common values for all households of the marginal rates of substitution. If, in terms of these prices, the marginal value productivity of a factor were larger in one industry than another, this would mean that by a shift in resources it would be possible to realize an exchange of consumers' goods which would enhance the utilities of some or all households without there being any concomitant losses.

In the case of capital goods, it is supposed that the "prices" represent "present values," where the present value of any particular capital good is the discounted value of its marginal value productivity in the consumers' goods industries. The rate of discount is the rate at which the Board discounts future in comparison with present income.[25] This presupposes

[24] See A. P. Lerner, "The Concept of Monopoly and the Measurement of Monopoly Power," *Review of Economic Studies,* June 1934, I, pp. 157–175; *idem,* "Economic Theory and Socialist Economy," *ibid.,* October 1934, II, pp. 51–61; *idem,* "A Note on Socialist Economics," *ibid.,* October 1936, IV, pp. 72–76; *idem,* "Statics and Dynamics in Socialist Economics," *Economic Journal,* June 1937, XLVII, pp. 253–270; *idem, Economics of Control.* Also Bergson, *op. cit.;* Hicks, *op. cit.;* Lange, "Foundations of Welfare Economics," *Econometrica,* July–October 1942, X, pp. 215–228.
[25] If it is assumed that the capital goods are used up fully within one accounting period, these conditions lead to a very simple relation, namely that the marginal product

of course that the Board has a fixed single rate of discount. One might more realistically conceive the case where the Board's rate of time preference varies with the amount of savings undertaken; or there might be multiple rates, each relating to a comparison of present income with income at some specified future date. This latter case has been treated in detail by F. P. Ramsey.[26]

(d) *In the optimum, there must be no possibility of shifting a worker from one occupation to another to increase the value of output by more than would be required to compensate the worker for the change.* This assumes that all commodities are valued according to principles already stated and that consumers' preferences govern not only as between consumers' goods but also as between jobs.

(e) *Occupational wage differentials must correspond at one and the same time to differences in marginal value productivity and, for marginal workers, to differences in disutility.* When the marginal worker is shifted from one job to another, then, he *actually* is paid the amount that is necessary to compensate him for the change in jobs. If freedom of choice prevails this must be the case; but it is not clear that this is desirable. The desirability of this principle of wage determination follows from the assumed ends. Given that the marginal welfare per dollar for a given household is unaffected by any change in its budget position which leaves its total utility unchanged, the worker must be compensated fully for any extra disutility incurred as a result of a change in jobs.[27]

(f) *The social dividend or tax, however, must be determined independently of the worker's occupation or earnings.* This principle, ad-

---

of an increment of a capital good employed in the industry producing this capital good must equal the increment of the capital good employed plus interest on this increment. Let $A_C \Delta C$ be the marginal product of an increment of capital good in consumers' good industry A, P_A be the price of the consumers' good A, $C_C \Delta C$ be the marginal product of the capital in the industry producing this capital good, and P_C be the price of this capital good. It is required that

$$(2) \quad P_A A_C \Delta C = P_C C_C \Delta C.$$

Since $P_C = \dfrac{P_A A_0}{1 + r}$, it follows at once that $(1 + r)\Delta C = C_C \Delta C.$

Since the marginal value productivity of capital is the same in every use, it follows also that the rate of interest earned on marginal investments of capital is the same in every use, and equal to the rate established by the Board.

[26] "A Mathematical Theory of Saving," *Economic Journal*, December 1928, XXXVIII, pp. 543–559.

[27] In theory, though hardly in practice, the possibility is not precluded by the foregoing considerations that different wages be established for workers in the same occupation, workers who are not on the margin of choice between occupations being paid less than those who are. In this way, the household's "producer's surplus" would be extracted for distribution in the community at large. This in no way would conflict with the principle of consumers' sovereignty.

vanced by Lerner,[28] also follows directly from the principle that marginal economic welfare per "dollar" is unaffected by any budget change which leaves the total utility of the household unchanged. Given any initial allocation of "profits," no change is called for if a marginal worker is shifted from one job to another for which the additional wage just compensates him for the extra disutility. An attempt to offset the established wage differentials by the use of the tax or dividend would be out of place. The amount of the dividend or tax might be established on any of a variety of principles: e.g., it might be fixed as an equal lump sum for all households; it might be made to vary with the size of the household, and so on.

In the foregoing we have made use of the distinction, which Lange recently has clarified,[29] between "consumers' sovereignty" and "freedom of choice." Consumers' sovereignty is an "end." Freedom of choice may also be an end, in and of itself, but is also an administrative procedure. The principle of consumers' sovereignty might conceivably be accepted, while some procedure other than freedom of choice was used to ascertain consumers' preferences (e.g., statistical inquiries); to distribute goods among the different households (e.g., rationing); and to recruit workers for different jobs (e.g., conscription). Under what circumstances, if any, this might be advisable is a matter for consideration. Conceivably also, freedom of choice might prevail without the acceptance of the principle of consumers' sovereignty. While households might be permitted to spend their incomes as they wish, at established prices, their demands might be disregarded in decisions on production.

Though it is not always made clear in the writings under review, for the purposes of *defining* the optimum position the assumption of consumers' sovereignty alone is sufficient. For the sake of logical clarity, the conditions are formulated here on this assumption and without regard to whether freedom of choice also prevails.

Lange has discussed also the case where consumers' sovereignty is abandoned or modified.[30] Conceptually, this case is readily disposed of. All that needs to be done is to rephrase the preceding argument to take into account the fact that the pertinent marginal rates of substitution are those

---

[28] In the original version of his essay, "On the Economic Theory of Socialism" (*Review of Economic Studies,* October 1936, IV, pp. 64, 65), Lange assumed that the dividend should be distributed proportionately to wages. The objectionable character of Lange's solution was pointed out by Lerner in a note appended to Lange's article, and Lange has since corrected his argument. Both Lange and Lerner assume freedom of choice as well as consumers' sovereignty. As a result, it is not brought out clearly that the stated principles of wage determination and taxation follow from the principle of consumers' sovereignty alone.

[29] *On the Economic Theory of Socialism,* pp. 95–96.

[30] *On the Economic Theory of Socialism,* p. 90 ff.

decided on by the Board rather than by individual households. Thus, in terms of *these rates,* the requirement that the marginal value productivity of a factor be the same in every use still holds.

If consumers' sovereignty were abandoned, however, it is open to question whether the Board would be concerned to elaborate its preference scale with any great precision. Very possibly there would be significant ranges of choice within which the Board itself would be indifferent as to allocations. To whatever extent that this is so, the optimum position is in the last analysis indeterminate.

III. "Marginal Cost" vs. "Average Cost"

It is an easy matter to restate the foregoing optimum conditions in terms of "costs." The total cost incurred in the production of the optimum output must be at a minimum and, in the optimum, price must equal marginal cost (since we say nothing about rent, costs may be understood here to comprise material costs, interest, and wages). The reader may readily verify that if the stated requirements regarding costs are met the following optimum conditions will be satisfied: the condition that the factors employed in each firm be combined in a technologically optimum manner, the condition that the marginal value productivity be the same in every use, and the condition that differences in the wages of different kinds of labor equal differences in their value productivity. Conversely, it can readily be shown that if the stated requirements do not hold for all firms alike, one or another of these optimum conditions will be violated.[31]

The requirement that the total cost of producing the optimum output be a minimum means, of course, that the average cost incurred in the production of *this* output is a minimum. If there is no barrier to using at one scale of output the same combination of factors that may be used at any other, then presumably one and the same combination of factors will be the most efficient at all scales of output. We deal then with the case of *constant costs.* Marginal and average cost are constant and equal for all levels of output.

For various well known reasons, however, the case of constant costs may not prevail in the real world. For one thing there is the case of the so-called "fixed factors"; for another there is the case of indivisibilities in

---

[31] At this stage where no specific planning scheme is in mind, it is a matter of convention just where the line is drawn between wages and dividends or taxes. As long as *differences* in wages correspond at one and the same time to *differences* in marginal value productivity, all is well. For our present purposes the convention may be adopted that in some one firm and for some one occupation, wages *equal* marginal value productivity. A similar assumption is needed in respect of the prices of capital goods.

the factors employed or in the production unit (e.g., bridges, railways, utilities, etc.). These two cases pose a variety of theoretic questions, which recently have been discussed in some detail by Lerner[32] and Lewis.[33] What is of concern here is that in both cases—in the former case, for the duration of the service life of the "fixed" factor; in the latter case, indefinitely—only a relative optimum combination of factors can be attained at any level of output, i.e., only the amounts of factors other than those that are fixed or indivisible can be adjusted as output varies. It is usually assumed that under these circumstances the average cost will vary with output according to a familiar U-shaped pattern, and, hence, that marginal and average cost will be equal only at one scale of output, that for which average cost is at a minimum. In the case of indivisibilities, however, the possibility has to be reckoned with also that because of the very heavy overhead and the relatively limited importance of variable costs, average cost per unit will not follow the familiar U-shaped pattern, but instead will continue to decline for a wide range of output variations. Marginal cost may be below average cost for the entire relevant range of operations.

To repeat, however, the rule for the attainment of the optimum is that price must equal *marginal* cost. This principle is perfectly general: it holds regardless of the relation of marginal and average cost, regardless of whether price is above average cost and there are "profits" (as might be so in the case of "fixed factors") or below average cost and there are losses (as might be so also in the case of "fixed factors," and very likely would be so in the case of large indivisibilities).

For this very fundamental proposition, we are indebted chiefly to Marshall and Pigou, who long ago advanced it boldly even for cases of decreasing costs. In recent years, however, the rule has had to be defended and reaffirmed on a number of occasions in the face of recurrent confusion. In this connection, mention should be made of the contributions of Lerner[34] and Hotelling.[35] Both writers, Lerner with special vigor, have championed the Marshall-Pigou position against doctrinal deviations.

---

[32] *Economics of Control,* Ch. 17.

[33] W. A. Lewis, "Fixed Costs," *Economica,* November 1946, XIII, pp. 231–258.

[34] "The Concept of Monopoly and the Measurement of Monopoly Power," *loc. cit.;* "Statics and Dynamics in Socialist Economics," *loc. cit.; Economics of Control,* particularly Ch. 15, 16, 17.

Lerner takes pains to make clear that "marginal cost" must be understood as the increment of costs at *given* factor prices. Only on this understanding does the condition that price equal marginal cost correspond to the optimum conditions set forth in Section II. Only then is it assured that any factor will be equally productive in every use. Lerner's stipulation, however, requires elaboration. If variations in output that are very small in relation to the supply of factors are under consideration, then for all practical purposes factor prices will be constant anyhow, so the stipulation is not necessary. On the other

Part of the confusion seems to stem from the fact that the distinction is not always kept clearly in mind between the definition of the optimum allocation and the problem of realizing this optimum in practice. As Schumpeter has observed, the stated principle follows from the general logic of choice;[36] its validity does not depend at all on the possibility of devising an administrative procedure under which the optimum might be approximated in practice. One important question posed by indivisibilities in the latter connection is referred to in Section V.[37]

---

hand, if there are large indivisibilities, so that the changes in output do affect factor prices, the changes in factor prices would have to be taken into account. The special problems arising when large variations in output are under consideration are discussed below in the text.

The foregoing refers to marginal variations in the output of a given production unit, as distinct from variations in output due to the opening up or shutting down of the production unit itself. For purposes of formulating optimum conditions, the concept of a production unit as distinct from an industry is purely conventional—except in the case of large indivisibilities, it is always possible to conceive of an industry as comprising a large number of very small production units, so that within the scale of operations of this production unit, no variations in output, whether marginal or total, have any significant effect on the prices of factors. If, however, the production units are taken to be large —let us say there is only one production unit in the industry—one must add one more item to the list of causes of a departure from constant costs, the rising supply prices of the factors. Average and marginal costs will diverge on this account even if there are no fixed factors or indivisibilities. But the optimum condition still is as before, that prices equal the marginal costs incurred at *given* factor prices.

These remarks, of course, bear directly on the controversy stirred up by Pigou, concerning the case of increasing supply price. This controversy seems no longer to be active, but it is perhaps just as well for us to go on record here concerning the main issues. First, so far as the nature of the optimum is concerned (this seems to have been one of the questions arising), our view is as above. Second, so far as concerns the question of whether the optimum would be realized under perfect competition (this apparently was the main issue), the logic, as Pigou himself came to recognize, is overwhelmingly in favor of the affirmative as advanced by Young and Knight and against the negative originally advanced by Pigou. Regardless of whether factor prices rise with increasing output in the industry, the relevant marginal cost under perfect competition necessarily is one for which factor prices are given for any one firm. The optimum condition that price equal marginal cost *in this sense* is satisfied. Any divergence that persists in the long run between price and average cost, of course, will be absorbed by rent.

A brief review of the literature in this controversy is presented in Howard S. Ellis and William Fellner, "External Economies and Diseconomies," *American Economic Review*, September 1943, XXXIII, pp. 493–511.

[35] Harold Hotelling, "The General Welfare in Relation to Problems of Taxation and of Railway and Utility Rates," *Econometrica*, July 1938, VI, pp. 242–269.

[36] J. A. Schumpeter, *Capitalism, Socialism and Democracy*, 2nd ed. (New York, 1947), p. 176, note 5. Schumpeter should have said that the principle follows from the logic of choice *and* given ends (see below, p. 430, note 44).

[37] Attention may be called here, however, to the article of E. F. M. Durbin ("Economic Calculus in a Planned Economy," *Economic Journal*, December 1936, XLVI, pp. 676–690) which raises several practical objections to the Lerner-Hotelling condition; to the article of Lerner just cited ("Statics and Dynamics in Socialist Economics," *loc. cit.*) which disposes very effectively of these objections; and finally to the recent article of R. H. Coase ("The Marginal Cost Controversy," *Economica*, August 1946, XIII, pp. 169–182), which again raises practical objections to the Lerner-Hotelling condition.

While Coase accepts the Lerner-Hotelling condition as a valid principle, he argues that in practice it might be desirable to use a multi-part price system, in which con-

The confusion concerning the principle of equating price and marginal cost seems to stem also from a further confusion as to the fiscal implications of the welfare principles. In particular it often is suggested that if losses are not offset by profits elsewhere, the stated principle could not be applied.[38] The optimum conditions that have been outlined, however, are fully consistent with either "profits" or "losses" for the system as a whole. The fiscal counterparts of these "profits" or "losses" are the subsidy and tax that have been mentioned. On a theoretic plane, a logically satisfactory fiscal device for financing the losses or disposing of the profits of the socialist economy is always at hand.

In the long run, of course, "fixed factors" too become variable and mistakes in investments may be rectified. The rule is the same as before: price must equal marginal cost. Now, however, it is "long-run" rather than "short-run" marginal cost that is of concern. Account is to be taken of whatever increment of cost is incurred in producing an increment of output under the condition that the "fixed factors" too are variable.

All of this is to say, of course, that in practice what we have to reckon with is not a unique marginal cost for a given level of output, but a complex of marginal costs, each of which is pertinent to a particular period of time. As a longer period of time is considered, more of the "fixed factors" become variable. Because of this greater flexibility in the production process, long-run marginal cost will generally be less than short-run marginal cost. Lewis discusses in detail the complexities that would be encountered on this account in determining marginal costs in the real world.

In the case of the indivisible production unit, the stated rule has to be reformulated. If the production unit is large, its introduction may affect the structure of prices (marginal rates of substitution) and wages. The optimum conditions listed in Section II all are formulated in terms of the prices and wages appropriate to a *given* allocation of resources. In the case of indivisibility this is no longer possible.[39]

---

sumers are charged one price to cover overhead and another to cover marginal costs. While in the special case he considers (where the overhead actually can be imputed separately to different households) his scheme is unobjectionable, our impression is that in any more typical case of indivisibility the lump sum tax scheme we have discussed would be a preferable means of covering overhead costs.

Incidentally, under socialism this tax might readily be used without ill effect to offset any important unfavorable effects on income distribution such as Coase argues would result from the charging of prices below costs to some consumers. In the same way, the Board might decide to pay an extra dividend to spaghetti eaters in seasons when the price of spaghetti was abnormally high.

[38] See Durbin, *op. cit.*, p. 685.

[39] Cf. Lerner (*Economics of Control*, p. 176): "The indivisibility is significant when it is large enough to destroy perfect competition."

How is it to be decided whether to introduce the production unit to begin with? In place of the requirement that price equal marginal cost, one may advance here the more general requirement that the social value yielded must equal the additional social cost. But how is it possible to tell when this condition obtains?

The solution of this problem advanced by Pigou still is generally accepted. This involves the use of the dubious consumers' surplus concept,[40] and so seems methodologically objectionable, but it is hardly likely that subsequent work will overthrow Pigou's important conclusion that it might pay to introduce the production unit even though it were known in advance that losses would be incurred. Lerner presents a very systematic exposition of this aspect of the problem of indivisibility.[41]

The general rule, we have said, is that price equal marginal cost. What if prices are merely proportional to marginal cost? Would this not suffice? In the face of a good deal of authority for the affirmative, the present writer[42] has argued that the correct answer is in the negative. If prices are proportional but not equal to marginal costs, the optimum conditions listed in Section II will be violated. In particular, the differences in value productivity of different types of labor will no longer equal differences in wages, and hence will not correspond to differences in disutility. A reallocation of resources, involving the shift in marginal workers from one occupation to another, would be in order.

IV. The Conceptual Framework

Before going further, let us try to understand the contribution that the foregoing analysis might make to the solution of the Board's task. As we see it, what has been done is to construct a conceptual framework which might serve two purposes. On the one hand, it in effect poses for the Board a series of questions on ends, i.e., on consumers' sovereignty, saving and investment, communal consumption, and income distribution. In this way the analysis might assist the Board to formulate a conceptually satisfactory scale of values to guide the economy, one that is internally

---

[40] A. C. Pigou, *Economics of Welfare*, 3rd ed. (London, 1929), p. 808. It should not be difficult to handle this question without using the consumers' surplus concept. Essentially what is involved is an index number problem, the objective being to compare the community's real income in two different situations with different price structures.

[41] *Economics of Control*, Ch. 16.

[42] See A. Bergson, *The Structure of Soviet Wages* (Cambridge, Mass., 1944), pp. 19-22, which also refers incidentally (p. 21, note 16) to the writings of Lerner and Dickinson on this question. Lerner, who is cited here as having supported the erroneous view that proportionality is sufficient, has since corrected himself (*Economics of Control*, p. 100 ff.).

consistent and in principle at least covers the bill. Insofar as the particular questions posed are such as the Board might be expected intelligently to deal with, this would be all to the good.

On the other hand, the analysis establishes the implications of the given ends. These implications are the optimum conditions. In this way the analysis might assist the Board to allocate resources consistently in accord with the given ends. The establishment of these implications would seem to be a prerequisite for the construction of a planning scheme which might approximate the given ends in practice. It happens that the criteria for the optimum that have been set forth are conceptually simple and, for the cases where small adjustments are possible, require for their application only facts which actually might be experienced in a given situation (the marginal rates of substitution, marginal productivities, etc.). For purposes of planning, this too is clearly all to the good.

How useful this particular conceptual framework might be, however, evidently would depend on whether the Board would feel that the particular questions posed are the right ones for it to decide, that is, whether in this sense the underlying aim is welfare. A somewhat different conceptual framework might be needed if the Board's aim were, say, to build up military potential. In this case, it might be necessary at least to pose for the Board a series of questions concerning the amounts of subsidies to be allowed to particular heavy industries. If the Board took a more or less absolutistic view on such matters, it might find these questions also unsuitable: in view of the uncertainties that inevitably would surround any attempt to control output *via* taxes and subsidies, the Board might wish to fix directly specific goals and priorities for key industries. In the case considered, moreover, the question at issue might not be what was good for the consumers from either their point of view or the Board's, but their efficiency, which need not come to the same thing.

The possibility also is to be reckoned with that there might not be any one set of questions which was right for any length of time. We have phrased the foregoing discussion as if the decisions on ends were taken by the Board. Whether this is so or the ends are formulated through democratic political processes, they hardly will reflect ethical considerations alone. Questions of power relations inevitably will obtrude. Probably such questions would be the more important the greater the division of opinion on ends in the community. Under certain circumstances, the Board might be compelled to do a good deal of the work of planning on an *ad hoc* basis.[43] In the light of changing political conditions, the Board

---

[43] The problems that arise for planning as a result of the existence of divisions on ends are one of the principal grounds for the argument, made familiar by F. A. Hayek, that

might find it expedient to give a higher priority to the manufacture of farm implements one day and to the production of automobiles another day.

What has been said as to the limitations on the relevance of the ends necessarily applies also to the optimum conditions which are deduced from the ends. Any particular optimum conditions are relevant only in contexts to which the corresponding ends are relevant. Thus the proposition that the marginal value productivity of a factor must be the same in every use—it being understood that values are proportional to the marginal rates of substitution of the individual households—clearly obtains only if the principle of consumers' sovereignty prevails as an end.

Of course, if, as is often the case, the optimum conditions are formulated in more abstract terms, the context in which they are relevant is broadened correspondingly. The condition that the marginal value productivity of a factor must be the same in every use might be formulated without specification of whether the marginal rates of substitution are those of the household or of the Board. This precept for socialist economic calculation is valid, then, no matter whether the principle of consumers' sovereignty prevails or not.[44]

In saying that the analysis outlined in preceding sections poses questions on ends for the Board, we do not mean to imply that the Board would not be interested in the views that the various writers have themselves expressed on these ends. No doubt the Board would be glad to have the advice of economists on the basic question of ends. No doubt it would wish to hear also from sociologists, dieticians, psychiatrists, et al. Whether in offering such advice economists are acting in their capacity

---

democracy and planning are incompatible. *The Road to Serfdom* (Chicago, 1944), Ch. V.

[44] It still does not follow, however, that this is a universally valid precept, or what comes to the same thing, that it is, as often is supposed, a matter of pure logic. The point is that the derivation of the optimum conditions that are listed in Section II requires a set of valuations not yet specified, namely that a shift in any factor from one use to another does not make any difference from the point of view of welfare, except in respect of the resulting difference in the value of output. In other words, a zero social value is assigned to such phenomena as "factory smoke," differences in a worker's attitude toward different jobs (as distinct from different occupations), etc. Only in this case is it rational to determine the allocation of any factor simply on the basis of a comparison of the value of output in different uses. The condition of equality of marginal value productivity, far from being universally applicable, applies only where the foregoing values prevail.

The prevalent confusion on this matter seems to have arisen in part from a tendency, for which I believe Robbins is chiefly responsible, to speak of alternative uses of a factor as if they always were alternative *indifferent* uses. Unless there are alternative *indifferent* uses, in the sense that nothing but differences in the value of output counts for welfare, there is no basis at all to speak as Robbins does of "ends" as distinct from "means." Insofar as "factory smoke," etc. have a negative social value, the optimum conditions that have been outlined must be reformulated along the familiar lines marked out by Pigou.

as *economists* or in some other capacity (which is the issue raised by Robbins[45]) is a question not necessary to debate here.

V. The Problem of Administration

The foregoing analysis in itself provides a conceptual basis for the use of a method of successive approximations to the optimum position, at least to the extent that small adjustments are in order. On the basis of the stated criteria for the optimum allocation of resources it is readily possible to establish whether and in what respects any given allocation deviates from the optimum position. Provided it had at its disposal the necessary facts, the Board might focus attention first on one pair of alternatives and then on another, and, on the basis of these criteria, try to distribute any given resources to the best advantage between each pair of alternatives in turn. There is no need even at this stage to suppose, as sometimes is suggested, that the Board would have to solve at one blow "millions of equations."[46]

That there is facing the Board any substantial administrative task is due to several facts. First, the vast stock of detailed knowledge that would be needed to decide on the myriads of alternatives that have to be dealt with is not immediately available to the Board; to the extent that it is available at all, it is scattered throughout the community—and indeed the amount of knowledge actually available will depend on the particular administrative procedure used. Second, even if such knowledge were available to the Board, it would be physically impossible for the Board within any finite period of time to decide successively on all the alternatives to be dealt with. Finally, even if the Board could specify how every sort of resource should be used, the task of controlling the execution of its directive would still remain.

It is necessary then to devise a planning scheme to approximate the optimum allocation in practice. This must take into account: the basic limitations on the knowledge and executive capacities of the Board and of any other decision-making units under it, the cost of running the planning scheme itself (some procedures might be too costly to operate), and finally the fact that "means" are also "ends." The choice of administrative procedure (e.g., as between rationing and freedom of choice) cannot be made solely from the standpoint of efficiency.

A number of recent writings on socialist economics grapple with this interesting administrative problem, though without always making clear its precise nature. To these writings we now turn.

---

[45] *Nature and Significance of Economic Science*, Ch. VI.
[46] L. C. Robbins, *The Great Depression* (London, 1934), p. 151.

VI. The Competitive Solution: Main Features

The optimum conditions that have been devised for the case of consumers' sovereignty will be familiar to the reader of any elementary textbook on economics. With certain exceptions, they are the same as the equilibrium conditions of "perfect competition" under capitalism. The exceptions are (1) the conditions relating to income distribution and the rate of investment (insofar as this is determined without regard to the time preference of households), and (2) the case of decreasing cost, where as the textbooks show competition breaks down.

For well-known reasons revolving partly around the exceptions just stated, this limited correspondence of the optimum with the competitive equilibrium does not in itself provide the basis for policy conclusions concerning perfect competition. It is the basis, however, for one much-discussed solution of the question in hand. This is the so-called Competitive Solution.

The correspondence of the optimum and the competitive equilibrium was noted in all the early writing to which we have referred. Indeed, this was one of the main points of Pareto and Barone. However, Pareto and Barone did not follow out this lead. The Competitive Solution is the work of a number of later writers, of whom the chief are Taylor, Dickinson, and Lange.[47]

The essentials of this planning scheme may readily be set forth. Reference is mainly to the very systematic exposition of Lange, and, for the moment, to the case where consumers are sovereign.

(1) All transfers of goods and services among production units and between production units and households are recorded in terms of an accounting unit, all goods being valued at established prices, and services at established wages. Both the prices and wages initially are arbitrary. In the case of transfers of goods and services between households and production units there may be a transfer of "cash."

(2) Freedom of choice is allowed the households in respect of both the work they do and the goods they consume.

(3) Each production unit is instructed to conduct its operation in

---

[47] F. M. Taylor, "The Guidance of Production in a Socialist State," *American Economic Review*, March 1929, XIX, pp. 1–8, reprinted in Lange and Taylor, *op. cit.*; H. D. Dickinson, "Price Formation in a Socialist Economy," *Economic Journal*, December 1933, XLIII, pp. 237–250; *idem, The Economics of Socialism* (London, 1939); O. Lange, "On the Economic Theory of Socialism," *loc. cit.*

In this connection mention is to be made also of the studies of A. P. Lerner, cited above, p. 421, note 24; and of E. F. M. Durbin, "Economic Calculus in a Planned Economy," *loc cit.*

accord with two basic rules. For any given scale of output, it must seek to combine the factors of production in such a way as, at the established prices, to minimize the average cost per unit of output. Second, it must seek to fix its output at the point where the established price for its goods equals marginal cost.

(4) The capital that is required for these purposes is made freely available to the production units at an established rate of interest, which is to be reckoned among the elements in cost.[48]

(5) On the basis of well-known theoretic arguments, it can be shown that, at the established prices, wages, and rate of interest, the aggregate demand for and supply of each and every sort of goods and services on the part of *all* households and production units is determined. There also will be some given demand for capital at the established rate of interest. One of the functions which the Board itself must perform is to adjust prices and wages from time to time in order to bring the demand and supply of goods and services into line. Where the demand for a product exceeds supply (this would be evidenced in the case of goods by a depletion of stocks), the price must be raised; where supply exceeds demand (as evidenced in the case of goods by an accumulation of stocks), the price must be reduced. The Board is also supposed to determine the rate of investment. The rate of interest is fixed so that the aggregate amount of new capital demanded equals the aggregate amount of new investment that the Board wishes to have undertaken. The Board allocates the dividend, and presumably decides on the amount of resources to be devoted to communal consumption.

Under this scheme, then, socialist households, like those in a perfectly competitive capitalist system, are autonomous in respect to the acquisition of consumers' goods and sale of their services. Accordingly they may be expected to act in accord with the same principles in these respects as apply under competition. Likewise, under the established administrative rules, the socialist production units are called upon to act in the same way, in respect of the purchase of factors and the determination of output, as enterprises in perfect competition. Under perfect competition each enterprise is such a small element of the market that it has no power over prices and accordingly must take prices as given so far as its own decisions on production are concerned: it seeks to maximize profits at the established prices. Under the established rules, the socialist production unit would tend to do likewise.

This is as far, however, as the analogy goes. Under the Competitive Solution, the Board supplants the capitalist marketplace as the integra-

[48] See Lange, *On the Economic Theory of Socialism*, p. 84.

tor of the decisions of the households and production units. The Board rather than the market adjusts prices to bring supply and demand into line.

Lange considers that the Competitive Solution might be adapted also to the case where the Board undertakes to determine what is good for the households.[49] In this case, the Board might introduce a system of taxes and subsidies on consumers' goods, to express the divergencies between its preference scale and those of consumers. In other words, there might be a two-price system in the consumers' goods market, one for the purpose of distributing goods to households and the other, based on the Board's preference scale, to guide production. Freedom of choice would still prevail, even though consumers' sovereignty had been abandoned. Alternatively, freedom of choice might be abandoned also, and consumers' goods rationed and jobs filled by assignment. For the rest, the scheme would be as above.

VII. The Competitive Solution: An Appraisal

Assuming that the socialist economic system were administered in accord with the very general principles and procedures outlined, to what extent might an optimum allocation of resources be approximated? For the moment we try only to provide a brief inventory of the more important considerations which might have to be taken into account in forming a judgment on this central question:

(a) Managerial Controls and Incentives. To begin with there is the fundamental question of how the success of the managers of the production units is to be tested. Lange does not deal explicitly with this question. Dickinson refers to it briefly.[50]

The obvious test is profits. As Dickinson recognizes, however, this is not an altogether satisfactory criterion. For one thing, there is the case of decreasing cost due to large indivisibilities. If the scale of operations for which price equaled marginal cost were one for which price was below average cost, there would be losses, and the manager would be disinclined to engage in any additional investments, even though they might be socially desirable. The maximization of profits (or minimization of losses) in this case would lead in the long run to the restriction of output below the optimum. If profits were the test of success, managers in order to succeed would be compelled to violate the rules. (The case of decreasing cost, then, constitutes an exception to the statement that has been made

[49] *Ibid.*, p. 90 ff.
[50] *The Economics of Socialism,* pp. 213–219.

that under the established rules the socialist like the competitive firm maximizes profits.)

Managers would be tempted to violate the rules also if their production units were large in relation to the market served by them. In order to make a large profit they might try to take into account the effects of their actions on the Board's decisions on prices. In this case they might restrict output in much the same way as monopolists do in a capitalist economy. The Competitive Solution might not be so competitive after all.

In such cases, then, there might be no alternative but for the Board to do as Dickinson suggests: to look into the cost records of the individual production units. This, however, would raise an administrative question of some dimensions. Clearly, if carried to any length, this practice would be in conflict with an essential aim of the Competitive Solution, to decentralize decision making.

Hayek[51] seems to argue that in fact the Board would have to look into the cost records of individual firms in any and all circumstances. This will not be a "perfunctory audit," but a full-fledged study to check whether the managers have operated as efficiently as possible. It would seem to the writer that this exaggerates the difficulties of the problem. Where, for example, profits might be used effectively as a control, probably much could be accomplished by tying incentives to profits and by comparing the profit records of similar firms and of one and the same firm over time. A detailed examination of the costs of each and every firm would not seem to be essential.

Provided the question of controls could be disposed of satisfactorily, our impression is that the question of managerial incentives would not present any serious difficulties. Given the possibility of fixing policy on dismissals on the one hand and on rewards on the other, it should be feasible to establish a climate in which the managers evaluate risks in whatever is considered to be the proper manner. There is no reason to suppose that they would necessarily be too venturesome or, as Hayek argues, too cautious.[52]

(b) ERRORS IN FORECASTS OF MANAGERS. Lange refers to his method as a "trial and error" method. Dobb[53] considers that an important source of error would be the forecasts made by individual managers concerning future market conditions. Even supposing that profits were the test of success, that there were no cases of decreasing costs, and that the man-

---

[51] "Socialist Calculation: The Competitive Solution," *Economica*, May 1940, New Series VII, p. 141.

[52] *Ibid.*, pp. 141–142.

[53] M. Dobb, "Saving and Investment in a Socialist Economy," *Economic Journal*, December 1939, XLIX, pp. 726–727.

agers did not seek to influence prices, they still would have to estimate their prospective behavior. This is necessary for purposes of deciding on investments. Under conditions of perfect competition, managers are supposed to take prices as "given" (parameters) insofar as their own actions are concerned; but they still must form estimates of future market conditions in deciding on investments.

Errors in forecasts presumably would be the greater the more dynamic the economy. In considering their possible magnitude under socialism, however, account must be taken of the fact that the Central Planning Board might run a very comprehensive information service for the benefit of the managers. In supplying this service, the Board would presumably not hesitate to express its own opinion and sentiments on market conditions, in much the same way as Central Banks of capitalist countries have been doing for the markets they control.

(c) RIGIDITY; UNDUE STANDARDIZATION; OTHER ERRORS OF THE BOARD. In the article already cited, Hayek[54] argues that the Board itself would be unable to cope effectively with its responsibilities. For one thing, it would be impracticable for the Board to adjust prices promptly in accord with the ever-occurring changes in supply and demand. Prices will be adjusted only periodically or from time to time. For a longer or shorter period of time, then, they will not correctly measure the "true" values of alternatives. For another, the Board hardly will be able to fix in detail prices for all the infinite varieties of goods produced in a modern industrial society. Inevitably, there will be a tendency to fix prices only for broad categories of goods, with the result that on this account also the prices will not provide an accurate measure of alternatives in particular circumstances.

Both these deficiencies apparently would stem from two limitations on the Board's executive capacities: its limited physical powers, which restrict the number of decisions it might deal with effectively, and the limitations on the amount of detailed knowledge of time and place which can be placed at its disposal. In another article,[55] Hayek emphasizes this latter limitation. He explains that

the sort of knowledge with which I have been concerned is knowledge of the kind which by its nature cannot enter into statistics and therefore cannot be conveyed to any central authority in statistical form. The statistics which such a central authority would have to use would have to be arrived at precisely by abstracting from minor differences between things, by lumping together, as resources of one kind,

---

[54] *Op. cit.*, pp. 135–136.
[55] "The Use of Knowledge in Society," *American Economic Review*, September 1945, XXXV, pp. 519–530.

items which differ as regards location, quality, and other particulars, in a way which may be very significant for the specific decision.[56]

These remarks of Hayek's would seem to provide a wholesome anti-dote to the tendency among many writers on socialism to regard the Central Planning Board as a committee of Supermen. In judging how important these limitations might be in practice, however, attention must be given to the fact that the Board could set up a more or less elaborate administrative apparatus just for the purpose of fixing prices. The apparatus might be broken down functionally and geographically; it might even have regional offices to take local conditions more fully into account.[57] Presumably the Board would establish general directives to guide its subordinates.

(d) INEQUALITY OF INCOME. Lange[58] argues that under his scheme income might be distributed on essentially egalitarian principles. While there would be differentials in wages to accord with differences in marginal value productivity, these differentials would correspond at the same time to differences in disutility. If the dividend itself were, say, equal for all households, then aside from differences in well-being due to personal variations in need, all households would in reality be equally well off. It is understood that education and training would be free for all.

Lange recognizes that there would be an exception to this in the case of persons with unusual natural talents (artists, musicians, etc.). For these persons, payment on the basis of value productivity might lead to differences in income all out of proportion to differences in disutility. Our impression is that these exceptions might be more numerous than is commonly assumed, e.g., what of the personnel in high level jobs in the bureaucracy? But in any event, Lange observes correctly that in such cases a high tax might be levied without any adverse effect on the supply of these services. There would be no conflict (such as was noted above, p. 423) with the principle of consumers' sovereignty.

It ought also to be observed, however, that disparities of this sort might be widespread purely as a result of dynamic factors. Workers in occupations where there is short supply might for protracted periods receive a "rent" over and above what is required to attract them into these occupations. If freedom of choice prevails, it would be out of the question to extract this rent by taxation devices. Also, as we already have observed, the equation of disutilities and value productivities holds strictly only for persons on the margin of choice between occupations. Depending

[56] *Ibid.*, p. 524.
[57] This, of course, is what is actually done in the Soviet Union.
[58] *On the Economic Theory of Socialism*, pp. 100–103.

on their preferences, intra-marginal workers would likewise receive a rent, which it probably would be administratively impractical to extract if freedom of choice prevailed. Thus, given freedom of choice, the departures from egalitarian principles might be much greater and more numerous than Lange envisages.

(e) INSTABILITY; UNEMPLOYMENT. Dobb[59] raises and answers the question as to whether under the Competitive Solution there might be any high degree of instability and large-scale unemployment of resources. He observes that a reduction in the rate of interest designed to encourage investment on the part of managers of firms might lead to a cycle of expansion and contraction: as the investments take place, there is an expansion in purchasing power, the prices for consumers' goods rise, there is a secondary increase in the demand for capital, and so on. An attempt to put an end to this process by increasing the rate of interest might lead to a cumulative movement in the opposite direction, resulting in unemployment. Dobb recognizes, however, that the Board would be able to control the volume of purchasing power directly through its fiscal powers. The Board presumably would plan its policy on taxes and dividends to assure as far as possible that the volume of purchasing power in the hands of consumers was just sufficient to buy at prices covering marginal costs the volume of consumers' goods it was desirable to produce.

Errors certainly would be made here as elsewhere in the operation of the Competitive Solution. Whether these errors would be so serious as to constitute a telling point against the Competitive Solution, as Dobb implies,[60] is open to question.

Referring to socialism in general and not to any particular planning scheme, Wright[61] argues that there might be cyclic disturbances because of a tendency to overbuild the durable goods industries. The capacity required to build up stocks of durable goods might exceed that required to maintain these stocks after they were built up. Insofar as the conclusion is that at one time or another there might be excess capacity in one or another durable goods industry, there can be no dissent from this argument. It is difficult to see, however, why this necessarily entails "waste" in any economic sense, as Wright implies. If the capacity is built up with a full knowledge of the implications, including the fact that at some future date it will be excessive, then presumably this represents an optimum use of the resources in question: the "value" of the

---

[59] "Saving and Investment in a Socialist Economy," *loc. cit.*
[60] *Ibid.*, pp. 723-726.
[61] D. M. Wright, *The Economics of Disturbance* (New York, 1947), Ch. VI.

capacity would be fully written off by the time it is released. Furthermore, it is not at all clear why the release of capacity in different industries should tend to occur merely simultaneously and thus engender a general cycle. The release of excess capacity in one industry or another might be entirely consistent with a balanced and even development of the economy as a whole. Finally, the workers released from one or another durable goods industry would be unemployed only during the time needed to retrain them for employment elsewhere. For this reason it is difficult to see why there should be the mass unemployment which Wright would expect.

(f) TRANSITION PROBLEMS. Lange[62] seems to argue that the Competitive Solution would work not only in an established socialist society but also in the period of transition. The proviso is made that the private sector of the economy must be small, that competition must reign in it, and that small-scale production must not in the long run be more expensive than large-scale production. (This last condition is to assure presumably that the private small-scale enterprise can survive; why this is desirable or necessary under socialism, however, is not clear.) Lange hints that political and other factors also might raise special problems for planning in this period.

In a more adequate treatment of this very important question, the present writer suspects that the difficulties in applying the Competitive Solution would loom a good deal larger than Lange implies. For one thing, insofar as, in the years following the transfer of power, political considerations might have an overwhelming importance, the usefulness of the conceptual framework that has been outlined (and by the same token the usefulness of the Competitive Solution) might be seriously impaired. The reasons for this have already been stated in Section IV. For another thing, there is the important question of the loyalty of old and the efficiency of new managerial personnel, which would have to be taken into account in deciding on the responsibilities to be delegated to them. This would presumably be a pressing problem in the transition period.

Schumpeter[63] argues that the political problems of transition would be more or less difficult according to whether the capitalist society from which socialism emerges is in an early or late stage of development. Thus, it is said that in a late stage of capitalist development resistance is likely to be weak and the revolution might be accomplished in an orderly

---

[62] On the Economic Theory of Socialism, p. 121 ff.
[63] Op. cit., Ch. XIX.

manner. My impression, based on the Soviet experience, is that a most favorable moment for the socialist revolution is at an early stage of capitalist development, when the middle class still is weak and the proletariat has not yet tasted the fruits of capitalism.

But certainly in this case, if the Soviet experience serves at all, there would be pressing economic as well as political problems to deal with after the seizure of power and it is easy to see that on account of the economic as well as political problems there might be very real difficulties in the way of applying the trial and error Competitive Solution. Consider only the matter of high-tempo industrialization, and the rapid shifts in demand and production schedules that would be associated with this process. In such a situation, the errors involved in the operation of the Competitive Solution might well be formidable; and evidently experience could not be very helpful in rectifying them. Whether there is any alternative planning procedure that might work more effectively in such circumstances is a question that has to be considered.

In referring to the foregoing considerations under the heading of transition problems, it is not implied that there ever would be a period in which they would be entirely absent, or at any rate, that there ever would be such a period short of the era of unlimited abundance. Lange is not explicit on this matter.

VIII. An Alternative Approach to Socialist Planning

It is necessary to refer here to the special case of "fixed coefficients" dealt with by Pareto and Barone: for technical reasons and regardless of their relative values, the different factors must be employed in amounts that bear a constant relationship to output.[64] In this case there is no basis for speaking of the marginal productivity of any one factor. It is necessary to formulate the analysis of the optimum conditions, as Pareto and Barone originally did, in terms of the fixed coefficients and without the use of the marginal productivity concept. With fixed coefficients, as in the case where the coefficients are variable, a scale of values is needed to decide on optimum output and the distribution of income; it turns out, however, that, for the rest, the allocation of resources is entirely a technical question.

It is easy to see that, if this case obtained, the practical work of plan-

---

[64] "Fixed coefficients" is itself a special case of the genus "limitational factors." Lange (On the Economic Theory of Socialism, p. 67, note 15; p. 94, note 46) distinguishes two types of limitational factors, according to whether the amount of the limitational factor that must be employed is a function of output or of the amount of another factor employed. If all factors are limitational in the first sense, we have the case of fixed coefficients.

ning might be simplified considerably. Lange[65] says that here "no prices and no cost accounting whatever are needed" in allocating resources. All is decided by considerations of technical efficiency. This is true only if, as Lange assumes, the demand for consumers' goods is in the form of fixed quotas. If demand is variable, prices and costs still would have to be taken into account in the allocation of resources among different consumers' goods industries. There would be no need, however, to rearrange production methods in the different industries in response to each and every change in the relative scarcities of the different factors of production.

If the Competitive Solution were in operation in this case, the managers of the individual production units would not have to change their production methods in response to changes in the price structure. On this account it might seem that the process of trial and error would be shortened appreciably. So far as the Competitive Solution is concerned, however, this case has an important adverse feature. If the coefficients are fixed, marginal and average costs are constant. The administrative rules established by Lange no longer provide a definite basis for managerial decisions. If prices were above marginal costs, for example, the managers would know that they should expand, but would be quite in the dark as to how much. The possibility is still open that by the manipulation of prices the Board could assure that the total output of the industry was brought in line with demand; there might be a "neutral" equilibrium such as it is supposed might be attained under capitalist perfect competition in the case of constant costs. But there would be no satisfactory basis for moving toward the equilibrium by successive approximations. As a result, the trial and error process might turn out to be very protracted, despite the simplification in the work of choosing between different production methods.

We may now consider an alternative planning scheme which seems to be inspired in part by emphasis on this case of fixed coefficients.

The alternative planning procedure, which may be referred to as the Centralist Scheme, has been sketched only in very general terms. Under the Competitive Solution the operations of individual production units and households are integrated through a market process. Under the Centralist Scheme it is proposed that, to a greater or lesser extent, these operations be integrated directly by the Board. The managers of individual production units, it is supposed, will submit to the Board the data required for this purpose. Under this scheme the process of trial and error takes place on paper rather than in the market place.

A planning scheme of this sort is suggested by Dickinson, who presents it merely as a possibly practical alternative to the Competitive

---

[65] *Ibid.*, p. 94, note 46.

Solution.[66] Dobb, however, advocates it as a preferable procedure.[67] It is in Dobb's writings that the case of fixed coefficients seems to be linked with the Centralist Scheme. Dobb emphasizes the importance of technological factors in the determination of the optimum allocation.[68]

The advocates of the Centralist Scheme, no doubt, have drawn their inspiration partly from the Soviet planning procedure, the distinguishing feature of which is a comprehensive plan that purportedly integrates the whole economy. This integration is accomplished by the so-called "Method of Balanced Estimates," by which the planned requirements of different commodities and services are checked against planned supplies.[69] Soviet economists have published very little in a theoretic vein concerning their planning system[70]—perhaps because they are too much preoccupied with practical work. From scattered writings, however, one gains the impression that they emphasize the importance of technological factors in resource allocation, and that this emphasis plays a part in their thinking about planning procedures.

It is not surprising, then, that another well-known feature of the Soviet economic system is incorporated in Dobb's program. Dobb contemplates that there might be numerous cases where the Board would overrule consumers' preferences.[71] This seems to be a prevailing practice in the USSR. It should be observed, however, that the Centralist Scheme itself is not tied logically to a system in which consumers' preferences are overruled or indeed tied to any particular ends. Dickinson has in mind a system designed to satisfy the demands of consumers as they see them.

The main objection raised against the Centralist Scheme is that it imposes an impossible administrative burden on the Board. It is said that large-scale waste is inevitable if planning is on this basis. We find ourselves again confronted with the problem of solving "millions of equations."

In general much weight would seem to attach to this objection; but clearly the difficulties are reduced in the case of fixed coefficients. Rela-

---

[66] *The Economics of Socialism*, pp. 104–105. Dickinson's position on this scheme in this book seems to represent a retreat from the rather positive views he expressed earlier in "Price Formation in a Socialist Community," *loc. cit.*

[67] M. Dobb, "Economic Theory and the Problems of a Socialist Economy," *Economic Journal*, December 1933, XLIII, pp. 588–598; *idem*, "A Reply," *Review of Economic Studies*, February 1935, II, pp. 144–151; *idem*, "Saving and Investment in a Socialist Economy," *loc. cit.*; *idem*, *Political Economy and Capitalism*, Ch. VIII.

[68] See especially *Political Economy and Capitalism*, p. 331 ff.

[69] For a brief description of this procedure, see Alexander Baykov, *The Development of the Soviet Economic System* (Cambridge, England, 1946), Ch. XX.

[70] For references to some of the Soviet sources on planning, see *ibid*.

[71] "Economic Theory and the Problems of a Socialist Economy," *loc. cit.*, p. 591 ff.; *Political Economy and Capitalism*, p. 309 ff.

tive prices then do not make any difference for much of the work of planning. It is not necessary to suppose that the case holds strictly. To whatever extent it is approached, any technologically feasible allocation will, to that extent, approach the optimum.

Insofar as the Centralist Scheme is feasible, the choice between it and the Competitive Solution presumably would revolve about the nature of the ends sought and the stage of political, social, and economic development that has been reached. One might imagine, for example, that in a highly dynamic economy a Centralist allocation of investment might lead to fewer and smaller errors than a Competitive allocation. While under the Centralist Scheme the Board might err, there would seem to be a better prospect of meeting the requirements of technical consistency with respect to complementary industries. If technical rigidities are present, the chances are diminished that under the Competitive Solution the errors of individual firms would cancel out.[72] In other words, the Centralist Scheme might be able to deal more effectively than the Competitive Solution with the problem of bottlenecks and excess capacity.

To what extent does the case of fixed coefficients hold in a modern industrial society? Lange considers it to be very exceptional.[73] The writer suspects that this is the view also of most "orthodox" economists. Lange seems to refer, however, only to situations where the case holds strictly. Clearly, it is a matter of very great interest how closely it is approximated: the more nearly it is approached the more limited is the range within which price calculations matter. On the basis of numerous recent cost studies,[74] it would appear that for a considerable range of short-run output variations marginal costs for the individual firm tend to be constant. This suggests that at least in the short run the proportions are indeed fixed between labor and other variable elements in marginal costs. Mention is to be made also of Leontief's study of the structure of the American economy.[75] Leontief found it practicable to assume that for broad industrial groups the production coefficients are constant. The prevailing preconception on this whole question may have to be revised as more empirical data become available.

The degree of emphasis on technological as compared with economic factors in resource allocation, by the way, might be one basis for a dis-

---

[72] This point was suggested to me by A. Erlich, with whom I have had many profitable discussions.

[73] On the Economic Theory of Socialism, p. 94, note 46.

[74] See the very careful evaluation of these studies issued by the Committee on Price Determination (E. S. Mason, Chairman) of the National Bureau of Economic Research, Cost Behaviour and Price Policy (New York, 1943), Ch. V.

[75] W. Leontief, The Structure of the American Economy, 1919–1929 (Cambridge, Mass., 1941).

tinction which is now rather difficult to make, between the "orthodox" and "Marxian" theory of planning.

There is no need here to go into the question of the validity of the labor theory of value as a basis for socialist calculation. Mises[76] has shown clearly enough its deficiencies in this respect. What is to be noted is that there now appears to be a diversity of opinion even in Marxian circles as to the applicability of the labor theory to socialism. Indeed, it is difficult to find in any quarter unqualified support for the labor theory in this connection.

Dunayevskaya[77] and Sweezy consider that the labor theory of value does not and was not intended by Marx to apply to socialism. On the question of what theory of value does apply, Sweezy has taken in turn two different positions. At one time, he argued that orthodox economics holds under socialism:

> Marxian economics is essentially the economics of capitalism, while "capitalist" economics is in a very real sense the economics of socialism.[78]

More recently, he seems to have taken the position that orthodox economics does not apply either; he now advances in its place the "principle of planning."[79] The nature of this principle is not explained. Presumably the Board is to work out the logic of choice on its own.

Dobb[80] is also difficult to classify. On the one hand, he makes free use of orthodox value theory in the analysis of socialist resource allocation. On the other hand, he seems to be unwilling to accept the necessary implication that rent and interest must appear as accounting categories in socialist calculation.[81] By a well-known and very awkward adjustment for differences in the organic composition of capital, Dobb formulates optimum conditions in terms of the labor theory.[82] One gains the impres-

---

[76] Op. cit., p. 112 ff.

[77] R. Dunayevskaya, "A New Revision of Marxian Economics," American Economic Review, September 1944, XXXIV, pp. 531–537. In this article Miss Dunayevskaya comments on the much-discussed Soviet article "Some Problems in the Teaching of Political Economy," Pod Znamenem Marksizma (Under the Banner of Marxism), No. 7–8, July–August 1943. A translation of this article also appears in the American Economic Review, September 1944. See also the comments on the article by C. Landauer, "From Marx to Menger," ibid., June 1944, XXXIV, pp. 340–344; P. A. Baran, "New Trends in Russian Economic Thinking?" ibid., December 1944, XXXIV, pp. 862–871; Oscar Lange, "Marxian Economics in the Soviet Union," ibid., March 1945, XXXV, pp. 127–133; R. Dunayevskaya, "A Rejoinder," ibid., September 1945, XXXV, pp. 660–664.

[78] P. M. Sweezy, "Economics and the Crisis of Capitalism," Economic Forum, Spring 1935, III, p. 79.

[79] Idem, The Theory of Capitalist Development (New York, 1942), pp. 52–54.

[80] See above, p. 442, note 67.

[81] See especially Political Economy and Capitalism, pp. 308–309, 326 ff.

[82] Ibid.

sion that in Dobb's analysis the labor theory is not so much an analytic tool as excess baggage.

According to a recent Soviet article already cited,[83] the labor theory of value continues to operate under socialism. As the article explains, this represents a change in position from the view formerly held in the USSR, according to which the labor theory referred only to capitalism. In judging the portent of this doctrinal change, however, account must be taken of the fact that here, as in so many spheres of the Soviet system, there seems to be a wide gap between theory and practice. The existence of such a gap is acknowledged in the article; it is explained that

The prices of commodities are set with certain deviations from their values, corresponding to the particular objectives of the Soviet state, and the quantity of commodities of various kinds which can be sold under the existing scale of production and the needs of society.

IX. The Debate

To come finally to Mises, there are two questions to ask: What does he say and what does he mean?

On the first question, let Mises speak for himself:

And as soon as one gives up the conception of a freely established monetary price for goods of a higher order, rational production becomes completely impossible. Every step that takes us away from private ownership of the means of production also takes us away from rational economics . . .

The administration (of the socialist state) may know exactly what goods are most urgently needed. But in so doing, it has only found what is, in fact, but one of the two necessary prerequisites for economic calculation. In the nature of the case, however, it must dispense with the other—the valuation of the means of production . . .

Where there is no free market there is no pricing mechanism; without a pricing mechanism, there is no economic calculation . . .

Exchange relations between production goods can only be established on the basis of private ownership of the means of production.[84]

As to what Mises means, there appear to be two views. According to that which seems to have gained the wider currency, Mises' contention is that without private ownership of, or (what comes to the same thing for Mises) a free market for, the means of production, the rational evaluation of these goods for the purposes of calculating costs is ruled out

---

[83] Above, p. 444, note 77.

[84] L. von Mises, *op. cit.*, pp. 104–111. Essentially the same argument is repeated in Mises, *Die Gemeinwirtschaft*. An English translation of this work has been published as *Socialism* (London, 1936).

conceptually. With it goes any rational economic calculation. To put the matter somewhat more sharply than is customary, let us imagine a Board of Supermen, with unlimited logical faculties, with a complete scale of values for the different consumers' goods and present and future consumption, and detailed knowledge of production techniques. Even such a Board would be unable to evaluate rationally the means of production. In the absence of a free market for these goods, decisions on resource allocation in Mises' view necessarily would be on a haphazard basis.

Interpreted in this way, the argument is easily disposed of. Lange[85] and Schumpeter,[86] who favor this interpretation of Mises, point out correctly that the theory is refuted completely by the work of Pareto and Barone. As the analysis of these writers shows, once tastes and techniques are given, the values of the means of production can be determined unambiguously by imputation without the intervention of a market process. The Board of Supermen could decide readily how to allocate resources so as to assure the optimum welfare. It would simply have to solve the equations of Pareto and Barone.

According to the other interpretation of Mises, which has the authority of Hayek,[87] the contention is not that rational calculation is logically inconceivable under socialism but that there is no practicable way of realizing it. Imputation is theoretically possible; but, once private ownership of the means of production has been liquidated, it cannot be accomplished in practice.

Hayek's[88] own thinking and that of Robbins,[89] seems to be along these lines. Lange, who interprets the views of Hayek and Robbins as being in reality a retreat from the original position of Mises, considers that his own analysis refutes their argument:

As we have seen, there is not the slightest reason why a trial and error procedure, similar to that in a competitive market, could not work in a socialist economy to determine the accounting prices of capital goods and of the productive resources in public ownership.[90]

Hayek apparently is not entirely convinced:

Whether the solution offered will appear particularly practicable, even to socialists, may perhaps be doubted.[91]

---

[85] On the Economic Theory of Socialism, p. 51 ff.

[86] Op. cit., Ch. XVI.

[87] "Socialist Calculation: The Competitive Solution," loc. cit., pp. 126–127.

[88] Collectivist Economic Planning, Ch. V, "The Present State of the Debate"; "Socialist Calculation: The Competitive Solution," loc. cit.; "The Use of Knowledge in Society," loc. cit.

[89] The Great Depression, p. 151.

[90] Lange, On the Economic Theory of Socialism, p. 89.

[91] "Socialist Calculation: The Competitive Solution," loc. cit., p. 149.

Which of these two interpretations of Mises is correct, we leave the reader to decide. The issue between Hayek and Robbins on the one hand and Lange on the other, however, calls for further consideration.

Operationally, how is it possible to tell whether any given planning scheme is "practicable" or not? (We pass by the question of how to tell whether a planning scheme is "particularly practicable.") Here again, it seems to be necessary to deal with two different views.

According to one, expressed most clearly by Schumpeter,[92] the question is not how well or ill socialism can function, but whether a planning scheme can be devised such that it can work at all. If there is no "practicable" basis for rational calculation, the economy presumably would break down. The symptoms would be waste on a vast scale and even chaos.

Clearly, if this is the test of practicability, there hardly can be any room for debate: of course, socialism can work. On this, Lange certainly is convincing. If this is the sole issue, however, one wonders whether at this stage such an elaborate theoretic demonstration is in order. After all, the Soviet planned economy has been operating for thirty years. Whatever else may be said of it, it has not broken down.

According to Hayek, the test is this:

. . . it was not the possibility of planning as such which has been questioned, but the possibility of successful planning . . . There is no reason to expect that production would stop, or that the authorities would find difficulty in using all the available resources somehow, or even that output would be permanently lower than it had been before planning started. What we should anticipate is that output, where the use of the available resources was determined by some central authority, would be lower than if the price mechanism of a market operated freely under otherwise similar circumstances.[93]

In familiar terms, the question for Hayek is: Which is more efficient, socialism or capitalism? This, of course, is the question which all the participants in the debate eventually come to face anyhow. As we see it, it is now the only issue outstanding. The discussion in preceding sections, it is hoped, will provide a partial basis for judgment on this important matter. For the rest, with the following few cautions, we leave this issue too for the reader to decide.[94]

First, in order to reach any conclusion on comparative efficiency, it is necessary to agree on the test of efficiency, i.e., on the ends according to which the optimum allocation of resources is to be defined. A compari-

---

[92] *Op. cit.*, p. 185.
[93] *Collectivist Economic Planning*, pp. 203–204.
[94] In addition to the studies already cited, mention must be made of the very balanced study of A. C. Pigou, *Socialism versus Capitalism* (London, 1944).

son of the total market value of the consumers' goods produced in the rival systems, such as Schumpeter proposes,[95] already implies the acceptance of the principle of consumers' sovereignty. It is necessary to decide, too, whether the egalitarian principle of distribution is one of the ends, whether consumers are to be sovereign in respect of decisions on investment, and so on.

Second, one must distinguish between blueprints of economic systems operating in hypothetical worlds and rival economic systems in the real world. There seems to be very little point, for example, in a comparison of perfect competition in a capitalist world that never existed, on the one hand, and socialism in Russia, on the other; or, alternatively, of the Competitive Solution in an established socialist state where there is a unanimity on ends, on the one hand, and monopolistic and unstable capitalism in the United States, on the other. We must compare ideals with ideals or facts with facts. Participants in both sides of the debate have erred in failing to observe this elementary rule.

Finally, it is necessary to bear in mind that in the real world the question of comparative efficiency cannot be divorced altogether from questions of politics. In this connection it suffices only to allude to the matter of working class co-operation and discipline, which Schumpeter[96] rightly emphasizes, and the question of social stratification in relation to the problem of assuring the effective use of natural talents.

---

[95] *Op. cit.*, pp. 189–190.
[96] *Ibid.*, p. 210 ff.

13

THE PROSPECTS FOR CAPITALISM

David McC. Wright

"WE CANNOT absolutely prove that those are in error who tell us that society has reached a turning-point, that we have seen our best days. But so said all who came before us, and with just as much apparent reason." —T. B. Macaulay, January 1830.[1]

Literature on the prospects for capitalism must in the nature of things be predominantly "liberal" or right-wing, and this is the case during the period under review.[2] The majority of socialists and all communists assume that if any important time-span is to be considered capitalism has no prospects, therefore the left tends to concern itself at most with the problems of the transition. Only those, broadly speaking, who have some remnant of capitalist values will trouble to ask whether the system might not pull through after all.

It would be a mistake, however, to take too seriously any superficial appearance of a community of standards derived from the American literature of the last ten years. Close inspection will soon reveal deep conflicts in social attitudes, methods of analysis, and resulting prognosis. Some come to help Caesar, others merely to bury him, while a few combine praise for past achievement with pessimism for the future in nearly equal parts.

The writing of the last decade on capitalist prospects can be loosely grouped under four heads: (1) Socialist discussions of the transition.[3] These are largely outside the scope of the present paper. (2) A vast Keynesian and near-Keynesian literature of varying degrees of optimism and pessimism, making heavy use of quantitative estimates, and generally embodying various suggested "modifications" needed to "save the system." Here, of course, the best-known name is Hansen.[4] (3) A more

---

[1] T. B. Macaulay, "Southey's Colloquies," in *Miscellaneous Works* (London, 1875). The quotation begins: "The present time is one of great distress."

[2] We shall not attempt in this essay to give a complete bibliography. Such a list on the present topic would run into thousands of titles. Only typical samples therefore are given, and nothing invidious is to be inferred from the omission of a particular book or article.

[3] On the border line between Marxist and Keynesian literature is Dr. P. M. Sweezy's *Theory of Capitalist Development* (New York, 1944).

[4] For example, A. H. Hansen, *Fiscal Policy and Business Cycles* (New York, 1941); also his essays in *Post-War Economic Problems*, S. E. Harris, ed. (New York, 1943);

sociologically orientated non- or anti-Keynesian group, rather further to the right, as Professors Frank Graham, Schumpeter, and Frank Knight.[5] (4) A small but vehement group of almost completely uncontaminated, non-Keynesian advocates of virtually pure *laissez-faire,* as Mr. Henry Hazlitt in his *Economics in One Lesson.*[6]

From this rather heterogeneous collection certain basic issues may be developed: First, what *is* capitalism? Next, how shall we predict its future? Will statistics suffice or must we consider cultural and ethical currents? What do we mean by an investment "outlet"? Are there limits to the amount of investment a system can currently absorb? If the system fails, will it be because of its own inherent weakness; or because its adherents have made mistakes; or simply because we do not like it?

I

"Since 1932," writes Dr. Bissell, "socialism, under that name, has not been a live political issue in the United States."[7] The influence of the Keynesian school has worked on the whole toward a blurring of the distinction between capitalism and other systems. This tendency is most strongly marked in Mr. A. P. Lerner's *Economics of Control,*[8] but somewhat the same attitude is traceable in Lord Beveridge's *Full Employment in a Free Society*[9] and underlies—though in very much less degree—the writing of Professor Alvin Hansen.[10] Certainly if one is to restrict the term capitalist to those who believe that the system can operate with adequate stability totally without help, the number of "capitalist" economists (or any type of capitalist) would be very small. But are there not deeper issues at stake?

idem, Economic Reconstruction (New York, 1945). For critical discussion of this line of thought, see A. F. Burns, "Economic Research and the Keynesian Thinking of Our Times," *Twenty Sixth Annual Report of the National Bureau of Economic Research* (New York, 1946); also *idem* and A. H. Hansen, "Two Interpretations of Keynesian Economics," *Review of Economic Statistics,* November 1947, XXIX. As samples of the more hopeful literature influenced to some degree by Keynes, see Howard S. Ellis, "Full Employment Through Competitive Markets," in *Financing American Prosperity* (New York, 1945); and M. G. de Chazeau, A. G. Hart, G. C. Means, et al., *Jobs and Markets, How to Prevent Inflation and Depression in the Transition* (New York, 1946). These titles are not listed as exhaustive. It would be impossible to give a complete bibliography in the limits of the present essay.

[5] F. D. Graham, *Social Goals and Economic Institutions* (Princeton, 1942); J. A. Schumpeter, *Capitalism, Socialism and Democracy,* 2nd ed. (New York, 1947); Frank H. Knight, *Freedom and Reform* (New York, 1947).

[6] Henry Hazlitt, *Economics in One Lesson* (New York, 1946).

[7] Richard Bissell, "Post-War Private Investing and Public Spending," in *Post-War Economic Problems,* p. 83.

[8] A. P. Lerner, *The Economics of Control* (New York, 1944).

[9] Lord Beveridge, *Full Employment in a Free Society* (New York, 1945).

[10] Cf. A. H. Hansen, *Economic Policy and Full Employment* (New York, 1947).

A fundamental cleavage centers about the attitude toward property. Is the survival of capitalism merely the survival of the vested interest—in other words of a "reasonable" number of property rights—or does it refer to a regime of competitive adaptation? To Professors Graham, Knight, and Schumpeter—as also to Mr. Thurman Arnold—a prime feature of the system lies in the existence of such flexibility of competition and such incentives, cultural and otherwise, as would induce and permit relative freedom of the entrepreneur in the initiation of new technical combinations.[11] These new combinations, furthermore, are expected and encouraged to break down old income claims (destroy the "dead hand") and open new horizons. Property therefore is regarded as an institution which constantly destroys itself in the particular instance in order to survive in the general.[12] Here is a thread which runs through the whole history and fabric of orthodox liberalism.[13]

Many modern liberals and extreme conservatives share, however, in paradoxical agreement, an entirely different approach. Those capitalists who are interested primarily in preserving an established routine rather than creating new paths are apt to take the attitude that capitalism survives as long as they "own" "their" factory. If they can persuade their competitors to combine with them to stabilize the market, so much the better. And if planning makes possible the perpetuation of this arrangement, even at the price of considerable taxation, it may seem not too bad an idea.[14] Furthermore under many modern standards such individuals may derive considerable social- and self-congratulation from their "liberal" and "forward looking" outlook. In fact, however, they are mere apologists for the vested interest. Nevertheless both in right- and left-wing literature it is frequently assumed that a system which does not directly confiscate anyone's property, but merely taxes wealth and income severely, while licensing and directing in advance the flow of net new investment, can be called capitalistic. Professor Schumpeter, however, has referred to such schemes as "guided capitalism" or "capitalism in the oxygen tent" and has shown that whatever their merits or demerits, they contain little or nothing of the essential qualities of what has hitherto been known as capitalism.[15]

---

[11] F. D. Graham, op. cit.; J. A. Schumpeter, op. cit.; Thurman Arnold, *The Folklore of Capitalism* (New York, 1939); *idem, The Bottlenecks of Business* (New York, 1940).

[12] Cf. Professor Schumpeter's phrase "creative destruction," op. cit.

[13] For example, Francois Bastiat's *Sophisms of the Protective Policy* (New York, 1848).

[14] Similarly liberals anxious to "plan" will be willing to settle for control on the basis of recognition of many vested interests.

[15] J. A. Schumpeter, "Capitalism in the Post-War World," in *Post-War Economic Problems*, p. 125. "On the understanding that the essence of the bourgeois economy will be absent from the picture, we may call this system guided capitalism."

We shall, therefore, use in the remainder of this essay the following definition: "Capitalism is a system in which, on average, much the greater portion of economic life and particularly of net new investment is carried on by private (i.e. non-government) units under conditions of active and substantially free competition, and avowedly at the least, under the incentive of a hope for profit."

Adoption of this definition entails certain consequences. Though the concept selected does not imply that capitalism survives only as long as "pure" or "perfect" competition survives (and we shall discuss this point later), nevertheless our definition does mean that if capitalist or other pressure groups have log-rolled themselves into an industrial stalemate with (in the most likely case) adequate employment ensured only by a permanent special flow of government war or welfare expenditure, such a system can no more by our terminology be called capitalist than socialist. In this essay we will be discussing the prospects for the survival of the regime of creative competitive adaptation.

II

Three principal lines of thought can be found in the literature, all of which lead to a pessimistic conclusion. First, it may be said that from the point of view of mechanical stability the system is inherently unable to "work." Next, that the competitive system is ugly or immoral and that however stable or prosperous it may be, its repugnance to our moral standards will eventually lead us to *stop* it from working. Third, some will say that though a competitive system could be adequately stabilized, and does not offend moral values while it is competitive, nevertheless the system "automatically" transforms itself into monopoly, and when it has done so will cease to be tolerated.

It might at first seem that the ethical issues could be left to one side. Thus the Keynesian "political arithmetic" of the last few years displays an apparent rigid "scientific" neutrality. The procedure used is quite simple in basic logic and will be found explained a hundred times over in popular as well as academic writing during the last ten years.[16] Estimates are made first of all of the output (gross national product) which could be produced if there were full employment. This would seem to be a purely technical matter. Next statistical records are used to estimate the proportion that society is likely to try to save of money payments cor-

---

[16] Among many popular expositions may be named Henry A. Wallace, *Sixty Million Jobs* (New York, 1945); Stuart Chase, *Where's the Money Coming From?* (New York, 1943); Robert R. Nathan, *Mobilizing for Abundance* (New York, 1944).

responding to a full employment output. Finally the estimated proportion of attempted saving is compared with the number of investment outlets believed to be available. If attempted saving shows a tendency to exceed investment outlets, a case is made out for intervention to stabilize the economy and prevent unemployment. And since the resulting policy measures believed necessary are frequently, though not inevitably, incompatible with capitalism, as we have defined it, the presence or absence of adequate estimated "outlets" for investment, or "offsets" to saving, is sometimes taken as being, in itself, a sufficient basis for forecasting the future of the capitalist system.

We shall shortly see that the economic logic behind the Keynesian approach just sketched is not as simple or self-evident as might appear. Nevertheless there is *prima facie* no objection to the income method as a means of organizing and clarifying economic data, *provided* all the relevant considerations are kept in mind. Relevant considerations, however, are frequently much broader than many purely quantitative theorists are likely to recognize. Thus Professor Marshall Stone of the University of Chicago mathematics department writes:

> On the theoretical side I would anticipate that the demands of statecraft would greatly accelerate the introduction of scientific method into the social studies. It is quite clear, I think, that once the social studies truly commit themselves, in accord with the exigencies of our times, to a serious attempt at prediction in the field of social phenomena, they will incline to loosen their ties with the fields of belles-lettres and moral philosophy—to their own considerable advantage.[17]

Unfortunately life is not so simple. Unless the "scientific" or "mathematical" economist also predicts the *cultural atmosphere,* and allows for changes in it, his statistical work is always apt to be upset. Investment "outlets" available under one outlook may not be available under another.[18] Should hostile propaganda lead a people to repudiate the essentials of a system as immoral, they will not follow the necessary policies; and quantitative forecasts, however carefully made and apparently favorable, will not be verified. The reverse is also true. The estimation of every value used in the Keynesian income calculations is liable to a tremendous (albeit frequently unconscious) personal bias and even if personal bias is substantially avoided the results yielded—for example, the number

---

[17] M. H. Stone, "Science and Statecraft," *Science,* May 16, 1947, CV, p. 309.

[18] Cf. Dr. E. E. Hagen's excellent and straightforward article, "The Reconversion Period: Reflections of a Forecaster," *Review of Economic Statistics,* May 1947, XXIX, pp. 95, 101, "I suspect that . . . I was bemused by my preconception of a deflationary period during the reconversion interval. More critical and imaginative self-analysis would probably have considerably improved my forecasts." Cf. D. McC. Wright, "The Great Guessing Game—Terborgh versus Hansen," *ibid.,* February 1946, XXVIII, pp. 18, 21, "Many people do not *want* to see other possibilities beside stagnation."

and type of individuals who "ought" to have jobs—depend very largely on the prejudices of the time.[19] Among the given data of the quantitative economist is the ethical attitude of a people, and this is not the less important because so frequently forgotten. We shall first discuss the ambiguities of the Keynesian forecasting method from the point of view of purely economic logic; but before a final summary can be made, ethical and cultural issues will have to be considered also.

III

Recent economic developments, as well as recent literature, have shown clearly that the reliability of Keynesian forecasting methods, and the pessimistic results often yielded by them, largely depends on the stability and predictability of two "schedules"—the consumption schedule and the investment schedule.[20] Expressed less technically this means that in order to make reliable predictions by the Keynesian method we must be able to draw up a graph showing the percentage of gross national product which people will try to save at each supposed level of output and project these estimates into the future without fear of serious discrepancies. In the same way the investment outlets appropriate to various output levels should also be accurately foreseeable, and when the two sets of estimates are compared we get a forecast of the level of activity which the community is likely to experience, barring intervention of some sort.

But fairly early in the "Keynesian Revolution" it was discovered that the consumption schedule, at the least, was not as stable as supposed nor could we be quite so dogmatic concerning its (long-run) shape. Keynes' "normal psychological law" of consumption behavior was that as income rose consumption would rise, but not as much.[21] Thus there would be a progressively greater gap between consumption and the output needed for full employment—necessitating a constantly increasing rate of investment if deflation was to be avoided. However, by 1942–43 Professors Samuelson and Hansen were obliged to concede that in the past at the least the consumption schedule *must* have risen spontaneously.[22] Other-

---

[19] For example, how many women should work? At what age should one start? What wage shall we take as basic?

[20] Dr. Lawrence Klein draws a distinction between the equating of savings and investment as "observables" where the Keynesian definitions are tautologies and as "schedules" where they are not. He does not appear to notice that if the schedules are not independent and stable they also become tautologies. Lawrence R. Klein, *The Keynesian Revolution* (New York, 1947), p. 110.

[21] J. M. Keynes, *The General Theory of Employment, Interest and Money* (New York, 1936), pp. 96–97.

[22] A. H. Hansen, *Fiscal Policy and Business Cycles,* p. 233; P. A. Samuelson, "Full Employment After the War," in *Post-War Economic Problems,* p. 35.

wise we would by now be requiring a flow of investment of astronomical magnitude.

This concession has done much to destroy the conciseness and precision of the Keynesian schema. Immediately the question arose of when and under what circumstances the schedule would shift. Dr. Gardiner Means and others suggested that an increased quantity of money would change the attitude of the public toward spending, and Dr. Lawrence Klein blamed the sudden upward shift of the postwar period upon increased "liquid assets" plus a "dearth of durable consumer goods."[23] Also Professor Pigou pointed out that though reduction of interest rates and other incentives toward accumulation might not at first appear to affect consumption habits, the long-run effects might well be most important.[24] Whatever the reasoning one employs, however, there can be little dispute that objectively the consumption schedule has shown itself to be much less stable than was at first supposed. We have barely scratched the surface of this problem and it is one of the most urgent fields now open for further research.

Turning from the consumption schedule to the problem of forecasting investment, we encounter a similar collapse of the simplified or "streamlined" Keynesian dogma. Keynesian theory has many versions,[25] but in its simplest and most rigid form the outlook toward investment seems to be about as follows: A "given" amount of equipment is needed to produce, in conjunction with labor, a "given" output of consumers' goods.[26] The relation between the two is apparently assumed to be predominantly a technical one and comparatively stable. In other words investment is assumed only to be made more or less directly to produce consumers' goods. Consequently if the demand for consumers' goods is not rising the demand for investment goods must soon fall.[27] The conclusion is therefore that there is an appropriate stock of capital—no more and no less— for each level of consumption, and once investment has built the capital stock to the appropriate figure no more can be "absorbed." Thus in ex-

[23] Gardiner C. Means, "The American Economy in the Inter-War Period," *American Economic Review* (Proceedings), May 1946, XXXVI, p. 32. D. McC. Wright, "Professor Knight on Limits to the Use of Capital," *Quarterly Journal of Economics*, May 1944, LVIII, p. 331; L. A. Klein, *op. cit.*, p. 61.

[24] A. C. Pigou, "Economic Progress in a Stable Environment," *Economica*, August 1947, XIV, p. 180.

[25] The writer's version, which undoubtedly colors this essay, will be found in his "Future of Keynesian Economics," *American Economic Review*, June 1945, XXV, p. 284. It may be of interest that I have personal letters from Keynes approving its general argument.

[26] See, for example, L. A. Klein, *op. cit.*, pp. 110, 196, 197.

[27] Compare P. A. Samuelson, *op. cit.*, p. 45. "Only where consumption demand is high are large savings and investment possible." As will be seen from the text, this statement is not correct as a universal proposition.

pounding the simplest version of the Keynesian system some writers speak of the consumption and investment schedules as "smooth" stable curves.[28]

Many Keynesians, however, including Professor Hansen, have pointed out that there is often in fact a large number of investments not geared directly, or not geared at all, to the current level of consumption.[29] The economy may be dragged out of depression by that section which belongs to the future. Also net new investment to improve efficiency is clearly possible even when consumption is shrinking; while a sufficiently favorable change in expectations could temporarily, at the least, call forth adequate investment.[30] Professor Fellner's "investment for further investment" sums up this strain of thought very neatly.[31]

Extreme Keynesians, however, while conceding the possibilities just named, consider them as more or less spasmodic accidents and would say that the simplified Keynesian view, directly linking investment to consumption levels, is normally the most accurate. Thus, using Klein's *Keynesian Revolution* as an expression of extreme Keynesianism in its later forms, we find investment outlets conceived of in three ways: (1) in direct technical relationship to consumption levels; (2) as influenced *spasmodically* by "innovations," arising from "sociological" forces "outside" the normal pricing system; (3) as "autonomously planned" by some central board without any necessary immediate reference to consumption levels—for example, as in Soviet Russia.[32]

Curiously enough one looks in vain for a comprehensive theory of investment outlets in Keynes' *General Theory*.[33] He does not even mention the work of authorities such as Professor Frank Knight who maintain that there is no limit to the amount of investment currently possible. Indeed Keynes treated Knight in much the same manner for which he himself criticized the Victorian treatment of Malthus. Also in this country the Keynesians have tended to follow Schumpeter's sharp distinction between the circular flow on the one hand, and "innovations" on the other, and to apply it, as in Klein's case, with uncritical literalness.

[28] L. A. Klein, *op. cit.*, p. 110.

[29] A. H. Hansen, *Fiscal Policy and Business Cycles*, pp. 39, 45.

[30] The Keynesian reply to this would be that, unless we assume a simply perverse optimism, expectations contrary to fact will not endure forever. However, if one follows Schumpeter in believing that there are a number of new possibilities "always present," then a change in expectations (confidence) inducing new entrepreneurial activity could have the necessary effect. See below, note 33.

[31] William Fellner, *Monetary Policies and Full Employment* (Berkeley, 1946), pp. 24, 25.

[32] L. A. Klein, *op. cit.*, pp. 75-80.

[33] Sometimes Keynes speaks of "stationary population," *op. cit.*, p. 106, and sometimes, as in Ch. 11 of the same book, of increasing uncertainty.

The truth is, however, that while Schumpeter's distinction is a valuable device for isolating an important factor, it can be extremely misleading.[34] Professor Knight's views have been discussed at length by Lange, Samuelson, the writer, and others.[35] If one *assumes* unchanged tastes and unchanged techniques the rigid Keynesian conclusions appear to the writer to follow.[36] However, they are based upon a distinction between growth and change which in fact does not exist. The mere fact of growth, in and of itself, "spontaneously" induces a constant shift in the pattern of taste and technique. Furthermore, in a purely and perfectly competitive world, the assumption of "perfect knowledge" involved in the concept of "perfect" competition might be said to include, by definition, an ability of business men to read off and anticipate all changes in taste as fast as they occurred. On that basis Professor Knight's ideas become correct and there is virtually no limit to the absorption of current investment. If growth-induced changes in the pattern of wants and production create a sufficiently rapid rate of obsolescence, there is no problem.[37]

This concession is of more than theoretical significance. Gustav Cassel in reviewing the *General Theory* in 1937 objected that on the basis of past trends wealth doubled every twenty-five years, and if wealth were to double again in the future, savers would be hard put to it to find the necessary saving.[38] This criticism seemed absurd during the 'thirties, but makes more sense today. If the competitive order is not persuaded or forced into ossification during a depression, it is submitted that we have a right to rely upon the institutional environment to produce "spontaneously," after an interval, new techniques and new wants.

It is nevertheless possible to reconstruct an approach to the Keynes-

[34] I wonder if Professor Knight and Professor Schumpeter are really as far apart on this point as they appear. For example, see J. A. Schumpeter, *The Theory of Economic Development* (Cambridge, Mass., 1934), p. 88. "It is no part of his (the entrepreneur's) function to 'find' or 'create' new possibilities. They are *always present,* abundantly accumulated by all sorts of people" (italics added). Does not this amount to a concession of the idea of boundless uses followed (in the remainder of the book) by an analysis of the social obstacles to the carrying through of the needed alterations?

[35] See F. H. Knight, "Interest," *Encyclopaedia of the Social Sciences* (New York, 1930-35), VIII; idem, "The Quality of Capital and the Rate of Interest," Parts I and II, *Journal of Political Economy,* August and October 1936, XLIV; idem, "Diminishing Returns from Investment," *ibid.,* March 1944, LII; idem, "Note on Dr. Lange's Interest Theory," *Review of Economic Studies,* June 1937, IV; Oskar Lange, "Interest in the Theory of Production," *Review of Economic Studies,* June 1936, III; P. A. Samuelson, "Dynamics, Statics, and the Stationary State," *Review of Economic Statistics,* February 1943, XXV; D. McC. Wright, "Professor Knight on Limits to the Use of Capital," *loc. cit.;* idem, *The Economics of Disturbance* (New York, 1947), Ch. IV.

[36] See articles cited in the preceding footnote.

[37] But of course the *whole* national income could not be saved and "invested," for more than a few hours, without everyone's starving to death.

[38] G. Cassel, "Mr. Keynes' 'General Theory,'" *International Labor Review,* October 1937, XXXVI, p. 437.

Hansen outlook, but in far less precise and dogmatic form. It may be said that whatever may be conceded regarding the mere unorganized whims of an individual, his *market habits* of preference change much more slowly than is postulated in theoretical models implying boundless outlets, and that the process of anticipating and creating wants is not an automatic one. The actual rates of obsolescence are thus not infinitely great, and an expanding society, as a result of the minimum friction inherent in any organization, may pass through periods of temporary glut in which tastes and technique may be taken, for practical purposes, as temporarily given.

The stagnation thesis may thus be re-formulated as follows: it may be said that there are observed *customary* rates of institutional response to various stimuli, and that these rates of response appear to have a certain degree of stability over time. Such a formulation resembles Professor Pigou's explanation of the rhythm of the cycle.[39] On the basis of customary institutional rates of response one may then ascribe a certain proportion of investment to population growth, to great new industries, etc., etc. But it is obvious that the Keynesian theory thus re-assembled has lost most of its definiteness and rigidity. The case for average stability of response is debatable, and clearly the influence of *policy* upon the institutional rates of reaction could be very great. So far as the stagnation thesis and population growth are concerned, what warrant is there for leaving aside foreign investment and foreign population growth? Even if we grant his statistics and arithmetic, the ultimate basis of Professor Hansen's thesis is the assumption of an invincible stupidity in international economic relations. Such an assumption may be justified, but in discussing it we come a long way from the rigid Keynesian outlook.[40]

It is interesting to apply the principles just worked out to the general method of forecasting used in the early nineteen-forties. Professor Hansen was the most cautious of the stagnationists in that his estimates ran in terms of long-run *proportions*—90 *per cent* consumption from disposable income, etc. Less cautious forecasters tended to extrapolate absolute schedules, or at least to carry forward wartime saving ratios, and thus made the problem seem much more severe.[41]

Probably the most interesting case was that of Dr. George Terborgh. Terborgh's *Bogey of Economic Maturity* represented almost an official

---

[39] A. C. Pigou, *Industrial Fluctuations,* 2nd ed. (London, 1929). Pigou suggests that one explanation of the so-called periodicity of the cycle may be a certain stability of institutional reaction.

[40] D. McC. Wright, "The Great Guessing Game," *loc. cit.*

[41] For example, compare Professor S. E. Harris' introduction to *Economic Reconstruction* with Hansen's estimates in the same volume.

answer of American capitalism to the stagnation thesis, yet Terborgh adopted much the point of view toward investment outlets just sketched as a possible formulation of the Keynes-Hansen outlook.[42] Furthermore his estimated long-run rates of institutional response did not appear widely different from those of Hansen.[43] Despite dogmatic language, Terborgh, in no place in his book, added up the components of the national income and compared them with expected saving. The fact is that if one attempts to follow Terborgh's analysis his various components do not quite make up full employment, and his model, in effect, leads to much the same conclusion as Professor Hansen's. In the writer's opinion, however, both Terborgh and Hansen, even if one should concede the validity of their quantitative estimates, were at fault in dismissing the possibility of foreign investment. In passing foreign trade over with a bare mention, Terborgh reflects the insular bias, and, by inference, the tendency toward die-hard protectionism, which is one of the most alarming characteristics of American conservatism.

IV

Undoubtedly it requires a good deal of faith to maintain in the depths of a depression that, if the system is not made too rigid by mistaken policy, new wants and new methods will soon appear. But if we consider the historical record of capitalism over an adequate length of time—say 150 years—is not its technological creativeness quite as stable a basis for prediction as the Keynesian "normal" law of consumer's behavior? Indeed for reasons given it seems more so. Furthermore, the association of competition with scientific growth can be shown to be no accident. The matter may be put as follows: If we make men free they become creative, and from their creations flow new wants and new techniques. "Innovations" are not therefore unrelated accidents but an inherent *and* recurrent characteristic of a given cultural atmosphere. So long as that atmosphere is not too much impaired, one has a right to expect from it certain results. In 1904 Henry Adams wrote, "Fifty years ago science took for granted that the rate of acceleration would not last. The world forgets quickly but even today the habit remains of founding statistics on the faith that consumption will continue nearly stationary."[44] Many of the economic forecasters of 1944 would have done well to remember his observation.

On the other hand, modern urbanized populations are pretty clearly

[42] George Terborgh, *The Bogey of Economic Maturity* (Chicago, 1945).
[43] Cf. D. McC. Wright, "The Great Guessing Game," *loc. cit.*
[44] Henry Adams, *The Education of Henry Adams* (New York, 1918), Ch. XXXIV, "A Law of Acceleration."

not going to submit again to the degree of unnecessary insecurity and poverty experienced in the "lamentable 'thirties" of this century—or the 1870's or the "hungry 'forties." Our challenge, therefore, is whether we can evolve techniques of stabilization adequate to keep depression within bounds, without too greatly impairing the factors making for *further* economic growth and development. To answer this challenge we must try to see what are the growth-making factors.

Attempts by academic economists during the period under review to defend the ideology of capitalism revealed a deeply seated conflict in radical philosophies. Thus Professor Frank Graham in his *Social Goals and Economic Institutions* converts Veblen's distrust of the "vested interest" into an argument for competitive capitalism, by insisting that competition best overcomes the power of the vested interest and the "dead hand" and hence is the freest and most productive form of economic organization.

One soon discovers, however, that many radical writers object to competition, *as such*, and that some of them do not even want technical change—though this last issue is seldom squarely faced. The ideal of a "conflict-free" world—also a strong element in Veblen's teaching—is developed, particularly by trade union economists, in ways opposed to the whole competitive ideal—no matter how pure or perfect. An interesting example of this side of Veblen is found in Dr. Gambs' most illuminating little book, *Beyond Supply and Demand.*[45]

The anti-competitive gospel is today reinforced by semantic associations easily linking the idea of competition with the idea of war.[46] Thus it might be said that the "spontaneous" rise in wants and technique earlier referred to is really spontaneous combustion. In other words the deadlock of stagnation can only be terminated by war.[47] This hypothesis gives a good apparent fit for World War II. It cannot be applied universally, however, without much tortuous logic. Spontaneous rise in investment and consumption schedules has occurred without the warlike

---

[45] J. S. Gambs, *Beyond Supply and Demand* (New York, 1946). This book suffers from an unwillingness to face the connection between change and conflict. And is not competition after all (no matter how "pure") another form of rivalry?

[46] We need to remember the differences between "competition" in the sense of a form of economic organization and "competition" in the general sense of rivalry.

[47] It is noteworthy, however, that evidence has been marshalled to show that the incidence of war was lighter in the nineteenth century than the eighteenth. See P. A. Sorokin, *Social and Cultural Dynamics* (New York, 1937), pp. 342, 345-346. Mr. Toynbee seems to feel that war has become more savage. But this, if true, applies only to a relatively short span of Western history. Anyone who reads of the Tartar invasions, for example, will obtain a different perspective. It seems to be an incurable and childish habit among Western intellectuals to assume that abolishing one set of forms of conflict will abolish all.

stimulus. Yet it may be further said that living in a competitive *market* makes us naturally competitive (combative) personally and therefore more open to the idea of solving the problem of maintaining investment flow by bombs rather than by slum clearance.

This issue may be argued indefinitely. Even on its own terms there are many other obstacles to constructive action in depression. What of the influence upon policy responses of a century and a half of literal teaching of Say's Law? Is the vested interest problem confined to capitalism? One point at least may be definitely disposed of on objective grounds: the idea that removing the competitive market will remove competition. At the bottom of most attacks upon the basic structure of the competitive ideal will usually be found the assumption that if market competition were abolished we would also abolish rivalry and frustration. It has been frequently pointed out in the last few years that this idea is absurd, for example, by Professor Frank Knight in his *Freedom and Reform*. If a man wishes to avoid the possibility of frustration or disappointment, he must become a meditating ascetic. The idea of rivalry is inherent in the nature of an integrated social life. A nation of completely moral and unselfish, self-sufficient farmers might need no government and have no rivalry or conflicts save in the home. But in a technically integrated economy—even if the political state has nominally "withered away"—there must remain a hierarchy of responsible technical operatives. Furthermore, some at least of the people must have some desire to hold responsible positions in the technical hierarchy or the machine will collapse. Yet the combination of ambition—if only ambition to do a good job for the State —plus the need for selection among candidates—inevitably involves some possibility of disappointment. Furthermore, if technical change, or scientific discovery, is still going forward, the possibility of conflict is greatly increased. For, if a man believes, however sincerely, unselfishly, and patriotically, that he has discovered valuable new truth, he is bound to oppose those who disagree with him. Economic peace is at best a generally agreed-upon way of settling conflicts *after* they have arisen—a generally accepted code of emulation and selection.

By a similar line of reasoning, attacks upon the distribution of wealth are also apt to presuppose that if wealth is equalized a general equality will ensue. But, as Hicks and Hart point out in *The Social Framework,* what of equality of power?[48] Inequality of power is inevitable in integrated social life. Democracy does not avoid the necessity of rulers. It only alters the way in which they are chosen and controlled. Furthermore, granting

---

[48] J. R. Hicks and A. G. Hart, *The Social Framework* (New York, 1945), pp. 231–232.

that inequality of power is inevitable, it follows that abolition of inheritance, and income differences, will not suffice to give everyone an equal start. What would be needed would be to destroy the family. For strategic position may be transmitted quite as well as money. And the commissar's son, no less than the boss's nephew, may get the "breaks." In sum we do not have a choice between a world of complete equality and a world of inequality. We can only choose among various forms of inequality. We do not have a choice between a world free from conflict and a world of conflict. We can only choose among various forms of conflict. Once this point is grasped, the case for capitalism becomes much stronger.

The writer bases his argument for the competitive economic market upon the principle of the decline of self-perpetuating groups, and the narrowing of the self-selecting elite.[49] This is a point of great importance in the theory of comprehensive planning. When planning ceases to be mere stabilization, or "filling in," and passes over into general licensing, or *ex ante* control of economic life, an institutional framework is set up which almost inevitably leads to self-perpetuation. For in planning what industries are to expand we almost inevitably plan what groups are to hold power. The consequences are twofold: first, technological progress, and with it the rise of the standard of living, will be hamstrung. For each entrenched vested interest will be able to log-roll with others, in approved N.I.R.A. style. Socialism does not avoid the pressure group problem.[50] Next, political democracy is endangered. The naïve supposition that mere possession of a vote, in a large electorate, is a sufficient protection for the individual cannot be substantiated. What counts is not merely a vote but power or influence with the organization. If the organization is able to pick off or neutralize its opposition *before* it has been organized, it can hold office more or less indefinitely. And when the ruling clique is in a position to administer suave but effective economic reprisal—even though for ends which *it* conceives to be good—there will probably come to be no way of getting rid of it short of violent revolution. Arthur Koestler complains that the Soviet bureaucracy is following the history of "all self-perpetuating groups" and becoming a regime of entrenched privilege.[51] But Koestler remains a socialist and does not notice that in the fabric of his own type of society there is a similar self-perpetuating mechanism, which, as far as the writer is concerned, will eventually yield similar results.

---

[49] D. McC. Wright, *Democracy and Progress* (New York, 1948); *idem, The Economics of Disturbance; idem,* "Hopes and Fears," *Review of Economic Statistics,* November 1944, XXVI.

[50] *Idem, The Economics of Disturbance,* Ch. III.

[51] Arthur Koestler, *The Yogi and the Commissar* (New York, 1946).

V

"All this," it may be said, "is very well, but we do not have competition any longer and there is no hope for reviving it." From such a point of view the writer dissents vigorously, and it is time to examine in more detail the contention that the system is automatically transforming itself into collectivism *via* monopolistic restriction.

The idea that the system is becoming relatively more monopolistic derives most of its self-evident character from an important semantic confusion which underlies two-thirds of the popular thought on the question. When most people say "monopoly" they only mean large-scale business. And it is undeniable that individual business units have become larger. But the mere fact that individual business units are becoming larger tells us almost nothing about changes in the degree of purity or perfection in their competition. What is needed is to compare the size of the individual concern with the size of the *market*. It is a far cry from selling buggies at the county seat to selling automobiles over the whole world. But whether competition is any more "monopolistic" is, at the least, debatable. Clearly we do have a serious trend toward monopoly today but its roots are quite different from those usually supposed. The basic modern difficulty lies not in the usual arguments, but in the fact that the *slogan* of planning has made the *fact* of monopoly respectable. The "good" monopoly arguments, so popular in British thought, are in the writer's opinion the most dangerous aspects of the problem.

Behind the "good" monopoly argument, in popular thinking at the least, often lies the idea that monopoly is needed in order to help avoid the business cycle. This view is rather popular in English circles. On the other hand, in the United States certain groups have made a determined effort to convince the public that monopoly is a chief cause of the business cycle.[52] Both sides cannot be right, but the writer does believe that they can be, and are, both wrong.

---

[52] The argument usually given in recent years in this country is that "big business" by raising prices "too high" "prices consumers out of the market," and causes deflation. While it is difficult to find explicit statement by an academic economist of this argument as the main cause of depression, an incautious reader might deduce something of the same idea from Edwin J. Nourse, *Price Making in a Democracy* (New York, 1944), Ch. X, "The Timing of Price Changes."

Such analysis, however, has many limitations. In addition to other sources of cyclical disturbance mentioned below in the text, there is the fundamental force of inflation itself. Much journalistic propaganda written today should be read in connection with Lord Keynes' remarks after the last war: ". . . The Governments of Europe, being many of them at this moment reckless in their methods as well as weak, seek to direct on to a class known as "profiteers" the popular indignation against the more obvious consequences

It should be clear that we cannot possibly agree upon an adequate anti-competitive policy until we know what approximate degree of competition we are seeking, why we are seeking it, and how much we are going to expect of it after we get it. For all these purposes the academic theory of pure or perfect competition seems to the writer hopelessly inadequate. The clue through which we find our way to some alleviation of the fearful semantic confusion now enfolding the subject is found, I submit, in Professor Chamberlin's distinction between "pure" and "perfect" competition.[53]

Under Chamberlin's terminology "purity" of competition means merely a perfect elasticity of the individual demand curve. This in turn reflects two requirements: (1) the consumer is completely indifferent between sellers; (2) each seller *believes* (he may be wrong) that, by himself, he has no influence on price and that his price policy will not provoke retaliation. Numbers are a necessary but not a sufficient condition for pure competition, and, granted a homogeneous product, the actual occurrence of a pure market may be as much the result of the competitive psychology of the entrepreneurs involved as it is of large numbers in the field. In other words, the more competitive the attitude of the entrepreneurs the fewer the numbers needed for pure competition.

"Perfect" competition, on the other hand, is sharply distinguishable from "pure" competition. It refers to "perfect" knowledge, "perfect" adaptability, frictionless adjustment. The mere durability of equipment, for example, or the existence of a given space-time system, could be considered "imperfections"—for they prevent instantaneous and perfect adjustment. A third term is really needed, and we will call it "absolute" competition. This would apply to conditions of both pure *and* perfect competition. But such a concept would imply its own special problems since without *some* friction things would be infinitely unstable—an infinite rate of vibration.

---

of their vicious methods. These "profiteers" are, broadly speaking, the entrepreneur class of capitalists, that is to say, the active and constructive element in the whole capitalist society, who in a period of rapidly rising prices cannot but get rich quick whether they wish it or desire it or not . . . By directing hatred against this class, therefore, the European Governments are carrying a step further the fatal process which the subtle mind of Lenin had consciously conceived. The profiteers are a consequence and not a cause of rising prices. By combining a popular hatred of the class of entrepreneurs with the blow already given to social security by the violent and arbitrary disturbance of contract and of the established equilibrium of wealth which is the inevitable result of inflation, these Governments are fast rendering impossible a continuance of the social and economic order of the nineteenth century. But they have no plan for replacing it." J. M. Keynes, *Essays in Persuasion* (New York, 1932), pp. 78–79.
    [53] E. H. Chamberlin, *The Theory of Monopolistic Competition*, 5th ed. (Cambridge, Mass., 1946) Ch. II, Appendix.

Fortunately we need not linger in these metaphysical regions. The important practical point is that, while pure competition is sometimes approximated, perfect competition is absolutely impossible—not from the nature of capitalism, but the nature of the universe. The best we can ever have is pure but imperfect competition. This is a qualification of the utmost importance, and one almost wholly overlooked in the recent literature. For as soon as we begin to consider pure *but* imperfect competition in a dynamic state—i.e., one in which constant readjustment is being made to technical change, and other disturbing factors—then virtually every statement usually made concerning the contrast between pure and *monopolistic* competition ceases to be necessarily true. Prices under pure competition need not be lower, output need not be greater, and profits need not be lower (though this last qualification of course also holds true in the static state). Furthermore, all these things—super-normal profit, for example—could occur though there was atomistic competition.[54] Economists have been trying to apply to the real world mathematical demonstrations which assumed static, "absolute" (or near-absolute) competition, when the most rigorous possible standard is dynamic, pure, but imperfect competition. No wonder we have been confused.

As soon as these distinctions are grasped the absurdity of blaming all business cycles on "monopoly" is readily apparent. Under the usual textbook illustration the confusion is easily understood. For the implication usually is that if we had pure competition everything would be all right. It follows logically, then, that, if everything is not all right, it must be the fault of "monopoly"—*ergo* "business" is responsible for the business cycle.

One of the most important problems underlying the business cycle concerns the durability of equipment plus the discontinuity of changes or expansion in demand and technique. These forces would exist even if every industry in the world were pulverized into 100,000 purely competing units. Furthermore, the basic problem cannot be completely solved by *ex ante* planning alone. There is an insoluble conflict of standards. When a massive change in wants, or increase in the level of demand, is found, plus durable equipment, plus slack in the productive system, the planners would have to choose between giving the consumer what he wanted *when* he wanted it (thus over-building the industry), or else of rationing consumers, sabotaging invention, and thus giving planned *ex ante* stability. If we restrict ourselves to *ex ante* planning, the conflict

---

[54] In other words, super-normal profit could exist even though there was free entry and a perfectly elastic individual demand curve, simply because the system was imperfectly competitive—i.e., had not yet had time to adjust itself.

is not socialism vs. capitalism but rationing vs. speed. The only way to reconcile, within limits, the demands of consumers (in their temporal as well as their absolute aspects) with stability, would be the despised capitalist policy of "filling in" or public works, when temporary collapse came in the market for durables.[55]

The results of our analysis are both favorable and unfavorable. We see that neither super-normal profit nor a business cycle are necessarily the results of monopoly. The welfare equations worked out, for example, by Mr. Lerner in his *Economics of Control* are derived from long-run static "absolute" competition and are almost useless in an actual situation. For example, if we did not at times have super-normal profit the probabilities are that we would never get adequate incentive for risky new investment.[56] If there were no advertising, how could a genuinely valuable new invention ever get before the public? And so on.

On the other hand, showing the irrelevance of pure competition, as an immediate standard, throws us back on relatively vague concepts as "workable" or "reasonable" competition and this does not satisfy those who demand a precise slogan and formula for everything. Yet is "planning" any more inevitably likely to give *always* an ideal solution? Does it, in itself, contain any definite criteria?

We come back then to the basic questions: Why do we try for competition, how much competition shall we seek, how much will we expect of competition? On balance it seems more nearly correct to say that monopoly is the result of the business cycle than that the business cycle is the result of monopoly. Monopoly, precisely because it does often sabotage rapid change, could make for greater stability. Yet these concessions do not seem to me to lead to an advocacy of "planned" monopoly on the English or European pattern.

---

[55] See D. McC. Wright, *The Economics of Disturbance,* Ch. VI and VII.

[56] This, it seems to me, is what Professor Schumpeter has in mind when he speaks of a certain amount of "monopoly" being necessary. Would it not be better to say a certain amount of imperfection? A sufficient "bonus" for the new venture might well be forthcoming under "pure" competition, if friction prevented immediate adjustment.

Many modern economists have been loath to recognize the paradox that investment, under the competitive profit system, is often undertaken, by the lender at the least, in *hopes* of something which the system itself is supposed eventually to prevent—namely, the hope of obtaining a *permanent* net value return. Even the entrepreneur expects super-normal profits for several years. The paradox can be solved "by definition" but it remains true in ordinary parlance to say that if the system worked absolutely perfectly, it would not work at all!

The attempt, furthermore, in recent years to regularize and limit this temporary bonus on the new venture and the new idea is bound to be a restraining influence on new investment. As long as the theoretical *possibility* of the glittering prize remains, men may work harder for it than if they know in advance they cannot possibly make more than a certain definite amount. The expectation of profit needed to start a new business is very different from that needed to keep one going.

The impressive thing about "good monopoly" and comprehensive planning arguments is their institutional naïveté. One may grant that, so far as economic stability is concerned, a program of holding back new inventions until just the right time could probably give a smoother flow of investment. But have we any guarantee that the inventions thus held back would *ever* be introduced? Inventions do not introduce themselves. They depend upon a social environment hospitable to change. Considering the universal presence of pressure groups, and of security sabotage; considering the decline of the self-perpetuating group, the chances are the new idea would never be used at all. Planning and rationalization can often serve as convenient social rituals for burying change, rather than implementing it.

Should we not, under the circumstances, therefore, try not for "pure" competition but for "workable" competition? Our reason for doing so will not so much be to meet mathematical standards of optimum output as to preserve the technological creativeness and personal democracy of our social structure. We want to keep an "open society"—to give the new man a fair chance to rise on independent terms. The standard for such competition would run not so much in numbers as in the frequency distribution. Does a new firm really have a chance in the field?

The aim of anti-trust action furthermore is not to establish a purely self-adjusting society. It seems unlikely that any degree of competition within the realm of possibility could be so flexible as to avoid the need, sometimes, for measures to prevent secondary deflation and maintain purchasing power. This means that anti-trust action, to be effective, must be underwritten by appropriate fiscal policy when necessary. And also that we be careful to see how our other policies—for example, labor and taxation—affect the new business venture.

VI

From the foregoing discussion, policy standards may be derived by which we may judge the remedies for deflation suggested during the past ten years. Generally speaking nearly all of the policies urged to maintain demand and increase consumption have had a tendency, if too literally applied, to backfire in the direction of restricting the margin of independent change and competition upon which so much has been seen to depend. Leaving aside the so-called "non-competitive" ideal already spoken of, three basic attitudes may be pointed out the application of which appears incompatible with continued creative development. First, insistence upon an *advance* guarantee that the economy shall never be in any danger of more than a minute fall in money income. Next, the implication that demand is self-satisfying and that obstacles to investment are a relatively minor matter. Third, the confusion of individual and social security.

There is a great difference between keeping deflation within tolerable bounds by compensatory action in a dynamic economy, and mechanically ensuring advance stability by putting investment flow in a strait jacket. The shift in emphasis which lies between Professor D. H. Robertson's *Banking Policy and the Price Level* and Lord Beveridge's *Full Employment in a Free Society* is something more than a technical matter of aiming for greater stability. It is a qualitative shift in social ideals.[57] Ninety-seven per cent stability cannot be achieved without putting an end to that development on relatively independent terms which is needed to implement invention and permit adequate innovation.

In the same way American redistributive policy has been shown by Butters and Lintner and others to bear with disproportionate weight against the *new* man and the *new* firm and thus to be a force making for monopoly.[58] The same is also true of certain aspects of labor's wage policy.[59]

Even disregarding the effects upon the new firm, redistribution to raise proportionate consumption has certain self-defeating qualities. It is a cardinal doctrine of the Keynesians, though Keynes himself was never as certain of the matter as some of his disciples seem to be, that entrepreneurs need little or no net profit incentive in order to initiate new enterprises. This doctrine seems to the writer to be based upon a confusion between marginal and absolute incentive. Because *some* people will do *some* work with little or, indeed, no profit incentive, it is assumed that *all* people will do *as much* work with little or no profit incentive. Kenneth Boulding in an outstanding article in the *American Economic Review* has done much to dispel this confusion.[60] There are possible cases in

---

[57] D. H. Robertson, *Banking Policy and the Price Level* (London, 1926); Lord Beveridge, *op. cit.*

[58] For example, see J. K. Butters and John Lintner, *Effect of Federal Taxes on Growing Enterprises* (Cambridge, Mass., 1945); also the writer's "Income Redistribution Reconsidered," in *Income and Employment, Essays in Honor of Alvin Hansen*, E. D. Domar and R. A. Musgrave, eds. (New York, 1948).

[59] R. A. Lester, "Shortcomings of Marginal Analysis for Wage Employment Problems," *American Economic Review*, March 1936, XXXVI; *idem*, "Marginalism, Minimum Wages, and Labor Markets," *ibid.*, March 1947, XXXVII; Fritz Machlup, "Marginal Analysis and Empirical Research," *ibid.*, September 1946, XXXVI; *idem*, "Rejoinder to an Anti-Marginalist," *ibid.*, March 1947, XXXVII; G. J. Stigler, "The Economics of Minimum Wage Legislation," *ibid.*, June 1946, XXXVI; *idem*, "Professor Lester and the Marginalists," *ibid.*, March 1947, XXXVII.

[60] K. E. Boulding, "The Incidence of a Profits Tax," *American Economic Review*, September 1944, XXXIV, p. 567. For Keynesian writing on the other side see Mrs.

which a high profits tax might actually produce more entrepreneurial effort, but the reverse may well be more generally true. The truth is that the Keynesian analysis, uncritically applied, contains an implicit stalemate. Taxation to raise the propensity to consume may indeed raise attempts at consumption; but, if supply is simultaneously discouraged, increased spending may be wasted in higher prices without any proportional increase in production or employment.

The final force likely to make for eventual cultural stagnation, if we do not control it, is summed up in Thurman Arnold's phrase, the "security economy." Economists have talked of *social* security, and probably most of them have realized that that is the only kind of security they can give without general cultural stagnation—if indeed even then—but most of their lay audiences have taken the slogan of social security to mean *personal* security and this attitude has been a most potent weapon for *de facto* monopoly whether from right or left. To it is due at once the restrictive policies of many unions and the opposition to freer trade of many industrialists. The "vested interest" of all classes combines to choke off expansion.

Certain further arguments have been given during the past ten years which would attribute a hopeless ideological instability to capitalism. Thus it may be said that the unemployment benefits and public works of a stabilization program will lead the unions to throw discretion to the winds and stop the system by inordinate wage demands. This seems to be substantially Professor Pigou's view—or nearly so.[61] In its Marxist version the argument runs that only the discipline of unemployment can reconcile the "workers" to "exploitation." To those, of course, who believe that the capitalistic system *is* a systematic exploitation this argument has great cogency. The writer entirely disagrees, but a treatise on value theory is out of place at this point. However, something should also be said concerning those more "moderate" persons who, while believing in the justice and usefulness of capitalism, feel that we must have socialism because, without the semantic hypnosis of collectivist slogans, the workers will act unsocially. To these it may be replied, first, that the effects of the slogans in overcoming pressure-group problems do not always seem to be very great, and, second, that their argument is not merely one for the end of capitalism but also for the end of democracy. For, if the people are in fact too shortsighted to follow, in the main, their own best interests, *no* democratic system is going to survive under any form of economic

---

Robinson, *An Essay on Marxian Economics* (London, 1942), p. 74. See also A. P. Lerner, *The Economics of Control.*

[61] Cf. A. C. Pigou, *Income: An Introduction to Economics* (London, 1947), p. 88.

organization. The same comment is also appropriate to those who maintain that we can never again have an intelligent tax policy.

A second point frequently made concerning capitalism involves the bias toward shortsighted action inherent in the capitalist "myth." The myth of capitalism is the doctrine of the invisible hand. But if the invisible hand really took care of everything why should we ever need action to stabilize the economy, or remedy abuses? Undue stress on *laissez-faire* may thus keep the capitalist from taking appropriate action to save his own system when action is needed. On the other hand if the invisible hand is totally discarded, the "good-monopoly" arguments are uncritically accepted and the capitalism of competition yields place to the protection of the vested interest. The moderate view that, on balance, the myth of the invisible hand is more nearly correct than the radical myth of the tender and omniscient mother-state, does not satisfy the emotional yearnings of those who are determined to find in economic doctrines an *ersatz* religion.

VII. Conclusion

What are the prospects regarding the future of capitalism to be derived from the literature which we have been discussing? First of all, circumstances themselves have exploded the drastically simplified outlook toward investment outlets with which the period began. We no longer regard the consumption function as stable and invariate, and our attitude toward new industries has undergone considerable modification. The needs of foreign nations are impinging more and more upon our economy; and, unless we become a hermit nation like Japan in the seventeenth century, it is difficult to see how we can avoid the conclusion that foreign investment and foreign trade will play a significant role in domestic economic and employment problems. This may be expected to aggravate the cyclical and ameliorate the secular problem.

The writer does not therefore see that capitalism is now suffering from any basic functional weaknesses in the sense of immutable laws preventing it from working. Actual results, however, depend upon the adoption of reasonably intelligent policy. Since it is likely to be more influential, the extreme right is as likely to be dangerous as the extreme left—perhaps more so. Over the long run, monopoly, high tariff, a generally insular bias, and fundamentalist public finance can scarcely be combined with a sufficiently stable system.

On the other hand the "liberal" emphasis on security easily degenerates into a system of general direction, accompanied by drastic redistribution and an excessive tenderness for industrial pressure groups quite as restrictive as "capitalist" "monopoly" (even though different).

The question of the capitalist future seems therefore to rest upon acceptance of the following conclusions: (1) We must secure relative stability. (2) We cannot attain *complete* stability and keep a system which is either technologically progressive or politically democratic. (3) We must recognize "security sabotage," whatever its label. (4) We must allow an adequate incentive to the entrepreneur. Capitalism can be stabilized far beyond anything that has been done so far. But, as Lord Beveridge amply demonstrates, we cannot give 97 per cent security and keep any genuine approach to our present system.

The next point is, how far do we really want capitalism? Are ideological frictions going to be overwhelming? Investment "glut" may be taken in two senses. Either it may mean that, objectively speaking, investment cannot be "absorbed" or it may mean that institutional frictions are too great to permit it. On this latter theory of an insuperably hostile ideology Professor Schumpeter bases the pessimistic conclusions of his *Socialism, Capitalism and Democracy.* It would be easy to make out a similarly pessimistic case. The writer, however, does not do so. Since the matter is not one of inexorable economic law, but rather of the degree of intelligence exercised in future economic policy, we are still left with a choice, and in this connection there is one factor which those who imply a permanently hostile ideology need to consider: That is the superior productivity of capitalism when sufficient demand is forthcoming.[62] It is difficult to escape the conclusion that under present conditions capitalism, economically speaking, once more makes sense. In the light of world conditions, what we need now is saving and production, and what can do a better job in these respects than capitalism? Were I a member of a socialist government, whether of a communist or a much milder persuasion, I should be seriously uneasy. For governments only stay in power by the means by which they achieve it. Yet the left wing today does not promise to the people a regime of secure poverty. That would be a promise which they could meet. They promise instead to have an economy which will grow and change as fast or faster than capitalism, and *yet* be more secure than capitalism. This is a promise which cannot be kept. Whether the frustrated masses will turn back to capitalism, or whether they will adopt—or, more likely, be compelled to adopt—regimes of increasing repression, one cannot say; but the only hope for a democratic liberalism lies in the

---

[62] In this connection see the last few pages of the second edition of Schumpeter, *Capitalism, Socialism and Democracy.* In the writer's opinion liberal socialism suffers from a fatal ideological instability in that it promises a rise in standards of living incompatible with the cultural stagnation which its institutional framework would entail.

first alternative. If enough people really come to believe this, then the prospects for capitalism are extremely favorable. After all, did not even Lenin himself say in his speech to the first congress of the Third International, March, 1919: "To believe that there is no way out of the present crisis for capitalism is an error. No situation is ever absolutely hopeless."[63]

---

[63] This quotation will be found in Mr. William C. White's *Lenin* (New York, 1936), p. 45. If the quotation is wrong, Mr. White, and not myself, is at fault. Of course Lenin was referring to the postwar crisis of the *first* World War. But still "no," to me, means "no."

INDEX OF NAMES

473

INDEX